A compr(
Church of G(

THE QUEST
for Holiness & Unity
Second Edition

A comprehensive history of the
Church of God Reformation Movement

THE QUEST

for Holiness & Unity
Second Edition

By John W. V. Smith

Revised & Expanded by
Merle D. Strege

Warner Press

Anderson, Indiana

Coordinator of Communications and Publishing
Church of God Ministries, Inc.
PO Box 2420
Anderson, IN 46018-2420
800-848-2464 • www.chog.org

To purchase additional copies of this book, to inquire about distribution and for all other sales-related matters, please contact:

W Warner Press, Inc.
PO Box 2499,
Anderson, IN 46018-9988
800-741-7721 • www.warnerpress.org

Scripture quotations marked KJV are taken from the King James Version of the Bible.

Scripture quotations marked NASB are taken from the *New American Standard Bible*, © Copyright 1960, 1962, 1963, 1968, 1971, 1972, 1973, 1975, 1977 by the Lockman Foundation. Used by permission.

Scripture quotations marked RV are taken from the Revised Version of the Bible.

Cover design by Carolyn Frost and Mary Jaracz
Layout design by Mary Jaracz
Production Editing by Stephen R. Lewis

ISBN-13: 978-1-59317-373-9

Printed in the United States of America.
09 10 11 12 13 14 15 /VP/ 10 9 8 7 6 5 4 3 2 1

CONTENTS

PREFACE TO THE SECOND EDITION

Ever since graduates of the School of Theology conferred on me in good humor the first—and as far as I am aware, the only—"John W. V. Smith *Pregnant Pause* Award," it was probably inevitable that one day I would revise and enlarge his most extensive work since our respective academic journeys frequently intersected. He was my principal professor at the School of Theology in the late sixties and early seventies. In the summer of 1978 John and his wife Margaret graciously opened their home while I spent several weeks gathering research materials for my doctoral dissertation, which—like John's—studied an aspect of the history of the Church of God. After he retired and I joined the faculty of my *alma mater* I was assigned some of his courses, notably the course in the history of the Church of God. Finally, after his sudden and untimely passing I succeeded John as the church's historian and soon after began publishing essays and articles of my own. In many respects my academic career has followed a trail blazed by John W. V. Smith.

The Quest for Holiness and Unity was originally published in 1980 as the centennial history of the Church of God reformation movement. Nearly three decades have passed since that celebration, and the memorable events and people of those ensuing years are sufficient in themselves to require additions to Professor Smith's book. Alongside momentous events and influential people, however, over these years the history of the Church of God has benefitted from a keener interest. This interest has produced numerous books and articles on the Church of God movement, not to mention the creation of a spacious archives on the campus of Anderson University, the founding of the *Historical Society of the Church of God*, and developing plans for a center that will historically interpret the movement's mission. This interest also has yielded significant additions to the Church of God Archives. Some of this new material contains information in the form of meeting minutes, correspondence, and other records that forces historians to reconsider and in some instances re-write episodes in the history of the Church of God. Since the publication of the first edition of this volume light has been shed on some critical moments in the movement's life, and a comparison of that edition with this will make quite apparent the places where new light now shines.

As almost always is the case with a project of this scope, so also here many must be acknowledged for their contributions to this updated version of what was from the first a valuable book. From the minute the project was first broached to her, Margaret Smith gave it her blessing. Much of my work was completed during a sabbatical leave from my teaching duties at Anderson University. Once again I am in debt to my academic home for releasing me from teaching and other duties in order to edit, research, and write. Joe Allison lent the material and technical support of Church of God Ministries' Publishing and Creative Services Team to the project. Special mention must be made of the patience and extremely competent work of Mrs. Marcia Lund, who transcribed my marginal notations and insertions—often little more than scribbles—into an electronic text version of the original. Vivian Nieman, Anderson University archivist, speedily and cheerfully answered every request for materials. I also wish to thank Russell Burk, Matthew Preston, and Keith Sayer, student assistants in the Department of Religious Studies, for resourcefully handling some last-minute research tasks. Spencer Spaulding, Cole Dawson, and Arthur Kelly read portions or all of chapters 18, 19, and the "Concluding Semi-historical Postscript." As with my previous work, their suggestions once again proved invaluable; in one or two cases following them to the letter produced a much better sentence than mine. I am indebted to these good friends for many improvements in the additions; any shortcomings remain my responsibility alone. Finally I must express once again my dependence on Fran, my wife of more than thirty-nine years, who encourages me with her questions and insistence that I tell any story clearly and well.

Merle D. Strege
Anderson University
Advent 2008

PREFACE TO THE FIRST EDITION

There is always drama in the search for beginnings. Whether family or fad, nation or notion, gulch or gadget, factory or faith, there is forever the lure of pushing through another layer of the unknown until one finally reaches the point where it can be said, "Here is where it all began!" Equally fascinating is the question of how the object of the query journeyed from its beginning to its present location. Combine these quests together and the road to finding the answers is history. That is what this work purports to be—a history of the beginning and the first one hundred years of development of the religious movement known as the Church of God (Anderson, Indiana).

Preparation for this search began over a third of a century ago. As a second-generation participant in the movement, as a person with graduate degrees in history, as the professor of church history in the church's seminary since 1952, and as the designated historian by the General Assembly since 1957, I had little choice but to attempt a general history of the Church of God as its centennial anniversary approached.

Others began to speak of the need for such a history several years ago. In the initial meeting of a Special Committee on Centennial Proposal on June 2, 1966, Adam W. Miller suggested that even though it was too early to make specific plans for the observance of the centennial of the Church of God it was not too early to project "certain anniversary volumes to be published, one of which could be a documented history of our movement." In a very practical vein he quickly added, "This might need to be subsidized in order to make it available at a popular price for general distribution."

In subsequent meetings of the Centennial Committee the need was reiterated. After attempts to commission the work failed to materialize, the matter was left to the writer and the publisher. The present volume is the result.

The purpose of this book is to highlight the rich heritage from those nineteenth-century people who received divine insights regarding the nature of the church, assembled them and published the results with such dedication and vigor that a self-conscious worldwide movement for the promotion of these concepts emerged within a few short years. The focus is primarily historical and informational. It is neither possible nor desirable, however, to avoid some interpretation and evaluation of people, past events, and points of emphasis. The author writes with unabashed basic agreement with and appreciation for all these pioneer leaders of the Church of God reformation movement. He is also aware that *heritage* is a constructed concept—a blend of what actually happened in the past with what the later inheritors perceive to have happened long ago. There is, thus, the possibility that a historical study will be colored by contemporary understandings of previously affirmed values and truths.

With these awarenesses in mind the writer admits there may be some reading back into the past, some giving credit which is not due, and possibly some romanticizing about very ordinary men and women. On the other hand there also has been a deliberate attempt to avoid idealizing and idolizing the pioneers or canonizing their teachings. They were very human and subject to mistakes in judgment and limitations in knowledge. But the insights into spiritual truth that were opened to them were timeless, and the vigor with which they expounded them should be a model for all who follow after. The heritage from them is rich in both content and example.

A word must be said about sources. The Church of God has not been very record conscious; primary historical materials are very scant for the early years. The few diaries and personal accounts are very helpful but the most valuable sources are the news and letter sections of the *Gospel Trumpet*. In all cases an attempt has been made to utilize original or earliest accounts rather than rely on secondary sources. Even so, the work of former historians has been helpful. Special mention should be made of Henry Wickersham's *History of the Church* (1900), Andrew L. Byers's *Birth of a Reformation* (1921), and Charles E. Brown's *When the Trumpet Sounded* (1951).

The various autobiographies, biographies, congregational histories and state histories have immensely enriched the primary resources. For the later years there are minutes, reports, and a multitude of printed and duplicated materials that are of great value but complicate the task of sorting and selecting. The *Yearbooks* since 1917 and Ministerial Lists from some earlier years contain much more data than just names and addresses. Considerable information has been secured through interviews, correspondence, and the many people who simply found something they thought might be valuable and sent it to the Church of God Archives. Speaking of the Archives, this is really the mine from which all the material has been dug. Without this collection, writing a history of the present scope would have been impossible.

There are some regrets. Even in a fairly voluminous book there is much that has to be left out or referred to only briefly. This is especially painful in regard to people. A great many people have played very significant roles in the development of the Church of God and it has not been possible to include their names or tell their stories. Dozens of other books need to be written to preserve the record of the countless people—laypeople and ministers, women and men, young people and older ones, black and brown and red and white people—who have worked, sacrificed, supported, and promoted the Church of God through all its hundred years around the whole earth. They have brought the movement, under God, to this milestone in its history. Omissions and slight mentions are regretted, and apologies here are offered beforehand for these deficiencies.

Acknowledgements are especially in order for a work of this kind. So many people have contributed to the whole process that it is dangerous to attempt to list them lest the name of some important contributor be omitted. Even so, the author must express special thanks—

To Dr. Aaron K. and Margaret J. Warren, whose interest in this project was great enough to endow the Leonard K. and Zella Warren Research Fellowship in Church of God history since 1976.

To the recipients of the Warren Fellowship—G. Lee Wallace, Betty Ruth Jones, Robert W. Palumbo, and Kenneth R. Tippin—whose research assistance made this volume possible.

To the several hundred students in twenty-eight years of the Church of God Backgrounds class in Anderson School of Theology, who have researched and written about almost every conceivable aspect of the history of the Church of God.

To Delena Goodman and the staff of Byrd Library in Anderson School of Theology, who have allowed the writer unlimited privileges and have been most helpful.

To Joyce Krepshaw, faculty secretary at the School of Theology, who typed the manuscript in the midst of and beyond all her other responsibilities.

To Harold L. Phillips, whose sharp eye and keen editorial sense have contributed in proofreading and polishing the copy.

To Warner Press Editor in Chief Arlo Newell and his staff, whose patience, faith, and prodding eventually brought the project to completion.

And finally, to Margaret, who quit nagging and continued to encourage, support, and love both the manuscript and the writer.

PROLOGUE

On the cornerstone of a church building in Michigan there is an inscription that reads, "The Church of God, Founded A.D. 30." Obviously that modest edifice could not accommodate even a small portion of the great assembly of believers who comprise God's universal church, and the architecture of the building quickly reveals that it is of much more recent vintage than the announced date. Apparently the inscription writer was not attempting to make any exclusive claims or report historical information about the congregation's origins. Rather, the writer intended to convey a message about the character of the people who gathered in that building and to identify the point in time that marks the beginning of that kind of fellowship. The message is evident. The cornerstone really was saying, "Herein meets a group of people who claim a direct link between their fellowship and that first community of followers of Jesus Christ, which originated on the Day of Pentecost. They declare themselves to be a visible local manifestation of the universal church which Christ founded and kept in the name of his Father."

On the surface this would appear a rather presumptive assertion for a group of fewer than a hundred people in a small city in the Upper Midwest of the United States. In the judgment of many it would be so. Audacious or not, the concept of such a church does exist. Extending beyond that small company, it represents the ideology of a worldwide fellowship of almost half a million Christians who seek to embody the goals suggested on that cornerstone. Over four thousand local congregations around the world call themselves by the biblical name "Church of God" because that is what they seek to be. Collectively they are known sometimes as the Church of God reformation movement but more often as the Church of God (Anderson, Indiana) because that is where their North American general offices and publishing house are located.

There is nothing unusual or unique, of course, in looking to the first Christian century for a model of what the church ought to be. Christian people and groups have been undertaking such a search ever since the passing of the first generation of Jesus' followers. To preserve both the record of events and the thought and practice of that early period was really the goal of second and third generations of Christians when they gathered and preserved those precious documents that became the New Testament. In selecting those writings that were considered to be authentically apostolic and canonizing them, these later Christians really were saying that the leaders and communities of earliest reference set standards and provided an example for all subsequent Christians to follow.

This concept of looking back to the primitive church as a point of basic reference has flowed through Christian history in all its centuries. Some individuals and groups emulate this primitive period consciously and deliberately; others do so unconsciously but just as overtly. In some sense all of Christianity, from high church to lowly sect, seeks to be apostolic. Those who make a major point of idealizing the first Christians are sometimes called primitivists, restitutionists, or radicals (in the sense of stemming from the *root)*. The most common label, probably, is restorationist. Within this general framework, with particular delineations that will be noted, the Church of God movement is most compatibly classified.

Before further clarification of this designation it is well to note the almost universal use of this concept of perpetuating or returning to this earliest period in Christian history. The doctrine of apostolic succession, for instance, obviously dramatizes this ideology with reference to clergy. In giving careful attention to the process of laying on of hands in ordination procedures there is at least theoretical validation of the symbolic image of a physical chain of hands being laid by persons on whom hands have been laid all the way back to the apostles. A kind of restoration of the apostolic tradition occurs each time this event takes place.

Millions of Christians find great meaning in the regular recitation of the Apostles' Creed or other early affirmations of faith—which is really a verbal act of restorationism. The value of such a practice lies both in reviewing the content of the statements and also in creating an awareness on the part of the worshiper that he or she is bridging the centuries and relating directly to an ancient formulation. Each repetition restores a primitive understanding of the faith. Such a relationship is even more pronounced among those noncreedal Christians who recognize "no creed but the Bible" in that they have an even firmer anchor in the first century. The more ardent the biblicism and the more literal the interpretation of Scripture, the sharper the focus on a documentary approach to restorationism.

A restorationist concept also is involved in the continued observance of certain practices of the primitive Christian community. Christians have sacralized some of these to the point of being considered means of grace. Whether sacrament or ordinance, these acts become a very overt and tangible link to the early church. Whatever other symbolism may be attached to baptism or the Lord's Supper, for instance, its meaning is enhanced by its relationship to the early church. Still other Christians identify additional practices mentioned in the New Testament as necessary to measure up to the model of the primitive church. Such cultural styles as communal living, distinctive dress, avoidance of any contamination by "the world," and similar practices are regarded by many as important for the faithful restoration of the primitive community.

There is yet another approach to restorationism which, like most of the other types, presumes that somewhere in the unfolding centuries there have been departures or neglect of some of the essential aspects of that primitive community. Therefore an attempt is made to reconstitute the early church—not literally—but in spirit, quality, and purpose. It is in this category of restorationists that the Church of God would find the best description of its reason for being.

In analyzing the scriptural accounts of that early church, the pioneer leaders of the Church of God saw that the two most emulated qualities of the New Testament church were holiness (purity) and unity (oneness). In their contemporary churches they saw these as the qualities most lacking; with such an apparent need, their objective snapped into focus quickly and sharply—to proclaim the one holy apostolic Church of God. It was that simple. In the context of late nineteenth-century Midwestern America, however, it became very complicated, polemic, and difficult as the specific steps to the achievement of this worthy goal began to unfold. The story of those specifics is the burden of this book, but more needs to be said about the objective.

Anyone reasonably acquainted with the records of the early centuries of Christianity, especially the documents of the New Testament, knows, of course, that regarding either holiness or unity, the situation during that period that is often described as "pristine" was far from perfect. Nevertheless, these are the qualities that are most often cited as essential marks of the ideal church, and the early Christians were the first to launch the quest for this ideal. Church of God movement writers and preachers adopted the New Testament church as the standard by which all churches should be measured. Their consistent use of this standard suggests that those early leaders overlooked the fact that the Corinthian church also was the New Testament church.

It would be possible, and probably profitable, to write the whole history of Christianity within the framework of this centuries-long struggle in the church with the interrelated problems of contamination and division. Pollution and dilution in both doctrine and practice have been constant threats, and the menace of dissension seldom has been absent. It was against the backdrop of these two issues that the canon was developed, the authority of bishops and eventually the papacy was augmented, and the formulation of creedal affirmations was furthered. For centuries the Montanists, Donatists, Monastics, Cathari, and other reform groups sought to purify the church, and councils and popes tried to preserve its unity.

The sixteenth-century Reformation was essentially a massive effort to restore the purity of the church. Even in the midst of this intense struggle to restore holiness, the reformers were not unmindful of the charge that in separating from the Roman Catholic Church they were guilty of schism. In order to live with their own consciences, both Luther and Calvin were compelled to develop their own internal rationales for separating from Catholicism. Luther eased his own mind by declaring that the papal institution was apostate and had actually ceased to be the church as early as the eighth century. In departing from it he reasoned that he was not really dividing the church. Calvin employed the ancient Augustinian argument against the Donatists, who objected to sinners in the church: the invisible church, he affirmed, is holy—and one; the visible church is imperfect—and divided.

By these and similar intellectual devices the existence of a divided church was rationalized and the denominational system became the developmental pattern for Protestantism. Although the established churches made a noble effort during the latter part of the sixteenth and through the seventeenth centuries to curb enthusiasm and enforce conformity, they were unable to prevent the rise of independent movements and "sectaries." During the eighteenth and nineteenth centuries denominational proliferation accelerated, especially in America, and the already sundered body of Christ exploded into hundreds of fragments. At the beginning of the nineteenth century, the restorationist Stone-Campbell Movement stood out as an exception to the growing divisiveness.[1] The closing years of the nineteenth century saw Christian rivalry accentuated, competition and proselytism rampant, and very few prophets to raise a voice against the scandal of division.

At this same time, however, there was a considerable company of widely scattered people who were lifting a strong voice in support of the purity of the church. They were banded together in a loosely structured organization that was known as the Holiness Movement. Their effort toward restoring the doctrine and practice of holiness in the church was both extensive and intensive. In the process of pressing for this emphasis, however, they, like other reformers before them, pushed unity to a very low priority item on the scale of desirable characteristics of the church. But some participants noted the sense of unity manifest in camp meetings sponsored by the national Campmeeting Association for Christian Holiness. Like other reformers, they were willing to settle for a rationalization of the divisions that were the norm in nineteenth century American Protestantism.

Certainly there is nothing inherent in the doctrine of holiness that would lead to separateness or division among Christians. On the face of it, quite the opposite should be true. Such terms as *perfect love, Christian perfection,* and *sanctification,* suggest anything but dissension and disunity. The fact is, as any student of the Holiness Movement knows well, holiness teaching has been the occasion for a considerable amount of bitter debate and many severed relationships. The "saints" not only fought their adversaries, but they also battled each other. Even in an era when harsh polemic was in style, they often exhibited a caustic vocabulary of notable and graphic castigation. Their deep commitment to the doctrine and their intense fervor in propagating it made holiness proponents not only strong protagonists but also formidable adversaries.

It was at this point that the early Church of God reformers were essentially unique in that they gave central attention to *both* of these characteristics of the church and related each to the other as being inextricably bound together in producing the Church Christ intended. It was for this reason that Daniel S. Warner and others withdrew from the structured Holiness Movement although they had no disagreement whatsoever regarding the doctrine of holiness. They believed that failure to separate the holiness emphasis from the "sinful" sectarian system was to negate its whole thrust

---

1. Among the churches that trace their roots to this movement led by Alexander Campbell and Barton W. Stone are the Churches of Christ, the Independent Christian Churches/Churches of Christ, and the Christian Church (Disciples of Christ).

and presented only a partial witness to the obvious divine intention for God's people.

The major emphasis of the Church of God reformation movement thus became a renewal of the centuries-long quest for the holiness and unity of the church. Their central focus is best summed up by Warner in his classic belief that neither holiness nor unity can be achieved unless both move together:

> It is, indeed, my honest conviction that the great holiness reform cannot go forward with the sweeping power and permanent triumph that God designs it should, until the Gospel be so preached, and consecration become so thorough, that the blood of Christ may reach, and wash away every vestige of denominational distinction, and *"perfect into one"*—yea, *one* indeed and in truth—all the sanctified.[2]

The account that follows is the story of the pursuit of that vision.

---

2. Daniel S. Warner, *Bible Proofs of the Second Work of Grace* (Goshen, IN: E. U. Mennonite Publishing Society, 1880), 436.

CHAPTER 1

IN THE FULLNESS OF TIME

"Christianity," says Williston Walker, "entered no empty world."[1] In his *History of the Christian Church* the noted church historian describes the various aspects of the world of the first century in which Christianity began. He points out that the political, social, economic, and cultural setting of the Roman Empire provided something other than virgin soil in which the new faith would take root and grow. The thoughts that already filled people's minds, their manner of living, and, most of all, their religious concepts had a great deal to do with the understandings and applications they brought to their encounter with Christianity. The new converts, whose inner lives were changed by accepting Christ and his way, still lived in the context of their culture. Consciously or unconsciously, they brought much of it with them to the church then forming. The record of this encounter of faith with environment is the story that is told in the documents found in the New Testament and in other early Christian writings. To really understand early Christian history it is necessary to examine both the content and the context of the faith at that moment.

What is true of the beginnings of Christianity also applies to its development and expansion through the centuries. Kenneth Scott Latourette's monumental seven-volume *History of the Expansion of Christianity* is built around this principle of interaction.[2] As he tells the story of the penetration of the faith to new continents, new countries, and the islands in the oceans, it is always with specific reference to the impact of Christianity on those environments and the ways each influenced Christianity. The basic faith is the same around the world, but its character, its methodologies, and its relationships vary greatly in the many different cultures in which it functions.

---

1. Williston Walker, *A History of the Christian Church*, 3rd ed. (New York: Charles Scribner's Sons, 1970), 3.

2. Kenneth Scott Latourette, *A History of the Expansion of Christianity*, 7 vols. (New York: Harper and Brothers, 1943).

This same principle applies to the historical study of any great movement within Christianity—monasticism, scholasticism, the Protestant Reformation, puritanism, pietism, revivalism, and many others. Each is fully understood only in relationship to its setting in time and place. In making these observations, however, it must be understood that such an approach in no sense negates the belief that God is at work in history. There is no way to ignore God's continued presence, God's guidance toward the accomplishment of the divine ultimate will, God's penetration and, sometimes in very dramatic ways, God's intervention in the course of events. That is part of the content of the faith that interacts with human cultural situations. Sometimes these are aligned with the purposes of God and speed the accomplishment of divine will; sometimes they blow as contrary winds that thwart and even destroy the work God would do. And even beyond the human factor, most Christians would recognize the presence of the demonic as a part of the context of life on the earth. So God is very present and is actively at work in history but, by choice, deigns to work through imperfect human instruments and is not unopposed.

With these thoughts in mind we now turn our attention to a particular movement in Christian history that has called itself, among other titles, the Church of God reformation movement. The first task is to locate it in time and geographical setting and to examine the external conditions and factors that had some bearing on the nature of the movement, its points of particular emphasis, its methodologies, and its relationships. Like the early church, the Church of God reformation movement entered no empty world; some analysis of that world is necessary. In the total course of Christian history the Church of God is a recent development. It arose in the last quarter of the nineteenth century. In terms of geographic location it began in an area that also was in a stage of relatively recent and very active development, the United States of America. More specifically, the movement originated in the period immediately following the American Civil War in the region commonly known as the Midwest.

Historians and analysts of American history have been hard put to find an adequate label to describe this period. One rather widely used designation is "The Gilded Age," implying a glittering overlay for a less valuable reality.[3] Another description labels this as the period of "American Victorianism" and highlights the cultural and other associations with England during the long reign of Queen Victoria.[4] The most common name applied to the era is "The Period of Reconstruction," referring to the necessarily long time of readjustment to the ravages of a devastating war. Still other designations are such terms as "a grim generation" and "the wild seventies."[5] A popular reference called this the age of "The Great Barbecue." All of these are apropos to a very diverse and volatile period in American history.

Rather than attempt to expound at length on any of the labels, it is more conducive to a general understanding of this period to call attention to the chief characteristics of the times and place. The most obvious of these is the simple observation that this was a time of very rapid development and change, producing a condition of unrest and even alarm on the part of those who cherished the values of an older order. This anxiety is perhaps nowhere better expressed than in an address by Methodist Bishop Edward Gayer Andrews at the 1887 General Christian Conference in Washington, DC, sponsored by the Evangelical Alliance. He expressed his concern about the new national dangers in these words:

> That American Christianity and American Society are confronted with perils, new, various, organized and gigantic, is obvious. The city disproportionately enlarging; immigration increasing beyond our power of assimilation; wealth accumulating rapidly in a few hands; monopolies repressing individual enterprise; a foreign church, hostile to American principles, fortifying itself among us; the saloon, threatening every interest of the home and the state; illiteracy overshadowing a large part of the body politic; socialistic tendencies among the laboring classes; crimes multiplying with extraordinary energy; sexual vice patent everywhere, attended by a loosening of the marriage tie and the growth

---

3. In 1873 Mark Twain and Charles Dudley Warner captured the national mood in a satirical novel, *The Gilded Age*, which introduced "Colonel Beriah Sellers," a seedy but magnificently undismayable promoter whose head teemed with get-rich schemes.

4. The application of the term *Victorian* to American life and culture of this period has been common. Two examples are Daniel Walker Howe, ed., *Victorian America* (Philadelphia: University of Pennsylvania Press, 1976) and H. Wayne Morgan, *Victorian Culture in America, 1865–1914* (Itasca, IL: F. E. Peacock Publishers, 1973).

5. These designations were used by Denis T. Lynch, *"Boss" Tweed, The Story of a Grim Generation* (New York: Boni and Liveright, 1927) and *The Wild Seventies* (New York: Appleton-Century, 1941).

of Mormonism; the alienation of great masses of the people from the Church, with a startling increase of Sabbath desecration; corruption among the makers and administrators of law—these are facts portentous of disaster and, if unchecked, of ruin.[6]

The rapid changes suggested by the bishop's enumeration of perils were almost all associated with three massive and simultaneous shifts in population that were in progress at that time. The first of these was a resumption of the westward movement of people that had been interrupted by the Civil War. This internal migration was encouraged considerably by the passage of the Homestead Act in 1862, which offered 160 acres of land in the western areas to those who would develop it. This was especially attractive to immigrants, ex-soldiers, and others whose lives and vocations had been disrupted by the war. In 1869 the completion of the first transcontinental railroad made the journey west, even to the Pacific Coast, much easier. The lure of striking it rich in western mines also attracted many, and the prospects of becoming a rancher or a cowboy led many others westward. Colorado became a state in 1876; the Dakotas, Washington, and Montana were admitted in 1889, and a year later Idaho and Wyoming achieved that status. After considerable controversy Utah became a state in 1896. America was rapidly fulfilling its promise and status as a continental nation, and many were moving west to join the action.

An even greater migration occurred during these years, however. The last quarter of the nineteenth century witnessed dramatic growth in American cities. In 1870 the population of the United States was about thirty-eight and a half million with 74 percent of the people living in rural areas and 26 percent in the cities. By 1916 the population was nearly 100 million people with only one-half of them rural.[7] Table 1 shows the increase in the population of some leading Midwestern cities.

Urbanization was occasioned by the rapid development of business and industry. The demand for war material had sparked the growth of the factory system especially if not exclusively in the North. The rise of industrial and business tycoons such as Andrew Carnegie, J. P. Morgan, James J. Hill,

---

6. Edward G. Andrews, "Address of Welcome," in *National Perils and Opportunities, The Discussion of the General Christian Conference Held in Washington, D. C, December 7th, 8th and 9th, 1887,* under the auspices and direction of the Evangelical Alliance for the United States, 13 (New York: Baker and Taylor, 1887).

7. *World Book Encyclopedia,* 1979 ed., s.v. "United States History."

TABLE 1: Population of Leading Midwestern Cities[8]

City	1850	1900
Chicago	29,963	1,698,575
Detroit	21,019	285,704
Toledo	3,829	131,822
Cincinnati	115,435	325,902
Indianapolis	8,091	169,164
Louisville	43,194	204,731
St. Louis	77,860	575,238

and John Weyerhauser who built their own empires pushed the process even faster. The invention of new technological marvels such as Alexander Graham Bell's telephone in 1876 and Thomas Edison's electric light bulb in 1879 ushered in a new age of advances in manufacturing and communication. As a result of this growth the nation's rich resources of coal, iron, lumber, and petroleum were increasingly exploited. Most of this action was taking place in the cities, so people flocked to these urban centers to find jobs, but also excitement. Within a generation after the Civil War the United States was transformed from a predominantly agricultural society to an emerging industrial nation. The factory had outdistanced the farm as a producer of wealth by 1890.

The third aspect of the great population shift was a great wave of immigration from Europe. In 1882 over three-quarters of a million people crossed the Atlantic to make America their home, and by 1907 a half million more than that were arriving annually. Approximately one-third of these settled on farms and in rural areas and the remainder crowded into the already teeming cities. Especially after 1880 many immigrants stayed in the East, which meant that the Atlantic seaboard cities such as Boston, New York, and Philadelphia grew even more than the Midwestern urban centers.

Industrialization, urbanization, and immigration combined to create tremendous social and cultural change. The effect of massive dislocation was to disrupt all systems of societal solidarity that had operated in the past. Even though community life was still oriented around the basic institutions of family, church, school, the professions, and government, there was such an expansion of the range that even longstanding institutions were not

8. George E. Delory, ed., *The World Almanac and Book of Facts* (New York: Newspaper Enterprise Association, 1978), 194.

effective social controls. In the words of Robert H. Wiebe, "America in the late nineteenth century was a society without a core. It lacked those national centers of authority and information which might have given order to such swift changes."[9]

The immediate result was a shift in values. It was at this point that the American Victorian cultural outlook would have an impact. One value they prized highly was that of competitiveness, "an attitude reflecting the excitement and sense of power with which Victorians faced the world."[10] This attitude can be seen in the acceptance and rise of party politics. It can also be seen in denominationalism, where Christian groups retained a great sense of rivalry. Daniel Walker Howe expressed the Victorian balance between order and competition, "Just as they valued rational order in the individual, the Victorians valued it in society at large. Within the order, they hoped, competition might be structured and contained."[11]

Victorians were also very conscious of the importance of time. In fact they were more concerned about saving time than saving natural resources. They destroyed topsoil and forests, slaughtered whales and bison to build their civilization. Labor was expensive and raw materials were cheap. They were more interested in accounting for time than in husbanding materials. Conspicuous consumption came to be a hallmark for the lifestyle of many of them.[12]

One of the Victorians' most notable characteristics was their future orientation. This is illustrated by their great interest in education, their readiness to reinvest profits at a risk, and their ambition. Each characteristic underscored the importance of planning and the wise use of time. Howe commented, "It is no accident that their great civil war was fought between American Victorians over rival visions of the future of the country, over the expansion of slavery into new territories, rather than over the actual presence of the institution."[13]

Alongside these characteristics Victorian Americans in general possessed a sense of morality sound enough to establish procedures for teaching it to the young but too weak for application to the new situations created by the monumental changes of the late nineteenth century. This moral condition

---

9. Robert H. Wiebe, *The Search for Order, 1877–1920* (New York: Hill and Wang, 1967), 12. This is a most incisive analysis of this period in American history.

10. Howe, *Victorian America*, 18.

11. Ibid.

12. Ibid., 19.

13. Ibid.

gives substance to the stereotype of narrow-minded hypocrisy so often attributed to the Victorians.

One other aspect of the era is noteworthy in relation to the setting for religious reform. New and uncontrolled developments in business and industry widened the gap between the rich and the poor. Many made fortunes, but many more were thrust into poverty. In between was a new middle class made up largely of wage earners who were beginning to organize themselves into labor unions in order to establish a position of strength in dealing with the industrialists. Laborers participated in the new wealth, but they were far from being among the rich. In this whole process class lines came to be more sharply drawn than they had been in the previous, predominantly agrarian society.

The improved economic status of those who acquired this new wealth created a changed climate of consumption as they looked for ways to spend their disposable income. A growing desire for the finer things of life began to find extensive expression in nineteenth-century America. Nevertheless, a contrast of lifestyles developed between the upper and lower class. The lower class labored long hours often with several family members working to make ends meet. They often lived in crowded city tenements with poor diets and inadequate sanitation. The elite, upper class developed a showy culture termed by Mark Twain as "The Gilded Age." They enjoyed such entertainments as the opera, luxury resorts, and antiques. This was one of the most apparent manifestations of Victorian culture in America. As H. Wayne Morgan put it, "The industrial growth that produced a great economy also made many Americans aware of and eager to acquire cultural status. The leaders of brawling and dynamic cities endowed museums, symphony orchestras, opera houses, and libraries. They planned cities, and collected paintings and statuary."[14]

For most Americans a culture was developing that was more sophisticated than that of previous years. It also produced greater contrasts between the rural and urban areas since much of the new culture was generated in the cities. One aspect of this was the rapid rise of the entertainment business—a development that many regarded as an inordinate increase in alluring opportunities for sin. Annual county fairs had been around for some time but to these were added extravaganzas such as the 1876 Philadelphia Centennial Exposition. Vaudeville shows, athletic games, and

14. Morgan, *Victorian Culture in America*, xi.

especially circuses increased in popularity. The circus, of course, owed its rise primarily to the period's greatest promoter, P. T. Barnum, who through massive publicity, unusual attractions, and well-trained animals grabbed the attention of the American people as few others had done. The circus was frowned upon by many church people, however; it was a show and thus either sinful or frivolous.

The rise of the theatre and other art forms were also characteristic of this era. Architecture, the public arts, and music were each brought to a higher degree of sophistication. Many American students studied in Paris or England, but the number of good American universities also increased. The development of high culture came with a price. As Morgan described it, "The sudden influx of ideas, increased wealth, and the need for durable artistic forms all inevitably produced confusion."[15] It was a time of readjustment as the goals of society and the centers of power determining these goals mixed, clashed, and effected cultural change. This enhanced the quest for money, power, and influence over the shape American society would take.

Still another fruit of this confused culture was the appearance of a number of challengers to the most fundamental of all religious beliefs—the existence of God. Some of these "infidels," as they were frequently known, traveled widely and invited the public to attend their lectures. The most famous of these was Robert G. Ingersoll, a former Protestant minister who made eloquent attacks on the clergy, the Bible, and the Christian faith. An even more bizarre lecturer is mentioned in an 1879 account reported in the *Herald of Gospel Freedom* edited by Daniel S. Warner:

> Geo. W. Burleigh, of Capron, Ill., gave an exhibition of the fruits of modern skepticism. Having previously announced that on Tuesday night, July 23d, he would deliver an infidel lecture, after which he would kill himself by shooting himself in the forehead. Admission, $1, proceeds to pay funeral expenses, and purchase the works of Huxley, Tyndal and Darwin for the town library. The hall was crowded at the appointed time, and the programme was carried out.
>
> Those books are then purchased of blood, but the darkest stains on them are under the covers. The infidelity which they encouraged has nothing better than suicide to offer for the disappointments of life. *(Christian Advocate)*[16]

---

15. Ibid., xii.
16. *Herald of Gospel Freedom*, February 1, 1879, 3.

These changes in the American ethos loosened the moorings that had held society together and preserved order. In an age that on the surface accepted the Victorian values of honesty, modesty, rectitude, thrift, sobriety, and hard work, it is amazing how graft, immorality, drunkenness, and waste became so pervasive—especially in government and business.

Corruption in government undoubtedly had its roots in the disruptions of Civil War and Reconstruction. In that agonizing period policy manipulations and even distortions seemed to be required to deal with extraordinary circumstances. In the process corrupt bargains, crude pressure tactics, and all kinds of extra-legal actions threatened to become the new standard. From the Grant administration in Washington to the smallest hamlet there were deals, special favors, and collusions for profit. The burgeoning cities were especially vulnerable and became an easy prey for the "boss" system. From Tweed in New York City to Pendergast in Kansas City, urban centers were caught in a web of cronyism and unprecedented corruption. At all levels controls were largely in the hands of the political machine, and ordinary folk were the victims. Small wonder that one scholar has observed, "Never had so many citizens held their government in such low regard."[17]

A similar climate prevailed in business. Often government officials and the leaders of industry were partners in exploitation. The railroads were perhaps the earliest participants in collusion since they needed land for a right-of-way to lay tracks, and the government owned more land than anyone in the country. Other industries—especially mining, oil, and timber, which involved natural resources—soon became involved after the pattern set by the railroad magnates. In the business world itself the great goal was "bigness." To achieve this any semblance of morality or ethics was forgotten. The creation of monopolies, the formation of trusts, cutthroat tactics to eliminate competition, and other tooth-and-claw methods were freely utilized. Phrases from Darwin's *Origin of the Species* such as "natural selection" and "survival of the fittest" were lifted out of biology and applied to the business world as a rationale for the competitive advantage of the large over the small. Marketing was involved as well as production. The forming of "pools," "cornering," and other kinds of deals worked toward the advantage of the big and the exploitation of those too small to compete. Specific examples of all these tactics—and more—are innumerable. For purposes of this study, however, it is sufficient to note the existence of these

---

17. Wiebe, *Search for Order*, 5.

conditions as a part of the context for the beginning of a new religious movement. In view of the facts, however, it is small wonder that Bishop Andrews continued the review of his times by saying:

> The situation is grave beyond question. The forces of evil are alert, aggressive, and in many quarters victorious. They imperil the most precious interests of ourselves and our posterity. They imperil our institutions and our civilization. They imperil the souls for which Christ died. They summon all right-thinking men to conflict severe, long-continued, and costly in every sense.[18]

As might be expected, while people were uneasy with apparent social ills they also found it difficult to find handles to correct the situation. When corruption becomes so pervasive that even many of the churches are caught having been recipients of the generous philanthropies of the rich, it is not easy to identify leadership for broad reform. To enact laws that would correct and control was nearly impossible since many government officials were part of the problem. The victims of the system were powerless. There was really no individual or group in the power structure who was inclined to act against the system even though many held an uneasy conscience toward it.

Despite these conditions there was a rising mood of reform. On the political front a major protest of the situation was known as Populism. Although it never became a viable rival of the Republicans or Democrats, it did function as a political party in some of the western states. Rooted in agrarian culture it became a very vocal opponent of land-grabs and special subsidies to industry. With the Great Commoner, William Jennings Bryan, as their chief spokesperson, Populists cried out against exploitation of farmers and laborers. Some attempted to link these concerns with the plight of blacks in the South and the ethnic groups in the cities, but the mixture never quite jelled and Populism became more of a prelude to reform than a reforming movement itself. It did meet with some political success in the 1890s, but eventually many Populist themes were absorbed by major parties. The rise of labor unions and the use of the power tactics available to them was also an evidence of the reform spirit being expressed in the cities and in mining communities. Some labor groups advocated a more

---

18. Andrews, "Address of Welcome," 13.

radical reform under the label of socialism. Following the lead of the workers there were other special interest groups who banded together to preserve or promote their own interests.

Another very significant move toward reform was initiated by newspaper journalists who began investigating the operations of both business and government and exposing them in print. "Muckrakers" like Ida M. Tarbell, Upton Sinclair, and Lincoln Steffens exposed the inner corrupt workings of factories, large corporations, state houses, cities, and Washington itself, laying the groundwork for the subsequent legislation and housecleaning of progressivism.

Along with all the organized and group protests in America at this time there was also a great deal of individual "anti" feeling in regard to many things. Western and rural areas were characterized by strong anti-intellectual sentiments—a carryover from the ethos of the frontier.[19] In such a climate, the vigorous emphasis on "heart" religion by the American revivalists found a ready response. By 1875 the revival or "protracted meeting" had become a regular feature of rural and small town America. Before the end of the century the famous evangelist Dwight L. Moody carried revivalistic Protestantism to large cities. The content may have been urban, but the dynamic of Moody's campaign was revivalism, a tribute to the enduring power in the American heart and mind. The concomitant apprehensiveness about creeds and formal liturgies placed the older mainline churches under some degree of judgment. The "called" minister was often regarded more highly than the formally trained clergyman, and the spontaneity of a camp meeting was regarded a more spiritual experience than repetition of traditional rituals. This notion did not often take the form of opposition to all education but it did object to the rising sophistication becoming evident in some segments of society, including the churches. Moody was an ordained layman—a shoe salesman. After him, no big-name American evangelist was graduated from a mainline seminary. The image of the intellectual was that of an impertinent snob—and there was little respect for such in rural Midwestern America.

One other factor with regard to the reforming spirit deserves mention—that of methodology. When individuals or organized groups became convinced that a certain course of action was the proper one there was a strong preference for direct attack. Whether a Carry Nation as a lone woman with

---

19. A Pulitzer Prize–winning work on the topic is Richard Hofstadter, *Anti-intellectualism in American Life* (New York: Random House, 1963).

a hatchet chopping up the furniture in saloons on the Kansas prairie or a labor union on strike in Chicago that set off the bloody Haymarket riot, the approach to problem solving was straightforward and artless, and violence was no deterrent to accomplishing a desired end. This was sometimes also true for religionists who had strong feelings about new movements that threatened their own solidarity; attitudes toward the Mormons would be a case in point.

There was one very great problem area, however, toward which little reform effort was being directed. That was the race issue. Whatever else was done to assist the freed slaves in the South or the free blacks in the North during Reconstruction, it was clear that integration of the black people was not one of American society's goals. The fourteenth and fifteenth amendments to the federal constitution gave some legal rights to blacks but did not guarantee social rights or equal opportunity. Already prior to the Civil War American society was segregated, even in the North. Even the churches did little to stem the tide. In the first year after the close of the Civil War two "colored" Baptist AME/AME Zion conventions were formed, and the Southern Methodists released their black members to form their own Colored Methodist Church in 1870. By 1869 the Presbyterians were in the process of doing likewise. Many black Methodists, however, found a new home in the older African Methodist Episcopal and African Methodist Episcopal Zion Churches. The Northern Methodist Church made provision in its structure for a separate black conference. Segregated churches enjoyed rapid growth and performed many valuable functions for black people, but they were still separate.

It is difficult to sum up a diverse and complicated period like the 1870s and 1880s in American history. It was a time when Americans, says one scholar, "came to discover a painful paradox of progress. Their prodigious achievements had been largely the product of a social and political system that gave a maximum of equality, mobility, and opportunity to all men. Yet, in a huge, complex and maturing industrial order it was increasingly difficult to preserve these virtues."[20] Historic values and virtues were still proclaimed, but their meanings were distorted and bent to fit the expediencies of a changing society. Tensions between the rural and urban, the East and West, and the black and the white were added to the lingering division of the North and South. The competitive style of business and industry

---

20. Bernard A. Weisberger, *The Age of Steel and Steam* (New York: Time, Inc., 1964), 29.

permeated the rest of society—including religion—and the wonder of it all sent people in almost every walk of life reaching for some order in the pervasive confusion. Reform in many areas was in the air but no one seemed quite able to put it all together. Yet, just as "when the fullness of time was come, God sent forth his Son" (Gal 4:4), so when the time was right some people began to speak to this confused age and put the church in proper perspective.

CHAPTER 2

RELIGIOUS REACTION: CONFUSION, ACCOMMODATION, AND REFORM

Harvard professor Arthur M. Schlesinger, Sr., a noted historian, labeled the years 1875–1900 as "a critical period in American religion."[1] Writing in retrospect some eighty years after the aforementioned Bishop Andrews's on-the-scene description of the time, Schlesinger sounded a familiar tone when he declared:

> Perhaps at no time in its American development has the path of Christianity been so sorely beset with pitfalls and perils as in the last quarter of the nineteenth century. The validity of the Bible itself seemed at stake in the light of new pronouncements of science and scholarship. Darwinism, the emerging science of biblical criticism, the increasing knowledge and study of other great religions—such threats to orthodoxy could not be ignored, yet how were they to be met? But this was not all. In an age of rapid, not to say fearful, urban and industrial development, the church was fast losing its appeal for the wage-earning masses, though such folk asked emotional, not intellectual, satisfaction of their spiritual guides. Was Protestantism to be sequestered in the small towns and rural districts, or could it adjust itself to the requirements of megalopolis?[2]

Schlesinger then proceeded to examine each of these great challenges to organized religion, noting that both the Christian system of thought was being questioned and the church's role in society was also being placed in jeopardy. He described how Darwinism challenged the biblical image of

---

1. Arthur M. Schlesinger, Sr., *A Critical Period in American Religion, 1875–1900* (Philadelphia: Fortress Press, 1967).
2. Ibid., 1–2.

creation but found acceptance by noted preachers like Henry Ward Beecher and Lyman Abbott. Biblical criticism called into question the infallibility of the Scripture but was embraced by many respected scholars. A new interest in world religions, culminating in the World's Parliament of Religions during the Columbian Exposition in 1893, undermined the concept of Christianity's uniqueness. New thought movements like Ethical Culture and Theosophy appeared, and Christian Science also attracted a following. The growing secularization of the Sabbath was evident on every hand, especially in the cities, and many states relaxed laws regarding Sunday observance. A multitude of Protestant churches fled their parishes in the city and were replaced by the Salvation Army, rescue missions, and secular settlement houses. To stem this tide and to serve human need the social gospel arose with the goal, in Walter Rauschenbush's words of "Christianizing the Social Order." Tensions between Catholics and Protestants mounted, sometimes to the point of violence, and controversy within and among Protestant groups often resulted in acrimonious debate and even further schism. The label of "critical period" was amply substantiated. For American religion the times were challenging as well as changing.

Despite monumental changes in American life and culture in the late nineteenth century and despite the avalanche of evil forces that were unleashed by the disruption of traditional modes in society, there was still a sufficient degree of stability to avert chaos and to notice at least a moderate amount of progress in some areas other than wealth and technology. Even Bishop Andrews, whose peril-laden picture of the era already has been cited, was willing to admit there were some brighter aspects of the religious situation in 1880:

Nor must we forget some striking signs of Christian progress with which the nineteenth century is closing: as, for instance, the better apprehension in the Church of personal Christianity as summed up in love and loyalty to Christ; the greater unity of Christian people as against the divisive tendency of dogma, organization and rite; the proven power of voluntaryism, by which Church provision, the edifice, the preacher and the school, have kept even pace with the westward march of our population; the probable decline of skepticism from that prevalence at the opening of the century…that gracious growth of the Evangelical Church in the United States, by which it includes in its membership one in five of the people as against one in fourteen in the year 1800; and finally that new aggressiveness of modern Christianity by which, from us as from Christian Europe, the Gospel sounds out into all heathen and Mohammedan lands.[3]

The bishop's catalog of positive indicators suggests that many areas evidenced improvement in regard to religion in general and Protestant Christianity in particular. Closer scrutiny might reveal that in some of his categories, such as "the greater unity of Christian people," overall advance was slight even if some progress is conceded. Even so, the list validates the fact that many churches were capable of adapting reasonably well to the transformations in the culture and were able to function somewhat successfully. The popular ideals of the American nation already had been easily incorporated into the thought and practices of mainstream Christianity and, since these ideals were still outwardly professed, there was little cause for ideological conflict nor much reason for churches to assume an antagonistic role toward society. Along with other Americans they kept busy adapting both faith and practice to the rapidly changing social context.

In the last quarter of the nineteenth century many religious people, however, were not able to accommodate either beliefs or lifestyle so readily and found themselves in conflict with prevailing societal standards and consequently also with mainstream Protestant Christianity. Sydney E. Ahlstrom has identified five groups, some already existing and others born in the era, who were left dissatisfied with or were openly hostile to the progress that they saw in the standard brands of evangelical faith.[4] The first groups were the agnostics, free religionists, socialists, and others who left the churches and adopted alternative forms of thought and value. The second consisted of the more moderate liberals and social gospelers who sought to adapt Christian faith and practice to what they considered urgent modern needs. A third group included a variegated cluster of those who, either because of ethnic background or some special revelation, had never been included in the old Protestant mainstream. One finds here Mormons, Christian Scientists, Mennonites, Unitarians, Roman Catholics, Jews, some Lutherans, some blacks, and others who had never been assimilated into

3. Edward G. Andrews, "Address of Welcome," in *National Perils and Opportunities, The Discussion of the General Christian Conference Held in Washington, D. C, December 7th, 8th and 9th, 1887*, under the auspices and direction of the Evangelical Alliance for the United States, 14 (New York: Baker and Taylor, 1887).

4. Sydney E. Ahlstrom, *A Religious History of the American People* (New Haven, CT: Yale University Press, 1972), 805–6.

the American religious ethos. Ahlstrom's fourth group was a large trans-denominational movement that resisted all innovation in religion and was troubled by the advance of theological liberalism (especially biblical criticism) and the passing of Puritan moralism. This group came to be known as fundamentalists.

In moving to the last of the groups of the dissatisfied or hostile, Ahlstrom expanded his description as follows:

> The fifth and final group effected a more distinct separation from mainstream Protestantism than most fundamentalists sought. A desire for a rebirth of life in the Spirit often led its adherents to schism and sectarian withdrawal. Its chief doctrinal concern was sanctification, and the "gathered" communities which it founded were Holiness or, if more radical in their innovations, Pentecostal churches. Finding its adherents chiefly among the disinherited and the uneducated, this movement was primarily a protest against birthright church membership and a Protestantism that had settled for a religion of conformity, middle-class respectability, and self-improvement. Since the Wesleyan emphasis on Christian perfection was very prominent in its teaching, the Methodist church was deeply involved in the attendant strife. Many of these sectarians, however, came to share the Fundamentalist's concern for biblical inerrancy, and Christ's Second Coming often loomed large in their thought.[5]

It is with this group of dissenters and reformers that the Church of God reformation movement would be most closely identified. Further elaboration and certain delineations are necessary, however, in order to understand more precisely the religious roots and relationships of this group. Ahlstrom's reference to "Holiness churches" actually describes a later phase (after 1890) of what was earlier a rather extensive transdenominational movement in American Protestantism. That movement had its beginnings before the Civil War but did not formally institutionalize until after the war's conclusion. The movement focused on what its members considered to be widespread neglect of holiness as a doctrine, experience, and way of life. The immediate background of this movement is summarized by Elmer T. Clark:

---

5. Ibid., 806.

At the close of the Civil War…there swept over the country a wave of immorality, secularism, and religious indifference. The spirit naturally affected the churches, bringing about what many believed to be a lowered moral tone, compromise with "the world," weakening of the insistence on definite religious experience as a condition of membership, with the consequent influx of unconverted persons into the fold, and a general decline of vital piety and holiness of life. As a result, by the familiar process of sectarian psychology, the humbler Christians with emotional temperaments and perfectionist leanings began to feel uneasy, to protest against the abandonment of earlier practices, and to seek wherever it might be found the experience of perfect love.[6]

Along with Ahlstrom, most religious historians describe the holiness agitation as largely stemming from Wesleyan teaching regarding perfection and the lack of emphasis that this doctrine was receiving within Methodism. While it is true that many of the Holiness groups had a Methodist background and several were direct offshoots of the Methodist body, it is also true that the Finney revival and the Oberlin theology of the period following the Civil War emphasized holiness. Furthermore, several German groups with a Lutheran and Reformed tradition, such as the Evangelical Alliance and the General Eldership of the Churches of God in North America, embraced the doctrine, though not all gave it strong attention.

Even though other groups were preaching holiness it is still true that the rise of the Holiness Movement was both inspired by Wesleyan theology and in its early stages encouraged by Methodist bishops such as L. L. Hamline and others. As Methodism increased in size, wealth, and social prestige, however, and as it found itself a victim of the post-Civil War forces noted above, a new generation of bishops gave less attention to "second-blessing" holiness. Those who upheld the doctrine began to drawing closer to each other by forming "holiness bands" and promoting their beliefs through establishing Holiness periodicals and Holiness camp meetings. Clark observed that when these developments came about:

The great denominations became alarmed and endeavored to bring the movement under control, making verbal gestures to the doctrine of entire sanctification but showing no sign of returning to it as a vital

6. Elmer T. Clark, *The Small Sects in America* (New York: Abingdon Cokesbury, 1950), 71.

experience. Controversy and mutual recriminations ensued, and the holiness people became more and more alienated from the churches. The small "bands" and groups declared independence in large numbers and in every part of the country.[7]

Although the formation of holiness bands and the publication of Holiness periodicals had begun before the Civil War, it was not until after the war that the movement reached any great proportions.[8] Gaddis set the birthdate of the National Holiness Association in 1867 when the first general Holiness camp meeting was held in Vineland, New Jersey.[9] Though professing to be interdenominational in scope, this camp meeting, said Clark, was essentially a Methodist institution.[10] It was here that the National Camp Meeting Association for the Promotion of Holiness was formed. One writer described the function of this loose associate of preachers and evangelists:

> Camp Meetings were organized on various bases—national, sectional, state, local; union, denominational, independent. They served to strengthen the morale of adherents to holiness who were outnumbered at home, they instructed and inspired leaders who would carry the message into other areas, and they served as a door through which new converts entered into the state of perfect love.[11]

Gaddis divided the history of the Holiness Movement into three periods. The first of these is from the beginning to around 1893 and is designated as the stage of undenominational movements. Characterizing this period, he wrote:

> Up until [this time] the holiness movement expressed itself mainly in bands, conventions and camp meetings of a more or less spontaneous

---

7. Ibid., 72.

8. *Guide to Holiness*, perhaps the oldest of the Holiness periodicals, started publication in 1842. Others that appeared after the Civil War were the *Christian Witness and Advocate of Bible Holiness, Banner of Holiness, Texas Holiness Advocate, Herald of Holiness, Pentecostal Herald, Gospel Trumpet,* and others.

9. Merrill E. Gaddis, "Christian Perfectionism in America" (PhD diss., University of Chicago, 1929).

10. Clark, *Small Sects in America*, 73.

11. Valorous B. Clear, "The Church of God: A Study in Social Adaptation" (PhD diss., University of Chicago, 1953).

and extra-denominational character...To call these loose organizations and gatherings "union" meetings is somewhat misleading, since they were for the most part mere aggregations of holiness people drawn from holiness factions of the various denominations of perfectionistic tradition. Most of the quasi-sects formed prior to the early nineties were of a sort which protested most vigorously against being called sects at all—a trait more or less characteristic of holiness groups in general. They preferred that their local organizations should be thought of as small units of a restored universal or catholic church, fragments of the kingdom of God, reformation movements, and so on.[12]

The second period extends from about 1893 to 1907. "This is the stage of sect formation in the holiness movement," said Gaddis.[13] No less than twenty-five Holiness sects sprang into existence in various parts of the country during this period. The third period is labeled "the stage of consolidation."[14] Around 1907 various independent groups began to bind together into larger denominations. The Church of the Nazarene and the Pilgrim Holiness Church are examples of this amalgamation. Consolidation was also advanced by the formation of Holiness colleges and the unification of some of the independent periodicals.

According to Gaddis's analysis, the Church of God should be classified as one of those quasi-sects formed during the first period of the Holiness Movement that protested vigorously against being called a sect at all and preferred to be designated as a "reformation movement." By his thoughts the Church of God was not an isolated protest but rather one of many manifestations of the widespread religious dissatisfaction of its time.

This period of reform, like those that preceded it, produced its extremists. The Church of God was, and remains faced with the problem of distinguishing itself from more fanatical groups that voice essentially the same protest but engage in practices and other beliefs rejected by the movement itself. The extremists of the nineteenth-century Holiness Movement were of the familiar types—those with a strong chiliastic emphasis or who judged the genuineness of religious experience by the

---

12. Gaddis, "Christian Perfectionism in America," 449.
13. Ibid., 458.
14. Ibid., 460.

presence of accompanying psychological phenomena. From the very beginning the Church of God movement has been faced with the necessity of differentiating itself from other groups. Many of those other groups carried the same name but either set their theology in the framework of millenarianism, insisted on the glossolalia and perhaps some unusual motor phenomena as evidence of the presence of the Holy Spirit, or a combination of the two.

The Church of God failed to find a strong feeling of kinship with right-wing Holiness groups either, such as the Church of the Nazarene.[15] This distinction is explained by Aubrey L. Forrest by the fact that the Church of God was one of the Holiness groups that was largely unrelated to Methodism. Of these non-Methodistic groups it is said:

> There appeared at this time some movements which later crystallized into church bodies which, while holding the Wesleyan "second blessing" teaching, were unrelated to the Methodist church families, and as a result did not express their agitation of this doctrine in the same manner that these other groups did. To such groups, the restoration of old Methodistic class meetings, policies and institutions did not elicit emotional warmth and nostalgic longing. As a result, they did not unite with such movements as the Church of the Nazarene…or other "right-wing" holiness bodies which were attempting to construct a rejuvenated Methodism.
>
> …These groups, in general, were made up of persons who had experienced a radical "second blessing" experience such as was taught by Wesley, but who had a background in older established churches which discountenanced such experiences. Some were from Baptist groups, others from the Lutheran bodies, some from Mennonite bodies, while others came from Reformed groups.[16]

Forrest concludes that there was a third type of group in the Holiness Movement, non-Methodistic in its background and expressing its longing

---

15. In addition to Gaddis and Clark, this distinction in holiness groups is also made by Harold W. Reed, "The Growth of a Sect-Type Institution as Reflected in the Development of the Church of the Nazarene" (PhD diss., University of Southern California, Los Angeles, 1943) and by Melvin E. Dieter, *Revivalism and Holiness* (Ann Arbor, MI: University Microfilms, 1973).

16. Aubrey L. Forrest, "A Study of the Development of the Basic Doctrines and Institutional Patterns in the Church of God (Anderson, Indiana)" (PhD diss., University of Southern California, 1948), 64–65.

for holiness in terms observably different from the Methodist-rooted groups and generally urging a return to what they conceived to be the New Testament pattern of local autonomy for the individual congregation. "These groups," says Forrest, "are not premillennial nor given to ecstatic forms of worship, and express their pietistic teaching in modern psychological terms."[17] It is into this category that the Church of God falls.[18]

There are solid explanations for the non-Methodistic character of the Church of God. Many of its early leaders, including Daniel S. Warner, previously had associated with the Churches of God of North America, a religious body that began in 1825 in Harrisburg, Pennsylvania. John Winebrenner, a German Reformed Church pastor of a circuit of four churches in and around that city, was greatly influenced by the effects of revivalism and ecumenism in the Second Great Awakening in the pietistically oriented German population in that area in the early 1820s.[19] He himself professed a conversion experience and his preaching reflected his recently acquired revivalistic concern.

Not all Winebrenner's parishioners were pleased with this emphasis and some of them began to complain. It was said that he sometimes attended Methodist meetings, occasionally preached for them, and even advised people in his congregations to attend when it did not conflict with their own services. He was also accused of holding too many prayer meetings and "anxious" meetings and conducting them with too much noise and confusion. In the new revivalist style he invited those who sought prayer to come forward to the "anxious bench"; he allowed people to groan during prayer and to respond audibly to the sermon with amens. He also continued the meetings until a late hour of the night, and he opened his pulpit to unordained ministers. A more serious charge among the German Reformed was Winebrenner's refusal to baptize infants.[20]

The local vestry presented Winebrenner with a list of demands regarding his behavior and practice to which he refused consent. The following

---

17. Ibid.

18. The non-Methodistic character of the Church of God is substantiated in a survey made by Clear, "The Church of God," 130, of the denominational background of ninety-three correspondents to the *Gospel Trumpet* during the first five years of its publication. Almost half (forty-five of the ninety-three) were from non-Methodistic bodies. Included were four Mennonite and two Quaker.

19. An excellent biography of Winebrenner is that of Richard Kern, *John Winebrenner, Nineteenth-Century Reformer* (Harrisburg, PA: Central Publishing House, 1974).

20. Adapted from the account by S. G. Yahn, *History of the Churches of God in North America* (Harrisburg, PA: Central Publishing House, 1926), 28.

Sunday he found himself locked out of the church building and he soon received similar treatment from the other churches on his charge. He had lost his churches but retained a strong following among some of his people. Subsequent events led to the establishment of several congregations and the organization of the first eldership in 1830. His evangelistic efforts were fruitful and many more congregations were organized under the name Church of God, later (1896) to be changed to Churches of God. Other elderships were formed in western Pennsylvania, Ohio, and in Indiana, and the first General Eldership meeting was held in 1849. By that time the group had twelve thousand members.

Theologically, the Churches of God were basically orthodox Protestant. They abandoned the Calvinist stance of the German Reformed Church and declared themselves Arminian. Intensely biblical, they adopted no written creed but affirmed that the Word of God was their only rule of faith. In his sermon at that first eldership meeting Winebrenner stressed the centrality of the doctrine of the church. Afterward he stated:

> It was agreed, as the unanimous sense of the meeting: First. There is but one true church; namely, the Church of God. Secondly. That it is the bounden duty of all God's people to belong to her, and none else. Thirdly. That it is "lawful and right" to associate together for the purpose of cooperation in the cause of God.[21]

To the ordinances of baptism and the Lord's Supper the Churches of God added the practice of foot washing.

By the last quarter of the nineteenth century the group had become mostly English-speaking, expanded westward, and organized new elderships in Kansas, Nebraska, and Oklahoma. Winebrenner had begun a periodical called the *Gospel Publisher* in 1833, which became *The Church Advocate* in 1846. The church eldership had founded Findlay College in Ohio in 1882. This vigorous group had a formative influence on the basic concepts and practices of the later reform movement that would carry the same biblical name—the Church of God.

Another originally German-speaking religious group quite active in the Middle West was the Evangelical United Mennonite Church, a group that had separated from the main body of Mennonites for essentially the

---

21. As quoted by Christian H. Forney, *History of the Churches of God in the United States of North America* (Harrisburg, PA: Publishing House and Book Rooms of the Church of God, 1914), 313.

same reasons Winebrenner had been disfellowshiped by the German Reformed Church. Little is known about this group except that it was quite active in northern Indiana in the late 1870s, operated a publishing house in Goshen, and had an organized conference. The group is significant in consideration of the roots of the Church of God reformation in that Warner's, and perhaps others', brief but intimate contact, provided an influential exposure to the basic tenets of the Anabaptist tradition.[22] Warner and other Church of God leaders found great affinity with such beliefs as believers' baptism, voluntary submission to Christian disciplines, the rejection of "worldliness," the dual authority of the Bible and the Holy Spirit, the Church as a holy community with its members committed to a life-embracing discipleship, and strong eschatological emphasis for life on earth as well as hereafter.

Still another aspect of the period's religious climate must be mentioned for its significance to the Church of God reformation. This is the theme of Christian unity. Reports on the importance of this theme are mixed. Bishop Andrews's statement about "the greater unity of Christian people" was noted earlier. The fact that he was speaking at a meeting under the auspices of the Evangelical Alliance further illustrates that at least some divided denominations were friendly enough to join in common concerns. The Holiness Movement also transcended party lines and brought people together from different groups. Indeed, Holiness people sometimes testified to the experience of unity they put in the camp meetings of the National Association. The voluntary organizations like the Bible societies, the Young Men's Christian Association, the temperance societies, and many others functioned as bridges across denominational lines.

Some Christian groups, the most notable of which is the Christian Church and other spiritual descendants of Alexander Campbell and Barton W. Stone, made Christian unity one of the primary reasons for their existence.[23] The Sunday school movement also was interdenominational. Through a dynamic new agency, the International Sunday School Association, attempts were made to establish Sunday schools in every community in the nation and to establish uniform lesson outlines. The social gospel,

---

22. Warner spoke of "these beloved brethren" with great affection, noting a "feeling that our hearts are wonderfully knit together in love" (Diary, September 26, 1879).

23. An excellent treatment of this tradition is Lester G. McAllister and William E. Tucker, *Journey in Faith: A History of the Christian Church (Disciples of Christ)* (St. Louis: The Bethany Press, 1975).

likewise, functioned without reference to denominational affiliation and many camp meetings were nonsectarian.[24] All these movements and efforts would indicate that the boundary lines between denominations were crossed at many points and in significant ways.

On the other hand there is an even greater volume of evidence that denominational rivalry was intense, acrimonious, and sometimes even violent. Theological debate was a mainstay of nineteenth century American Christianity. Protestant-Catholic relationships were worsening, and many denominations were experiencing internal tension and even schism. One example of the kind of competitive spirit that prevailed in the Middle West is the treatment accorded some of the leaders of the Holiness Movement. As groups that were challenging the condition of society and the failure of existing churches to speak to that condition, Holiness people found that the strongest opposition often came from the clergy of established denominations. The very existence of the Holiness Movement implied a serious indictment of the spiritual state of the main Protestant bodies. Almost all of the holiness bands were forced to leave their denominational homes. Like other adherents to the doctrine of holiness, D. S. Warner and other leaders in the Church of God were subjected to ridicule and often denounced publicly. They were attacked not only by the long-established churches because of teaching holiness but also by their fellow holiness associationists for their stand on antidenominationalism. Warner's first biographer, A. L. Byers, described conditions in this fashion:

> Satanic forces were arrayed against the reformation work in every conceivable way, not only by mobs and undisguised, professional evil (though this form of attack was usually instigated by the sectarian element), but also by deception—by teachers and editors who were apparently right on some main question in order to deceive, but wrong on some other vital points.[25]

---

24. A report in the *New York Times*, September 5, 1880, indicated that a very successful "camp-meeting season" had just closed. Mention is made of the well-known camps at Ocean Grove, Shelter Island, Sea Cliff, Round Lake, Martha's Vineyard, Chautauqqua, and Thousand Islands. The story reported that such meetings were increasing in popularity and that facilities were being greatly improved.

25. Andrew L. Byers, *Birth of a Reformation, or the Life and Labors of D. S. Warner* (Anderson, IN: Gospel Trumpet Co., 1921), 286.

It is quite apparent, then, that the Church of God movement began in an atmosphere of intolerance and sharp polemic. To identify with such a group often was to abandon social status and suffer the severing of relations with former friends and relatives.[26] Those who followed did so because they were among the convinced; there was little chance for personal gain of any kind. Persecution and suffering of one kind or another could almost be guaranteed.

No review of the period's religious influences on the Church of God would be complete without mention of the great revivalists. Charles G. Finney had refined the evangelistic techniques of the frontier and moved the action to the rising cities even before the Civil War. Later his interests turned more toward teaching and writing, but his zeal and methods were picked up by an even more colorful evangelist by the name of Dwight L. Moody. A shoe salesman turned preacher and with burgeoning Chicago as his initial territory he teamed up with Ira D. Sankey as a singer. The revival had become routine by the time of the emergence of the Church of God movement; in the hands of the Moody-Sankey team revivalism was professionalized. Starting in 1873 in Great Britain they conducted evangelistic campaigns in London and in many of the great cities of America—Brooklyn, Philadelphia, New York, St. Louis, and on to the Pacific Coast. Audiences numbered into thousands, and the meetings were carefully orchestrated from preparation to follow-up. In essence his message was a simple declaration of the saving work of Jesus Christ and a call to the sinner to repent. He avoided controversial theological issues and showed no partiality of one denomination over another. His advice to all who repented, "Join some church at once," kept him out of sectarian crossfire. When Moody retired in 1892, there was really no one to take his place, but several successors continued to ply the city circuit. Among these were J. Wilbur Chapman, R. A. Torrey, Sam Jones, Benjamin F. Mills, and, after the turn of the century, Billy Sunday. These revivalists, however, had little effect on those groups that emerged from the Holiness Movement. The "big" evangelists concentrated on the cities while movements like the Church of God were digging their roots into the soil

---

26. The late Robert Reardon observed, only somewhat facetiously, that the Anderson Country Club members once denied membership to three groups in town: blacks, factory line-workers, and Church of God people. Current membership indicates that attitudes have changed at the Country Club.

of rural America.[27] However, revivalism's rhetorical style, which conceived and delivered sermons as persuasive speeches, profoundly shaped Church of God preaching for three generations.

It is difficult to put any final order to the religious situation in this period. As Ahlstrom said, "No aspect of American church history is more in need of summary and yet so difficult to summarize as the movements of dissent and reaction that occurred between the Civil War and World War I."[28] In seeking to explain the difficulty, he noted:

After 1865 the problems of Reconstruction, urbanization, immigration, natural science, and modern culture destroyed the great evangelical consensus, leaving a situation wherein dissenters were merely angry and frustrated. Increasingly, conservatives and liberals simply lost contact with each other, both culturally and religiously. Social and economic factors also seem to loom larger as divisive forces.... The older middle-class churches, whether countrified or urban,...alienated many and simply failed to attract others—who then sought religious solace where more earnestness and old-time fervor prevailed. Others...sought to reverse the tide of "apostasy" within their own Communions or...join[ed] more militant groups. Whether these conflicts, secessions, and new church formations were occasioned by doctrinal or more institutional forms of discontent, they all revealed deep fissures in Protestantism.[29]

In this context of religious confusion and accommodation to a new and changing cultural situation a new movement was born. Drawing heavily on a heritage of faith from the past and responding specifically to the concerns and needs of that present, a small group of reformers sought to follow their conception of God's will to bring the church out of confusion, revealing it in resplendent glory.

---

27. There were only occasional references to Moody and other revivalists in the pages of the Church of God's chief periodical, the *Gospel Trumpet*, during the years when they were so popular. They were not criticized but neither was there any great rejoicing about what was happening. The reform movement was interested but was working on its own important agenda.

28. Ahlstrom, *Religious History of the American People*, 823.

29. Ibid., 824.

CHAPTER 3

SORTING OUT THE ISSUES
(1880–1890)

In reviewing significant events in the religious world for 1881, the *New York Times* noted that the unquestionably chief event of the year had been the publication simultaneously in England and America of the Revised Version of the New Testament. After elaborating on the general reception and import of this scholarly achievement mentioning other notable religious events in Britain, the commentator turned his attention to America and observed, "The Churches of the United States have been little disturbed by controversy or by unusual movements of any kind. Moody and Sankey worked rather quietly in San Francisco, but there has been no general revival excitement."[1]

The *Times* assessment was accurate; there was not a great deal of religious excitement in 1881. The great revivals in Brooklyn, New York, Philadelphia, Boston, and Chicago that had attracted so much attention in the 1870s were past, and there was even some evidence of reaction in the mainline churches against these extraordinary efforts of former years. The *Times* editor expressed his personal hope that "the operation of the ordinary and quieter methods have produced quite as favorable results."

The *Times* editor was incorrect, however, when he noted the year had produced no "unusual movements of any kind." There was no way for him to have known of two related events taking place in the American Middle West in October of 1881. These events marked the beginning of an unusual movement that soon characterized itself as a religious reform affecting the whole of Christianity.

The setting for the first of these events was a small frame country church on the outskirts of the lakeside village of Beaver Dam in Kosciusco County

---

1. *New York Times*, January, 1882, 6.

This building in the village of Beaver Dam, Indiana, housed the congregation of the Northern Indiana Eldership of the Churches of God from which D. S. Warner withdrew in 1881.

in north central Indiana. The occasion was the annual meeting on October 1, 1881, of the Northern Indiana Eldership of the Church of God, a small denomination that had been formed in 1876 to protest the failure of the parent denomination, the Indiana Eldership of the Churches of God (Winebrennerian), to pass a resolution denouncing freemasonry and other secret societies. Unlike its parent body, the new group was open also to the "second blessing" teaching of the Holiness Movement. The new denomination had experienced modest growth in five years and additional elderships had been established in Michigan, Missouri, and Kansas. The number of congregations was still small with probably no more than a dozen located in the northern Indiana geographic area. It is likely that fewer than thirty people attended the Beaver Dam Eldership meeting.[2]

There would have been little to note in this Saturday meeting had it not been for some proposals presented by Daniel S. Warner, editor of the

2. *Gospel Trumpet* (September 1, 1881), 2 announces there will be a general meeting of the Churches of God in Indiana, Michigan, Missouri and Kansas on October 4, 1881, at Beaver Dam, Indiana, this indicating expansion to three additional states. Data has been gathered from a number of subsequent references, most notably Byers, *Birth of a Reformation*, 282–85.

denomination's periodical, the *Gospel Trumpet*.[3] Warner had been associated with this fellowship for three years and was a minister in good standing. He had been appointed pastor of a congregation in Indianapolis and his position as editor marked him as a respected leader. Most members of the Eldership were not quite prepared, however, for the changes he proposed for the denomination's structure and mode of operation. Although the exact wording of his proposals has not been preserved, his intent is indicated in biographer A. L. Byers' statement that Warner set forth "some measures by which that body might be made to conform more perfectly to the Bible standard with reference to government."[4] It is likely Warner proposed (a) that the Eldership abandon the practice of granting ministerial licenses and simply recognize all preachers who bore the fruits of their call and (b) that established procedures for admitting church members be eliminated with each congregation opening its fellowship to all persons who had been truly regenerated and evidenced a sincere desire to do the will of God.

After some discussion the Eldership rejected Warner's proposals. His response was quick and deliberate. He stood to his feet and announced that he was convinced that sectarian division of the church was sinful and that he could no longer continue his affiliation with a religious body that persisted in maintaining the characteristics of a humanly formed sect; he was taking his stand with Christ alone, free from all encumbering party labels and human constructions. Apparently the negative vote on his proposals had not been unanimous, so he was encouraged to go further and ask if there were others who would take the same bold step with him. Five individuals rose to their feet—David Leininger, Mr. and Mrs. William Ballinger, and Mr. and Mrs. Fred Krause. Later, several others declared their freedom from "sect

---

3. By March 1, 1881 (the earliest available edition), the *Gospel Trumpet* did not carry in its masthead a designation that it was the official organ of the Northern Indiana Eldership of the Church of God, but the various announcements regarding Eldership affairs would indicate that the paper continued to have the same function as the *Herald of Gospel Freedom*, which Warner had edited and which did contain a statement of sponsorship, a term which apparently did not imply ownership of the equipment by the denomination or the obligation to subsidize the costs. The Eldership simply gave its blessing and moral support and the editor was responsible for the whole enterprise. On December 23, 1880, the Board of Publication and the Standing Committee of the Eldership approved a merger of the *Herald* with another paper, *The Pilgrim*, edited by G. Haines and published in Indianapolis. The merged periodical was given a new name, the *Gospel Trumpet*, and the first issue appeared January 1, 1881, from Rome City, Indiana, with Warner and Haines listed as joint editors. By June 1, 1881, Warner had bought Haines' interest for $100.00 and became the sole owner and editor of the publication. In separating from the Eldership on October 1, 1881, Warner lost only the blessing of that denomination and continued to publish the paper.

4. Byers, *Birth of a Reformation*, 282.

Babylon" and joined the five in a new kind of open fellowship that they envisioned as a prototype for the whole of God's Church in the world.[5]

Later that month, on October 15, about 160 miles to the north in Carson City, Michigan, at the annual meeting of a sister dissident group, the Northern Michigan Eldership of the Churches of God,[6] a similar confrontation occurred with almost parallel results. Warner was not a member of this Eldership, of course, but his good friends, Joseph C. and Allie R. Fisher who were members, had invited him to come to their hometown to conduct Holiness revival services for two days prior to the Eldership meeting. The Fishers had affiliated with the Michigan group in the fall of 1878, and Joseph had met Warner on a business trip to Indiana in the spring of 1880. The Fishers had heard him preach at that time, had accepted the doctrine of holiness, and received the experience of sanctification. In the fall of that year they had invited Warner to come to Michigan and preach holiness. During the summer of 1881, after Warner had been forced to buy out a partner's interest in the *Gospel Trumpet,* J. C. Fisher apparently had given Warner sufficient financial assistance to be considered a new partner in the enterprise, for the masthead of the September 1 issue of the paper reads, "Edited and Published in the name of the Lord Jesus Christ, by D. S. Warner and J. C. Fisher."[7] By the fall of 1881 Warner and the Fishers had found considerable common ground in their theological perspectives.

The obvious strategy in preparation for the Michigan Eldership meeting was to have Warner come early and through his preaching on holiness and the evils of sectarianism try to convince the voting members that they should do away with human machinery in the church and adopt proposals similar to those presented to the Indiana group. The Fishers' hopes for such an outcome were crushed, however, when strong opposition arose and the vote was again negative. Following this defeat the Fishers, along with about eighteen other individuals, followed Warner's example and withdrew from the Northern Michigan Eldership, declaring themselves to be free from the shackles of sectarianism.

---

5. Ibid., 285.

6. The Northern Michigan Eldership had been formed at Pompeii, Gratiot County, Michigan, at about the same time (1876) as the Northern Indiana Eldership, withdrawing from the Michigan Eldership of the Churches of God for the same reasons—secret societies, which they opposed and holiness, which they espoused.

7. *Gospel Trumpet* (September 1, 1881), 1. Fisher never moved to Indianapolis to actually assist in the editorial work, but he frequently wrote articles and letters. By early 1882 his title was changed to "Corresponding Editor."

The Michigan group apparently had anticipated the need of a precise definition of the issues involved and had given more thought to clarifying and specifically stating their views than the earlier cluster in Indiana. They declared their common convictions in the form of a series of resolutions:

Whereas we recognize ourselves in the perilous times of the last days, the time in which Michael is standing up for the deliverance of God's true saints (Dan. 12:1), the troublesome times in which the true house of God is being built again, therefore,

Resolved, That we will endeavor by all the grace of God to live holy, righteous, and godly in Christ Jesus, "looking for, and hastening unto the coming of the Lord Jesus Christ," who we believe is nigh, even at the door.

Resolved, That we adhere to no body or organization but the church of God, bought by the blood of Christ, organized by the Holy Spirit, and governed by the Bible. And if the Lord will, we will hold an annual assembly of all saints who in the providence of God shall be permitted to come together for the worship of God, the instruction and edification of one another, and the transaction of such business as the Holy Spirit may lead us to see and direct in its performance.

Resolved, That we ignore and abandon the practice of preacher's license as without precept of example in the Word of God, and that we wish to be "known by our fruits" instead of by papers.

Resolved, That we do not recognize or fellowship any who come unto us assuming the character of a minister whose life is not godly in Christ Jesus and whose doctrine is not the Word of God.

Resolved also, That we recognize and fellowship, as members with us in the one body of Christ all truly regenerated and sincere saints who worship God in all the light they possess, and that we urge all the dear children of God to forsake the snares and yokes of human parties and stand alone in the "one fold" of Christ upon the Bible, and in the unity of the Spirit.[8]

On the surface there appears to be nothing unusual about these two related instances of broken fellowship in a church organization. On hundreds of other occasions in Christian history, particularly since the

---

8. As quoted in Byers, *Birth of a Reformation*, 289.

sixteenth century, a group of disaffected members of some particular religious body have identified what they deemed important differences with the parent organization and, finding the mainline party unwilling to change, have withdrawn and formed their own groups. The two elderships here described were themselves prime examples of the splintering process. Taking a stand that resulted in separation was nothing new in 1881; it was already commonplace in Protestantism and has often been repeated since.

Just what, then, was either different or significant in these unheralded incidents in rural Indiana and Michigan? In the light of subsequent developments in both thought and deed at least three important distinctives seem to be evident.[9] (1) Although the separations took place in relation to particular religious sects each was in fact a rejection of *all* religious sects. The issue was not just a quarrel with either of the elderships involved but a challenge to the whole denominational system. (2) In each case those who separated deliberately avoided the formation of a new organization. In keeping with their concept of the Church they refused to substitute their own inventions for those they had rejected. In the words of the Carson City resolutions, they identified themselves only as an open fellowship of "all truly regenerated and sincere saints who worship God in all the light they possess." (3) They resisted the temptation to define their identity in terms of a creedal statement that would segregate them from other Christians; their reliance on the Word and the Holy Spirit was affirmed but the specifics of belief were left open.

Against the backdrop of Christian history these distinctives have a familiar ring. In early nineteenth-century America the Stone-Campbell movement, which produced the Christian Church (Disciples of Christ, Church of Christ, and so forth) sought to transcend the denominational system. The sixteenth-century Swiss Brethren (Anabaptists, Mennonites, and so forth) had envisioned the Church as a voluntary fellowship of the truly regenerated. Quakers and many other groups have rejected formal creeds and emphasized the Bible and the Holy Spirit as sufficient guides to all truth. The one distinguishing feature of these 1881 declarations lay in their combination of all these emphases in a single package that they then wedded to the Wesleyan doctrine of holiness. In this form these convictions formed the ingredients of a cause that could not be restricted to an obscure rural setting.

9. A more complete discussion of the theological rationale for the movement follows in chapter 4.

Quickly they were conceived in global terms and described by these devotees as a "mighty reformation."

To adequately understand the events of that October in 1881 and the subsequent development of this religious reform movement it is necessary to review the spiritual pilgrimage of D. S. Warner. He was the person primarily responsible for developing and articulating the concepts around which the new movement came to be focused.[10] Daniel Sidney Warner was born June 25, 1842, in a small town in eastern Ohio, now known as Marshallville. The following year his father, David Warner, sold the tavern that he had operated for eight years and moved the family to a 140-acre farm in Crawford County near New Washington. It was here that Warner spent his boyhood and youth. During the Civil War in 1863 the Warner family made another westward move to Williams County, Ohio, in the northwest corner of the state near the town of Montpelier. After brief service in the Union army, Warner spent parts of two years (1865–1866) attending Oberlin College, and also teaching in the public schools.[11]

Daniel S. Warner (1842–95), cofounder and first editor of the *Gospel Trumpet*. In the autumn of 1881, his calls to forsake denominations, first at Beaver Dam, Indiana, and subsequently at Carson City, Michigan, led to the formation of the Church of God reformation movement.

During this postwar period, while Warner was in his early twenties, he became genuinely concerned about religious matters. Having been reared in an almost completely irreligious atmosphere, it is small wonder that his first reaction to things of the spirit was almost entirely negative. He revolted

---

10. Because of a strong conviction regarding the divine origin and restoration of the church, there has been resistance from the earliest days of the movement to the present to designate Warner or anyone else as the founder of the Church of God. Even so, there is little doubt that Warner's beliefs and activities were the major catalyst in bringing the movement into self-consciousness.

11. For more complete biographical treatments of Warner, see Byers, *Birth of a Reformation*; John W. V. Smith, *Heralds of a Brighter Day* (Anderson, IN: Gospel Trumpet Co., 1955), Chapter 2; John A. Morrison and Joseph Allison, *Vital Christianity*, successive issues from June 9, 1974, to January 19, 1975; and Barry L. Callen, *It's God's Church* (Anderson, IN: Warner Press, 1995).

against the prevailing form of religion that he found in his community and for a time declared himself an infidel.

His rebellion, however, was apparently only superficial, for he never lost a keen sensitivity of conscience. Little by little he began to ask questions that only Christianity can answer. In February of 1865 a series of protracted meetings was being conducted in a schoolhouse near his home. The evangelist was from the Churches of God in North America, and Warner attended several services with some of the other fellows in the community. One night he announced to his friends that he was "going forward." They thought he was joking and expected him to pull some prank. But Warner was in dead earnest. He did go forward as he had promised, but not to pull any pranks. He earnestly sought to make his peace with God and was genuinely converted. This experience changed the whole course of his life. "Thank God for that step," he later wrote. "Oh, how glad I am that it was ever my lot to become a Christian!"[12] From that time on he never ceased to be a sincere seeker for divine truth and a fearless follower of the will of God as he understood it. For some time Warner struggled with the question of how God wanted him to spend his life. By the fall of 1866 he was convinced that he was being divinely called to the Christian ministry. He began his preparation immediately by arranging for a room at his parents' home where he spent most of the winter in private study of the Scriptures and other books he had at his disposal.[13] It was not until the following spring that he had the opportunity to do any preaching. The Methodists were holding a protracted meeting in the Cogswell schoolhouse near Warner's home. When they learned he was entering the ministry, they invited him to preach an evangelistic message. On Easter night 1867 he delivered his first sermon.

Warner's choice of a religious body with which to affiliate was a deliberate matter. He examined the beliefs and practices of several of the denominations that had churches in his neighborhood and compared them with

12. Warner Diary, June 17, 1874. Warner kept a diary from November of 1872 to January of 1880, the original of which is in the Anderson University and Church of God Archives. Since this diary exists only in manuscript form (except for a typescript) and is not arranged according to volumes, all citations will be given by date of entry.

13. Whether Warner realized that he was then located in one of the strongest ministerial training centers in America, it is hard to surmise. Charles G. Finney, the great evangelist, was just retiring as president of Oberlin and continued to teach in the seminary for several years. Warner undoubtedly had opportunity to hear him preach, if not to sit in his classes. His lack of understanding of the usual requirements for ministerial preparation and his desire to get started as soon as possible apparently led him to reject the opportunity available to him at Oberlin.

the interpretation of biblical truth he had acquired from his own study. He eventually chose to join the group officially known as the General Eldership of the Churches of God in North America, though the more common designation was the Winebrennerian Church of God. Warner was licensed to preach by the group's West Ohio Eldership in October 1867. The next ten years of his life were crowded with the kind of activities demanded by Christian ministry of that day. He served pastorates in northwestern Ohio for six years, spent two years in pioneer mission work in southeastern Nebraska, and then returned to Ohio for another pastoral appointment. He was hard working, diligent, conscientious, and more than moderately successful in his ministry.[14]

Unity and Holiness

During this decade of ministry in the Churches of God in North America Warner had the opportunity for close involvement in the give and take of religious competition in America. He also experienced the internal tensions of ecclesiastical institutions. In this context the two foci of his later reforming work were formulated and sharpened. The first of these, Christian unity, was already an important emphasis in the General Eldership, and here Warner found encouragement and support for his attacks on the sectarian system. John Winebrenner himself had called on all "Christians and Christian ministers…to rally and unite the children of God, who are now divided and scattered abroad, into one body, according to the form and manner of the apostolic church."[15] Furthermore, Winebrenner had laid down a challenge: "If the doctrine of Christian union is true, then division and sectarianism are a great and prodigious evil, and therefore ought to be abolished. Who then will lay the axe at the root of this corrupt tree, to help to cut it down?"[16]

In choosing to affiliate with the Churches of God after his conversion, Warner had noted the biblical name and even then was impressed by the group's claim to be a scriptural church rather than a sect framed by beliefs of a person or party. One of his earliest diary entries refers to a schoolhouse

---

14. See Christian H. Forney, *History of the Churches of God in the United States of America* (Harrisburg: Publishing House of the Churches of God 1914).

15. John Winebrenner, *Doctrinal and Practical Sermons* (Lebanon, PA: General Eldership of the Church of God, 1868), 256.

16. Ibid., 257.

meeting near Holland, Ohio, in which a man had left his sect amid a storm of persecution. Warner's comment was, "But he was firm and now commands the position. Every foe had fled and all that truly fear God join in to encourage the truth. Some will doubtless soon cut loose from sectarian bondage."[17] A few months later Warner preached two nights in Larue, Ohio, and reported:

> It had been announced in the Larue Citizen that I would speak on the Church of God. This brought out quite a large congregation. Both nights I spoke plainly and boldly against the evil of sectarianism and other abominations. Many were ill at ease. Some preachers were present. The Lord gave me good liberty.[18]

In the pioneer work of his Nebraska mission Warner continued his affirmation of the one true Body of Christ. His 1874 Easter sermon was on the theme of the church. He observed that, "the truth was well received."[19] After noting various responses, he wrote, "Another good old Methodist Episcopal brother who preaches some sanctioned my sermon all through, even my strongest denunciation of creeds, sects, etc."[20] Not always was the reception so favorable. A year later Warner reports preaching a sermon in which he "proved the oneness of Christians; the fact that this oneness is not manifest in the world; that it should be; and how." In response one man got up, he said, and "harangued in favor of sects....After meeting, Brother B _____, another poor sectarianized soul, pitched into me."[21] Even a good friend expressed fear that Warner had spoiled the good feeling of the meeting by preaching on the church. His response was a prayer: "Oh that the world were freed from the curse of human creeds, that men could be at liberty to obey God!"[22] Even on the sparsely settled Nebraska prairies Warner found numerous occasions to voice his great concern for Christian unity and his abhorrence of the divisive forces in institutional Christianity. His return to Ohio by the fall of 1875 did not lessen this concern. Illustrative of his continuing concern is Warner's response to a call in the spring of 1876 to go to Upper Sandusky, where some sectarians were causing trouble.

17. Warner Diary, November 13, 1872.
18. Warner Diary, May 30, 1873.
19. Warner Diary, April 5, 1874.
20. Ibid.
21. Warner Diary, March 14, 1875.
22. Ibid.

After observing some blatant, overt proselytizing activities and sizing up the situation, he lamented, "O Sectarianism! thou abomination of the earth, thou bane of the cause of God, when will thy corrupt and wicked walls fall to earth and cease to curse men to hell?"[23]

The other focal point in Warner's reforming emphasis—holiness—was later in developing. He had encountered some proponents of Wesleyan teachings along this line early in his ministry and had reacted very negatively. In 1872, for example, he reported attending an evangelistic meeting:

> Nearly all blew loudly the horn of sanctification but manifested little of its fruits, such as travail of soul for the sinner and sympathy for the one soul at the altar, to whom none gave a word of encouragement, but each in turn arose and boasted of his holiness. Oh the delusions of Satan! How manifold they are![24]

Just over four years later, however, Warner had become positively interested in the doctrine of holiness and sanctification as a second work of grace. A number of factors entered into this change of attitude. His father-in-law was active in the Holiness Movement, and Warner's wife claimed the experience of sanctification. Through them Warner met others associated with the Holiness cause and had opportunity to discuss the doctrine. By early 1877 he was at least willing to begin a reexamination of his previous judgment. He studied the Scripture passages used to support the belief, and he sought counsel from those who preached it. The person who was, perhaps, most influential in leading him to full acceptance of the doctrine was a Baptist minister by the name of C. R. Dunbar who was at this time working with the Ohio Holiness Alliance.[25]

Warner and Dunbar talked through April 1877. By the summer Warner was preaching sermons on holiness, and by the first part of July he was so thoroughly convinced that the Bible taught entire sanctification as a second work of grace that he began to seek the experience for himself. He had been an evangelistic preacher for ten years and had seen over seven hundred people bow at the altar as a result of his ministry, but Warner himself walked around to the public altar on the night of July 5, following one of his own sermons. Neither that night nor the next did he feel the assurance that he

---

23. Warner Diary, April 2, 1876.
24. Warner Diary, November 11, 1872.
25. Warner Diary, April 13, 1877.

had found the experience that he sought, but on the third night he was able to record triumphantly in his diary, "Hallelujah, it is done!"[26] It did not take long to shift the major emphasis of his ministry to the proclamation of this doctrine. Not only did he preach it; he also began to write about it. Within a week of receiving the experience, he noted, "Commenced article for the *Advocate* on sanctification."[27] Two weeks later he said, "Finished my second article on sanctification."[28] Within months he was at work on the manuscript of a book on the same subject titled *Bible Proofs of the Second Work of Grace.*[29] It is small wonder that he quickly acquired a reputation as a preacher and writer on holiness.

In many ways, the period 1877–78 was probably the most crucial in Warner's life. In July 1877 he had received the experience of entire sanctification. His enthusiasm in proclaiming this doctrine and his cooperation with other ministers in the Holiness associations soon brought criticism from some of his colleagues in the West Ohio Eldership. By September formal charges were brought against him by W. H. Oliver, who accused Warner of inviting a "sect of fanatics calling themselves the Holy Alliance Band to hold meetings in the local Churches of God," of bringing schism among those churches, of slighting the ordinances of the Lord's Supper and foot washing by taking less than one hour to observe them, and of stating that he had been preaching his own doctrine even prior to his experience of sanctification.[30] His case was heard by the Eldership and the charges were sustained, but Warner was recommended favorably for renewal of his license on the condition that he not bring Holiness workers to hold meetings in the Churches of God without their consent. He agreed to the restriction and was assigned a circuit in the Canton area.[31]

Hardly had Warner arrived on his circuit when he began to feel that it

---

26. Warner Diary, July 5, 6, 7, 1877. In these three lengthy diary entries, Warner described in considerable detail both his thought and feelings as well as the events, indicating the depth of intensity and the import of this experience for the rest of his life and ministry.

27. Warner Diary, July 14, 1877.

28. Warner Diary, July 28, 1877.

29. D. S. Warner, *Bible Proofs of the Second Work of Grace* (Goshen, IN: E. U. Mennonite Publishing Society, 1880).

30. Warner Diary, September 16, 1877. He reproduced the contents of a formal letter dated September 15, 1877, stating these changes, which were not reviewed until the Eldership meeting on October 1, 1877. He also gave his own explanation and defense against these changes.

31. Warner Diary, October 1, 1877. Forney, *History of the Churches of God*, 567, confirms this action by reporting: "D. S. Warner's case was acted on charitably. His 'license was renewed with certain restrictions—that he cease to spring this so-called Holiness Alliance Band or any other outside party he may stand connected with, upon the churches of God.'"

was not God's will that he should be there. He was strongly impressed to spend full time in evangelistic work. He resigned his appointment in November and moved his family to Upper Sandusky to the home of his wife's parents. By December he was in a revival in Findlay, Ohio, which had been moved from the Church of God Bethel to the courthouse after the second night because the local elders would not approve the use of their facilities for a "holiness meeting."[32] The fact that he continued the meetings at another location in the same city was regarded by certain members of the West Ohio Eldership as a breach of the agreement he had made the previous year. It did not take long for the Standing Committee to act. On January 30, 1878, he was accused and expelled. The formal charges were: (1) transcending the restrictions of the Eldership, (2) violating rules of cooperation, and (3) participating in dividing the church.[33] In Warner's words, however, he was disfellowshiped "for preaching full salvation, for following the Holy Spirit, and for helping to save over 150 souls" in Findlay.[34]

Upon hearing that his license had been withheld, Warner expressed the feeling that, from the standpoint of his attachment to the Church of God and its principles, this decision was a "dreadful calamity and intolerable to bear." He had the sweet assurance that "my dear Father, to whom I belonged, would turn this and everything else (as long as I lay on the altar) to my good and his glory. Praise his holy name!"[35] As Warner thought further about the meaning of this action in relation to his own ministry he began to see the implications of his ideas not only for the Eldership but the whole of Christianity. That this light began to dawn on him on that crucial day is indicated by a diary entry written over a month later when he recalled:

On the 31st of last January the Lord showed me that holiness could never prosper upon sectarian soil encumbered by human creeds and party names, and gave me a new commission to join holiness and all truth together and build up the apostolic church of the living God. Praise his name! I will obey him.[36]

---

32. The events of the Findlay meetings are given in considerable detail in Warner's diary entries from December 24, 1877, to January 3, 1878. Also forced to move from the courthouse, he received a promise of use of "Reform House," but this was also closed. He then went to a United Brethren church to conclude the meetings.

33. Warner Diary, January 30, 1878.

34. Ibid.

35. Warner Diary, January 31, 1878.

36. Warner Diary, March 7, 1878.

Not yet did Warner realize the full import of his insight. At that moment he had no strategy for carrying out his resolution, and he had no way of knowing that others whom he had yet to meet were beginning to think along similar lines. The new commission was interpreted strictly in terms of his own ministry. No reformation was launched, but apparently some consideration was given to the identification of independent congregations. One 1878 diary entry written following an evangelistic meeting notes, "Fellowshipped some fourteen souls in the Church of God formed on a congregational basis, with holiness the principal foundation stone."[37] No further reference is made to any similar action. He had no specific plans for developing a personal following.

The years following that "dreadful" January day in 1878 were by no means idle. He had made up his mind to be a Holiness evangelist, and set himself to that task. He went wherever he had calls, and these were not lacking. He went from city to city and from one country schoolhouse to another, preaching holiness. Sometimes he did not wait for a call but made his own opportunity. He took advantage of every situation. Warner was not content, however, to continue as a lone preacher. He definitely could not be called an independent. He had prayed, "God save the church," too many times to sever connections with his brothers and sisters. His main concern at this time seems to have been to find a group with which he could affiliate and where he would be free to preach the message on his heart.

Calls for evangelistic meetings in Indiana in the spring and summer of 1878 brought him in contact with a group that seemed to answer this need. It was the Northern Indiana Eldership of the Churches of God, the already mentioned severed branch of the same denomination from which he had been expelled and a fellowship open to the preaching of holiness. The better acquainted Warner became with this group, the more convinced he was that there he could feel at home. Accordingly he made a great effort to attend their Eldership meeting in October 1878 even though he was still weak from an illness. At this meeting he was both accepted into their fellowship and made associate editor, along with editor I. W. Lowman, of the group's authorized periodical, the *Herald of Gospel Freedom*, published at Walcottville, Indiana.[38]

Warner's connection with the *Herald* soon developed into a very significant relationship. By March 1879, he had entered into full partnership

_____

37. Ibid.
38. Warner Diary, October 5, 1878.

with Lowman and was listed as the magazine's joint editor and publisher. A little over a year later he become sole editor and was seeking to consolidate with some other Holiness publication in order to expand. An offer came from a G. Haines in Indianapolis who was publishing a paper called *The Pilgrim*. On December 23, 1880, the Northern Indiana Eldership voted to merge their paper with Haines's magazine, with the two men forming a partnership in the venture. Instead of taking the name of either, the new paper, at Warner's suggestion, was given a new name. The first issue of the *Gospel Trumpet,* published in Rome City, Indiana, appeared on January 1, 1881.[39] It was largely through the medium of this paper that the impact of his subsequent work was to be felt.

While affiliated with the Northern Indiana Eldership Warner continued his battle against the evil of division in the church. Because of the premises on which it had been founded, he perceived his new group to be nonsectarian in character and saw no inconsistency in attacking other denominations while defending his own. Likewise, he apparently believed it possible to mitigate the sin of sectarianism by the merger of like-minded groups. In 1879, along with his evangelistic and editorial pursuits, he became the chief promoter of a proposal to merge the Eldership with the Evangelical United Mennonite Church. He had come in contact with some of the ministers of this Mennonite group and was impressed with the similarity between their ideas and the Eldership's. In speaking of one such contact, he said, "I pray God we may become one fold."[40] In September he visited the meeting of their conference and was instrumental in arranging for Northern Indiana Eldership's reception of the Mennonite delegate to their meeting. By December a joint meeting of official representatives from the two groups had been arranged and resolutions for a merger were formulated.[41] The records do not indicate the final outcome of this proposal, but the two bodies apparently never worked out a suitable arrangement. Warner, however, remained on friendly terms with the Mennonites, for his book *Bible Proofs of the Second Work of Grace* was published at Goshen in 1880 by the E. U. Mennonite Publishing Society.

---

39. Byers, *Birth of a Reformation*, 237–38.

40. Warner Diary, August 6, 1879.

41. Warner Diary, December 5, 1879. Warner quoted in full a two-paragraph preamble and three resolutions that were designed to form the basis for a consolidation of the two groups. A joint convention to consider these was held at Hawpatch, Indiana.

Another venture in formal ecumenical relations developed in the spring of 1881 with the Salvation Army in Indianapolis. A news item in the *Trumpet* under the heading of "Salvation Army Notes" reports an April 16 business meeting in which new officers for the Army were named. The account reads, "Eld. C. C. Bogert was continued General in command. D. S. Warner was elected Adjutant-General." The names of other officers follow, and the article concludes with the statement that, "each *Trumpet* will give reports of the battles and conquests of the Lord's Salvation Army."[42] Events of the next few months cut short this congenial relationship, for by early 1882 he wrote,

> O how the enemy of God tries to get God's little ones to looking at something else besides the body of Christ. "Our Church," "Eldership," "Salvation Army," or anything that he can get the people to "join," instead of simply being "joined to the Lord," is a trick of satan [sic] to rob God, and separate souls from Christ the "head and only name."[43]

During his years with the Northern Indiana Eldership, Warner also accelerated his participation in the Holiness associations. Both the *Herald* and the *Trumpet* contain frequent announcements and reports of both local and regional Holiness meetings with an indication that he attended many of these. One meeting of particular import was the Western Union Holiness Convention held at Jacksonville, Illinois, December 15-19, 1880. This was a general meeting with participants from "all of the great West."[44] Warner was one of the speakers at this convention, and his name is listed as a member of the General Committee charged with the responsibility of calling future Union Holiness Conventions.

During the years after his expulsion from the General Eldership ministry Warner never lost sight of his new commission, as he continued to oppose sectarianism and uphold holiness. He was still floundering, however, as to the proper method for accomplishing what he felt God had called him to do. Although he was never free from misgivings, his dual affiliation with the Northern Indiana Eldership and the National Holiness Association seemed to provide a satisfactory arrangement, at least for a

---

42. *Gospel Trumpet*, May 1, 1881, 2.

43. *Gospel Trumpet*, February 8, 1882, 2.

44. *Proceedings of the Western Union Holiness Convention* (Bloomington, IL: Western Holiness Association, 1881), 16, 30–33.

time. Neither of these groups attempted to throttle either his preaching or his editorial activity, and so he had no cause to be particularly unhappy with either of them. By early 1881, Warner was beginning to feel uneasy about these relationships. The first to be called into question was his membership in the Indiana State Holiness Association. He was especially concerned about the clause in the organization's constitution that stipulated that "it shall consist of members of various Christian organizations and seek to work in harmony with all these societies."[45] One day in April, while in Hardinsburg, Indiana, with two of his colleagues, he spent a day in prayer about this matter. He came out of that prayer meeting with some definite conclusions. "The Spirit of the Lord showed me," he said, "the inconsistency of repudiating sects and yet belonging to an association that is based on sect recognition. We promised God to withdraw from all such compacts."[46]

On May 20–21 Warner went to the annual meeting of the association in Terre Haute and introduced a resolution to have the "sect-endorsing clause" removed from the constitution. He suggested a substitute wording that would make membership in the association open to "all true Christians everywhere." The substitute clause was defeated. Warner reported this incident in the *Gospel Trumpet* and then declared, "And now we wish to announce to all that we wish to co-operate with all Christians, as such, in saving souls—but forever withdraw from all organisms that uphold and endorse sects and denominations in the body of Christ."[47] In the months that followed, his affiliation with the Northern Indiana Eldership came in for the same kind of scrutiny, as already noted, and he was soon free from affiliation with any organized ecclesiastical institution.

These incidents mark the beginning of a new era in Warner's career. His inward struggle with inconsistencies was resolved. He quit looking for a suitable church home. His spiritual floundering was past. He had found the freedom in Christ for which he had so long sought. A new ingredient entered his life. It was as if he had been released from a great burden and for the first time was able to stand erect. He felt as though he had stepped from the condemnatory shadow of his own and all other sectarian walls and now stood in the full light of truth—the "evening light" of which the

---

45. As quoted in an editorial, *Gospel Trumpet*, June 1, 1881, 2.
46. Ibid. The meeting took place on April 22, 1881.
47. Ibid.

prophet Zechariah had spoken.[48] There was indeed cause for rejoicing. God, he believed, had begun a new day for the church.

Almost immediately a new note of exuberance and a new sense of urgency were evident in all that Warner did. He turned to the Scriptures for further corroboration of the truth he comprehended. He had studied the Bible for years, but now he began to see in its pages a great unfolding drama of revealed truth, and he sought to grasp it more perfectly. His writing changed as a result. Warner had long been a proficient writer, but now he wrote with a vigor of expression and a positiveness previously unseen. The *Gospel Trumpet* was not only the vehicle for expressing his own views, but it also became the instrument for identifying and communicating with others who shared his convictions. Identify themselves and communicate they did. Even before Warner's contact with the Fishers and others in Michigan, there were congenial encounters with and between several people in Ohio, Indiana, and Illinois who were to become leaders in the new enterprise. By the middle of the decade of the eighties a new movement was under way, and by the end of another decade the shape of its future was largely formed.

---

48. Zechariah 14:6–7.

CHAPTER 4

THE FLYING ROLL
AND THE FLYING MESSENGERS
(1880–1895)

It is something of an anomaly that neither of the geographic locations where the saints first took their stand became a center from which the movement spread. Congregations were gathered in the areas of both Beaver Dam, Indiana, and Carson City, Michigan, and annual camp meetings later developed near each, but the generative forces for the new movement were not attached to either a geographic locale or a colony of committed adherents. Without benefit of any strategic plan, the two chief instruments for propagating this new found truth were very mobile: (1) *The Gospel Trumpet,* a magazine sometimes referred to as "the flying roll," whose existence was so tenuous that its place of publication changed six times in its first seven years,[1] and (2) an increasing number of wide-ranging itinerant ministers whose travels were so deliberately persistent and extensive they referred to themselves as "flying messengers."[2] Flying roll and flying messengers were so intertwined that it is impossible to separate them functionally. The itinerants used the magazine to bolster the content of their message, to keep them in touch with each other, and to receive direction for future travels. The magazine depended on the traveling messengers to boost circulation, write

---

1. In the mid-1880s, the *Gospel Trumpet* carried in its heading a line-drawing depicting an angel blowing a trumpet from which hung a scroll inscribed with verses from Zechariah 5. This flying roll drawing was interpreted in the July 1, 1884, issue as representing "the many printed heralds of God's salvation and straight truth that so vividly 'go forth over the face of the whole earth,' in this age of lightning speed." See Harold L. Phillips, *Miracle of Survival*, Warner Press, 1979, 31–32.

2. This descriptive term apparently was derived from the language of Revelation 14:6: "And I saw another angel fly in the midst of heaven, having the everlasting gospel to preach unto them that dwell on the earth, and to every nation, and kindred, and tongue, and people." An article, "God's Messengers," by Isaac Key (*Gospel Trumpet*, February 1, 1888) explained that angels are messengers or ministers.

articles, and supply inspirational news of the success and expansion of the work. Writers and preachers both were referred to as "publishers" of truth.

In October 1881, the *Gospel Trumpet* was edited and published in Indianapolis by D. S. Warner and J. C. Fisher.[3] Its masthead declared it to be a "Holiness Journal," which identified it as one of the several dozen such publications, most of them independent, then in circulation. The thirteen-by-twenty-inch four-page, five-column paper contained articles on Bible subjects (mostly on holiness and the Church), notices and reports of meetings, testimonies, letters, and sometimes material reprinted from other publications. Its stated object was, "The glory of God in the Salvation of men from all sin, and the union of all saints upon the Bible."[4]

In the earliest issues of the *Gospel Trumpet* one senses a growing enthusiasm on the part of those who were to become the leaders in a new religious reform movement. Not only was the content of their message beginning to

J. C. Fisher (1854–c.1950), evangelist, publisher, and songwriter. Fisher and his wife Allie were D. S. Warner's partners in the first years of the *Gospel Trumpet*. Warner dissolved their partnership in 1887 when Fisher divulged his desire to divorce his wife for another woman. Despite this estrangement, some of Fisher's songs continued in the songbooks and hymnals of the Church of God, including "I Ought to Love My Savior" and "I'm Redeemed."

take shape, but the elements of their methods of propagation also were becoming apparent. Warner, for instance, had a great burden for writing and editorial work, but he never saw himself as a desk man. He was an evangelist who felt the Lord strongly calling him to continue traveling in revival campaigns and Holiness meetings. That the two callings of manager and leader were not exactly compatible never seemed to have occurred to him. He

---

3. Fisher still resided in Michigan, and so his involvement at this time was as financial partner and frequent contributor of letters and articles. It was not until the publishing operation was moved to Williamston, Michigan, in 1884 that Fisher became an active publisher and associate editor.

4. Masthead, *Gospel Trumpet*, March 1, 1881, 2. Same in subsequent issues published in Indianapolis.

clearly intended to be both resident editor and itinerant preacher, setting a pattern for himself and many others over the next several decades.

The pilgrim ministry envisioned by the movement's earliest leaders is dramatically portrayed in an idea conceived during the summer of 1881 and described in the *Gospel Trumpet* a full month before the historic event at Beaver Dam.[5] Under the title "The Salvation Car," Warner elaborated on a dream that apparently had been developing in his mind for some time and also suggested by a "Bro. Pelton" of Ashland, Illinois. The idea was to fit out a railroad car as a traveling evangelistic center with "part partioned off for an office and the rest for the band and equipments." "The band," he explained, "we expect will consist of about four sisters and six brethren, whom the Spirit shall select." The equipment would include a "Tabernacle and a few good tents for the campaign," plus a printing press to "publish our bills, tracts, and possibly a paper as we go."

After assuring readers that the *Trumpet* would continue publication even if the salvation car were not secured, and suggesting the possible alternative of moving the office to Illinois on property offered by Pelton, Warner continued with vigor:

> BUT THE CAR is what is needed, not only for the sake of the office, but to enhance the comfort of the company—to enable us to carry provision, that the Lord may give us, and to travel with a great deal less expense. Let it also be remembered that once on the track for Jesus, we shall continue to go winter and summer, withersoever the Lord will.

Warner was not unaware of the great cost of realizing this dream, but he felt encouraged to pursue the project since "our dear Bro. Pelton has offered to invest his whole 40 acres of good Illinois land in Tabernacles for the Lord, which will enable him to fit out three or four companies." With only the unmentioned price of the railway car(s) yet to be secured, he then launched an appeal for large contributions. "O, ye rich," he pleaded, "how hardly shall ye enter the Kingdom of heaven if ye will not give your hundreds to speed this last, midnight cry." Hundreds became thousands before Warner finally asked, "Who will make haste to sell, if need be, the best land he has to send out this first salvation car for the glory of God? Speak out quickly lest God pass you by and another take your crown." Despite this

---

5. *Gospel Trumpet*, "The Salvation Car," September 1, 1881, 2. Subsequent quotations on this matter are from the same article.

impassioned appeal the needed support apparently did not materialize, and so the idea was set aside. Likewise, Warner and Fisher did not accept Pelton's invitation to relocate the *Trumpet's* home in Illinois. The salvation car idea, however, did portend a widespread pattern of ministry for the next quarter century and beyond.

Indianapolis was the *Trumpet's* home through September 1882, but only with increasing hardship and difficulty. The downtown office over 70 North Illinois Street was abandoned in the summer of 1881 in order to save money—$5.00 monthly rent. Warner hoped to build a small office building on a lot shared with his house at 625 West Vermont Street. He had secured most of the lumber for the project by dismantling a stable on his property.[6] He did manage to raise the shell of the building but was unable to raise sufficient funds to finish it before cold weather. Reporting this failure, he both explained and exulted:

> We did not move, neither were we able to plaster our office. How then do you think we managed to get out this paper? We will tell you. Dear Wife tendered her kitchen to the Lord for the use of publishing salvation. Praise the Lord! By thus crowding in a sufficient amount of the office to get along for the winter we shall save fuel, and the expense of finishing the office until next fall. Thank God, we are willing to get along any way for Christ's sake, so that we may fulfill our mission and publish truth and righteousness. We are not at all mortified at these humble facilities from which the Trumpet goes forth to its readers. Christ started his earthly mission from a manger. Oh no, we are not ashamed to let all men know that the Trumpet is published in the rear of a small cottage. God's presence makes the whole domicil [sic] sacred. Oh, how wonderfully he pours out his glory on our souls in this work![7]

Despite discouragements Warner was able to modify his equipment so as to enlarge the pages to fifteen by twenty inches and in February 1882 he reported a press run of two thousand papers which, he observed, "is quite a task with our hand press." Without complaint he continued, "But praise God he gives me blessed health and strength, and I am perfectly satisfied

---

6. *Gospel Trumpet,* June 1, 1881. For further details of the story of the paper and the whole publishing enterprise of the Church of God see Harold L. Phillips, *Miracle of Survival* (Anderson, IN: Warner Press, 1979).

7. *Gospel Trumpet,* November 1, 1881.

to work on with the means the Lord has furnished, until He sees proper to give me others."[8] In fact the means furnished were very inadequate, and the winter in Indianapolis was bleak and desperate. But the Warners never lost hope.

In the early autumn of 1882 the way opened for them to move to what promised to be a more favorable location—the town of Cardington in Morrow County, Ohio. A "glorious" revival meeting had been conducted there in August and the presence of "a precious band of saints" promised a much more supportive environment for the publishing work.[9] With the support, however, came more problems. The financial crunch was worsened by the breakdown of the printing press and the necessity to publish the paper in a reduced size done in a job press format. The subscription price was reduced to seventy-five cents and later to fifty cents per year. Even more devastating was the overt opposition that arose in the community. Under a heading of "Salt in Cardington," Warner reported:

> God's cause has passed through a terrible sifting in this place. All the powers of darkness and of Satan's hellish rage have been let loose upon the few loyal, holy little ones here. Wicked sect members have boasted that this cause was crushed out....But bless God, the devil's sadly mistaken. Several souls have recently become established, unblameable in holiness. The Lord is with us in power, the hidden ones have four meetings every week, and God is wonderfully blessing us.[10]

By June 1883 the publishing operation was moved again, this time just twenty miles away to Bucyrus in neighboring Crawford County. A generous benefactor, D. D. Johnson, had purchased a lot and furnished the material to erect a building. In August his name appeared on the masthead as publisher. Likewise, Warner arranged to purchase his first good press, a rebuilt Country Campbell, for approximately $600.[11] Prospects were brightening, and for a few months the publishing work and Warner's ministry experienced considerable success. Two developments over the next few months, however, were to bring new destructive threats to the nascent reform movement and to Warner's personal well-being.

---

8. *Gospel Trumpet*, February 8, 1882, 2.
9. *Gospel Trumpet*, September 22, 1882, 2.
10. *Gospel Trumpet*, May 1, 1883.
11. Byers, *Birth of a Reformation*, 250–51.

The first of these devastating events was a meeting called by Warner that he intended to be the first general assembly of the saints in Ohio. The meeting was announced for November 9–12, 1883, at Annapolis, about seven miles northeast of Bucyrus. In issuing the call he opened the door for any persons who were dissatisfied with either themselves or the church they attended. In impassioned tones he wrote:

We expect to see a large turnout of the saints of the living God from Van Wert, Paulding, and Wood counties, and some from eastern Ohio; and come ye, dear ones, from Pennsylvania. Come, O ye sanctified hosts of the Lord! Let us eat together in the name of our Chief Shepherd and only Head and Leader. Come in the power of the Spirit; come to have the spiritual gifts stirred up and strengthened; come to sharpen each other as iron sharpeneth iron and to have the faith once delivered to the saints developed in us up to the Bible standard; come to make a more perfect consecration. Come, O ye lame and halt and blind and deaf, for the power of the Lord will be present to heal all who believe on him. Come, O ye sufferers, and give yourselves up to the mighty God and be made whole. Come, poor sinners, and be saved in the day of his power. Come, O ye poor and wayward Christians, and have your hearts established unblameable in holiness. Come, ye who are in bondage of sect captivity, and learn your way out of the wilderness unto the city that is set upon a hill, which hath foundations, and whose builder and maker is God. Come from far and near, whoever seeks the old paths and the peace of Jerusalem. Come, for the little ones will make you welcome; yea, the Spirit and the bride say, Come, and whosoever will, let him take of the water of life freely.[12]

The plea apparently was effective, for many did come, but the meeting that Warner expected to be "a sample of the reign of heaven" did not materialize. Instead, "Satan was…loosed and a terrible conflict ensued."[13] Early in the meeting three men from northwestern Ohio who believed it was wrong to wear collars, collar buttons, lace, and eyeglasses created considerable disturbance by insisting that all the participants who were wearing these articles should remove them. Warner rebuked them as fanatics, but they continued to disrupt the meeting by prostrating themselves on the floor at

12. As quoted in Ibid., 289.
13. Ibid., 291.

the front of the hall and moaning and groaning during Warner's sermon. By the second evening another detractor, L. H. Johnson of Toledo, who published a paper called *The Stumbling Stone,* showed up and began to harangue the participants from the back of a wagon as they entered the meeting place. Decidedly antisectarian, Johnson however also opposed the doctrine of holiness and rejected the New Testament ordinances. He followed the people inside and repeatedly interrupted the proceedings throughout that day and the next. Other disturbances vexed the remaining days of the assembly. Efforts to move the meeting to a different location in order to escape the "confusing and delusive elements" were unsuccessful. Warner commented, "How apt we are to forget that we are still in the field of battle, and Satan is now loosed for a little season, having great wrath because he knows his time is short!"[14] In reflecting later on this meeting Warner was able to see that some good came from it: "This providential bringing together of the children of light and the powers of darkness has proved a great blessing to the saints in that it has already brought to light which side men occupy."[15]

An even harder trial, however, was yet to come. Following the Annapolis assembly several ministers supported Warner's views and subsequently identified themselves with the cause. Among these was R. S. Stockwell and a man by the name of Rice. Stockwell came to Bucyrus and began assisting in the publishing work, quickly gaining the Warners' respect and friendship. Soon, however, he began advocating an interpretation of holy living, contending that the sex relation was carnal even in marriage. This marital purity doctrine was held by an extreme fringe of the Holiness Movement. The doctrine held that a husband and wife who were "entirely" sanctified would have only the same bond of love for each other as they would have for all the other saints. Warner's wife Sarah accepted Stockwell's teaching, putting something of a strain on their marriage.[16]

In January 1884 Stockwell became the principal instigator of another crisis. He declared that God had revealed to him that Warner should sell the publishing work to Rice, who had agreed to buy it. On this point he also had the concurrence of Sarah. One night the three of them, and possibly others, subjected Warner to a long and grueling harangue trying to get him to submit to their "leading." Finally they secured his agreement to sell the *Trumpet,* and all of them retired with great satisfaction—except Warner. The

---

14. As quoted in Ibid.
15. Ibid., 292.
16. Ibid., 292–93.

next day he informed them that he could get no divine confirmation of the previous night's agreement, and so he was going to continue publication. The consequences were devastating. Stockwell, of course, left, but so did Sarah, returning to her parents' home in Upper Sandusky with the Warners' three-year-old son Sidney.[17] Sarah's motives are unclear. It may have been that the Annapolis fiasco had so alarmed her that in securing ownership she wanted to steer the *Trumpet* message away from its church radicalism back toward the Holiness Movement mainstream. Warner was distraught. His mental and spiritual agony kept him from publishing a single copy of the *Gospel Trumpet* for almost four months. Repeatedly he tried to win back his wife, but without any success. Through letters to rival Holiness papers she denounced him and criticized his teachings. Within two years she returned Sidney to Warner's custody, obtained an uncontested divorce, and later remarried.[18]

In April 1884 some friends and supporters in Michigan arranged to move the publishing operation to Williamston, about twenty miles east of Lansing. Thomas Horton, a businessman of that area, traveled to Bucyrus and had all the equipment loaded in a freight car and shipped to the new location. A more commodious building, some new equipment, and particularly the coming of J. C. and Allie Fisher, already part owners of the enterprise, rekindled hope and opened many new opportunities for advancement.[19] It was during the two-year stay in Williamston that the publishers launched a new venture that would prove to be one of the most important factors in propagating the movement for many decades. Nothing spectacular—just a small book titled *Songs of Victory.*[20] It was the first book to come from *Gospel Trumpet* presses and contained words and music of ninety-four new songs written mostly by Warner and Fisher. Warner had been writing poetry for many years. He was also interested in music and sang a good tenor. Fisher likewise was poetically gifted and possessed some talent for musical composition. By combining their skills they not only produced some singable gospel songs, but they also lyricized the theology and the spirit of the movement in such a way that it became more joyful, inspiring, and contagious than before. As Fisher wrote in the preface:

17. Ibid., 295–97.
18. Ibid., 297–303.
19. Phillips, *Miracle of Survival*, 27–29.
20. Joseph C. Fisher, ed., *Songs of Victory* (Williamston, MI: Gospel Trumpet Co., 1885).

It is a fact well known, and felt by the saints, that the hymns of the past fail to express the glorious Light and Liberty, Grace, Truth and Power, the Free and Holy Church has attained in this blessed evening light. Hence the Lord has marvelously given us these NEW SONGS, that we may more fully sing the Joy and Victory we have in the Lord Jesus Christ.

The songs caught on. Most of them were exuberant expressions of gladness with titles like, "I'm Redeemed," "I'm Reigning in This Life," "Blessed Salvation," and "Praise the Lord!" Some were quiet admonitions such as, "I Ought to Love My Savior," "Come, Jesus, Reign in Me!" and "Don't Resist the Holy Spirit." Many of the songs were evangelistic, with warnings against sin and invitations to repentance: "Come Home, Poor Sinner," "Christ Is Calling," "The All-Cleansing Fountain," and "Sinner, Christ Is Waiting." Of particular significance were several songs expressing their composers' vision of the church: "The Holy Church of God," "The Bride of Christ," "The Gospel Trumpet," and "The Evening Light." The lyrics of the last hymn, based on Zechariah 14:7, gloried in the restoration of the one holy church:

Free from babel, in the Spirit,
Free to worship God aright;
Joy and gladness we're receiving,
O how sweet this evening light![21]

It was also during the two-year stay at Williamston that Warner and Fisher instituted a deliberate policy of enlisting workers in the publication enterprise without any compensation except board and room, supplying personal necessities as needed. The two-story facility at Williamston had sufficient space to house several individuals, and by January 1885 eight people were assisting Warner in the publishing work: the Fishers, William N. and Jennie Smith, Jeremiah Cole, John Spaulding, Rhoda Keagy, and Celia Kirkpatrick.[22] This communal arrangement was the beginning of what came to be known as the "Trumpet Family," an institution that continued for thirty-two years, at times including as many as three hundred people.

In 1886 the publishing office made yet another move, this time to Grand Junction, Michigan, in the southwestern part of the state. This

---

21. Ibid., no. 58.
22. Noah H. Byrum, *Familiar Names and Faces* (Moundsville, WV: Gospel Trumpet Company, 1902), 82.

time the saints in the area apparently had begun to feel some responsibility regarding this part of the work, for the record indicates that the recommendation for the move came from those assembled at the camp meeting in nearby Bangor. They were able to secure a very adequate building for $800. Sebastian Michels of South Haven provided a portion of the funds necessary to make the move, earning the appearance of his name on the paper's masthead as publisher.[23] The enterprise now designated itself as the Gospel Trumpet Publishing Company.

In Grand Junction the publishing work experienced its first real success—but not without weathering another severe trial. In early 1887, J. C. Fisher, Warner's partner since the company's early days and a capable colleague at Williamston, became convinced that a man had a scriptural right to divorce his wife. Warner sensed that Fisher had fallen in love with a younger woman by the name of Alice Davis and was preparing to divorce his wife Allie. He warned Fisher that he would have to repent of this evil interpretation or leave. Fisher refused to repent, got a divorce, and married Miss Davis.[24] Fisher's departure from the company required his replacement, and that meant someone with sufficient money to buy Fisher's share of the partnership. In early June 1887, at the Grand Junction camp meeting, on the recommendation of Henry Wickersham, Warner approached Wickersham's cousin, Enoch E. Byrum of Randolph County, Indiana, and asked him to consider becoming a partner and functioning as the company's publisher and business manager. Byrum later recalled his reaction:

> Three or four days after my arrival at the meeting, Brother Warner came to me and asked me to accept the position as publisher and business manager of the Gospel Trumpet publishing work at Grand Junction, Michigan, as H. C. Wichersham had recommended me as one suitable to fill that position.
>
> As I had never spent two hours in a printing office and knew nothing about the publishing business, my first plea was my inability and incompetency for such an undertaking. Immediately there was a sudden check of my presentation of excuses as the Lord by His Spirit vividly reminded me of the consecration I had made a few years before while plowing the field, when I had promised that if he would open the way for me to go to school whenever he called me into the work, whatever

23. Ibid., 86.
24. Byers, *Birth of a Reformation*, 308ff.

Gospel Trumpet Publishing Company buildings in Grand Junction, Michigan. Other than Anderson, Indiana, the publishing house stayed in Grand Junction longer than at anywhere else, from 1886 to 1898. The years at Grand Junction witnessed the first extensive growth in the company's capital equipment.

it may be, I would go. That was a call to preparation and now came a call for active service.

I had not been trained in business, was unacquainted with the art of printing and publishing work, and knew but little about the Bible doctrine. To accept such a position with my inexperience and lack of knowledge in regard to such things was like taking a step into the unknown, so far as responsibilities were concerned....The next morning I met with the Brethren again and told them that I felt clearly led of the Lord to accept the position and was ready to begin at any time.[25]

On June 21, 1887, E. E. Byrum became the publisher and business manager of the Gospel Trumpet Publishing Company, having purchased J. C. Fisher's share of the company. Warner, Michels, and Allie Fisher were the other partners. Byrum's younger brother Noah came to work in the office later that summer, and he too became an important part of the publishing venture.[26]

Despite their youth and inexperience, the Byrum brothers proved to be excellent business partners for Warner. Enoch's managerial personality

---

25. From the Diary of Enoch E. Byrum in the Anderson University and Church of God Archives. Also published in Noah H. Byrum, "Early Days of Our Publishing Work: God Called a Farmer Boy," *Gospel Trumpet*, April 5, 1941, 7.
26. Byrum, *Familiar Names and Faces*, 98.

nicely complemented the older man's visionary but peripatetic leadership. Warner now was free to tour the country on evangelistic missions while Enoch Byrum stayed home and answered the mail. The number of workers increased and Enoch purchased a house across the street to accommodate the growing publishing family. The accomplishments during the eight remaining years of Warner's life make an impressive list. A new song book, *Anthems from the Throne,* with ninety additional songs, was published in 1888 and was followed by another, *Echoes from Glory,* in 1893. A new semimonthly paper for children, *The Shining Light,* began publication in January 1891, and the *Gospel Trumpet* became a weekly periodical a year later. The printing of religious tracts was greatly accelerated with press runs of thirty thousand to forty thousand copies. Other books appeared, such as E. E. Byrum's *Divine Healing of Soul and Body* and *Biblical Trace of the Church* by William G. Schell.[27] In December 1892 Warner announced his desire to start a German paper.[28] On March 23, 1893, the *Gospel Trumpet* appeared with two columns in German, a feature that was repeated periodically for the next year and a half. On January 1, 1895, a new German periodical, *Die Evangeliums Posaune,* began to be issued from the Trumpet offices in Grand Junction.[29] Fred L. Hahn, a former Baptist minister of Milwaukee, Wisconsin, was its first editor. The addition of new presses and other equipment made the printing operation a decided success.

The significance of the publishing work in the development of the Church of God movement certainly warrants space devoted to telling the story of its problems and progress up to this point, but the *Gospel Trumpet* was but a single segment of what was happening across the nation and beyond as the flying messengers took their message to the crossroads of the countryside and the streets of the cities. The number and names of all these people will never be known, for no rosters or registers were kept. It is possible, however, to arrive at a general idea of the scope of activity by examining some of the available data. If a head count of all the writers of articles, testimonies, notices, and letters to the *Gospel Trumpet* for the first two decades were made, for example, it would total many hundreds of active participants. A sample tally of names appearing in a single eight-page weekly issue of the paper in early 1898 counted more than fifty individual

---

27. Summarized by Phillips, *Miracle of Survival,* 38–40.
28. Charles E. Brown, *When the Trumpet Sounded* (Anderson, IN: Gospel Trumpet Co., 1951), 337.
29. Ibid.

writers or reporters.[30] The 1902 publication titled *Familiar Names and Faces* contains pictures, mostly three-by-four-inch bust photographs, of 216 people identified by name whose travels or writing made them well-known leaders in the movement.[31] Some Ministerial Lists compiled in the late 1890s and early 1900s contain up to 422 names. Still, they fall short of telling the whole story, since many of the itinerant messengers were unordained gospel workers who gave full time to ministry as laypeople.[32]

The identity of these earliest leaders and the nature of their work was given considerable attention about forty years following these labors when some attempts were made to identify and pay tribute to the most prominent of the pioneers. Andrew L. Byers wrote a series of twenty-four biographical sketches of "Pioneers of the Present Reformation,"

Andrew L. Byers (1869–1952), minister and song-writer. In addition to writing the first biography of D. S. Warner, *Birth of a Reformation*, Byers collaborated on many gospel songs, including "Fill Me with Thy Spirit, Lord," "The Reformation Glory," and "The Church's Jubilee."

which were published in the *Gospel Trumpet* from February through July of 1920. The first sketch, a biography of Warner, is prefaced with an introductory tribute to "those. . .pioneer exponents. . .who were baptized" with the "burning truth" of "the present religious reformation" who "were willing to brave the necessary hardships in blazing the way for the establishment, once more in the earth, of the New Testament church in her undivided wholeness."[33]

---

30. *Gospel Trumpet*, January 13, 1898.

31. Byrum, *Familiar Names and Faces*.

32. Later these laypeople were encouraged to register in the *Yearbook* with the designation of "gospel workers." It was not until 1967 that the number of persons registering under this caption had become so few that the practice was discontinued.

33. A. L. Byers, "Pioneers of the Present Reformation," *Gospel Trumpet*, February 5, 1920, 18. Three years later the 1923 *Yearbook of the Church of God*, 12–13, listed the names of twenty-one preachers, mostly the same ones who were subjects of the sketches, who, the editor said, should be "classed as pioneers of the work."

One really cannot understand the mood of excitement, the spirit of involvement in a great work, and the sense of dedication to a cause felt by these initial leaders without some acquaintance with a few of the flying messengers. One of the earliest of Warner's fellow reformers was Alexander J. Kilpatrick. Born in Hancock County, Ohio, he became a public school teacher and taught for twenty-two terms, with about four years out for military service during the Civil War. In 1870 he was converted in a protracted meeting held by a United Brethren circuit preacher, and within a year he himself had been granted a ministerial license by that denomination. After preaching for about eight years, in 1878 Kilpatrick attended a meeting held by a band of Holiness workers in Payne, Ohio. There he received the experience of sanctification and began preaching the doctrine. Soon thereafter the United Brethren church was shaken by a schism, so Kilpatrick severed his connection with them and refused to join any other church. His explanation: "Every person that has salvation and belongs to a denominational church belongs to two, and Jesus built one church."[34] About this same time he heard of Warner, arranged to meet him, and discovered that their views on the church were identical. The next year (1879) Warner went to Payne and joined Kilpatrick in a series of evangelistic meetings. In the course of conversations during these meetings, both men renounced their sectarian ministerial credentials and, in a small log house about two miles southwest of the town, they reordained each other.[35] Kilpatrick spent the rest of his life, almost forty years, as an evangelist traveling in twenty-two states and Canada, proclaiming the message of freedom from sectarianism that had first brought him and Warner together.

Jeremiah Cole, his sister Mary, and younger brother George all became vigorous proponents of the reform movement. The family moved from Ohio to Missouri, where Jeremiah was converted, joined the Methodist Episcopal Church, and became an exhorter. He later was led into the experience of sanctification and participated in Holiness meetings. He

---

34. A. L. Byers, "Pioneers of the Present Reformation: A. J. Kilpatrick," *Gospel Trumpet* (March 25, 1920), 22.

35. It is difficult to assess the import of this incident. Kilpatrick had already severed his denominational connections, and so he was an unaffiliated evangelist and remained so. Warner continued his relationship with the Northern Indiana Eldership for two years, so the renunciation and re-ordination did not change his actual status. Moreover, there is an account of a meeting in Williamston, Michigan, in 1884 that states that Warner and others were ordained by the laying on of hands of those assembled.

attended the Western Union Holiness Convention at Jacksonville, Illinois, in December of 1880, where he met D. S. Warner. They discovered their common belief in divine healing but did not discuss the church question. A year or so later a friend handed Jeremiah a copy of the *Gospel Trumpet*, and he recognized Warner's name. He wrote to him and, after several exchanges of letters and some difficulties with the Methodist Episcopal and Free Methodist Churches, he renounced denominationalism as sinful and separated himself from all. Already he and Mary were traveling in evangelistic work, and she also was led to proclaim independence from sectarianism. Later she also traveled with her younger brother, George. She and George were responsible for beginning the work of the Church of God in Chicago. The Coles were all strong preachers, and Mary pioneered the way to an open door for ministry by many women in the movement. Jeremiah and Mary both experienced miraculous healings, and so they also gave great emphasis to prayer for the sick. Mary authored a book on the subject. They traveled all across the United States, sometimes in pairs and sometimes separately, often meeting vigorous opposition but always proclaiming the message with power and vigor.[36]

Among the more colorful individuals associated with the movement in its earliest days was Sarah Sauer Smith. Born of German parentage in Summit County, Ohio, she was baptized and reared in the Lutheran Church. At age twenty she had a conversion experience and became so fervent in her prayers and expressions of spiritual joy that she was opposed and eventually rejected by her church. In 1859 she sought and received an experience of sanctification four years before she ever heard a sermon on the doctrine. Both the Evangelical Alliance and the Methodists sought to enlist her as a minister, but she wanted to be free to go when and where God would lead. She did join a small Holiness band in Jerry City, Ohio, near her home. In one of these meetings she was handed a copy of the *Gospel Trumpet* containing an article on the one church, and she realized she had found other people who shared the concerns she had felt for some years. When D. S. Warner came to the neighborhood in early 1882 and A. J. Kilpatrick somewhat later, they found a receptive audience. Along with about twenty others Sarah declared her freedom from sectarian division. Soon she felt God calling her to begin an active ministry, and at age sixty-one she left her husband in the care of their eldest son and went out to hold revival

---

36. Byers, "Pioneers," *Gospel Trumpet* (February 12, 1920), 17, and (February 19, 1920), 22.

meetings. Early in 1885 Warner asked her to join a company of traveling singers and workers he was assembling for evangelistic work. She accepted the invitation and for more than five years she was a vital and necessary member of Warner's company, singing tenor in the quartet, testifying, praying, and sometimes preaching. Mother Sarah Smith never lost her heavy German accent, her faith and exuberant enthusiasm for the work of God, or the message of the movement.[37]

Mention of Warner's company highlights one of the most unique and productive means of evangelism developed during the period of the flying ministry. Warner's invitation to Mother Sarah Smith was designed to round out a group of five individuals who would travel together and cooperate in conducting revival campaigns. Although Warner did most of the preaching, the other members of the company sang, gave their testimonies, counseled the seekers, distributed literature, did visitation work, and often conducted children's meetings. The most important qualification, however, was to be able to sing one of the four parts to form a quartet with a harmonious blend so that the listeners could hear and learn the new songs that were being composed and published—songs that preached a message identical to that proclaimed by the ministers. In addition to tenor Sarah Smith, Warner enlisted two younger women, Nannie Kigar of Payne, Ohio, and Frances (Frankie) Miller of Battle Creek, Michigan. For the bass, over the objections of the lad's father, Warner took along eighteen-year-old Barney Warren of Geneva Center, Michigan. This company traveled together for over five years. Mostly they evangelized in the Midwest but went as far south as Mississippi, west

Courtesy of Anderson University and Church of God Archives

D. S. Warner's evangelistic company: Barney Warren, of Geneva Center, Michigan; D. S. Warner, of Grand Junction, Michigan; Nannie Kigar, of Payne, Ohio; "Mother" Sarah Smith, of Jerry City, Ohio; and Frankie Miller, of Battle Creek, Michigan. Beginning in 1886, the group traveled together for five years throughout the Midwest, South, and east to Pennsylvania.

37. *Gospel Trumpet*, February 26, 1920, 5–6. Also Byrum, *Familiar Names and Faces*, 182–248 contains Sarah Smith's autobiography.

to Missouri, and east to Pennsylvania. Like the others, they encountered considerable opposition, endured persecution, and held many wonderful meetings. Of them the fourth editor of the *Gospel Trumpet*, C. E. Brown said, "The record of the travels and work of this company are worthy of a book."[38]

Warner's company became a model for others. For the next quarter century and more the Field reports in the *Gospel Trumpet* are often signed with the name of a minister with "and company" to indicate he or she was accompanied by a group of assistants in itinerating evangelistic work. This technique opened the way for many more people to be involved in the flying ministry, especially women. Although many women were preachers and carried on their own evangelistic campaigns, hundreds of others joined these companies

Barney E. Warren (1867–1951), composer and songwriter. A native of Michigan but a longtime fixture at Springfield, Ohio, Warren was the most prolific of Church of God composers and writers. Among his best loved songs are "What a Mighty God We Serve!," "The Bond of Perfectness," "A Child of God," and "There Is Joy in the Lord."

as singers and assistants. This development gave rise to the designation of such unordained persons as "gospel workers," a descriptive title that was utilized three decades later in the first issue of the *Church of God Yearbook* in 1917 and was continued in this annual publication for three more decades.

Young Barney Warren's enlistment proved very opportune. Not only did he sing a good bass for the quartet, Warren also had musical skills in composition and harmony. Fisher's defection in 1887 created a great need for someone with these abilities, and Warren proved to be that person. Warren coedited the second songbook, *Anthems from the Throne*, in 1888 and also wrote music for seventy-eight of the book's ninety songs.[39] Warren also possessed poetic skills, for he wrote the lyrics for twenty-three of these songs. As the book title suggests, most of these were songs of praise. War-

---

38. Brown, *When the Trumpet Sounded*, 126.

39. Daniel S. Warner and Barney E. Warren, eds., *Anthems from the Throne* (Grand Junction, MI: Gospel Trumpet Publishing Co., 1888).

ner's titles, such as "Complete in Christ," "Living for Jesus," and "Forever Thine," reflect this theme. Other songs were evangelistic in tone and a few, like the following, expressed his vision of the church.

> See the Church in heaven's beauty,
> With her spotless robe of white;
> She is marching on to vict'ry
> In Jehovah's wondrous might.
>
> Chorus:
> In her walks the holy people,
> And her walls are glory bright;
> "On the arm of her beloved,
> Forth she came in dazzling light."[40]

Warren was a major contributor to the music of the Church of God for more than half a century. He was a coeditor with Warner for the next songbook, *Echoes from Glory*, which appeared in 1893 and was involved in the publication of almost every other songbook and hymnal produced by the movement until the 1940s. The most prolific of Church of God songwriters, Warren is said to have composed the music for more than seven thousand songs.[41]

George T. Clayton was another of the early leaders who "saw the light on the church" before he had heard it preached by anyone else. Born in West Virginia, he endured a period of severe spiritual struggle during his early years but eventually experienced both justification and sanctification without establishing a relationship with any denomination. Later he affiliated with the Methodist Episcopal Church and preached for them. But he concluded that the scriptures taught believers' baptism, and so he was rebaptized and joined the Churches of God in North America. Internal problems led him to separate from this group in 1883. He then became convinced that denominationalism itself was contrary to God's will, and for four years he and his wife, Lizzie, held meetings in western Pennsylvania without church connection. Through the *Gospel Trumpet* he came in contact with Warner, and after a lengthy meeting they concluded they were of one mind. From that time until Clayton died, he and his wife were

---

40. Ibid., "The Church of Christ," no. 24.
41. W. Dale Oldham, *Giants Along My Path* (Anderson, IN: Warner Press, 1973), 103.

The Floating Bethel. In 1894, G. T. and Lizzie Clayton converted an unpowered river barge into a floating chapel. They called their boat a *bethel*, from the Hebrew word meaning "house of God." Winebrennerian Church of God people commonly referred to their churches as bethels, and early Church of God preachers who had come out of that communion continued the use of the term. The *Floating Bethel* left Pittsburg in 1894 with plans to drift down the Ohio and Mississippi; however, the barge was destroyed by fire while moored at Moundsville in 1898.

evangelists in the Church of God, traveling in nineteen states and Canada. As evangelists in the Church of God, the main focus of their ministry was in western Pennsylvania, West Virginia, and Ontario.[42]

The most dramatic aspect of the Claytons' evangelistic work was the *Floating Bethel.* In 1893 Clayton conceived the idea of a meeting house on an unpowered barge that could be launched at Pittsburgh and floated down the Ohio River to the Mississippi and on to the Gulf of Mexico, evangelizing at every landing along the way. He brought the dream to reality by securing a river barge and constructing a chapel and living quarters on its flat deck. Leaving Pittsburgh in early 1894, the *Bethel* was an effective, and sometimes dangerous, instrument of evangelism for over four years. Its downriver mission ended far short of its intended destination, however, when the boat was destroyed by fire in December 1898, while docked at Moundsville, West Virginia. The Claytons were instrumental in establishing several new congregations and leading others such as Herbert M. Riggle, William Drew, W. W. Titley, and Harry Rogers into the work of the move-

---

42. A. L. Byers, "Pioneers," *Gospel Trumpet*, March 4, 1920, 9–10.

ment.[43] A second floating chapel was purchased by L. C. and Jennie I. Mast and was operated farther down the Ohio at the same time as the Claytons' *Bethel*. The Masts had secured a former showboat requiring considerable renovation and had christened it the *Gospel Ark*. It was put in commission at Parkersburg, West Virginia, by May 1895 and continued to be used for evangelization at the various river landings down to Point Pleasant, West Virginia, by 1898.[44]

All of the earliest leaders were "come-outers." They had been affiliated with some other group and forsaken it to take their stand with the Church of God. Many were already licensed or ordained preachers in the denominations from which they came. Among those was Alfred B. Palmer, who was born in Cass County, Michigan. After graduating from high school Palmer became a teacher in the country schools of that area and continued in that profession for twenty years. During all this time he was a member of the Methodist Episcopal Church, serving as a class leader, steward, Sunday school superintendent, and eventually being licensed a local preacher. In 1877 he heard some preaching on sanctification and received the experience. Six years later a neighbor by the name of Lottie Blackwood told him that she heard some ministers around Bangor preaching that sectism was sinful. He began to study the Scriptures on this matter and concluded they were right—without having, in his own words, "ever heard a sermon preached on the church question." By the end of 1883, at age forty-eight, he had joined the ranks of the flying messengers. As an evangelist he was quite successful; in one series of meetings near Allegan, Michigan, he witnessed 156 conversions. Like the others Palmer traveled widely and never lacked for calls as long as he was able to be active. He enjoyed excellent health and lived to be eighty-six.[45]

Another minister who was delivered from sectism before he was aware that others even in his own community had taken a similar stand was Jasper N. Howard. Born in Harlan County, Kentucky, and growing up in northwestern Ohio, he was converted in 1875 and joined the United Brethren Church. He felt a call to preach but did not actively respond until after 1881 when he sought and received an experience of sanctification. At the same

43. Ibid. There are frequent reports from the *Floating Bethel* in the News from the Field section of the *Gospel Trumpet* from 1894 to 1898.

44. The *Gospel Ark* never received as much publicity as the *Bethel*, but reports indicate it was at least moderately successful even though the Masts suffered considerable hardship and privation. Reports appeared periodically in the *Gospel Trumpet* from May 9, 1895, to June 16, 1898.

45. A. L. Byers, "Pioneers," *Gospel Trumpet*, March 11, 1920, 5–6.

time he rejected denominationalism, withdrew from the United Brethren, and began traveling as an unaffiliated holiness preacher. About 1884 he read a copy of the *Gospel Trumpet,* made contact with Warner, and became an enthusiastic Church of God evangelist, traveling mostly in the early years with his wife, Martha, by team and wagon throughout Ohio, Indiana, and Michigan. Through his efforts others who became prominent leaders, such as Emma Myers of Louisville, Kentucky; Edgar A. Fleenor of Tampico, Indiana; and John Turner of Dayton, Ohio, were brought into the work of the movement. The Howard's daughter Mildred also became a minister.[46]

Sebastian Michels was one of the pioneers whose ministry began as an itinerant one but later moved toward an institutional type of service that was not highly regarded by his fellow ministers. Born in London, Ontario, he was educated in a Lutheran school and was converted at age nineteen after his family had moved to southwestern Michigan. He joined the United Brethren Church and became a steward. In the autumn of 1882 he met J. C. Fisher, who answered many of his questions and later led him to an experience of sanctification. After a miraculous healing in 1883 Michels began preaching, first in company with other ministers and later with his own family as assistants and singers. Under his leadership, the Joseph Smith family, parents of later *Gospel Trumpet* editor Frederick G. Smith, was led into the work. William Hartman, Lodema Kaser, and S. P. Strang were also converts through Michels' ministry. Because some of his financial investments were profitable, he was able to supply needed funds for the publication work and was listed as its "publisher" for a number of years. He developed a particular interest, however, in a children's home ministry, first in Grand Junction and later in South Haven, Michigan. It began as a means of caring for the children of ministers who were travel-ing in evangelistic work. Later the home was expanded to include some orphans, also. Michels' proposal to add an old people's home encountered great opposition; his colleagues felt the call to preach could only be the call to "go." Because he insisted on "staying" he was considered out of harmony for a number of years even though he never officially was disfel-lowshiped. Michels operated his old people's home in South Haven for twenty-five years. Even after his health failed and the home closed, he built a little chapel near his home in order to have a place for Sunday school and the preaching of the Word.[47]

46. *Gospel Trumpet,* March 18, 1920, 5–6.
47. *Gospel Trumpet,* April 1, 1920, 22–23.

To write biographical sketches on each member of the flying ministry during the first decade of the movement's history would be impossible. The story of that fresh and vibrant period would not be complete, however, without mention of a dozen more individuals who were significantly involved in ceaseless itineration prior to 1895. There was Lodema Kaser who came from a Mennonite home in northern Indiana and joined with Mary Cole in meetings in Missouri, Kansas, and Nebraska. She was a strong advocate of divine healing and spent several years in mission work in Chicago.[48] William N. Smith, formerly a United Brethren member, first met Warner in Ohio in 1882. In 1884 Smith and his wife moved to Williamston, Michigan, to assist in the publishing work. After nine months there, they began a nineteen-year traveling ministry that took them to twelve states.[49] Henry C. Wickersham was a native of Indiana and an ordained minister in the United Brethren Church. When the Warner company visited his Randolph County community in 1886, he and his wife declared themselves free from sectism. Wickersham ministered in his own locality until family responsibilities permitted him to travel; after 1891 he itinerated widely, journeying to the Deep South, the East, and the Pacific Northwest. Wickersham was also the first church historian in the movement.[50] David Leininger was one of the five who stood up with Warner at the memorable meeting in Beaver Dam, Indiana. A former Winebrennerian, he became a farmer preacher who did not travel widely but ministered in his own community. Leininger became one of the first settled pastors, serving at the rural Olive Bethel Church about a half mile from his home. He was the major promoter of a camp meeting in that area that later became a state camp meeting for Indiana at Yellow Creek Lake.[51]

Jacob W. Byers and his wife, Jennie, hailed from Illinois where they were members of the Brethren in Christ (River Brethren) Church. Byers was an ordained minister in that denomination when Warner and his company held meetings in their community in 1888. After the Byerses took their stand, Warner ordained both of them and immediately they began a traveling ministry. In 1890 they moved to the West Coast and were responsible for starting much of the work in California.[52] A. Leroy Sheldon was from

---

48. *Gospel Trumpet*, April 22, 1920, 5–6.
49. *Gospel Trumpet*, April 8, 1920, 5–6.
50. *Gospel Trumpet*, April 15, 1920, 7–8.
51. Obituary in *Yearbook of the Church of God*, 1926, 15–16.
52. A. L. Byers, "Pioneers," *Gospel Trumpet*, May 13, 1920, 7–8.

Michigan and began his ministry around 1886. He also traveled first in Michigan and later in Ohio, Indiana, and Illinois. He and third wife Delia eventually settled in Flint, where they were responsible for the beginning and development of several churches there.[53] William G. Schell began his ministry in 1886. C. E. Brown described him as "a man of an unusually fertile and brilliant mind, a magnetic and eloquent preacher, and a voluminous and interesting writer."[54] His travels took him to most states east of the Mississippi. Although he later was removed from fellowship—twice—he was a very able and effective evangelist. Samuel L. Speck was Canadian-born but moved to Michigan and later Chicago where he was converted from a very rough life in 1882 under the preaching of J. C. Fisher. Ordained to the ministry in 1884, he traveled with other ministers and later with his wife in evangelistic work in eleven states and the province of Ontario.[55]

George E. Bolds began his ministry in Illinois around 1881 and continued to be active for more than forty-two years. Four of his children also became preachers in 1888 and each carried on a fruitful ministry,[56] some in turn influencing their children to become preachers also. William Hartman was a staunch member of the Salvation Army in Kalamazoo, Michigan, when he attended a revival in 1887 held by Sebastian Michels and his company. Hartman and six others took their stand and he became the leader of the group. He did not travel, since he had to work for several years in a factory to support his family, but he became the pastor of the Church of God in Kalamazoo and remained a fixture in the Southwest Michigan church for fifty-four years.[57] A. J. Shelly, a Pennsylvania Lutheran, moved to Michigan, joined the Methodists, and subsequently came in contact with the Church of God through the *Gospel Trumpet*. In 1884 he and his wife became team-and-wagon traveling evangelists, first in Michigan and later in the Pacific Northwest.[58] A singularly noteworthy evangelist was Fred N. Jacobson, a blind man from Chicago who attended the 1884 Bangor camp meeting, stayed briefly to work in the *Trumpet* office and then launched a long career of pioneer evangelism. Most of his work was in the Pacific Northwest, where he was instrumental in opening the work in many new places.[59]

53. *Gospel Trumpet*, May 20, 1920, 7.
54. Brown, *When the Trumpet Sounded*, 124.
55. Ibid., 116–17.
56. Ibid., 137.
57. Ibid., 116.
58. Ibid., 118. Also *Gospel Trumpet*, July 15, 1920, 5.
59. Ibid., 119.

Many more flying messengers could be mentioned. The pages of the *Gospel Trumpet* during these formative years contain the names of dozens who were on the move in witness to their new found freedom from sin and sectism. No attempt was made during this early period to tabulate either the extent or results of this breathless rush of evangelistic activity and literature distribution. A general excitement pervaded the new movement because it was evident that a great many things were happening in a large number of places. At the end of 1894, E. E. Byrum could well write, "The Lord has wonderfully shown his favors and approval upon the work: while croakers and wicked men have howled against it, he has only increased the volleys of truth against the strongholds of Satan."[60] Byrum referred primarily to the publishing work, which by then involved some thirty or forty workers, but the same spirit of enthusiasm permeated the whole movement.

A further indication of the extent of the movement's reach can be gleaned from a regular feature of the *Gospel Trumpet,* the section under the caption "News from the Field," which sometimes made up almost one-fourth of the copy in the weekly magazine. It consisted of letters from various itinerants and evangelistic companies traveling about the country. They reported their meetings, successes, and difficulties. Hardship and opposition seemed only to spur them on. During 1895, the last year of Warner's life, 384 of these field reports were published, most of them containing accounts of several series of meetings, each lasting from one to six or eight weeks. Published letters came from thirty-three states, Canada, and two European countries. The largest number came from Ohio (47), Michigan (44), Missouri (36), Indiana (26), and Illinois (17). There were also many from Pennsylvania (35), California (18), Nebraska (17), Kansas (15), South Carolina (13), Washington (13), Oregon (12), and Ontario (10). There were at least four reports each from West Virginia, Mississippi, Arkansas, Iowa, Kentucky, Oklahoma, Wisconsin, Texas, and Tennessee. At this point the penetration of the movement was weakest in the eastern seaboard states, the Deep South, and in the less populated states of the West.

One additional indicator of the geographic extent of this flying ministry is found in an analysis of another regular feature of the *Gospel Trumpet* captioned "Calls for meetings." Under this heading letters were printed from individuals expressing a desire to have some evangelist or company

---

60. *Gospel Trumpet,* December 27, 1894, 2.

Denver Camp Meeting, 1900. The Church of God spread swiftly across the United States under the ministry of the flying messengers and others. By the turn of the century, there were camp meetings throughout the Western states.

come to their area and conduct a series of meetings. During 1895 a total of 196 such calls appeared. They came from thirty-two states, two provinces in Canada, and one from England. Most of the calls came from states where the work was most active, but almost without exception they were from localities where the message of the movement had not previously been preached. Requests came from individuals who had read some of the Trumpet literature or had otherwise learned of the success of meetings held elsewhere. Such printed calls kept the flying messengers on the move and opened doors even when they had no personal invitations.

There were those who later called attention to the weaknesses of the flying ministry, pointing out the obvious deficiencies of what sociologist Val Clear called "guerrilla" evangelism.[61] The hit-and-run tactics covered a great deal of territory but did not always leave lasting results. H. M. Riggle, one of the most vigorous and capable of the itinerants, expressed his own regrets by saying, "One of the greatest mistakes of my early ministry was to

61. Valorous B. Clear, *Where the Saints Have Trod* (Chesterfield, IN: Midwest Publications, 1977), 85–87.

open up new fields of work and then rush off and leave them."[62] He cited examples of his failure to stay long enough to ensure a continuing witness in places where his initial meetings had been very successful. It thus became necessary to restart a congregation several times before a permanent fellowship was established.

Despite some weaknesses, by 1895 a new movement was well under way. A struggling independent Holiness periodical had not only survived a precarious period of migration but had developed into a significant production and distribution agent for reformation literature. The number of individual and company itinerant evangelists had multiplied many times and by their deep commitment, enthusiastic efforts, and innovative methods had carried the message to the North American continent and across the oceans. The flying roll and flying messenger concepts did not die with Warner. Through modification and new methods of literature evangelism, the idea of pioneer evangelism continued in the movement's ethos for much of its history.

---

62. Herbert M. Riggle, *Pioneer Evangelism* (Anderson, IN: Gospel Trumpet Co., 1924), 85–89.

CHAPTER 5

A DEVELOPING REFORMATION CONSCIOUSNESS

(1880–1895)

No reform movement, religious or otherwise, is born full-grown. Of necessity it begins very simply as one or more individuals identify strongly felt dissatisfactions and articulate them. If some who hear or read the complaints respond approvingly, an initial group identity may be generated as people relate to each other. They realize they are all disturbed about the issue or issues. Grumblers are thus drawn together by common discontents and, often without any deliberate plan, they find themselves in a fellowship of protest.

Inherent in such protest is a belief or hope that remedies are available. These remedies need not be articulated or spelled out initially. At this point it suffices simply to cry out in opposition and only imply that *something* ought to be done. At least some suggestion of possible change is necessary, however small, for no reformation movement can grow out of a fellowship of those who despair of any solutions to their problem. Reformers must be able to see or feel that there is hope for a brighter day, articulating present problems and pointing out, however tentatively, the path forward.

Some movements never seem to get beyond this primarily negative focus and fail to articulate any commonly held remedies even though they may develop a fairly sophisticated structure, attract large numbers of followers, and continue for a considerable length of time. Eventually they fade and die. The religious reform movements that survive and make a significant contribution in the long haul, however, project some specific answers to the identified problems and build a strong theological base for the positions they espouse. They turn protest into positive affirmation, and in the process develop a valid supporting rationale for their own existence as a movement.

This raison d'être (reason for being) may be stated categorically or just be generally understood, but it must be present.

If one is to understand the dynamics of the Church of God, it becomes important to analyze the early years of the movement in order to discover, first of all, if leaders did indeed identify problems and propose solutions. Did they build a theological base for their points of protest, and then articulate positive purposes for their corporate cause? If so, it becomes necessary to examine the content both of their theological foundations and their understanding of the mission of the self-conscious group that developed.

The task is both difficult and simple. It is difficult because these early leaders were preoccupied with their "doing" and never really took the time to analyze the reasons, motives, and purpose of their activity beyond being convinced that their activities and course were God's will. Moreover, since both humanly devised creeds and ecclesiastical organization were specific items of protest, the earliest reformers were themselves reluctant to formalize either a statement of their beliefs or declaration of their objectives. On the other hand, they clearly articulated both their protests and convictions. It is not difficult to discover their stance on almost any theological or biblical issue. The particular matters of their major concern are conspicuously apparent in the literature they produced and in the records of their activities. The problem is to assemble this commentary in such a way that, looking back, observers may see matters or, as they would have put it, the leadings that brought them "into the light." By examing the literature from the first decade (1881–91), it shall be the concern of this chapter to analyze the ingredients of the developing "reformation consciousness" that provided both the initiative and the momentum for bringing the Church of God movement into being and sustaining its growth through that crucial early period.

What were the concepts that together formed the foundation of the early leaders' thought and action? What was their particular apprehension of Christian faith and witness that spoke meaningfully to both the unsaved and to those who were already members of existing churches? What were their unique perspectives? At least four basic concepts undergirded the reformation movement and brought it to realization. Each must be explored at some length.

As a prelude to this analysis, we highlight characterizations of the early period of this work of reform. In the first place, no one claimed to be a prophet who had received a special new revelation from God. The early leaders rejected the very thought of elevating *any* human being to a place of preeminence or authority. They believed in divine illumination, but it was a light that any truly redeemed person could see and understand. Secondly, from the standpoint of the historic Christian faith there was nothing heretical about the pioneers' thought or action. They had their own interpretations of biblical truth, but these lay quite within the bounds of historic Christian orthodoxy. Thirdly, they envisioned themselves as church reformers. They judged all the churches of their day as being weighed and found wanting. Not only did they see errors, abuses and neglected truth that required proclamation, but they also saw the whole structural system of their contemporary churches as contradicting the essential character of the fellowship of God's people on the earth. Consequently, the early reformers devoted considerable time and energy in the cause of reform—calling attention to the errors and abuses, lifting up the neglected truths, and challenging the ecclesiastical systems that they felt distorted God's clear intention for his people. With these understandings in mind, we can turn our attention to the basic theological presuppositions of these first messengers of what they called "this present truth."

First, they affirmed the basic Protestant precept that the sole foundation of the Christian faith is the Bible. In many ways the early leaders declared their commitment to the authority of Scripture. All their preaching was not only *from* the Bible but also *through* the Bible; every point was supported by a multitude of texts. The word *Bible* was attached to all the other important words in their theological vocabulary: Bible truth, Bible holiness, Bible salvation, Bible church, Bible standards, Bible ordinances, Bible organization, and many others. An example of this commonly expressed language comes from the words of Warner: "The lifting up of the pure standard of Bible holiness through the power of the two witnesses, the Spirit and the Word, strikes the seat of the dragon in the city of sect confusion, and arouses him to battle."[1]

Warner's first book, as its title indicates, followed in the same vein. *Bible Proofs of the Second Work of Grace* not only declared a biblical base for his favorite doctrine but also marshaled myriad texts to validate the teaching on sanctification.[2] The Carson City group, which took its stand for the truth

---

1. D. S. Warner, "The Two Witnesses," *Gospel Trumpet*, July 15, 1884.
2. Daniel S. Warner, *Bible Proofs of the Second Work of Grace* (Goshen, IN: E. U. Mennonite Publishing Society, 1880).

in October 1881, drew up a resolution to express their intention, which, among other things, declared "that we adhere to no body or organization but the Church of God, bought by the blood of Christ, organized by the Holy Spirit, and governed by the Bible."[3] Later book titles reflected the same fundamental focus on the Bible: *Biblical Trace of the Church* in 1893 by William G. Schell and *Holiness Bible Subjects* in 1894 by Henry C. Wickersham. F. G. Smith's *What the Bible Teaches* (1914) also epitomized this characteristic.

They further stated that the Bible was the only doctrinal and ethical authority. Though by no means original these reformers often reiterated the stance of "no creed but the Bible." The title banner and the masthead of the *Gospel Trumpet* contained scripture references and usually included a declared intention of promoting "the faith once delivered to the saints." Song lyrics also proclaimed the authority of Scripture. Each of the new songs in the first two songbooks carried a biblical quotation under the title; all were avowedly biblical.[4] D. Otis Teasley's 1901 song "Back to the Blessed Old Bible" encapsulates the theme:

> Back to the blessed old Bible, Back to the city of God,
> Back to the oneness of heaven, Back where the faithful have trod.
> Back from the land of confusion, Free from the bondage of creeds;
> Back to the light of the morning, Jesus our Captain leads.
> Back to the blessed old Bible, Back at the Master's call,
> Back to the words of our Savior, Loving, obeying them all.
> Never in sects to be scattered, Never again to do wrong.
> Unity, holiness, heaven, Ever shall be our song.[5]

Charles Naylor's later poetic expression put the premise of the authority of the Word even more explicitly:

> The Bible is our rule of faith and Christ alone is Lord,
> All we are equal in his sight when we obey his word;

---

3. Andrew L. Byers, *Birth of a Reformation* (Gospel Trumpet Company, 1923), 269.

4. Joseph C. Fisher, ed., *Songs of Victory* (Williamston, MI, 1885), and Daniel S. Warner and Barney E. Warren, eds., *Anthems from the Throne* (Grand Junction, MI: Gospel Trumpet Publishing Co., 1888).

5. First appeared as no. 110 in Warren et al, *Truth in Song* (Anderson, IN: Gospel Trumpet Co., 1907). The song has been included in almost all songbooks and hymnals printed since that time.

No earthly master do we know, to man-rule will not bow,
But to each other and to God eternal trueness vow.[6]

The authority of the Bible was based, of course, on the firm belief that it is the inspired Word of God. In general these early leaders were diligent students of Scripture, but they were not technical Bible scholars. It was sufficient for them to accept the fact of inspiration without delving into the various theories about it. One of the earliest writers, however, does deal with the issue and his definition is worthy of note:

> The Bible is the only authentic source from which instructions can be derived, in relation to the knowledge of God; his various dispensation to mankind, and the duties required of men by their Creator. As it claims to be regarded as the book of God, a divine authority, so it claims to be the only authority. It is not *a* rule, it is *the* rule both of faith and practice. The Bible, therefore, is the canon; that is the authoritative standard of salvation and morality.
>
> The different writers of the books of the Bible were inspired of God. It is not the words of the Bible that were inspired, it is not the thoughts of the Bible that were inspired; it is the men who wrote the Bible that were inspired. Inspiration acts not on the man's words, not on the man's thought, but on the man himself; so that he, by his own spontaneity, under the impulse of the Holy Ghost, conceives certain thoughts and gives utterance to them in certain words, both the words and the thoughts receiving the peculiar impress of the mind which conceived and uttered them.[7]

Emphasis on the preeminent authority of the Bible was also a negative judgment on all human creeds. There was no attack on any specific creedal formulations nor was there any attempt to prove that certain statements in the historic creeds were in conflict with the Bible. Early leaders simply rejected the whole idea of any person or group trying to condense all biblical truth into a small, neat package. Nothing but the whole Bible could contain all the truth; why should one settle for anything less? Creeds were

---

6. Verse 2 of "The Church's Jubilee'" by Charles W. Naylor. First published as no. 60 in H. A. Sherwood, comp., *Reformation Glory* (Gospel Trumpet Co., 1923).

7. Henry C. Wickersham, *Holiness Bible Subjects* (Grand Junction, MI: Gospel Trumpet Publishing Co., 1894), 18–19.

the creation of the sects and were the instruments of division. Only the whole Bible could unite the whole church.

The second major theological presupposition undergirding the developing Church of God movement was the basic conviction that *religion, for the Christian, is essentially experiential.* In this they were not especially unique, either in the concept or in its various elements. These nineteenth-century reformers stood squarely in the camp of the sixteenth-century Reformation in affirming justification by grace through faith—a viewpoint that rejected all schemes for justification by works, including participation in the sacraments. Early Church of God leaders also accepted both the premises and methodologies of nineteenth-century revivalism, which de-emphasized any kind of confessional approach to justification and elevated the necessity of a life-changing conversion experience—an identifiable occasion when the believer is born again through repentance, faith, and grace. Revival meetings and camp meetings provided frequent opportunities for people to repent, exercise their faith in Christ, and claim God's gracious salvation experience.

An important ingredient of their experiential emphasis was that it pinpointed a specific memory and place when "something happened." This memory provided internalized assurance of the forgiveness of sins and the reality of being a child of God. "Know-so" salvation was the occasion for great rejoicing. Public testimony regarding "what the Lord has done" was not only encouraged but expected of every believer. The *Gospel Trumpet* provided a special section for those who wished to share their witness in print. Almost all public meetings included a time for oral testimonies. Many song lyrics were written in the first person and provided opportunity for a whole congregation to join in declaring,

> I'm redeemed, praise the Lord!
> I'm redeemed by the blood of the Lamb;
> I am saved from all sin, and I'm walking in the light,
> I'm redeemed by the blood of the Lamb.[8]

Even in a social gesture like signing an autograph album, Warner always included his testimony by adding, "Your saved brother."[9] Joy in the Lord was a trademark of both public and private worship.

---

8. J. C. Fisher's lyric published in the first songbook continues to be widely sung in churches.
9. Warner also autographed his pictures and books with this phrase.

An additional aspect of this experiential emphasis was brought into focus by Church of God leaders and other Christians in America who espoused the doctrine of holiness. For them the word *salvation* was usually preceded by the adjective *full,* and *full salvation* was defined as the result of a "two-fold work of grace." In the words of Warner, "The great object of the Savior's death is to save men from all sin. And since sin exists in two forms, the word of God often presents salvation as a two-fold remedy for sin."[10] In the words of Charles Wesley "He breaks the power of cancelled sin; he sets the prisoner free…" The two forms of sin were described as "committed" sins and "inbred" sin or the unrighteous nature in fallen humanity. Thus a "double cure" was required to rectify the human condition—forgiveness for the sins of transgression and empowerment for victory over the sinful nature. Full salvation, then, would remove *all* sin and enable the believer to live free from sin because of having experienced both justifying grace and standing grace (Rom 5:1-2).

This theological line was followed by most of those who espoused the doctrine of holiness.[11] Many of the early leaders had been part of the Holiness Movement. Their standard presentation called for not just one but two spiritual crisis experiences—justification and sanctification. According to Henry C. Wickersham:

> Sanctification, in the economy of grace, is a distinct work subsequent to regeneration. Regeneration, the first work of grace, includes the pardon of all past sins; the removal of all guilt and condemnation; adoption into the family of God; the witness of the Spirit pardon and Sonship; spiritual life and a new moral nature, including all the Christian graces.
>
> Sanctification, the second work of grace, includes the destruction of all the works of the devil; the restoration of man to the state of holiness from which he fell, by creating him anew in Christ Jesus, and restoring to him all that image and likeness of God which he lost in the fall of Adam.[12]

---

10. Daniel S. Warner, *Salvation: Present, Perfect, Now or Never* (Grand Junction, MI: Gospel Trumpet Publishing Co., [1896]), 30.

11. This interpretation would describe all those who followed the teaching of John Wesley and the Methodists. A somewhat different, but not incompatible, view of holiness was held by Charles Finney and the Oberlin School, who did not make a sharp distinction between the two experiences of justification and sanctification.

12. Wickersham, *Holiness Bible Subjects*, 47–48.

Warner saw sanctification as a Holy Spirit-initiated experience granting perfection (understood as intentional moral purity) to the recipient because the old nature had been removed. Without sanctification one could not live up to the Bible standard, but with sanctification came "heart purity," "fullness of God," "fullness of joy," "assurance of faith," "full assurance of hope," "perfect love," "the more abundant life," and "the baptism of the Holy Ghost."[13] Thus the double cure was validated in a double experience resulting in full salvation. Who could do other than rejoice?

The importance of this experiential understanding of salvation in the minds of the pioneer leaders of the Church of God can hardly be overemphasized. It was related to all other aspects of their faith and practice, and especially to their view of relationships to each other, to the world, and to other Christians.

The third undergirding premise of these earliest reformers was their belief that God was calling them to proclaim and to model the visible earthly expression of his one holy catholic church. In point of fact this presupposition became the movement's central focus, and all other teaching came to have contingent meaning related to this understanding of the universal church. In response to this call as it related to the church of their day, a number of particular points emerged for both attack and affirmation. Although nobody drew up a campaign platform or manifesto, there does seem to be some design in their treatment of the church issue. In the first two decades at least seven facets shaped their perception of this "light on the church" that had been opened to them. A brief look at each of these is necessary for an understanding of the message that so excited the flying messengers.

The most elemental aspect of their view of the church was the conviction that indeed they were religious reformers because God had opened to them a vision of the Church as God intended it to be—a vision that contrasted sharply with the competitive picture of institutional Christianity they saw around them. "Seeing the light on the church" was, for them, more than a mere intellectual understanding. In their vision they saw the church as a visible universal spiritual fellowship of all the redeemed. It is visible, they said, because it is made up of living people who are redeemed by the atoning work of Christ—recognizable saints whose lives witness to their experience of rebirth. It is universal in that it includes *all* the redeemed, regardless of

---

13. Warner, *Bible Proofs*, 50–53.

whatever churchly affiliations they might or might not have. It is spiritual in that true membership is limited to the spiritually reborn; the Church can include *only* those who are truly saved. It is a fellowship in that this common experience in Christ brings together in a new and wonderful relationship all those so redeemed without the necessity of any human structure and without regard for any sectarian boundaries. All God's people are inevitably related simply because they are God's people.

The early saints found their vision of the Church to be supported by Scripture, making it clearly God's will for his people and, therefore, an achievable goal. They identified themselves as having been called to be God's messengers in proclaiming this ideal and in outlining the biblical means for its realization. They were challenged by this divine assignment and gladly put their whole lives into carrying out their commission to make the vision a reality.

The second facet of the early leaders' ecclesiology was the categorical rejection of any expectation that the true church could be identified with any existing sect or denomination. They saw no point in searching to find the one that most closely approached the ideal, for all groups calling themselves "churches" necessarily fell short of the vision. In some sense all were apostate; fallenness was clear. In the first place, every sect was guilty of dividing the church, and division among God's people is contrary to Christ's intention. Denominationalism itself is inherently a sinful system. As Warner put it, "If a sect organization were right in everything else, its actual existence is in opposition to the word, and is therefore wrong."[14]

The saints saw further evidence of the deviance of denominationalism in the practice of admitting as members, thereby labeling them Christian, individuals whose lives did not measure up to the Bible's standards. The sects were considered guilty of corrupting the church by permitting obvious sinners to enter into full favor and fellowship. The point of criticism was not just laxity in screening admissions but the practice of formal church membership itself, which seemed to imply a positive judgment on the spiritual condition of the candidate—a judgment that no finite human being was capable of making. The final flaw evident in existing sects was that all were locked into humanly made systems of organization and humanly devised creedal commitments. Without these they could not function or even exist. The true church, early leaders believed, could never be so shackled or

---

14. "Erroneous Sayings," *Gospel Trumpet*, February 18, 1892, 2.

alienated from divine direction. In the final analysis, then, no denomination could measure up to the stature of the church. The system itself was sinful, and since all existing groups adhered to that system all were participants in that sin.

The third aspect of the early reformers' understanding of the church concerned their response to denominations. The only viable solution to this massive distortion of the church, the pioneers said, is to reject and discard the sinful system in which the church had allowed itself to become ensnared. This rejection would entail eliminating the whole conglomerate of sectarian structures then in existence and calling out all the redeemed, the true church, into an open fellowship of "saints." This new community could then function corporately in ministry, service, and mission under the direct leadership of the Holy Spirit without lapsing into any humanly devised organization. Such a simplistic, even naive, solution to a monumental problem carried strong appeal for many people. Reflection on the magnitude of its implications excited them and generated considerable support. Likewise, advocating the dissolution of denominations naturally provoked many questions and raised no small amount of opposition. The early saints seriously advocated this dump-the-accumulated-excess-baggage-and-start-over-again approach, defending it as the only way to get "back to the blessed old Bible" and thus reconstitute the church.[15]

The fourth facet of "light on the church" was a particular point made of the generally accepted Christian belief that God intended the church to be holy. The reason for lifting up this affirmation was to emphasize the sense in which the holiness of the church should be made manifest. Church of God leaders rejected the view held by Roman Catholics and many Protestants that the church is holy because it has been entrusted with the ministration of the sacraments, which correspondingly become the means of grace. Likewise the saints negated the related doctrine of "apostolic succession" which supported the concept of a holy church by viewing its clergy as direct successors of Christ and the apostles, thus making clergy the authorized mediators of grace. These views were regarded as human inventions that encouraged a concept of salvation by works and populated the sects with unredeemed sinners. On the contrary, according to the pioneers the holiness of the church was based on two biblically supported premises: (a) The church is the body of Christ; he founded it and it continues as his presence

---

15. D. Otis Teasley, "Back to the Blessed Old Bible," 1901. First appeared as no. 110 in Warren et al, *Truth in Song* (Anderson, IN: Gospel Trumpet Co., 1907).

in the world; and (b) the members are holy people, the redeemed. Through empowerment by the Holy Spirit in the experience of sanctification even the human element of the true holiness of the church could be made holy.

Fifth, the aspect of the church probably most often mentioned in the early Church of God was unity. God does not have churches, they said, he has *a* church. God's ultimate will is a single, united, visible church. They made a special point that the unity of the church must be real, not a nebulous spiritual connection that actually was camouflaged division. They could not settle for an invisible unity that many found acceptable. Genuine unity must be apparent if Jesus' followers were to effectively witness "that the world might believe." Moreover, the saints could not accept a humanly contrived unity such as federations, councils, or associations of churches. These or denominational mergers might produce a semblance of union, but they could not create unity. All these were seen as attempts at rationalizing division or covering up the sinful disunity that was distorting and weakening the church. The unity of the church was linked with the doctrine of holiness and the experience of sanctification. The perfection of the saints was the only way to achieve the perfect unity of the church. In Warner's words, "Both Christ and all that are wholly sanctified by him are of one, yea, of one Spirit, of one mind, of one faith, of one heart and soul, and all in 'one body,' of which he is the head, and we are members in particular."[16] Holiness and unity were thus inseparably linked, with unity being the beautiful fruit of perfected holiness.

Sixth, to avoid the trap of forming another sect in their attempt to escape sectarianism, these reformers shunned any kind of organization other than governance by the Holy Spirit. *Human ecclesiasticism* was one of the most abominable terms in their vocabulary. "Succession of authority down through a course of ecclesiastical lords," wrote Warner, "is all a superstitious delusion, a dragon power." He continued:

> Those whom God saves, baptizes with power, and commissions by the Holy Spirit have the only ecclesiastical authority instituted of God, and this comes direct from heaven and not through any imaginary line of predecessors....
>
> The church, then, is organized by the Lord, who sets the members in the body as it pleases him and distributes the gifts and callings

---

16. Daniel S. Warner and Herbert M. Riggle, *The Cleansing of the Sanctuary* (Moundsville, WV: Gospel Trumpet Publishing Co., 1903), 262.

through his own wisdom to all the members of the body. Men may organize a human compact, but never the divine body of Christ which is the church....[17]

This vision of a divinely, charismatically organized church was expressed in many ways—including poetry and song. C. W. Naylor's 1922 lyric is a good example:

Divinely built, divinely ruled,
To God she doth submit;
His will her law, His truth her guide,
Her path is glory lit.

God sets her members each in place,
According to His will—
Apostles, prophets, teachers, all,
His purpose to fulfill.[18]

From a practical standpoint, *charismatic stance* meant the elimination of all offices, titles (except Brother and Sister), committees, boards, and any other procedures requiring elections or appointments. The one exception was the ordination of elders or ministers. While admitting ordination implied some human organization of the church, Warner insisted that this was simply a way of "recognizing the divine call and dedicating thereunto."[19] He substantiated this view in Acts 13:14. Operationally, action occurred—meetings, decisions, travel, publications, and all that was involved in the saints' intense activity—as "the Lord led." They sought and found the mind of the Lord through prayer, counsel, study of the Bible, and by being impressed that a certain course accorded with the Lord's will. It is notable that, as loose and subjective as this procedure might seem, it sustained the activity of the movement for almost forty years.

The seventh and final aspect of the church as perceived by these early leaders was the quality of openness. They believed that God, through the

17. Daniel S. Warner, *The Church of God, or What Is the Church and What Is Not* (Anderson, IN: Warner Press, n.d.), 11.

18. Stanzas 2 and 3, "O Church of God," in *Worship the Lord: Hymnal of the Church of God* (Anderson, IN: Warner Press, 1989), no. 289.

19. Warner, *Church of God*, 11–12. "Do Ministers of God See Eye to Eye?" *Gospel Trumpet*, December 14, 1893, 1.

Holy Spirit, continues to reveal knowledge of himself and his will to those followers who are faithful, diligent, and seeking. While all divine truth is contained in the Scriptures, human understanding of that truth can and should increase. All individuals do not begin at the same level of knowledge or grow in understanding at the same pace. It is only natural therefore, that there would be some differences in the way parts of the Word might be interpreted by finite human beings. The important thing was that each person should be open to "light" and then be willing to walk in that light. This principle allowed for a great deal of flexibility in doctrinal and practical belief. At the point of application to everyday circumstances, however, there was a strong insistence that there be no disharmony in teaching. In late 1892, for instance, there seems to have been some noticeable diversity regarding the interpretation of Matthew 19:24. Warner raised the question whether ministers should be in total agreement concerning Scripture. He wrote a series of three articles elaborating a proper view of the points at issue. In stating his general premise he wrestled with the apparent paradox of rigidity versus flexibility. He put it this way:

> On the authority of God's word we affirm that it is the privilege and solemn duty of all God's messengers to understand and teach the word of God in perfect harmony. This does not however, imply that they all have the same gifts or abilities, nor yet that they have all attained unto the same degree of knowledge in sacred truth; but "whereunto we have attained we walk by the same rule," and what we have not learned of the Lord we do not presume to teach. Hence there is harmony in all that is taught, so long as each teacher is confined within that measure of truth received by the Holy Spirit."[20]

By the third article in the series Warner seemed to have moved more toward the rigid side of the spectrum in that he changed the title from a question to a statement, making it read, "The Ministers of God Must See Eye to Eye." Even so, as he closed this final article reaffirming the basis on which all may ultimately arrive at the same understanding of divine truth, Warner still left the door open for some variance as long as harmony prevailed. He concluded:

---

20. "Do Ministers of God See Eye to Eye?" *Gospel Trumpet*, December 14, 1893, 1.

And now beloved, if we are going to fulfill the prophecy of a holy ministry returned from Babylon confusion, to see eye to eye, and teach the same things, be sure that you take up and teach nothing that only has the traditions of sectism to sustain it. Only teach what you know by the sure Word and Spirit of God, and there will be harmony.[21]

These seven facets of early Church of God ecclesiology demonstrate the pioneers' deep sense of mission in reforming the church. Their ecclesiology colored much of their theology. It is not much of an overstatement to say that in the Church of God underneath almost any theological dispute one would find that the real issue is ecclesiology.

The fourth, and last, major concept undergirding the Church of God reformation movement was the belief that they were participants in the fulfillment of a segment of divine destiny for all humanity. They understood their role as being heralds of God's ultimate will for his church. All the rest of their beliefs took on a special significance in this light. The concept itself had several facets and developed in stages over more than a decade. One caution is in order. This sense of destiny did not provide the initial impetus for the movement. As it developed, however, it provided new and strong incentives to proclaim the original concepts and certainly accelerated the development of the movement's self-consciousness among both leaders and followers.

There were three aspects to the concept of divine destiny—aspects that almost become sequential stages, although they cannot be delineated quite that simply. First was the belief that the end of time was near. While not particularly distinctive, since many contemporary groups operated from a "last days" understanding, the Church of God leaders made this a very prominent aspect of their teaching. Nobody set the time of Christ's return, but Warner is reported to have said that he expected the end of the world during his lifetime.[22] Written confirmation of such a view is absent, but it is not inconsistent with related statements made by him and others that indicate an expectation that the second advent was imminent.

Along with many others who claimed an adventist emphasis, Church of God leaders pointed to certain world events as signs of the times and indicators of the approach of the end. In addition to the usual references

---

21. "Ministers of God Must See Eye to Eye," *Gospel Trumpet*, December 28, 1893, 4.

22. Charles W. Naylor, *The Teachings of D. S. Warner and His Associates* (Anderson, IN: privately published, n.d.), 6.

to "perilous times" they noted that the organized church was fallen and sinful,[23] that the Jews were returning to Jerusalem,[24] and that many of them were accepting Christ.[25] Unlike others, the pioneers saw their own work toward the restoration of the church as a sign of the approaching end.[26] Also, unlike most others who emphasized an imminent second advent, these early leaders rejected millennialism in any form and saw Christ's return as the occasion for final judgment and the end of the world. Verses and phrases from many early songs indicate the prominence of this emphasis. For example, Warner wrote:

> Are you ready waiting for the Lord?
>   See, the signs proclaim Him near;
> In the awful thunders of His word,
>   Now His coming steps we hear.
> Soon we'll hear the trumpet's sound!
> Judgment's coming, O how soon!
> Christ is coming, O the heavenly sight!
>   Our beloved can't delay;
> For His bride is robed in snowy white,
>   Ready for the crowning day.
> Quickly coming in Thy Glory![27]

The belief that time was short and the urgency of the message drove the early reformers to become flying messengers, willing to accept persecution and hardship to fulfill their God-ordained mission. In reporting one meeting Warner observed, "The number of those that are separated wholly unto the Gospel of our Lord Jesus Christ, is rapidly increasing. God is evidently making a 'short work upon the earth,' and He wants 'Many to run to and fro.'"[28]

The second aspect of this destiny consciousness expressed itself in the terminology of apocalypticism to describe the current condition of the

---

23. D. S. Warner, "Woe to the Inhabiters of the Earth," *Gospel Trumpet*, September 1, 1884, 1.

24. D. S. Warner, "The Jewish Exodus," *Gospel Trumpet*, January 1, 1885, 2.

25. D. S. Warner, "Present Awful Truth—The End Drawing Nigh," *Gospel Trumpet*, November 15, 1881, 1.

26. D. S. Warner, "The Glorious Return," *Gospel Trumpet*, June 1, 1885, 1–2.

27. "The Lord Is Coming," in Joseph C. Fisher, ed., *Songs of Victory*, (Williamston, MI: Gospel Trumpet Co., 1884), no. 7.

28. "The Glorious Assembly," *Gospel Trumpet*, October 15, 1884, 4.

church. As early as March 1878, just two months after his expulsion from the Ohio Eldership, Warner referred to those in the sects as "Babylon's children," and then elaborated by noting, "Babylon properly includes about all protestant churchism."[29] In April he made another reference to Protestant denominations as "formal Babylon."[30] One of the earliest full-length *Gospel Trumpet* articles based in apocalyptic interpretation was written by Warner and appeared in October 1883. Titled "Babylon Leaders and Dragon Authority," this article dealt with Revelation 13 and equated the first beast with Roman Catholicism and then distinctly identified the second or two-horned beast with those churches that sprang from the Roman Catholic Church. He wrote:

> Now who will tell us what this second beast is? There is absolutely nothing on earth that corresponds with it but protestant sectism. The sects are closely related to Rome, their mother. So the second beast [is] allied with the first. They exercise the same kind of authority, namely that which [was] conferred by the dragon, an ecclesiastical authority, constituted by humanly created offices.[31]

Early leaders equated apocalyptic literature with prophecy, understood primarily as foretelling the future. A significant aspect of the prophetic emphasis was the identification of those last days as the "evening time," a phrase drawn from Zechariah 14:7 which states, "It shall come to pass, that at evening time it shall be light." Early leaders came to interpret this text as projecting their own work. In sermon, in tract, and article, and as usual, in song, they heralded the evening light. The exhilaration of this thought is reflected in one of Warner's lyrics:

> Brighter days are sweetly dawning,
> O the glory looms in sight!
> For the cloudy day is waning,
> And the evening shall be light.
>
> Lo! the ransomed are returning,
> Robed in shining crystal white;

---

29. Warner Diary, March 26, 1878.
30. Warner Diary, April 5, 1878.
31. *Gospel Trumpet*, October 15, 1883.

Leaping, shouting home to Zion,
Happy in the evening light.

Free from babel, in the Spirit,
Free to worship God aright;
Joy and gladness we're receiving,
O how sweet this evening light![32]

A component of this cluster of beliefs was a call to all the truly redeemed to abandon the sinful sects and to come out of spiritual darkness into the light. Although the early leaders denied the charge of preaching "come-outism" because the term was generally understood at that time to mean "come out of one group and join another," there is no denying that they gave a great deal of emphasis to 2 Corinthians 6:17: "Come out…and be ye separate." In calling the faithful out of sectarian bondage they strongly insisted they were not asking the redeemed to join another sect but were inviting them to participate in the free fellowship of the Spirit. In response to the accusation of being a sect founder Warner replied that it was not so; such an act would only multiply sin:

> God forbid that any more of the harlots should be "conceived in sin, and shaped in iniquity." If that were so sectism were a sin from which there would be no escape. But the voice from heaven says, "Come out of her, my people." So there is a way out of her, "and it shall be called the way of holiness."[33]

All true Christians were expected to recognize and accept God's call to leave their sects when they saw the light. Those failing to answer the call would remain in darkness and ultimately be lost.

The third and latest aspect in developing the destiny concept was the interpretation of apocalyptic literature in the Old and New Testaments in a church-historical framework that projected the date for a new—and final—reform of the church. This date coincided, not accidentally, with the approximate date of the beginning of the movement in which they were involved. There was nothing new about such efforts, of course, for they had been made throughout the centuries by some of Christianity's most

---

32. D. S. Warner, "The Evening Light," in Fisher, *Songs of Victory*, no. 58.
33. Warner, *The Church of God?* 29.

able scholars. Jonathan Edwards, the great eighteenth-century preacher and theologian, had developed his own scheme for matching the symbols in the Book of Revelation with events in church history.[34] Contemporary with the early Church of God, extensive use of this method had been made by the Seventh-day Adventists. Although the earlier predictions by founder William Miller had fallen into disrepute, the methodology had survived, and modified applications were made by Ellen White and scholar Uriah Smith. Warner and other early leaders in the Church of God were acquainted with these writings. Smith's writings were frequently referenced, usually disputing his conclusions but not in opposing his method.[35] The use of a church-historical method by Church of God writers represents a later stage in the development of their concepts about the divine destiny of their work.

The earliest published reference in Church of God literature to the dating of events in church history by interpretive apocalyptic literature is found in 1884. Warner wrote two articles in expositing Revelation 11. In the first he interpreted the 1,260 days referred to in verse 3 to mean 1,260 years of tyrannical papal rule and paralleling the "time, times, and a half time" of the little horn of Daniel 7:25.[36] No beginning or terminus date for the period is suggested. In the second article Warner made a special point of the two witnesses—the Word and the Spirit—rising three and a half days later and striking terror into those who saw them. This, he said, prophesies the "great special holiness reform."[37]

It was not until 1887 that the first article appeared in the *Gospel Trumpet* that developed from biblical apocalyptic chronology for the renewal or reformation of the church. Based on an interpretation of the eighth chapter of Daniel, the article bore the same title as the book that Warner was to begin later, "The Cleansing of the Sanctuary."[38] Here Warner dealt specifically with the sanctuary that is to be cleansed at the end of the 2,300 days. In rather complicated fashion he wrestled with the writings of other prophets, events, and dates, eventually concluding with the year 1882, which, he wrote, "better accords with the facts." He found the whole

---

34. Jonathan Edwards, *Apocalyptic Writings*, ed. Stephen J. Stein, vol 5, *The Works of Jonathan Edwards* (New Haven: Yale University Press, 1977).

35. Uriah Smith, *Thoughts on the Prophecies of Daniel and the Revelation* (Battle Creek, MI: Review and Herald Publishing Co., 1897). This was a major work of Smith's. Earlier writings were available.

36. *Gospel Trumpet*, April 15, 1884.

37. *Gospel Trumpet*, June 1, 1884.

38. *Gospel Trumpet*, June 1, 1887.

experience of prophetic inquiry to be a stimulating exercise with exciting ramifications:

> Praise God! We see something grand in this, which we can only here take time to hint at. There is an exact parallel between the description of Nehemiah 2-6 and the present work of cleansing the sanctuary, or restoring the complete walls of salvation, and gates of praise, to the Heavenly Jerusalem, or Church of First-born.

Warner was excited and yet tentative about this line of thought. "There are many particulars connected with Gabriel's revelation that we cannot now speak of. As the Lord continues to enlighten our mind, we will give to you as He gives to us."

Later in 1887 additional information and a somewhat different conclusion appeared in the *Gospel Trumpet* concerning the two witnesses of Revelation 11. Warner frequently was asked by readers to answer or explain doctrinal questions. In one such instance he responded:

> The papacy was not set up until the 4th century, but the same ecclesiastical beast authority that formed into the papacy was set up about the year 270. So the 1260 years beginning at that time expired in 1530. That was just the time the second beast appeared on earth—see Rev. 13—namely protestantism. The Augsburg Confession, the first protestants' creed was made and adopted in that year. Also the Smolcald [sic] league of protestants was made and subscribed to in the same year. That is when the devil, having failed to destroy the Church by persecution and martyrdom, conspires against her by his second counterfeit, protestantism, and by this more deceptive policy these two witnesses are killed and their dead bodies lay in the street of the great city....
>
> "Three days and a half," the Spirit interprets to us as 350 years of protestantism, beginning 1530 and ending with the evening light in 1880. In the evening light, the two witnesses rise up again in power.[39]

In this article Warner outlined the dating schema that was to become standard in the movement for several decades. It is notable, however, that practically no further mention is made of this interpretative method until

---

39. *Gospel Trumpet*, September 15, 1887, 4.

1890. By then other writers had taken up the study, and it became a matter of general interest. Henry Wickersham wrote an article making use of the types-and-shadows method of interpreting the Old Testament, which covered much of the same ground Warner had covered earlier. The first major work that developed this apocalyptic identity of the Church of God was William G. Schell's, *Biblical Trace of the Church*, published in 1893, although parts of the book had been printed earlier in the form of *Gospel Trumpet* articles. Warner was working on a major manuscript in this area at the time of his death—a work that was later edited and completed by H. M. Riggle, *The Cleansing of the Sanctuary* (1903). Still later (1908) F. G. Smith, in *The Revelation Explained,* became the chief authority and spokesperson for this church-historical interpretation applied to the Church of God. Across the movement Smith became the recognized expert on the church in prophecy and history. His talent as a writer, lecturer (with illustrative charts), editor, and preacher helped to solidify this framework for validating the group's self-consciousness. The conclusions of church-historical interpretation provided an accepted central rationale for the movement's existence for more than a third of its life.

In summary, it must be noted that the Church of God reform movement did not find the basis for its self-consciousness in any one of the basic concepts herein delineated but in a combination of all four. Each depends on the other three, and all give support to each. None of them have any meaning, for instance, without the principle that the sole foundation of the Christian faith is in the Scriptures. The personal experiential interpretation of the Christian life is necessary to understand the nature of the church and the unity of believers. The sense of destiny involves the Christian individually and also corporately in the church. The interlocking themes that tie them all together are holiness, unity, and mission. Of such was the Church of God made as it emerged from a loosely associated, but sincere people to become a united movement aware of its purposes in the accomplishment of God's divine will for all his people on earth.

CHAPTER 6

TOWARD A WORLDWIDE FELLOWSHIP
(1882–1909)

It could be expected that the initial evangelistic efforts of the flying ministry were concentrated in the United States. Calls for meetings were so numerous that every available worker constantly traveled in response to these requests. There was little time to sit and dream of new worlds to conquer. However, even during the first decade of the movement's history there were several contacts and some overt efforts to extend the reform work beyond the national borders. By the turn of the century international activity was extensive, and by the time of the first organization of missionary work the work had expanded to a global reach. The years from 1888 to 1909 marked a period of the movement's spontaneous, unstructured expansion to worldwide proportions.

Canada

Since a great deal of the activity of the publishing work and the itinerant ministry was centered in the upper Middle West, it was only natural that the first international extension of the message was to Canada. The first contact made by the movement to America's northern neighbor came through the printed pages of the *Gospel Trumpet*. It is not known exactly how the *Trumpet* made its way into Canada, but there is evidence it was read in Ontario as early as 1882.[1] Apparently there were already those in Canada who held

---

1. The first letter received from Canada was sent from Ontario by Eliza J. White and printed in the February 15, 1883, issue of the *Gospel Trumpet*, 2. In it she writes, "We received your paper three times, so far like it very well. My husband, myself, and a few others are outside of denominations, have been so for about two years, cannot submit to idolatry and man's yoke. We have Christ's yoke which is better: it is easy and light. We meet in private houses excepting one place where is built a hall for us to worship in. Pray for us that we may stand firm for God's truth and that nothing of the world be bound upon us, that our master be but one, and that the great God of heaven."

views similar to those found in the *Trumpet's* pages and, after reading of the truth that Warner proclaimed, these Canadians wanted to hear more.[2] Correspondence indicates that the *Trumpet* played a major role in introducing Canadian people to the Church of God reformation movement and was a welcome source of encouragement to those with compatible theological views and insights. The message was spread initially through the individual efforts of readers in Ontario. Some requested sample copies to distribute to potential subscribers.[3] One reader simply states that he would do his best to get subscribers for this paper.[4]

The *Gospel Trumpet* thus preceded any evangelistic visit to Canada from the United States, but there are indications as early as 1883 that such visits were desired.[5] A number of people were by then familiar with Warner and his publication and had already been involved in raising up groups that were free from sectism. A lay preacher who had written the first letter to the *Trumpet,* Eliza J. White, held evangelistic meetings assisted by Thomas McClive in Fulton, Castorcenter, and Attercliff in 1886.[6] In January of that same year, White had corresponded with Warner and communicated her interest in inviting him to come to the area.[7] Another person involved in these early developments, John E. Smith, also expressed hope that Warner would visit Canadian brothers and sisters.[8]

The first recorded evangelistic visit to Canada occurred in 1888. Eliza White is credited for arranging this visit by Warner and his evangelistic company. The company, consisting of Warner, B. E. Warren, Mother Sarah Smith, Frankie Miller, and Nannie Kigar, spent the summer of

---

2. Beverly Carvin Anderson, "A History of the Church of God in Ontario," BDiv thesis, Anderson College and Theological Seminary, 1955, 6. Anderson observes that the *Gospel Trumpet* served more as a reinforcing agent or an encouraging agent to those who had already realized for themselves the truth that D. S. Warner was preaching then as an evangelistic tool to lead people out of sectism and into the Church of God reformation movement.

3. *Gospel Trumpet*, November 1, 1883, 4.

4. *Gospel Trumpet*, August 15, 1883, 4.

5. In a letter from Thomas R. Wilson in Brace Ridge, Ontario, Wilson states, "May God raise up someone to preach Christ in all his fullness in these parts" (*Gospel Trumpet*, December 1, 1883, 4).

6. Anderson, *History of the Church of God in Ontario*, 9.

7. In Eliza White's correspondence printed in the *Gospel Trumpet* on January 15, 1886, 4, and directed by Warner, she stated, "We have started a special work for the Master in my neighborhood... Will be glad when God says to you, go to Canada."

8. In a letter printed in the May 1, 1887, edition of the *Gospel Trumpet*, 4, Smith related how he came into the fellowship of the "true saints" and gave indication that there was a need to have certain areas of the church's needs "set in order." It is in this context that he said, "My prayer is that God will send Bro. Warner out here to set in order the things that are wanted in the church."

1888 attending camp meetings and visiting churches located in Michigan, Indiana, Ohio, and Pennsylvania. They arrived in Welland, Ontario, on November 24, 1888, and remained on the Niagara Peninsula until March 1889. Warner held meetings in Welland, Fenwick, Crowland, St. Ann, and Vineland and encountered much opposition because of his antisectarian preaching. Despite this religious conflict, Warner secured many new subscribers to the *Gospel Trumpet,* ordained leaders to carry on the work in Ontario, made plans for a camp meeting, and established three congregations in Crowland, Fenwick, and Welland. A few months after Warner's departure, George T. and Lizzie Clayton moved to Welland, Ontario. The Claytons were great contributors to the early development of the Church of God movement in Canada. Along with a Mr. Evans, like the Claytons from Pennsylvania, they were in charge of the first Ontario camp meeting, held two miles north of Welland from August 30 to September 6, 1889. Clayton and Evans held meetings at Chippewa and Crowland following the meeting. Evans returned to the United States, but the Claytons set up residence in Welland, holding meetings there and in the surrounding area. Clayton was assisted at times by John E. Smith, William Thomas of Fenwick, Mary Pack, the Shivelys from Buffalo, and the Patchens from Welland.

A Canadian publishing venture is one of the notable aspects of the early work of the Church of God in Ontario. C. L. Kaumeyer of Chippewa, Ontario, perhaps on the direct suggestion of D. S. Warner, began to print a children's paper titled *The Guide.*[9] A June 1889 issue of the *Gospel Trumpet* announced:

> We are happy to announce that a paper for the children is about to be started. Many have been writing to us encouraging us to publish such a paper. We were thinking of doing so, when we doubt not that the Lord directed our minds to Bro. C. L. Kaumeyer of Chippewa, Ont., as one we thought well qualified for this calling and being provided with a competent printing office. We wrote him about the matter, and he is willing to publish the same, and expects to start it soon.[10]

The following month the *Gospel Trumpet* advertised: "We are in receipt of a number of copies of the first issue and can heartily recommend it to

---

9. Anderson, *History of the Church of God in Ontario,* 35–36.
10. *Gospel Trumpet,* June 1, 1889, 2.

all our friends, as a valuable publication filled with Gospel truth, and is interesting to both old and young and it should be in every family for the benefit of the children."[11] Later, in reference to *The Guide's* second issue, Warner wrote, "There is a great difference between its tone, and the trashy Sunday School sheets in popular circulation. But we regret that so few have sent in orders. Brethren this is sheer neglect. I know you want the paper, and many of you intend to send for it. For Jesus' sake attend to the matter at once."[12]

The Guide subscribers received bimonthly issues for thirty cents a year. Later, in an effort to increase circulation, Kaumeyer announced that the paper would be free. In May 1890, he conceded that he was unable to keep his paper going regularly and would print it only as funds were available. Eventually the paper succumbed to financial woes. A final report from Kaumeyer appeared in an early 1893 issue of the *Gospel Trumpet:* "We have not been able to get out another number of the 'Guide' since July. We have received about $1.40 toward printing the next issue, which would make it appear to be a failure."[13]

Warner visited Ontario again for a camp meeting in the late summer of 1891.[14] Clayton returned with the Warner company to the United States for some meetings in Pennsylvania and went back to Canada about January 1, 1892. Mary Sowers and Emily Dunmyer accompanied the Claytons on their return to Canada and assisted them in meetings at Fenwick and the Townline Bethel. It was during this time that the Claytons sought to launch the *Floating Bethel* evangelistic boat. The *Gospel Trumpet* carried many requests for the project's assistance, and Canadians were interested in helping. The Patchens of Welland advertised their house and lot for sale in order that they might contribute toward the barge's purchase. They later worked with the Claytons on the *Floating Bethel.* During the summer of 1892,

---

11. *Gospel Trumpet*, July 1, 1889, 2.
12. *Gospel Trumpet*, July 15, 1889, 3.
13. *Gospel Trumpet*, January 5, 1893, 3.
14. In a letter published in the October 15, 1891, edition of the *Gospel Trumpet*, Warner expresses his disappointment in the camp meeting: "The camp meeting in Canada was scarcely entitled to the name. It came in the busy time of seeding besides, most of the people know nothing about camp meetings, hence scarcely any of the brethren provided ways to camp on the ground....Part of the time the weather was cold and wet, which prevented many from attending. On favorable nights, and on the Sabbath there were large crowds of people present. There were but few souls saved during the meeting. We were happy to meet nearly all we left clear in their souls three years ago yet saved and rejoicing in the Lord," 2.

Clayton and W. J. Henry held meetings throughout the Ontario province.[15] By late summer, the Claytons left Ontario to work in Pennsylvania and to launch their long-planned Ohio River campaign. G. T. Clayton returned to Ontario in 1899 and spent nine months strengthening established areas and holding evangelistic meetings. In the spring of 1893, A. J. Kilpatrick held meetings at Fenwick and Crowland.

Growth of the local ministry in Ontario at this time was noticeable. S. M. Birdsall took active leadership once he came into the movement and is listed as the "correspondent" in the camp meeting notice for 1893. He and John E. Smith were very active in evangelistic work. Birdsall, a medical doctor, was ordained as a "minister to preach the gospel" at the 1893 camp meeting along with David Moyer. Moyer went to Berlin (now Kitchener), Ontario, to conduct services during the winter of 1893–94. He was assisted by William G. Schell who arrived in the spring of 1894. William Deachman held meetings in eastern Ontario and J. C. Blaney was converted through the indirect influence of Deachman's ministry.[16] Blaney later became one of the strongest leaders in the work in southern Ontario.

In 1894 a camp meeting was held near Fenwick from August 23 to September 2. It was during this camp meeting that John A. and A. J. Dillon arrived in Ontario. They served as provincial evangelists until 1898. Like the Claytons, the Dillons established residence in Welland and from that base held many evangelistic meetings during their four-year stay. Although they left for a brief period during the winter of 1895–96 to visit Pennsylvania, the Dillons returned to Ontario later in 1896 to continue their work. During the Dillons' ministry a permanent campground was developed in 1895 near Fenwick, and the first camp meeting there was held August 29 through September 9. The Dillons' evangelistic ministry was characterized by what were called tabernacle meetings. A large tent, thirty by fifty feet, was purchased and meetings were held in it at Welland, Berlin, St. Thomas, Attercliffe, and Winona. Abram M. Bixler joined Dillon during the summer to assist him in these meetings, and they were also the principal speakers at the 1895 camp meeting. While the Dillons were in Pennsylvania, John E. Smith, S. M. Birdsall, and other local leaders carried on the work in Ontario.

15. During one of these meetings, Dr. S. M. Birdsall of Fenwick was saved. Birdsall later became quite active in evangelistic work.

16. "Deachman, assisted by a Mr. Scobbie, held a revival in the town of Pendleton. This was the home of the Blaney family. Fred Blaney was converted at a time when John was away from home. When John returned he was won to Christ through the influence of his family" (Charles E. Brown, *When the Trumpet Sounded* [Anderson, IN: Warner Press, 1951], 327).

The Church of God movement in Canada received a major setback during the 1897 camp meeting. Birdsall began to preach a doctrine during this camp meeting similar to the anti-cleansing heresy or Zinzendorfism that was to affect the rest of the Church of God two years later. J. A. Dillon and J. C. Blaney spoke out against Birdsall's error and he was eventually disfellowshiped.[17] Several followed him when he left, one of these being a Mr. Swayze, the campground owner. Besides losing the campground, the work in Canada also lost a meeting hall in Fenwick owned by Birdsall. He later moved to Niagara Falls to continue his medical practice. The loss of both a competent leader and a campground was a severe blow to the movement's progress in Canada. Following the 1897 camp meeting, Dillon and Blaney held a meeting in Welland and then split up, Blaney going to Fenwick and Berlin and Dillon going to Sherkston where, he said, "we found things not in a good condition." He reported a good meeting that left "the little ones in better condition."[18] Soon afterward he returned to the United States.

The rather discouraging condition of the work in Ontario in late 1897 and 1898 is revealed in a report from Blaney dated August 10, 1898, in which he reviews his labors for the previous half year:

We greet you all once more in the name of Jesus, with a heart full of gratitude to God for his wonderful care over us since we started out to serve him. Blessed be his name! As I thought the saints would be glad to hear how God is dealing with us I determined to send a report of the same through the TRUMPET. There are a few of us here who are serving God in this blessed evening light, which is very much opposed in this vicinity. After visiting the saints in western Ontario last autumn, I came home to prepare for winter, and then left my wife and family (Feb. 14) to go in search of lost souls, in company with one of my brothers. We went from place to place for nearly a month holding a meeting or two here and there without much encouragement from the people whom we met, and encountered many false prophets on the way. Finally while visiting some places in the vicinity

---

17. In a letter sent to the *Gospel Trumpet* concerning the Birdsall developments, Dillon said the following: "Look out for false revelation and new light in these last days of peril, and pray for the dear man spoken of, that he may find repentance and humbly come before the church and acknowledge his error. Until this is done, receive him not."

18. *Gospel Trumpet*, April 14, 1898, 5.

of Osgoods, Ont., the morning of March 11th, the Spirit plainly spoke to us to go to Bancroft, a distance of over 180 miles. At first we thought we must be deceived, as we did not have the means to carry us there; but after communing with God we were satisfied he wanted us there. So we started to walk, and got there after seven days. We found a few saints out of Babylon at that place, and labored in the vicinity for over three months; and quite a number received the word and are standing out for God. On July 20 I started in the direction of home, a brother from Bancroft driving me, and came to Plevna in two days. This brother had sent some TRUMPETS to that place which had faithfully performed their mission, and some were prepared to receive Bible salvation. I held meetings in a schoolhouse for three weeks, which resulted in about twelve souls making their escape out of Babylon. Free Methodists tried hard to defend their creed, but it was of no avail, for the people came out of her, because they were honest. I bade them all farewell and started home July 25 and arrived home next day, where I was gladly received by my family, after being absent for nearly five months and a half. As soon as circumstances permit, I will be out again.[19]

Despite problems the congregations in Ontario continued to function and hold area meetings. The loss of the campground forced them to move the 1898 camp meeting back to the old grounds near Fenwick. David H. Moyer of Vineland and John E. Smith were in charge.[20] Newsworthy activity and evangelistic campaigns seem to have slowed during the next several months, for very few reports from Canada appeared in the *Gospel Trumpet* for the remainder of that year.

During the last year of the nineteenth century some new leaders arose and were successful in establishing a church in Peepabun. In 1899 Harry Nelson, his sister Annie, and George P. Tasker started this new work. Born in the United States, Tasker had been raised by relatives in Montreal. As a young adult he moved to Chicago where he came in contact with the Church of God then under the leadership of Gorham Tufts. Nelson and his sister also had come into contact with the church in Chicago.[21] In the spring of 1900 William E. Warren came to Ontario and held meetings in

19. *Gospel Trumpet*, August 25, 1898, 6.
20. *Gospel Trumpet*, August 11, 1898, 7.
21. Anderson, *History of the Church of God in Ontario*, 42.

Bright and Berlin. While in these meetings, Warren was stricken with severe congestion but was miraculously saved through prayer. There were reports of many conversions. Emma Tufford writes this account of the work done with Warren:

> We had the most glorious meeting I have ever attended. The truth went forth in a very radical manner on all points of doctrine, and it appears that is just what the people needed; for the straight truth drew large congregations, and several souls were saved and the sick healed.
>
> Our co-worker Brother Warren was raised from death's door. He was stricken down with congestion of the lungs in very serious form. We realized at one time that the powers of death were in the room, determined to snatch our brother away from us.[22]

With the new century some other new leaders came into the movement who were to go on and have a tremendous effect on the ministry of the church. Among these was William Neff, a Methodist minister. Through his outreach the David Zinn family of Bright, Ontario, was converted and began evangelistic work in the province.[23]

Early in the twentieth century Americans of both heterodox and orthodox stripes continued traveling north.

J. C. Blaney reported on the 1901 camp meeting in Jordan Harbor:

> Sister Delia Fry came about the beginning of the meeting and was used in setting forth the gospel. Two of the anti-cleansing heresy, W. A. Haynes and E. G. Masters came from Fenwick to the grounds. We gave no place to their doctrine or spirit but resisted their foul influences, and soon they, with all their poor deceived souls who follow them, took their departure and did not return.
>
> Brother J. R. Hale from the Trumpet office was also with us through most of the meeting, and was used of God in encouraging the church. We were treated to an unexpected and joyful surprise near the close of the meeting by the coming of Bro. E. E. Byrum. Some of us had never met him before, and we praised God for the privilege of meeting with the much esteemed editor of the Lord's paper, the *Gospel Trumpet*....

22. *Gospel Trumpet*, April 5, 1900, 5.
23. *Gospel Trumpet*, January 17, 1901, 6.

We had a precious ordinance service Saturday evening before the meeting closed, and as near as can be ascertained about seventy-five happy saints washed each others feet and ate the Lord's Supper....[24]

In the first years of the decade, the Canadian movement expanded geographically and numerically. In 1902 H. A. Brooks joined J. C. Blaney to hold meetings in eastern Ontario and Quebec. These were the first recorded Canadian meetings held outside Ontario.[25] The camp meeting of 1902 again was held at the campgrounds in Jordan Harbor. During that meeting three individuals, William Neff, Annie Neff, and Mary Mayer, were ordained as overseer and deaconesses respectively. Twelve people were also baptized there.[26]

The 1903 camp meeting was moved to Peepabun with J. C. Blaney chosen to report the events. He reported that "it was the best ever held in Canada." Over a thousand attended the last service. Eight hundred dollars was raised to help retire the debt on the Trumpet offices. Visiting ministers were E. E. Byrum, J. W. Daugherty, A. D. Khan, and Delia Fry.[27] The 1903 midwinter assembly meeting was held near Drumbo, December 24–26. "Over one ton of books and tracts were on the way from the Trumpet office, donated by the bretheren there to be distributed by the ministers and workers in Canada."[28] All of the national leaders were in attendance and shared in the encouraging of the saints.

In the summer of 1904 two camp meetings were held in Canada. The first was at the Peepabun campgrounds. H. W. Nelson reported, "About fifteen or more followed the Lord in baptism. Sister Clayton was ordained into the eldership through the laying on of hands. Brother H. M. Riggle, J. C. Blaney, H. A. Brooks, William Deachman, and H. W. Nelson were the full-time ministers at the meeting."[29] The second meeting convened at the old campground in Fenwick. It was announced in the *Gospel Trumpet* as follows: "Campmeeting is to be held in the old campgrounds. This is the first place campmeeting was ever held in Canada, and was the place of the general meeting for some years until unhappily false teachers arose and heresy given a place."[30]

---

24. *Gospel Trumpet*, September 26, 1901, 6.
25. *Gospel Trumpet*, July 17, 1902, 6.
26. *Gospel Trumpet*, September 25, 1902, 6.
27. *Gospel Trumpet*, July 23, 1903, 6.
28. *Gospel Trumpet*, January 7, 1904, 6.
29. *Gospel Trumpet*, July 21, 1904, 5.
30. *Gospel Trumpet*, August 25, 1904, 7.

In 1905 Josephine McCrie left Peepabun for Moundsville to prepare to go to India as a missionary. She was the first Canadian missionary to be sent to the field. Annie Nelson wrote a letter soliciting support for Josephine McCrie: "Let us pray and give. Her traveling expenses alone will be $250.00. Let us freely and gladly give it."[31] Ten people were saved at the 1905 camp meeting at Peepabun. The meeting was reported to be a very precious time of testimony and mutual exhortation. A very bad windstorm tore down the tabernacle, and so the meeting was held in the dining room on Sunday evening.[32]

In 1905 the movement's first known Church of God contact in western Canada occurred when Hiram A. Brooks left Ontario to visit relatives in Saskatoon, Saskatchewan.[33] At a Salvation Army meeting there he met Fleming May and Alex L. Stevenson, who were won to the movement's message and through them a small congregation was formed. Because of homesteading opportunities, three more Church of God families moved to Saskatchewan. Later Dr. L. H. Morgan and R. D. Brooks held meetings near Saskatoon and reported many conversions. The work remained small, however, until 1912 when L. E. Millensifer became the pastor of the Saskatoon Church and asked Ethel Williams of Ontario to come and help care for the congregation.[34]

One would expect that the growth of the Church of God in the Ontario sector would produce programs and leaders who would evangelize the provinces to its west. This was not the case. The spread of the Church of God message developed, except for Saskatoon, independently of the work in eastern Canada. The person primarily responsible for the beginning of the movement's work in Alberta was William H. Smith, a black minister from Denver, Colorado, who moved to Edmonton on April 28, 1906.[35] For the first five months he worked with his hands assisting masons, preaching on the streets at night. The corner of McDougal and Jasper Avenues was a favorite spot for Smith's preaching. In October 1906 a building was rented for ten dollars per month.[36] When that building was sold by the owners, another was rented for fifteen dollars per month until the warm weather of 1907 arrived and tents could be used. When the cold weather returned, the

31. *Gospel Trumpet*, October 27, 1904, 4.
32. *Gospel Trumpet*, July 13, 1905, 5.
33. Brown, *When the Trumpet Sounded*, 329.
34. Ibid., 330.
35. *Gospel Trumpet*, October 7, 1909, 12.
36. *Gospel Trumpet*, January 30, 1908, 13.

group moved back indoors for twenty-five dollars per month. In early 1908 a permanent place consisting of two lots, a five-room house, and a barn was purchased as the new mission property.[37] Smith explained his objectives:

> The object of the purchase is: First, that the ministers and workers might have a stopping place in the city when called to work in this part of the country, without paying such high rent. Second, as this is the most central city in Western Canada, it is a very good distributing point. We can send papers, tracts and books to all parts of Western Canada from Edmonton. Third, to have a permanent meeting place in a good locality. Nearly all nationalities are represented here. They are still coming from all parts of the world, it seems.[38]

In that same letter, Smith expressed three needs: (1) more workers, (2) more literature, and (3) the need to pay off the debt on the purchase.

Later, Anna L. Huntington, in a letter to the *Gospel Trumpet,* praised the Lord for financial assistance and stated, "The Lord furnished us with a gospel wagon to take the workers to different places for street-meetings, as they are usually too tired to stand on the street during the service. We hand Trumpets from the wagon, and the people come to the wagon and get the papers, and seem very much interested."[39]

This is just one example of many reports appearing in the *Gospel Trumpet* confirming Edmonton as the center for evangelistic efforts in all of Alberta.

Smith's leadership abilities were described by the later Canadian leader, H. C. Heffren:

> Evangelist Smith possessed great personal charm which enabled him to make friends. He was a gifted speaker and like so many colored people he could sing well. Although he was single he was an expert cook as well as a good gardener. Crowds of people were attracted on Jasper Avenue to listen to this earnest man proclaim the gospel, after which he would invite his listeners to attend the evening meeting at the mission.[40]

---

37. *Gospel Trumpet,* October 7, 1909, 12.
38. Ibid.
39. *Gospel Trumpet,* August 11, 1910, 13.
40. Henry C. Heffren, *Voices of the Pioneers* (Camrose, AB: privately published, [1968]), 4.

A woman from Bullocksville, Alberta, about one hundred miles from Edmonton, wrote in the *Gospel Trumpet* that the Edmonton work was influential at Bullocksville.[41] This is just one example of many reports appearing in the *Gospel Trumpet* confirming Edmonton as a center for evangelistic efforts in all of Alberta.

Not all ministry in these early years was in English. In 1908 J. G. Neff and Smith tell of some meetings that made them aware of the need for preachers who could speak the languages of Russian-Germans, Swedes, Poles, and Austrian-Germans. They appealed for a Swedish or German preacher who could take advantage of this opportunity.[42]

The work at Edmonton apparently grew rapidly, for on July 1, 1911, it was reported that the trustees put the mission property up for sale and new construction was either in the planning stages or actually building at that time.[43] For several years after, however, there were few reports in the *Gospel Trumpet* about the Edmonton work. Perhaps E. E. Byrum's somewhat cryptic comments following a visit in 1915 explain: "The work of the mission at 313 York St., Edmonton, has been unsatisfactory during the past few years, and the brethren have withdrawn their support and recognition of the work in that place. Bro. L. E. Millensifer and R. W. May are opening the work in other parts of the city."[44]

Other sources report that the mission was heavily in debt. Smith personally held the deed to the property, and that inhibited contributions. Smith later left the movement to join a missionary group that sponsored a journey to Africa, his long held ambition. However, Smith refused to be inoculated against tropical diseases and succumbed to illness shortly after his arrival.[45] There is no doubt that William H. Smith was very instrumental in the initial rapid development of the movement in Edmonton from street corner preaching to a mission center for evangelistic outreach. It is also apparent that Smith was instrumental in the decline of the Edmonton work.

Another person who began his work in the early part of the century and later was to play a very significant role in the development of the Church of God in Western Canada was Leonard E. Millensifer. Millensifer did not move to Canada as an evangelist or a missionary, leaving the United States

---

41. *Gospel Trumpet*, March 19, 1908, 7.
42. *Gospel Trumpet*, July 9, 1908, 13–14.
43. *Gospel Trumpet*, November 2, 1911, 13–14.
44. *Gospel Trumpet*, August 12, 1915, 11.
45. Heffren, *Voices of the Pioneers*, 5.

shortly before his conversion. Born in Oxford, Nebraska, on October 18, 1882, he married Emma Stoll from Kansas in 1905 and shortly thereafter homesteaded in Alberta. On a trip to Edmonton for supplies, Millensifer heard W. H. Smith preaching on the street and eventually committed himself to serve God.[46] Millensifer wrote a personal testimony on Christmas Day of 1907 that subsequently was published in the *Gospel Trumpet:* "I thank God that my beloved companion and I can celebrate our first Christmas being happy in Christ Jesus and having fellowship with the dear saints of God."[47] Soon Millensifer gave up his homestead and began to devote full time to preaching. He was ordained into the ministry at the January 1911 assembly meeting held at Edmonton.[48]

Mexico

Benjamin F. Elliott (1859–1926) extended the Church of God reformation movement beyond the southern border of the United States. In 1889 Elliott, a former Methodist preacher and professor of Greek at the University of Southern California, began preaching in the streets of Santa Barbara, California. Around 1891 he became impressed with the need to spread the gospel to Spanish-speaking people. Along with others, he cleaned and repaired an old house in Santa Barbara and opened up a "Faith Mission in Spanish."[49] He learned the Spanish language through a loaned Spanish grammar book and New Testament and within a week's time was preaching in Spanish in Santa Barbara.

In the fall of 1891 Elliott was led to go into Lower California (Baja California), Mexico. He was accompanied by another brother from Santa Barbara and Elliott's five-year-old son Clark. As the trio began their journey they stopped at Los Angeles, California, where they met D. S. Warner. They accompanied Warner to San Diego and then departed for Ensenada, Baja California.[50] When they arrived they had only three or four dollars in

---

46. Ibid., 11–12.

47. *Gospel Trumpet*, January 16, 1908, 11–12.

48. *Gospel Trumpet.*, April 6, 1911, 13–14.

49. Benjamin F. Elliott, *Experiences in the Gospel Work in Lower California, Mexico* (LaPaz, Mexico: Office of "The Gospel," 1906), 8.

50. Elliott commented on his meeting with Warner: "In taking our leave of Bro. Warner he looked me full in the face and said, 'How much is your fare on the boat?' I told him. He said, 'Do you lack any of that amount, if so, how much?' We told him we lacked two dollars. He quietly slipped the two dollars in my hand" (Ibid., 10–11).

Mexican money. Elliott and his company found Ensenada to be very much Americanized, but this was true of other towns they visited.[51] The company set out on a flying ministry that took them up and down the Baja peninsula. They traveled to towns such as Mandero, Santo Tomas, San Ramon, San Telms, and Tijuana, preaching, praying, laying hands on the sick, and selling and giving away Testaments and Gospels. When funds ran out, Elliott twice interrupted this journey to return to southern California.

It was about August 1892 that Elliott took a two-year furlough in the United States. In 1894 he visited the *Gospel Trumpet* office in Grand Junction, Michigan, where his son remained for three months attending Sebastian Michels' school for ministers' children. Elliott left Grand Junction by himself in December 1894 and arrived in Los Angeles, California, on July 3, 1895. That December he returned to San Diego, where he was later reunited with his son, who traveled from Grand Junction with Georgia Cook. Elliott remained in San Diego for a while, and in 1896 he and Georgia Cook were married.

The family returned to Ensenada in August 1896 and became involved in another flying ministry, again supported by freewill offerings and secular employment. There were times when he had to withdraw from full-time ministerial work and take employment in places such as a match factory. At one point, the whole family was put to work manufacturing baskets. He soon felt led to go south into Mazatlán, on the Mexican mainland. A letter was sent to the *Gospel Trumpet* stating his intentions with a request for support from the brethren. Support came, and the Elliotts arrived in Mazatlán, Sinaloa, around October 1897 and remained there for a little over one year.

In 1898 the family was back on the Baja peninsula at La Paz. In a letter sent to the *Gospel Trumpet,* Elliott expressed a need for a printing press, and soon a donor sent money for the purchase. Another friend from New York sent a letter saying he was sending a foot-powered press that was to arrive in Guaymos, Mexico. Elliott took his family to Guaymos to meet the shipment and they remained there for three years. The family finally settled down in LaPaz, where he purchased a lot and built a small house and

---

51. "Ensenada had perhaps 2,000 inhabitants. It is beautifully situated on the slope of a range of foot hills, on a cove rather than a bay (Ensenada means cove). It is lighted with electricity and is the capitol and chief town of the Northern District of lower California. It is more Americanized in its manners, customs, etc. than any other town we have visited in Mexico. Really the chief interests are American or English" (Ibid., 11).

printing office. For eight years Elliott printed tracts and papers in Spanish to be distributed up and down the coast of Mexico and into some South American countries.[52] The Spanish counterpart to the *Gospel Trumpet, La Trompeta Evangelica,* and some Trumpet books he translated into Spanish also came from Elliott's press. The printing work increased to the point where he had to hire help.

Elliott spent a total of thirteen years in Mexico, but rumors of revolutions forced him, his family, and other American workers to leave. The congregations he established were not strong enough to survive without his leadership. Political policy after the revolution of 1910 prevented any further evangelization in Mexico for the following two decades.

Overseas

Alongside its extension to these North American neighbors, by 1909 the Church of God had spread to or had significant contacts in at least seventeen additional countries. In the British Isles the movement was evangelizing in England, Scotland, and Ireland. On the European continent there were congregations or known adherents in Germany, Switzerland, Denmark, Sweden, Poland, and Russia. In Asia either missionaries or native pastors were at work in China and Japan, and in India significant works were developing in four widely separated geographic centers. Egypt was the only African nation represented. The continent of Australia also had been reached, and congregations had been established on at least three islands in the West Indies: Jamaica, Trinidad, and Bermuda.

The year 1893 marks the beginning of Church of God activity in spreading the true gospel beyond North America. The initial concern for involvement in overseas work seems to have come from W. J. Henry. He reported that in the spring of 1892 he had felt led to serve in a foreign field.[53] Evidently George R. Achor developed a similar interest at about the same time, for by December of the same year he departed from the *Gospel*

---

52. This information and much in the previous paragraphs are from a typed account by Georgia C. Elliott, "Early Spanish Work," in the Anderson University and Church of God Archives.

53. The January 12, 1893, *Gospel Trumpet* contained this testimony from Henry: "Last spring the Lord wakened me one morning and requested me to make a deeper and more settled consecration… asking me if I would give up certain things, and do certain things. And in the long line of questions that the Lord asked me was this one: Are you willing to go to the foreign fields if the Lord would call you, and you would get a letter and the means would be furnished; without going home to bid your friends good–by?…I received a letter and the means to start with."

Trumpet office in Grand Junction for New York City with the intention of journeying across the Atlantic to England. Henry and Achor met on the East Coast and planned to sail for England by December 21, 1892, but failed to embark at that time.[54] The pair finally sailed from New York harbor on January 7, 1893, and arrived in Liverpool on January 17. They began holding meetings in this English port city and established there the first Church of God in Europe. This initial overseas missionary enterprise was short-lived, however, for Achor returned to the United States in June of 1893 and Henry was in Walkerton, Indiana, by October of that same year.

William J. and Mollie Henry, pioneer ministers. W. J. Henry was associated with the Holiness meeting in Jerry City, Ohio, out of which emerged several prominent early Church of God leaders, including Mother Sarah Smith and A. J. Kilpatrick. Henry married Mollie Byers, sister of J. W. and A. L. Byers. The Henrys were key leaders in the early work of the Church of God around Springfield, Missouri.

Before the close of 1893, however, Church of God missionaries were again on English soil. Among these were Achor, Lena Shoffner, J. W. Daugherty, James Kriebel, and J. H. Rupert. When Achor returned to England with his wife Mary they were accompanied by Shoffner. The trio arrived in Liverpool on November 12. Shoffner remained in Liverpool at least until September of the following year. The Achors were in London for a time, but they and Shoffner returned to the United States in 1895. J. W. Daugherty and his wife ministered from 1893 until 1895 and returned again in 1896 with Bertie Cresswell. The Daugherys are known to have done some work also in Bolton. J. H. and Hattie Rupert traveled to England in 1893 with the intention of strengthening the congregation established in Liverpool on the original trip made by Achor and Henry. Their work also took them into Warrington and some rural areas.

In a letter to the *Gospel Trumpet* published in March 1894, the Ruperts announced that they had begun to feel a call to extend the work into

---

54. *Gospel Trumpet*, December 29, 1892, 2.

Germany.[55] Rupert left for Hamburg alone since he did not have sufficient funds to take his wife. Almost immediately, however, the money was provided and Hattie left London on April 24, 1894, to meet her husband. During their eight-month stay in Germany the Ruperts were not without real difficulties. They faced opposition to their work from the Salvation Army in Germany and also ran into serious financial problems. In August of 1894 the Gospel Trumpet Company decided to send Rupert money from missionary funds to help him pay off his debts. The Ruperts returned to England in late 1894 and the congregation they had established in Hamburg fell dormant for almost a decade.

Back in England Rupert got the idea for a "gospel van" ministry and wrote to the *Trumpet* of need for a horse-drawn enclosed wagon fitted out for literature display as well as travel.[56] By July 1895 the gospel van was in operation. It also provided living facilities for missionary personnel and cooking facilities to provide food for the hungry. Rupert thought that it was the church's responsibility to provide food for the poor before talking to them about salvation. The gospel

The Gospel Van. England was a target for some of the first Church of God missionaries. The first contingent arrived early in 1893. Later the same year, J. H. and Hattie Rupert arrived. Liverpool was an early center of missionary activity. In 1895, the Ruperts fitted out a horse-drawn wagon christened the *Gospel Van* and used it as a traveling base of operations up and down the Wirral Peninsula.

van proved to be a very effective tool for the missionary effort in England as it was pulled along the streets and roads with its lettering on the side, "Non-Sectarian Gospel Van. Tracts and Pamphlets Free. Christ the Only Remedy."[57]

In 1906 W. H. and Anna Cheatham left Illinois for the British Isles to begin a ten-year ministry, principally in Ireland. In 1909 Adam Allan (1865–1946) and his family left their home in Portland, Oregon and

---

55. *Gospel Trumpet*, March 1, 1894, 2.

56. *Gospel Trumpet*, February 8, 1895.

57. From a photograph of the gospel van in the Anderson University and Church of God Archives.

returned to his native Aberdeen, Scotland, beginning a gospel literature ministry that resulted in the establishment of a congregation there. He also later evangelized in Ireland. Others who ministered in the British Isles (some only while enroute to other places) during this early period were: C. E. Orr, Jennie C. Rutty, E. E. Byrum, G. P. Tasker, A. D. Khan, E. A. Reardon, F. G. Smith, and H. M. Riggle.

After Rupert's departure from Germany in 1894, the small congregation in Hamburg disbanded, but one woman, Johanna Nieman, continued to maintain a concern for the work of reformation. She wrote a letter to the Moundsville office of the *Gospel Trumpet* requesting a minister to come. This letter came to the attention of George Vielguth of Slate, Kansas, a German by birth and an evangelist for several years. He felt a call to respond, and on February 7, 1901, he left for Germany and made contact with Nieman. Once again regular meetings were started and a literature distribution campaign was initiated.[58] He also held meetings in Riga, Latvia, and in Quickborn, Germany, near Hamburg. Vielguth returned to America in April 1902. In the next few years the evangelistic work of the Church of God in Europe began to accelerate. By 1903 several congregations were established.[59] More workers came from America. Vielguth returned in October, followed by Karl Arbeiter. By 1907 the William Ebels and the Otto Doeberts arrived, and the Vielguths had established a missionary home in Essen where a camp meeting was held that year. After the meeting the Ebels journeyed to Riga, Doebert went to East Prussia and from there to Poland and Russia. Vielguth and Arbeiter went to Hungary, and Arbeiter came back to Switzerland when the Vielguths returned to the United States. The following year more evangelistic trips were made to eastern Europe, making many contacts and recruiting local leaders to carry on the work.[60]

The beginning of the work of the Church of God in the Scandinavian countries came just at the end of the period. About 1905 the O. T. Rings, who were natives of Sweden, went back to their homeland to do evangelistic work for a brief time. Later, Carl J. Forsberg followed and planted churches in Gothe and Karlstad. In 1909 the Nels Renbecks and Morris C. Johnson became the first Church of God evangelists in Denmark. A great revival is

---

58. *Gospel Trumpet*, February 14, 1901, 4, reported his departure, and March 21, 1901, 4, his arrival and the beginning of his work. He had stopped in Moundsville on his way to New York and was given a large supply of German literature.

59. Gerhard Klabunde, letter to Kenneth Prunty, May 15, 1953.

60. Brown, *When the Trumpet Sounded*, 338–40.

reported to have swept the northern part of the country as a result of their work and several congregations were established.[61] Within a short time the clouds of World War I forced most American workers to leave all of the European countries, but by then the Church of God was quite firmly established.

Previous to 1895, the international thrusts of the movement had occurred in countries where Christianity was the dominant religion. In that year the *Gospel Trumpet* office received a request for some literature from a young convert from Islam, and contact was made for the first time with a non-Christian land.[62] John A. D. Khan (1877–1922), who was first converted to become a Baptist during his teen years, requested this material while he was engaged in study at the University of Calcutta. Khan had a deep desire to learn all he could about the Christian faith and read all the material he could find. He responded to an advertisement in a newspaper stating that "a man in Texas was offering to send samples

John A. D. Khan (1877–1922), pioneer church leader in India. Converted from Islam to Christianity by Baptist missionaries in East Bengal (his middle initials stand for Allah-ud-Din), Khan affiliated with the Church of God in 1896 while a university student in Calcutta and along with a few like-minded converts pioneered the work of the Church of God in India. His book *India's Millions* and a tour of American churches in 1903 fired the movement's imagination for world missions.

of Holiness papers published in America, on receipt of a silver dime."[63] Among the items sent to Khan was a copy of the Gospel Trumpet Company catalog of books. Consequently he sent for material and read it with great interest. In studying the Church of God literature he found that it was in agreement with conclusions at which he already had arrived in his own

---

61. Corinne and Jens N. Ikast, "A Brief History of the Scandinavian Work," a two-page typed copy in the Anderson University and Church of God Archives.

62. It might be noted here that as early as 1892 D. S. Warner sent over one thousand tracts to Bombay, India, for free distribution, according to the "Editorial News" contained in the February 4, 1892, *Gospel Trumpet*. The 1895 date, however, is widely accepted as the beginning of the Church of God influence in India.

63. A. D. Khan, *India's Millions* (Moundsville, WV: Gospel Trumpet Co., 1903), 214.

personal reflection on the Scriptures. These conclusions had isolated him from all denominations,[64] and he was in the process of searching diligently to find someone who upheld what he had come to believe as truth.[65] On July 7, 1896, at nineteen years of age, Khan wrote from Calcutta to the Gospel Trumpet Company requesting a subscription to the *Gospel Trumpet*. During this time, Khan also had become acquainted with R. N. Mundal, a Calcutta businessman who held similar beliefs, and they began to hold meetings in Calcutta. Others soon joined, and worship and regular public meetings were held at Number 3 Bowbazaar in Calcutta.

In 1897 a severe drought and famine was raging across India. It began in 1896 and continued until 1900. A Church of God minister in the United States, Charles J. Blewitt, who was then the superintendent of the missionary home and pastor of the Grand Avenue Church in New York City, made a speech at the 1897 Grand Junction Camp Meeting. Blewitt's speech expressed his great interest in the missionary work of the Church of God, and apparently it was effective. The crowd was moved by the story of need and plans were made to raise an India relief fund. Many appeals were made through the *Gospel Trumpet* to raise funds to be sent to India.

Gorham Tufts, leader in the Chicago work, was chosen to carry the gift to India and supervise its distribution. Tufts left in July 1897 and arrived in August with nearly $2,100 to relieve the famine sufferers. He also carried great quantities of Gospel Trumpet literature for distribution. Tufts remained in India for only a short time, so he and Khan never had an opportunity to meet personally during this trip.[66] However, Tufts did contact some of Khan's co-workers in Calcutta.

Tufts was instrumental in arranging the shipment of two printing presses and one thousand pounds of literature to India by the Gospel Trumpet Company.[67] Prior to this gift, Khan and Mundul had felt the need to pub-

---

64. Concerning this, Khan wrote, "When I came to these conclusions from the Word of God, I found myself in an isolated place; I could not join any of the denominations then. I became peculiar in every way." A. D. Khan, *From Darkness to Light: The Testimony of A. D. Khan—Converted Mohammedan* (Anderson, IN: Mission Board of the Church of God, 1954), 20.

65. Khan said of the Gospel Trumpet Company materials, "I found in these books just the things that the Lord was teaching me all those days. I saw how the Lord leads all his children by His own Holy Spirit, no matter where they may be irrespective of their color and creed" (Ibid., 7).

66. Tufts returned to the United States on October 26, 1897, to begin work again in the Chicago area (*Gospel Trumpet*, October 28, 1897). In a letter from Khan printed in the *Gospel Trumpet*, he states, "I am sorry I could not see Bro. Tufts, for I was away in South India when he came to Calcutta. Our brethren saw him and got a great blessing by his visit" (October 18, 1897).

67. Editorial, *Gospel Trumpet,* December 18, 1897.

lish their beliefs in order to reach those who otherwise would go without any contact with Christianity. They already had begun to publish *The Fire Brand,* a monthly magazine, in both English and Bengali. The presses from America arrived but were not put into immediate use. The Indian work did not possess type and other necessary materials. When these were obtained, the presses were put to work printing tracts, books, and *The Fire Brand.*

In 1898 Khan left the University of Calcutta to engage in full-time preaching and publishing. In a letter published in the June 23, 1898, edition of the *Gospel Trumpet,* Khan expressed his deep concerns for India and shared with American brothers and sisters his strategy for spreading the gospel in his native land. This strategy included a goal of spreading the gospel to areas where it had not yet been preached and, in particular, establishing a Bible training home in Bogra. Bogra was a district two hundred miles northeast of Calcutta with a population of approximately 800,000 souls.[68] Khan and M. Naug went to Bogra before the year ended and laid the foundation of what would eventually develop into a Bible class for young people and a Sunday school for boys.

Khan came to the United States in 1903 and stayed for several months, visiting many meetings and congregations. Broad exposure to a flesh and blood convert from a non-Christian religion dramatically stimulated an already developing world consciousness. When Khan returned to India in January 1904 he was accompanied by E. E. Byrum, the G. W. Baileys from Washington, and Evalyn Nichols from Idaho and Los Angeles.[69] The Baileys remained for a year and Nichols married Indian pastor J. J. M. Roy, continuing to live and work there. Later that year the Robert Jarvises were in Lahore operating a faith home and orphanage, and Josephine Mc-Crie and Edith Ashenfelter were on their way to India as missionaries. By 1909 the number of American workers there had increased to at least eight including Ira Zaugg, Thaddeus Neff, Alice V. Hale, Victor C. Maiden, and George S. Williams. Four centers of outreach were established: Lahore in North India, Shillong in Assam, Cuttack, and Kurseong. Except at Lahore, native leaders guided the work. By the turn of the century a contact had also been established in Travencore in South India. P. J. Philip, through reading a copy of the *Gospel Trumpet,* found his own convictions being expressed in the paper and made contact with Khan, who visited South India several times. A solid work was established there without the aid of missionaries.

---

68. *Gospel Trumpet*, June 23, 1898, 6.
69. *Gospel Trumpet*, January 21, 1904, 4.

In 1906, Church of God missions were extended to the West Indies. In that year the George H. Pyes, Lydia Yoder, and N. S. Duncan went to Trinidad. By 1909 the work had strengthened sufficiently to leave it in the hands of native workers until other missionaries arrived over two years later. Duncan also preached on the island of Barbados in 1906, but no permanent work was established until 1912. In 1907 the George W. Olsons and their daughter Mary went to Jamaica where they, along with others, were to labor for forty-six years. At the 1909 Anderson Camp Meeting reports were also given of work in Bermuda and British Honduras in Central America.[70]

Egypt was first visited by representatives of the Church of God in 1907 when G. P. Tasker and H. A. Brooks stopped on their way to India and wrote back that the opportunities for evangelization in Egypt were promising. By November of that year E. A. Reardon had arrived and remained for a year. When he returned home in 1908 he left the work under the care of G. K. Ouzounian, an Armenian who had been led into the Church of God from the Adventist church. Ouzounian carried on, almost alone, for the next fifteen years until additional missionary help arrived.[71]

Nineteen hundred and eight is also the year when the work of the Church of God began in Japan. The person responsible was not a missionary but a young Japanese layperson by the name of Ukichi Yajima, who had been converted to Christianity and ordained as a Presbyterian minister. On a trip to the United States in 1905, he came across a copy of the *Gospel Trumpet* on a San Francisco interurban train. What Yajima read interested him, and he wrote to editor E. E. Byrum, who directed him to contact some of the churches in California. Yajima did and liked what he found. In 1908, he returned to Japan as a Church of God evangelist. The next year he was joined by three missionaries from America: J. D. Hatch and the W. G. Alexanders. Most of this early work centered in and around the city of Tokyo.

The movement's beginning in China occurred in 1909 when William A. Hunnex and his wife Gloria sailed for Shanghai and then on to Chinkiang. Five years earlier Hunnex and his brother Charles, who were both born in China and were sons of English missionaries, had moved to America and come in contact with the Church of God. Both worked for a time in the missionary homes in Chicago and New York but then felt they should return to China. Charles Hunnex and Pina Winters followed William and

---

70. *Gospel Trumpet*, June 17, 1909, 9.
71. Ibid. Reardon gave the report of the work in Egypt at the 1909 Anderson Camp Meeting.

Gloria in 1910. Within four years there were four mission stations operating in China.

Contacts in Australia took the form of responses to literature that had been randomly sent there. Occasional reports of letters received mention these inquiries. By late 1909, however, J. M. Philpott of Arncliffe, Australia, had developed a sufficiently strong center for the work there to have it listed in the roster of "Missions and Homes" published weekly in the *Gospel Trumpet*.[72] It would be another decade before any missionary effort extended to this continent; the work in Australia in this early period was not substantial.

The Church of God expanded worldwide without benefit of a sending agency and without assured methods to underwrite missionary expenses and income. While it is true that there was a certain "naturalness" about much of the international activity—German immigrants went to Germany, Scots to Scotland, Swedes to Sweden—there was more than a desire to share the good news with kith and kin. The same spirit that drove the flying messengers to crisscross the North American continent also motivated global itinerants. They possessed a message that they believed all people in the world should hear. Any place on the earth was a potential field for witness and evangelization simply because people in that locale had not yet heard. While being burdened for or led to a given place often related to previous contacts or information, the call was considered to be from God. Early missionaries eagerly responded in faith that their needs and means would be provided.

It cannot be said that these faith ventures were entirely without method. A person who felt a leading to go abroad as a missionary would make that feeling known—among friends, in public meetings, and by a letter to the *Gospel Trumpet*. Sufficient responses that yielded funds for travel were considered a confirmation of the call. Once on the field there were rather frequent letters that served as reminders for continuing support. Money could be sent directly to individuals or to the missionary fund held by the Gospel Trumpet Company. Undesignated contributions were distributed at the discretion of the committee of company personnel who handled the fund. This policy allowed J. H. Rupert to get some help in clearing up his debts in Germany, but nothing of this sort was guaranteed. There were no continuing commitments to anyone; those who went out did so on faith

---

72. *Gospel Trumpet*, November 4, 1909, 12.

that God would supply the needs of those doing the Lord's will. By 1909 more than two dozen people were "out there," by faith, sharing the message in at least twenty countries around the world.

CHAPTER 7

STRENGTHENING THE OPERATIONAL BASE
(1890–1917)

In the quarter century from the early 1890s to 1917 the Church of God was moving in many directions, but the most significant of these was in stabilizing, regularizing, and enhancing the achievements of the movement's first decade. There was no modification of the message and no abatement in vigor or dedication, just subtle changes in method and focus that made considerable difference in the specific directions the group would take in the future. These were moves toward broadening, improving, and strengthening the various points of activity from the central publishing work to the many locations across the country and around the world, commonly were referred to as "the field."

Flying Ministers and Settled Congregations

The primary focus of the flying ministry period had been to proclaim the message quickly before the anticipated end of time and to lead as many people as possible out of sectism into the light of the one true church. This overarching eschatological context meant very little emphasis on the formation of continuing local groups; there were even warnings against organizing anything—including congregations. Despite this guerrilla-type preach-and-run style, there were bands of saints, composed of those who had taken their stand for the truth, who continued to meet together for worship and further evangelism after the preachers departed. Thus, local congregations began to develop even though they were not part of a master plan.

As the decade of the 1890s opened there is evidence that many of these loosely structured local groups existed, especially in the middle western states, but most of these bands functioned without benefit of a regular preacher. In fact, a resident preacher contradicted the general understanding of ministry. Preachers were warned against settling down, and congregations were urged to avoid tempting them to do so. In 1892 a *Gospel Trumpet* editorial admonished local groups not to lure preachers by offering to build a home for them. "Beware," said Warner, "how you through selfish motives of having frequent preaching lay a snare to entangle God's flying messengers....This is the time of the end, and God's messengers must run to and fro."[1] However, that Warner took such a stance in print suggests that some congregations were feeling the need of a settled pastor, and that some of the itinerants were beginning to consider the benefits of folding their wings and roosting for a season.

Local groups also faced the problem of an adequate meeting place. Usually groups of saints first met in homes. As numbers increased they often sought some other available building—a schoolhouse, a courtroom, or some other public facility that could be secured at little or no cost. When such arrangements were unavailable or outgrown it became necessary either to rent a meeting place or to procure one of their own by building or purchase. The latter option had become sufficiently common by 1893 that the editor of the *Gospel Trumpet* was prompted to advise congregations so that they might hold corporate title to property without violating the principle of "no man-made organization." After cautioning that specific legal requirements in each state should be checked before proceeding, he recommended that in a meeting of the congregation "a minister or any brother" may suggest the names of individuals who would be approved by the group as elders or deacons (the only titles designated in the New Testament). These and their successors could be considered as the trustees that most laws required. The congregation could approve them by saying "amen," thus avoiding the practice of voting, which was considered "contrary to the principles of the body of Christ."[2]

This naturalized process of congregation planting and development began modestly and grew quite slowly through the decade of the 1890s and on into the early years of the twentieth century. All during this time the traveling campaign procedure was still the prevailing mode of ministry. Even so, more congregations were being born, and small ones were growing. By the second decade of the 1900s the momentum in this direction began accelerating markedly. In the words of Quaker historian Howard Brinton,

---

1. *Gospel Trumpet*, March 10, 1892, 2.
2. *Gospel Trumpet*, November 23, 1893, 2.

"The burning zeal which flames out in the market place must sooner or later become the warm glow of the household hearth."[3] A good example of this transition from bonfire to hearthfire is the development of the Church of God in the area of Meridian, Mississippi.

About 1889 two local holiness preachers, W. W. Bradley and Samuel H. Bozeman, both of whom had learned about the Church of God movement only a few months earlier, began holding meetings in the Spring Hill community a few miles south of Meridian. There was only one church in that neighborhood, and its leaders did not agree with the sermons they heard. Soon all those who believed in holiness were ordered to leave that church. The expelled believers had no place to meet, so they decided to construct a new building. This they did—a small frame house of worship for the new group. In late 1889 or early 1890 D. S. Warner and his company arrived and began preaching the message of holiness and sin-free living even more vigorously than Bradley and Bozeman. Immediately there was no small amount of trouble, including violent opposition. Opponents and believers threw rocks into the wagons as members left the church. Trees were cut down and pulled across the road, and hindrances of every sort were created. One night a heavy rain kept people from the church, and they later learned that a disguised group had been hiding in the church waiting for the members to arrive. Another night, while Warner was preaching, someone let go with a slingshot full of buckshot, missing his face by inches. The velocity was so great that the buckshot deeply embedded itself in the wall behind him. He continued his sermon as if nothing had happened. The company was staying in the home of J. M. Smith. A mob of seventy-five to one hundred men armed with guns came to Smith's home. Warner was beaten but managed to escape into the woods, and the mob left.[4] Despite this opposition the church continued to grow. Out of this tumultuous beginning five strong Church of God congregations were later to develop in Meridian and the surrounding area.

Certain other characteristics of congregation founding and building are illustrated in the experience of another early local fellowship, which became the First Church of God in Rolla, Missouri. In this instance the initial impetus came from ministers in a neighboring community about ten miles away. Jeremiah Cole, then of St. James, Missouri, and one of

---

3. Howard Brinton, *Friends for 300 Years* (New York: Harper and Brothers, 1952), 181.

4. Essie Lee McDonald Sorrell and Mae McDonald Frazier, "Prologue to History of First Church of God, Meridian, Mississippi," Anderson University and Church of God Archives.

that state's earliest Church of God ministers, had brought the message of divine healing to his handicapped sister, Mary. She had believed, was healed of her maladies, and then became one of the early woman ministers of the Church of God. Through the efforts of this brother-sister team—Jeremiah and Mary Cole—along with Julia Myers, another Church of God minister in that area, the church came to Rolla sometime prior to 1892. Driving from St. James to Rolla with horse and buggy, the three contacted a few people and began conducting weekly prayer meetings. Thus began the Rolla Church of God.

Julia Myers, pioneer evangelist in Missouri. Along with the Cole siblings—Mary, George, and Jeremiah—Myers traveled extensively throughout the state in evangelistic work.

One of the early locations of the church was a building at Fourth and Walnut Streets. This building was far from comfortable; its main convenience was a potbellied stove that was closely patronized during wintertime services. Another place of meeting was the upstairs of Schuman's Produce Building at Sixth and Pine. In 1892 the founding ministers attended a camp meeting in Grand Junction, Michigan. At that meeting they were able to interest Adelbert Bixler and his wife, the former Kitty Warren, in the Rolla work. This young couple with their infant son came as the first pastors of the Rolla Church of God. The Bixlers pastored the church for two years and then returned to Michigan.

After the Bixlers left Rolla, the church became more of an evangelistic center than a nurtured fellowship. During this period of intense evangelism, many ministers held meetings in the town. Some of the remembered names are George Bolds, D. S. Warner, Samuel Ford, and members of the Bennett family. Each meeting seemed to open up new areas of advance as ministers inspired the local congregation to move forward. Land for the Flat Camp Meeting, donated by a Brother Vance, illustrates this pattern and response. Vichy Campground, also, was established through inspiration of the Rolla congregation. It would be another decade and a half before this church would have another settled pastor, but the group continued to function and grow. Exact dates are not known, but it is believed that Joe Payne and S. R. McElmmerry pastored the Rolla congregation from 1912 until 1915. Since 1915, when J. C. Woods became the pastor, the congregation has continued its ministry with strong leadership.[5]

Most of the congregations formed in this early period were in the rural areas of America. Sometimes they were in small towns like Rolla, but often the churches they built were in the open country in communities like Spring Hill, Mississippi. The roadsides of Indiana, for instance, became dotted with small meetinghouses with such lyrical names as Praise Chapel, Brush College, County Line, Olive Bethel, Block Chapel, and Valley Bethel. Similar developments were taking place in other Midwestern states as well as in the South, the North, and the West.

A third example of congregational formation is the Redline Church of God near Palco, Kansas. In 1896, Mr. and Mrs. Andy Jones of Smith County came to the Redline community to visit the George Brown family. Mrs. Jones was a half sister of Mrs. Brown. It was a pioneer farming community where some of the people had acquired their land by planting trees (called timber claims) and others by homesteading. They made their living mostly by farming.

Andy Jones had been a Methodist class leader, but he had left the Methodist church and accepted the Church of God after hearing a Nebraska evangelist by the name of Charles Bowers who was preaching at Cedar Fork Schoolhouse in Smith County in 1893. While visiting their relatives, the Joneses arranged some group gatherings in different homes to tell people of the "new" doctrine. Later meetings were held in several schoolhouses. Since no preacher was available, these meetings consisted mostly of singing, praying, and testifying. Some of the first families to follow Andy Jones's teaching were the Columbus Cox, Hayden Bass, L. W. White, Oscar Gustafson, John Eakes, and the Jackson and Brown families.

The schoolhouses were not convenient for worship services, so the small group decided to construct a church building of their own. Columbus Cox gave them an acre of ground one mile south and four miles west of Palco on which to build a church. The church was constructed and dedicated in 1906. It was built in a fashion very similar to the country schoolhouses of that time. It was set level with the ground on a cement foundation with a cement step in front and hitching posts for horses on the west side a short

---

5. Marianna House, comp, "A Historical Sketch of First Church of God" (Rolla, Missouri), Anderson University and Church of God Archives.

distance from the building. Inside, a coal stove was set in the middle aisle and short pews were put on either side of the stove so as to get past the stove to the front of the church. (The stove was removed in the summertime.) There was a small rostrum in front with a homemade pulpit. Behind the pulpit on the wall was a blackboard for ministerial use in illustrating sermons. The building was first lit with kerosene lamps and lanterns, later replaced by gasoline lamps. These big double lights held by a rod from the ceiling were regarded as an improvement.

The church functioned for several years without a full-time pastor. A local preacher by the name of Wilson served on a part-time basis. Evangelists J. W. Daugherty and Charles Mayfield stayed for short periods of time at the Columbus Cox home and served as temporary pastors. The George T. Neals came down once a month from Norton. Not until Lilburn Neal came in 1917, followed by J. G. Gordon in 1918, did the congregation enjoy continuing ministerial leadership. The church had been started, grown, and functioned for twenty years largely through the efforts of dedicated lay leaders in a community of farmers.[6]

Not all of the congregations developing in the early 1900s, however, were in rural areas. This also was the era of beginnings for the missionary home work in Chicago, New York, Kansas City, Oakland, and other cities. These "homes" eventually produced congregations; their development followed a pattern different from the usual small town and rural congregations. There are examples, however, of city churches that began in this era and developed along more traditional lines. One of these is found in Oklahoma City.

J. A. Carter lived on a farm not far from Oklahoma City. He had heard and accepted the message of the Church of God through a traveling evangelist who held a revival meeting in his community.[7] Carter subsequently felt that God was leading him to move into the city even though he knew no one and had no promise of a livelihood. With his young wife and children he made the move in autumn 1903. They arrived in a horse-drawn wagon, found a house to rent, and his wife started a home laundry to earn their living. By chance Carter met Ewald ("Ed") Matthesen and his in-laws, Pow-

---

6. Margaret Gustafson, a history of the Redline Church of God, Anderson University and Church of God Archives.

7. In a 1949 letter from Shipman in Bellingham, Washington, to G. W. Johnson in Whittier, California, he says he held the first Church of God meeting in Oklahoma City, which would have been in the late 1890s. It is logical to assume that Carter heard him at this meeting or another in the general area. The letter is in the Anderson University and Church of God Archives

Camp meetings took place across the nation. This photo captured the Church of God camp meeting in Oklahoma City in 1920.

hatan ("Pappy") and Elizabeth ("Mammy") Yeaman, and talked to them about the Church of God. Elizabeth Yeaman had already heard about the movement. Earlier she had met evangelist Lena Shoffner and knew what an outstanding preacher she was; so there was a readiness to accept Carter's message. All of them became interested in starting a regular meeting in Oklahoma City, even though Matthesen and the Yeamans lived a few miles south in Moore. (Matthesen's wife had died and the Yeamans were living with him to help care for his children.) Accordingly, they invited Shoffner to hold a series of evangelistic meetings.

Lena Shoffner and her friend and fellow worker Mabel Ashenfelter arrived in the spring of 1904. A hall on California Avenue just west of Harvey had been rented and nicely furnished, mostly through donations by Matthesen. It was well located and easily accessible, so they were expecting large crowds. In this expectation they were keenly disappointed. Often a dozen people were present and that included the workers. At the first service, there were barely more inquirers than ministers and workers. On weekends more would come in for the services. The greatest excitement came in the form of severe opposition. A band of Holiness people known as the Firebrand came to cause trouble. One night a member of this opposing group walked up on the platform and said to evangelist Shoffner, "I rebuke thee in the name of the Lord;" furthermore, he told her she was out of order and not preaching correct doctrine. Then he commanded her to leave the pulpit. Lena Shoffner was not easily intimidated. She stopped her sermon long enough to place her hand on her hip, fix a cold eye on the opposer and tell him that they had paid rent on the hall and furnished it. If he did not like what he was hearing he could rent his own place and preach as he wished. She continued with her sermon as he walked back to his seat. That was not the only time the Firebrand interfered, but eventually they gave up.

The meeting continued for four weeks until at last a break came. There were twenty-five or more in the service one evening, and every unsaved person came to the altar along with others who needed spiritual help. The Church of God in Oklahoma City was born that night. At the close of this four-week revival the church decided to continue services in the hall. They chose Lena Shoffner as pastor and Mabel Ashenfelter as her assistant. Later the church moved from the hall to an old German Methodist church located just across

Mabel Ashenfelter Hale (1879–1961), pioneer evangelist. A Kansas native, Hale was won by the preaching of Clarence and Nora Hunter in 1897. Prior to her marriage to Jesse R. Hale in 1910, Mabel was a gospel worker in Topeka, worked in the Chicago missionary home, and along with Lena Shoffner started a congregation in Oklahoma City. J. R. and Mabel Hale were typical of many husband-wife gospel teams in the first half of the twentieth century.

the street and one block west. Erastus Morgan was pastor of the church for a while. In 1908 they moved to a larger upstairs room known as Redman Hall located on the southwest corner of Main and Harvey Streets. While in these quarters A. L. Hutton was called to assist as pastor, continuing until 1909. This congregation grew to become the four hundred-member Capitol Hill Church of God, which spawned most of the other congregations in the area. It attracted the leadership of such noted individuals as evangelist H. M. Riggle; Steele C. Smith, who later became president of the Gospel Trumpet Company; and Lawrence J. Chestnut, who served as pastor and builder for over forty years.[8]

8. "History of the Beginning and Early Years of the Church of God in Oklahoma City, Oklahoma," Anderson University and Church of God Archives.

A footnote to that Oklahoma City revival is the story of the forming of another husband-wife ministerial team. During the meeting Lena Shoffner made trips to Moore to visit Elizabeth Yeaman, who was caring for the Matthesen children. Shoffner became burdened about Matthesen's responsibility for the children since "Mammy" Yeaman could not stay there long. Shoffner became so concerned that she went down on a nice secluded creek bank for secret prayer. One day as she was there praying she told the Lord about Brother Ed, his problem regarding the care of the children, and his need to be married. She asked the Lord to send him a good wife. Shoffner did not know that Matthesen was close by in the field working and had heard her praying. He did not tell her until later that at that time he decided she was the Lord's answer to her prayers for Ed. Sometime after the revival they were married and both continued in a fruitful ministry for many years.

Courtesy of Anderson University and Church of God Archives

Lena Shoffner Matthesen (1869–1937), evangelist. Influenced by D. S. Warner's preaching, Lena Shoffner affiliated with the Church of God in 1890 and began evangelistic work in 1892. She spent a year in England as a missionary, 1893–94. After her marriage to Ed Matthesen in Moore, Oklahoma, Lena Shoffner was the lone woman on the committee of seventeen progressive ministers behind the influential *Our Ministerial Letter*.

Accounts such as these of new congregations being formed could be multiplied by the hundreds, each with its own story of exciting meetings, hardships, opposition, and determined effort. The names attached to a dedicated cast of characters are different in each place and specific events are unique, but the plot is very similar. In spite of the fact that not every act had a happy ending, the Church of God movement was becoming settled in America as well as in the world, establishing a base of operation in multiple hamlets, towns, and cities across the land.

For the period prior to 1897 there is really no way of knowing the number of ministers and workers active in the movement or the number of established meetings. The first attempt at any sort of tabulation occurred when E. E. Byrum asked all ministers in the movement to send in their names and addresses for the purpose of compiling a *bona fide* list to send to the railway clergy bureaus, which issued certificates for clergy rates.[9] The first annual list was compiled in 1897 and contained slightly more than three hundred names. The last "Ministerial List," published in 1916, included 985 people.[10] Understanding the purpose of these lists and that no recognition was involved, they tell us little beyond the fact that in twenty years the number of individuals desiring clergy rates increased by over 300 percent. Even so, this is one indication that the movement was growing and extending its witness nationwide.

In turning to consider the growth of the publishing work one is struck first of all by the fact that like a growing number of ministers, the migrating magazine had finally settled in one location. Facilities were sufficiently adequate and the community climate generally compatible enough that the Gospel Trumpet Company remained in Grand Junction, Michigan, for twelve years. The moves from two locations in Indiana and two in Ohio in less than four years made the two-year sojourn in Williamstown, Michigan, seem like a long tenure; settling in at Grand Junction was the epitome of stability. In the first few years partners and assistants had turned over rapidly. Even Warner's wife Sarah and the capable and loyal J. C. Fisher had fallen by the wayside. Much of what happened in the period up to 1917 can be attributed to a new team of leaders who joined in the publishing enterprise soon after the move to Grand Junction. Like the company, they stayed put and set the tone and guided the development of this most central operation.

Two of the most important new leaders were Enoch and Noah Byrum. These brothers were actually in charge of the Gospel Trumpet office almost from the time they arrived at Grand Junction in 1887. Warner was away on evangelistic tours most of the time, and in his absence the Byrum brothers had a relatively free hand both to manage and to enlarge the publishing work. Both were dedicated energetic men with good business sense. One of the first steps Enoch Byrum took as managing editor of the *Trumpet* was to put the company on a cash basis. Warner had been hounded by creditors in the past, and misunderstandings over paying debts had nearly destroyed the company at Indianapolis and Bucyrus. Byrum's policy was that the

---

9. "To Ministers and Gospel Workers," *Gospel Trumpet*, December 17, 1896, 2.

10. To give this list an official character for the railway clergy bureaus, the Gospel Trumpet Company designated one of its staff workers as registrar. In 1916 this was J. W. Phelps, who also compiled the first *Yearbook of the Church of God* in 1917.

company should pay for everything on delivery.[11] Warner supported him in this, but Byrum went further: the publishing company should buy whatever it needed and then trust God to provide the payment when it was due. So it was that the Byrum brothers repeatedly ordered new equipment and materials on a thirty-day cash basis and then began praying that sufficient money would arrive before the bill. Apparently their prayers were answered, although sometimes not until the last minute. The phenomenal growth of the publishing work and of the Church of God in this period is a striking witness to the trusting faith of these men.

The Development of the Gospel Trumpet Company

During the 1890s the *Gospel Trumpet* became an ever more important vehicle for expanding the movement. It traveled where the flying messengers could not—from the Atlantic to the Pacific, from Canada to Mexico, and to many foreign countries. In March 1896 E. E. Byrum began raising money to send a roll of *Gospel Trumpets* to every post office in the United States.[12] By June of that year the *Trumpet* was read in every state of the Union and twenty foreign countries.[13] During the 1890s the Trumpet office received letters from readers in Jerusalem, Copenhagen, London, Alaska, Australia, New Zealand, Africa, Persia, Egypt, India, Norway, France, Germany, Russia, Austria, Bulgaria, and other countries. This scope of readership in conjunction with the foreign missionary efforts of the movement make it apparent that by the turn of the century the Church

Courtesy of Anderson University and Church of God Archives

Enoch E. Byrum (1861–1942), editor of the *Gospel Trumpet* from 1895 to 1916. Byrum was particularly dedicated to the ministry of divine healing and in 1892 published *Divine Healing of Soul and Body*. Byrum's conservative mentality and managerial acumen enabled him to steer the Church of God through its most serious theological crisis, the "Anti-Cleansing Heresy" of 1898–99.

11. *Gospel Trumpet*, January 31, 1942, 6.
12. "Who Will Help to Spread the Gospel?" *Gospel Trumpet*, March 12, 1896, 2.
13. "The Publishing Work," *Gospel Trumpet*, June 25, 1896, 2.

of God had made contact with every continent except Antarctica and South America.

Circulation figures for the *Gospel Trumpet* give some indication of numerical growth during this formative period. At the beginning of 1890, five thousand copies of the paper were being printed.[14] By August of 1892 the number had jumped to nine thousand.[15] In the next few years the circulation figures vary considerably because large quantities of the *Trumpet* were occasionally distributed free of charge. In 1896, for example, Byrum reported that twenty-five thousand free copies were being distributed in a single week.[16] By March 1900, the big rotary press at Moundsville, West Virginia, (after 1898 the company's new home) was turning out two and a half tons of printed material every week.[17]

Growth in production required the physical growth of the movement's publishing work. When the Byrum brothers arrived in Grand Junction in 1887 fewer than a half-dozen individuals were at the publishing house, all without pay. Work was being done in an old store building. They had a dilapidated flatbed Campbell press that printed only two pages at a time and was run by a three-horsepower steam engine. All of the type was set by hand. E. E. Byrum recalled that in the winter the uninsulated building was so cold that the ink would not spread evenly.[18] Often kerosene lamps were put under the press just to keep the ink warm.

The threadbare operation quickly changed for the better after the Byrums began their purchase-and-pray plan. In 1890 they bought their own stereotyping equipment, which allowed them to make their own printing plates.[19] In 1891 they bought an automatic addressing machine.[20] The following year they bought a larger press.[21] In 1893 they built a boiler-and-engine room and purchased a job press for printing tracts.[22] They acquired their own bookbinding equipment and automatic typesetting machinery in

---

14. N. H. Byrum, "Early Days of Our Publishing Work," *Gospel Trumpet*, September 13, 1941, 18.

15. *Gospel Trumpet*, May 23, 1942, 18.

16. *Gospel Trumpet*, April 23, 1896, 2.

17. S. L. Speck and S. Strang, "A Visit to the Gospel Trumpet Pub. Co.," *Gospel Trumpet*, March 15, 1900, 4–5.

18. Enoch E. Byrum, *Life Experiences* (Anderson, IN: Gospel Trumpet Co., 1928), 90.

19. N. H. Byrum, "Early Days of Our Publishing Work," *Gospel Trumpet*, October 11, 1941, 17.

20. *Gospel Trumpet*, February 12, 1942, 16–17.

21. *Gospel Trumpet*, March 7, 1942, 18.

22. *Gospel Trumpet*, July 25, 1942, 19–20, and August 29, 1942, 20.

1897.[23] Then, in the summer of 1898, they left Grand Junction and moved the whole company to Moundsville, West Virginia. The relocation demonstrates the Byrums' business sense. As facilities grew so did the company's dependence on steam power. Gospel Trumpet Company boilers were fired by coal, which could be purchased at a much cheaper price in West Virginia than in Michigan. There they set up operations in a three-story factory building with their own electric generator in the basement and plenty of room for the new rotary press.[24] When S. L. Speck and S. P. Strang rode into Moundsville at midnight on March 5, 1900, they found that the lights were still on at the Trumpet Company building.[25] In just over a decade, the company grew under the Byrums' management from less than six workers to more than one hundred. The presses were running twenty-four hours a day, printing more than two million sheets a day. Even at that rate the company was not able to fill all the orders.[26]

The most important publication, of course, was the *Gospel Trumpet*. Frequently people would pick up a copy of the paper or a tract printed by the company and become so vividly impressed with the truth of these publications that they would write to the Trumpet office for more literature or perhaps ask for a team of gospel workers to visit their area. For example, there is the story of Al Peterman, who came into contact with the movement in 1893 through a copy of the *Gospel Trumpet* that had been stashed away in an old trunk. After reading the paper Peterman became so excited about its contents that he gave it to his United Brethren pastor, G. W. Bailey, who wrote to Warner and asked for a team to come to their part of the country. That invitation began the work of the Church of God in eastern Washington.[27] The *Trumpet* planted a seed that later sprang up in new congregations. This sequence of events would be repeated hundreds of times in the years ahead.

Another important type of literature produced in massive quantities was tracts. Among the many hundreds of these small messengers was one published in 1890 titled *Must We Sin?* It had been written by Warner and was a very effective presentation of holiness doctrine. Hundreds of thousands of

---

23. "For the Book Bindery," *Gospel Trumpet*, May 6, 1897, 2.

24. Noah H. Byrum, *Familiar Names and Faces* (Moundsville, WV: Gospel Trumpet Publishing Co., 1902), 152.

25. Speck and Strang, "Visit to the Gospel Trumpet," 4.

26. E. E. Byrum, "Words of Greeting," *Gospel Trumpet*, December 28, 1899, 1–2.

27. Charles E. Brown, *When the Trumpet Sounded* (Anderson, IN: Gospel Trumpet Co., 1951), 319–20.

copies of these leaflets were distributed during the decade. They were selling for thirty-five cents a pound.

Yet another important aspect of the publication ministry was books. *Divine Healing of Soul and Body* by E. E. Byrum was published in 1892. As F. G. Smith was recognized as the movement's leading authority on the church in prophecy and history, so E. E. Byrum came to be the authority on divine healing both as a writer and as an individual with special gifts for intercessory prayer on behalf of the physically ill. Another book on the same subject, *The Great Physician*, was published in 1899. Other ministers joined the list of authors. William G. Schell became an important doctrinal writer of this period. Among his most influential books were *The Biblical Trace of the Church*, published in 1893, and *The Better Testament*, which appeared in 1899. By the end of 1900 the company advertised fourteen clothbound book titles and eighteen additional paperback books and booklets, all from its own presses.[28]

Songbooks played an important role in the growth of the movement. After Fisher's defection, gifted songwriters and editors appeared to take his place. Warner and B. E. Warren edited *Echoes from Glory*, which was published in 1893. That was followed by *Songs of the Evening Light*, edited by Warren and A. L. Byers, in 1897, and *Salvation Echoes*, printed in late 1900. In addition, the first Church of God songbook for German-speaking people was published in 1899, and *Den Evangeliske Sanger*, the company's first Dano-Norwegian songbook, appeared the same year.[29]

Clara M. Brooks (1882–1980), songwriter. Early Church of God songbooks largely comprised songs written by men and women of the movement. They sang their faith to such an extent that it is a commonplace that the theology of the Church of God was conveyed through song rather than formal confession of faith. Clara Brooks collaborated with Barney Warren on "What a Mighty God We Serve!," with A. L. Byers on "By Faith and Not by Sight," and W. H. Oldham on "Draw Me Close to Thee."

28. *Gospel Trumpet*, January 3, 1901, 7.

29. Letter from Thomas Nelson, *Gospel Trumpet*, March 23, 1899; and an editorial, *Gospel Trumpet*, October 12, 1899.

Some children's publications were also placed on a firm footing in the 1890s. After the demise of C. L. Kaumeyer's periodical for juveniles, *The Guide*,[30] in 1891, the Gospel Trumpet Company took a step of faith in starting a new youth paper, *The Shining Light*. This illustrated magazine was issued semimonthly at first and after 1897 every week until 1952, when it was supplanted by *Stories for Children*. Youth-oriented books like *The Boy's Companion* also appeared in this decade.[31]

A significant move during this period was the publication of Sunday school cards beginning in April 1896.[32] This seems to be the first material in this movement published specifically for the Sunday school. A Sunday school had been organized on the Grand Junction campgrounds in the summer of 1892 with E. E. Byrum as the superintendent and Isabel Coston, A. L. Byers, Gideon Detweiler, and Byron Wooden as teachers.[33]

One of the most unusual aspects of the publishing work was the continuing development of the communal lifestyle that Byrum found when he first joined the Gospel Trumpet Publishing Company. In the beginning at Grand Junction there were only five workers. This small working family grew close together, ate their meals around a common table, and prayed together for requests sent in by readers and for the needs of the publishing work. By 1891 the work force had increased to fourteen. As the enterprise grew the different functions began to become more specialized and departments were formed. At certain times, however, the total group joined together to accomplish a given task. One of these common tasks was the folding by hand of the *Gospel Trumpet* in preparation for mailing. N. H. Byrum described the procedure:

> Generally on Wednesday or Thursday this would be done, as these were mailing days. A number of tables would be arranged, the work in other departments would sometimes be dropped, and a number of hands would set to work folding papers. This would make a busy scene, all in one large room; and, with the singing of songs, it generally would be a pleasurable change of employment for the workers.[34]

---

30. N. H. Byrum, "Early Days of Our Publishing Work," 16.

31. Enoch E. Byrum, *The Boy's Companion, or a Warning Against the Secret Vice and Other Bad Habits* (Grand Junction, MI: Gospel Trumpet Co., 1893).

32. "News: Sunday School Cards," *Gospel Trumpet*, April 17, 1896, 2.

33. N. H. Byrum, "Early Days of Our Publishing Work, 18.

34. N. H. Byrum, *Familiar Names and Faces*, 102.

By 1892 the number of workers had increased to the point that specialized help was needed for the mundane task of meal preparation. The following appeal illustrated the method of recruiting individuals with special qualifications:

> As there are now nineteen persons in the Trumpet family, besides the many visitors, a good sister, strong in faith and strong in body, to take charge of the kitchen, is very much needed. We deem it proper to speak of this, because we had spoken that probably enough help was at hand, and on that account persons might not be free to follow the Spirit when led to offer themselves. We want God to make the selection. Other kitchen help will be furnished, but one to take the lead is wanted. Who is it?[35]

By 1894 the Trumpet family membership numbered twenty-five and was attracting the attention of southwestern Michigan. The *Kalamazoo Weekly* reported the existence of a "queer religious sect over at Grand Junction" composed of people who dressed plainly so as not to be overtaken in pride by the devil. The Trumpet family, living in two "commodious dwellings," greeted each other, it was stated, by saying "Praise the Lord" instead of "Good Morning" or "Howd'y do."[36] Historian Henry Wickersham contends that the Trumpet family was not fanatical in regard to simple dress but did admit some tendencies in that direction:

> When zealous children of God see by the Word that it is their duty to dress plain, the devil pushes them over the mark, and they become slovenly and slouchy in their appearance—this is fanaticism…[which] is one of the counterfeits of reformation. It runs parallel with reformation, but is not part of it. The world sometimes mistakes the one for the other.…This reformation has not been free from persecuting neither has it been free from the effects of fanaticism.[37]

In a later news story titled "Our Strange People at Grand Junction," it is related how a labor bureau inspector found this group of people who were

---

35. *Gospel Trumpet*, January 14, 1892, 2.

36. "The Saints," *Kalamazoo Weekly*, July 4, 1894.

37. Henry C. Wickersham, *A History of the Church* (Moundsville, WV: Gospel Trumpet Publishing Co., 1900), 293.

giving all their earnings to the Church of God. The article states that the inhabitants, about 115 in number, were interested in a concern known as the Gospel Trumpet Publishing Company. The meager earnings were barely enough for food and clothing, and all profits were used for the enlargement of the plant and establishment of new churches.[38]

Income from subscriptions and the sale of other printed materials was never sufficient to cover the costs of new equipment, supplies, postage, and living expenses for the Trumpet family. The pages of the *Gospel Trumpet* made it known that donations of money, commodities, and clothing would be accepted in order to keep the work going and growing. Each issue of the paper reported names of donors and items received such as buckets of honey, clean wheat, cabbage, meat, and cloth. There seemed to be a fairly regular inflow of this kind of support, but when extraordinary expenses, such as payment for a new press, came along the only recourse was prayer—and they did a great deal of praying. E. E. Byrum told of one particular financial crisis that really tested their faith. At the busiest hour of the day on a Tuesday, he reported, the machines were stopped and all workers gathered for prayer. By Tuesday of the following week, no more than the usual amounts of money had been received. They held another prayer meeting at the same hour. Still the results were the same.

> So we gathered together the third time for prayer; we realized that over thirty workers sacrificing an hour in the busiest part of the day, and meeting with one accord, would surely move God to answer, and we announced that we would spend the hour in a praise meeting, thanking God for hearing and answering prayer....A few minutes later the mail train came in and soon a letter was brought in that read as follows: "Enclosed find a bank draft for $100.00 to be used to the glory of God." This also soon followed by other donations, orders for books, etc.... Within the last few months we have had a new engine and boiler room and a ten-horsepower engine and a fifteen-horsepower boiler, and other machinery, and steam heating, which has all been paid for.[39]

The Trumpet family grew with the needs of the company. As some workers would leave others would arrive to take their places. Especially after the June camp meeting people stayed on to work and thus added their names to

---

38. From a detached clipping, probably from a Kalamazoo paper also around 1898.
39. N. H. Byrum, *Familiar Names and Faces*, 110–12.

the Trumpet family. Usually there was a sufficient number of volunteers, but at times a plea was sent out for some particular need at the company. In November 1895, this notice was published: "At present we are in need of some carpenters, woodcutters, and someone to set type. The workers here give their services free. Has not the Lord been talking to some consecrated persons on this line?"[40]

Charles W. Naylor (1874–1950), minister, songwriter, and author. Two accidents in the 1920s left Naylor nearly completely bedfast for the rest of his life. He nevertheless continued to write devotional books and some of the most theologically profound and hauntingly beautiful songs of the Church of God, including "Spirit Holy" and "I Am the Lord's."

One person who responded to such a call was Charles W. Naylor, who later became one of the movement's most prominent writers, poets, and songwriters. His account gives an idea of the everyday work and general attitude of the office:

On Jan. 10, 1896, I stepped off the train at Grand Junction, Mich., with the intent of becoming a worker in the Trumpet Office. I saw an old store building not far away with the words, "The Gospel Trumpet Publishing Co.," painted on its side. A large addition was under construction adjoining it.

I went into the building and was shown into a small room cut off from the main room. In one corner at a desk sat E. E. Byrum. In another corner was N. H. Byrum, and on the side next to the street John White was wrapping books and tracts ready for mailing.

After introducing myself and telling them that I had come to be a worker I was invited to have a chair, and they all continued their work, paying no further attention to me. I sat there, becoming more and more embarrassed, for perhaps an hour, when E. E. Byrum turned to me and said a few words then remarked: "You have come to be a worker? Well, you may begin by taking up the carpet of this room."

---

40. *Gospel Trumpet*, November 7, 1895, 2.

That carpet had more holes and more dirt in it than any I had ever seen, but in spite of having my best clothes on, I did the job. Next I helped stick postage stamps on 11,000 catalogs. My next job was to clean a lot of frozen and rotten potatoes and cabbage out of the cellar, then to crawl under the floor of the building amid the cobwebs and paste asbestos paper on the steam pipes, meantime bumping my head and elbows on the timbers and burning my hands on the hot pipes again and again as I worked in the semidarkness for several hours.

That was my introduction to life as a Trumpet Worker. It also marked the beginning of some wonderful friendships…memories of Grand Junction, of Moundsville, and of Anderson; of names, faces and incidents; of work, play and meetings; of joys, sorrows, difficulties, trials and victories.[41]

Like Naylor, most of the family members were young and single people. A few married couples either set up their own housekeeping or lived with the Trumpet family in the Trumpet Home. By the nature of the work, and because of the circumstances under which they all came together, the workers developed a precious camaraderie growing out of the common task in which all worked for the spreading of the "pure evening light." A. L. Byers wrote, "They lived together in a peaceable way, which has long been a marvel to sinners and to those who do not understand how God makes his people of one heart and soul."[42]

The "peaceable way" among the workers did not happen automatically. As the Trumpet family grew it became necessary to establish some procedures for the preservation of harmony. During 1895, a tradition began that was to continue for the duration of the communal lifestyle. That was the "Monday Night Meeting." This gathering was established as a time when the entire Trumpet family could join together for the purpose of "considering and praying for the needs of the work, and for discussing family affairs in general."[43] The Monday night meeting was held in the Trumpet Home parlor and provided ample opportunity for the necessary sharing and airing to preserve good group relationships. Later, in Anderson, the Monday night meeting of a much larger Trumpet family became popularly known by the workers as "The Dos and Don'ts Meeting."

41. "Trumpet Family," *Workers Bulletin*, September 1947.
42. In N. H. Byrum, *Familiar Names*, 140.
43. Ibid., 120.

The Trumpet family rapidly increased in size. By the end of 1896 it included fifty workers. Four months later there were over sixty. In early 1898 there were ninety workers and by midyear over one hundred. The number of gospel workers had become so large they could not all eat at the same table or even worship together. It also meant that, in addition to the weekly meeting, there had to be some regulations regarding the common life and work of such a large group. One of the problem points, for instance, was that some of the workers spent so much time on the job that, says Byers, "there was some danger of their zeal causing them to work harder than their physical and mental powers would long permit."[44] For this and other reasons, rules were established. Byers explained the evolution of those rules in this way: "The confining labor of some of the departments would tell on the general health, and those members of the family who had spent years in the work were compelled to observe some regulations pertaining to diet, sleep, working hours, recreation, etc., and see the necessity of advising all to do the same."[45] He went on to state, "Seldom was there any sickness, and then it was perhaps caused by a weakening of the body through protracted and confining work. They knew how to trust the Lord for their healing, and there were many instances of their being touched with his healing power."[46]

Despite the press of unfinished work and the unstinting dedication of the workers to their task, time was available for recreation and fun together. Opportunities in Grand Junction were quite limited, however. The terrain was not suitable for many forms of outdoor recreation. There were not many trees, and scenic areas were almost nonexistent. The only places for relaxation and fun were the numerous lakes around Grand Junction, and Trumpet family members found occasion to utilize the opportunities they offered. "These afforded opportunity for boat riding, fishing, swimming, or enjoyment of the pleasant shade of the trees growing on their banks."[47] Saddle Lake must have been their favorite spot, for during one of their busiest times the entire family took one entire day off to enjoy the place that had shared their joys, trials, and tears. Byers wrote, "Busy as they were…they could afford to spend a day of recreation by the lakeside that had so often refreshed their weary spirits. They took their dinners and spent a profitable day."[48]

---

44. Ibid., 138–40.
45. Ibid., 138.
46. Ibid., 140.
47. Ibid., 144–46.
48. Ibid.

What motivated the workers to so willingly expend themselves in united effort? Obviously, these people were completely dedicated to Christ and the cause. A major contributing factor to this zeal was their awareness that the *Trumpet* message was not only being sent to the entire world but also was bearing visible fruit. The office constantly received testimonies describing how a publication or tract found in an unexpected way had led to conversion or to acceptance of the truths of sanctification and separation from sectism. Coupled with this the family was aware of the establishment of new Church of God congregations throughout the world and the launching of other projects such as children's homes, the *Floating Bethel,* book and tract distribution offices, and foreign-based activities. The family members considered themselves to be part of a successful and exclusive reformation. E. E. Byrum spoke for them:

> …Many wonder why we say so much about increasing the work, and are constantly pushing forward to greater things. In places churches have been raised up through reading the TRUMPET, without a sermon being preached, and in hundreds of places it has as John the Baptist prepared the way for Him who should come after. We are doing all we can…[49]

In February 1898 an editorial announced that the management of the publishing work was considering a move to Moundsville, West Virginia. The facilities at Grand Junction had reached their capacity. A larger office building would have to be built and coal used for fuel was costing almost six dollars a ton. The new location could supply coal at anywhere from thirty-five to seventy cents a ton. In addition, George Clayton informed them of the availability of a large new brick building complete with engine, boiler, shaftings, and other machinery which was ready for occupancy. The cost, $2500, which included a beautiful campground, was less than half the cost to construct such a facility. Moundsville, it was thought, would be a more central spot for distribution of the publications.

Since the publishing operation was the common concern of the Trumpet family and all those who supported the work, those interested were given considerable opportunity to express themselves. There seemed to be general satisfaction concerning the move, and so on June 28, 1898, a train

---

49. E. E. Byrum, "Only A Trumpet," *Gospel Trumpet*, October 14, 1897, 2.

containing two passenger cars, one baggage car, and nine freight cars left Grand Junction. Sixty-nine people were on board; two were bicycling the distance, and thirty who were on vacation found their own way to the new location.[50] Even the train ride was employed in evangelizing. One hundred large scriptural placards were attached to the train and about one hundred thousand tracts were distributed along the route.[51] When the train arrived at Moundsville, the company learned that a fire started by embers from a passing train had burned the Grand Junction office building and two large dwellings. The loss amounted to between three and four thousand dollars. Proceeds from the sale of these buildings had been intended for the purchase of the property at Moundsville. After the initial shock, the family realized they were fortunate to have all their equipment; they would just have to pray harder to secure the funds for the new site.[52]

The publishing plant moved into its new facilities and soon was busily involved in expanding publications. The Trumpet family was temporarily headquartered in an empty planing mill across the road from their property. Here meals were served and worship was held, but lodging had to be found in nearby rented houses. In the spring of 1899 a nearby tract of almost six acres was purchased as the site for a home for all the workers. The site included a large "Prohibition" tabernacle, built to house anti-liquor meetings and seating for over four thousand people.[53] A Moundsville

Courtesy of Anderson University and Church of God Archives

In 1898, the Gospel Trumpet Company relocated to a converted shoe factory in Moundsville, West Virginia. An inexpensive source of energy, coal, to fire its steam-powered equipment was a key factor in the company's decision to move to West Virginia, where it remained until 1906.

newspaper, referred to the proposed "mammoth building on the assembly grounds" (the future Trumpet Home) as the largest lumber contract ever to come to Moundsville. The shipment of lumber, it was noted, would amount to over thirty-five carloads and cost about $600. Another newspaper article

---

50. N. H. Byrum, *Familiar Names*, 154–56.
51. Ibid.
52. Ibid., 150.
53. Ibid., 168.

described the three-story veneer brick building as a hundred-room hotel that would accommodate two hundred people. (It actually contained 104 rooms plus a large dining room.) The article continued, "The company with the help they have and what donations have been received have been able to build the new home without having to touch any of their other money."[54] In November 1899 the Trumpet family moved into the new Trumpet Home. To facilitate the monumental task of meeting the family's needs, the home was organized into departments—kitchen, dining room, baking, sewing, laundry, janitor, shoe mending, general housework, and general outside work. A matron was responsible for these departments. Visitors were welcomed at both the home and office. The Trumpet family now numbered over one hundred.[55]

The communal character of the Trumpet family continued to attract public attention. A Philadelphia paper ran a story in July 1900 reporting that the Church of God held much valuable property in Moundsville. This, the account stated, included an enormous auditorium, a large three-story home that "houses people who publish the church paper and conduct business of the Lord." The printing plant was described as having modern machinery and equipment on which "the colony turns out three weekly papers of a 60,000 copy circulation, tons of tracts and pamphlets as well as books." E. E. Byrum is quoted as saying, "We believe the whole Bible… we have not attempted to make the Bible suit our moods but have tried to make our moods suit the Bible."[56] It is noteworthy that the article does not describe the company as eking out bare survival, as earlier reports were prone to emphasize.

Not all public impressions were favorable, however. *The Wheeling Intelligencer* stated that rumors were circulated that the Gospel Trumpet colony was Mormon, a frequent confusion since both the Church of God and the Mormons referred to their adherents as saints. This article sought to set the facts straight.[57] Another account the following month printed E. E. Byrum's reply to a Mr. Allinger of the German Methodist Episcopal Church who had been critical of the *Gospel Trumpet,* inviting him to spend two weeks as a guest at the Gospel Trumpet Publishing Company.[58]

---

54. Detached clippings.
55. Byers, in N. H. Byrum, *Familiar Names*, 176.
56. *North American Philadelphia*, July 11, 1900.
57. *The Wheeling Intelligencer*, April 16, 1900.
58. "Gospel Trumpeters Reply," *The Wheeling Intelligencer*, May 16, 1900.

At Moundsville the publishing work grew extensively. The first linotype machine was purchased in December 1901 and a second one in 1903. New presses, bindery equipment, and other machinery speeded up processes and increased production. During 1903 a total of 76,950 books were published, with ten new titles added. That same year, with the help of a special subscription campaign, the circulation of the *Gospel Trumpet* reached a temporary high of 35,500 copies a week. More workers were recruited and a night shift was added. By 1905 the building was crowded to capacity and there was talk of new additions or even new buildings. Certain circumstances, however, began to turn the talk in another direction—toward the possibility of another relocation.[59]

Company managers discovered that Moundsville was not quite the central location for the work of the Church of God that they had anticipated. Most of the congregations were developing in the Middle West. Moreover, cheap coal was becoming less and less a factor because most of the new machinery ran by electricity rather than steam. At this point the Byrums decided to locate elsewhere. They had requested the city of Moundsville to run an electric power line to their property, but the request was denied. By the summer of 1905, despite the size and prosperity of the establishment in Moundsville, these circumstances sparked a decision to begin a search for a new location further west.

After investigating several sites they eventually selected Anderson, Indiana, where suitable rental facilities were immediately available. A well situated forty-acre tract of land for future development could be purchased for a reasonable figure, and the city was willing to offer certain inducements, including an electric power line, to attract new business. In the words of A. L. Byers, "It seemed to be in the order of God that the move to Anderson should be made."[60] Apparently it was considered a good move also by the news media in Indiana, for an August 1905 article in an Anderson newspaper reported an investigative visit by "President Byrum" and others of the "Gospel Temple [*sic.* Trumpet]" who were looking for "30 to 50 acres of woodland near a traction line and convenient to the city. For this they will pay spot cash if a price can be agreed upon."[61] The article continued by reviewing the economic advantages to Anderson for such an enterprise as

59. Harold L. Phillips, *Miracle of Survival* (Anderson, IN: Warner Press, 1979), 84–100.

60. Andrew L. Byers, *The Gospel Trumpet Publishing Work* (Anderson, IN: Gospel Trumpet Co., 1907), 32.

61. As quoted in Phillips, *Miracle of Survival*, 103.

Courtesy of Anderson University and Church of God Archives

The Gospel Trumpet Family Home in Anderson. Trumpet workers lived a semi-communal lifestyle in this building until the arrangement was abandoned in 1917. In that year J. T. Wilson founded Anderson Bible Training School, which moved into the recently vacated home. Generations of Anderson College students remember the building as Old Main.

Byrum described, and it expressed hope the arrangement could be made. By year's end a firm decision was reached, and on February 1, 1906, the first fourteen members of the Trumpet family left for Anderson. Their assignment was to begin construction of a new Trumpet Home. By late September the last of twenty-six freight-car loads of machinery and inventory plus two passenger cars had left Moundsville. The September 27, 1906, issue of the *Gospel Trumpet* was datelined Anderson, Indiana, and a new era for both the publishing work and the Church of God had begun.

The first task, in addition to moving ahead with expanded printing operations, was the construction of facilities. In the next four years they raised four major buildings plus a three-story barn and some smaller structures on the campground. All of this was done with a labor force acquired for the most part by enlarging the family to include a construction crew in addition to the publication workers. Three of the large buildings were constructed of sculptured-face concrete block, hand-poured in molds on the site. The fourth was of reinforced concrete with stucco exterior. The first to be completed, in December 1906, was the Trumpet Home, an imposing

H-shaped edifice of three stories plus attic and basement[62] that housed all facilities necessary to accommodate over two hundred people, including living rooms, kitchen, dining room, bakery, parlor, library, sewing room, music room, laundry, and a large chapel.

The next two buildings, both begun in 1907, were an auditorium and an old people's home. Construction began on the latter first, but the structure was mostly destroyed by a fire in December 1907, and had to be rebuilt. It was completed in 1908. This was also a three-story building to be used, "as a home for aged saints who from a spiritual as well as a temporal standpoint do not have proper support elsewhere."[63] Construction of the auditorium was authorized after a severe storm during the 1907 Anderson Camp Meeting created some major problems with the canvas tabernacle that was used that first year. The new facility was ready for use by the June meeting of 1908.[64] The fourth building was the new publishing plant, the first building the company had ever occupied that was constructed specifically for publication work. Until its completion the company rented a production building in downtown Anderson. Begun in 1909, parts of the facility were in use by the fall of 1910 and the inner core was finished in 1911.[65] With approximately fifty thousand square feet of floor space the publishing work finally had sufficient room to carry on and expand.

Expand the company did, both in volume as well as in products and services offered. A new monthly periodical, the *Missionary Herald,* was launched in 1910 and continued until 1913 when it was merged with the *Trumpet.* The whole area of foreign missions had increased to the point that a special missionary committee had been formed in 1909 to give direction and guidance to this work and to properly distribute funds designated for this purpose. Publication work for the blind in Braille was begun in 1913. Art-velvet mottoes, scripture-text calendars and postcards, children's books and stationery were added to the line of items being produced and marketed. Another new periodical, *The Helper,* was launched in 1915 and contained articles designed primarily for laypeople. Failure to get and maintain a sufficient number of subscribers to cover costs forced discontinuation the following year.

---

62. Byers, *Gospel Trumpet Publishing Work,* 32.

63. Ibid., 71.

64. This is the only one of these first three buildings still standing. It was restored by Anderson College as a performance center and is known as Byrum Hall.

65. Phillips, *Miracle of Survival,* 107.

Camp-meeting revivalism shaped the early ethos of the Church of God. Several early Church of God preachers had been associated with the camp-meeting circuit of the National Camp-meeting Association for the Promotion of Christian Holiness. The photo pictures the first camp meeting (1907) held in Anderson, Indiana, after the relocation of the publishing house in 1906.

The first tabernacle built in Anderson, Indiana. Constructed in 1908 to house the general services of the Anderson Camp meeting, it still stands on the campus of Anderson University, known today as Byrum Hall.

The Gospel Trumpet Company headquarters and publishing plant in Anderson, Indiana. After relocation in 1906, until construction of this building was completed in 1911, the publishing company operated in leased facilities in downtown Anderson.

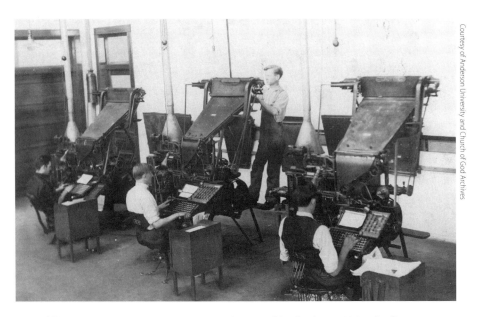

Gospel Trumpet compositors setting type. Invented in the late 1800s, the linotype machine vastly speeded up the typesetting process. Linotype machines were used by the Gospel Trumpet Company and Warner Press until the late 1970s.

Two very significant books were published during the first decade in Anderson: *What the Bible Teaches* (1914) by F. G. Smith and *Select Hymns* (1911), edited by Barney Warren and others. Smith had earlier served as E. E. Byrum's personal secretary and later took a missionary assignment in Syria. Written in Syria as a teaching tool, Smith's book became the most widely circulated standard work on biblical interpretation the movement would have for many decades. *Select Hymns* was the first attempt at publishing a general purpose hymnal that contained many commonly used hymns and gospel songs as well as songs written by the movement's own writers. The first of several general purpose hymnals, *Select Hymns* embodied the musical tradition so important to the Church of God. Both books remained in publication for many years.[66]

Another significant addition to company products was the beginning of Sunday school lesson helps, published for four different age levels. Starting in July 1910, the first regular quarterlies appeared for primaries, juniors, intermediates, and seniors. All were based on the International Uniform Series outlines. An additional story paper, *Our Little Folks,* had been started earlier (1907) and was recommended for use with children under six. This curriculum material was augmented by a 1912 book written by D. Otis Teasley titled *How to Conduct a Sunday School.* Despite continuing reservations the movement was becoming much more amenable to Christian education.[67]

Even with all its growth the publishing work continued to operate on a volunteer basis with communal living in and around the Trumpet Home. The increase in numbers, sometimes well above three hundred, necessitated some modifications and more detailed rules of conduct. The chief change came in 1912 when each worker was allocated a four dollar per month allowance in order to eliminate the great number of requests for small personal items. The greatest personnel change came in 1916 when E. E. Byrum, in response to some rather extensive criticism of his leadership methods, resigned as editor in chief after an association with the company of almost thirty years. He was succeeded by his former secretary, F. G. Smith. Byrum continued to keep an office in the company from which he conducted a personal service and healing ministry until his death in 1942.

---

66. Smith's book, in a condensed form, continues in publication to the present time.
67. Phillips, *Miracle of Survival*, 122–29.

Rudimentary Organization

The stabilizing process was manifested in a third sphere—the development of rudimentary organizational structures beyond the local congregations. The need first became evident when those who had been attending the camp meeting near Bangor, Michigan, decided to purchase their own meeting site on Lester Lake just north of Grand Junction. This decision was reached in 1891 and arrangements were made to buy the land before the year was out. From early spring until the meeting in June a great deal of work went into constructing some necessary facilities to accommodate the meeting. All of this took place before the purchase had been finalized. It became the task of those who assembled to decide how they could hold corporate title to the property without resorting to "human organization." It was a difficult problem but finally they agreed by consensus and without voting to form the Grand Junction Camp Meeting Association with nine brethren suggested by Warner as the trustees.[68] In case a vacancy occurred, the remaining trustees would agree upon a successor. By avoiding any voting procedures and limiting the trustees to the management, improvement, and maintenance of the property, they believed they had avoided sectarian ecclesiasticism. Similar agreements were made later regarding campgrounds in Indiana, West Virginia, Pennsylvania, and Alabama.

The most natural point at which any general organizational structures developed, of course, was in the publishing work. It was after all, a business as well as a mission. The early pattern of individual and/or partner ownership was not actually formalized in a written agreement until just two days before Warner's death. On December 10, 1895, Warner, E. E. Byrum, Sebastian Michels, and N. H. Byrum signed an Articles of Agreement. In this document they recognized Christ as head of the church and bound present and future members of the Gospel Trumpet Publishing Company to certain rules and principles. Each agreed to give his complete labor to the publishing work in exchange for only food and clothing. All income was to be reinvested in the work and any partner or his heirs could draw out only what the member had originally invested, without interest.[69]

Shortly after the move to Moundsville in 1898, the business was reorganized as a stock company. At that time the Byrums were paid back the actual

---

68. *Gospel Trumpet*, July 7, 1892, 2. Other sources indicate there were eight trustees instead of nine as reported in this article.

69. Phillips, *Miracle of Survival*, 46.

amount of money they had put into the company (Michels had already withdrawn his investment) and the business was controlled by a board of seven trustees. The purpose of such a move was to increase the operating capital by selling shares of stock. The shares were to pay no dividends and would not increase in value as the company grew. The arrangement was essentially a means of requesting interested people to loan money interest free for the work of the Lord.[70]

The idea of a stock company did not attract sufficient capital to accomplish the desired goal. In 1903 this stock corporation was dissolved, and all its assets were assigned to a new corporation organized under a West Virginia law designed for not-for-profit religious and charitable institutions. A charter and bylaws controlled the operating procedures. The incorporators constituted a self-perpetuating board of company members.[71] After relocating in Anderson the company reincorporated under a similar Indiana law.

The most crucial aspect of the stabilizing and indigenizing process was the establishment of these continuing local groups without which the movement could not move. The number of permanent propertied congregations continued to increase as did the percentage of ministers who retired from their itinerant evangelistic endeavors to pastor these congregations. The earliest of the ministerial lists to designate a ministerial title was the one for 1916, which contained data for the previous year. This list included the names of 985 ministers; of these, 467 designated themselves as "pastor" or "assistant pastor." By 1915, 47 percent of Church of God preachers had shifted from the flying messenger role and were engaged primarily in pastoral ministry in a single location—a considerable change from a quarter century earlier when the call to preach was equated with a call to go forth across the land.[72]

By the time the first *Yearbook* appeared in 1917 listed ministers resided in 852 different locations in the United States and 22 in Canada. This does not mean there were congregations in each of these places, but the likelihood was great. The effectiveness of the itinerant evangelists and the literature outreach is indicated by the fact that these locations were in forty-three states plus the District of Columbia, and four provinces of Canada. About one-third of them were in the middle western states and another

---

70. Ibid., 64.
71. Ibid., 91–92.
72. Data processed from the 1915 Ministerial List and the 1917 *Yearbook*.

third were in the South. The West Coast states and the northeastern region each had about 8 percent, and the balance were in the northern and central plains and Rocky Mountain area.

In summing up, it becomes evident that by 1917 the Church of God movement had reached a stage of relative stability. Small bands of saints were becoming solid congregations, and they were growing in both number and size. Sufficient structure had developed to secure and extend their existence and enable them to cooperate with other congregations. The publishing work was serving the needs of the movement as a whole and providing rudimentary vehicles for overseas expansion. The major shortcoming was the absence of any means for ministers in general or for laypeople to have any voice in the processes of decision making at the national level. That was also to come in that very year, 1917, with the formation of the General Ministerial Assembly.

CHAPTER 8

ETHNIC OUTREACH
(1885–1920)

The Church of God reform movement began at a very volatile and transitional moment in the history of the United States. Two of the most
unsettling social issues at the nation's centennial were the integration of
emancipated black slaves into the national economy and social structure
and the absorption of the vast numbers of peoples from foreign lands who
came to America with varying customs, languages, and distinctive ethnic
characteristics.

The Church of God reformation movement proclaimed a message for
all people, so it was not unexpected that movement pioneers would extend
their evangelistic endeavors to various ethnic groups. Significant efforts to
reach at least five of these groups—African Americans, Germans, Slovaks,
Scandinavians, and Greeks—took place early in the movement's history,
and major segments of the work of the Church of God developed among
blacks and European ethnics in the United States and Canada. These efforts
occurred just as Americans were in their second period of nativism. The
story of the beginnings and progress of the ethnic ministries is an important
part of the movement's history.

The Blacks

The beginnings of the Church of God reformation came in the middle of
the second decade after the slavery era. In the wake of the painful period of
Reconstruction there was a considerable amount of racial unrest. The freed
blacks were thrust into new social predicaments with new responsibilities
of a totally different lifestyle. The numerous social and political restrictions
placed upon blacks made for further tension.

During the slavery era and afterward African Americans were a religious people. Thousands of slaves were active Christians, worshiping in services approved by their masters or not infrequently slipping off to unauthorized "hush-arbor" meetings led by slaves themselves. The collective experience of slavery sometimes lent a peculiar twist to slaves' reading of the Bible. If the masters could whip their slaves or break up families through the sale of a husband, wife, or child, from the slaves' point of view stealing eggs or a chicken from the master's henhouse did not seem a terrible moral lapse. Before the outbreak of the Civil War, Northern blacks formed independent denominations. Under the leadership of Richard Allen the African Methodist Episcopal Zion Church was founded with James Varick its first bishop. The Civil War and emancipation brought a new context. Antebellum paternalism was no longer acceptable. The prewar tendency to begin separate black congregations exploded in the formation of new, separate churches and denominations, often retaining the name of the parent body but with additional modifiers to affirm the new groups' ethnic distinctiveness. New church bodies such as the National Baptist Convention appeared as segregated black denominations, many of them founded in the period 1865–1895.

The Civil War ended slavery, but not racial discrimination and segregation, which were practiced formally or informally in the North as well as the South. The Church of God reformation's message of unity of all believers, however, implicitly contained a commitment to interracial and ethnic unity. It is notable, however, that in the first decade no special point was made of the racial issue; the message was preached and black people responded and were accepted.

Very little was written in the early *Gospel Trumpet* about racial issues or evangelism to blacks. By the end of the second decade, however, there appeared articles with a strong disdain for racial prejudice. In 1901, for instance, F. G. Smith wrote: "May God hasten the time when all race prejudice may be obliterated, and every soul for whom Christ died be recognized as precious in his sight, and a worthy recipient of the redemption grace purchased in the death of our Savior."[1] Smith wrote this in his preface to a very forthright, antiracist affirmation in the form of William G. Schell's book *Is The Negro a Beast?* Schell's book was a reply to *The Negro a Beast* by Charles Carroll. Carroll's position attempted to prove that blacks were actually subhuman; indeed, no more than beasts. Schell refuted Carroll's

---

1. F. G. Smith, in the preface to William G. Schell, *Is the Negro a Beast?* (Moundsville, WV: Gospel Trumpet Co., 1901), 10.

argument point by point and, in fact, supported the full equality of blacks and whites in the sight of God. Schell's book suggests a concerted effort by some early white leaders to support and uphold their black brothers.

The identity of the first black converts to the Church of God reformation is unknown. Some testimonies indicate there were blacks working in the Trumpet family very early in the movement's history. One of the earliest congregations of blacks grew under the labors of Jane Williams in 1886 in Charleston, South Carolina. James Earl Massey, in his book *African-Americans and the Church of God,* reported that this group came to function as a sort of headquarters for the movement's black work, which spread from there to Alabama, North Carolina, Georgia, and Florida. He stated that black and white leaders worked hand-in-hand in the establishing of churches throughout the South."[2]

Williams also spent considerable time in Georgia. In August of 1888 she wrote from Augusta:

> O Brother Warner I pray the Lord to send yourself and company to this wicked city. The Lord has a few blood washed ones here, and we long to see your faces in the flesh, so you could more fully establish the little Church of God at this place, in the true faith of the Gospel.[3]

Still in Augusta later in that same year Williams wrote:

> I have just returned from a place in the dark swamps of S.C. where darkness covers the earth, and gross darkness the people; but the Lord tells me to ask of Him what I will and I shall have it. O dear saints of the living God plead with me that the glorious light of the Gospel may shine in that dark place.[4]

Ten years later Jane Williams was either again or still in Augusta and reported on a recent assembly meeting there:

> As to the assembly at this place, we can never thank the dear Lord enough for that meeting, and we can truthfully say that every honest soul

---

2. James Earl Massey, *African-Americans and the Church of God, Anderson, Indiana* (Anderson, IN: Anderson University Press, 2005), 31.

3. *Gospel Trumpet,* August 1, 1888, 3.

4. *Gospel Trumpet,* December 15, 1888, 3.

was truly blessed of the Lord at that glorious feast. The Lord's anointed ministers were used in preaching the Word. We ask the saints to join in prayer with us for our meeting-house which we intend to build here.[5]

Five years after this assembly, W. Thomas Carter and A. J. Kilpatrick, both white, spent about six weeks in Augusta in evangelistic work during the winter of 1893 working with both blacks and whites. Historian C. E. Brown reported: "It seemed there were more colored people interested in Salvation. A church was established for each, but there were more colored people who took their stand for the full Gospel of the one Church of God."[6] This meeting sufficiently increased the number of adherents to realize Jane Williams's dream. The meeting house in Augusta was probably the first real property owned by a black Church of God congregation.[7]

As blacks began to encounter the Church of God reformation movement, many more of them found truth in its basis and began to identify themselves with the group. From the beginning the early reformers' doctrine of unity was a strong invitation to blacks as well as whites. This doctrine was applied to racial lines as well as other divisions in the church. Both blacks and whites sought to realize the ideal of unity, and their dedication to this goal is evidenced by the many meetings held throughout the South with both black and white people not only present, but actually worshiping together as equals! Open and full racial integration in worship services demonstrated the commitment of the participants to unity, for these interracial meetings were held in defiance of the prevailing customs and laws throughout the South that prohibited such integrative practices.

Jim Crow laws permitted blacks and whites in a common worship service, but the races had to be divided by some physical barrier. In buildings with a balcony, that was the part of the church reserved for blacks. The early Church of God refused to acknowledge this social custom. One example of this dedication can be given in the story of the Alabama State Camp Meeting in 1897, which was held in Hartselle, Alabama, and attended by both races, with only a rope stretched down the middle of the tent as a recognition of the legally required segregation. Among the ministers at this meeting were J. B. Collins, Lena Shoffner, L. L. Porter, Otto Bolds, N. S.

---

5. *Gospel Trumpet*, March 3, 1898, 5.
6. Charles E. Brown, *When the Trumpet Sounded* (Anderson, IN: Gospel Trumpet Co., 1951), 264.
7. Massey, *African-Americans and the Church of God*, 19–20.

Duncan, and J. F. Lundy. One day Lena Shoffner preached a sermon about tearing down the "middle wall of partition." Her sermon was apparently so moving and so convincing that Duncan felt led to take down the rope that separated the blacks from the whites. Once the barrier had been removed whites and blacks knelt together at the same altar. That night a mob came to the campground in wild fury. They threw dynamite under the boarding house and camp houses and searched out each of the preachers and evangelists, most of whom had already fled into the night. One of the men stood in a creek all night. Another preacher put on a woman's clothes and escaped. The next night, however, the mob followed them to the homes where they had sought refuge, in some cases up to fifteen miles away from the campgrounds.[8]

D. S. Warner also suffered persecution for preaching the doctrines of Christian unity and holiness with their strong racial implications. In November 1890 he was preaching at Beech Springs, Mississippi, where there was a group known as "Straight Holiness" people. Regarding the group A. L. Byers wrote, "Its teachers failed in the South to be uncompromising against tobacco and other evils and they incited no little opposition and prejudice against the New Testament standard held by Brother Warner."[9] In addition, as C. E. Brown reports, "It seems Warner and his company were far more rigid and stern in their stand…for justice to the Negro" than the Straight Holiness people were.[10] As a result of Warner's uncompromising preaching in Mississippi there was a serious clash that resulted in a mob attack in their second night of services at Beech Springs. Warner reported:

> Several pieces of brick and clubs came crashing through the window, all doubtless hurled in wrath at us. Nearly half the sash was broken in and the glass flew over the house. The unsaved were frightened, and the whole house was thrown into confusion. The glory of God was greatly upon us through the evening, and with the cowardly onslaught the heavenly tides so wonderously swelled in uproar. Oh, the mighty river of peace and joy![11]

---

8. Brown, *When the Trumpet Sounded*, 266.

9. Andrew L. Byers, *The Birth of a Reformation* (Anderson, IN: Gospel Trumpet Co., 1921), 365–66.

10. Brown, *When the Trumpet Sounded*, 156.

11. As quoted in Byers, 366.

Shortly after Beech Springs, Warner's group met further opposition at Oak Grove, Mississippi, near Meridian. A letter from another state had been received by someone in that community who misrepresented the saints as believers in racial amalgamation. The evangelistic company found their meeting house locked and for one night were forced to hold their services on the road in the moonlight.[12]

It was not unusual for others of the reformation's early preachers to endure persecution for racial openness. J. E. Forrest, a white Southerner who began preaching in 1901, strongly proclaimed the doctrine of unity. He traveled in twenty-one states enduring the stress of persecution and rigorous working conditions. He preached under brush arbors, in streets, cabins, theatre buildings, and on creek banks. Once he was preaching to blacks in Sanderville, Georgia, in 1909 when he was arrested and endured a severe inquisition and lecture at the sheriff's office. After his release Forrest returned to the church and that night enjoyed one of the most glorious meetings of his whole experience. After the meeting, however, he was reprimanded for his actions. He said concerning that night after the meeting, "I was gathered by the collar, shaken a little, kicked a little, and loaded onto a freight train and sent out of town at midnight."[13]

Despite these bold efforts to overcome racial barriers the movement did fall under the influence of segregationism in the North as well as the South. Speaking of the situation in the South, C. E. Brown observed, "The Church of God preachers and leaders probably suffered more for their friendship with colored people in the South than the leaders of any other religious work who ever operated there. Nevertheless open and bold denial of the refusal of the color line in the southern states was deemed impossible."[14]

The inevitable mounting of tensions came forward and forced the editor of the *Gospel Trumpet* to make a statement. In 1897, E. E. Byrum wrote a long article giving the following advice:

> There are no certain rules that can be laid down nor lines drawn that will govern every community, except those set forth in the word of God, as customs in various places widely differ, and often times it is wisdom, and to the glory of God to follow customs of the country, though they differ from those of our native place.

---

12. Byers, 367.
13. Brown, *When the Trumpet Sounded*, 267.
14. Ibid., 360.

However, when the customs of the people conflict with the word of God, then Peter's advice should be followed—obey God rather than man; forsake the customs of the people rather than forsake God. We do not believe in white and colored people mixing in marriage, or in any other way that is unnecessary. We believe it would be better if it were convenient to have it so, that they meet in separate meetings; but there are places where it is almost necessary for them to meet together and they do in many places harmoniously and to the glory of God.

But when all prejudices between the race is removed, that does not give them liberty to intermarry, but if custom is not too strong against them they can meet together in harmony.

There is nothing wrong in them meeting separately, where it can be done for the glory of God; or, on the other hand, there is nothing wrong in them meeting together where it can be done for the glory of God. All we desire is to see the word of God fulfilled. We do not require the white brethren to greet the colored brethren with the Holy kiss. If they feel it is a duty according to the word of God, let them fulfill the word, and God will get the glory.[15]

The zeal that the pioneers had held concerning the ideal of racial unity began to wane after the turn of the century. The pressures of society finally became so great that the worthy goal that was originally pursued began to crumble. Evidence of this is apparent in a 1909 issue of the *Gospel Trumpet*. There Lena (Shoffner) Matthesen, the preacher at Hartselle, Alabama, twelve years earlier, wrote concerning the Oklahoma Assembly, "The meeting was somewhat hindered because of the color question. At the ministers' meeting it was decided that investigations be made in Guthrie to find out whether or not it would be better to have separate meetings there. This must be mutually agreed on by both colored and whites of the congregation."[16]

This is but one indication of the growing concern with the question of racial unity. Oklahoma was not the only place where racial separation was being considered. In fact, some places in the North had already taken more purposeful steps toward segregation. Also in 1909 legal and cultural pressures eroded the ideal of unity as two interracial congregations divided along the color line in Pittsburgh and New York City. In 1910 the same division occurred in St. Louis, and by 1915 there were similar separations

---

15. *Gospel Trumpet*, September 2, 1897, 2.
16. *Gospel Trumpet*, February 25, 1909, 10.

in Chicago and Detroit. Thus was begun a pattern of modified unity that developed over the next several years.

Racial issues were not confined to local levels. By 1910 the *Gospel Trumpet* was publishing articles that indicated an emerging separatist attitude among some white church leaders. While race certainly was no issue regarding salvation, C. W. Naylor made a concession to "social differences that we cannot ignore without serious consequences. These social differences in no way affect the spiritual unity or fellowship. Both white and colored are better off as a result of social separation than they would be mixed together in these relations."[17] Soon the *Trumpet* took the view that racial separation advanced evangelism better than did integrated congregations. The paper's views were given concrete expression in a 1913 request from the committee that managed the Anderson Camp Meeting. On the example of a separate German language service held during the annual meeting, the committee directed E. E. Byrum to consult with leading black minister Daniel F. Oden about black leaders' willingness to hold a separate worship service on the Anderson grounds. Blacks were cool toward the proposal, and the matter was dropped for that year. Over the next few years similar requests were made and always met with the same demurrals. Finally, and over the blacks' expressed reservations, the committee proceeded with plans for a separate service as an experiment. The confrontation did not divide blacks from whites within the Church of God movement, but it did contribute to a growing climate hospitable to the beginning of a separate organization of blacks within the movement.[18]

Daniel F. Oden (1871–1931), missionary and pastor. In the late nineteenth and twentieth century, African Americans migrated from the South to great industrial centers in the North, such as Chicago, Pittsburgh, and Detroit. Oden's ministerial career followed this pattern. During a pastorate in Bessemer, Alabama, he was sent by the missionary committee on trips abroad. In 1917, Oden came to Detroit, where he founded the largest Church of God congregation in the city, which he pastored for fourteen years.

Courtesy of Anderson University and Church of God Archives

---

17. *Gospel Trumpet*, March 11, 1910, 10.

18. Merle D. Strege, *I Saw the Church: The Life of the Church of God Told Theologically* (Anderson: Warner Press, 2002), 147–48.

Obviously the stage was set for splitting the movement along racial lines, and that is what almost happened. Without any deliberate planning or design, however, an informal arrangement emerged that preserved the concept of an open fellowship with unrestricted participation by all, white or black, in the general work of the movement. At the same time, the blacks were free to develop their own structures, which they did. The result was rather complex—a church body segregated locally but unified at the national level, with a satellite national structure by the segregated black churches and independent of the general national structure. In addition, separate black and white ministerial assemblies developed in most Southern states as well as some in the North.

The black satellite national structure, The National Association of the Church of God, emerged from a camp meeting organization in western Pennsylvania. Shortly after the turn of the century Earnest E. Wimbish, a black Baptist from Cleveland, Ohio, had a vision "of crowds and crowds of real happy people having church out in the woods where there were beautiful buildings among the trees."[19] Full of religious zeal, Wimbish searched at every opportunity for the place in his vision but could not find it. After Wimbish married, he moved to Sharon, Pennsylvania, continuing his association with the Baptist church and also his search for his place in the woods. After a time Wimbish and his wife disassociated themselves from the Baptist church in favor of a small prayer band they had formed called the Brothers and Sisters of Love. Shortly thereafter, a representative of the Church of God reformation movement attended their services and told them that their teaching was identical with that of the Church of God. After pursuing the matter they decided to associate themselves with the Church of God.

J. A. Christman, a minister who was working with Wimbish, is credited with finding the place of the latter's vision. He was out hunting one day when he came across a tract of land that resembled the one in Wimbish's description. He brought Wimbish back to the spot, and he verified that it was indeed the site. They made arrangements to purchase the land and soon began holding meetings there. In 1917, this property at West Middlesex, Pennsylvania, which was to become the official campgrounds of the National Association of the Church of God, was purchased when Wimbish and some others mortgaged their homes to secure the necessary funds.

19. Katie R. Davis, *Zion's Hill at West Middlesex* (Corpus Christi, TX: Christian Triumph Press, n.d.).

While these developments occurred over some time it is important to note 1917 as a key date in black-white relations in the Church of God. Not only was this the year for the purchase of the campgrounds at West Middlesex, but it was also the beginning of a separate national organization of blacks in the movement. Initially it was called the Western Pennsylvania and Eastern Ohio Campground Association. The organization was later renamed the Gospel Industrial Association of the Church of God Evening Light. Still later it became the National Association of the Church of God.[20] In this same year the Church of God movement as a whole brought into being in Anderson, Indiana, its first national organization, the General Ministerial Assembly. The West Middlesex structure in many ways paralleled developments in Anderson, providing for various boards to be responsible for various cooperative functions. The founding of a black national organization was not considered a breakaway action, and later years proved this to be a viable working relationship.

While perhaps appearing strange to non-adherents, this unique arrangement served to help keep the African-American constituency of the Church of God within the general group at percentages higher than in other Holiness bodies.

The Germans

From the very beginnings of the movement there had been a concern for sharing the message with the German-speaking people. Warner himself could preach in both English and German, and his ten-year association with the German-rooted Churches of God in North America (Winebrennerian) brought him into contact with many German-speaking people.[21] Numerous other leaders were of German descent, such as David Leininger and Mother Sarah Smith, both of whom spoke with heavy German accents. An overview of the early history of the movement reveals a German relatedness of significant proportions. Three of the five who took their stand with Warner at Beaver Dam in the fall of 1881 were of German descent. All five were associated with the Northern Indiana Winebrennarian splinter group that was very active among German-speaking people. Among the other

---

20. Ibid.

21. John Winebrenner, founder of the Churches of God in North America, was a pastor in the German Reformed Church in Harrisburg, Pennsylvania. For several decades after his new group was formed in 1825, it was almost entirely German speaking.

Ethnic language ministries flourished in the Church of God from the last decade of the nineteenth century. Perhaps the most extensive work developed among German language immigrants in the United States and Canada. Two years before D. S. Warner's death, the *Gospel Trumpet* published a two-column feature in German. In 1895 a new periodical, *Die Evangeliums Posaune*, began publication from the Trumpet offices. Soon a German department was organized at the publishing house. Pictured here are a group of workers in that department.

denominations from which many of the Movement's early brethren came out were Lutheran and German Baptist. These early connections make it impossible to fix an exact date for the beginning of outreach to German-speaking people in the United States.

In the early 1890s key events occurred that mark a particular thrust toward the German-speaking populace. By 1892 there was increasing concern for a German-language publication. In September of that year at a camp meeting held in a beautiful grove just outside the city of Wichita, Kansas, two men pledged twenty-five dollars to purchase German type. The *Trumpet* mentioned this donation, along with the notice that it would be enough to start publishing in German.[22] Prospects for the German work looked good, and in November the paper announced that a tract already had been translated.[23] By December some people were so anxious for a German *Gospel Trumpet* to be published that they already had mailed in

22. *Gospel Trumpet*, October 6, 1892, 2.
23. *Gospel Trumpet*, November 24, 1892, 2.

subscriptions.[24] Progress toward this goal was rapid and before the end of the year an enthusiastic report appeared in the *Gospel Trumpet*:

> Praise God! The Lord is moving the work along. Since our last writing, the Lord has sent Bro. M. De Derer of Louisville, Ky. who came over from Germany a few years ago and now comes to aid in the great work of sending forth the gospel in its purity to the German races. He is now translating *Divine Healing of Soul and Body* and will soon have other books and tracts translated into the German and French language.[25]

The paper also pled for a worker who could set German type. Very soon William Ebel came from the West Coast to learn the art of typesetting. "In a few days, if God wills," the editor wrote, "German tracts will begin to go forth…teaching the way of full salvation."[26] Soon several doctrinal tracts were being published that greatly helped the cause of German outreach.

Early in 1893 a column in the German language appeared in the *Gospel Trumpet*. The article was titled "Das Volle Heil" ("The Full Gospel").[27] In 1894 another article titled "Glauben" ("Beliefs") appeared.[28] In the latter half of 1894, a word edition of *Echoes from Glory*, a popular songbook of the movement, was printed in German. By year's end, the joyous announcement was made of a subscription drive for the German *Gospel Trumpet*: "We are very thankful to God for his blessings upon this work. Many of his children are becoming interested in the spread of the Gospel to the Germans. A number of subscriptions have already been received, and almost enough means to publish the first issue of the paper, which will soon be ready, the Lord willing."[29] On January 1, 1895, the semimonthly periodical *Die Evangeliums Posaune* (*The Gospel Trumpet*) began publication, edited by Fred L. Hahn. The first issue was given a good sendoff with a run of eight thousand copies. The eventual paid subscription list totaled about three thousand. The paper did well under his leadership. From Milwaukee, Wisconsin, Hahn had been a prominent minister among the Baptists before he had "come out."

---

24. *Gospel Trumpet*, December 8, 1892, 2.
25. *Gospel Trumpet*, December 22, 1892, 2.
26. *Gospel Trumpet*, February 23, 1893, 2.
27. *Gospel Trumpet*, January 5, 1893, 4.
28. *Gospel Trumpet*, March 23, 1894, 4.
29. *Gospel Trumpet*, December 6, 1894, 2.

Editor Hahn published an article in the *Gospel Trumpet* later in 1895 expressing his strong desire to reach the German people. He said, "I was over sixty years old when God gave me to see…his call.…I stretch forth my hands to plead that he may let his grace appear unto younger brethren among my German countrymen, that are more fit by his manifold gifts to go forth into the harvest among the Germans." He went on to say how well the work was going. He mentioned the church in Milwaukee and said that the work was progressing very slowly, yet steadfastly. "I could hold meetings night after night, most times preaching in both English and German to houses filled with seekers after the truth, who stayed often till after midnight." He mentioned a "Brother Halbesleben," in Sauk County, Wisconsin, who was doing the work of God there. He closed the article with an urgent call to "raise up German laborers and to send them into the harvest."[30] A report on "The German Work in Wisconsin" appeared in the *Gospel Trumpet* in late 1895. The article contains several German testimonies translated into English. Fred L. Hahn stated, "Our number is still small but very slowly increasing." Further in the article he said, "Brother Halbesleben is still at work there at date of writing, having labored three or four weeks in Baraboo, the county seat of Sauk County."[31]

The ready availability of Church of God literature in the German language greatly facilitated the spread of the movement among German-speaking people both in America and in the European homeland.[32]

From 1895 until the beginning of World War I, leaders of the German work shuttled back and forth across the Atlantic. In some cases, converts in Europe emigrated to America and started new congregations where they settled. One such instance involved the Gottfried Kohns, who were converted in Hamburg under the preaching of American evangelist J. H. Rupert. In 1899 they moved to Philadelphia and started a German-language congregation in that city.[33] George Vielguth of Logan, Kansas; Karl Arbeiter of Medicine Hat, Alberta; William Ebel of Grand Junction, Michigan; Otto Doebert of Wiley, Colorado; and others made frequent trips to Germany, Switzerland, Latvia, and other European countries. The enthusiasm and dedication of the German-speaking leaders stimulated progress on both continents.

---

30. *Gospel Trumpet*, September 5, 1895, 2–3.

31. *Gospel Trumpet*, November 21, 1895, 2.

32. The development of the movement in Germany, already noted in chapter 6, was greatly abetted by American-produced literature until they were able to acquire their own publication facilities in 1922.

33. Brown, *When the Trumpet Sounded*, 338.

By the publication of the first *Yearbook of the Church of God* in 1917, the ethnic presence in the movement was sufficient to list any languages spoken by each minister. Of the approximately twelve hundred ministers listed that year, around seventy individuals (6 percent) in over twenty states and provinces indicated they spoke German.[34] Eventually, no fewer than twenty-six German-speaking congregations developed in the United States and Canada.[35] The outbreak of war in 1914 and the rise of strong anti-German sentiment in America seriously curtailed both travel and expansion of the German work in the United States and Canada. Most congregations either weakened, changed to English, or entered a holding pattern for the next decade.

The Scandinavians

The work of the Church of God among Scandinavians in the United States began in the north central states where there were large concentrations of immigrants from these European countries. Earlier in the nineteenth century a spiritually-rich religious revival under the preaching of Hans Nielsen Hauge had swept across Norway and left much discontent with the Lutheran Church. Religious awakenings had also occurred in Sweden and Denmark. Many of the Scandinavian immigrants, influenced by these pietist movements, were ready for the Church of God message. Sven Olsen Susag, for example, a Norwegian immigrant who had been converted in 1895 and later became one of the most outstanding evangelists in the Church of God both in America and Europe, gave this testimony:

> The Lord spoke peace to my wife and me at the same time in our home, and called us into the ministry. He brought us out of darkness through three visions and showed us the evil of all sectarian division [sic] all this was giving us light on the beautiful Church of God. Without our having heard any preaching on the subject nor did we know anyone who believed as we did.[36]

---

34. *Yearbook of the Church of God*, 1917, 44–131.

35. Known German-speaking congregations were in the following cities: Buffalo, New York; St. Joseph and Benton Harbor, Michigan; Chicago, Illinois; Milwaukee, Green Lake, and Sheboygan, Wisconsin; Portland, Oregon; Lodi and Fresno, California; Shattuck, Oklahoma; Wiley, Colorado; Durham and Herrington, Kansas; York, Nebraska; Cleveland, Ohio; Philadelphia, Pennsylvania; Kitchener and Toronto, Ontario; Winnipeg and Worden, Manitoba; Biggar, Saskatchewan; Calgary, Edmonton, Medicine Hat, and Bruderheim, Alberta.

36. S. O. Susag, *Personal Experiences of S. O. Susag*, (Houston, TX: Ambassador Press, n.d.), 9.

One of the most significant of the Scandinavian leaders was Thomas Nelson (1872–1946). Though his work is well known, there is little personal information about his early life. It is generally supposed he was born on Mors Island, Denmark, and emigrated to the United States at an early age. When or where he was converted and how he came into contact with the Church of God is unknown. The first reference to his church activity is in 1895 when it was reported he left Denver to take the message of the Church of God to Denmark.[37]

In 1899 Nelson published a songbook in Norwegian, *Den Evangeliske Sanger*, containing 178 songs, 79 of which he had composed himself.[38] Around 1900 he began publication of the *Den Evangeliske Basun (Gospel Trumpet),* a Dano-Norwegian periodical, in Muscatine, Iowa. In 1901 he moved his equipment to Grand Forks, North Dakota, in the Grand Forks steam laundry, and in 1903 moved again to St. Paul Park, Minnesota, where publication continued for another twenty years.[39]

Nelson's contribution to the Scandinavian work in the Church of God is well summarized by Anna Koglin:

> The prodigious talent and capacity of Brother Nelson can be seen in an overview of what he accomplished. He not only directed the publishing of the *Evangeliske Basun,* he also directed the printing of the Swedish periodical, *Den Evangeli Trumpet.* Thomas Nelson edited the *Basun.* His most astonishing accomplishment was the composition of 171 songs which entered the hymnody of the Church of God.…Ninety of the 178 hymns in *Zions Seier Sange* (1906) were written by Thomas Nelson.…He also wrote four books: *Frälsnings Hemlighet*; *Hjem, Helbred Og Lykke*; *Väsentliga Bibelämnen*; *Veien Til Frelse Og Det Aandelige Liv.* The second one was translated into English—*Home, Health and Success*—and had a wide sale.
>
> Thomas Nelson was also the moving spirit in the construction and operation of the Old People's Home in St. Paul Park in 1907. This home

---

37. Brown, *When the Trumpet Sounded*, 173. In a letter from Denmark dated June 6, 1895, and printed in the *Gospel Trumpet*, July 4, 1895, 3, Nelson reports he has held no meetings, since he can find no meeting place, but he has been writing, having translated and composed eighty songs.

38. Anna E. Koglin, *History of the Church of God in Minnesota* (n.p., privately printed, 1976), 72.

39. The work of the Church of God by and among Scandinavians in the United States and Canada is the subject of Merle D. Strege, "Where Scandinavian Is Spoken" (ThD diss., Graduate Theological Union, 1982).

was intended principally for elderly Scandinavian people, but was open to others as well.

Besides these many activities and responsibilities Nelson also served as the pastor of the St. Paul Park congregation.[40]

Along with Susag and Nelson, other strong leaders in the Scandinavian work included Otto T. Ring, C. J. Forsberg, Charles A. Grant, Nels Renbeck, Olaf Lundy, and Olae Christopherson. Among English and German-speaking ministers who also worked with the Scandinavian people were G. W. Bailey, George Vielguth, W. J. Baldwin, J. B. Peterman, and C. H. Tubbs. Lundy of Norway Lake, Minnesota, and Ring of Belgrade, Minnesota, were both introduced to the Church of God through reading the *Gospel Trumpet* around 1898. Likewise, Grant , who was converted in his native Sweden, came across a copy of the paper in Hoboken, New Jersey, and contacted C. J. Blewitt in New York City, who led him into an active ministry. Forsberg emigrated from Sweden in 1901 and in 1904 was converted in Stoneboro, Pennsylvania, under the ministry of Herbert M. Riggle and John L. Williams. Renbeck and his wife Edel, who had emigrated from Denmark in 1889, came in contact with the Church of God in 1897.[41] Some of these later individuals were to become evangelists for the Church of God in their native Scandinavian countries.

So it was that many who heard the Church of God message responded quickly and enthusiastically. Much of the early work among Scandinavians took place in Grand Forks, North Dakota. It was there in November of 1895 that George W. Bailey from Spokane, Washington, began holding meetings. Bailey had just come out of the United Brethren denomination earlier that year. Grand Forks proved to be a fruitful area of ministry and Scandinavians who lived in the area were included. In 1896 C. H. Tubbs and his wife Mary stopped briefly in Grand Forks to help with the work there before proceeding to Minnesota. Bailey pastored this church in Grand Forks until his resignation in 1897, after which C. H. Tubbs returned to take charge of the work.

In 1897 a camp meeting was held in Grand Forks with services for Scandinavians in their own languages. In 1899 a plot of land near the town

---

40. Koglin, *History of the Church of God in Minnesota*, 74–75. *Zions Seiers Sange* was edited by Thomas Nelson and D. Otis Teasley and published by Evangeli Basun Publishing Company in St. Paul Park, Minnesota.

41. Biographical data secured mainly from autobiographical sketches prepared for C. E. Brown in 1950. On file in Anderson University and Church of God Archives.

on the banks of the Red River was secured for a permanent campground. From 1901 to 1903 Nelson headquartered his publishing work there in the basement of C. G. Niels' steam laundry.

In 1903 the center of the Scandinavian work shifted to St. Paul Park, Minnesota, about 12 miles down the Mississippi River from St. Paul, when Nelson moved his publishing work there. Also in 1903, a Swedish version of the *Gospel Trumpet* was started by O. T. Ring and Charles Grant. The name of this paper was *Evangeli Trumpet,* and O. T. Ring became the editor. This work was also located in St. Paul Park and the integrated structure of the publishing and evangelistic work there followed the same basic organizational patterns as the Gospel Trumpet Company followed in Moundsville and later in Anderson. *Den Evangeliske Basun* and *Den Evangeli Trumpet* were sent throughout the United States and into Europe. In addition to the periodicals, a large number of books and tracts were printed and distributed, often by colporteurs like Anna Koglin and Olae Christopherson. As a result of the literature, congregations were established in several states, especially in Minnesota and North Dakota.

Even though the Scandinavian languages were used as a primary vehicle for reaching the immigrants from these countries, there was always close cooperation with the English-speaking work. All general meetings were attended by people from both language groups and services would often be conducted in more than one language. The first Church of God camp meeting in Minnesota, for instance, which was held in 1902 near Paynesville in a grove owned by Scandinavian-American Hans Hansen, held services in both English and Scandinavian languages.[42] S. O. Susag and his wife, Martha,

Courtesy of Anderson University and Church of God Archives

Anna Koglin, educator. A native of Minnesota, Koglin worked as a colporteur for the Scandinavian publishing house in St. Paul Park, Minnesota. Koglin studied at Anderson Bible Training School and at the University of Berlin and then taught German at Anderson College. She also taught at Fritzlar Bible School in Germany.

---

42. Koglin, *History of the Church of God in Minnesota*, 52.

were among those present. Susag was greatly impressed with this meeting and reports it in his memoirs:

> Warning was sent around the neighborhood to lock their chicken coops, for the campmeeting was financed by only two poor men, who were giving free meals to all who came....It was a wonderful meeting; many souls were saved and sanctified, devils were cast out and some were healed. The ministers present were Brother and Sister Tubbs, Brothers Enos and Elihu Key, and Brother Thomas Nelson. The country around was stirred and a number of people tried to hinder the meeting. Some businessmen in Paynesville hired a team, borrowed a three-seated platform-buggy from the implement company, and placed a small cannon on it. They drove within a few rods of the tent and fired the cannon. However, this turned out to the dismay of the persecutors, for as they shot off the cannon the horses took fright and ran away into the timber, smashing up the new buggy and tearing the harnesses to pieces. There was no more harassment.[43]

By 1909 the Scandinavian congregations in America were sufficiently strong to finance the sending of missionaries to their homelands. O. T. Ring was the first to go, followed by Carl J. Forsberg, Nels Renbeck, Morris Johnson, the Ikasts, Lars and Ellen Olsen, and others. It was only in its first years, however, that this missionary work was purely a project of the Scandinavian Americans. After the organization of the Missionary Board in Anderson, much of this European work was encouraged or sponsored through that agency. In the meantime, St. Paul Park developed into a flourishing Scandinavian center. In addition to a well-equipped printing plant there was a home for the workers, most of whom were young people who came to assist in the publishing endeavor without wages, as was the custom in missionary homes. At the opposite end of Broadway, on a hill above the village the group operated the Church of God Old People's Home of the Northwest. The two periodicals flourished, with the Dano-Norwegian publication becoming a weekly and the Swedish a semimonthly. People from five states gathered at this headquarters for two large conventions each year, and several Scandinavian-speaking congregations were organized.

---

43. Susag, *Personal Experiences*, 46–47.

The Scandinavian work was always closely allied with the total church. After 1923 and the passage of immigration restrictions, it seemed advisable to concentrate on the missionary aspect of the Scandinavian-language project. The publication and mission interests were moved to Denmark and Sweden under the general supervision of the Missionary Board. The benevolent interests, including the old people's home, were taken over by the Gospel Trumpet Company in Anderson. The Scandinavian groups in the United States in towns like St. Paul Park and Montevideo, Minnesota, eventually changed their services to English and found their place in the ongoing life of the church. However, as Koglin observes, "a large percentage of the people of Minnesota who are affiliated with the Church of God today are of Scandinavian background. Their parents or grandparents were nurtured in the faith by reading the Scandinavian periodicals and attending the Scandinavian services at the camp meetings."[44]

Slovaks

The year 1905 marks the date of the beginning of the movement's influence among Slovak immigrants in America. In Sharon, Pennsylvania, several Slovak people were worshiping in a Winebrennarian church pastored by Jacob Luchansky. Luchansky had been converted in 1902 in Mt. Pleasant, Pennsylvania, and had moved to Sharon in 1903 to begin his work among Slovaks there. In 1905 J. Grant Anderson and H. M. Riggle, both of whom had extensive ministries in western Pennsylvania, held a tent meeting in which many of the Slovak people associated with the Winebrennarian and other churches were greatly interested and influenced. That summer Luchansky attended the camp meeting in Emlenton, Pennsylvania, and began cooperating with the work of the Church of God. However, it was another man from the Sharon Winebrennarian congregation, Samuel Fabry, Sr., who emerged as the movement's key leader in work among the Slovak people.[45]

In addition to Anderson and Riggle, several other English-speaking ministers—I. S. McCoy, C. M. Boyer, G. H. Pye, and J. L. Williams—preached to the Slovak people through interpreters. As a result a number of other individuals from eastern Pennsylvania and western Ohio severed their connections with the groups with which they were affiliated. Among

---

44. Koglin, *History of the Church of God in Minnesota*, 75.

45. A substantial portion of the material relating to the Slovak work in the Church of God is adapted from Paul Yanik, *Through the Years* (Sharon, PA: Hlasnik Publishing Co.), 1956.

these were John Cerbus, John Horevay, John Racketa, and Anna Uram, all of whom joined Fabry in the development of the Slovak work. Racketa ministered to new converts to the movement in Sharon and in the organization of a Sunday school that greatly enhanced the work. Uram was extremely gifted in soul winning. Horevay starting churches in New Kensington, Johnstown, and Smithfield, Pennsylvania, and in Campbell, Ohio. Fabry himself launched a congregation in Torrington, Connecticut, and later, in 1919, went to Akron, Ohio, and started a new church there. Cerbus took over the work in Sharon and, while pastoring there, also preached in Butler and Arnold, Pennsylvania.

I. S. McCoy (1867–1955), evangelist and pastor. McCoy traveled throughout Pennsylvania and also worked in New Jersey. He was a regular speaker at the large camp meeting at Emlenton, Pennsylvania, and instrumental in beginning the ethnic ministry among the Slovaks of western Pennsylvania and eastern Ohio.

Courtesy of Anderson University and Church of God Archives

Samuel Fabry (1864–1944) fluently spoke five different languages and was a highly educated man. It is no small wonder that he and his family would play such a key role in the publishing and evangelistic development that followed.[46] Two years after the Fabry family had settled in Akron, their teen-age son Michael felt a call to the ministry and shortly afterward, even though he was not then proficient in the Slovak language, became assistant pastor of the Slovak Church of God there. At the time he also worked in the printing department of the Diamond Salt Factory and was very interested in the printing trade. When young Michael asked his father to purchase a small hand press for him, the elder Fabry readily complied, not only for Michael's benefit but with the intention of printing a few tracts and eventually a Slovak hymnal. From that time Samuel Fabry spent most of his spare time translating Church of God hymns into Slovak. Soon afterward the

---

46. A great deal of the work among the Slovak people, including the publishing enterprise, developed after 1920. The arbitrary cutoff date for data is included in this chapter. In order to keep the story intact, these further developments are reviewed here rather than in a subsequent chapter.

174 / **Quest for Holiness and Unity**

printing program was under way, and with the help of others, Michael was delegated to do the work. The first project was a hymnbook that contained only the words without the music but was widely used in the early Slovak congregations. Printing that first book was an unforgettable experience for its publishers. The lights burned late into the night in the attic of the Fabry residence, where the text was hand-set and the pages printed singly on the small hand-powered printing press. This 1923 project was the beginning of the Slovak publishing work.

In 1927 many of the Slovak constituents thought that a new and better hymnal should be published—this time with the music. This seemed like a tremendous undertaking to the half dozen or so small groups of worshipers, but after some consideration they decided to attempt the project. At a special meeting an appeal was made for at least $2,000 seed money. Pledges were taken that were to be paid within one year. The total amounted to more than was solicited, and the new project was under way. Since this was a group undertaking, a committee was selected to supervise publication. Samuel Fabry was named editor and translator of the hymnal, with Michael Fabry and A. Hanak assisting in an advisory capacity. The small hand press was exchanged for a power jobber and printing plates made in Chicago. The book's pages were printed in the basement of the church building in Akron and then shipped to the Gospel Trumpet office in Anderson, Indiana, for binding. The hymnal was published as *Melodic Sionske* (*Songs of Zion*) in 1929. The first edition was sold quickly in various parts of the United States, Canada, and Europe. A second edition was printed in 1950 and combined into a large new 354-page hymnal widely used in Slovak services in America and abroad.

Meanwhile, Michael Fabry's interest in printing grew until the possibilities of the printed page challenged his mind. He began to pray earnestly that the Lord would send a man learned in the language to edit a Slovak periodical. The answer to his prayers came in a way he least expected. While he waited, he himself became seriously interested in the Slovak language and set out to study it thoroughly. Fabry mastered the language without the aid of a teacher, and he himself became the first editor of the *Hlasnik* (*Herald*). The periodical was born in the midst of the Great Depression, the first issue appearing in 1930. A Youngstown, Ohio, firm printed the paper while foundry type and some additional equipment were being accumulated for use in the church basement print shop.

It was about this time that Paul Yanik, Jr., the grandson of Samuel

Fabry, Sr., entered the history of the work. His first adventures in printing were his rather innocent investigations of the type cases in the printery, where he mixed up many a box before he learned that each letter had a place. As a penalty for his curiosity he had to study and learn the type cases and thus began to serve his apprenticeship in the printing trade. By thirteen or fourteen Yanik was spending more and more of his spare time in the printery, where he became a keen observer as Michael Fabry, A. Uram, A. Hanak, and others prepared the publication. In just a short time he became a useful member of the small staff of the Hlasnik Publishing Company.

The name of Michael Fabry will never be displaced from its central significance in the Slovak work. Through his tireless efforts, the printery grew in his lifetime from a small hand press and a few cases of foundry type to an automatic press and a linotype. In addition to the monthly periodical, tracts, Sunday school lessons, pamphlets, mottoes, and Bible stationery were printed on this machinery. In 1935, however, tragedy struck. On February 15, 1935, Michael Fabry, who had been in poor health for some time, died at the age of twenty-nine. The elder Fabry filled in the gap and assumed the editorship, and Paul Yanik continued in the shop with the composition and printing. Samuel Fabry had already passed his seventieth birthday when he accepted the editorship of the *Hlasnik,* and continued in that work until his death some years later.

The passing of Samuel Fabry dealt another heavy blow to the church in Akron and to the whole Slovak work. For a time it seemed that the impact would prove too great for the work to survive. However, Paul Yanik, Sr., accepted oversight of the work in Akron and the congregation chose Paul Yanik, Jr., as the assistant pastor after his ordination in 1942. The two Yaniks shared the pulpit, with the father preaching in Slovak and the son preaching in English. In addition the Slovak brethren asked the younger Yanik to assume editorship of the periodical. The publishing work continued, and in subsequent years the printery was enlarged and remodeled. More modern equipment was added and the facilities came to include a large cylinder press, a new linotype, an automatic folding machine, a stitcher, paper cutter, two job presses, and other smaller equipment to complete the efficient little plant. The *Hlasnik* was reaching people throughout America and Canada, South America, various parts of Czechoslovakia and Yugoslavia, and even a few readers in Africa. At one time there were almost two thousand subscribers in Czechoslovakia alone.

Camp meetings were of particular importance to the Slovaks. The first annual meetings were one-day grove meetings held east of Sharon, Pennsylvania. There was a considerable amount of interest in finding a good location for a campground, and finally a suitable site was found in a wooded section of the Fedor farm near Hubbard, Ohio. Until the 1940s all services were in Slovakian. Gradually more and more of the meetings were held in English. By 1970 Slovak was no longer used in any of the general meetings. The campground then came to be used by all the Church of God congregations of the area. When the sweep of communism following World War II closed the door of literature evangelism in eastern Europe, Slovak-American congregations made the final transition from Slovak to English. This change was inevitable; the printery was closed, the equipment sold, and publications ceased. The last few issues of the *Hlansik* were printed at Warner Press in Anderson, in 1958. Slovak-speaking fellowships quickly adopted English or merged with nearby English-speaking congregations.

Greeks

The work of the Church of God among Greek-speaking Americans began, interestingly enough, in Egypt. E. A. Reardon had visited there in the period 1907–8 while on an extended missionary tour. He was introduced to an Armenian doctor of medicine, G. K. Ouzounian, who was also a Seventh-day Adventist minister. Reardon left several doctrinal books with Ouzounian that were to have a great influence on his life and lead him into the Church of God. He became a leader of the movement's work in Cairo, and among the people he influenced was a Greek visitor to Egypt in 1915 by the name of Constantine (Gust) Nicholaou (1884–1948). Nicholaou was from Salt Lake City and had been converted from Greek Orthodoxy to Mormonism. Ouzounian led him to embrace the message of the Church of God and enlisted him as an assistant in the mission work in Egypt.[47]

Nicholaou felt a call to the ministry and returned about 1916 to his home in Salt Lake City. He began a ministry there to a small group of Greek immigrants and in the next several years engaged in wide ranging

---

47. There are variant versions of Nicholaou's pilgrimage. Data used here is derived largely from letters quoted by John Pappas, of Detroit, Michigan, from several of the early Greek leaders. The account by Pappas, written around 1950, is in the Anderson University and Church of God Archives. There also are brief descriptions of the Greek work in the 1924 and the 1925 *Yearbook of the Church of God*.

evangelistic activity that included many places in the Far West and Middle West. By 1919 he was also the leader of a small group in Provo, Utah.[48] In 1920 he enrolled as a student in Anderson Bible Training School. In 1922 Nicholaou was again in the West as pastor of a congregation in Spanish Fork, Utah.[49]Among other places he ministered, either starting or pastoring churches, were Detroit, Michigan, and four locations in California: Lodi, Fresno, Oakland, and Bay Point.

One of Nicholaou's most significant contributions was the great number of young Greeks he recruited who became future leaders in the movement. Among these were Constantine Stavropoulos, Sam Lellos, Michael Stergiou, and Nick Stergiou. Indirectly many other leaders felt the impact of his ministry.[50] Among these early Greek converts was a zealous young worker named Nick Zazanis, who shortly after his conversion in Detroit felt a call to the ministry. He graduated from Anderson Bible Training School in 1922. While in school, Zazanis began editing the Greek *Gospel Trumpet*. He moved to Chicago in 1922 where he pastored a church and continued publishing the twenty-four-page monthly periodical. Zazanis also translated several tracts and books, including F. G. Smith's *What the Bible Teaches.* Zazanis' fruitful ministry in America and in Greece extended for more than another half century.

The printed word facilitated the spread of the reformation's message to Greek-speaking people not only in America but around the world. Greek-speaking congregations developed in perhaps a dozen or more cities in the United States, with Chicago and Detroit becoming the chief centers of activity. Additional major leaders included George Dallas, William Conkis, Chris Angelos, Athanasius Chionos, Anestes Karamitros, and John Pappas. Through the efforts of these congregations and leaders, extensive missionary effort was directed toward Greece and Egypt, with some activity among Greeks in Brisbane, Australia, and Bombay, India.[51]

---

48. *Yearbook of the Church of God*, 1920, 87.

49. *Yearbook of the Church of God*, 1922, 114.

50. Pappas' sources indicate Nicholaou left the movement in 1924 and joined with a Pentecostal group.

51. *Yearbook of the Church of God*, 1924, 29.

CHAPTER 9

FACING DIFFICULT ISSUES
(1896–1917)

Rapidly growing movements, religious or secular, are vulnerable to internal disagreement and tension. That possibility of dissension is considerably heightened in the absence of formal written guidelines or a leader whose arbitration is final should divergent opinions arise. The Church of God reform movement found itself in just this situation in the years immediately following D. S. Warner's death. From the outset the movement's hostility toward written creeds had precluded the composition of a doctrinal statement. Although he had never thought of himself or acted as the ultimate authority regarding to either belief or practice, Warner was highly respected and his opinion settled almost any disagreement that might arise.

After Warner's death in December 1895, no candidate appeared, not even E. E. Byrum, on whom his mantle of spiritual authority in the movement could immediately fall. This authority vacuum left the way open for divergent views to gain a foothold. Such divergent views produced two serious internal crises, each of which resulted in numerous defections and one of which spawned the only major continuing schismatic offshoot in the movement's history. In one instance a divergent view developed and gained momentum until it reached the crisis stage; in the other a particular teaching snowballed to the point of rebellion on the part the movement's central leadership, leaving a minority to continue the emphasis and separate.

The point at issue in each crisis related to one of the central teachings that had brought the movement into being—the doctrine and practice of holiness. The first crisis was theological, arising from a divergent understanding of the doctrine of sanctification; the second was practical, resulting from variant views on behavioral standards for a holy life. The doctrine of sanctification was one of the key teachings stressed by the earliest leaders of the Church of God. Warner had been disfellowshiped by the Ohio Eldership of the Churches of God largely because of his commitment to this doctrine and his activities related to propagating it. When the *Gospel Trumpet* was launched the title banner heading the first page included the word *sanctification,* and almost all issues of the paper contained articles or editorials that dealt either directly or indirectly with this doctrine.

The specific understanding of sanctification held by movement pioneers closely resembled that taught by Holiness people generally. The often repeated definition stated: Sanctification is a second definite instantaneous work of grace, subsequent to justification, wrought by faith through the Holy Spirit, which frees human beings from their inherited or Adamic nature, cleansing them from all desire or love for sin and enabling them to live a life free from sin in this present world. It was the second cleansing aspect of this understanding that came into question. The issue was not new or unique. Others in the nineteenth-century Holiness Movement espoused a similar viewpoint, contending that a person was *completely* cleansed from sin in the experience of justification, since Christ's redeeming work was not partial. While a second work might add such graces as sealing, empowering, and deepening of consecration it really did not accomplish any further cleansing because no need for such remained. The origin of this view goes back another 150 years to John Wesley (1703–91). One of Wesley's contemporaries was Count Nicholas von Zinzendorf (1700–1760), a leader of the Moravians, the group whose piety exerted considerable influence on Wesley. The two men sharply disagreed on this issue of cleansing.

Zinzendorf held that "the best men are miserable sinners"[1] and that from "the moment one is justified, he is entirely sanctified."[2] Wesley disputed Zinzendorf on this point. He asked Zinzendorf, "The true believer grows daily in his love of God, doesn't he? Is he, then, entirely perfected in love when he is justified?"[3] Zinzendorf replied, "He is. One does not grow in God's love. From the moment of justification he loves as entirely as he is also entirely sanctified."[4] Never far from Luther's strong emphasis on human depravity, Zinzendorf essentially regarded sanctification as forensic as justification: God declared the sinner sanctified as well as justified. The

---

1. Albert C. Outler, ed., *John Wesley* (New York: Oxford University Press, 1974), 367.
2. Ibid., 370.
3. Ibid.
4. Ibid., 371.

proponents of the traditional view in the Church of God referred to it more often, however, as the "anti-cleansing heresy."

Zinzendorfism posed problems for the Holiness Movement in general, not only the Church of God. Among the latter, however, the most articulate of the anti-cleansers were W. A. Haynes, W. J. Henry, and George P. Keeling. Haynes often wrote in the *Gospel Trumpet* between 1894 and 1898. Many of his articles expounded the Wesleyan view of sanctification, but Haynes apparently had a change of mind some time in 1898. Henry was one of the earliest leaders in the movement, having taken his stand along with Mother Sarah Smith and a group of about twenty others in Jerry City, Ohio, in 1882. He was in the vanguard of overseas missionary work when he went to England in 1893. Keeling had also been won to the movement in its early days through the efforts of the Cole evangelistic team. As late as April 1899 an article of his had appeared in the *Gospel Trumpet* defending the orthodox view of sanctification. Each of these, and many others, were highly respected leaders who until the late 1890s apparently shared the second cleansing view of sanctification.

In his *Life Experiences,* E. E. Byrum recalls that his first intimation of trouble came within the Trumpet family at Moundsville, West Virginia. Three young men who worked there had troubled an established young lady with the Zinzendorfian view. She experienced doubts about her own experience after they shared this new light with her. Around one hundred people were present at the Thanksgiving Day service of 1898 where the "false teaching and false spirit" that had been privately spread abroad were publicly exposed. According to Byrum, shouts of victory and a service of healing concluded the time of worship during which it had been stated that there was "no place in our midst" for this false doctrine and teaching.[5] The three young men vowed to stick together and fight it out. They were promptly relieved of their duties. Two of them had managed the subscription department and one had been assistant to the secretary of the company.

In the late 1890s the major leaders began to publicly oppose and warn against proponents of Zinzendorfism. Many articles appeared in the publications reaffirming sanctification as a second definite cleansing work of grace subsequent to justification. By 1898 the *Gospel Trumpet* began to deal with the issue very pointedly. Byrum's editorials as well as articles by a variety of writers explained sanctification in detail. The editor was

---

5. Enoch E. Byrum, *Life Experiences* (Anderson, IN: Gospel Trumpet Co., 1928), 152.

undaunted by the threats of those (themselves anti-cleansers) who advised him not to oppose the anti-cleansing doctrine. He seemed to operate on the assumption that this controversial issue could best be resolved by open exposition of the issues at hand and, if necessary, the expulsion of those causing division. Byrum expounded the orthodox holiness by affirming that people must first be forgiven of their sins before presenting themselves for sanctification. Regarding Romans 12:1–2, he wrote, "Sinners can not fulfill this scripture and become justified and sanctified all at the same time, because they cannot present their bodies a living sacrifice, as they are dead in trespasses and sins. They cannot present themselves a holy sacrifice, because they are unholy."[6] Byrum also said that oneness comes as a result of the cleansing power that removes all divisive elements from the heart. For Byrum, the anti-cleansers' denial of this experience threatened the basis of Christian unity and itself indicated a divisive spirit.

One of the *Trumpet's* clearest statements on the issue came from the pen of W. G. Schell in a two-part series titled "Zinzendorfism Refuted," published in March of 1899. Schell viewed the "one-work theory" as heresy. He then laid out the premises of the reformation movement, summarized as follows: (1) Every person born in this world possesses the "germ of sin"; that is, Adamic sin or sin inherited. (2) When one matures to the point of comprehending good and evil and then chooses to do evil, it is an act of sin. This is sin acquired. (3) Spiritual birth cleanses one from all sin acquired and brings about the restoration to infantile innocence. This new birth includes the grace to refrain from committing actual sins. (4) However, sin inherited remains in the heart and is manifested in anger and other passions. The second cleansing—sanctification—coincides with the baptism of the Holy Ghost. This is the cleansing from sin inherited that restores the self to Adam's state before the Fall. Schell emphasized cleansing by the Holy Spirit as a part of sanctification. To be sanctified was to be consecrated, but it was more than that. In Schell's terms it was also to be cleansed by the Holy Ghost.[7]

This was possibly the issue disputed by the anti-cleansers. George P. Keeling spoke for them when he wrote: "But after they have been converted there still remains in them this fallen nature. For man to dispute this is to dispute not only his own experience (if he has been converted) but

---

6. E. E. Byrum, "The Two Works of Grace" (editorial), *Gospel Trumpet*, November 17, 1898, 4.
7. William Schell, "Zinzendorfism Refuted," *Gospel Trumpet*, March 16, 1899.

the experience of all the children of God."[8] Less than three months later Keeling himself would reject Schell's orthodox view and leave the reformation movement.

The anti-cleansing challenge severed the link between sanctification and Christian unity. Holiness, including the removal of carnality, was the prerequisite for unity. As Warner had written, "O Brethren how this perfect love unites us all in Jesus." A. L. Byers spelled out the implications of Zinzendorfism: "To remove the doctrine of the second cleansing would simply be to quickly bring this reformation to naught, because it is just what the Church of God has needed to bring her out of spiritual Babylon into the glorious unity with Christ, and her members with one another.[9] Byers later summarized the *Trumpet* position in an article titled "The Second Cleansing Scripturally Considered."[10] He affirmed that sanctification is indeed a cleansing, not merely a setting apart; that it is an experience that perfects God's people; and that it is a filling with the Holy Spirit. The differences had been made quite clear.

The anti-cleansing proponents were not silenced by the barrage of defenses of orthodoxy, and by early summer of 1899 the intensity of disagreement had heightened considerably. An encounter in the June camp meeting in Moundsville seemed inevitable. Byrum was aware of this and sought a strategy that would reaffirm the traditional position without a confrontation and, most important of all, without giving further opportunity for the heretics to proclaim their teaching.

In a post-encounter editorial titled "The Camp Meeting," Byrum recounted the events. Over one hundred preachers and a large number of gospel workers were present. Byrum said that it was "a real battle against the powers of darkness, as we read in the book of Job that where the sons of God gathered together Satan came also." Byrum's report explained that no place was given for public discussion of the issue because (1) it had been exposed before most of those involved over one year earlier; (2) at different times since then the doctrine had been exposed; (3) those involved had been warned in private of the false spirit behind the anti-cleansing heresy; (4) some of the ministers had spent more than two days with them in recent

---

8. George Keeling, "Sanctification," *Gospel Trumpet*, April 6, 1899, 1.

9. A. L. Byers, "The Second Cleansing on Established Scriptural Doctrine," *Gospel Trumpet*, May 4, 1899, 4.

10. A. L. Byers, "The Second Cleansing Scripturally Considered," *Gospel Trumpet*, May 11, 1899, 4.

discussions; and (5) there is no wisdom in publicly discussing a known heresy.

The proponents of this new light were not about to be silenced, however. They met together and put their teaching in writing. This document was prepared by W. A. Haynes, W. J. Henry, J. A. Smith, J. E. Chase, E. G. Masters, E. S. Sloan, E. W. Durkee, S. C. Dickason, and Frank McCann. Following two days of negotiations, the statement was allowed to be read before the ministers and assembled saints. It was then "publicly refuted by the Word of God showing its falsity in doctrine and in spirit."[11] Byrum then observed:

> The meetings had been very much hindered on account of permitting this element to have influence without a public exposure, but when it was given God witnessed the same at the close of the service by an outpouring of his Spirit and about forty persons flocking to the altar seeking salvation and deliverance through Jesus Christ.[12]

Observers noted that most of the anti-cleansers soon left the grounds, and the work of God continued with power.

During the refutation session, W. J. Henry made a public statement on the issue of Zinzendorfism being refuted by the Word of God. Henry confessed that he saw the doctrine was false and renounced it as "being founded upon scientific and philosophical principles and reasoning," but not Scripture.[13] The spirit of what he said was rebuked. Henry later returned to the anti-cleansers.

In addition to those present at the meeting in Moundsville, Byrum listed individuals "in the West" who had taken a stand for the doctrine: Fred Husted, J. M. Harrington, A. A. Kenzie, Price McCully, and W. Christ. In conclusion, Byrum warned: "To receive such persons or any one else teaching such who have been faithfully dealt with is to receive them and their doctrine and spirit at the peril of your souls. When they have seen the error of their way and turned from it we shall be glad to inform our readers of the same."[14]

The import of this 1899 meeting was soon apparent. The anti-cleansers now clearly understood they were not welcome either in the meetings or

---

11. E. E. Byrum, "The Camp Meeting," *Gospel Trumpet*, June 22, 1899, 4.
12. Ibid.
13. Ibid.
14. Ibid.

in the movement. The only alternatives were to recant or leave. Many did the latter. The exact number who withdrew from fellowship is not known. Some estimates of defections run as high as 50 percent of the ministers.[15] Although that figure is probably much too high there is no question that the number was considerable. It is also true that the dissidents included some of the most able and eloquent speakers in the movement.

There is evidence that some attempt was made to gather the anti-cleansers into a new fellowship. Haynes and Keeling began publication of a rival periodical called *The Messenger of Love*. In the first issue in January 1900, Haynes stated the purpose of the paper:

> The object of sending forth this letter *Messenger of Love* is to give the honest searcher for truth the chance to observe the old maxim, *audi alteran partem*—hear both sides. The saints are aware of the controversy in the church at present regarding the doctrine that teaches two cleansings of the soul in the plan of salvation.[16]

Haynes contended the anti-cleansers were not denying the reformation; they believed it was of God. "We acknowledge this reformation," he said, "but deny some errors that still cling to many."[17] The paper upheld the anti-cleansing position with various articles and also jabbed at Holiness preachers in the Church of God.

Some meetings were held to promote Zinzendorfism. One of these was noted in the *Gospel Trumpet*. William T. Whaley reported on an assembly of the anti-cleansers held at Flat Creek in Pike County, Indiana, during November 1899. The meeting lasted for ten days. It was well attended but Whaley described it as "dry and dead" with no converts to the cause. The meeting closed with a "disgusting" public collection for W. A. Haynes and George P. Keeling, who were also present.[18]

Hopes for regrouping apparently were soon abandoned, for many began to affiliate with other compatible denominations. Haynes, for instance, joined the Disciples of Christ. However, a large group had second thoughts about their departure and returned to fellowship in the Church of God.

---

15. Charles E. Brown, *When the Trumpet Sounded* (Anderson, IN: Gospel Trumpet Co., 1951), 364.

16. *The Messenger of Love.* 1, no. 1 (January 1900), 4.

17. Ibid.

18. William T. Whaley, "Zinzendorfism in Indiana," *Gospel Trumpet*, Feb. 8, 1900, 4.

Among these were W. J. Henry and George P. Keeling. Prior to the 1900 Moundsville camp meeting Henry had written a letter from Springfield, Missouri. It was published in the *Gospel Trumpet* under the heading "Anti-Cleansing Doctrine Renounced." He explained his short-lived defection as due to the pressure of others and at that time, he had not yet been fully convinced himself. Henry pictured the past year as one of a soul in the midst of a storm. He concluded with a penitent plea: "Dear ones, will you please. . .pray for unworthy me that God may in his mercy once more fully restore me to his love and favor?"[19]

With the contents of this letter already widely known, Henry appeared at the Moundsville meeting. Great rejoicing took place upon his arrival. Byrum reported, "He had already renounced that doctrine and was making desperate effort to get an experience to the satisfaction of his soul."[20] The saints prayed for Henry, and he testified to the joys of salvation and deliverance from the spirit of error. W. J. Henry needed acceptance by the brethren as well as God. Apparently he received both at Moundsville in 1900. Byrum also reported that he had received a letter from George P. Keeling renouncing the anti-cleansing doctrine. He desired to get "in line with God" and was sorry he was the means of leading souls astray during the previous year.[21]

The controversy subsided and the original theological position of the Church of God reformation movement on sanctification thus remained intact. This did not mean, however, that all the questions were answered in regard to this doctrine, particularly its implications for daily living. Within a decade definitions of the outward signs of a sanctified life were to bring in a new round of internal debate, conflict, and eventually schism. Specifically the crisis occurred in a dispute over the wearing of neckties.

In the interlude between these two periods of tension, and even within them, the movement continued to grow and make progress. The publishing work expanded so rapidly as to render inadequate the new facilities in Moundsville. A new, more central location was sought and the move to Anderson, Indiana, was made in 1906. The overseas work was developing at a rapid rate. Perhaps the most significant aspect of growth during this time, however, was in the number of new localities in America where the movement gained a foothold and increased the strength of its base of operations.

---

19. W. J. Henry, "Anti-Cleansing Doctrine Renounced," *Gospel Trumpet*, June 21, 1900, 4.
20. E. E. Bryum, "Moundsville Campmeeting," *Gospel Trumpet*, June 21, 1900, 4.
21. Ibid.

Many local congregations sprang up during this period, but there is no way to tabulate the number since this growth occurred prior to the publication of the *Yearbook*. Often these were started as a result of evangelistic meetings held in homes, groves, halls, schoolhouses, or wherever else anyone would come to listen. Typically the work was carried on with unsalaried pastors, little or no organization, and leaders who possessed little education or worldly possessions but were rich in dedication and faithful prayer. A local congregation that exemplifies many of the typical characteristics of congregations beginning during this period is the Floyd Church of God, located in a small rural community about ten miles from Midland, Michigan.[22] Although some new congregations grew in cities the majority of Church of God congregations were still located in small towns or the countryside. There was also at this time a higher percentage of women ministers in pastoral leadership positions than in later years. Such was the case at Floyd where Mrs. Frances Eastman was the founding pastor. In March 1911 A. J. Shelly held the first evangelistic meetings in the old Gleaner Hall. He was a fiery evangelist who specialized in holding revivals and raising up congregations. He traveled by horse-drawn wagon and was once reported to have had no clothes other than those on his back. He traveled by faith and great sacrifice. Two couples were converted in the Floyd revival and a new congregation was under way.

The church continued to meet at Gleaner Hall. They preached against secret societies, antagonizing local lodge members in the process. As a result the church was denied the use of the hall. They moved to the Floyd School and held meetings there during the summer. In the fall they moved out of the school and held prayer meetings and Sunday school in homes or wherever possible. Finally, Eastman bought an old log house on the corner of Pine River Road and Eight Mile Road, and the congregation began meeting there.

The pastor came to be known for her rich prayer life, hard work, and faithful piety. One of the earliest members, Mary Mashue, gave this account of her first encounter with "Sister Eastman," at Hitsmans' small country store at the Floyd corner:

I couldn't help but notice her as she wore a sun bonnet and apron. Her [sic] and Sister Beebe were there together. They looked different than

---

22. Information obtained from a history of the Floyd Church of God in the Anderson University and Church of God Archives.

ordinary people, as if they had something in common, different from the rest. I didn't know they were Christians, but thought it by their looks. Afterward she told me she was the one that got Brother Shelly to come to the Gleaner Hall to preach. That was where I first heard of the Church of God.[23]

The saints at Floyd as elsewhere were noted for their plain dress, and there continued to be strong teaching against wedding rings and worldly apparel even after the critical battles with the necktie controversy were a dim memory. The church in its earliest days also did not believe in human organizations, so there was no financial officer or board of trustees. Eastman made the church's purchases, and she was always given money to pay its expenses. However, throughout her pastorate, 1911–34, Eastman received no salary. When Blaine Varner succeeded her as pastor in 1934, he was paid five dollars a week.

By 1914 the congregation's influence in the community was growing, and they continued their evangelistic thrust. In that year W. H. Clingenpeel reported: "I was in a good meeting near Floyd with Bro. A. J. Shelly and others. The Word went forth in power, some were saved, sanctified, and healed; and some things were made right, for which we give the Lord all the praise."[24] The log house was not suited to congregational growth, and the members eventually concluded they needed a new meeting house and that it should be located on the Floyd corner at the intersection of Eight Mile and Chippewa River Roads. All of them prayed to this end, but the owners refused to sell. After further prayer and fasting, a piece of land next to the corner lot was leased to the congregation by Henry and Mary Mashue, Sr. on the condition that they build within two years. The offer motivated them for a seemingly impossible task for a congregation of only about twelve members. The saints prayed and fasted for building supplies, and construction began in October of 1914. They served as their own contractor and builder, and constructed a building that served the church well for approximately twenty-five years.

The congregation grew but maintained a close fellowship through numerous family ties and a rewarding rural camaraderie. The women formed a sewing circle that predated the formation of the National Woman's Missionary Society. The congregation enjoyed some humorous experiences, including the time when they were singing "Let the holy fire from heaven

23. Ibid.
24. W. M. Clingenpeel, Field Reports, *Gospel Trumpet*, March 12, 1914, 14.

fall on me" and the stovepipe fell down. Membership doubled between 1920 and 1930 and nearly doubled again in the following decade, which was typical of the growth pattern of many of the movement's churches during the period. The church was not exactly on the corner until many years later when the corner lot next to the church property was finally purchased by the church and cleared. At last the church building stood on Floyd corner as Pastor Eastman and the others long since departed had prayed for more than fifty years.

As the Floyd church and many others across the country were getting under way, the Church of God movement nationally was becoming preoccupied with questions relating to the outward signs of holiness. The prevailing pietistic taboos against worldliness had been standard in the movement from the beginning. In addition to such obviously sinful practices as using tobacco, drinking liquor, and taking drugs, the Holiness people also forbade amusements such as dances, shows and "play parties" and had much to say about modesty and unnecessary adornment in dress. In all these things the Church of God leaders sought to hold as high or higher standard as anyone else, including very strict groups such as the Dunkards. About 1881, for example, D. S. Warner and two other preachers held a meeting at Bucyrus, Ohio. There were some sectarians present, including a tobacco-using Dunkard preacher who was "indoctrinated with creeds" and the "sin-you-must" belief. In E. E. Byrum's words: "The Dunkard preacher, with his long hair parted in the middle, full beard except the shaved upper lip, peculiarly cut coat, flap trousers, and broad-brimmed hat, all as a part of his religion, and with his love for tobacco, was told to clean up and get rid of the 'mark of the beast.'"[25]

The competitive spirit was evident in all the groups associated with the Holiness Movement as they sought to outdo each other in practicing the signs of a sanctified life as they understood it. No group wanted to be accused of being less holy than another. The Free Methodist Church, for example, which began in 1860, was particularly strict in teaching that clothing should be plain, modest, and never costly. They condemned all adornment such as pearls, gold, and other jewelry, and in some parts of the country they preached against neckties. When one group placed specific items such as these on the forbidden list others quickly adopted the same emphasis in order to avoid accusations of letting down the standard.

---

25. E. E. Byrum, "Customs and Traditions," *Gospel Trumpet*, July 1, 1915, 3.

Sometimes encounters led to bargaining between the parties involved. On one occasion Warner and a few colleagues were harshly condemning sectarianism and creedalism when some other Holiness people present responded by accusing Warner and his friends of conforming to the world, "demanding that they lay aside their collars, cuffs, and neckties as 'superfluities,' quoting James l:2l."[26] The sectarians refused to listen to the come-out message unless the Church of God preachers measured up to their holiness standards. Recounting the incident, E. E. Byrum said, "The ministers and brethren without further consideration removed their collars, cuffs, and neckties, and cast them into the stove, in order that the people they were trying to reach might be without excuse."[27] C. E. Brown reported a similar incident when Warner was challenged by a Free Methodist who agreed to give up his membership in the Free Methodist sect if Warner would give up his necktie. Warner quickly removed the offending article of clothing.[28]

Although the major portion of attention to these ascetic legalisms was directed toward items associated with women's dress and adornment, the focus of discussion and debate turned more and more toward one item of men's clothing—the necktie. From the time of Warner the movement took a stand against neckties. Warner, however, according to E. E. Byrum, never did make the absence of the tie a test of fellowship. Byrum later mentioned he knew an individual closely associated with Warner "who was by him recognized and fellowshipped as a true saint of God," and who "wore a tie until the day of his death."[29] Even so, from the time of the 1880s it can be said that the necktie was regarded as an unnecessary superfluity and a symbol of pride.

Leaving off the necktie was not without its problems, however, especially when the detachable collar was also removed. Soon men found their suit-coat collars were being soiled quickly and ruined. They concluded that God would be glorified more if they wore a collar and thereby observed cleanliness. However, the collar without a tie, exposed a collar button which was usually brass. Since it resembled gold, which was also forbidden, men had to find a source for securing white bone buttons. Soon men also began wearing high-cut vests which almost took the place of a tie but did not carry the same stigma. Within a few years they were also wearing shirt cuffs

---

26. Ibid., 11.
27. Ibid.
28. Charles E. Brown, *When Souls Awaken* (Anderson, IN: Gospel Trumpet Co., 1954), 77.
29. E. E. Byrum, "A Warning to the Church," *Gospel Trumpet*, February 19, 1914, 3.

again, but the tie remained stigmatized as an unnecessary article of worldly adornment and the indication of a proud heart.[30]

In the years following Warner's death, and especially in the first decade of the new century, the emphasis on abstaining from worldliness increased and the number of items to which that label was attached multiplied, running all the way from gores and pleats to feathers, lace, and corsets. The concern over this matter seemed to become almost a preoccupation.

In 1903 the Gospel Trumpet Company published a book by C. E. Orr titled *Christian Conduct*. In it Orr made a strong plea for strict asceticism and urged the readers to persist in the fight against worldliness:

Extravagance in dress is indicative of a proud heart....Any article of dress put on merely for adornment can only be the fruit of pride in the heart. Some may wear adornments by way of jewels, pearls, rings, necklaces, etc., and still say that they are not proud. But the Bible says: "By their fruits ye shall know them." These facts are plain, no matter how much man or woman may deny them.[31]

In these years the ministers began to preach more and more sermons on prohibitions associated with holiness. Practically every issue of the *Gospel Trumpet* carried articles upholding rules and regulations of one form or another. The theme of this period was, "Wherefore come out from among them, and be ye separate" (2 Cor 6:17 KJV), and this applied to both human-made sects and the behavioral standards of the world. The following quotations represent the tenor of the age:

What I wish to mention will more particularly concern the sisters, because it is regarding dress, and they have more temptation on this line than the brethren.[32]

The society leaders and their devotees will have to bid farewell forever to their jewels of gold, pearls, and costly array of gaudy clothing and ornamental dress.[33]

---

30. Byrum, "Customs and Traditions," 11.

31. Charles E. Orr, *Christian Conduct, or the Way to Heaven* (Moundsville, WV: Gospel Trumpet Co., 1903), 59.

32. Opal F. Brookover, "On Dress," *Gospel Trumpet*, February 27, 1908, 133.

33. J. C. Blaney, "Love Not The World," *Gospel Trumpet*, November 22, 1906, 3.

I was saved from sectism, horse-racing, ball playing, secret orders, fairs, shows, picnics, dances, worldly amusements of all kinds, jestings, light and foolish talking, immodest apparel, superstition, etc. Now, I can see plainly that if I go back to any of these things, I make myself a transgressor.[34]

Even such an extreme emphasis was not altogether out of place in the context of the time and place. In general, the Church of God movement from its beginning to the turn of the century was concentrated in the rural areas and small towns of the Midwest. There was little need for fine dress and adornment since all were expected to toil with their hands from sun up to sun down. Therefore, there was little objection in regard to prohibitions of such things as neckties and jewelry. In fact, there was a certain amount of glee in hearing castigations from the pulpit of the fancy and extravagant ways of the affluent citified dudes and damsels.[35] With the passage of time, however, the movement began to win converts in the towns and cities; some of these were professional people such as teachers, doctors, and bankers who were accustomed to urban styles of dress and found it difficult to abide by rural standards. Their questions about these matters opened the door for discussion, and eventually sides were taken and a schism occurred. By the end of the first decade of the twentieth century the debate was in full heat. The area of concern was worldliness, but the topic was the necktie.

In 1910 editor Byrum presented his position in a significant article titled "Marching Along the Bypath":

At the present time the enemy has laid a snare for the people of God.... The object is to destroy the spirit of this reformation, by getting it on the side-tract of compromise....In a shrewd manner he seeks to gain the conflict by stealthily turning the people of God into drifting into worldliness of dress, and on other lines.[36]

Byrum observed that two or three ministers had put on the tie and worn it into the pulpit, even at a camp meeting, and then had proceeded to label

34. C. E. Orr, "Self-Examination," *Gospel Trumpet*, November 29, 1906, 7.
35. E. V. Patterson, "Ornaments," *Gospel Trumpet*, June 4, 1908, 1.
36. E. E. Byrum, "Marching Along the Bypath," *Gospel Trumpet*, September 15, 1910, 9.

A group of flying messengers: John E. Roberts, Enoch E. Byrum, Hiram Brooks, H. M. Riggle. Even before the necktie controversy of the early twentieth century, some Church of God ministers favored the use of a clerical collar, as worn by Byrum and Brooks. Roberts and Riggle wear the cellulose collar, sans tie, customary of many movement ministers during the era. The necktie was considered a symbol of pride and worldliness. Hats, even fashionable bowlers, obviously did not come under the same strictures.

as fanatical those who would not do the same. He held no brief for these rebels, but he did make room for some possible exceptions: "There may be circumstances where such an article of dress would not be objectionable when required in holding a business position, but it is a superfluity in the assemblies of the saints."[37] This is consistent with Byrum's own practice in business affairs, according to his daughter. She reported seeing her father return from a business trip during this time wearing a necktie.[38] His article "Marching Along the Bypath" was quoted by the necktie opposers, however, for many years to come. Byrum's centrist position was that "fanaticism and compromise are equally dangerous; neither of them belong to the highway. Beware of both!"[39] Neither side heeded his advice.

H. M. Riggle (1872–1952) sounded a further note of caution. He pointed out the advantage of dropping certain practices, especially in city work. He said the movement had held on to customs that were hampering the work with higher classes of people. However, he called for people to wait for God to bring about the change in his good time. "There is no need of

37. Ibid.
38. Interview with Harold L. Phillips, March 1979.
39. Byrum, "Marching Along the Bypath," 10.

agitating these things....But if some brethren with more impulsiveness than good wisdom, will run ahead of the Lord, and push upon the church something it is not prepared for, a good thing will be spoiled, and the desired results will be entirely defeated."[40] The pressure to relax the stern asceticism of the pioneers began to increase. At the Anderson Camp Meeting, on June 7, 1911, a resolution in this direction was unanimously adopted by twenty-five ministers representing eighteen states:

1. That there is no good reason for a change in what for years has been the general attitude of the church in this country in regard to the matter, namely, that the wearing of the tie is a thing to be discouraged as being unnecessary and as tending to the spirit of the world.
2. That liberty be given to its being worn by those whose consciences do not forbid their doing so on occasions when their business or other extreme circumstances require it.[41]

Among those present and notable for their approval of this compromise were Willis M. Brown, N. S. Duncan, J. E. Forrest, C. E. Orr, H. M. Riggle, F. G. Smith, and E. E. Byrum.

Two years later, however, at the Anderson Camp Meeting of 1913, some felt it necessary to present another resolution opposing the necktie. A meeting was held in the tower of the Gospel Trumpet building at which a resolution calling for a holding to the standard teaching was passed. Among those present then were A. L. Byers, H. M. Riggle, C. E. Orr, D. O. Teasley, N. S. Duncan, and W. M. Brown. The new affirmation on holding the line turned out to be little more than window dressing. It was this resolution against wearing ties, on the one hand, but the failure to carry it out, on the other hand, that resulted in an open revolt and a schism. The *Gospel Trumpet* maintained silence concerning this action at the camp meeting of 1913.

Byrum attempted to steer the paper on a middle course during these rocky times. Proponents of both positions—liberal and anti-compromise—were alleged to have plans for beginning a new paper if the *Trumpet* did not speak out on their behalf. Byrum indicated that his stand would be upon the weighty matters of the Word of God and not upon such a minor issue

---

40. H. M. Riggle, "Compromise—Be Careful," *Gospel Trumpet*, September 1, 1910, 2.
41. Brown, *When the Trumpet Sounded*, 362.

as "the tie." His preferred position was to be on the Lord's side in all such questions. He wrote, "It is a shame and a disgrace to the cause of Christ that ministers whom God has called should turn aside and so fall under the power and influence of a factious spirit as to undertake to bring division among the brethren over such trifling matters."[42]

The dispute divided the ministry of the Church of God. Prominent and rising younger ministers were ranged against each other. The liberal camp included D. O. Teasley, H. M. Riggle, A. T. Rowe, J. Grant Anderson, J. T. Wilson, C. W. Naylor, B. E. Warren, and E. A. Reardon. In addition to those mentioned earlier who would eventually break with the movement, J. E. Forrest was also a part of the radical camp. Forrest did not break with the movement, however.

The most prominent figure among the necktie opposition was C. E. Orr. Orr was a former school teacher who had entered the work of the Church of God in 1891. He was a man of mystical and poetic mind. Being a person of such sensitive spirit, he was also inclined to a sensitive conscience. A very small offense often placed him under a burden of guilt. Following his conversion, Orr became an evangelist in the Midwest and traveled by faith. Many stories were told of the miraculous ways in which food and money were provided to sustain his evangelistic labors. He was a gifted writer who was competently able to bring the things of the Spirit to life. But by December 1913 Orr was dropped from the *Trumpet* as one of its contributing editors. That month, in Aberdeen, Scotland, the first issue of Orr's paper, *The Herald of Truth,* was published. Schism had come.

Others who followed in Orr's footsteps were Willis M. Brown, N. S. Duncan, and W. H. Shoot. Shoot was converted in Missouri at the age of fourteen and began preaching at sixteen. Duncan came from Alabama. He had been converted under the ministry of the Bolds family in 1893. He evangelized widely in the South and was under persecution most of the time. Duncan's preaching was reported to have "literally broke(n) the hearts of some of the bitterest and most cruel persecutors, and often led them to Christ."[43] W. M. Brown was converted from a life of drink and gambling in southern Illinois. In the summer of 1895 Brown began to preach. He was a fiery preacher and a strong advocate of divine healing.

The new paper, the *Herald of Truth,* contained many articles relating to worldliness and was particularly concerned about dress and worldly

---

42. E. E. Byrum, "'Liberals' and 'Radicals'," *Gospel Trumpet,* September 11, 1913, 12.

43. Brown, *When the Trumpet Sounded,* 223.

amusements. Orr wrote an article titled "Salvation" in one of the early issues: "The Bible is silent so far as directly condemning shows, fairs, baseball games, picnics, etc. but there is a law written on the soul of every holy man and woman which does forbid going to such places."[44] He also spoke against socials, festivals, and Fourth of July picnics in this article. Orr described his paper as "definite and radical for the truth in the fullness of love."[45] He further elaborated:

> The good old truths that separated this reformation and the Church of God from sin and sectism will still be taught through these columns. Candidly this paper sees no reason why we should be any more afraid to speak out plainly against wearing gold, pearls, feathers, flowers, neckties, corsets, and using tea, coffee, organs in worship, going to Fairs, picnics, picture shows, etc., than we have been all down through this blessed reform.[46]

In this same issue Orr contributed another article titled "Innovations Cause Division." He stated simply, "Keep out all innovations and division *can not come in*."[47] He further stated, "Brethren who are standing by the doctrine and practice of any reformation should steadfastly oppose all innovations and never allow men nor devils accuse them as being the cause of division."[48] He got very specific at the end of this article:

> For some to believe in using organs in worship, in life insurance, in visiting ball games, picture shows, in lecturing on politics, introducing novelties in meetings, and some not believing in such things and all agreeing to give the others liberty of opinion. Such will do very well for Sectarian union but not the Holy Spirit unity.[49]

Christy Mathewson may have been known as the "Christian Gentleman," but Orr was not about to buy a ticket to watch Christy pitch for the New York Giants.

Another Orr article in this same issue condemned the titles "Reverend" and "D.D." (which stands for doctor of divinity). Orr wrote, "The only

---

44. C. E. Orr, "Salvation," *Herald of Truth* 1, no. 3 (December 1913) (Aberdeen, Scotland), 3.
45. Ibid.
46. Ibid.
47. Orr, "Innovations Cause Division," *Herald of Truth* 1, no. 3 (December 1913), 7.
48. Ibid.
49. Ibid.

place in the Bible we find anything standing for D.D., is found in Isa. liv. 10 'His watchmen are blind; they are all ignorant, they are all *dumb dogs* that cannot bark.'"[50]

Finally an editorial Orr replied to commented on a minister who said, "The days of preaching against ruffles and tucks are past in this reformation." Retorted Orr, "They may be past with him, and he may be, and no doubt is, well-nigh past being a reformer, but the days of preaching against such things are by no means past in this reformation."[51]

Early in 1914, E. E. Byrum went on an extended tour of congregations in the United States. In February he wrote from Oakland, California:

Many false reports are told and written from place to place, also, Scotland. Literature has been sent out, to lash the innocent and unsuspecting into believing such, with a fear that everything is going to smash. We cannot doubt the sincerity of some, but almost every deceived person is sincere.[52]

Byrum's rebuke did not deter Orr, who continued his campaign. In June 1914 he complained of compromise:

The sisters are dressing like the world in many ways. Some have ribbons sticking up on their hats "as long as a mule's ears." They wear not only a tie but a clasp to hold it to the shirt. They use slang and chew gum. Some of the young saints go courting every other night. The true saints are suffering, and are called fanatics and told to keep still and not oppose these things.[53]

By September, Orr was becoming shrill. He published another article titled "What Shall We Sing?" in which he asserted "The Bible tells us not only how to talk and what to think about, but also what and how to sing." He went on to condemn such songs as "My Old Kentucky Home" and "Bring Back My Bonnie To Me." He stated, "No one can sing 'Casey Jones,' unto the Lord with grace in the heart.…We cannot sing or play rag-time

---

50. Orr, "Rev. and D. D.," *Herald of Truth* 1, no. 3 (December 1913), 8.

51. Ibid.

52. E. E. Byrum, *Gospel Trumpet*, February 5, 1914, 10.

53. C. E. Orr, "Not the Compromiser But the Compromise," *Herald of Truth*, (Memphis, TN), June 15, 1914, 6.

music to the glory of God any more than we can smoke a cigar to his glory."[54]

In Scotland, Orr also published a tract titled "The Rule of a Saintly Life." While he conceded that the Bible said nothing specific about the necktie and several other outward adornments, he did base his position on a viewpoint that gave it a tenuous biblical platform: "Beyond the letter of the law there is an unwritten law upon the soul that is in fellowship with God which interprets the rule of a saintly life to a much wider circle than the letter of the word can possibly cover."[55] To worldliness Orr added the sin of schism. Principles coming out of the Word of God were not to be violated. Transgressing them would damage one's communion with God. Departure from the standard first laid down when the reformation movement began was tantamount to starting a new movement and thus bringing division. Orr contended that his intent was not to begin a new movement,[56] but remain true to the old one. He had high praise for D. S. Warner and his teaching. Further, he asserted that his doctrine and practice did not differ from Warner's. In Orr's mind, if there had been a departure from truth, it had been made by the *Trumpet* and the others who remained in the movement. He and they had formerly shared the same footing, but they could no longer do so because of new "innovations." In other words, in Orr's view the movement's moderates were the schismatics, not he.

One of the moderate voices, D. Otis Teasley, reviewed Orr's *The Rule of a Saintly Life* in the *Trumpet*. He prefaced his review with some thoughts about C. E. Orr as a person:

He has been a man loved by all, and his writings have had a fascination. To those of us who know him best, however, his tendencies have been too idealistic. Through an overwrought imagination he can paint fanciful pictures of an ideal life more easily than he has able at all times to live to his ideal....To us who are intimately acquainted with him, therefore his present strenuous position is only one phase of his personal history repeating itself. Heretofore, he has always been able, after a time, to

---

54. C. E. Orr, "What Shall We Sing?" *Herald of Truth* (Los Angeles, CA), September 1, 1914, 6.
55. C. E. Orr, *The Rule of a Saintly Life* (Aberdeen, Scotland: Herald of Truth Publishing Co., n.d.), 7.
56. C. E. Orr, *Not a New Movement* (Guthrie, OK: Faith Publishing House, n.d.), 5.

recover himself, and it is sincerely hoped that this aspect also of his personal history will repeat itself.[57]

Teasley's major criticism of Orr was the way he elevated inner revelation over Scripture. The great majority of Church of God ministers were said to stand upon the written Word as the standard, with the Holy Spirit as the guide to that Word, and a clear Christian conscience being the result of obedience. The bottom line for Teasley was that *The Rule of a Saintly Life* was the quintessence of sectarianism and contained the rank seeds of error.

One week following Teasley's review of one of Orr's tracts, E. E. Byrum sent out "A Warning to the Church." Likening himself to a "watchman on the wall of Zion," Byrum warned against the spirit and propagators of the *Herald of Truth*. With regret, Byrum said that C. E. Orr "is under a spirit of heresy."[58] In effect, Orr was said to be out of line with the principle of unity among believers and had set up his own opinion as *the* rule of conduct. Orr was finally stung by the criticism of his former associates.

D. Otis Teasley (1876–1942), minister, author, and songwriter. In the era of the necktie controversy, Teasley was a voice for moderation. (He is pictured here wearing a clerical collar). In addition to writing the movement's first book on hermeneutics, he also collaborated on a ministerial correspondence course and wrote such gospel songs as "I Will Praise Him, Hallelujah" and "God Is Love."

The January 13, 1915, issue of the *Herald of Truth* still listed C. E. Orr as editor, but by then Orr had begun to regret some of his actions. Two months later the *Gospel Trumpet* published this note from him:

I have had a sad, bitter experience and can not feel clear before God and man until I make a clear, clean confession. For some time my eyes have been gradually opening to see my mistake in starting the publication of "The Herald."…Last December I saw things going out of God's order and resigned the editorship, and should have never taken it back.… There is, beyond question, a bitter spirit of prejudice at work, which has

---

57. D. O. Teasley, "The 'Inner Word' Heresey," *Gospel Trumpet*, February 12, 1914, 6.
58. E. E. Byrum, "A Warning to the Church," *Gospel Trumpet*, February 19, 1914, 3.

grieved me many times. I saw this spirit at work in many of the *Herald* supporters. If one did not see things as they saw them they denounced him at once as a compromiser. I also saw that many of the fanatics who had been dissatisfied with *The Trumpet* for the past twenty years and were ready to rally round "The Herald."...If "The Herald" had been of God it would not have agitated and confused honest souls as it did.

When I took my stand I expected God to pour out his Spirit upon us in a wonderful way, but after waiting for a year it has not come.[59]

After Orr's letter appeared, some of his writings were printed in subsequent issues of the *Gospel Trumpet* and his name appeared in the *Yearbook* through 1926.

The *Herald of Truth* continued for several months without Orr as editor and persisted in causing much agitation. Some were still confused about the controversy. Fred Pruitt, who later became the editorial spokesperson for the dissidents, told the story of succeeding events:

I was taking the "Herald of Truth" paper printed at Carthage, Missouri, and was also reading the "Gospel Trumpet" paper. I was much puzzled about which was right, and being much in earnest about the matter I sought the Lord in prayer that He would keep me in the right way. I told the Lord I would be satisfied if I only knew I was pleasing Him. The Lord gave me another vision.

I was standing in the edge of a river. The water was some above my ankles. Out in the middle of the river was a man and a boy in a buggy, driving up stream. The water in the river began to rise and I at once began to call to the man and boy to get out of the river, because it was rising. They would pay no attention to me, but just kept driving up stream. Pretty soon it occurred to me that I had better get out or I would drown with them. I got out on the bank and stood and looked at the man and the boy in the buggy. The water got higher and higher, and they were swallowed up and drowned. I began to travel, and had a hard, rough, winding road to go over. It seemed to me that the man represented the "Gospel Trumpet" and the boy, the "Herald of Truth."[60]

---

59. C. E. Orr, "A Note From C. E. Orr," *Gospel Trumpet*, March 18, 1915, 12.
60. Fred Pruitt, *God's Gracious Dealings* (Guthrie, OK: Faith Publishing House, 1955), 31–32.

Pruitt's vision came true, partially. The *Herald of Truth* did die. Pruitt eventually came in contact with L. Y. Janes' tracts, which were printed at Guthrie, Oklahoma.[61] He also took Janes' paper called *Field Views and Testimonies*, visited Janes in Guthrie, and then decided to move there. The Pruitts arrived on June 13, 1918, and helped Janes at his print shop. Janes also printed a paper called the *Christian Triumph*. Janes, Pruitt and his wife were joined by Robert Longley, who also helped in the printing work. As the work increased a few more came to help, but after a time Janes and Pruitt separated. Janes took the *Christian Triumph,* the subscription list, and all his machinery and moved out, later to reestablish his operation elsewhere.

Fred Pruitt had worked about four years in the pressroom and with his experience he began, with the help of Longley, to print tracts. They subsequently started a paper called *Faith and Victory* and mailed six thousand copies of the first issue in March of 1923.[62] *Faith and Victory* took up the banner dropped by Orr and spoke out against worldliness and superfluities, including the necktie. In the meantime, C. E. Orr became editor of a paper called *The Path of Life*, which he felt led to merge with *Faith and Victory*. In December 1932, he began to edit the last six pages of *Faith and Victory*. He became a staunch supporter of the paper and the other printing work at Faith Publishing House until his death in 1933.

Orr continued to be listed in the Church of God *Yearbook* through 1926, and his death was mentioned in the 1934 *Yearbook*. L. Y. Janes moved his paper to Corpus Christi, Texas, where he published the *Christian Triumph,* books, and tracts. He had a mission outreach to Spanish-speaking people and was listed in the Church of God *Yearbook* from 1945 until his death. Fred Pruitt continued editing *Faith and Victory,* tracts, and doctrinal books. After his death his son Lawrence continued as editor, still making occasional anti-Anderson comments and preaching against the necktie.

---

61. Ibid., 29.
62. Ibid., 28–46.

CHAPTER 10

BREAKING THE ORGANIZATIONAL BARRIER (1916–1928)

The years from 1916 through 1928 proved to be a period of dramatic change in the polity of the Church of God reformation movement. The organization of the General Ministerial Assembly with a written constitution and bylaws, major corporate changes in the Gospel Trumpet Company, the establishment of Anderson Bible Training School, the printing of the *Yearbook of the Church of God,* the formation of boards for foreign missions, church extension, and religious education, respectively, and the beginnings of Associated Budgets highlight the changes of this twelve-year period. The contrast between the movement's polity in 1895 and the bureaucratic organization thirty-three years later is so great as to be difficult to comprehend. Of even greater significance is the modification of theological views that allowed change to take place. The inevitable alterations of perspective that accompany growth, frustrations with the inadequacies of the old pattern of charismatic organization, and new problems with the increasing variety and expansion of work of the Gospel Trumpet Company combined to permit and compel consideration of bureaucratic organizational structures that would have been rejected in Warner's day. Circumstances thus forced the leaders to search diligently for a better way to carry on the corporate work of the church and opened the door to organizational innovation.

D. S. Warner strongly opposed all human ecclesiastical organization. He lashed out with harsh words against denominationalism, creeds, and sects. He was adamantly opposed to committees, formalities in worship, and ecclesiastical machinery. In all his writings Warner taught against voting for church offices, all bureaucratic systems, and any form of human rule. He wrote, "All organisms that make their own laws, creeds, disciplines, and systems of cooperation, 'do not hold the head'—Christ. Their law-making synods and general conferences ignore the Divine Lawgiver, usurp the place of Christ and sit in the stead of God, and are not Christ's church, which is subject to him."[1]

Until his death Warner personally handled most problems related to the preservation of orthodoxy and correct teaching. As editor, he, of course, controlled the contents of the *Gospel Trumpet*, which was the chief medium for expressing commonly held views. He was very articulate and widely respected, and almost everyone who remained prominent in the movement for very long agreed with him on major issues or else said very little. This is not to say that Warner was completely inflexible or that he had ultimate control regarding the movement's beliefs and practices. He did not. Rather, he was regarded as a trusted person who was richly gifted with insight and discernment in spiritual things. His motive for holding strongly to that which he believed, taught, and practiced was simply that he sincerely believed in all of it as truth. His fellow workers accepted what he taught not merely because he taught it but because they also believed it was right.

The organizational changes that developed after Warner's death were made to extend decision-making control to a larger part of the church and to enhance the growth of a movement that was changing its perspective in regard to its own mission and role in Christian history. To better understand this national situation, it is helpful to note the change taking place all over the country in the ascending importance of local congregations. In the beginning of the movement's history there was the romantic era of the itinerants. Those were the years of the flying messengers when ministers who devoted their lives to the church were traveling evangelists, either alone or as part of a company. Few if any pastors were supported by local churches. This was due to two factors: the doctrine of walking by faith limited congregation size, and a minister was not to be a "hireling" and depend on others for material support of food, shelter, and other necessities. This would be a violation of faith and would give the minister's supporters control over her or him.[2] Christians, moreover, were not encouraged to give regularly or systematically; on the contrary, prospective givers and donors

---

1. D. S. Warner, *The Church of God, or What Is the Church and What Is Not* (Anderson, IN: Warner Press, n.d.), 4.

2. Charles E. Brown, *When the Trumpet Sounded* (Anderson, IN: Warner Press, 1951), 356–57.

were to wait on miraculous leading by the Holy Spirit to give the preacher a gift. The urge to give a dollar or two was not only a credit to the piety of the preacher, but also an indication that the giver was close enough to God to receive a personal message of this kind.[3]

After the romantic era came the missionary homes period, which represented the beginning of the church's involvement in the cities. Until 1893 most Church of God ministers avoided large towns and cities. But Warner himself caught a vision of the opportunities for evangelizing in the rising urban centers, and he encouraged other ministers to enter the cities and start working there. The missionary homes, which eventually numbered several dozen, indicate a further stage in organizational development. Even though they were faith-based homes they did require a structure with someone recognized as in charge and others assigned to designated responsibilities. Second, the homes required continuing arrangements for facilities; people had to either rent or buy property and arrange for the care of the property. Third, the homes required longer range planning and programming related to both their hospitality function and the mission enterprise. They had to be prepared to receive any of the flying ministers who might alight for a time and also to direct their evangelistic activity while on site. Moreover, home managers created programs to help people improve their ministry by offering classes in practical home missionary work and in preaching. In most instances the homes became the impetus for developing permanent Church of God congregations.[4]

The early 1900s saw a shift further away from the flying ministry to a settled pastoral ministry. By 1915 the *Church of God Ministerial List* recorded 468 pastors and assistant pastors but only 344 evangelists. This statistical data, of course, is not a complete record of the movement's entire ministry, since there was considerable resistance even to filling out the registration form. The incomplete data does show, however, a trend toward an established pastoral ministry as opposed to the flying ministry of the late 1800s.

During this transition there was a very high turnover rate among ministers. Often a minister would move on before a congregation was sufficiently established for survival. C. E. Brown commented on the effect of the anti-organization emphasis of the movement's early years:

---

3. Ibid., 357.
4. Ibid., 357–58.

When I collected data on the various congregations, I sometimes found many different reports of the time when the work was started in a certain locality. The solution was simple. In that district a congregation had been founded, died out, started again, and so on, often repeatedly. There is no doubt that the antiorganization theory was one of the principal causes of repeated failures. So far as I know, Warner himself never found the solution to this problem although he undoubtedly was hampered, if not frustrated, by it repeatedly.[5]

As local congregations became better established they encountered issues concerning how they should own property and handle their corporate business affairs without organizing. A related issue was financial support for pastors. Faced with these and other needs, the sentiment against bureaucratic organization began to shift. Many congregations, as early as the mid-1890s, found ways to carry on their business but with informal procedures. The Pauline admonition that "all things be done decently and in order" (1 Cor 14:40) was used as a rationale for many arrangements. Then, too, by 1916 many of the pioneers who would have opposed changes that seemed to conflict with the earlier antiorganizational theology had died or left the movement. Some had departed in 1899 during the anti-cleansing heresy debate, while others left between 1910 and 1914 during the necktie controversy. Thus many of the most conservative had disassociated themselves from "Anderson." Without specifically rejecting Warner's views, willingness emerged to refer to principles rather than specifics. Particularly precious was the principle of Holy Spirit leadership in the church. The generally accepted Spirit-led or charismatic organization was showing them the need for a type of Spirit-led organization that could last for years with stability. This insight further enhanced aversion to bureaucratic organization.

The history of the Missionary Board provides a very good example of the early aversion to organizational structure and the myriad of difficulties that resulted from such a stance. The first overseas missionary recorded as being commissioned was Gorham Tufts, who was sent to India in 1897 to distribute famine relief funds solicited through the *Gospel Trumpet* and to make contact with some known native converts.[6] Other individuals had begun cross-cultural missionary work as early as 1892, but without official commissioning. Until 1909 the missionary work was unorganized

5. Charles E. Brown, *When Souls Awaken* (Anderson, IN: Gospel Trumpet Co., 1954), 113.
6. Ibid., 122.

and almost entirely individualistic in nature.[7] Aspiring missionaries decided on their own to go to a particular field, raising funds for their passage among friends and relatives. After arrival these early missionaries published field reports in the *Gospel Trumpet* and mentioned their financial needs. The Gospel Trumpet Company served as a relay to receive funds designated for individuals and distribute the money to them. Eventually, certain individuals in the company were appointed to handle this growing business, and these employees functioned until a Missionary Committee was organized.

On June 12, 1909, H. M. Riggle addressed the ministers at Anderson Camp Meeting on government in the church. He presented plans for a missionary paper to be called the *Missionary Herald*[8] and then recommended that "certain brethren" should be recognized by common consent to have responsibility and care of the foreign missionary work.

George Pease Tasker (1872–1958), pioneer missionary to India. About 1910, Tasker joined the Trumpet family in Moundsville. In 1912, he and his first wife, the former Minnie Criswell, answered a missionary call to India, where Tasker was to labor for thirty-four years. Tasker formed a close friendship with A. D. Khan, and their approach to missions and church work in general stood in opposition to the theology of F. G. Smith and his supporters. After publicly challenging Smith's views, Tasker was recalled in 1924, but he remained in India as an independent missionary until his retirement.

Their job description included the tasks of "advising, instructing, encouraging, and restraining." The men who were recognized for this committee were D. O. Teasley, J. W. Byers, E. E. Byrum, E. A. Reardon, G. P. Tasker, H. A. Brooks, and D. F. Oden. Riggle then gave this charge: "It is intended that the entire ministry should cooperate with these brethren." There was a hearty "Amen" in response. Thus was the Missionary Committee created.[9]

---

7. Ibid.

8. *Missionary Herald* was published from 1910 to 1913 and was then merged with the *Gospel Trumpet*.

9. J. W. Phelps, "Our Mission Work," *Our Ministerial Letter,* November 1912, 9.

Reflecting upon that decision, in 1912 several leaders felt impelled to further explain the formation of the committee. Apparently there had been some strong opposition to the "organization" of this committee. Leaders addressed the question from the Bible, noting that the early church had some structured patterns in its form. They also attempted to dissociate organization from sectarianism, a distinction that earlier writers had not affirmed. As one writer put it:

> We hold sectarianism to be antiscriptural, and claim that sectarianism has resulted from two things in particular: (1) the teaching and practice of unscriptural doctrines, and (2) the substitution of the human for the divine in schemes of church government. We regard every effort to organize the church of Christ humanly as being denominational and sectarian.[10]

Without challenging this viewpoint, in 1912 leaders showed themselves more favorably disposed to organization:

> It will be seen that sectarianism results, not from attempts on the part of God's children to plan to do the work of the church in an orderly, systematic manner, but from attempts to bind upon men as doctrines things not required by the letter or spirit of the Word, or to release men from obligations which the letter or the spirit of the Word requires.[11]

These early proponents of organizing at least certain aspects of the work of the church cited the Holy Spirit organization of the first century as a precedent for meeting organizational need in the Church of God. They set forth the following rationale: When the number of believers was small the efforts of the ministry were kept unified by personal contact, by letters from the leaders to the congregations, and by frequent visits from the apostles. However, as the church grew and problems arose it was necessary to appoint individuals to look after the business of the church. The naming of the seven deacons in Jerusalem was the first such instance. This organization of a working force did not at all interfere with the functioning of the Holy Spirit in their midst.[12]

---

10. Frederick G. Smith, "The Church of God Reformation Movement," in Warren Roark, comp., *The Church* (Anderson, IN: Warner Press, 1946), 78.

11. Phelps, "Our Mission Work," 8.

12. Ibid.

H. M. Riggle gave a new twist to an old argument, turning it in the direction of positive support for organization. In preaching at the Anderson Camp Meeting in June 1912, he said, "Government and system need to be recognized in the church. Such recognition will not show that we are a sect; on the contrary, these things being God's order, our recognition of them will be one of the surest signs that we are the Church of God."[13] The Missionary Committee was the embodiment of Riggle's "signs that we are the Church of God."

The function of this committee was to collect and distribute the Home and Foreign Missionary Fund. They did this, but the committee did not limit itself to this task. Another area in which they began to work was the obtaining of general and special information concerning ministers and missionaries. One can only surmise the specific information requested. Generally the concern was the character and ability of the ministry. To justify this effort the Missionary Committee wrote:

> Experience shows that there is need for the ministry to look after the standing of those who are preaching. Certain ones are reported to be tearing down the work faster than the true ministry can build it up.... Since last June we have been informed of three reprobate ministers— one a tobacco-user, one a horse-jockey, and one a libertine. Since the names of two of these appear on the ministerial list, we would have recommended them as suitable persons to hold meetings, had no one informed us...[14]

The developing organizational pattern took a giant stride in the direction of being more fully answerable to the entire church with the appearance of the General Ministerial Assembly in 1917. A very simple original motion in the informal Ministerial Assembly meeting at Anderson Camp Meeting began a more organized effort to perform the work of the church: "A motion was made that in the temporary organization only ordained ministers of the Church of God have the right to vote. Motion seconded. Motion carried."[15] Almost from the very beginning of the movement there had been General Assembly meetings, but they were informal, inspirational gatherings. C. E. Brown reported his memories of one early Assembly:

---

13. Ibid., 3.
14. Ibid., 21.
15. Minutes of the General Ministerial Assembly, June 14, 1917.

The first Assembly that I remember attending took place at the Yellow Lake Camp Meeting in 1902. The ministers present at the camp meeting assembled in the men's dormitory and sat around on the beds and talked. The only touch of a formal organization in this meeting was the appointment by this informal gathering of one man to represent the group in talking to the railroads concerning the availability of clergy rates.[16]

As early as 1907 there was a General Assembly meeting, which continued annually in connection with the camp meeting at Anderson. Preaching, encouragement, and exhortation highlighted these meetings. Occasionally, controversial subjects would arise concerning which varied opinions were expressed. Often the result would be that "one of the more influential brethren would stand and say, 'Now, brethren, this is the way we believe the question.'"[17] Usually that settled the matter.

Why then the need for the formalization of these meetings? One possible answer deals with the question of clergy rates on the railroad. A. T. Rowe expressed the opinion that the formalization of the Assembly would provide an official body to make acceptable arrangements for giving the railroads a listing of ministers in the Church of God.[18] Another reason given for formally organizing the General Ministerial Assembly was the need to legally tie the publishing work and the missionary outreach to the whole church. From Warner's days the Gospel Trumpet Company had been operated as a nonprofit business, owned and controlled by the church in spirit but not in actuality. To give the church actual control of the operation, the Gospel Trumpet Company consented to relate itself to the General Ministerial Assembly. The Missionary Committee's association with the General Ministerial Assembly was not so distant in time. Only eight years before, in 1909, a Ministerial Assembly had brought this committee into being by common consent. Its operation, however, had continued to reside within the company. Like the publishing house, the committee was also willing to be related to general ministerial control.

The *Gospel Trumpet* gave considerable space to the creation of the 1917 Ministerial General Assembly. Absentees needed a precise, careful

---

16. From a personal interview with C. E. Brown, October 15, 1957, as quoted in Marvin J. Hartman, "The Origin and Development of the General Ministerial Assembly of the Church of God, 1917–1950" (BDiv thesis, Butler University, 1958), 21.

17. Ibid.

18. Ibid., 25–26.

explanation, and the danger had to be minimized that opponents would misrepresent the real facts. The core of this explanation merits quotation:

> The business interests of the church are receiving more careful attention than ever before. The Lord has given the ministry a larger vision of our unparalleled opportunities for spreading the pure gospel to the end of the earth….In order to insure a sound financial basis for these increased activities, better business methods are being considered for the future than we have been accustomed to in the past.
>
> It has also been felt for some time that there should be a more direct legal relationship existing between the publishing work and the general body of the ministry. Steps have been taken to place this great work in more immediate touch with the ministry….[19]

During the next several years the General Ministerial Assembly moved slowly in defining its territory and working out the logistics of its assignments. By 1920 the Assembly seemed to be quite well accepted and functioning with reasonable smoothness. That year also marked a sharpening of focus for all future development. The underlying principle to guide the Assembly became "organization as needed."[20] Marvin Hartman made this observation: "From this period on, time and time again as the Assembly spread its organization and sharpened its lines of responsibility, it is apparent that these advancements came purely as a result of need."[21]

The organization of the General Ministerial Assembly in 1917 was preceded by a significant change in leadership in the Gospel Trumpet Company. In mid-1916, Enoch Edwin Byrum somewhat reluctantly resigned as editor of the *Gospel Trumpet*. Frederick George Smith was named to be his successor. Several national leaders were very concerned that the editor had been wielding too much power both within the company and in the church at large. For instance, the general approval of ministers across the country depended a great deal on the say of the editor, who controlled the chief medium of publicity. There was a great desire to remove some of Byrum's power and give more to other capable individuals. Was the opposition personal? Byrum's power could have been distributed without his resignation.

---

19. "The Anderson Campmeeting," *Gospel Trumpet*, June 28, 1917, 10.
20. Hartman, "Origin and Development," 38.
21. Ibid.

Announcing Byrum's resignation as editor, the *Gospel Trumpet* issued the following statement:

> Brother Byrum became associated with the Gospel Trumpet publishing work on June 29, 1887. For about nine years he served as publisher, business manager, and managing editor. At the death of D. S. Warner in December, 1895, he became editor-in-chief of *The Trumpet* and president of the company. As the years passed by and the publishing work grew larger and larger, his duties and responsibilities so increased that he could no longer bear up under them all. Consequently he specially requested that he be relieved of the editorship. He was also anxious to be relieved of the presidency of the company, but this request could not be even considered at this time, so he continues as president.[22]

The Gospel Trumpet Company always had been integral to the movement. Ties were strong but informal. The company really was an independent entity. It elected its own officers and members and was free to make any decision regarding publication policy or management of the company's assets. Although the company was sensitive to the movement it served, the church had no formal means to exercise authority over the company. Many people believed this made for too much independence. In the 1917 action the General Ministerial Assembly was given the responsibility of electing the twenty-four members of the Gospel Trumpet Company and

Frederick G. Smith (1880–1947), third editor of *The Gospel Trumpet* (1916-1930). Smith's books popularized a church-historical interpretation of Daniel and the Revelation and raised him to prominence at a comparatively young age. In 1930, the Publication Board failed to reelect him to the editorship, whereupon he moved to the pastorate of McKinley Avenue Church of God in Akron, Ohio. Some of the issues that Smith championed were part of theological and political conflict in the church from the mid-twenties to 1934.

22. *Gospel Trumpet*, June 15, 1916, 12.

also was authorized to ratify the person elected by company members as editor in chief.

In addition to changes in its relationship to the church, the company underwent important internal changes. Until 1917 the company had operated as an extended family, a kind of religious commune using volunteer labor and providing food, clothing, and shelter but no monetary wages. This had been a happy relationship when the company and its work were small. But the work had grown so large after the move to Anderson that there were many complex situations to handle not directly related to the publishing work.

> By the time the family came to Anderson it had become too large to eat at one table any more or even to be housed all together in one home, however large. The whole operation of providing all the needs of such a large group became incredibly complex—farming, gardening, laundering, shoe cobbling, garment making, food services, a commissary, an Old People's Home, a cemetery, a campground, plumbing, heating, lighting, livestock—all this in addition to printing or publishing.[23]

As a means of dealing fairly with this situation company leaders in 1917 decided to pay employees a cash wage.

These structural changes did little to reduce the role of the Gospel Trumpet Company in the general work of the church. Although the Missionary Committee separated, within the next few years several new significant church functions were added. The first of these was the formation of the Anderson Bible Training School. It was begun in 1917 with Joseph Turner Wilson (1876–1954), general manager of the Gospel Trumpet Company, serving as principal. The school operated as a department of the company and offered no degrees or diplomas until 1923. The company's board of directors appointed a Managing Committee and was also responsible for the selection of the school's principal. In 1925 Anderson Bible Training School became independent of the Gospel Trumpet Company, and a fifteen-member board of trustees was elected by the General Ministerial Assembly. That year the trustees elected John A. Morrison, president; R. R. Byrum, vice-president; Russell Olt, dean; Oscar J. Flynt, treasurer.

---

23. Harold L. Phillips, *Miracle of Survival* (Anderson, IN: Warner Press, 1979), 149.

Several other agencies and organizations had their beginning under the auspices of the Gospel Trumpet Company. Others that began as independent organizations also eventually came under the company's supervision. The old people's homes at St. Paul Park, Minnesota, and Anderson were established to provide for elderly people in the church who had no friends or relatives to care for them. Those who were financially able to support themselves were expected to pay an amount equal to the expense incurred in caring for them. Others had to depend on the charity of the church. For several years these homes were managed by separate organizations known as "old people's home associations," but by 1922 both had become one division of the Gospel Trumpet Company's work, a move that simplified management and made for more economical operation. Each of these homes was directed by a superintendent appointed by the general manager of the Gospel Trumpet Company.[24]

Another organization that came to function out of the Gospel Trumpet office was the publishing work for the blind. Grace DeFore, herself sightless, believed that the more than one hundred thousand blind people in the United States needed the gospel as much as others. With the aid of one or two others she established the blind publishing work. They first printed the *Gospel Trumpet* in raised type in Pomona, California. Later the plant, which consisted of a little hand machine, was moved to Anderson, where it operated as a department of the Gospel Trumpet Company's business, with the founders of the work still in charge. By 1922 the department was provided with a modern power press and other equipment whereby output could be greatly increased.[25]

In November 1920 a corporation by the name of Commercial Services was created as a subsidiary of the Gospel Trumpet Company. William H. Bowser was instrumental in the development of this corporation, the purpose of which was to print commercial jobs on the Trumpet presses.[26] Its purpose was to produce revenues by using the company's printing facilities, which otherwise would not have been running at full capacity. This helped generate extra income for the financially pressed Gospel Trumpet Company, but much criticism was aimed at the company for printing secular literature.

As far back as the late 1890s the Gospel Trumpet Company had published lists of Church of God ministers. These were needed for clergy

---

24. *Yearbook of the Church of God*, 1922, 10–11.
25. Ibid., 13.
26. Phillips, *Miracle of Survival*, 166.

permits for reduced fare on the railroads. The lists were also helpful as mailing address files for workers at the Trumpet office. By 1916 a need began to be felt for a more complete listing that would include congregations, pastors, and "isolated saints." J. W. Phelps, who later was designated the registrar, reported the process by which the first *Yearbook of the Church of God* was created in 1917:

> At the last international camp meeting of the church held at Anderson, Ind., in June, 1916, it was decided that instead of a Ministerial List a Yearbook of the church should be published, including the names of all the ministers and missionaries of the church, the location of all congregations of the church that have no pastors, the location of isolated saints, the location of all property of the church, chapels, campgrounds, etc.[27]

Some feared that the volume would be misused by those wishing to send a general mailing of literature with false teachings. Less than two decades had elapsed since the anti-cleansing heresy that had so riled the church. In spite of these reservations, it was decided to publish the *Yearbook*, and the Gospel Trumpet Company was initially assigned to the task. After the formation of the General Ministerial Assembly, however, this function came under its jurisdiction.

Another not-so-subtle issue was associated with the publication of a yearbook. It was feared that such a publication would stimulate ecclesiasticism. The determination of which ministers and congregations to list required human judgment. An official listing would have a tendency to place borders around what is a Church of God congregation and what is not. It would also tend to place these same borders around the process of determining who is or is not a true minister of the Church of God. Since the beginning of the movement it had been affirmed that only God could truly judge who is a minister or whether a congregation was in harmony with God. Theological issues thus inevitably raised their heads in the printing of a book that was the source of considerable discussion for several years.

The power of the *Yearbook* was tested in 1925 when the General Ministerial Assembly adopted a new constitution. The Constitution and Bylaws Committee had voted unanimously to strike a proposed sentence in

---

27. *Yearbook of the Church of God*, 1917, 4.

the bylaws that would have placed heavy authority on the *Yearbook*. The stricken sentence read, "The official Yearbook of the Church of God shall be made a test of membership, in case of contest by any member of the Assembly."[28] F. G. Smith was chairperson of that committee and was very sensitive to the dangers of developing a bureaucratic organization. In 1921 he had written a one-page publication titled "Organization Dangers."[29] He warned of the peril of making ministerial assemblies legislative and pointed out the difference between a "conference" and a voluntary assembly.

> Do I believe in ministers' meetings? Most assuredly I do—if they are the free voluntary kind, where advice, admonition, and instruction consti-tute the only ecclesiastical functions. But when a conference assumes a legislative and judicial character and begins to pass laws and regulations to bind upon the disciples of Jesus, or to enforce ministerial relations and operations by corporate authority then there is to be found the sect principle of man-rule.[30]

Smith also issued a warning in regard to preservation of the subservient nature of boards.

> If there is need of the organization legally of a board of trustees to hold church property, or of some other board to raise funds for supplying the needs of some other line of work undertaken by the ministers of the church, they may be properly legally organized; but the corporate function of such boards *are of a business nature.* THEY HAVE NO ECCLESIASTICAL AUTHORITY WHATSOEVER and they are entirely subservient to the spiritual leadership of the church.[31]

Clearly Smith expressed the fear that with the new organization could come a surge of human rule that would destroy the very precious concept of Holy Spirit church government.

The Gospel Trumpet Company also managed the annual national camp meeting in Anderson. Responsibilities included planning the program as well as arranging for facilities. Program planning was not an especially arduous

---

28. Minutes of the General Ministerial Assembly, June 17, 1925.
29. F. G. Smith, "Organization Dangers," (Anderson, IN: Gospel Trumpet Co., 1921).
30. Ibid.
31. Ibid.

task. Except for working out a schedule of meetings and other events, very little work was done regarding the selection of speakers because there was the generally accepted opinion that the Holy Spirit would inspire whoever was to preach without any advance planning. It was expected that the Lord would lead when the announced time for a meeting arrived. As might be expected with several hundred preachers present, problems arose when several felt led to speak at the same service. By 1918 it was felt expedient to name a speakers committee, which first functioned as a clearing house but later became a program planning committee selected by the General Ministerial Assembly.

Prior to 1920 there was no organized agency specifically designated for promoting general cooperative home mission work in the Church of God. When the Missionary Board was reorganized under the General Ministerial Assembly in 1917 it was assigned both home and foreign missionary work and was called the Board of Home and Foreign Missions of the Church of God. As the foreign work expanded people began to see that the two functions were very different in nature, and so the very next year the Missionary Board asked to be relieved of responsibility for the home work. In 1918 the General Ministerial Assembly gave its consent for this board to confine its work to foreign missionary fields alone.[32]

The assembly's action meant there was no systematic or cooperative home missionary effort. The need still existed and the burden for extending the work in the homeland and building up a stronger home base grew heavier on the hearts of some leaders. They could see great cities into which the message had not been taken at all. Some were particularly concerned about the vast territories in the United States where the witness of the movement was very weak, such as New England, the South, and the great regions of the West. Therefore, it seemed imperative that some national agency be created to carry on a strategized program of evangelism and home missions.

In June 1920 the Ministerial Assembly created a new agency known as the Board of Church Extension and Home Missions. This Board initially consisted of nine members chosen from different sections of the country and was thus intended to be representative of the entire church. In the words of a later leader, they were "men of vision and leadership, who would plan and direct the great program of cooperative evangelization and missionary

---

32. Minutes of the General Ministerial Assembly, June 21, 1918.

work at home."[33] The next year this Board was enlarged to fifteen members and incorporated as an Indiana not-for-profit religious organization.[34] Its original purposes were stated in the enabling motion: "…first to establish work at strategic points where there is no local agency sufficient to establish a work, a second to assist struggling congregations by lending them money for the erection of necessary church buildings."[35]

At its inception the Board was focused more on church extension than home missions. Immediately the Board began to function along these lines. The Benevolent Budget approved by the 1922 Assembly included $50,000 for church extension as well as $35,000 for the publishing work, $10,000 for Anderson Bible Training School, and $144,000 for foreign missions.[36] Each agency was responsible for soliciting their own funds; the budget was more a target than an assured amount.

The 1922 Assembly took some further steps in regularizing its own functions by providing for "a nominating committee of 15, who shall nominate a pulpit committee, a business committee on ordination, and a chairman and secretary for the General Ministerial Assembly."[37] Cautiously the Assembly built structures to enhance and strengthen the cooperative work of a movement that was expected to grow.

Throughout the early stages of the Assembly's development there was a latent hesitancy to allow the active choosing of individuals who were to hold various offices. Until 1921, the term *elect* really meant *ratify*. This was true both for the twenty-four members of the Gospel Trumpet Company and the fifteen members of the Missionary Board. When the first Board of Church Extension and Home Missions was chosen in 1920 the Assembly approved a committee of twenty-five to select the nine members, then the Assembly elected (ratified) the nine. However, by the following year the process of

---

33. Elver Adcock, *Our American Missions* (Anderson, IN: Board of Church Extension and Home Missions of the Church of God, [1934]), 23–24.

34. The first Board of Church Extension and Home Missions was composed of the following members: Earl Martin, Houston, Texas; L. W. Guilford, Los Angeles, California; A. T. Rowe, Akron, Indiana; J. T. Wilson, Anderson, Indiana; C. E. Brown, Detroit, Michigan; A. C. Harrison, Wichita, Kansas; R. R. Byrum, Anderson, Indiana; W. D. McCraw, Ashland, Kentucky; A. F. Gray, Clarkston, Washington. Wilson and Byrum served respectively as president and secretary-treasurer. These two men, along with H. A. Sherwood of Anderson, composed the first executive committee. Only three of these—Rowe, Wilson, and Byrum—were renamed when the Board was increased to fifteen members the following year. Lists are in *Yearbook of the Church of God*, 1921, 21, and *Yearbook of the Church of God*, 1922, 10.

35. Minutes of the General Ministerial Assembly, June 25, 1920.

36. Minutes of the General Ministerial Assembly, June 24, 1922.

37. Ibid., June 18, 1922.

electing from among nominees and for specific terms began taking root. Another result of this interest in home missions and evangelism was the formation of the Spanish Evangelical Association in the early spring of 1920 to "promote the work among Spanish-speaking people" and "to encourage the preparation of persons for service in connection with gospel work in the Spanish language."[38] The Spanish Evangelical Association brought into being another organization called the Spanish Literature Company. B. O. Bertelson was in charge of this work, and J. W. Byers was the editor of the monthly periodical *La Verdad Apostolica (The Apostolic Truth)*. The Evangelical Association was based in Anderson, and the Literature Company was located in Los Angeles, California. The officers and workers were D. W. Patterson, president; Bruce R. Corey, vice-president; B. O. Bertelson, secretary; H. H. Dillard, general manager and treasurer; J. W. Byers, editor; E. F. DuCummon; Myrl Byrum; M. F. Tafolla; and E. L. Martin.[39]

Christian education and Sunday schools represented yet another area of church life that called for the creation of a national agency. From its earliest days the Church of God movement generally was hostile toward Sunday school. This attitude, which took years to be fully changed, existed for several reasons. First, some saw the Sunday school plainly as against the gospel and the will of God. Second, some people feared that the Sunday schools might become a substitute for revivals. Third, "they were associated with the sects, and whatever represented sectarianism was to be discarded."[40] Fourth, the schools were "educational in their approach and thus long-range in their results. The pioneers were interested in accomplishing the most possible in the shortest time."[41] This latter attitude stemmed from their belief in Christ's imminent return. Another reason for the anti-Sunday school sentiment was the organizational structure associated with such programs. Early movement leaders did not believe in any form of organization that might hamper the proper callings and leadings of the Holy Spirit, and Sunday schools seemed to require elected officers and teachers.

In 1885 Warner wrote that the Sunday schools "as ordinarily conducted in Babylon, are schools of vanity, and hotbeds of pride and false religion. Let all saints keep themselves and children out of all such fashionable and

---

38. *Yearbook of the Church of God*, 1922, 14.
39. Ibid.
40. John W. V. Smith, "Mileposts of Multiplication," *Planning Creatively*, October 1956, 3.
41. Ibid.

worldly gatherings."[42] He added, however, that they were permissible for children and youth if all the teachers were holy elders who were willing to let the "Holy Spirit preside instead of a voted in superintendent."[43] Warner also stated that there was a great need for teaching the children. Out of this need Sunday schools began to spring up. In 1889 one article in the *Gospel Trumpet* reported that the "brethren write us from different localities stating that they have good Sabbath schools. Many more should be started."[44] Many more were started. By 1910 the International Uniform Lesson outlines were adopted, and quarterly lesson booklets were being printed by the Gospel Trumpet Company. (It was not until 1926, however, that the first graded materials were published.) In 1911 D. Otis Teasley published a book titled *How to Conduct a Sunday School* dealing with the philosophy and methods of what once had been labeled "child of Babylon," but now was welcomed as an instrument of God.

As the movement grew, the number of Sunday schools continued to increase and the need for promoting this aspect of God's work was gradually conceded. Six years after the organization of the General Ministerial Assembly, that body voted into existence the Board of Religious Education and Sunday Schools (more commonly called the Board of Sunday Schools and Religious Education). Elected on June 22, 1923, the Board was originally composed of R. L. Berry, O. A. Burgess, Nettie Berghouse, Jennie M. Byers, W. B. McCreary, Mrs. A. T. Rowe, Earl Martin, F. C. Blore, and Bessie Byrum.

The constitution and bylaws were approved just four days later with the following stated objectives:

> The objects of this board shall be the promotion of Religious Education. It may promote religious education generally, the establishing and conducting of Sunday schools, weekday schools and Daily Vacation Bible schools. It may seek to establish Sunday schools through its agents in congregations of the Church of God that have none and in other places where no such congregations exist. Also it may represent the religious education work of the Church of God in international conventions, fix

---

42. *Gospel Trumpet*, December 1, 1885. As quoted by John W. V. Smith, *Truth Marches On: A Brief Study of the History of the Church of God Reformation Movement* (Anderson, IN: Gospel Trumpet Co., 1956), 63–64.

43. Ibid.

44. Correspondence, *Gospel Trumpet*, June 15, 1884, 2.

Sunday school standards for those it represents, plan curricula for the various phases of religious education including teacher training, Sunday school, weekday church school, and Daily Vacation Bible School. It may issue certificates and diplomas in recognition of satisfactory completion of prescribed courses and for other work, and it may recommend the publication of such books, papers, quarterlies, and other literature needed for the aforementioned phases of religious education.[45]

Approximately five hundred Sunday schools existed in the Church of God movement at the time of the Board's creation. During its first years the Board chose to tackle the task of leadership training, mostly by qualified national leaders, congregation by congregation. However, in 1927 (the year Bessie Byrum became board president) the executive committee decided that the board "might be able to get various communities of the Church of God to go together and conduct teacher training classes. It was also thought that this would be good work for the state committees to carry on."[46] It was becoming clear that the large number of small congregations with limited financial and human resources meant it was impossible to do all this training from a national office. A shortage of funds and capable volunteers seriously limited the expansion of this training program in the early years.[47] Despite all the handicaps, Church of God Sunday schools were on the upswing. President Bessie Byrum wrote in 1928,

> It is encouraging to note the progress we are making in religious educa-tion. The Yearbook shows an increase the past year of nearly 9,000 pupils….The number of Daily Vacation Bible schools conducted last year was a half more than the previous year.
>
> The ministers are showing a marked increase of interest in the re-ligious educational phase of the work….There is an increasing sense on the part of teachers for the need of training….More than 500 are pursuing the Standard Training Course….We are eager to have more schools, bigger schools and more powerful schools.[48]

---

45. "Constitution of the Board of Sunday Schools and Religious Education of the Church of God," Article II, Minutes of the General Ministerial Assembly, June 23, 1923.

46. Minutes of the Board of Religious Education and Sunday Schools, June 14, 1929.

47. It would be almost another twenty years before the Board of Christian Education had sufficient budget for a full-time staff executive.

48. Bessie Byrum, "Report of the President of the Board of Sunday Schools and Religious Educa-tion," Minutes of the General Ministerial Assembly, June 1928.

Closely related to the field of religious education was youth work. Although many young people were involved in the early period of the movement's history there was no planned program for youth until the early 1920s when camp meeting programs included special meetings for young people.

In 1924 the first International Young Peoples' Convention was held during the Anderson Camp Meeting. This activity marked the beginning of a more diversified ministry in the movement. In 1927 a committee was chosen to study the church's program for youth, and finally, in 1929, the young people themselves voted to hold their convention away from Anderson and at a time other than camp meeting.

In 1925 the Constitution for the General Ministerial Assembly adopted in 1917 was replaced by a more developed constitution, and bylaws were added. In this action the structures that had been created were confirmed as good and necessary.

The twelve years from 1916 to 1928 represent a remarkable organizational evolution. In that brief time the tradition of the previous third of a century had been changed. An assembly had been organized, officers were elected, and boards and committees had been established to take care of the church's general corporate responsibilities. Perhaps an even greater change than the more sophisticated organization itself was the financial system made necessary by the budgets of these developing agencies. The power structure shifted from Holy Spirit leadership with only minimal informal organization to what was hoped to be Holy Spirit leadership with formal organization. By 1927 the general agencies were seeing the need to work together in the financial area instead of competing with each other, and when a proposal for a cooperative plan of fundraising was made most of them were ready to act upon it.

At that time there were five general church agencies that depended upon support from the churches to carry on their work. These agencies were the Missionary Board, Board of Church Extension and Home Missions, Board of Sunday Schools and Religious Education, the Gospel Trumpet Company, and the Anderson Bible School and Seminary. As early as 1923 R. L. Berry had suggested a joint meeting with the directors of the church agencies for the purpose of discussing the possibility of combining the benevolence askings into "one general budget."[49] Nothing was immediately done regarding

49. Phillips, *Miracle of Survival*, 191.

this suggestion. Each board continued to arrive at its own budget and bring it directly to the General Ministerial Assembly for ratification and then set about to raise that amount by soliciting the churches. The problems of such a system for both agencies and churches became increasingly apparent.

In June 1927 the five agencies voluntarily agreed on a plan for fundraising and budget making. The proposal was described as follows:

> According to this new plan a committee of ten are appointed in the following manner: each of the three boards and the School and Company appoints one of its own members to serve on this committee, and the other five are appointed from the church at large by the General Ministerial Assembly. To this committee each agency presents a budget estimate for the fiscal year, based on needs of the already existing work and extension prospects. The committee goes over these estimates and determines just what each budget shall be. Of course the action of the committee must be ratified by the General Ministerial Assembly.[50]

This breaking of the organizational barrier also had its effect on the local congregations. They also began incorporating and using committees, budgets, and voting procedures.

The General Ministerial Assembly's establishment of bureaucratic organization did nothing to interfere with local congregational autonomy. R. R. Byrum's *Problems of the Local Church* was written in 1926 and provided guidelines for leading a congregation to a more sophisticated system of church organization—a system considerably different from the traditional structure commonly followed in Church of God congregations prior to 1916. In it he discussed officers of the church, membership, budgeting, bylaws, business meetings, planning, erecting church buildings, pledging, offering envelopes, and how to conduct a church trial.

Breaking the organizational barrier was a controversial issue for many years because of a deep concern that the Holy Spirit's place in the church might be usurped by human rule. The twelve years from 1916–28 were marked by fears that the movement would develop denominational tendencies at the local level as well as nationally and internationally. While a new style of administration emerged for the movement and for the local congregations, the principle of the divine origin and governance of the church

---

50. *Yearbook of the Church of God*, 1928, 30.

remained. Warner's words were still sung with dignity and conviction in local churches and in camp meetings across the country as congregations lifted their voices to enthusiastically extol "The Church of God":

Church of God, thou spotless virgin,
Church of Christ, for whom he died,
Thou hast known no human founder,
Jesus bought thee for his bride.
Sanctified by God, the Father,
Built by Jesus Christ the Son,
Tempered by the Holy Spirit,
Like the holy Three in One.

God himself has set the members
In his body all complete,
Organized by Jesus only,
Oh, the union pure and sweet!
Church of God, the angels marvel
At the music of thy song;
Earth and hell in terror tremble,
As thy army moves along.

Church of God, in heaven written,
Thine the risen life of Christ;
And the treasures to thee given,
Never, never can be priced.
Far above this world's confusion,
Walking close by Jesus' side,
Leaning on his loving bosom,
In the church, his chosen bride.[51]

---

51. "Church of God," in H. A. Sherwood, comp., *Reformation Glory* (Anderson, IN: Gospel Trumpet Co., 1923), no. 33.

CHAPTER 11

REASSESSMENTS REGARDING METHODS AND MINISTRY (1917–1935)

The period that witnessed the changing climate of opinion about church organization also saw shifts in attitude toward other matters. Positions and practices that formerly had been negated came to be viewed in a different light, and the case against certain beliefs was opened for reevaluation. Early saints had rejected almost all sectarian church practices simply because of association with the sinful denominational system. Salaried preachers with seminary degrees, planned programs for meetings, fine organs with robed choirs and other practices were denounced as evil because they were both condoned and promoted by the sects. In the pure church all such things were to be avoided, and the faithful were warned against the temptation to let down the standard on any of these matters. These generally accepted procedures in denominational churches were judged to be expressions of sinful pride and otherwise evidence of an even more serious fault: they substituted human initiative and planning for the direct leadership of the Holy Spirit. However, between 1915 and 1935 many of these negative judgments were reexamined, and new attitudes and practices emerged—but not without considerable trauma.

At no point are changes more evident than in the area of ministerial training. D. S. Warner had not been opposed to education as such. He was a schoolteacher before his conversion, and had attended Oberlin College and Vermillion College. By the time of his conversion, he was better educated by far than most of his peers in western Ohio. As an Oberlin student he probably was acquainted with the standard programs of training for ministerial preparation even though he was not enrolled in the seminary. Despite this background much of Warner's early writing and preaching was antagonistic, if not inflammatory, toward formal ministerial education. Such is clearly seen in his 1884 article titled "The Devil's Preaching Factory":

Colleges are necessary to fit men for the work of the devil, and the business of this world, but instead of fitting men for God's work of saving souls, they (such as they are) are the devil's device to transform them into spiritual blindness, to do his work of soul-damning. They are but satan's playhouses.... The parents offer up their children as a sacrifice to parental and sectarian pride, the priests teach them for hire, and hell reaps the fruit of the whole business.[1]

Earlier, Warner had stated in response to a question from a reader that the "ability to talk the English language is all the education a soul needs to present Christ to dying sinners...."[2] He believed "no amount of education can make a minister of the Gospel."[3] It is clear that at this point in his ministry he was adamantly opposed to seminary training for ministers; it was both unnecessary and detrimental. On the surface this view seems inconsistent with his own experience. At a deeper level, however, he was faithful to his fundamental convictions. The negative emphasis on human training was one side of a coin, the other of which gave emphasis to Holy Spirit empowerment. Like many before him, Warner stressed the wisdom that comes from above rather than through book learning. Preaching should spring from a spiritual dynamic rather than a cognitive one. The qualification for ministry was not a seminary trained mind but God's divine call and preparation of the heart. In Warner's words, "The Holy Spirit of God gives both the saving word, the most faithful thought, and the most effectual 'mouth,' or language, to express it. For both preparation of the heart, and the answer of the tongue, are of God."[4]

Like church organization, formal ministerial training substituted human learning for the work of the Holy Spirit. Warner was also opposed to expensive college buildings, "hireling" professors, and the whole ecclesiastical network associated with the sectarian institutions. After a few years, however, his negative judgment in this regard softened. There is, however,

---

1. D. S. Warner, "The Devil's Preacher Factory," *Gospel Trumpet*, October 15, 1884, 3.
2. *Gospel Trumpet*, December 1, 1883, 1.
3. Ibid.
4. Warner, "Devil's Preacher Factory," 3.

no indication that his attitude changed regarding the work of the Holy Spirit in ministerial preparation.

In a very real sense Warner himself became a theological educator. He took an active personal interest in the training and care of younger, inexperienced workers. He frequently took them along on his evangelistic tours, in the process providing a model for the time-honored apprentice method of education. In 1895, however, Warner became burdened to formalize the educational process and provide a facility in Grand Junction for study "preparatory to labor in the vineyard of the Lord." In the fall of 1895 he wrote,

> "A few days ago our heart was stirred very much with the duty of making an effort in this direction. Last Lord's day we confessed our convictions, and a general impression has since then rested on the hearts of many of the brethren here that we ought to make a beginning of some kind. We have had a consultation before the Lord, and find all of one mind. And so we are safe in saying something will be done in this good work."[5]

Space was available for approximately twelve students, but not just anyone would be allowed to attend. Only those fully consecrated, dead to sin and particularly to "youthful lusts" were welcome. Furthermore, prospective students needed to exhibit a blameless life established in Christ. To instruct budding ministers, "the Lord will need about three teachers, who will divide the work into,

1st. Bible history and perhaps archeology.
2d. The critical study of the New Testament, and lectures on prophecy.
3d. Experimental and spiritual truth. It is also hoped that music and elocution will be added."[6]

"Subjective Bible Study"[7] was scheduled to begin on Thursday night, December 5, 1895, but Warner fell gravely ill, and the group of students did not meet. He died on December 12, and two weeks later the *Gospel Trumpet* announced:

---

5. D. S. Warner, "Instructions in the Bible," *Gospel Trumpet*, October 17, 1895, 2–3.
6. Ibid.
7. "The Saints' School," *Gospel Trumpet*, December 5, 1895, 2.

Some have asked if we have a theological school here. We answer, No. Neither do we expect to have. We have Bible readings and special faith meetings almost every evening which are wonderfully blessed of God by way of spiritual advancement and real soul food, and holiness is lifted up to the Bible standard.[8]

E. E. Byrum, the new editor, believed that a training center was inconsistent with the previous position. This is not to say, however, that Byrum was opposed to all forms of ministerial training. The Trumpet family home provided a rich atmosphere for Bible study and the cultivation of many ministerial skills. Moreover, the prevalent feeling in the years to follow was that young ministers should spend some time working in the company of an older, better established minister and "improve their gifts" under supervision—a reversion to Warner's apprentice method.

The communal-style living arrangement of the Trumpet family became the prototype for a national network of training centers. Other homes began to be organized, specializing in various types of ministry and outreach other than literature publication. These became known as *missionary homes*. They offered special opportunities for beginners in the ministry to work in a controlled setting under the supervision of well-established, experienced ministerial leaders. These homes offered food, clothing, shelter, and most importantly, training in ministry and an opportunity for experience in service for the participants in the various corps of volunteer workers. The missionary homes became one of the most common ways for new ministers to get started and were the forerunners of most of the church's colleges.

The development of missionary homes in the Church of God represented a shift from the predominantly rural focus of the earliest years and an awakened awareness of the growing importance of cities in American life. The homes became a unique Christian response to the great needs and opportunities placed before the church in the burgeoning urban centers in America at the turn of the century. The impetus for this type of ministry seems to have come out of Warner's reactions during a trip to the West Coast in 1892–1893. While in San Diego, California, he was made acutely aware of both the human distress crying out for ministry and the spiritual timeliness of evangelizing in concentrated population areas.[9] He developed a vision

---

8. *Gospel Trumpet*, December 26, 1895, 2.
9. Charles E. Brown, *When the Trumpet Sounded* (Anderson, IN: Gospel Trumpet Co., 1951), 357.

of the urgency of launching some kind of effort among the vilest of sinners, the greatest sufferers of hardship, and those least aware of the love of God.

The missionary home era in the Church of God covered a span of approximately three decades, beginning in the 1890s and continuing into the 1920s. Although each home had its own distinctive characteristics they all developed as large multi-purpose residences whose occupants engaged in rescue mission work, colportage, community service, evangelistic work, and hospitality for visiting ministers and missionaries. They operated on a faith basis; none of the workers was paid and expenses were covered by freewill gifts from the "saints" and other interested persons.

Exactly when the first missionary home was started cannot be determined. In early 1893 a Mrs. E. C. Dunham of Waterloo, Ontario, wrote of her work in the "Faith and Works Mission," but there seems to be no evidence that this mission was operated in the manner of the later homes.[10] Over a year later there was a report from "The Woman's Faith Home" in Danville, Illinois.[11] There is little likelihood that this operation would fit the later pattern either. Probably the earliest missionary home operation was the work of Jacob W. and Jennie Byers in San Diego, the same city where Warner's concern for city work was awakened. Even here not all the ingredients of the later pattern were present, but the method is clearly indicated. After Warner's departure there were numerous reports of what was being done there. A March 1893 account gave an outsider's description of the manner in which the Byerses were carrying on their evangelistic work:

> They go out on the street every evening and sing and pray and talk to the people, and by the time they get through they generally have a crowd around them, when they invite them into their hall for further services....Numbers are rescued from drunkenness and other vices....[12]

The San Diego mission ceased to function for a period of time, but a new home started in Oakland when the Byerses moved there in 1906.

Among the largest and most successful of the early missionary homes was the one in Chicago. Its beginning dates to January 8, 1895, when Gorham Tufts arrived in the city and two days later preached at the Open Door

---

10. *Gospel Trumpet*, April 20, 1893, 2.

11. *Gospel Trumpet*, November 15, 1894, 1.

12. Samuel Zook (as quoted from *Evangelical Visitor*, February 15, 1893), *Gospel Trumpet*, March 23, 1893, 2. Byers would later go to Oakland, California, and establish a missionary home there.

Mission at 396 Dearborn Street. This facility was soon turned over to him and a full-scale rescue mission operation was carried on in a large six-story building with other facilities nearby for industrial work; another building served as a home for the workers. It was a large enterprise. Tufts reported, "From January 1 to March 10, 1896, we have kept and fed 10,172 poor men and preached the gospel to them."[13] The mission moved several times, and the character of its work was modified considerably with the coming of George and Mary Cole in

Chicago Missionary Home. Beginning in 1892, Church of God leaders developed the missionary home as an element of their flying messenger evangelistic methods. Although some of the homes were located in large cities, they were not conceived as conventional urban missions. Missionary homes served as resting places for traveling evangelists and colporteurs, as well as early training centers for people called to the ministry. The home in Chicago was a major center of such activity.

1898 and Eugene A. Reardon a short time thereafter. Eventually they built their own facility in 1903–4 at 300 West Seventy-Fourth Street.

The Chicago home became a model for all the other missionary homes that were to develop. The rescue mission aspect of the work diminished and greater emphasis was placed on evangelism, literature distribution, teaching, and hospitality to traveling ministers and missionaries.[14] Such an extensive operation obviously required the enlistment of many people involved principally in temporal duties such as cooking, housekeeping, and building maintenance. However, even these people did some spiritual work. Spiritual workers were occupied in circulating books from the free library, which involved delivering the books to homes and picking them up later. Others distributed literature in house-to-house visitation. Still others were busy

---

13. *Gospel Trumpet*, March 19, 1896, 3.

14. Brown, *When the Trumpet Sounded*, 198–201. One cannot avoid noting the similarity between the Church of God missionary homes and the settlement house movement popularized by Jane Addams with her famous Hull House in Chicago, which had been established only a short time before in 1889. These houses also had multiple functions, serving as residences, schools, and activity centers. The obvious differences would be the religious factor and the communal living style of operation.

holding cottage prayer meetings, which were found to be a very convenient and effectual means of reaching people. Besides all this, the ministers were kept busy in pastoral work, visiting and praying for the sick, encouraging the people of God, and preaching at regular and special services. Besides the regular meetings at the chapel on the south side and a general gathering in the central part of the city on Sunday, there was also a German-language mission on the north side and an African-American mission on State Street. The Chicago home was among the first of the prominent missionary homes to get started and the last to close.[15] It later became the base for launching the first Church of God congregation in Chicago.

After 1900, the missionary home methodology for city work began to gain momentum. By late 1906 the *Gospel Trumpet* started running a list of such homes in each issue. The first list noted five locations: New York, Chicago, Kansas City, Oakland, and Portland.[16] Twelve years later, under a heading of "Abridged List," the number had increased to thirty.[17] This may well be near the greatest number of such homes operating at any one time. By 1920 the homes were no longer listed in the *Gospel Trumpet,* but their locations were included in the *Yearbook of the Church of God.*

Apparently not all of the attempts to start missionary homes were successful. In 1912 J. W. Phelps, who had a great concern for missions both domestic and foreign, felt the need to give some guidance regarding procedures, facilities, worker recruitment, and programs to be implemented. In a long article, he outlined the difficulties and opportunities for city work of this kind.[18] Among other requirements he pointed out the need for both spiritual and temporal workers, and made a special appeal for the latter. He pointed out that the spiritual workers were occupied with meetings, visitation, prayer for the sick, and need for study and preparation, and required freedom from household responsibilities. Consequently, individuals who would dedicate themselves to domestic work were encouraged to volunteer on the same basis as those carrying out the spiritual duties. Phelps noted that these functions would provide opportunity to exercise faith, forbearance, and self-denial and develop a strong spiritual character. It was a good way for an untrained person to learn to do spiritual work; Phelps cited one prominent leader who began as a missionary home janitor.

---

15. *Missionary Herald,* November 1910, 16.
16. *Gospel Trumpet,* November 15, 1906, 12.
17. *Gospel Trumpet,* July 18, 1918, 13.
18. J. W. Phelps, "Our Mission Field," *Gospel Trumpet,* April 25, 1912, 5–6.

Despite their similarities each of the missionary homes was distinctive, and many of them developed unique special ministries. For instance, the New York City home became the departure and return point for all the movement's trans-Atlantic travelers and missionaries. These sojourners often stayed for a while to assist in the city ministry. Under the capable leadership of individuals such as D. Otis Teasley, George P. Tasker, C. J. Blewitt, and Axchie A. Bolitho, workers developed a comprehensive program of meetings in various sections of the city and among the many immigrant groups in this great cosmopolitan "gate-

The New York Missionary Home. Because New York was a major port of embarkation for ocean travel, the New York home routinely hosted missionaries traveling to and from Europe and other foreign ports. Additionally, under the leadership of D. O. Teasley and with the assistance of George Tasker and A. D. Khan, the New York home started a Bible institute and a ministerial correspondence course.

way of the nation." The home sponsored three big events each year: a spring convention, a summer tent campaign during July and August, and a Christmas week convention. Most significantly, they developed an educational program for workers. The New York Bible Training School offered "exceptional opportunities for personal work, visitation and contact with all nationalities." By 1919 more than a dozen courses in biblical and doctrinal subjects were taught in regularly scheduled classes. The school also offered correspondence courses "covering the essential phases of religious instruction."[19] The New York correspondence course provided ministerial training for many, most notably the young A. F. Gray, who became the president of Pacific Bible College and author of a major theological textbook.

---

19. *Yearbook of the Church of God*, 1919, 229.

The missionary home in Oakland was begun by J. W. and Jennie Byers. First located at 721 Sixteenth Street, it was known as the Gospel Healing Home. Special emphasis was given to prayer for the sick, and many testimonies of healing were reported in a monthly publication, "Tidings of Healing." In 1906, shortly after the San Francisco earthquake and fire, another location was secured at 719 Fifty-Fourth Street and the program was broadened. Centrally located in the Bay cities and within sight of the Golden Gate, they found opportunity to minister to people of many nationalities as well as to devotees of a wide variety of sects and cults. They operated a free circulating library of about two hundred books and distributed many tracts and papers in a continuing visitation program. The home published a Japanese periodical called *The Pure Gospel* and distributed it on the docks as Asian ships arrived and departed. They found many people receptive to the message but also encountered a great deal of opposition.[20] Many young people got their start in gospel work in the Oakland missionary home, including John D. and Pearl Crose, who later served as missionaries for over a half century in the Far and Middle East.

The missionary home in St. Paul Park, Minnesota, was the center for the Scandinavian publishing work. In the fall of 1905, Thomas Nelson, O. T. Ring and others, purchased a two-story factory building on the banks of the Mississippi to accommodate an already functioning publishing enterprise. It was remodeled and fitted out as a printing plant, furnished with machinery—printing press, linotype, folder, stitcher, two job presses, two gasoline engines, and a stereotype outfit. From this facility a great deal of gospel literature in the Scandinavian languages was published. In 1910 there were approximately twenty workers in the home and office who devoted their entire time to the mission work, trusting the Lord to supply their needs. The home also served as a training center to prepare workers for even greater fields of labor and usefulness. Eventually this center became the St. Paul Bible Academy. Several students felt called to missionary work and later went to fill places of responsibility in foreign lands. The St. Paul Park home had a free literature fund from which they supplied missionaries and gospel workers with tracts, periodicals, and books for distribution. Through this fund they were able to respond to the many calls for Scandinavian-language literature, which came in the mail from both the United States and abroad. They published two papers, one weekly in Dano-Norwegian and a semimonthly in

---

20. "The Church of God Missionary Home, 719 54th St., Oakland, California," *Missionary Herald*, April 1910, 6.

Swedish. Aside from these papers, many tracts and books were printed, some of which were translated from the English literature published in Anderson, Indiana.[21] An old people's home similar to the one located in Anderson was also a part of the St. Paul Park operation. With accommodations for more than fifty people, they admitted applicants of all nationalities.

The missionary home in Spokane, Washington, was another characterized by distinctive ministries, particularly its training program for young people. In 1905, George W. Bailey returned to the United States from India, where he had served as a missionary for several years, and became pastor of the Church of God in Spokane. Within a few years he had gathered a corps of workers to visit prospective converts, distribute literature, and help in the Sunday school. Most lived in a home provided by Bailey. For the workers' benefit, he began holding classes in music, Bible geography, Bible history, and similar subjects to help them in their ministries. By 1913–14 the missionary home had developed into an established school known as the Spokane Bible Institute. The student body consisted of forty students, and the school was supported by the ministers of the Pacific Northwest District of the Church of God.

Ministerial preparation was addressed in a variety of special training sessions throughout most of the decade. In addition to the Spokane Bible Institute, a ten-day training session for gospel workers was held in 1914 on the campgrounds at Edmonds, Washington. Courses included homiletics, pastoral methods, missions, Bible geography and history, music, English, speech, and lectures on the Book of Revelation. The institute was directed by E. G. Masters, who was assisted by Bailey, O. A. Burgess, and A. F. Gray. The same type of gospel workers' institute was also held the following year. In 1916, a similar institute was held following the Colfax camp meeting. In 1917 all these institutes were cancelled because the men were serving in the armed forces in World War I. After the war Gray held a school at Clarkston, Washington, for gospel workers.

In 1920, the Spokane Bible Institute reorganized and moved to Boise, Idaho. The school was then renamed Pacific Bible Institute. A. F. Gray was appointed the principal, assisted by O. A. Roush. In 1922, the ministers who supported the school decided to move it to Seattle, Washington. At this point, due to the lack of adequate facilities and a small enrollment the Pacific Bible Institute was forced to close. The desire for a Church of

---

21. "Scandinavian Publishing Work," *Missionary Herald*, May 1910, 11–12. Also *Yearbook of the Church of God*, 1919, 231.

Kansas City Training School 1919   Stultz Digital

Kansas City Training School Students, 1919. Between 1910 and 1917, four Bible institutes were founded at missionary homes: New York, Spokane, Kansas City, and Anderson. The Spokane institute was the precursor to Pacific Bible College. Although the New York institute developed a correspondence program, it soon closed, as did the Kansas City institute, in favor of the more centrally located Anderson Bible Training School, the last of the four schools to be started.

God training school in the Northwest did not die, however. In 1935 the ministers of that district decided to reopen the school. After much work, the needed funds were raised and plans were developed. The old missionary home building in Spokane was repurchased, and early in 1937 Pacific Bible College was incorporated. Fourteen students were admitted the first year with two faculty members, A. F. Gray and Daisy V. Maiden. In 1940, the school moved to Portland, Oregon.[22]

The missionary home in Kansas City, Missouri, was another that rather quickly developed into a center for training young people in gospel work. James B. Peterman was superintendent of the home and assumed charge of the developing training school. They declared their program to be "A Training School for Young Men and Women Who Feel the Call of God to the Spiritual Work."[23] Course offerings included a synthetic Bible course, doctrines of the Bible, rudiments of music, voice culture, homiletics, sermonizing, grammar and rhetoric. The *Yearbook* profile indicated:

22. Brown, *When The Trumpet Sounded*, 382–83.
23. *Yearbook of the Church of God*, 1919, 230.

The strength of this school lies in its ability to develop the students, to bring out what is in them, to fit them to know themselves and to fill a place in the church.

An immense advantage is the field of labor, where each student finds plenty of work to develop his natural abilities, under competent and sympathetic supervision.[24]

The school's stated plan was to develop the person, teach doctrine clearly, encourage spirituality, and let the worker learn by doing. It helped the students learn the theoretical and then apply it in practical ways. Students were given spiritual work that varied according to their ability. Such work as visitation, mission work, cottage meetings, and Sunday school were among the opportunities.

The school was located in a house that could accommodate up to twenty-five students. Like the New York school correspondence courses were offered in such areas as Bible history, Old and New Testament studies, Jewish institutions, training for service, and geography.[25]

While the missionary home movement was gaining popularity in most circles, not everyone favored the idea of starting a home in every city. As early as 1907, H. M. Riggle wrote an article in which he discouraged this method of ministry:

Sometimes there is a tendency in some to fall in line and pattern after others. The thing spreads till nearly everybody becomes affected. Then the Spirit of God has to call a halt. Faith missionary homes are all right and a good thing. But because they are needed and a success in New York City, Chicago or Kansas City, is no reason to suppose that God wants all his ministers to locate in some city and start a missionary home.[26]

Riggle objected to erecting a building before a congregation was established because it could easily end up as a useless effort. He believed the congregation's work should be fairly well established first. There are hints that Riggle still favored the idea of a flying ministry as he continued, "The

---

24. Ibid.
25. Ibid.
26. H. M. Riggle, "Faith Missionary," *Gospel Trumpet*, January 3, 1907, 9.

Lord has called some to take charge of and settle down to city work, but…
he has not called all to it, but wants a host of ministers to go 'to and fro'
and scatter the present truth in hamlets, villages, country places, as well as
cities."[27]

In 1908 Riggle repeated his concern, this time more extensively in a
two-week series of articles. In the first he wrote:

> Of late, there has been a craze for faith homes in many different towns
> and cities. The time has come when the Spirit of God must call a halt.…
> There is positively no need further to burden the church financially,
> by erecting a host of so-called "faith homes," "training homes," etc. in
> towns and cities all over this land.[28]

Riggle objected to the creation of more homes on several grounds. They
diverted money that could have been better spent for foreign missions.
Homes concentrated ministers in limited geographical centers, limiting the
spread of the message.[29] Moreover, the denominations had training schools,
and Riggle also expressed reservations about these homes as a vehicle for
training ministers.

> The Lord has never got many Holy Ghost ministers out of these places.
> I have carefully watched to see how many real efficient gospel ministers
> are raised up in such homes, and I find them very few.[30]

Known as the "Boy Preacher of the Reformation," Riggle had a marked
preference for revivals as the place for young ministers to learn their craft.
Revivals in the rural countryside remained his favorite venue.[31]

Despite Riggle's objections, the trend still held steady. Some missionary
homes did close, but many more opened. A composite of all published lists
shows a total of at least forty-five homes in operation at some time during
the three decades of their popularity. (See table 2.)

---

27. Ibid.
28. H. M. Riggle, "Faith Homes," *Gospel Trumpet*, December 17, 1908, 10.
29. Ibid.
30. H. M. Riggle, "Faith Homes: Article II," *Gospel Trumpet*, December 24, 1908, 10.
31. Ibid.

TABLE 2: MISSIONARY HOMES

City	Address	Principal Leaders
Akron, Ohio	Church of God Chapel Second Ave. & Chittenden St.	Calvin B. Hines D. T. Koch
Baltimore, Maryland	Hall 211 S. Highland Ave.	W. D. McCraw Lottie F. Charles
Bangor, Maine	Church of God Mission 54 Main St.	J. P. Anderson
Bellaire, Ohio	4452 Noble St.	C. O. Dodge
Bessemer, Alabama	Mission Home of the Church of God 1710 Arlington Ave.	D. O. Teasley
Boston, Massachusetts	Church of God Mission 14 Hanover Street	G. W. Doyle
	Mission 70 Humphreys St.	R. R. Byrum
Chicago, Illinois	Faith Missionary Home 400 W. 74th St.	G. L. Cole E. A. Reardon
Cleveland, Ohio	Church of God Meeting Place Auburn Ave. & 25th St.	J. N. Worden C. A. Warnock
Denver, Colorado	Church of God Chapel 3626 West 32nd Ave. (Later address: 2459 West 38th)	T. A. Phillips H. A. Brooks C. H. Tubbs
Detroit, Michigan	Church of God Mission Benitea & Goethe Ave.	Charles E. Brown
El Paso, Texas	601 S. Oregon St.	B. F. Elliott
Flint, Michigan	Chapel Mabel & Minnesota Aves.	Leroy Sheldon

Fort Wayne, Indiana	709 Home Ave.	C. E. & Nora Hunter
Grand Forks, North Dakota	Church of God Chapel Second Ave. & Cottonwood St.	A. G. Ahrendt
Houston, Texas	Bishop St. & Fletcher Ave.	S. W. Joiner Earl Martin
Indianapolis, Indiana	Northside Chapel 1240 Roache St.	W. H. Oldham
	Westside Chapel Ray & Warren St.	W. H. Oldham
Kalamazoo, Michigan	Church of God Chapel 310 West Ransom St.	William Hartman
Kansas City, Missouri	6241 Lee St.	James B. Peterman H. A. Swecker
Lansing, Michigan	Church of God Mission South St. Chapel	C. S. Sisler
Los Angeles, California	1121 Migonette St.	O. A. Chapman Alvin Ellison L.W. Guilford
Louisville, Kentucky	Chapel Queen & Central Aves.	Emma A. Meyers
Martins Ferry, Ohio	1019 Zane St.	C. O. Dodge
Minneapolis, Minnesota	Church of God Faith Home 521½ Cedar Ave.	E. G. Masters
	Charity Mission 205 Cedar Ave.	E. G. Masters

New York, New York	2450 Grand Ave.	D. O. Teasley G. P. Tasker C. J. Blewitt
Oklahoma City, Oklahoma	Missionary Home Capitol Hill	A. L. Hutton A. B. Stanberry
Oakland, California	719 54th St.	J. W. Byers
Philadelphia, Pennsylvania	Allegheny Ave. & Cedar St.	J. Grant Anderson
	Church of God Meeting Place 3005 Frankford Ave.	John. C. Blaney
	Church of God Meeting Place (German) 121 E. Allegheny Ave.	Adolph Ast
Pittsburgh, Pennsylvania	Church of God Missionary Home ("colored") 149 Julius St.	R. J. Smith
Portland, Oregon	430 Hawthorne Ave.	G. T. Neal
	361 Failing St. & Garfield Ave.	Harry & Hazel G. Neal
Roswell, New Mexico		Willis M. Brown
St. Joseph, Michigan	Church of God Faith Home (German & English)	August F. Schmitz David Koroch

St. Louis, Missouri	Church of God Mission and Home 2939 Olive St.	P. O. Purcell Merton M. Merica
St. Paul Park, Minnesota	Evangeli Basun Pub. Co.	Thomas Nelson
San Diego, California	Chapel 537 13th St.	W. A. Warner
Seattle, Washington	3906 Woodland Park Ave.	James Bamford Simon Decker James R. Tallen S. W. Woods
South Bend, Indiana	Church of God Chapel Harrison & Lindsey Sts.	Otis Austin
Springfield, Missouri	845 N. Grant St.	W. J. Henry
Springfield, Ohio	Chapel 1227 Maiden Lane	C. E. Byers
Spokane, Washington	Church of God Chapel E. 1101 Olive Ave.	G. W. Bailey
Tacoma, Washington	Church of God Mission 2501 Tacoma Ave.	William Strong
	Missionary Home 2510 S. G St.	William Strong
Toledo, Ohio		J. N. Worden
Wichita, Kansas	Mission Chapel Wabash & 12th St.	A. C. Harrison

The training of young people became a standard feature of almost all of the missionary homes. The promise of an opportunity for self-improvement undoubtedly was a strong inducement, along with the challenge to service, for the enlistment of capable and dedicated young workers. In some locations, such as Spokane and Kansas City, the training school superseded other aspects of the work and this was the only aspect that continued. The development of institutes at several homes indicates that the movement's earlier aversion to formalized training for religious service was diminishing. The missionary homes provided a temporary measure for those who desired such training.

By the early 1920s the era of missionary homes began to wane as some of their major functions began to be carried out by other means. As solid congregations were established in the various cities, it became apparent that the ministry in that location could best be handled through resident members rather than by visiting workers. The hospitality service for going and returning missionaries became increasingly the responsibility of the Missionary Board. Probably the most significant factor in the decline of missionary homes, however, was the beginning in 1917 of a centrally located and more prestigious training school in Anderson, Indiana, under the auspices of the general manager of the Gospel Trumpet Company.

The idea of a Bible training school in Anderson was a long time in process and developed more slowly than in other places already noted. In fact the school at Anderson was the last of four such schools to be founded between 1910 and 1917. The Gospel Trumpet family arrangement, however, did include training as one aspect of its program, but not religious training. Even after Warner's dream of a Bible school in the Trumpet Home in Grand Junction had been aborted there were continuing classes in skills such as penmanship, spelling, shorthand, and other subjects. At Moundsville, George Tasker taught a class on the Bible that inspired young Russell Byrum to further biblical and theological study. Then in late 1909 a "Missionary Bible Class" was formed in Anderson, apparently without any direct sponsorship by the Gospel Trumpet Company, but including as many workers as wished to attend. The first class, "Outline of Bible Geography," enjoyed an enrollment of seventy students.[32] Other classes were projected. This was at least a beginning of a shift in attitude toward formal religious education for leaders in the church.

In 1912 an article by H. A. Brooks with the surprising title "Advantages and Value of Education" appeared in the *Gospel Trumpet*. Brooks responded

---

32. "A Missionary Bible Class," *Missionary Herald*, February 1910, 8.

to current arguments against education in the light of obvious positive values of specialized training. He concluded:

> Men and women upon whom God lays his hand for the ministry in their youth must be public speakers, singers, readers, and writers all the days of their life. Both God and man require this duty of them. They should qualify themselves to meet ably every obligation and to fulfill properly each duty required of them in their calling.[33]

Brooks' article set a new tone. In 1917 a regular column in the *Gospel Trumpet* known as Observation of Our Times included in at least two issues favorable statements concerning education. One of the articles, titled "Girl Student and Modern Dress," said, "Ideals gained in high school or college influence our lives long after we have quit the classroom, and it is through teaching that most reforms are brought about."[34] Another article stated, "Our Schools should not be the means of creating wrong ideals concerning honest toil, but should help us to do our work more intelligently."[35] The clearest illustration of changing attitudes occurred in November 1917, just one month after the formal start of a new venture, the Spiritual Workers Training School at Anderson. An article by Robert L. Berry appeared in the *Gospel Trumpet* under the unlikely title, "Go to School." He counseled potential gospel workers, "My advice to all such is 'Go to school.' There is no logic nor reason in the idea that uneducated persons are more spiritual than educated ones."[36]

James Turner Wilson, Gospel Trumpet Company general manager, conceived the idea of a company-sponsored Bible school at Anderson. Interest in education was increasing across the country, and a very adequate facility for a school in Anderson became available in the summer of 1917. The Gospel Trumpet Company had decided to discontinue the communal living arrangement and began paying salaries and wages to its workers. This meant the company was no longer obligated to provide a home for members of the Gospel Trumpet family. Those who desired to continue in the Trumpet Home could do so by paying rent and board, but they were

---

33. H. A. Brooks, "Advantages and Value of Education," *Gospel Trumpet*, June 20, 1912, 4–5.
34. Observation of Our Times, *Gospel Trumpet*, January 11, 1917, 16.
35. Observation of Our Times, *Gospel Trumpet*, February 8, 1917, 16.
36. Robert L. Berry, "Go to School," *Gospel Trumpet*, November 1, 1917, 8.

not required to reside there. Additionally, most of the personal services once provided were discontinued. It was soon evident that the changes would make possible a different type of facility, and Wilson had a proposal.[37] Well aware of the interest in training, both on the part of young people and also of many ministers concerned about the need for more capable leaders, Wilson prevailed on the members of the Gospel Trumpet Company to name a managing committee to launch a school. Those selected were J. T. Wilson, chairperson; H. A. Sherwood, secretary; J. E. Campbell; R. R. Byrum; and F. G. Smith, with Wilson named principal. The first faculty consisted of: Henry C. Clausen, Mabel Helms, Russell R. Byrum, Bessie L. Byrum, and H. A. Sherwood. F. G. Smith, D. O. Teasley, and E. A. Reardon came in for occasional lectures. Classes began on October 2, 1917.[38]

The first program was intended to provide practical training for all varieties of gospel work. At Wilson's request the curriculum was designed by Russell R. Byrum, who had examined the programs of many other schools. Courses of study included Bible, English, history, music, practical theology, public speaking, and missions. Students who wished simply to enrich their knowledge of these subjects were not refused admission because of a lack of a definite call to Christian service. The school declared its express purpose to be the providing of instruction for those who had been divinely called to be ministers, missionaries, Sunday school superintendents or teachers, and song leaders. To meet this variety of callings Byrum designed a two-year program.[39]

Wilson and the school's early leaders also believed the school could serve an additional purpose. They saw the fledgling institution as a means of introducing the movement to those outsiders who were interested. They wrote: "There are many honest-hearted people who come to us from other religious bodies and are anxious to become better acquainted with the truth revealed in this last reformation."[40]

In its first few years the school bore little resemblance to a college. About fifty part-time students were taught by five teachers, most of whom were part time, and none with the academic training to qualify them as advanced instructors. Like most of their students, the faculty spent the majority of their time working for the Gospel Trumpet Company. Classes convened in the

---

37. First Annual Catalog of the Anderson Bible Training School, 1917–1918.
38. Ibid.
39. Ibid.
40. Ibid.

Trumpet Home. Dormitory rooms were in the same building directly above the classrooms. The Home was on the way to becoming Old Main.

Finances were a problem from the very beginning, not so much for the students as for the sponsoring institution. Tuition as such was not charged until 1925, except for private music lessons. In the beginning, furnished rooms could be had for $1.50 a week and meals were $3.00 a week. Economically-minded students could attend school for a full year for about $180.00.[41] With these meager sources the school closed its first year in the red and had to be subsidized by the Gospel Trumpet Company.

Despite the school's inauspicious beginnings, the enthusiasm of its first students compensated for many deficiencies. Receiving little recognition for their work and falling under the immediate suspicion of many movement leaders because they had deliberately enrolled in a school, the first students pursued their studies with remarkable dedication. In the midst of considerable controversy and heated discussion, they persisted in their pursuit of something they saw as essential to their growth as ministers and leaders in the church. A report near the conclusion of the first term indicated that even though a number of students were called out because of the war the majority "continued to the end, and it seemed that their interest did not flag during the entire term. In fact, the last of the term seemed to be the best, in some respects."[42]

After a full year of operation the church still had misgivings about the Bible Training School. The 1918 General Ministerial Assembly raised questions about the appropriateness of sponsoring such a school. A three-person

Russell R. Byrum (1889–1980), educator and theologian. While on the publication staff of the *Gospel Trumpet*, Byrum began offering courses at Anderson College. Eventually, he left the publishing house to teach theology. His book *Christian Theology* (1925) was the first systematic theology published by a Church of God writer. In 1929, Byrum was tried for heresy but acquitted of all charges. He nevertheless resigned his faculty appointment and went into the construction business.

41. Ibid.
42. News Note, *Gospel Trumpet*, June 6, 1918, 15.

committee, consisting of H. M. Riggle, J. C. Blaney and F. G. Smith, was appointed to define the function and scope of the new venture.[43] The committee reported their belief that the school should be kept within certain bounds: (1) attending it should not be made a requirement for recognition of young ministers; (2) the school should not replace other training schools of the church; (3) students should have the freedom to choose their own course of study; (4) no diplomas or degrees should be given; and (5) training should include more than intellectual development, namely personal enrichment in spirituality, gifts of the Spirit, and faith. The General Assembly accepted this report.[44]

Wilson's role as principal was over and above his regular responsibilities as general manager of the Gospel Trumpet Company. The position entailed many problems, some relating to the war economy and others to the transition in publishing house operations. At one point Wilson urged Russell Byrum to become principal, but Byrum never felt led to take on this responsibility. Instead Byrum suggested to Wilson that he ask young John A. Morrison to fill the position.[45] At the time Morrison was pastor of a small Church of God congregation in Delta, Colorado. He had been writing for the *Trumpet*, and Byrum, as managing editor, recognized Morrison's potential. Wilson contacted Morrison and invited him to Anderson. He accepted and joined the faculty as a teacher and assistant to Wilson.

Morrison began his first year at Anderson Bible Training School in October of 1919. He did not find a very promising situation. Prior to his arrival the school had suffered the loss of several students who were drafted into military service because of the growing American involvement in World War I. Severe financial problems continued, and an influenza epidemic in the fall of 1918 had closed the school for a time by order of the Anderson Board of Health. Wilson and Byrum kept the school alive, however, and as assistant principal Morrison was ready to share in the responsibility of helping move the school toward stability. He became principal in 1923, and in 1925 he became the school's first president.[46]

Upon assuming the principalship, Morrison began making changes. In 1923 he drafted a resolution to lift the ban on diplomas, but he experienced

43. Minutes of the General Ministerial Assembly, 1918.
44. Ibid.
45. Russell R. Byrum, "The Byrum Family," manuscript in the Anderson University and Church of God Archives.
46. John A. Morrison, *As the River Flows* (Anderson, IN: Anderson College Press, 1962), 142–46.

difficulties even in getting the resolution before the General Ministerial Assembly. Seeking out E. A. Reardon, the highly respected pastor of Park Place Church in Anderson, he persuaded him to present the resolution. Without the expected avalanche of opposition the vote was overwhelmingly positive. Granting diplomas was made retroactive so that even the earliest graduates had something to show for their achievement.[47] In 1925 the name of the institution was changed from Anderson Bible Training School to Anderson Bible School and Seminary. In that same year the school separated from the Gospel Trumpet Company, and was governed by trustees elected by the General Ministerial Assembly. The school's first executive committee consisted of J. A. Morrison, chairperson; Russell Olt, secretary; R. R. Byrum; E. A. Reardon; and Oscar J. Flynt. The board of trustees consisted of J. T. Wilson, chairperson; H. A. Sherwood, secretary; A. F. Gray; Earl Martin; Mrs. F. G. Smith; R. L. Berry; S. P. Dunn; R. R. Byrum; L. W. Guilford; Walker Wright; J. A. Morrison; O. A. Burgess; A. T. Rowe; Anna G. Koglin; and Russell Olt.[48]

After 1925 the pace and significance of change at the college grew. When school opened in October 1925 Russell Olt, formerly of Wilmington College in Ohio, was the new dean. In the same year Russell Byrum's *Christian Theology* was published. F. G. Smith had been a great help to Byrum in writing this volume for use in the college. Then in 1928 the General Ministerial Assembly authorized the school to offer a liberal arts program. Many assembly members were deeply opposed to this move, believing that the church had no business operating a school except for ministerial

Courtesy of Anderson University and Church of God Archives

S. P. Dunn (1881–1959), pastor. Born in Louisiana, Dunn attended Leland University in New Orleans. Ordained to the ministry of the Church of God in 1913, he came to Chicago in 1920 to take the pastorate of the congregation that became Langley Avenue Church of God. Dunn served on the Board of Church Extension and Home Missions and was also an Anderson College trustee. Dunn Hall on the Anderson University campus honors his memory.

47. Ibid., 147–50.
48. *Yearbook of the Church of God*, 1926, 27.

training. Morrison later described this opposition: "They yelled to high heaven that the church was selling out to the world. They wrote denunciatory letters, and passed red-hot resolutions, and prayed vehemently that the Lord would shut the flood gates of 'worldliness.'"[49] Reflecting the approved change in the curriculum, in February 1929 the name of the school changed again, this time to Anderson College and Theological Seminary.

Approval by the General Ministerial Assembly, however, did not eliminate all opposition to church sponsorship of a liberal arts college. Near the middle of 1929, Anderson College and Theological Seminary became the focal point for several theological differences that had been increasingly apparent in the movement for several years. Debate on some of these issues resulted in a direct challenge to faculty member R. R. Byrum in 1929, and some of the controversial points resurfaced as key issues five years later in the General Ministerial Assembly of 1934. In one sense the two events are separate and unrelated, but the theological issues existing at the time were implicated in each.[50]

Many Church of God leaders were shifting away from earlier teaching regarding the Book of Revelation. The earlier writings (e.g., *The Cleansing of the Sanctuary* by Warner and Riggle, Schell's *The Biblical Trace of the Church,* Riggle's *The Kingdom of God and One Thousand Years' Reign,* F. G. Smith's *What the Bible Teaches* and *The Revelation Explained*) had portrayed the Church of God reformation movement as a fulfillment of biblical prophecy. The Roman Catholic Church was identified as the "beast" and Protestant denominational churches were labeled as the daughters of "mystery of mysteries, Babylon, Mother of Harlots." Using a year-for-a-day formula to interpret symbolism, the year 1880 was identified as the prophetic date of the last reformation. However, Morrison had openly told F. G. Smith he did not agree with the positions set forth in Smith's 1919 book, *The Last Reformation.* Furthermore, regarding the year-for-a-day formula, R. R. Byrum had told his classes that this "interpretation cannot be proved true."[51] Others in the movement also questioned the church historical interpretive method. As a possible alternative, Byrum presented the position of A. T. Robertson of Southern Baptist Theological Seminary, a viewpoint

---

49. Morrison, *As the River Flows,* 154.

50. For a detailed account of one side of this period of conflict see Ibid., 163–82, and Robert H. Reardon, *The Early Morning Light* (Anderson, IN: Warner Press, 1979), 49–75. The "other side," being unsuccessful, has not been so adequately analyzed and reported.

51. R. R. Byrum, "The Byrum Family," 17.

far different from the position held in the earlier writings of the Church of God. R. R. Byrum also offered his students a basis for the doctrine of Christian unity different from that expressed in earlier writings.[52] His approach was founded primarily in the Gospels and Epistles and did not rely on the movement's traditional interpretation of the Book of Revelation. This alternative produced a different context for understanding and preaching the central doctrine of Christian unity.

Earlier writers of the movement used Scripture to buttress their understanding of the end-time role of the church. Robertson started with the Scripture text itself, delving into the root meaning of biblical terms, seeking to understand how early Christians had used these words to engage with the secular thinkers of their day. This was also Byrum's approach.[53]

In the spring of 1929 Byrum preached a sermon expounding his concept of unity at the meeting of the Indiana Ministerial Assembly held in Anderson. He declared:

> Few thinkers among us at present expect all true Christians to come to us, or to come into an operative unity with us as we as a group are with one another. Some still try to hold that position or shrink from recognizing that they no longer hold that narrow theory, because it would be unorthodox, and seems to them to be a surrender of the Bible doctrine of unity. Such brethren need to find a truer ground for unity.[54]

Numerous ministers took exception to Byrum's position. A complaint was filed complaining that Byrum's teaching was out of harmony with the reformation movement. His sermon on Christian unity was duplicated and sent to a number of ministers across the country by President Morrison with a request that they offer their opinions. Byrum's position was generally perceived as being out of harmony with past teaching, but many were of the opinion that the old view was far too narrow and preferred Byrum's viewpoint. Others had strong reservations about his views and expressed hope that he would conform to "standard" teaching. Another charge against Byrum was his reported statement that a person's salvation

---

52. R. R. Byrum "Christian Unity," duplicated paper presenting a position on unity and sent to various ministers in the movement in 1929.

53. Merle D. Strege, *I Saw the Church: The Life of the Church of God Told Theologically* (Anderson, IN: Warner Press, 2002) 156–58.

54. Byrum, "Christian Unity," 3.

did not depend on whether or not he could remember exactly when it occurred.[55]

Byrum's critics demanded a hearing to determine the validity of charges of heresy concerning his teaching. The college consented to conduct a meeting and hear testimony on both sides, with Byrum himself being given opportunity to defend himself. The event had the atmosphere and procedure of a courtroom. Three college trustees and a panel of fifteen ministers served as judges. After several days of hearings the ministerial panel, though not unanimously, supported Byrum and exonerated him of any charge of heresy. The next morning, however, the trustees produced a statement of belief that they proposed to ask all faculty members to sign. The trustees aimed to rebut criticism of the college, but Byrum thought such a statement would limit thought."[56] Since he saw himself as the cause of all the furor he felt the simplest solution was for him to resign. Somewhat to his surprise and J. A. Morrison's later regret,[57] the president accepted Byrum's resignation, and Byrum returned to the building trade he had learned from his father as a youth. Byrum later said, "Some might say I made a mistake. That could be. But there had been no anger or hate on my part. My feelings were only of much sadness at the loss of the fellowship of practically all of my best friends of a lifetime....But we survive these things."[58]

Byrum's departure in 1929 slowed but did not reverse the tide of criticism of Anderson College and Theological Seminary. Burning theological questions remained, and the liberal arts curriculum was a continuing point of disagreement. Opposing alignments had been drawn in the Byrum affair, and both sides actively fortified their positions and sought support. The first showdown came in 1930, when F. G. Smith's term as editor in chief for Gospel Trumpet Company expired and he sought reelection. Smith had opposed Byrum's openness to other interpretations of the Book of Revelation, since he believed the historic teachings of the movement were being challenged. Smith's opposition to Byrum and his views made him an adversary of the college. In return, college supporters opposed Smith and sought to prevent his reelection to the editorship. Their efforts were successful. After testing other possible candidates, the company named Charles E. Brown as editor, and he was ratified by the General Ministerial Assembly.

---

55. Reardon, *Early Morning Light*, 58.
56. R. R. Byrum, "The Byrum Family."
57. Ibid., and a reported oral statement by J. A. Morrison.
58. Ibid.

Smith may have been out of office, but he was not out of the picture. He found a new base for both ministry and influence as pastor of McKinley Avenue Church in Akron, Ohio.

The next real test came in 1934 when John Morrison's term as college president expired and he sought reelection. In the years since Smith's departure, opponents of a church-sponsored liberal arts college and of reported liberal teaching in college classes teamed up to force change. In 1933 the Ohio Ministerial Assembly passed resolutions and circulated them nationally that were critical of the content of certain courses and called for a return to a Bible training school program. A succession of similar resolutions followed from the other state assemblies. The college administration responded with mailings, a publication called *The Broadcaster*, and numerous appearances by college personnel at meetings all across the country. When the crucial vote came in June 1934, college trustees renamed Morrison as president. Now everything

John A. Morrison (1893–1965), educator. In 1919, Morrison answered J. T. Wilson's call to join the faculty of Anderson Bible Training School as a teacher and assistant principal. In 1923, Morrison became principal and two years later president of Anderson Bible School and Seminary. During his thirty-five-year tenure, the school grew from little more than a department of the Gospel Trumpet Company into a fully accredited liberal arts college and graduate seminary.

rested on his ratification by the General Ministerial Assembly. With a majority vote required, Morrison's position was retained by a margin of only thirteen votes. Despite the intensity of the conflict and the closeness of the vote, the breach healed quickly. In the process of this monumental internal debate the movement had worked its way through a very great crisis and had survived.

By 1934 the battle for education was mostly over, won by its proponents. Other educational institutions had appeared—and some disappeared—but not because of widespread opposition. Two schools began and closed near the time of the Great Depression. The first was a preparatory boarding school known as Winchester Academy. About ten years after Anderson Bible Training School was founded, a boarding school for Christian students was started in Winchester, Kentucky. W. H. Hunt had conceived the project in 1926, and one year later classes were first held for grades one through twelve in facilities on the Winchester campgrounds.

Academy courses were taught by "saved and sanctified teachers in full harmony with the truths of this present reformation."[59] The school was fully accredited in Kentucky, and most of the teachers held degrees from some of the best colleges of that time. Proponents of the school, such as Hunt and later W. T. Wallace and Z. A. Horton, wanted to provide both a good educational and spiritual environment for young students. Academy founders believed a child should develop spiritually as well as physically and mentally. They urged, "All parents and guardians seeking to protect their children at this critical age of their lives will do well to investigate the merits of this worthy school."[60] The slogan of the academy was "Where the Bible is taught." This boarding school was an ambitious project and the financial needs were great. Even though the school itself was a financial struggle from the start, the cost for students was kept at a modest $200 per year, thus enabling people of lower income to send their children to the school. Enrollment climbed to 136 by the second year, but the popularity of the school could not counterbalance the general economic crisis. The Great Depression was the greatest single factor in the school's closure in 1930.

In the American Southwest another school, an avowedly liberal arts university, was launched at about the same time as Winchester Academy. The idea for a Christian college in the Southwest had been discussed at the Texas State Camp Meeting in Gorman, Texas, in August 1927. The following year ministers from Texas, Oklahoma, and Louisiana approved the venture. A board of trustees comprised of prominent ministers of the Church of God in the Southwest was selected to organize the college. J. T. Wilson, then residing in Dallas, Texas, once again became the prime influence in a school's formation and eventually was named the first president of Warner Memorial University at Eastland, Texas.[61] Classes convened in September 1929 in temporary surroundings, but by the following year two new buildings had been constructed on a campus of sixty acres. Despite the ambitious beginning the timing was ominous for survival, let alone growth. The university was a victim of economic circumstances over which it had little control. The school had no established means of financial support,

---

59. Robert L. Berry, *The Golden Jubilee Book* (Anderson, IN: Gospel Trumpet Co., 1931), 30.
60. Ibid., 31.
61. Ibid., 30.

and in the small town of Eastland students could not find sufficient employment to meet living and tuition expenses. After three terms Warner Memorial University closed its doors, and later attempts to revive the school were unsuccessful.

In 1933 in the midst of the Depression, a more successful venture in ministerial training was inauspiciously launched in Gordon, Nebraska. It began when a group of local ministerial students who could not afford to leave home for school began meeting regularly in the church there for Bible study under the leadership of pastor R. A. Germany. Others joined the group, more teachers were added, and Gordon Bible School was born. In 1944 the name was changed to Midwest Bible School, and it continued to function until 1957. More than 150 pastors and laypeople and some national leaders such as Ralph V. Hatch, later of the World Service staff, and Elmer Case, a future staff member of the Board of Church Extension and Home Missions, received training at the school.

During this period the Church of God wrestled with some of its most fundamental premises. Believing as strongly as it did in divinely called and Holy Spirit-directed leadership, the pioneers rejected all human efforts to produce leaders in the church. Yet early leaders quickly learned that the skills of leadership did not necessarily come in the same package with a divine call. The journey through the ministerial apprenticeships, missionary homes, training schools, Bible colleges, liberal arts colleges, and later a graduate seminary represents a long struggle with a way to provide leadership that is both divinely empowered and humanly efficient. In the process of this journey there emerged an acceptance that formal education, both for ministry and for life, is not in itself an enemy of spirituality and in truth, is necessary for effective service. It also came to be recognized that the kind of education and the environment in which it takes place is an important aspect of the training experience, and so the church had an obligation to provide opportunity for its young people to pursue an education that enabled them to be both spiritually directed and trained.

Along the way the movement reaffirmed its original stance of openness to truth. It rejected the demand for adherence only to what had been published in standard literature. The Byrum hearing came close to snapping the lid shut, but the ministers presiding exonerated him even though his views were at variance with previous interpretations. In his resignation Byrum added to that principle of openness by rejecting the idea of requiring the signing of a creed by college faculty members, thus preserving not only belief in academic freedom but also the concept of bondage to the Word and the Spirit.

CHAPTER 12

THE GOLDEN JUBILEE
(1928–1935)

The conscientious celebration of the anniversary of a significant event tends to sharpen the meaning associated with it and to encourage assessment of present and future relationships to the remembered occasion. It is difficult to find references to any anniversary celebrations during the early decades of the Church of God. There was a strong consciousness of history, a general recognition of contributions made by the pioneers, but no specific events were recognized as the beginning of the movement, and so there were no commemorative occasions highlighting past events and dates. For the most part, even historically-minded adherents were content to state that the movement began around 1880.

The first deliberately observed movement-wide anniversary celebration was the marking of the half-century point in the movement's history. This fiftieth-year celebration was appropriately called "The Golden Jubilee," and 1931 was the year.[1] The particular events of that year have meaning, of course, in a larger context.

To begin with, it is appropriate to note that in 1931 it was difficult to find much in the general economy of the nation and the world that would warrant a celebration of any kind. That year and the one following were the darkest of the Great Depression. Widespread bank and business failures, massive unemployment, long breadlines, and low income even for those who were working, spelled financial trouble for all institutions that depended on gifts for support. This was especially true of small religious groups such as the Church of God, whose constituency came largely from

---

1. The selection of 1931 rather than 1930 as a time to celebrate was based on the date of the beginning of the *Gospel Trumpet* (January 1, 1881) rather than any event that would mark the beginning of the movement. As noted later, the major thrust of the Golden Jubilee celebration was carried by the Gospel Trumpet Company with other agencies of the national church cooperating.

the lower economic strata of society and whose institutions were not only unendowed but barely established. At the time of the stock market crash in 1929, none of the church's national agencies except the publishing work had been in existence more than twelve years, and most were younger than a decade. From a financial standpoint it is fortunate that plans for cooperative budgeting and promotion had been established in the years of economic prosperity before the Great Depression. Approved by the General Ministerial Assembly in 1927, the Associated Budgets' Plan became operative in 1928. In the years following 1929 general income was greatly reduced, but each national agency received a proportionate share. All suffered but all survived.[2] This might not have been true had each been on its own.[3]

Mutual fundraising became the chief point of emphasis for the next several years. Church leaders made extensive efforts to convince the church of the great need for cooperative financial effort. Promotion occurred frequently in the *Gospel Trumpet*, annually in the *Yearbook*, and repeatedly by personal contacts from agency leaders. These promotional pieces included information regarding distribution of funds, but a great deal of emphasis was also placed on procedure and reasons why the mutually established Associated Budgets was superior to the previous individual solicitations by each agency. For the Depression years it was particularly appropriate to emphasize the economy of such a plan. An ad from the 1932 *Yearbook* illustrates the story well:

> The Associated Budgets' plan will save the church thousands of dollars every year, dollars that should go directly into soul-saving channels.
>
> By the Associated Budgets' plan the costs of gathering the money necessary to the Boards can be cut to the minimum. Instead of several solicitors being necessary to go before the church one solicitor can do it all. Instead of five office forces to obtain and receipt monies, one agency can do it all. Then the various Boards can reduce their clerical help to that needed to carry on their particular work.

---

2. See chapter 10 for an account of the beginning of the Associated Budgets. Total budgets were cut from $237,000 in 1928 to $150,000 in 1935, a reduction of 37 percent.

3. Two of the church's educational institutions, Warner Memorial University and Winchester Academy, neither of which was supported by the national budget, did not survive the Depression. See chapter 11.

THE ASSOCIATED BUDGETS' PLAN

The Associated Budgets' plan is very simple.

The five Church Boards combine to raise their funds.

1. It calls for every local church to set aside a percentage of their income for the general causes, or to place in their budget certain amounts which they intend to send to those causes.

2. It calls for these monies to be sent to one central agency, the Associated Budgets, which will receive, receipt, and distribute the gifts according to the will of the givers.

3. It will save thousands of dollars to the church.

4. It permits designated gifts to any board, and there is no leveling off anywhere.

5. It affords an equitable, impartial, proportionate, regular, and systematic income for all the Boards.[4]

---

4. *Yearbook of the Church of God*, 1932, 22.

Courtesy of Anderson University and Church of God Archives

The interior of the wooden tabernacle constructed to replace the first tabernacle built in Anderson. The wooden tabernacle served as the primary meeting place for Anderson Camp Meeting until a section of roof collapsed under the weight of a heavy spring snow in 1960, forcing a rare cancellation of the camp meeting for the following June.

Despite the prevailing hard times, the Jubilee years were good ones for the Church of God. The movement not only survived—it grew, experiencing the highest growth rate of any comparable period in its history before or since. Membership totals based on the estimates in the yearbooks show an increase from 34,709 to 59,799, a gain of 72 percent. If one goes back two more years to 1926 when the membership was listed at 27,771, the ten-year gain was 115 percent. Overall Protestant membership in the United States for this same decade grew approximately 15 percent.[5] During these years one heard references to the Church of God as "the fastest growing religious movement in America."

Something of the general climate of interest and concern in the pre-Jubilee years is revealed in actions and issues before the General Ministerial Assembly. In 1928, for instance, the Assembly gave attention to the appropriateness of continuing to call the annual June meeting in Anderson a camp meeting. It was noted that the program of this convocation had expanded to include not only the evangelistic meetings and sessions of the

5. Statistics taken from respective yearbooks of the Churches of God and yearbooks of American Churches.

General Ministerial Assembly but also multiple conferences and conventions for special groups such as youth, Christian educators, and missionaries. The Assembly concluded that the meeting "has grown beyond what is commonly comprehended in the term camp meeting." Consequently, it adopted a resolution changing the name to International General Assembly of the Church of God.[6] Colloquially, however, the General Assembly continued to be known as camp meeting.

The General Ministerial Assembly also dealt with current social issues in the same fashion as other church bodies of that era—by passing resolutions. World War I and its attendant atrocities spawned a broad peace movement among American Protestants. The 1928 Assembly passed a strong resolution supporting all efforts to preserve peace: Groups and individuals other than the historic peace churches were concerned for World Peace. In this spirit:

> WHEREAS, it is an undoubted fact that warfare has caused untold misery and suffering to the human race, and
>
> WHEREAS, war as a method for settling international disputes is contrary to the principles and teachings of Jesus, and
>
> WHEREAS, it is a growing sentiment among Christians everywhere that war should be outlawed and abolished from the face of the earth as an enemy of the progress of the human race and a detriment to the propagation of the Christian religion; therefore
>
> BE IT RESOLVED, that we, the General Ministerial Assembly of the Church of God convened in session June 22, 1928, hereby declare ourselves in favor of every effort being put forward by our government and the government of other nations, and the various leagues that are organized to propagate the principles of peace, which have for their aim the outlawry of war.[7]

The same body, five years later, adopted an even stronger resolution that called for a personal commitment to peace on the part of each member of the Assembly. The resolution, in part, declared,

> War is unchristian, futile and suicidal, and we renounce completely the whole war system. We will never again sanction or participate in any war. We will not use our pulpits or classrooms as recruiting stations. We

---

6. Minutes of the General Ministerial Assembly, June 22, 1928.
7. Ibid.

set ourselves to educate and lead youth in the principle and practice of good will, justice, understanding, brotherhood, and peace. We will not give our financial or moral support to any war. We will seek security and justice by pacific means.[8]

It is interesting to note that many of the sons of those who said here that they would not again "sanction or participate in any war" found themselves less than a decade later engulfed in the greatest war that the world had ever seen, World War II. These peacetime resolutions, however, were to become the basis of support for young men of the Church of God who were conscientious objectors and asked to be so classified by their local draft boards.

Another issue familiar to church groups was the liquor traffic and the evils of alcohol. In 1919, after many years of effort, the prohibition of the sale, manufacture, and transportation of alcoholic beverages had been written into the United States Constitution. The eighteenth amendment was enforced by the Volstead Act and later by the Jones Act, which provided maximum penalties for violation of five years imprisonment or a fine of $10,000 or both. It appeared the battle against "Demon Rum" had been won. However, by 1928 Prohibition was being challenged by some prominent politicians, including a presidential candidate. Amid considerable propaganda promoting repeal of the eighteenth amendment, the 1928 Assembly passed a resolution strongly opposing both the propaganda and repeal:

> WHEREAS, we regard this propaganda as a challenge to the morality and public welfare, therefore
> BE IT RESOLVED, that we urge a strict enforcement of the present prohibition laws, and
> BE IT FURTHER RESOLVED, that we put ourselves upon record as favoring no candidate or political party that favors modification of the present prohibition law.[9]

In addition to the resolution many sermons and comments regarding the evils of alcohol were preached from the pulpits, and various articles were written in the *Gospel Trumpet*. A radio sermon prepared by W. B. McCreary titled "What About Prohibition?" and printed in the *Gospel Trumpet* is an

---

8. Minutes of the General Ministerial Assembly, June 23, 1932.
9. Minutes of the General Ministerial Assembly, June 22, 1928.

excellent example of the movement's attitude toward alcoholic beverages: "A gallon of misery to every half pound of comfort is exactly the wages a nation will receive that disregards the law of God and licenses stuff that is poisonous and damning to its people."[10] The movement definitely took its stand with the drys and continued to oppose the use of alcohol even after the eighteenth amendment banning its sale, manufacture, and transportation was repealed in 1933. Many of the women joined the Women's Christian Temperance Union (WCTU) to continue opposition to the liquor traffic.

Another matter of major concern during these years was leadership. The creation of the General Ministerial Assembly and the structuring of five subordinate boards defined the separate areas of the national work and delineated lines of responsibility and authority in ways different from when all operations had been contained in the Gospel Trumpet Company. In the process of redefining and clarifying it was almost inevitable that some conflicts and tensions would arise, particularly among strong leaders who headed the various general agencies. The focal point for many leaders was the editor in chief of the publishing company, a position which until 1917 was undoubtedly the most powerful office in the movement.

When the twenty-four Gospel Trumpet Company members met in 1930, the stage was set for a sharp debate on whether to reelect F. G. Smith as editor in chief. Rather widespread dissatisfaction with Smith had developed. Some felt he was wielding too much power. An editorial statement in a January 1930 issue of the *Gospel Trumpet* evidenced some awareness of these critical feelings:

> As to our EMPHASIS, some seem to feel that certain articles published in the *Gospel Trumpet* in recent months, particularly editorials and observations, have borne down too heavily in certain respects, casting undue reflection upon others and upon other departments of our own church work....We regret any misunderstandings or ill effects thus caused...[11]

Unpleasant feelings toward Smith also lingered in the wake of Russell R. Byrum's resignation from his teaching position at Anderson College after his heresy trial. Smith's relationship to some of the Anderson College people had become problematic. J. A. Morrison definitely favored Smith's

---

10. W. B. McCreary, "What About Prohibition?" *Gospel Trumpet*, September 24, 1931, 8.
11. *Gospel Trumpet*, January 2, 1930, 30.

removal from the *Trumpet* editorship because, in Morrison's words, "I felt that he was throwing the full weight of the paper against what we were trying to do in the College."[12] Smith also was criticized for a busy schedule that frequently kept him out of town on speaking engagements or other business. His staff had extra responsibilities when he was away.[13] Although the decision of the company members was far from unanimous, H. M. Riggle was elected to replace Smith as editor of the *Gospel Trumpet,* and his name was submitted to the General Ministerial Assembly for ratification. However, by a vote of 153 to 176 the Assembly had refused to ratify the elected *Trumpet* editor.[14] Riggle was a popular preacher and writer; his veto was due rather to the reluctance of the Assembly to oust Smith. Many Assembly members believed the Gospel Trumpet Company would respect the obvious desire of the Assembly and rename Smith, but the company refused. Several of the members "had pledged themselves to stand pat for a change."[15] Thirteen members flatly refused to vote for Smith. After it became apparent that the majority would not change, Charles E. Brown was elected as a compromise. Brown accepted only on the condition that Smith endorse him on the floor of the Assembly. Smith did so. In the June 17, 1930, Assembly session, F. G. Smith made a statement. The minutes read as follows:

> He called upon the Assembly to ratify the election of Charles E. Brown as editor in chief of the Gospel Trumpet Company, and stated that he willingly turned over the office of editor in chief to Charles E. Brown. The chair then announced that H. M. Riggle would make a statement. He did so, saying that he was perfectly satisfied with the results of the election, and also recommended to the Assembly that the election of Charles E. Brown by the Gospel Trumpet Company as editor in chief be ratified.[16]

The ratification vote was unanimous, and "a unanimous vote of thanks was given to F. G. Smith for his long service as editor in chief of the *Gospel Trumpet.*"[17]

---

12. John A. Morrison, *As the River Flows* (Anderson, IN: Anderson College Press, 1962), 171.
13. Harold L Phillips, *Miracle of Survival* (Anderson, IN: Warner Press, 1979), 201.
14. Minutes of the General Ministerial Assembly, June 17, 1930.
15. Morrison, *As the River Flows*, 170.
16. Minutes of the General Ministerial Assembly, June 17, 1930.
17. Ibid.

C. E. Brown, coming from a pastorate in Detroit, Michigan, brought his valuable perspectives as a preacher, church historian, and biblical scholar to the *Trumpet.* He had no illusions regarding the circumstances that brought him to this important office. He was aware that his predecessor had been removed because of his authoritarianism and an unwillingness to tolerate opposition. Brown also recognized that he had been selected for the position as a compromise and consequently had to steer a course acceptable to many strong people with varying viewpoints. Accordingly, he immediately declared his neutral position by notifying the leaders that the paper was not to be a "battlefield of debate—either one-sided or two-sided—but an instrument in the hands of God, for the promotion of deep spirituality and of the Great Revival of Holy Ghost religion for which humanity today languishes."[18] Brown also used this occasion to relinquish the editor's traditionally held power to determine the standing of any minister in the church:

Charles E. Brown (1883–1971), editor of the *Gospel Trumpet* from 1930 to 1951. After Midwestern pastorates, Brown succeeded F. G. Smith at the Gospel Trumpet Company. A prolific writer, Brown was a self-educated historian, and his historical and theological approach to the church was a principal influence in the church's departure from a self-understanding grounded in interpretations of the apocalyptic books of the Bible.

> Wherever any conflict arose or any minister's standing was in question, the accused minister would be tried by a local group of ministers, an informal ministerial assembly. Nevertheless, the editor of the *Gospel Trumpet* could always review the finding. If the editor continued to publish the accused minister's reports, then he would continue to retain his standing as a minister, and no one could prevent it.[19]

Brown decided not to take so much power upon himself. He said, "I announced promptly that every minister's standing would depend entirely

18. *Gospel Trumpet*, July 3, 1930, 24–25.
19. Charles E. Brown, *When Souls Awaken* (Anderson, IN: Gospel Trumpet Co., 1954), 120.

upon the judgment of his own state ministerial assembly."[20] Although throughout the church there was some hesitation in accepting this, the new policy quickly gained popularity and helped strengthen the role of the state assemblies.

The rapidity with which this change came about is illustrated by noting some of the actions of the General Ministerial Assembly in regard to ministerial standing.

In 1928 the Assembly voted to accept a report by the Committee of 14 regarding the standing of a brother against whom the Pennsylvania ministry had taken action. The committee concluded he "did not receive a scriptural or legal trial." They therefore recommended that he "be treated as a Christian minister in good standing until proved otherwise."[21] The General Ministerial Assembly thus overruled action by a state assembly. After C. E. Brown's announcement concerning his policy the situation changed quickly. In 1933 a committee appointed by the General Ministerial Assembly to investigate the qualifications of two individuals to be bona fide members of the Assembly gave their report and recommended that the matter be referred to the appropriate state ministerial assembly.[22] From that time the Assembly rarely took any action relating to ministerial standing, giving major responsibilities in this area to the state assemblies.[23]

At the time of Brown's appointment to the editor's chair, an important personnel change occurred in the business management of the Gospel Trumpet Company. Since 1919 D. W. Patterson had served as general manager. By 1930 the publishing work, along with many businesses, faced major financial problems. The company's fiscal situation had always been tight but the Depression brought even greater hardship, and a change seemed advisable. In 1931 A. T. Rowe, a pastor from Atlanta, Georgia, who had banking experience, was named general manager of the Gospel Trumpet Company. It was hoped that he would be able to help the company avoid financial disaster. There was great difficulty in trying to meet the payroll, and wage cuts were instituted. Most employees accepted the cuts, but workers in the composing room, who were all members of the typographical union, objected. Half of these did not accept the wage reduction and left the

---

20. Ibid.
21. Minutes of the General Ministerial Assembly, June 22, 1928.
22. Minutes of the General Ministerial Assembly, June 24, 1933.
23. Marvin J. Hartman, "The Origin and Development of the General Ministerial Assembly of the Church of God" (BDiv, Butler University School of Religion, 1958), 54.

company under protest. The company was picketed by the union for a little over a year. The other half of the composing room employees accepted the salary cut and stayed.[24] Despite the financial and labor struggles the printing work continued and survived the Great Depression. The management skills of Rowe and others contributed significantly to both survival and success.

The Golden Jubilee celebration in 1931 was originated, instigated, and engineered primarily by the Gospel Trumpet Company with other agencies cooperating and participating at appropriate points. The grand celebration was planned by a committee with R. L. Berry serving as director. Committee members included D. W. Patterson, Earl L. Martin, and Charles E. Brown.[25] The following large two-page advertisement was placed in an early 1931 issue of the *Gospel Trumpet*:

> For over a year it has been on the mind of the Gospel Trumpet Company how fittingly to celebrate this event in its history. Merely to celebrate is easy, and futile. It was felt that something more than looking upon the past—glorious as that past may have been—was essential. Above all it was felt—what will please God (whose paper the *Gospel Trumpet* is) most?[26]

Nine major efforts were planned for this celebration:[27]

1. *Publication of a Commemorative Book.* Robert L. Berry edited and was the primary author of the *Golden Jubilee Book,* which featured the fifty-year history of the Gospel Trumpet Company and the Church of God reformation movement. It contained photos of over twelve hundred ordained ministers and about 350 pictures of church buildings. The 152-page glossy paper book also contained brief accounts of the various national institutions of the church, including the Gospel Trumpet Company, Anderson College and Theological Seminary, Church Extension and Home Missions, Warner Memorial University, Winchester Academy, Overseas Missions, and Sunday School and Religious Education. With its hardbound blue binding and gold lettering it proved a fitting tribute to the occasion. A printing of fifteen thousand copies was planned.

---

24. Phillips, *Miracle of Survival*, 229–30.
25. *Gospel Trumpet*, January 22, 1931, 23.
26. Ibid., 22.
27. Ibid., 22–23.

2. Gospel Trumpet Jubilee Subscription Campaign. The plan was to double the subscription list within the year, setting up state quotas based on current subscription lists. Special offers to individuals and incentive rewards to states who met their quotas were announced as part of the campaign.

3. Unity Book Fund. The goal announced was to send one thousand copies of Charles Ewing Brown's new book, *A New Approach to Christian Unity* to one thousand Christian leaders throughout the world. The *Gospel Trumpet* announced, "A list of 1,000 Christian leaders in America, England, Germany, Scandinavia, Near East, Egypt, India, South Africa, China, Japan, and Australia will be compiled. These men and women will be the leaders of Christian thought in these lands, every one of whom is thinking about unity.[28] An appeal was made for $1,000 in contributions to carry out this project. "It is our belief," the announcement said, "that this book will take hold, that it will command the respect and attention of the greatest men in Christendom."

Brown's new book grew out of his deep concern for the emphasis on Christian unity, which had been central in the movement's teachings from the beginning. He articulated this concern in terms understandable to all and directed more to the outsider than to the already convinced. He addressed the problem of Christian division, stating, "Various denominations are just as independent of each other as England and America are at the present time."[29] He objected to the wasted "duplication of effort" put forth by denominations instead of united team work.[30] Brown maintained, "We need Christian unity in order to exert the proper Christian influence upon the social order of our time."[31] The general tone of the whole book was indicative of Brown's general acceptance of Christians in denominations but without condoning their denominationalism. The volume was advertised in the *Gospel Trumpet* as follows:

> There are two methods proposed: the Roman Catholic method—all unite under the Pope; the Protestant method—consolidate and federate. Or we might term them the imperial and democratic methods.

---

28. *Gospel Trumpet*, January 22, 1931, 22.
29. Charles E. Brown, *A New Approach to Christian Unity* (Anderson, IN: Gospel Trumpet Co., 1931), 18.
30. Ibid., 62.
31. Ibid., 64–65.

After all the shouting about it is over these two systems will be left standing and one or the other will have to be accepted—that is, if man is to do the uniting.

Is there not a shorter way to Christian unity, a way less full of thorns and briars of men's asking?

"A New Approach to Christian Unity" deals with the most delicate problems involved, sets one to thinking, and points out a way.[32]

4. Circulate Good Books. The company had thousands of valuable books on its shelves. Sales of some languished due to the Depression. The goal was to distribute 95,000 doctrinal books. The Jubilee Distribution Book Sale featured slashed prices and sales promotion through the *Gospel Trumpet.*

5. Camp Meeting, June 14-18. One advertisement in the *Gospel Trumpet,* stated, "This 1931 meeting is expected to be the most powerful meeting ever held on the Anderson Camp Grounds."[33] Camp-meeting services typically featured preaching, but on June 18, a pageant titled "Onward with Christ and Truth" was presented. Written by R. L. Berry, it included an orchestra, children's choir, college male quartet, and adult chorus. It presented the highlights of God's working through the many years of church history. Portrayed were various significant personalities including Phillip Melanchthon, Menno Simons, John Calvin, John Knox, William Tyndale, and John Wesley. The final segment presented a series of "eight speakers, one from each of the schools and one for each of the boards, including the blind work, Old People's Home and literature."[34] Over five hundred people were involved in the production.

6. A Campaign of Prayer and Spiritual Power. A committee chaired by E. E. Byrum was formed "in order that the main spring of prayer be kept wound up."[35] Other committee members included H. A. Sherwood, J. R. Tallen, M. A. Monday, and P. B. Turner.

7. Constructive Evangelism. A committee chaired by E. E. Perry was formed to enhance evangelistic efforts. The *Gospel Trumpet* announced it as follows:

---

32. *Gospel Trumpet*, February 12, 1931, 26.
33. *Gospel Trumpet*, May 21, 1931, 21.
34. *Gospel Trumpet*, June 4, 1931, 19.
35. *Gospel Trumpet*, January 22, 1931, 23.

It is hoped that the attention of the ministers and church will be focused during 1931 on how to reach more people. A committee that will do what it can to encourage constructive evangelism in every area consists of:

E. E. Perry, Chairman, Detroit, Mich.
C. A. Thompson, Hickory, N. C.
E. E. Shaw, Akron, Ohio
E. G. Masters, Long Beach, Calif.
M. R. Desgalier, Buffalo, N. Y.
H. A. Schlatter, Seattle, Wash.
E. A. Reardon, Denver, Colo.[36]

8. Golden Jubilee in Other Camp Meetings. The celebration was not to be limited to activities in Anderson. "The spirit of jubilee and of going forward should fire every camp meeting." A committee chaired by A. T. Rowe had as its objective "to get as much of this into all camp meetings."[37]

9. A New Awakening Everywhere. The final objective of the Jubilee took shape as a broadside for global spiritual renewal:

A new awakening everywhere, a quickening of evangelistic zeal in every area, in every congregation, is sought for. It is not intended that the Jubilee Celebration center in the Anderson Camp Meeting, but instead that there will be a mighty revival spring up in every minister, every saint, every congregation, and blaze forth with the glory of God.

We hope every corner of the world will feel the quickening, reviving Spirit of God moving upon us as never before, and that with a clearer, bigger vision and more constructive cooperation, we can fill the world with "this doctrine."[38]

Along with the Jubilee celebration the 1931 sessions of the General Ministerial Assembly gave attention to a matter that would have dramatically changed the character of the Assembly. The previous Assembly (1930) had authorized the appointment of a commission on reorganization. U. G. Clark was named as chairperson. The commission had met and had drawn up a proposed plan to reorganize the Assembly. A. F. Gray was called upon

---

36. Ibid.
37. Ibid.
38. Ibid.

to read the report, which included the affirmation that, "The plan does not involve the creation of a new body but a change in the makeup of the present Assembly."[39] The proposed change would have converted the Assembly from a voluntary body to a delegated body made up of "representatives selected by the various states and provinces."[40] Specifically the plan called for an Assembly of 112 members with 60 of them being congregational delegates and 52 ministerial representatives. Twenty-six were reserved for "colored" people and the remaining number white.

At the end of the report were the signatures of the members of the commission. Two of the signers appended comments. One was J. A. Morrison, who wrote, "Opposed to any change." After F. G. Smith's signature was the comment, "Opposed on Scriptural grounds to the changes proposed." Signatures without comment included those of A. F. Gray, C. K. Chapman, W. R. Abell, E. A. Reardon, J. T. Wilson, A. T. Rowe, Adam Miller, U. G. Clark, C. E. Byers, D. W. Patterson, Herbert M. Riggle, and W. E. Monk. The minutes record that after the report was read, "A. T. Rowe made the statement that this plan would disfranchise the majority of our ministers and moved that the plan be tabled."[41] The motion was seconded and carried.

The 1930 Assembly also had passed a resolution calling for a commission to give due consideration to the formation of a business body to manage the general interests of the church. This commission did not report in 1931 and apparently did not prepare an official report from the commission itself. In 1932, however, the Business Committee, chaired by W. E. Monk, presented a resolution calling for amendment of the Assembly's bylaws to provide for the creation and incorporation of the Executive Council of the Church of God. The council, to consist of fifteen members, was assigned the following functions:

> The objects and purposes of the corporation are hereby declared to be to promote the religious and benevolent work of the Church of God, and for such purposes such corporation shall have power to receive, take and hold real and personal property, donations of money and property, legacies and bequests, and to sell, transfer and otherwise convey such

---

39. "Report on Commission on Reorganization," Minutes of the General Ministerial Assembly, June 17, 1931.
40. Ibid.
41. Ibid.

property, on behalf of the Church of God, to sue and defend any and all actions in any court, and to have, hold and enjoy all the rights, privileges and powers of corporations at common law.[42]

The Executive Council thus became the legal arm of the General Ministerial Assembly and the legal entity for conducting the general business of the Church of God.

Even though the major impetus for the 1931 Golden Jubilee celebration came from the Gospel Trumpet Company, all of the other church agencies became involved and contributed toward the accomplishment of the celebration's objectives. It must be noted also that not all the special emphasis action was confined to a single year. Many projects initiated at that time continued. The Board of Church Extension and Home Missions, for instance, contributed greatly to the already noted tremendous thrust in church growth during the Golden Jubilee years, when the movement experienced its highest rate of growth ever. The Board was very active in planting new congregations and strengthening churches in need of assistance. It also sponsored efforts to reach Native Americans, the Spanish-speaking people of the Southwest, migrant workers, Asians in the United States, southern mountain folk, immigrants, and others in need of the gospel. Elver Adcock, executive secretary of the Board, published a book in 1934 titled *Our American Missions* in which he described systematic efforts of the Board to evangelize the nation. In many ways this Board helped to implement a great organized thrust for expansion.

Evangelism was an emphasis in almost every part of the work of the church. In the preaching particularly, this note was struck loud and clear in the Jubilee years. In the spirit of the Golden Jubilee, A. T. Rowe delivered a sermon titled "Stirring up the Spirit of Evangelism in the Church" to the International Camp Meeting in 1928. He urged listeners:

Go Out! Go Out! Go Out! It seems to me that that message ought to ring in the heart of every minister and every member of the church today. If we could burn by the power of the Holy Spirit, if we could burn that message—those two words "Go Out!"—into the heart of every individual here this morning, we would start the sort of evangelism working that we need....There are many methods....If one method

---

42. Minutes of the General Ministerial Assembly, June 20, 1932.

will not work, we ought to try another; if one of these methods will not work, try one that will.[43]

This message and many others were not forgotten. Articles and sermons on the growing church became a major emphasis in the *Gospel Trumpet*. Reports of new building, Sunday church growth, lay witness missions and revivals appeared in profusion and inspired even greater development. One letter among twenty or so in a 1932 issue reported such growth in Gloucester, New Jersey:

> Often our church in the Sunday evening service has been filled to overflowing. The Lord has enabled us to pay off an indebtedness on a lot and also to erect a foundation for a new place of worship.
>
> We are glad to report increasing spirituality and also a spirit of personal evangelism. We mean to spend this truth to every possible home within our reach. One of our reasons for being encouraged is a group of about fifteen saved young people who are fast becoming real workers with God.[44]

The key phrases of this short letter are "personal evangelism" and "workers together." From these two phrases one could sum up a good understanding of the church's method of outreach and its basic theology of evangelism.

Other articles used in the *Gospel Trumpet* ranged from ragtime evangelism to constructive evangelism. The goal for the church was every-member evangelism, to see that every person heard the gospel either through literature, preaching, or the Sunday school. A key motivator of evangelistic efforts in the Golden Jubilee period for the Church of God was R. L. Berry. His 1934 booklet *Constructive Evangelism* emphasized the fact that evangelism did not mean just revivalism. It was proclaiming the Christian message. In Berry's view, evangelism and church planting were the church's chief concerns. The need to develop a growing church arose out of the conviction that the world needed to know the truth of Jesus Christ. The gospel

---

43. A. T. Rowe, in *Select Camp-meeting Sermons: Preached at the International Camp-meeting of the Church of God, Anderson, Indiana, June 16–24, 1928* (Anderson, IN: Gospel Trumpet Co., 1928), 116–18.

44. Herman E. Beyer, quoted in "What Churches and the Ministers Are Doing," *Gospel Trumpet*, March 12, 1932, 25.

mandate was the starting point that opened the way to further development through church planting. George S. Cooper, also contributed in the building of a conscious concern for church growth when he described the task of the church to be the winning of souls, missions, and social service.[45]

With the task at hand, the church surveyed the needs and identified specific targets for evangelistic effort. It was found that of sixty-eight cities in the United States with a population of one-hundred thousand or more, less than half had Church of God congregations. Moreover, Church of God congregations could be found in fifteen hundred cities numbering five thousand or more.[46] It was apparent that the church needed to plant more congregations in the cities. More churches were also needed in the West and in states such as Wisconsin, Iowa, California, Oregon, Texas, Montana, Wyoming, Idaho, and Colorado. It was also found that in the deep South and the New England states there was a great need for churches to be planted.

In order for the goals to be reached, leadership was needed. Berry wrote:

> Every evangelist, every pastor, should do his best to train workers, give lessons on doctrine, on faith, on doing spiritual work, on healing the sick, on casting out devils, on constructive evangelism, on pastoral work, on religious music, so that the church may enjoy and profit by the labor of efficient ministers and workers.[47]

In emphasizing the training of laypeople to be evangelists, Berry was striking a familiar chord in the Church of God. From the days of the evangelistic companies of the flying ministry through the heyday of missionary homes, there had been a strong emphasis on gospel workers. Many of these laypeople continued to identify their sense of calling to this ministry by listing their names in the *Yearbook* with the designation GW.

It was on the local level, of course, that growth had to take place. A large number of very small congregations that had been struggling for survival found the evangelistic thrust of the Golden Jubilee period to be the needed impetus for finding new strength—and new people. Along with increases in existing churches many new congregations came into being. Between

---

45. George S. Cooper, "The Task of the Church," *Gospel Trumpet*, December 28, 1935, 5.
46. Berry, *Golden Jubilee*, 43.
47. Berry, *Constructive Evangelism*, 23.

By 1890, the Church of God had reached California. Jacob W. Byers and his wife Jennie, who moved to the West Coast in 1890, were responsible for much of the work in California. This photo captures a large Church of God camp meeting in Pomona, California, in 1927 or 1928.

1926 and 1935 the number of congregations in the United States and Canada increased from 635 to 1,352, a gain of 113 percent over the ten-year period.[48] To put it another way, during this decade new congregations of the Church of God were launched at the rate of one every five days. A few examples illustrate how this developed.

One of the new congregations was the Church of God in Lebanon, Ohio, which began in 1930 under the labors of James R. Hillard and Albert Bastin. Street meetings and tent meetings were held featuring the evangelistic efforts of such people as R. C. Caudill and the James H. Lear family. In January of 1931 services were moved to the former Church of Christ building on East Silver Street. Later the group moved to a vacated Presbyterian building on Main Street. A 1932 photograph pictured seventy-nine people attending there.[49]

Like many other churches, the Church of God in Bloomington, Indiana, began in a home. Seven people started meeting together for prayer. Everett and Marie McCurry opened their home to host the meetings in November 1929. Every Monday night from November through May the pastor at Bedford, Indiana, G. T. Neal, came to lead the meetings. In May the group began meeting in the Broadview schoolhouse for the summer. They organized a Sunday school and in June called Earnest Branam as pastor. A very fruitful revival was held soon after that and it was not long until

48. *Yearbook of the Church of God*, 1926, 189; 1935, 114.
49. "Lebanon First Church of God," a booklet describing the church's history.

The Golden Jubilee / 273

Sunday school attendance reached fifty. In September 1930 it was necessary to secure another place of worship. One of the members purchased a house on Rogers Street, and it was remodeled. Soon after the move Sunday school attendance reached ninety-four. Isaac B. Tucker became pastor in 1931 and the church continued to relocate several more times to accommodate the growth. By 1933 the average Sunday school attendance reached 208.[50]

Similar stories were repeated again and again across the continent. Through the efforts of traveling evangelists, by assistance from neighboring churches, and often by the witness and work of a single family who invited neighbors to their home, new congregations came into being. After they were started some were able to get assistance from the national Board of Church Extension and Home Missions. In the autumn of 1928, a Church Extension Tour was arranged to take a closer look at the local congregations' needs. A group of men traveled throughout America seeking to determine new ways of getting the gospel to unreached areas. One of those ways was loaning money to newly established churches. The first loan by the Board was for $300 to help erect a church in Oklahoma. By 1931 the fund had increased to over $600.[51]

In foreign missions the expansion was not so dramatic. In fact, the Depression years actually witnessed a decrease in the number of missionaries under appointment by the Missionary Board from forty-seven in 1926 to forty-three in 1935.[52] Even so, in the latter year the Church of God was at work in twenty-five countries (compared to twenty-two in 1926) outside the United States and Canada with 422 identified congregations or preaching places and an estimated constituency of over seventeen thousand.[53] Full-time missionaries were at work in only twelve of these countries, but

Courtesy of Anderson University and Church of God Archives

Hester Greer (1880–1976), pastor, evangelist, and missionary in the Caribbean.

---

50. Marie McCurry, "A Cherished Past."
51. Berry, *Golden Jubilee*, 26.
52. *Yearbook of the Church of God*, 1926, 180–86; 1935, 97.
53. *Yearbook of the Church of God*, 1935, 99.

national pastors and workers were given partial support in several of the thirteen remaining nations. The missionary work had not expanded, but the same could not be said of its supervising board.

In 1935 Charles E. Brown, president of the Missionary Board, described the role of the Board as follows: "The Missionary Board of the Church of God is merely the foreign evangelization committee of the church, charged with the responsibility of carrying out the church's work in sending the Gospel to the non-Christian world."[54] This description can be contrasted with the 1909 committee whose primary task was to distribute funds sent to the Gospel Trumpet Company for missions.

With the Golden Jubilee years came another significant change that would affect the reformation's missionary efforts for years to come. This was the formation of the National Woman's Home and Foreign Missionary Society. At the International Camp Meeting in Anderson in the year 1931, a conversation at lunch between Nora Hunter of California, Grace Henry of Ohio, and Evalyn Nichols-Roy of India turned to discussion of the field of service for the women of the church. This conversation resulted in a hastily arranged meeting for all women present on the campground. Only a few people responded. Another meeting was announced, but this time about two hundred women attended. Hunter served as chairperson. Some of the women urged that the group organize at once; however, Hunter in her wise and tactful way suggested waiting a year for prayer and research. A committee was appointed to research the possibility of a national organization the following year. Mrs. E. E. Byrum of Anderson, Indiana, Mrs. T. A. Berry of Indianapolis, Indiana, and Mrs. Olive Sheefel of Bellefontaine, Ohio, were appointed. The committee spent much time in prayer and research. Hunter worked with them and also corresponded with H. M. Riggle, secretary of the Missionary Board. Ministers and church workers were interviewed. The Missionary Board and many ministers felt there was a definite place of service for women.

The Missionary Board, in its meeting preceding the 1932 Anderson Camp Meeting, called Hunter in for a progress report. In relating this experience she said, "That meeting must be recorded somewhere upon the walls of heaven; I shall look for it when I arrive."[55] Albert F. Gray, president of

---

54. C. E. Brown, "Missionary Board of the Church of God," in *Yearbook of the Church of God*, 1935, 21.

55. Hazel G. Neal and Axchie A. Bolitho, *Madam President* (Anderson, IN: Gospel Trumpet Co., 1951) , 53.

the Missionary Board, said, "Are you ready to organize?" Hunter answered, "Yes, if you approve." The entire Board said, "We approve." Hunter replied, "At thy word I will let down the nets."[56]

Following this approval a preliminary meeting was held in Park Place Church to discuss and tentatively adopt the bylaws for the society. Many women and most of the members of the Missionary Board were present. Only one hour had been allotted on the Anderson Camp Meeting schedule for the organization of the Missionary Society. During this time the bylaws were read and approved unanimously, but not enough time remained for election of officers. A. F. Gray, C. J. Blewitt, Adam W. Miller, H. M. Riggle, and E. E. Byrum took into consideration the need for additional time and offered the women fifteen minutes of the Missionary Board's time the next day for completion of their work. The following day the women marched in a great throng from the tabernacle to the auditorium, singing "Onward Christian Soldiers," led by Rachel Lord. One name was presented for each office (the nominating committee being the research committee that had been appointed the year before), and on Saturday, June 18, 1932, at 1:15 in the afternoon, the first officers of the National Woman's Home and Foreign Missionary Society were unanimously elected. The Church of God, after functioning for over fifty years in this and other lands, had given birth to their first national woman's organization. Of this organization, H. M. Riggle wrote:

> We believe that this great national society of women will be a mighty inspiration and help to our foreign missionary work. The Missionary Board with its executive committee are 100 percent back of the move-ment....We hope that in every local church the women will organize local Home and Foreign Missionary Societies and help push the work of evangelizing the world.[57]

At the time of its inception, the objectives of the National Woman's Home and Foreign Missionary Society were as follows:

1. To cooperate intelligently with the Missionary Boards of the Church of God in helping promote missionary work in various fields at home and abroad.

---

56. Ibid.
57. H. M. Riggle, "Missionary Activities at the Anderson Campmeeting," *Gospel Trumpet*, July 9, 1932, 16.

2. To make the cause of missions a heart interest rather than a passing fancy.
3. To study social, spiritual and moral needs of the field—"the world."
4. To educate the young people and children of the church in home and foreign missions.
5. To train leaders to carry responsibility in teaching the Gospel of Christ to all nations at home and abroad;
6. To encourage liberality and wisdom in the true stewardship of prayer, the stewardship of responsibility, and in the stewardship of possessions.
7. To fulfill the Scripture, "The Lord giveth the word; the women that publish tidings are a great host." Psa. 68:11 R.V.[58]

In the early organization of the society, it was the desire of the research committee, led by Nora Hunter, to develop an organization that would make it possible to put every woman associated with the Church of God to work in some strategic spot—rather than placing the responsibility of the society in the hands of a dozen or so woman ministers. This organization was established in a meaningful way on the national, state, and local level. On the national level, each director had such committees as were necessary to carry on the various duties of her office. Similarly, state and local organizations were patterned after the national.

During the Jubilee years, a significant aspect of the growth of the movement was related to the development of Sunday schools both within and beyond established congregations. In 1935 there were 523 (almost 39 percent) more Sunday schools than congregations listed in the *Yearbook,* whereas in 1926 there were only twenty-four more.[59] The growth in the number of Sunday school students in this decade went from 53,113 to 86,900 or almost 64 percent. Christian education was finding a markedly increasing role in the development of the Church of God, and the Sunday school was a principal means of church growth.

A great deal of the credit for this progress must go to the work of the Board of Sunday Schools and Religious Education which had been authorized in 1923. For the first several years the Board operated without a paid

---

58. Hazel G. Neal, ed., *National History of the Woman's Home and Foreign Missionary Society,* vol. 1, 1932–1933 (unpublished material,), 35.
59. *Yearbook,* 1926, 189; 1935, 114.

staff, with the president of the Board and other volunteer workers taking the initiative in implementing the program. R. L. Berry, W. B. McCreary, Earl L. Martin, Walter Haldeman, Bessie L. Byrum, Anna Koglin, Adam Miller, Russell Olt, Esther Boyer, and others were active in the general work of Christian education. It was a major step forward when the Board secured in 1930 the services of Pearl Johnson as a field secretary.[60] She traveled the whole country, visiting many congregations, conventions, and camp meetings speaking on behalf of religious education. In her spare time she wrote Sunday school lessons. In 1934 Esther Boyer assumed this position and continued Johnson's work. The following year Amy Phillips became a part-time worker for the Board in its small office at the Gospel Trumpet Company.

The major portion of the Board's work was devoted to leadership development and teacher training. This work was accomplished in several ways but by the early 1930s most of it was being done by utilizing the Standard Leadership Training Curriculum outlined and standardized by the International Council of Religious Education. In 1932 the Board awarded approximately 450 credits.[61] These credits were graded at three levels and presented to individuals who attended the required number of classes and completed the specified assigned reading. To this program were added many conferences at camp meetings and other assemblies. Home study courses were also available. In 1933 the Board began to publish a mimeographed magazine called the *Church School Worker*. The publication was short-lived, however, being discontinued in 1934 due to lack of funds.

In the 1933–34 academic year, the Board launched the first intensive, nationwide promotion for starting new Sunday schools. The instigator of the program was A. T. Rowe, then general manager of the Gospel Trumpet Company. The project was a cooperative effort of the publishing house and the board. Rowe received help from the Board, and Lestie Pletcher, an employee of the Gospel Trumpet Company, was in charge of administrative details. The plan called for one thousand new Sunday schools to be started in one year. Free curriculum materials for one quarter were offered to any new school. Despite extensive promotion, the goal was not achieved, but the campaign was effective enough to account for the great increase in

---

60. Anna Koglin, "Report of the Board of Sunday Schools and Religious Education," Minutes of the General Ministerial Assembly, June 20, 1932.

61. W. B. McCreary, "Report of the Board of Sunday Schools and Religious Education," Minutes of the General Ministerial Assembly, June 19, 1933.

Sunday schools not attached to a local congregation. About six hundred new schools were started, and three hundred continued after the campaign was over. The number of Sunday schools jumped in one year to 1,585 in 1934 from 1,072 in 1933, while in that same year total enrollment increased by over 4,300 individuals.[62]

The name of the Board was changed to the Board of Christian Education of the Church of God by vote of the Ministerial Assembly on June 20, 1935.[63]

During the late twenties and early thirties increased efforts were made in ministry to youth. Youth camps were beginning to be set up. In 1930 at South Bend, Indiana, the International Youth Convention was held for the first time apart from the Anderson Camp Meeting. The 1931 Anderson Camp Meeting held six o'clock young people's services that broke previous attendance records. L. Helen Percy, editor of the *Young People's Friend,* the national youth paper of the Church of God, reported these meetings:

> The first service gave us a retrospective view of the past fifty years of work in which we are engaged. E. E. Byrum, who went to the Gospel Trumpet office a young man just out of college, told of the part youth played in the beginning of this publication work. All of the workers at the office except Bro. D. S. Warner, at the time Brother Byrum was there, were in their twenties or younger....Following E. E. Byrum, Bro. B. E. Warren spoke of the place youth had in the field in the early part of this work. Brother Warren himself started traveling with D. S. Warner when he was seventeen years old and continued with him for six years.[64]

Percy's report indicates strongly the increasing emphasis placed on youth and their sensitivity to the heritage that was being celebrated in the Jubilee. A camaraderie had developed that was plainly evident. She further reported, "Then the sections marched to the old auditorium where a mass meeting was held."[65] This mass meeting received an enthusiastic invitation to hold the 1932 International Youth Convention in Atlanta. Over one

---

62. *Yearbook*, 1933, 1934.

63. Minutes of the General Ministerial Assembly, June 20, 1935.

64. L. Helen Percy, "With the Young People at the Anderson Campmeeting," *Gospel Trumpet,* July 2, 1931, 15.

65. Ibid.

hundred young Southerners sang this song, ironically, to the tune of "The Battle Hymn of the Republic":

Way down in good old Dixie
    Where the watermelons grow,
We will have our next convention,
    And we want you all to go;
Feel our southern hospitality
    Our wondrous sunshine's glow
In nineteen thirty-two

Onward, onward to Atlanta
Onward, onward to Atlanta
Onward, onward to Atlanta
In nineteen thirty-two.[66]

Atlanta won the bid, and the eighth International Youth Convention met there September 1-4, 1932.

The *Young People's Friend* continued to publish articles of interest to young people including those of college age. Youth work was beginning to be mentioned in most of the Church of God *Yearbooks*. Some *Yearbooks* even listed the names of youth leaders. Mounting enthusiasm and national support and encouragement of youth ministry were some of the most shining characteristics of the Golden Jubilee years.

By the Golden Jubilee celebration many of the prominent leaders of the movement's pioneer period had passed from the scene. An unusually large number of them closed their earthly ministry during these Jubilee years. Among them were J. Grant Anderson (1873–1927), Allie R. Fisher (1854–1927), Frances Miller Warner (Mrs. D. S. Warner) (1853–1927), J. F. Lundy (1845–1928), George E. Bolds (1844–1929), A. LeRoy Sheldon (1854–1934), Nels Renbeck (1859–1934), Otto Bolds (1869–1935), and J. N. Howard (1859–1931). In this same period concern grew for creating formal assistance to families of deceased ministers. The Ministers' Benefit Association was launched at the International Camp Meeting in Anderson in 1929. Its purpose was to provide financial help for which most ministers had not been able to prepare. It was an assessment-type plan that called for

---

66. Ibid.

contributions when any member died. By 1935 death claims amounting to over $53,000 had been paid.[67]

During the Golden Jubilee years the Church of God reformation made great growth in the midst of great struggles. The Great Depression forced the closure of two academic institutions, but Anderson College and Pacific Bible College survived. The constituency of the movement grew at a record pace. Increased responsibility for the ministry passed to state and regional assemblies, and through the programmatic activities of the several boards the work of the Church of God expanded at home and abroad.

---

67. *Yearbook*, 1935, 26.

CHAPTER 13

A MOVING MOVEMENT
(1936–1946)

By the mid-1940s the world had been engulfed in war for almost six years. Global weariness, suffering, and anxiety remained intense, for despite Allied victories in Europe, in the summer of 1945 the outcome remained uncertain. The only really positive ingredient of life anywhere was the hope remaining that sometime, prayerfully soon, battles would cease, bombs would no longer fall, and blacked-out lights could switch on again all over the world. Only then, could definite plans be made and expectations realized. This was as true for institutions and groups as it was for individuals.

In the midst of this mood of pervasive uncertainty and remote beleaguered hope, it is somewhat strange to read the Church of God literature of the war years and find statements like these:

Everywhere there is optimism and enthusiasm....New Sunday schools are being organized, new church buildings are being erected, new congregations are being established, new ministers are entering the field, denominationalism as a sectarian principle is fading, the desire for unity is becoming more pronounced. Is there anything about which we should be discouraged? Not as we see it from here.[1]

Many new congregations are being launched in various parts of the country. THE CHURCH OF GOD IS A GROWING CONCERN.[2]

I doubt if there has ever been a time when the air has been so charged with expectancy and planning for the future as it is at the present time.[3]

---

1. A. T. Rowe, "The Work Moves On," *Gospel Trumpet*, July 7, 1945, 12.
2. Harold L. Phillips, "Photo-Editorial," *Gospel Trumpet*, May 20, 1944, inside front cover.
3. John W. V. Smith, "Except the Lord Build the House," *Gospel Trumpet*, July 22, 1944, 3.

For the Church of God the period between 1936 and 1946 was a time of rapid growth and extension; the rate of increase was greater during this decade than in any other ten-year period in the movement's history. Despite obvious wartime hindrances it was a very auspicious time for this particular group. The elements of the message were all in place along with an increasingly clear understanding of the church's task. The controversies of the early 1930s were fading memories, and positive momentum had begun to build. By 1936 there were signs of economic recovery, and the future had begun to brighten. The road to this point, however, had not been easy.

The Great Depression had left its scars. Times were hard for people, for congregations, and for the general work of the church. The Associated Budgets of the Church of God entered the period of 1936–46 with a proposed budget of $165,000. However, in each of the fiscal years 1934–35 and 1935–36, less than $30,000 was given to the general causes.[4] This meant that less than 20 percent of the proposed budget was raised—a real cause for discouragement.

By 1938, however, the tide had begun to turn. H. M. Riggle, president of the Gospel Trumpet Company, was able to report a company profit of $44,385 for that year. This picture of the previous bleak Depression years and the need for these long-awaited profits was described as follows:

1. During the severe depression years from 1931 to 1936, the Company, in common with most great concerns, whether industries in general or religious publishing concerns, operated most of the time at a decided financial loss. This was simply unavoidable.…Now in the more prosperous years of 1936–1937 we have been able to apply the profits in replacing the former losses and shortages.
2. During these years of depression some of our machinery wore out and some became obsolete or unfit to do the work necessary to carry on successfully. So in the last two years a good part of these profits has been used in installing new and up-to-date machinery.…
3. We have built up our inventories with new salable goods.…
4. From the profits in the Publishing Plant must also be deducted the losses sustained through our several church activities.[5]

---

4. *Yearbook of the Church of God*, 1937.
5. Minutes of the General Ministerial Assembly, June 13, 1938.

The Associated Budgets coordinated the fund-raising solicitations for the five general boards of the Church of God, thus unifying the giving and removing some of the possibility for jealousy and competition among the boards. Each board formulated its own budget; the total amount approved was then prorated. In June 1935, the General Ministerial Assembly approved the following percentage distribution for that year:

Missionary Board	52%
Board of Church Extension and Home Missions	17%
Anderson College and Theological Seminary	17%
Free Literature, Blind Work, Old People's Home, etc.	11%
Board of Christian Education	3%
	100%[6]

The name Associated Budgets was changed in 1941, but the method of functioning remained essentially the same. At that time C. W. Hatch, director of this operation, reported:

The name of the Associated Budgets has been changed to World Service, but this is a change in name only.

Due to the fact that the name Associated Budgets seemed to emphasize the method rather than the work which the method was to accomplish, there has been much study in recent years concerning the possibility of a more meaningful name—one which would more fully emphasize the worldwide missionary work of the church. Hence the general ministerial assembly in its June meeting at Anderson voted unanimously to change the name from Associated Budgets to World Service.[7]

Slowly, congregational giving to general causes began to rise. In addition to an improving economy the increase in giving was due to the leadership of Clarence W. Hatch. In 1938 Hatch had become the director of the Associated Budgets. He later became known as "Mr. Stewardship." By 1940 he was challenging each congregation to contribute 10 percent of their budget, or another designated amount, or a monthly offering to Associated Budgets.[8] In spite of his early efforts the church's giving, year

---

6. *Yearbook of the Church of God*, 1936, 11.
7. C. W. Hatch, "Notice of Change—Change of Name," *Gospel Trumpet*, July 12, 1941, 7.
8. *Yearbook of the Church of God*, 1940, 9.

after year, fell below the proposed budget of $165,000. This cycle of defeat was broken in 1940, however, with the institution of Christ's World Service Day on the last Sunday of the Anderson Camp Meeting. A reasonable goal of $10,000 was set to be received on that day; $12,000 came in response. Hatch reported, "It gives us great joy to announce that when all the offerings were in and the books were balanced at the end of June, there was a grand total in the WORLD SERVICE OFFERING of a little over $12,000. For this we humbly thank God."[9] World Service Day continued to be a successful experience, as Table 3 illustrates:

TABLE 3: World Service Day Contributions 1940–1946

Year	Goal Set	Approximate Amount Received
1940	$10,000	$12,000
1941	15,000	17,000
1942	20,000	28,000
1943	30,000	52,000
1944	250,000*	258,000*
1945	100,000	105,000
1946	no goal	225,000**

*Quarter Million Campaign funds added to World Service Day funds
**Million Campaign funds

Campaign victories multiplied as the goal was raised each year only to be exceeded by income. Sights were raised to include even such ambitious projects as the Quarter Million Campaign and the Million Campaign, which added capital fund amounts to annual program expenses. Giving to the regular budgets increased along with the special campaigns. The goal was raised from the usual $165,000 in 1940 to $250,000 for the proposed budget in 1944, and even this higher goal was exceeded. The success of the World Service Day and the strengthening economy were not the only factors that brought about increased giving to the general causes of the Church of God. Another force was at work.

After 1930 the Church of God movement adopted new attitudes toward stewardship. Before 1910 movement constituents heard sermons

---

9. C. W. Hatch, "Announcement," *Gospel Trumpet*, August 10, 1940, 3.

that attacked the practice of tithing as unbiblical. A decade later that view was eroding in favor of more conventional ideas. After 1930 movement leaders emphasized the importance of stewardship. That other force was an increasing awareness and emphasis on Christian stewardship. In 1936, the General Ministerial Assembly unanimously adopted the following resolution:

> WHEREAS, all our church boards are suffering because of insufficient funds due to a lack of cooperation of the churches, and
>
> WHEREAS, there is manifest dissatisfaction with "Drives" and "Special Appeals," that are in themselves inadequate,
>
> THEREFORE, be it resolved (1) that we reaffirm our approval of the Associated Budgets. (2) That we go on record as favoring the appointment by the General Ministerial Assembly, of a Finance Commission consisting of 7 men—2 laymen and 5 ministers, to make a three-year study of the problem of finance with a view to raising the Budgets, and report the results of their research annually, at each annual meeting of the Ministerial Assembly.[10]

It is of incidental interest to note that this finance commission probably was the first task force of the General Ministerial Assembly to involve laypeople. When the commission gave its report in 1938, the findings included the following list of obstructions to financial progress in the church:

1. Lack of thrift, and system in personal and family finance on the part of the individual members.
2. Prevalent lack of knowledge of the Christian standard of Stewardship as taught in the Scriptures.
3. The failure of pastors generally to understand, teach, and administer a scriptural and efficient system of finance in the local church.
4. The collapse and abandonment of many enterprises and projects of the church.
5. Inadequate administrative organization in local, state and national work, and a lack of agreement as to amount and kind of organization needed.
6. Lack of agreement, correlation and united promotion.[11]

---

10. Minutes of the General Ministerial Assembly, June 17, 1936.
11. Minutes of the General Ministerial Assembly, June 14, 1938.

R. L. Berry, C. W. Hatch, and other leaders prepared and gathered materials and planned a national program of stewardship emphasis. Berry wrote *Guide to Christian Stewardship,* which was published in 1940.[12] This book covered many facets of stewardship and money handling, such as the biblical teaching on the subject, the Christian way to acquire wealth, covetousness, sharing, and investing. Along with church-wide giving campaigns such as the Christ's World Service Day, C. W. Hatch promoted year-round programs on the theme of Christian stewardship.

Besides books and pamphlets, an effective means of stewardship education was through the pages of the *Gospel Trumpet.* Numerous stewardship articles were printed. Readers could hardly miss the many aspects of the theory and practice of good stewardship that were presented repeatedly.

As a by-product of the stewardship emphasis, the Church of God began to realize its obligation to older ministers. The General Ministerial Assembly authorized a Ministers' Pension Fund in 1937.[13] Three percent of the undesignated funds received by the Associated Budgets were to be allocated to a pension fund even though no plan had been formulated for disbursement. The following year the ministers' pension fund was added to the Associated Budgets with an increased percentage of 5.5 of total undesignated monies received. It would be another decade before a board of pensions was authorized and a stable plan initiated, but these early steps marked the beginning of this program.

Not only the Church of God at large, but also individual organizations within the church suffered from the hard times of the Depression. John A. Morrison, first president of Anderson College, recalled that the all-time low enrollment for those desperate years occurred during 1932–1933 when only ninety-one students were registered.[14]

Morrison described the hard times:

I can never forget the dedication of those teachers in those hard years. Their salaries were shamefully low to start with. Then as times grew tougher and tougher, we would call an occasional meeting of the teachers. We would recite how conditions were growing worse and worse, how money was harder and harder to get, and how students were

---

12. Robert L. Berry, *Guide to Christian Stewardship* (Anderson, IN: Gospel Trumpet Co., 1940).

13. Minutes of the General Ministerial Assembly, June 16, 1937.

14. John A. Morrison, *As the River Flows* (Anderson, IN: Anderson College Press, 1962), 159.

working for nine cents an hour when work could be had at all. Then the question would come up, What can we do about it? One by one the members of that faculty would rise and say, "I am willing to take another cut in salary."[15]

With the college desperate for money or donations of any kind, Morrison and some of the students would travel in search of contributions. He related:

> Getting into my 1929 model Durant car I drove thousands of miles in many states collecting foodstuff and a few dollars wherever such could be found....I asked the members of the church to give us whatever they felt they could. The largest single donation I got was $600 from a good old Methodist brother in Ohio. When I had his check safely in my pocket I wired the good news to Dean Olt. He announced the streak of luck in chapel and there was general jubilation…
>
> The college got hold of a used truck which was put into service in foraging for food. Bill Dudgeon, a student then, now a pastor, was the driver of the truck. He went into faraway places with that truck with uncertain tires to collect farm produce. He hauled food from as far away as Pennsylvania. Potatoes, corn, beans, canned and fresh fruits, pumpkins, and once in a while a hundred-pound bag of sugar would come in. One church made and sent to the college 500 quarts of sauerkraut. For a while the whole hill had a sour odor.[16]

Even after some prosperity returned, the tradition continued of donating food items to the college when money was lacking. The Alumni Association in planning the college's 1940 Harvest Festival urged, "Why not follow the good old custom of dedicating a pig, a calf, a dozen chickens, a plot of garden, an acre of potatoes to the Lord's work?"[17]

In addition to finances there was the continuing problem of public relations. Anderson College's liberal arts program had been approved by the General Ministerial Assembly in June 1928, but not without resistance and

---

15. Ibid., 159–60.
16. Ibid., 161–62.
17. Mildred M. Hatch, "The Alumni Association," *Gospel Trumpet*, May 25, 1940, 7.

some opposition. In 1936 and later, Morrison was still trying to convince various groups within the movement of the wisdom of a church-supported liberal arts college. For this task he often used his regular column in the *Gospel Trumpet,* titled "College Corner." There he argued:

> If the American of the future is to be blessed with leadership in statesmanship, in industry, in economics, in education, and in all other great realms of human endeavor, leadership must be developed in accordance with the principles of the Christian religion.
>
> Just here is where the Christian college stands forth in its high purpose....We must train missionaries, ministers, and religious education workers, to be sure, but our responsibility does not end there. We need Christian school-teachers. We need Christian lawyers. We need Christian business executives. We need Christian statesmen. These leaders need to be thoroughly committed to the principles of Jesus' way of life. Where is such a leadership to be gotten if it is not to be gotten in the ranks of the church? Who is to inculcate these Christian ideals and ideas if the church does not?[18]

Enrollment at Anderson College showed fairly steady growth during this period. By 1946 the student count was about triple what it had been in 1936, but there were some lean years in between. With an expanding program the very existence of the college depended on an increasing enrollment, and World War II took its toll. In 1943 Morrison reported that fifty male students had left during the prior semester, leaving 350 students on campus:

> In the interest of national well-being, the Government has seen fit to defer students falling within such categories as pre-medical, pre-engineering, and theological students. Students falling within these various classifications, together with many women students who are preparing for teaching, religious education work, and other lines of work, will constitute a student body large enough to insure this school's remaining open.[19]

The college needed recognition by the academic community as well as greater acceptance in the church. The college was inspected for accreditation in 1937 by the Indiana Department of Public Instruction and, as

18. John A. Morrison, College Corner, *Gospel Trumpet*, January 18, 1936, 10.
19. John A. Morrison, "Anderson College and the War," *Gospel Trumpet*, May 15, 1943, 3.

a result, was approved for the granting of degrees by the Indiana State Board of Education.[20] This meant that work done at Anderson College was validated for training public school teachers. State approval gave the college considerable academic credibility, but there remained the major hurdle of accreditation by the regional association.

By 1940 Dean Russell Olt decided to push for full accreditation by the North Central Association of Colleges and Secondary Schools. Four objectives were identified: (1) enrollment of 500 students, (2) North Central accredit-

After accreditation in 1946, Anderson College began a program of campus development that drew on civic as well as church leaders. The photo illustrates this widening circle of support. Standing are college trustee Wilbur Schield, assistant to the president Robert Reardon, and Dean Russell Olt; seated are President John Morrison, General Motors CEO Charles E. Wilson, and local banker Linfield Myers.

ment, (3) lifting all indebtedness, and (4) establishment of a loan fund for ministerial students.[21] In April 1942 Anderson College applied for admission into the North Central Association with the objective of meeting all requirements within four years.[22] The accreditation team spent several days in a preliminary inspection. Upon reading their assessment, Morrison remarked, "As Dean Olt and I pondered the report it seemed to us that what was wrong with us was a mountain and what was right was a molehill."[23] They set to work, however, and on March 27, 1946, the college was granted full accreditation. Morrison's diary recorded the following:

March 29, Friday. The Pennsylvania train from Chicago pulled into the Anderson station this morning at 2:00 a.m. Dean Olt and I got off and what did we see? Five or six hundred students and teachers with the College band—all jubilant over the fact that A. C. had been fully accredited.

20. Morrison, *As the River Flows*, 185.
21. *Yearbook of the Church of God*, 1941.
22. Morrison, *As the River Flows*, 185.
23. Ibid., 186.

We formed a long and noisy line up Eighth Street and College Drive to Old Main and hundreds of them crowded into the main lobby to hear short talks by the Dean and me. We went to bed at 4:00 AM…[24]

Classes were cancelled for that day. The following year Anderson College received further recognition when it was voted membership in the Association of American Colleges.

By the mid-1930s the ministers in the Pacific Northwest were considering whether to reopen the Bible institute that had functioned earlier in Boise and Seattle. In September 1935, the Northwest Ministerial Assembly met in Spokane, Washington, and unanimously approved E. V. Swinehart's motion to establish a college for training ministers. A special meeting was held in Portland, Oregon, in January 1936, at which the assembly decided to purchase the old missionary home in Spokane for the college. At its next regular meeting that September a board of trustees was elected and plans were made to incorporate Pacific Bible College. In February 1937 the school was incorporated and $700 was raised to purchase the missionary home and make necessary repairs.[25] Classes began on October 5, 1937, with eight regular and two special students. The faculty included Daisy Maiden, who taught on Monday and Friday, and A. F. Gray, who taught on Tuesday, Wednesday, and Thursday.[26] Gray served also as pastor of the Woodland Park Avenue Church of God in Seattle, and commuted Mondays and Fridays. He resigned his Seattle pastorate in 1938 to devote full time to the new school.

Courtesy of Anderson University and Church of God Archives

Albert F. Gray (1886–1969) minister, church leader, and educator. From humble origins in North Dakota, A. F. Gray became a pastor and in 1936 the founding president of Pacific Bible College, later Warner Pacific College. Gray also served as the chairperson of the General Assembly for a total of eighteen years, a record.

---

24. Ibid., 189. See also, "Thank God, Anderson College Is Fully Accredited," *Gospel Trumpet*, May 4, 1946, 3–5.

25. Albert Frederick Gray, *Time and Tides on the Western Shore* (N.p., privately published, 1966), 97–98.

26. Ibid., 98–99.

In 1940 the school moved to a larger facility in Portland. With borrowed money they bought a former sanatorium on the southern slope of Mt. Tabor in the southeast section of the city. By 1943 the school was free of debt. From the beginning the primary aim of Pacific Bible College was to train ministers and church workers. It was primarily supported by the churches of the Pacific Northwest until it came to be included in the national World Service budget in 1947. A great academic boost for the school came with the appointment of Otto F. Linn as dean in 1942. Linn held a PhD from the University of Chicago and formerly had been professor of New Testament and Greek at Anderson College.[27] He had resigned from the Anderson faculty in 1936 in a curriculum dispute with Russell Olt. From 1936 to 1942 Linn served as pastor of the Church of God in Dundalk, Maryland. A student of Edgar Goodspeed at Chicago, Linn was to serve on a translation subcommittee of the Revised Standard Version of the Bible. By 1946 the college had been accredited by the Oregon State Department of Education and had an enrollment of almost two hundred students.

In western Canada, the Alberta Bible Institute came into existence in the 1932–33 academic year; the first term began in January of 1933. The guiding personality behind what was at first called Alberta Bible Training School was Harry C. Gardner, its principal and president for twenty years. The school opened with two branches, one under Gardner in Edmonton and one under Jacob Wiens in Medicine Hat. The two branches were joined in Ferintosh, Alberta, in 1934 and the following year the school was moved to Camrose. In 1937 the name of the school was changed to Alberta Bible Institute. A year later it boasted an enrollment of sixty-four students. By 1947 it was incorporated with authority to train ministers, missionaries, and gospel workers.[28] Today, it is known as Gardner College.

Back in Anderson other changes were in progress. The Board of Sunday Schools and Religious Education had changed its name to the Board of Christian Education in 1935. This national agency had been staffed by volunteers and part-time help until 1940, when Irene Smith became the first full-time field worker for the Board; by 1944 she was the first full-time executive secretary. The Board of Christian Education found its greatest opportunity for service to the church through classes for laypeople and ministers, enabling them to acquire credits in leadership training. Over

27. Ibid., 100–103.
28. Alberta Bible Institute, *Catalogue 1976–77* (Camrose, AB: Gospel Contact Press), 4.

a thousand credits were issued in 1937 and three thousand in 1940; the number of credits issued increased more than 50 percent in following years.[29] The Board encouraged the formation of similar boards in each state. The 1942 *Yearbook* listed the chairpersons of boards of Christian education for twenty-nine states and a Sunday school convention calendar for conventions in eighteen states.[30] In 1938 a lending library was proposed. In addition, the Board supported committees on children's work, adolescent work, adult work, vacation church schools, leadership training, family and parent education, and conventions and institutes.[31] In 1939 the Board inaugurated a mimeographed quarterly for pastors titled "Planning Creatively," and in 1942, under the leadership of T. Franklin Miller they be-

Irene Smith Caldwell (1908–79), Christian educator. The author of several books in the field of Christian education and a curriculum consultant for the Gospel Trumpet Company/Warner Press, She served on the faculties of four Church of God colleges and the School of Theology at Anderson College.

gan publishing a periodical titled *Planning Creatively for the Church School.* It developed into a monthly periodical for leaders.

The Sunday school was the most prominent element in Christian Education. In late 1940 the following article appeared in the *Gospel Trumpet*:

In 1940...THERE has been a national demand that we launch a comprehensive Sunday-school campaign all over North America, and everyone seems to feel that if we are able to increase our church attendance and strengthen our churches we must do so by strengthening our Sunday-schools.

The Gospel Trumpet Company will celebrate its sixtieth anniversary in 1941, and as one feature of this anniversary celebration we have planned a campaign to increase our Sunday-school attendance at least 50 percent, and we are going to cooperate with every Sunday school

---

29. *Yearbook of the Church of God*, 1937, 7; 1940, 12; 1943, 13; 1944, 19.
30. *Yearbook of the Church of God*, 1942, 22–23.
31. *Yearbook of the Church of God*, 1938, 8.

of the Church of God in North America in this campaign. It can be done.[32]

Four weeks later A. T. Rowe, general manager of The Gospel Trumpet Company, repeated the first goal—and then added another feature to the campaign:

OUR great Sunday-school attendance campaign is on. It is not a contest; it is not one Sunday school trying to beat another; it is an effort to do two things; namely, increase the attendance of our present schools all over the country by 50 percent and, second, to organize 1,000 additional Sunday-schools….Let's go, Church of God Sunday Schools, and make 1941 a banner year![33]

Almost immediately local Sunday school leaders became aware of problems and situations hindering growth. Problems included inadequate buildings, lack of trained leadership, pastoral opposition to the Sunday school, transportation problems, and the cost of Sunday school literature.[34] Rowe offered help on the last problem by providing free literature to any new Sunday school for the first quarter. The report at the end of the campaign a year later showed these gains:

1. 391 new Sunday schools organized
2. 1184 schools enlisted
    a. of these, 434 reached a 50% increase on at least one Sunday
    b. of these, 9 schools showed a 50% increase for the whole year[35]

Another major effort in Christian education during this period was the United Christian Advance. This was a Church of God adaptation of the interdenominational United Christian Education Advance promoted by the International Council of Religious Education. The International Council had proposed this program as a means of reaching the unreached half of America's population through Christian education. The Church of God adaptation

---

32. A. T. Rowe, "Calling All Sunday-School Workers," *Gospel Trumpet*, December 14, 1940, 13.

33. A. T. Rowe, "The Great Sunday-School Attendance Campaign Is On," *Gospel Trumpet*, January 11, 1941, 17.

34. A. T. Rowe, "Some Questions Answered," *Gospel Trumpet*, January 18, 1941, 6.

35. Lestie Pletcher, "Report on the 'Forging Forward in '41' Campaign," *Gospel Trumpet*, May 16, 1942, 11.

of this five-year program (1941–45) initially included the following major aims: (1) reach the unreached; (2) train workers; (3) deepen spiritual life; (4) Christianize the home. A great number of printed materials were developed to support this program. The program was widely accepted in the Church of God because the Advance was viewed as a great opportunity for evangelism. By 1944 new aims were added: (5) launch new congregations; (6) promote Christian reading; (7) enlist youth.[36] Roughly half of all Church of God congregations in America actively participated in the Advance.

Both the Sunday School Campaign and the United Christian Advance helped raise the movement's consciousness level in the area of Christian education. In addition to courses by the Board of Christian Education and books published by the Gospel Trumpet Company, a wealth of Christian education resources was published in the pages of the *Gospel Trumpet*. Besides articles on doctrine, the magazine offered articles on family life, social problems, the use of music, pastoral responsibilities, pastor-people relationships, and relating the Bible to contemporary living.

Beginning with the church school quarterlies for October 1, 1936, the Gospel Trumpet Company began publishing a line of life-centered, graded curriculum materials. By December of the same year, A. T. Rowe could report that the response to the Christian Life series included encouragement from all the states and many foreign countries.[37] Several months later, Rowe again reported, "The new Christian Life series of Sunday-school literature is getting a fine reception from the field."[38] He based his opinion on the facts that several three-day Sunday school conventions were planned, that Lawrence Brooks was visiting churches to promote the series free of charge, and especially that larger orders were being received.

Later Lawrence Brooks offered an explanation for the enthusiastic use of the new curriculum. He stated that the Christian Life series had a good appearance for its price and was properly graded. He had confidence in the writers and editors of the materials and found the content safe and acceptable. Also, he thought it important to be loyal to the publishing house of the Church of God.[39]

---

36. Donald Addison Courtney, "A Study of the Development of the Sunday School in the Church of God," (BDiv thesis, Anderson College and Theological Seminary, 1954), 98.

37. A. T. Rowe, "New Sunday-School Literature Appreciated," *Gospel Trumpet*, December 12, 1936, 12.

38. A. T. Rowe, "Sunday School Notes," *Gospel Trumpet*, February 6, 1937, 7.

39. Lawrence E. Brooks, "Why I Use Church of God Sunday-School Literature," *Gospel Trumpet*, November 15, 1941, 3.

All of these developments were taking place in the context of World War II. The war may have boosted the economy, but it also cast a shadow everywhere. For at least ten years, the war and the events that led up to and followed it were newspaper headlines, topics of conversation, and sources of anxiety and speculation. References to the war were seen everywhere, and religious publications were no exception. For instance, the *Gospel Trumpet* ran an advertisement that pictured three warplanes. The message was a challenge for "spiritual rearmament."[40] Long before the United States became directly involved in the conflict the Church of God missionaries had an increased awareness of the war. Missionary Lester Crose wrote, "As we face world conditions today our hearts are grieved. No man dare foretell what the morrow will bring forth." He went on to say:

> While all around there is destruction and confusion, they [the missionaries] alone are the ones who can heal and unite. And yet it takes something for them to stay on the foreign field. Food has gone up three and four times higher in price. All other necessities for living are extremely scarce, and many missionaries are laboring under sacrifice.[41]

Already missionaries were being forced to return to the United States for their own safety. The following 1940 report preserves some of the flavor of the haste, danger, and uncertainty of the times:

> Two telegrams from New York City brought us the good news that our workers in the Scandinavian countries had arrived safely in New York. On Saturday morning, May 24, we received the first telegram. It came from Brother and Sister Lars Olsen. They had been fortunate enough to secure permission from the German government to travel from Denmark, through Germany and on to Genoa, where they were able to board the Italian liner, the S. S. "Conte de Savoia."
>
> Yesterday, May 27, we received the second telegram. It told us that Brother and Sister Ring had just arrived in New York from Sweden. By what line they came, and how they managed to get out of that war-torn area we do not know. Later on they will write a report that we shall publish in the Gospel Trumpet.

---

40. *Gospel Trumpet*, September 27, 1941, back cover.
41. Lester A. Crose, "What about Foreign Missions Today?" *Gospel Trumpet*, October 19, 1940, 11–13.

All of our readers will rejoice with us and them over their safe arrival in this country.[42]

Adam W. Miller, secretary of the Missionary Board, informed the church that instead of sending supplies to the missionaries yet remaining overseas, which was costly, uncertain, and subject to high customs charges, great efforts should be made to send full allowances to the missionaries—cash, not goods.[43] The missionary work also faced obstacles beyond financial consideration. C. E. Brown cautioned:

Not only have there been problems concerning the support of our missionary work, the anxiety concerning the safety of some of our missionaries, and the difficulty in keeping in touch with them, but the far greater question of how the changes brought about by the war will affect missionary work in these countries. We must prepare to meet these changes.[44]

As part of this preparation, the Missionary Board had already begun planning an emergency fund in case missionaries needed to be evacuated, and to help them withstand the higher prices caused by the war.[45]

In these troubled times one particularly poignant report by Adam W. Miller stated, "Missionaries and Christians in every country affected by the war have shown remarkable fortitude and courage, and have continued the saving ministry of Christ in spite of dropping bombs and the horrors of modern warfare." He continued by sharing a letter from Thaddeus Neff, then serving in Alexandria, Egypt. After a recent series of air raids that involved many deaths, including the deaths of everyone in a nearby maternity hospital, Neff poured out his heart:

We are very tired and nervous these days, and it is very difficult to get the rest one needs. We do hope and pray that the civilized and Christian people will become awakened and do something to stop this brutal aerial war on the civilian population. I cannot think nor write of what

---

42. Adam W. Miller, "Our Scandinavian Workers Arrive Safely in America," *Gospel Trumpet*, June 22, 1940, 21–22.

43. Adam W. Miller, "Notice Concerning the Sending of Supplies to Missionaries," *Gospel Trumpet*, December 7, 1940, 14.

44. *Yearbook of the Church of God*, 1941, 6.

45. *Yearbook of the Church of God*, 1940, 8.

happens, and how terrified children become, without weeping. To think that our so-called civilization seemingly has lost all its humane feelings! Please remember us in prayer.[46]

Besides the anxiety felt for the missionaries and the mission work, Church of God people responded to the developing war in other ways. For instance, antiwar sentiment was expressed by James T. Murray in his article "What War Means."[47] C. E. Brown's book, *The Way of Prayer,* was advertised as dealing with the question, "Why does God permit war?"[48] More information about the war was offered in the book *I Was in Prison,* by Charles S. MacFarland, which was advertised as containing suppressed letters by German pastors exposing Hitler's attack on Christianity.[49] One article simply dealt with the question, "What can we do about war?"[50] Others proposed to supply all new soldiers with a pocket edition of *The Christian's Treasure,* a compilation of Scripture passages. Part of the reasoning for this project ran along these lines:

> Sixteen million of our young men registered, subject to a call to army camps and from there to the battlefield. If called, some will never return; others will be in hospitals or will be prisoners of war. It may not be your son, brother, or husband, but some mother or relative of a young man will be praying and wishing that some kind friend will lend a helping hand for the spiritual welfare of that one.[51]

The expanding war posed many questions to all Christians, especially to those associated with groups having pacifistic tendencies such as the Church of God. At first, many warnings and negative speculations appeared in the *Gospel Trumpet.* Anderson College professor Earl Martin, after reviewing historic clashes between church and state, wrote concerning a more recent encounter:

---

46. Adam W. Miller, "In Spite of Bombs," *Gospel Trumpet*, August 16, 1941, 4.

47. James T. Murray, "What War Means," *Gospel Trumpet*, April 6, 1940, 14–15.

48. *Gospel Trumpet,* January 25, 1941, 21.

49. *Gospel Trumpet,* February 24, 1940, 22.

50. The Universalist Builder, "What Can We Do About War?" *Gospel Trumpet*, May 18, 1940, 1–2.

51. By One Who Cares, "Getting the Gospel to the Soldiers," *Gospel Trumpet*, November 8, 1941, 16.

The decision in the famous Macintosh Case in our Supreme Court may seem like past history, but it is not. Professor Macintosh applied for citizenship, but refused the oath to take up arms in war, which he believed to be contrary to the law of God. He thought that the Constitution of the United States granted him religious liberty, the right to serve God according to the dictates of his own conscience, but the court's decision said: "When he (Doctor Macintosh) speaks of putting his allegiance to the will of God above his allegiance to the government, it is evident, …that he means to make his own interpretation of the will of God the decisive test….We are a nation with the duty to survive; a nation whose constitution contemplates war as well as peace; whose government must go forward upon the assumption, and safely can proceed upon no other, that unqualified allegiance to the nation and submission and obedience to the laws of the land, as well as those for war as those made for peace, are not inconsistent with the will of God." Maybe you agree that this decision is just, but there can be no doubt that it means that the state, and not the individual, is to be the interpreter of the will of God.

Martin further clarified his own position in saying:

Bear in mind that we are not here talking against nationalism or patriotism. This is our country, and as long as my duty to my country does not conflict with my duty to God, I must serve my country.[52]

Another article published the same year counseled, "America, Stay Out of War." It appeared conspicuously on the first page of an October issue of the *Gospel Trumpet* and was written by Anderson College student Val Clear.[53]

One article dealt with the nature of conscientious objecting—whether to killing in specific or to war in general—and discussed the degrees to which objectors were involved in the previous world war. The authors were quite frank in revealing statistics reporting the severe mistreatment of conscientious objectors during World War I. They went further to state, "The importance of the conscientious objector must not be underrated. As long as the state is compelled to recognize the right of the individual to freedom of conscience the basic principles of democracy can be said to be still

52. Earl Martin, "Christianity and Nationalism," *Gospel Trumpet*, January 21, 1939, 3.
53. Val Clear, "American, Stay Out of War," *Gospel Trumpet*, October 14, 1939, 1.

alive."[54] The hope these writers offered the potential conscientious objector of the future was based on the actions of the past: "Special treatment for the conscientious objector in the last war was brought about not so much by their numbers as by their obvious sincerity, and by the existence of a very small but militant sector of public opinion in their favor."[55]

Despite the fact there was no official position stated by the Church of God regarding participation in the war, it was apparent that many individuals in the movement were conscientious objectors. They needed some kind of declaration from their church to support their position. It was time for the Church of God to take action, and the General Ministerial Assembly responded:

> ...in regular session on this 18th day of June, 1940, empower and direct the EXECUTIVE COUNCIL OF THE CHURCH OF GOD in Anderson, Indiana, to act for the Church in its relations with the Government of the United States, or with its appointed boards or agencies, if and when the need arises for the following purposes:
>
> 1. In securing for the members of the Church of God exemption from combative participation in war.
> 2. In securing exemption from such compulsory military training, in peace time or in war, as implies or involves combative participation in armed conflict.

F. G. Smith moved the adoption of the resolution. It was seconded and adopted without a dissenting vote.[56]

The assembly action reaffirmed the antiwar position of the Church of God. The Gospel Trumpet Company set up a "Peace File" for the depositing of signed statements by those who wished to register their objection.

As the United States readied itself for possible direct involvement in the war, it became apparent that not all the people in the Church of God saw the war issue from the same standpoint. The majority entered the military without qualms. In fact Church of God men entered the armed services at rates higher than the general population. Although not exclusively the case, the large majority of conscientious objectors in the

54. Lucille B. Milner and Groff Conklin, "Conscience in War Time," *Gospel Trumpet*, April 13, 1940, 3.
55. Ibid.
56. Minutes of the General Ministerial Assembly, June 18, 1940.

Church of God were ministers or ministerial students, not laypeople. Some objectors complied with the Selective Training and Service Act of 1940 and registered for the draft with a request for a CO classification; some did not register. Others decided on noncombatant military service as a kind of ministry rather than performing civilian work. One such was Dick Hendricks, who stated:

> There was much noncombatant work I could do in the army which would assist in no way in death or destruction. Rather, it would help greatly if a Christian would choose this field. What better place is there to bring the gospel of Christ than to an army camp, where at times there is no other hope except Him?…Yes, I decided, a Christian life lived there could be an influence for good while in an objectors' camp I would be among my own kind, for the most part.[57]

By the time the United States declared war on Japan it was reported:

> A LARGE number of graduates or former students of Anderson College are now serving their country in the various ways as their conscience directs. Some are chaplains; others are to be found in the air force, the navy, the army, and in C.P.S. camps.[58]

There were many other ways the war affected the Church of God. Foreign missionaries were most vulnerable to the war, especially those in Asia, Europe, and the Near East. The Church of God continued to be concerned about the missionaries and their work. The 1942 *Yearbook* reported that no news had been received from the European churches. The John Croses were forced to leave Syria, but soon began working in India. The Lester Croses began working in Barbados and Trinidad when it was found they could not go to Syria.[59] The 1944 *Yearbook* reported that the Hunnexes, missionaries in China, had been interned in a prison camp in Shanghai.[60] The Missionary Board was making plans for 1945 to set aside emergency funds to train new missionaries, begin new works, and rebuild churches.[61]

---

57. Dick Hendricks, "An Objector Chooses the Army," *Gospel Trumpet*, October 25, 1941, 20.
58. Frederick A. Schminke, "Serving Their Country," *Gospel Trumpet*, April 25, 1942, 17. CPS refers to the Civilian Public Service camps set up as "Alternative service" for conscientious objectors.
59. *Yearbook of the Church of God*, 1942, 15.
60. *Yearbook of the Church of God*, 1944, 15.
61. *Yearbook of the Church of God*, 1945, 17.

The Church of God saw many opportunities to minister during the difficult war years. The program of the Board of Church Extension and Home Missions included the Wartime Emergency Service, which involved ministry to soldiers and religious work in defense communities.[62] The Christian Crusaders, the youth organization of the Church of God, made an effort to stay in contact with all Church of God service members through quarterly mailings.[63] Ministering efforts continued to come to light, such as the military chaplaincy, ministry to the spouses of soldiers and sailors, or comfort and help to war widows.[64] The *Gospel Trumpet* helped direct the thoughts and actions of its readers. One article counseled, "Let Us Pray for a Just and Durable Peace."[65] Another sought to answer the questions many Christians were asking.[66] Still another sought to define the relationship between religion and patriotism. Editor C. E. Brown made the following observations:

1. Antipatriotism is rooted in sophistication
2. Patriotism does not endorse what is wrong in the nation
3. Patriotism is not the equivalent of state religion
4. One can love one's country without obstructing higher loyalties[67]

Congregations found it difficult to make long-range plans. Wartime building restrictions would not allow the construction of new church buildings. The Board of Church Extension and Home Missions advised congregations to take this time to create reserve funds for the future.[68] No General Ministerial Assembly meeting or Anderson Camp Meeting was held in the years 1943 or 1945 due to wartime travel restrictions. To compensate for the loss of the camp meeting, C. E. Brown suggested local World Service Days, a special week of services in local congregations, and

62. *Yearbook of the Church of God*, 1943, 11.
63. Ibid., 21.
64. Chaplain Byrum L. Martin, "The Chaplain and His Job," *Gospel Trumpet*, June 9, 1945, 12–13; Mildred M. Hatch, "Fellowship for Servicemen's Wives," *Gospel Trumpet*, June 16, 1945, 8; Harold L. Phillips, "A Letter to a War Widow," *Gospel Trumpet*, July 1, 1944, inside front cover.
65. Earl L. Martin, "Let Us Pray for a Just and Durable Peace," *Gospel Trumpet*, June 2, 1943, 3–4.
66. H. C. and Florence Heffren, "Why Doesn't God Intervene?" *Gospel Trumpet*, April 10, 1943, 18–19.
67. C. E. Brown, "Religion and Patriotism," *Gospel Trumpet*, July 1, 1944, 1.
68. *Yearbook of the Church of God*, 1945, 13.

a greater attendance at state camp meetings.[69] Brown reported concerning the camp meeting that was held in Anderson in 1944 that the presence of young men was sorely missed; his only son and two sons-in-law were among those away serving in the armed forces.[70]

As the Church of God anticipated an end to the war, speculation grew about post-war life. Predictions, positive and negative, were made as the Church of God anticipated an end to the war. Several *Gospel Trumpet* articles expressed the expectation that the boys who left for war would be changed by the suffering, homesickness, and evil they experienced as soldiers.[71] They would be different people, observed one writer, who would need many things, including jobs and love.[72] In fact, another wrote, one could expect the whole world to be changed—impoverished by war, full of hatred and psychologically damaged. To face this situation, the writer advised, "Organization and education, necessary as these may be, must never take the place of love in our ministry."[73] The challenge of the world's agony was evident to the Church of God. One bright spot was the anticipated possibility that Church of God service personnel who came into contact with foreign cultures and/or Church of God missionaries would become inspired to become missionaries themselves.[74]

With the war's conclusion, the Church of God sensed great opportunities for evangelism and ministry. Titles of *Gospel Trumpet* articles expressed this awareness: "Christianity, the Postwar Need," "The Church and Returning Service Personnel," and "The Dawn of the Atomic Age."[75] An unsigned article expressed the relief felt by all in a decidedly spiritual tone, "The War Is Over—Let Us Express Our Thanks with Giving." It was noted:

> The end of the war marks the return of our boys and girls to take again their places in the church congregations and choirs. It marks the

---

69. C. E. Brown, "How to Compensate for the Loss of the Camp Meeting," *Gospel Trumpet*, April 10, 1943, 1.

70. C. E. Brown, "Camp Meeting in Wartime," *Gospel Trumpet*, July 29, 1944, 1–2.

71. John A. Morrison, "Anderson College and Postwar Problems," *Gospel Trumpet*, May 6, 1944, 3, 12.

72. W. W. King, "When the Boys Come Home," *Gospel Trumpet*, March 3, 1945, 3–4.

73. Carl M. Kilmer, "The Minister in the Postwar World," *Gospel Trumpet*, February 27, 1943, 9–10.

74. Adam W. Miller, "Our Service Men Discover Missions," *Gospel Trumpet*, June 19, 1943, 13.

75. Carl M. Kilmer, "Christianity, the Postwar Need," *Gospel Trumpet*, September 30, 1944, 15; Denzel R. Lovely, "The Church and Returning Service Personnel," *Gospel Trumpet*, January 12, 1946, 5–6; Albert F. Gray, "The Dawn of the Atomic Age," *Gospel Trumpet*, October 26, 1946, 5–6.

reunion of families. The lifting of travel restrictions means we can drive to church not only on Sunday, but during the week; state and national camp meetings can be held.

The writer observed that missionaries could return to their posts, mission facilities could be replaced and enlarged, and workers could be trained.[76] Such dreams were quickly turned to action. In 1946 seventy-five missionaries were working with the Missionary Board; eleven new missionaries had been sent out; eighteen more would be sent within six months.[77]

Wartime suffering did not cease when hostilities ended. Church of God publications increasingly made their readers aware of the desperate plight of war's victims. Hundreds of thousands of war orphans in Europe were desperate for the basic necessities of life—clothes, medicines, milk and other foods, adequate shelter, even shoes. It was explained that, "The mass destruction of towns and villages, by fire or otherwise, the extermination of the adult population or its deportation explain the presence of millions of homeless children now."[78] The situation seemed terrible at the time, but the prospect for the long-term effects of malnutrition and homelessness seemed overwhelming.[79] Another article along the same lines dealt specifically with the plight of German orphans.[80]

Nora Siens Hunter (1873–1951), founder and president of the National Women's Home and Foreign Missionary Society of the Church of God from 1932 to 1948. From 1893 to 1896, Nora Siens teamed with Lena Shoffner to evangelize throughout the Midwest and Middle Atlantic states. After her marriage to Clarence Hunter in 1896, Nora took the lead in this husband-wife evangelistic and pastoral team.

76. "The War Is Over—Let Us Express Our Thanks with Giving," *Gospel Trumpet*, September 22, 1945, 13.

77. I. K Dawson, "High Lights from Annual Reports of Our General Church Boards," *Gospel Trumpet*, August 3, 1946, 17.

78. Bulletin of the Joint Relief Commission of the International Red Cross, "The Situation in Europe," *Gospel Trumpet*, October 12, 1946, 12–13.

79. Ibid.

80. Anna Koglin, "The Children! The Children!" *Gospel Trumpet*, March 16, 1946, 8–9.

Even more poignant sensitizing to needs across the world was evident. Nora Hunter's well-marked copy of *They Shall Inherit the Earth* (a book about the plight of children in wartime), and her notes between its pages attest to her role as a goad to the conscience of the Church of God as she traveled the country speaking to women's groups and churches.[81] Other heart-searching topics in the *Gospel Trumpet* included "Only God Can Save Japan," and "Millions Need Bread."[82] The Missionary Board reported:

> The churches in China need our assistance in rebuilding the churches destroyed and damaged. From Japan has come word that five of our six church buildings in Tokyo have been destroyed….In Germany the devastation has been beyond description. Brief reports indicate that nearly all of our churches were destroyed. Here is a great task ahead of us. In the Philippines, the two church buildings survived and the Christians are carrying on as best they can.[83]

Such reports caused some church leaders and laypeople to question their own consciences. After having participated in the destruction of churches abroad, how could an estimated 90 percent of Church of God congregations in the United States plan some kind of building expansion for themselves?[84] Many resolved the issue by doing both—building and helping to rebuild. The church also recognized new problems on the home front. Marital break-ups and juvenile delinquency became issues of the day. Marriages made in haste during the war and long separations frequently prevented relationships from flourishing. Extramarital romances, gossip, adultery, and other forms of immorality contributed to the instability of many marriages and added to a rising divorce rate.[85] A syndicated article by FBI Director J. Edgar Hoover in the *Gospel Trumpet* stressed parental responsibilities for the moral guidance of children. In support of his plea he cited a rise after the war in serious crimes committed by an increasing percentage of teenagers.[86]

---

81. See Nora Hunter biographical file, Anderson University and Church of God Archives. The book is Otto Zoff, *They Shall Inherit the Earth* (New York: John Day Co., 1943).

82. By a Young Japanese Woman in Tokyo, "Only God Can Save Japan," *Gospel Trumpet*, March 16, 1946, 12–13; T. Franklin Miller, "Millions Need Bread," *Gospel Trumpet*, December 21, 1946, 17.

83. *Yearbook of the Church of God*, 1946, 17.

84. C. W. Hatch, "Can We Build Greater While They Have None?" *Gospel Trumpet*, October 12, 1946, 17.

85. Carl Kardatzke, "Saving Our War Marriages," *Gospel Trumpet*, June 29, 1946, 17.

86. John Edgar Hoover, "Parents—Wake Up and Act," *Gospel Trumpet*, October 19, 1946, 7–8.

Despite paper shortages, the period 1936–46 was one of considerable activity in the Church of God in the area of publications. A list of some of the more significant books produced by the Gospel Trumpet Company during this time is impressive and includes the following:

1937: *The Christian's Treasure*, E. E. Byrum
       The New Testament Church, H. M. Riggle
       The Preacher of Today, J. A. Morrison
1939: *The Church Beyond Division*, C. E. Brown
       At Work with Young People, Ida Byrd Rowe
1940: *Guide to Christian Stewardship*, R. L. Berry
       The Way of Prayer, C. E. Brown
       Songs of Zion
       Thoughts on the Life of Faith, E. E. Byrum
1941: *Toward Understanding God*, Earl Martin
       The Secret of Being Strong, C. W. Naylor
       Gospels & Acts, vol. 1 of *Studies in the New Testament:*,
       Otto F. Linn
1942: *The Gospel of John*, Otto F. Linn
       Romans to Philemon, vol. 2 of *Studies in the New
       Testament:*, Otto F. Linn
       Hebrews to Revelation, vol. 3 of *Studies in the
       New Testament:*, Otto F. Linn
       To the Chief Singer, Axchie A. Bolitho
1943: *An Introduction to the New Testament*, Adam Miller
       The Way of Faith, C. E. Brown
1944: *The Gospel of Luke*, Earl Martin
       The Gospel of Mark, Otto F. Linn
       The Gospel of Matthew, Adam Miller
       Solving Church School Problems, Irene Smith
       The Meaning of Salvation, C. E. Brown
       Christian Theology, vol. 1, A. F. Gray
1945: *The Meaning of Sanctification*, C. E. Brown
       Divine Healing, Warren C. Roark
1946: *Adventures in the Spiritual Life*, C. E. Brown
       Christian Theology, vol. 2, A. F. Gray

One of the 1942 publications was particularly significant in that it presented a variant interpretation of the book of Revelation. In his preface to *Hebrews to Revelation,* the third volume of *Studies in the New Testament,* Otto F. Linn wrote, "Since there is a great deal of controversy centered around the interpretation of many of the symbols of this difficult book, the author submits this writing with reserve. It is hoped that those who differ will have as tolerant an attitude as the writer has toward their differences."[87] Linn's exegesis differed greatly from the so-called "standard" interpretation by F. G. Smith and other earlier writers. This variation explains the primary reason why the third volume of Linn's series was published for him by the Commercial Service Company (the job printing subsidary of the Gospel Trumpet Company), rather than by the Gospel Trumpet Company itself.

In dealing with the portion of volume 3 on Revelation, Linn stated:

We must ask ourselves the question: What would this particular passage mean to those to whom it was directly written? Otherwise, we might develop a technique of interpretation that is wholly acceptable to the Western analytical mind but entirely foreign to the poetical Oriental mind which served as the vehicle for the divine revelation. This is a common error of interpreters.[88]

He also made quite a point against the generally accepted church-historical interpretation of Revelation when he wrote:

It should also be observed that since historical situations are involved and history has a way of repeating itself, some of these symbols may find a striking fulfillment in events other than those originally intended. For this reason people of all ages have tended to interpret the Book of Revelation in the light of their own time, and we may have been startled by the apparent application of some symbols to current history. It is very important that we keep in mind that *history repeats itself* and that such repetitions are not to be confused with the original historical situations, although the moral or lesson intended may rightly be applied to every apparent repetition.[89]

---

87. Otto F. Linn, *Hebrews to Revelation,* vol. 3 of *Studies in the New Testament* (Anderson, IN: privately published, 1942), v.
88. Ibid., 80.
89. Ibid., 80–81.

Besides the regular publishing of the *Gospel Trumpet,* books, tracts, and curriculum materials, the Gospel Trumpet Company was also involved in a publishing work for the blind. The guiding spirit behind this work was Grace DeFore, who was herself blind. Three periodicals were published in Braille—the *Gospel Trumpet,* the *Sunday School Monthly,* and the *Junior Sunday School Monthly,* the former two also being published in point. It was the practice of this ongoing project to send a free copy of the Braille Christmas issue of the *Gospel Trumpet* to all known blind people.[90] De Fore's office also conducted a lending library by mail since postage was free for reading materials sent to the sightless. DeFore was pleased with an exhibit of handcrafted goods made by blind people on display in the blind printing office. "Many seem to think," she said, "that when one loses his sight he loses all, and we are glad to give such people a concrete example to disprove this theory."[91]

Otto F. Linn (1887–1965), educator. Linn was the first minister of the Church of God to earn an academic doctorate; he taught at Anderson College from 1930 to 1936. After a pastorate in Dundalk, Maryland, in 1942 Linn moved to Portland, Oregon, where he served as dean and professor of New Testament at Pacific Bible College. In addition to several commentaries published by the Gospel Trumpet Company, Linn also worked on a subcommittee that assisted with the translation of the Revised Standard Version of the Bible.

The wartime economy made possible two special fund-raising efforts. The Quarter Million Campaign, the first of these, grew out of the success of Christ's World Service Day. "The QUARTER MILLION CAMPAIGN was launched as an intensive effort by the Church of God to raise a quarter million dollars EXTRA by June 1944, mainly as a postwar reserve fund."[92] Movement leaders anticipated greater financial support for missionary endeavors after the war. The Church of God rose to the challenge and that year raised a total of $258,000. C. W. Hatch reported that regular World Service giving was estimated to have been $70,000, and so

---

90. Grace DeFore, "The Blind Included in the Last Commission," *Gospel Trumpet,* December 19, 1936, 7.

91. Grace DeFore, "A Visit to Braille Land," *Gospel Trumpet,* November 30, 1940, 3–4.

92. *Yearbook of the Church of God,* 1945, 5.

this was combined with the Quarter Million Campaign funds in order to reach the goal that had been set. A sign of longer-range growth was that in 1945 the church raised over $100,000 on Christ's World Service Day and recorded a total of $280,425 given that year for general causes.[93]

Close on the heels of this successful venture and in response to the great needs of the postwar world mentioned earlier, the Church of God in June 1945 began its second financial drive of the decade, the Million Campaign. Many projects were included in this ambitious project, including a national radio ministry, greater missionary expansion, the rebuilding of destroyed overseas church buildings, the first dormitory for Anderson College, expanded evangelism, and the urgent needs in a devastated Europe.[94]

The slogan of the Million Campaign was "The Truth to Millions." The goal of the two-year drive was $1,000,000 by June 1947. To accomplish this goal the campaign sought to have every congregation participating by Easter 1946, to challenge individuals to give a week's salary, and to challenge congregations to (1) increase the number of generous givers, (2) increase the size of the gifts, and (3) increase the total number of givers.[95] The campaign also encouraged fifty days of prayer before Easter for the needs that had been identified. The publicity affirmed, "Although the goal each year has been set in dollars, the real goal has been souls.... The war is over and doors of opportunity are opening on every hand."[96]

By June 30, 1946, more than $225,000 had been collected in the Million Campaign.[97] The stated objective was that the remaining balance would be pledged by Thanksgiving and that the total amount would be in hand by the following June.[98] A dramatic victory event was planned for Christ's World Service Day, June 15, 1947. A giant thermometer display registering $100,000 dominated the front of the large tabernacle. It was to be raised to the top and restarted ten times as gifts over the two-year period were recorded. Led by a group of well-known ministers, the entire audience, singing as they marched, passed by the altar and left their offerings. The crowd rejoiced as the thermometer went up again and again. The jubilation subsided, however, when the register stopped after the sixth climb. C.

---

93. C. W. Hatch, "Another Outstanding Victory," *Gospel Trumpet*, July 21, 1945, 3–4.

94. *Gospel Trumpet*, May 4, 1946, inside back cover (architectural drawing).

95. *The Million Campaign News*, April 1946, 1–2, 4, 6.

96. Ibid., 4.

97. C. W. Hatch, "Church of God Giving Reaches All-Time High," *Gospel Trumpet*, July 27, 1946, 7.

98. *Gospel Trumpet*, November 2, 1946, 22.

W. Hatch wrote, "Great was the disappointment. The church cannot go forward on disappointment. We must gird ourselves with renewed effort and vigor for the great task before us."[99]

The following day the General Ministerial Assembly, in a mood of "the work must go forward," adopted the largest annual budget to date—a half-million dollars. Part of this was allocated to some of the unmet needs resulting from failure to raise the total in the Million Campaign. "The great task," said Hatch, "is still out there yet to be done."[100]

In the midst of these campaigns, and even before, other special efforts were made for outreach and expansion. One of these projects was "A National Church in the Nation's Capital." This was first proposed in 1937 through an article by Earl Martin titled "Washington—The Religious Capital of the United States." He explained that many groups were represented in the nation's capital by a thriving congregation in a beautiful building. Martin asked for responses as to whether the Church of God desired a representative church building in Washington, DC.[101] His proposal became a project of the Board of Church Extension and Home Missions. A congregation of one hundred already existed in the city and a building lot was purchased by 1940. The drive was on in February 1940 to pledge money for the erection of a new building.[102] Under the local leadership of Pastor Esther Boyer, groundbreaking ceremonies were held during the International Youth Convention in August of 1940. Architectural plans were approved by the District of Columbia Building Commission and construction was begun in May of 1941. The project was culminated by the dedication of the new Gothic building in January of 1942.[103]

An interest in radio broadcasting also had begun to develop. In 1936 Warren C. Roark, pastor in Canton, Ohio, wrote of the success of his half-hour program on a local Akron station. This program was funded by area congregations, emphasized singing, and included a ten-to-twelve-minute message. Roark reported that the results from the program included many letters and increased attendance in area churches. He thought that broadcasting on local stations better served the interests of the church than a

---

99. C. W. Hatch, "Another Great Christ's World Service Day," *Gospel Trumpet*, July 26, 1947, 4.

100. Ibid.

101. Earl Martin, "Washington—The Religious Capital of the United States," *Gospel Trumpet*, August 14, 1937, 8–9.

102. W. T. Wallace, "Can a Church Be Built in Washington During February?" *Gospel Trumpet*, February 17, 1940, 15–16.

103. *Yearbook of the Church of God*, 1942, 11.

national network program because a national hookup was more expensive, the listening public knew the local congregation and its pastor, and the program would be better supported by the local church.[104] These factors were decisive in Roark's mind, even though a nationally sponsored program might be of higher quality.

Ten years after Roark's pioneering efforts however, a national broadcast was announced. Interest in and support of radio programming had grown. In 1938 there were twenty-two radio programs listed, and by 1946 there were forty-five broadcasts by local Church of God pastors. Sponsored by the Board of Church Extension and Home Missions, a coast-to-coast (soon around-the-world) broadcast, to be known as the *Christian Brotherhood Hour*, was slated to start, and did, in January 1947. The initial twelve sermons were delivered by W. Dale Oldham; the program's director and announcer was Richard Lee Meischke.[105]

The work of the Woman's Missionary Society in the period 1936–46 cannot be overlooked. In 1936 the bimonthly magazine *Friends of Missions* began publication; it included news of missionaries, promotional methods, and study guides on missions. It became a monthly publication in 1938.[106] The Missionary Society from its beginning in 1932 had always sought not to duplicate the work of any Board or agency or divert funds away from any worthy cause; most of the money they collected was dispensed through existing Boards.[107] Some of the large Society projects they completed during this period were: $4,000 for a church building in Shanghai (1936), $3,000 for the Ludwig residence at Kima (1939–41), and $25,000 for a mobile clinic and dispensary for Lalmanirhat station, Bengal, India (1942–46). Projects in progress in 1946 included a five-year plan to raise $25,000 for a hospital unit for Kima and a four-year plan to raise $12,000 for a school in Kentucky.[108]

Home missions involvement by 1946 included projects in Alaska (Anchorage, Palmer, Kodiak), Mexico, among Spanish-speaking people in the United States (Los Angeles, San Antonio), among Native Americans (Park Hill, Oklahoma; Lapwai, Idaho; Marysville, Washington; Wounded

---

104. Warren C. Roark, "Radio Broadcasting," *Gospel Trumpet*, January 11, 1936, 13.

105. "Church of God On the Air…Coast-to-Coast," *Gospel Trumpet*, September 7, 1946, 21.

106. Hazel G. Neal and Axchie A. Bolitho, *Madam President* (Anderson, IN: Gospel Trumpet Co., 1951), 70–71.

107. Axchie A. Bolitho, "National Woman's Missionary Society of the Church of God: A Brief Survey 1932–1946," (Anderson, IN: National Woman's Missionary Society, 1946), 6.

108. Ibid., 7–8.

Knee, South Dakota; Toppenish, Washington; Cody, Wyoming), among agricultural migrants, Japanese-Americans (Seattle, Los Angeles), and among mountain people of Kentucky and Tennessee.[109]

The many factors in the movement's development during this period naturally led to changes. Probably one of the most significant of these changes was a definite trend toward a more forward and businesslike approach to problems and situations that formerly had been handled by the decision of a small group or an individual. An article such as "How Should a Congregation Proceed in Regard to a Pastor's Resignation, Retaining Their Pastor, or Getting a New Pastor?" attacked old problems in a more formal, systematic fashion.[110] The practical application of the principle of Holy Spirit leadership had never been programmed and many were seeking some supplementary human help for divine guidance.

Editor Charles E. Brown emerged as an intellectual leader as he introduced fresh theological insight on organization's relationship to the church. He wrote a number of editorials about the functional aspects of the church. Brown commented, "Somehow there has gone abroad the idea that it is a mark of spirituality to be stubborn, non-cooperative, and independent in one's attitude toward the church."[111] Instead, he noted, there must be a reemphasis on the role of the Holy Spirit in directing the work of the church:

> In the Church of God at the present time we acknowledge only one ruler—the Holy Spirit. Holy Spirit rule in the church is within two spheres: first, it operates in the spiritual work of saving souls, sanctifying believers, healing the sick, and the like; and second, in the management of the temporal affairs of the church.
>
> It is in connection with this second sphere of Holy Spirit rule that the accusation of man rule is usually associated.[112]

In another article Brown reaffirmed the historic view in the movement that by its very nature the church is more than an organization:

---

109. *Yearbook of the Church of God*, 1946, 10–11.

110. R. L. Berry, "How Should a Congregation Proceed in Regard to a Pastor's Resignation, Retaining Their Pastor, or Getting a New Pastor?" *Gospel Trumpet*, February 20, 1937, 11–12.

111. C. E. Brown, "Our Duty to Work Together," *Gospel Trumpet*, October 2, 1943, 1.

112. C. E. Brown, "Man Rule in the Church," *Gospel Trumpet*, February 22, 1941, 1.

Just as the church is one, both visible and invisible at the same time, so the church is an organism. The church is not an organization. It cannot be organized.[113]

He then continued, with new perspective, by affirming,

True, we can organize the work of the church. We can systematize that work; we can appoint committees to carry out that work. That is what the church did in the apostolic age. That is what we have a right to do. But that is far different from organizing the church itself.[114]

Brown went further to explain traditional Church of God teachings about the organization of the church's work:

In this reformation we have always taught that men cannot organize the church. The church is the body of Christ, and we believe that denominationalism has perpetuated division in the body of Christ by seeking to organize the church and by this means creating organized divisions which bar some of Christ's people. We stand against this practice with all the earnestness and conviction that our leaders taught in this work more than sixty years ago.[115]

He then used the following analogy to reconcile the paradox of an unorganizable church being organized to accomplish goals:

But certain members of a large human family could organize certain business activities without impairing their relation to the family in any way. And this is what has been done in the pure church from the beginning.

In this reformation we have always taught that the church has the right to organize its business activities and its administrative work.[116]

He went counter to tradition, however, when he proposed that the way to ensure the will of the Spirit in decision making was the democratic method of voting. This he supported thusly:

---

113. C. E. Brown, "The Visible and Invisible Church," *Gospel Trumpet*, February 9, 1946, 1.
114. Ibid., 2.
115. C. E. Brown, "Working Together for the Lord," *Gospel Trumpet*, April 3, 1943, 1.
116. Ibid.

…since the church is the body of Christ, since each of its members is a priest and a king in its holy fellowship, therefore the safest way to obtain the guidance of the Holy Spirit and to submit our problems of government to His direction is by free vote of the persons concerned.[117]

Brown thought that self-appointed individuals had no more right to decide than those chosen by the group. Thus, "the only road of safety for the Church is that its gifted leaders shall appeal to the common consent and cooperation of the members of the church."[118] Thus he stated:

The *Gospel Trumpet* is not the personal mouthpiece of any one man. It is the voice of our Church and of the ministry everywhere lifted in a perpetual witness of the truth by the sacrificial and cooperative efforts of tens of thousands of self-sacrificing Christians.[119]

In this way, Brown eased the consciences of many people in the Church of God about organization in the life and work of the church. Acceptance of his teachings allowed for free development of organization as needed within the church.

During this era, state organizations also were emerging and, due to several factors, were encouraged to develop. The movement had grown large enough that it was not feasible for Brown as editor, or anyone else for that matter, to be knowledgeable concerning the character and standing of the many people sending in articles for publication and reporting their activities through the *Gospel Trumpet.* Brown clearly stated his policy:

In every issue of the *Gospel Trumpet* at the beginning of the "Church Notices" occurs this statement: "All names of ministers or workers appearing in these reports must have the endorsements of their State Registration Committee." …Undoubtedly the Lord knows us all, including the people in prisons and in editorial offices, but there is a moral problem involved for us.…

Now the rule in the Gospel Trumpet office is that the ministers of a district are the sole judges of whether a person is in good standing in the ministry. The editor of the Gospel Trumpet absolutely refused

---

117. Brown, "Man Rule in the Church," 2.
118. Ibid.
119. Brown, "Our Duty to Work Together," 2.

to decide any such question. No one at the editorial department could know a person's standing with the ministry as do the ministers among whom he labors constantly....We do not wish to recommend persons unknown or unacceptable to their own ministerial brethren and we wish no minister or worker would ask us to do so.[120]

This policy could not help but foster district and state cooperation while opening the door for stronger organization among ministers at this level. The ordination committee of the General Ministerial Assembly moved in the same direction when it suggested in 1938 that all candidates for ordination be referred to the state level for determination of eligibility and for certification. This obviously helped strengthen these regional organizations.

The General Ministerial Assembly also became more businesslike and organized during this period. In 1940 the term of office for the secretary of the Assembly was lengthened from one year to three, thus providing more stability and continuity of leadership. The chairperson two years later suggested that Boards print or mimeograph their reports instead of reading them to the Assembly. This practice would allow members of the Assembly time to study the reports more carefully and better use the time of the annual sessions.

In summing up it may be said that the decade of 1936–46 was a period of great growth for the Church of God. Despite the continuing economic uncertainty and all the disruption of a world war, membership in the movement in the United States almost doubled. There was a significant increase in the number of congregations, in the number and size of Sunday schools, in the number of ministers, and in the number of church buildings—even in a time of war-diverted money and restrictions on construction. With more people and more money there was a broader perspective on the total work of the church and a great increase in resources and fiscal responsibility. With new momentum and direction the Church of God in 1946 was truly a moving movement.

---

120. C. E. Brown, "Concerning Names in the Year Book," *Gospel Trumpet*, August 29, 1936, 4.

CHAPTER 14

MID-CENTURY PAIN AND PROGRESS
(1946–1954)

The sense of relief and yet also expectancy that accompanied the end of World War II was expressed by Elver F. Adcock, registrar for the Church of God Clergy Bureau:

> There have been great events and tremendous changes in the world. We have had the end of World War II, the atomic bomb, the return of millions of our men from the battlefronts of the world, and there is an attempt at the making of peace.... The tasks confronting the church today are greater than ever before....
>
> This is a year of decision for the Church of God. The call to greatness has come. We must witness with all that we have and all that we are if we are to stem the tides of disillusionment, despair, hatred, and violence that are still threatening to engulf all the world. Something of heroic service on the part of every minister and every layman is demanded in times like these.[1]

Adcock's statement was more prophetic than he knew. In 1946, but also for the decade following, the Church of God would be called upon to make many crucial decisions, not only about its witness in a peace-building, atomic bomb–frightened world but also in regard to the movement's own internal peace and unity in the context of a growing and more diverse constituency.

The first postwar concern, of course, was to complete some of the tasks begun during the conflict but which remained unfinished. In 1944 the General Ministerial Assembly in 1944 had created a World Peace and Post

---

1. *Yearbook of the Church of God*, 1946, 3.

War Problems Committee. Part of this committee's original assignment was to arrange alternative service opportunities for conscientious objectors from the Church of God. In large part the church had purchased participation rights in the program of Civilian Public Service Camps established by the Church of the Brethren. In 1946 Russell Olt, chairperson, reported to the Assembly that a balance of approximately $20,000 was still owed to the Brethren Service Committee under this arrangement. He noted that the Brethren were willing to accept payments in kind for distribution in their postwar relief program as well as cash in payment of the obligation. Congregations and individuals were thus urged to give heifers, clothing, or staple commodities for this purpose. Thus the Church of God could receive appropriate credit toward paying their debt and at the same time would be contributing to the desperate needs of people in devastated parts of the world. The committee report stated:

> We are sure the Church of God will not lag behind in doing its part at this critical time.
>
> Our relief effort, we believe, will do much to restore hope to a disillusioned world and will afford an opportunity for us to give the cup of cold water in the name of Jesus.[2]

In addition to chairperson Olt, other members of the World Peace and Post War Problems Committee were Carl Kardatzke, Irene Smith Caldwell, Ida Byrd Rowe, Adam W. Miller, A. Leland Forrest, and Elver F. Adcock. At that 1946 Assembly the name of the committee was changed to Church of God Relief Committee.[3]

Another postwar concern was to resume disrupted missionary activity around the world. Several missionaries serving in the war zones of the Middle East and Far East had been withdrawn. Charles and Annabel Hunnex, who had been serving in China, were interned in a prison camp in Shanghai but were released at the end of the war. Other missions activity was curtailed because of travel restrictions and shortages in both personnel and funds. In the midst of the war in 1943 there were forty-one missionaries under appointment by the Missionary Board of the Church of God. Nevertheless, the following year, with the war still on, this number jumped to fifty-one. By 1945 the Missionary Board had instituted a

---

2. Minutes of the General Ministerial Assembly, June 18, 1946.
3. Ibid., June 19, 1946.

Five-Year Program to strengthen the whole overseas operation, a new field had been opened in West China, and the number of missionaries had increased to sixty-five. In 1946 there were seventy-eight under appointment serving in twenty stations around the world, including Milton and Eleanor Buettner and David and Elsie Gaulke, who were assigned to the new West China outpost. It was not until 1949, however, that American missionaries returned to Japan with the commissioning of Arthur and Norma Eikamp to Tokyo.[4]

Other national agencies quickly responded to postwar needs and opportunities. The home missions emphasis shifted from attention to ministries in defense communities to more work among Native Americans and Spanish-speaking people. The colleges tooled up for an anticipated avalanche of veterans qualified for educational benefits under the GI Bill. Local churches launched into long-deferred building programs as soon as materials were available. By 1953 the Board of Church Extension decided to staff a new department of church architecture to meet the growing demand for this kind of service. Between 1944 and 1954 the value of local church property increased from $7,050,000 to $43,476,530. During the same period the national World Service budget grew from $250,000 to $1,139,260.[5] Freedom from wartime restrictions had opened the door to rapid expansion in both facilities and programs. All segments of the church were headed toward improvement and growth.

Despite this prevailing expansive mood, by the mid-forties internal rumblings and dissident voices became sufficiently loud and pointed to disrupt the work of all the national agencies and of many local congregations. The particular events that brought this disaffection into the open are readily identifiable, but the real reasons behind what ballooned into a major upheaval are more subtle and require some analysis.

Even before the end of the war the movement's national leadership had become the target of vocal criticism. Over a period of time a general feeling of uneasiness had developed toward the growing and bigger-spending agencies in Anderson. Questions were sometimes raised only to receive unsatisfactory answers. Many ministers and a few laypeople across the country harbored suspicions about the "big boys" who were "running things" in the church's national work. The specifics of this mistrust focused on five

---

4. All data secured from Missionary Board Reports and Directories of Foreign Missionaries in *Yearbook of the Church of God* for each of the years indicated.

5. *Yearbook of the Church of God*, 1945, 5, 111, 132.

general categories of criticism. These categories need to be identified before reviewing the details.

The first point of attack was the accusation that the national leadership was steering the movement away from its historic beliefs and practices. The chief target of criticism was a proposal coming out of a national agency office that was considered to carry the taint of ecclesiasticism and therefore contrary to the principle of Holy Spirit leadership. To some minds another evidence of departure was a 1944 General Ministerial Assembly resolution that seemed open to the possibility of the Church of God joining the Federal Council of Churches. For many even an exploration was abhorrent and a negation of the movement's concept of Christian unity.[6]

A second area focused in accusations that Anderson leaders were letting down the standards regarding various personal, social, and business practices. Rumors circulated that some people in high places were participating in worldly amusements and were resorting to doctors instead of upholding the practice of divine healing. Rumor also had it that the consecrated presses at the Gospel Trumpet Company were being used to turn out indecent literature for some of the job printing customers. Although untrue, in the absence of trust explanations or denials were of little avail.

Another point of concern about the "headquarters" operation was the apparent power bloc that had been allowed to develop as the various agencies were created and as they began to expand operations. The creation of the General Ministerial Assembly had put the agencies under the control of the church, but it had not really changed the earlier pattern of concentrating decision-making in the hands of a few influential leaders. Before 1917 they had simply assumed leadership; after 1917 they were nominated and elected to leadership. These few, through what the business world calls "interlocking directorates," were involved in several of the agencies at the same time. One person, for instance, in 1944 was on the executive committee for three general agencies. Another was a board member for two agencies, president of and a member of the board and board of directors for a third, and a member of the Executive Council.[7] As this condition became more and more apparent the level of dissatisfaction across the country increased.

---

6. Minutes of the General Ministerial Assembly, June 1944. The committee, chaired by Elver F. Adock, was to report back in 1945. Since there was no Assembly in 1945, the committee reported in 1946 that no full investigation of the Federal Council of Churches had been made, and so the committee was discontinued.

7. Data secured from rosters of members on the various boards, *Yearbook of the Church of God*, 1944, 29–31.

Corresponding to the interlocking directorates, a fourth aspect of the mid-forties situation was widespread frustration and feelings of powerlessness on the part of many ministers who envisioned themselves as the "little guys" whose voices were hardly heard. The structure really provided little opportunity for an outsider to challenge the system. The "big-name" pattern of leadership had been with the movement from the beginning, and there seemed no way within the organization to overcome it. Many were at the point of being willing to join in a protest outside the structure and attack the individuals involved directly—at every point where they might be vulnerable.

The final factor in the overall context of the period, but not specifically articulated by the critics of the Anderson establishment, was a sentiment growing out of the war itself. In this particular conflict the enemy had been dictatorships under the labels of Nazism, facism, and imperialism. There was great appeal for the perpetuation of the democracies that had just emerged victorious over the dictatorial ideologies of Hitler, Mussolini, and Hirohito. There was equal concern for democracy at other levels. Certainly no comparisons were made, but the value and pride in participatory decision-making was in the heady atmosphere of postwar victory. Individual ministers in the Church of God whose significance had been diminished by increasing numbers and the controlled character of the system were ready to assert themselves.

All of these feelings had been building up for some time, but the flashpoint of open controversy did not arrive until late 1944 when Muncie, Indiana, pastor and radio preacher L. Earl Slacum delivered a sermon at the annual meeting of the Indiana ministers under the title "Watchmen on the Wall." On September 19, 1944, Slacum preached the sermon that was to place him in the spotlight in the Church of God for the next several years as the key stimulus in a period of severe agitation. In this discourse he stated, "I know the cry comes that we should not be alarmists, but I am alarmed."[8] He continued by citing what he considered to be a previous serious departure from historic Church of God doctrine:

I remember very distinctly, when a gentle departure from what we have always believed and known took place in this very state, in a STATE MINISTER'S MEETING SOME FIFTEEN YEARS AGO.

---

8. L. Earl Slacum, "Watchmen on the Walls." Mimeographed copy of sermon delivered on September 19, 1944, to the meeting of the Indiana Ministerial Assembly of the Church of God, Terre Haute, Indiana.

It was the first liberalized statement of CHRISTIAN UNITY AMONG US. It was a departure from the clear vision that God has given us. Then like a stream, it has widened, until now it reaches the entire movement in spots.

The reference was to Russell R. Byrum's sermon on Christian unity, which had triggered the Anderson College controversy in the late twenties and led to Byrum's resignation from the faculty. Byrum had stated:

What is Christian unity?...Some think of it as being almost an absolute uniformity in doctrinal belief, in type of religious experience, and in conduct. The New Testament does not so represent Christian unity.... But what then is Christian unity if it does not consist in the foregoing particulars? Christian unity consists in loving fellowship.[9]

In addition to Byrum's alleged liberalism, Slacum cited examples of what he considered departures from the movement's additional earlier teachings. He saw signs of worldliness, failure to preach certain doctrines and, most of all, the growing power of the general agencies of the church in Anderson. The prime example was a booklet just released by the Board of Church Extension and Home Missions titled *Working Together in an Enlarged Program of State Evangelism.* Written by I. K. Dawson, secretary of evangelism for the Board, the thirty-two-page pamphlet outlined a plan for congregations in a state to join together in employing a state evangelist who would assist in and coordinate all evangelistic work in the state. To Slacum this was an "ecclesiastical octopus" (there were eight suggested officers who would constitute an executive council) that had the power of "entwining around the activities of all phases of the work." The balance of Slacum's sermon attacked this Dawson Plan specifically and decried trends that he had seen developing generally, with particular attention to the "man-made organizations" in Anderson. Slacum called for "a definite stand against the system."[10]

The remainder of the 1944 Terre Haute meeting was spent discussing both the plan and Slacum's attack. Opposing viewpoints were expressed and the debate was on with each side presenting its position and the other side rebutting. When the vote was taken, the plan and even a revised compromise

9. Russell R. Byrum, "Christian Unity," Anderson University and Church of God Archives.
10. Slacum, "Watchmen."

were both defeated. Unfortunately, the basic issues became lost in attacks on personalities. Personal differences were remembered long after the meeting ended and became major irritants as the controversy expanded. In fact, while growing ecclesiasticism within Anderson and a steady decline in doctrinal preaching were the original concerns of Slacum and his followers, as time passed personalities were attacked more often than principles defended.

Earl Slacum's role as a defender of the faith had begun much earlier. Born in Maryland and converted under the preaching of Emma C. Coburn in Federalsburg, he came to Anderson Bible Training School in 1923 and completed the three-year course. After pastorates in Illinois and Ontario he returned to Anderson in 1935 to begin a radio ministry. In 1938 he moved his "Bible Hour" program to Muncie and became pastor of a new congregation there. Known as a straight-line preacher, in the 1943 state ministers' meeting, he had vigorously challenged a speaker who depreciated doctrinal preaching and expressed a great concern for preserving the solid truths that brought the Church of God into being. [11]

In early 1944 Slacum published an article in the *Gospel Trumpet* titled "Doctrinal Dangers Facing the Church of God."[12] He expressed a fear that doctrinal preaching was being forgotten in the pulpits and asked the church to consider the effect this would have on the message and upon one's own spiritual life. Slacum also referred to a study done by Robert Reardon as part of his graduate thesis, which surveyed representative Church of God pastors and found them becoming less concerned about the doctrine of sanctification.[13] These and other signs were warnings to Slacum that something had to be done to correct a doctrinal slippage.

In September, the *Gospel Trumpet* published a second Slacum article. This one was titled "Is An Apostasy Emerging?"[14] It appeared just three days prior to the meeting in Terre Haute.

In the Terre Haute meeting and immediately following, Slacum received considerable affirmation, so he decided to go national in his campaign. He began publishing a paper under the same title as his sermon, which appeared in the first issue. *The Watchmen on the Walls* (later renamed *Church of God Watchman*) was sent to every minister listed in the *Yearbook*. He

---

11. Interview with L. Earl Slacum, April 1979.

12. L. Earl Slacum, "Doctrinal Dangers Facing the Church of God," *Gospel Trumpet*, February 19, 1944, 9–10.

13. Robert H. Reardon, "The Doctrine of the Church and the Christian Life in the Church of God Reformation Movement" (Master's thesis, Oberlin Graduate School of Theology, 1943), 128.

14. L. Earl Slacum, "Is Apostasy Emerging?" *Gospel Trumpet*, September 16, 1944, 7–8.

appealed for a response "so that some action may be taken...to correct this thing." In subsequent issues he delivered a frontal attack on many of the leaders and most of the agencies in Anderson. In addition to his own knowledge and suspicions about laxity and deviations, he received a great deal of his ammunition for these attacks through an anonymous informant who regularly sent unsigned, typewritten letters mailed with an Anderson postmark. Claiming neither time nor means to verify the allegations, Slacum nonetheless published what he received.[15]

Allegations, even unsubstantiated, often find an audience. Responses supposedly from hundreds of ministers and laypeople encouraged Slacum to continue with vigor, and he did. Other ministers, such as Samuel W. Joiner, E. A. Fleenor, and H. F. Allen from Indiana, W. G. Finney, Elmer Powell, and I. W. and Marie Gibson from Illinois, Peter Wiseman from Ohio, J. B. Brunk from Michigan, and African missionaries John and Twyla Ludwig either contributed to the magazine or allowed their names to be reported as supporters of the *Watchman.* It is not possible to determine either the geographical or numerical extent of Slacum's following, but it was considerable. Despite the fact that most of his specific charges were never substantiated, there was sufficient general dissatisfaction to keep the protest barrage alive. For seven years the whole Church of God movement was troubled with persistent internal agitation.

The movement's establishment reacted and rebutted, but Slacum's accusations resulted in no dismissals or resignations. The Anderson-based leadership did not panic. Indeed poet-preacher M. A. Monday expressed the tolerant and almost patronizing mood of many in a ten-verse poem, three verses of which follow:

I know a man who prints a sheet
But there's nothing in it that is sweet;
He calls it "Watchman on the Wall."
I think he must have had a fall.
He seems to think there's nothing right,
The church is in an awful plight.

All of the boards have gone astray
And are leading us the downward way.

15. Interview, April 1979.

He says we all have apostatized,
That all of us have compromised;
Of course, he is still ringing true
And wants to tell us what to do.

He says we must go back some years,
Because we've gone too far, he fears,
And let the "Watchman" pilot us.
We must ride the Reformation Bus;
Our model of nineteen and forty-five
Must count back years for sixty-five.[16]

Church agencies and their staffs made no attempt to defend their actions or answer Slacum's charges. Nonetheless they were concerned about the possible effect in the church. Rather than react personally, it was judged wiser to deal with their agitators only through official channels, the regularly constituted state and national ministerial assemblies.

The first formal responses did not occur until the 1945 Indiana Ministerial Assembly. That assembly passed a resolution expressing disapproval of Slacum's attacks and asking that he cease all opposition toward Anderson.[17] Slacum did not comply and more and more people seemed to be aligning themselves with him, two factors that, along with the resolution, led to the 1946 appointment of a committee of the national General Ministerial Assembly to investigate all charges. The committee's intent was to put an end to all unsupported allegations and to restore harmony within the fellowship. This committee, known as the Committee on Research and Improvement, was chaired by Indianapolis pastor W. W. King and was composed of seven members. They were to report their findings to the 1947 General Assembly. They met with Slacum and his group on several occasions and thoroughly investigated matters on their own.

Slacum's agitation had created a crisis of confidence. In response the church called upon one of its most stalwart supporters, F. G. Smith. After having been a central figure in the national work for almost three decades, he had been removed from his editorial post in 1930 and had become a pastor in Akron, Ohio. Smith proved to be a very capable parish leader, and from this base had continued to serve the church nationally as a lecturer

---

16. M. A. Monday. Entire poem in the Anderson University and Church of God Archives.
17. Minutes of the Indiana Ministerial Assembly of the Church of God, September 19, 1945.

and evangelist. Many Anderson leaders thought that Smith could render the national work a great service in helping to heal the eroded trust resulting from the Slacum agitation. In 1946 he was elected president of the Gospel Trumpet Company and was asked to return to Anderson as director of public relations. Smith threw himself into this assignment with zeal and energy, and there was evidence of progress. In this capacity Smith traveled across the country with a message of confidence. He answered questions, cleared up rumors, and listened to complaints. While in the midst of this challenging and important assignment, F. G. Smith suffered a fatal heart attack and died April 24, 1947.

When the General Ministerial Assembly met on June 16, 1947, chair-person A. F. Gray opened the session by stating that the Assembly was not an ecclesiastical court established to settle differences of opinion.[18] After one or two orders of business, the report from the Committee on Research and Improvement was called for. The committee reported they had found no basis in fact for most of the personal charges. To charges of doctrinal and behavioral laxity by certain agency personnel, the committee reported that there was no "habitual" relaxation. To the charges of ecclesiasticism within Anderson, the committee reported they found nothing to be out of harmony with accepted Church of God practices. However, they went on to recommend that an enlarged committee be appointed to further study agency structures.[19] This recommendation brought the Committee on Revision and Planning into existence.[20] Over the next several years this committee reviewed such structures as the Ministerial Assembly, the Execu-tive Council, the Gospel Trumpet Company, and various other agencies within the Church of God.

In the afternoon session there was more consideration of the report of the Committee on Research and Improvement. There was some heated discussion, the full text of which is not available, and Slacum took the floor. He began by asking forgiveness of anyone he had offended. He further apologized for any possible mistakes and false materials that he might have published in his papers. He then pleaded that corrective action be taken for those abuses he had uncovered.[21] He admitted his errors, but he likewise maintained that his attacks were not entirely without merit. Slacum felt that

---

18. Minutes of the General Ministerial Assembly, June 16, 1947.
19. Minutes of the General Ministerial Assembly, June 17, 1947, first session.
20. Ibid, second session.
21. Ibid.

if some of his allegations could effect a change for the better within agency structures, his entire effort would have been worth the price he had paid.

Unfortunately, in Slacum's opinion, the Assembly was not ready to admit to serious errors, and he regarded this inaction as an attempt to whitewash the entire episode.[22] It was this apparent cover-up that caused Slacum to continue the cause. The Assembly further confirmed his feeling of rejection and suspicion by formally reaffirming its faith in the agencies and condemning Slacum for his actions.[23] Furthermore, this resolution demanded that all disruptive activity immediately cease. A second resolution censuring the agitators was proposed but defeated. The defeat of this second resolution was of small consequence to Slacum's group, for in their minds the damage was done and the die cast. As a result of the Assembly's action, over the next few months a number of ministers and congregations withdrew their fellowship from Anderson. These dissident congregations rallied around Earl Slacum in a "reformed" reformation, which they called the Church of God but which became known colloquially as the Slacum movement or the Watchman movement. While division was never Slacum's intention, he took this road as a result of the Assembly action and pressure from those who sided with him.

An example of the withdrawals during this time is the action of a congregation in Bessie, Oklahoma. They voted to unite with Slacum and wrote a letter of disfellowship to Anderson from their congregation. In this letter the pastor, E. C. Tennant, stated that because of the apostasy within the Church of God in Anderson the church in Bessie must disfellowship that body. The letter goes on to state that whenever the body in Anderson is willing to repent the church in Bessie will gladly refellowship them.[24]

Since the 1947 action left Slacum with no plausible alternative but to withdraw himself from working relationships with Anderson, he moved out on his own. The new movement quickly developed its own organization for the promotion of those principles he was trying to defend. They assumed operation of a Bible school in Plymouth, Indiana. This school, the Ministers and Missionaries Training School, was begun in 1946 by Samuel Joiner but was not officially aligned with Slacum until late 1947. In Ashland, Kentucky, the group established the World Missionary Society of the

22. Taped interview, January 26, 1976, Anderson University and Church of God Archives.

23. Minutes of the General Ministerial Assembly, June 17, 1947.

24. Letter from E. C. Tennant and Marvin Reuber to Lawrence Brooks, March 15, 1950, Anderson University and Church of God Archives.

Church of God. Its purpose paralleled the Missionary Board in Anderson. The Ashland society recruited and supported John and Twyla Ludwig in Africa and E. Faith Stewart in Cuba.[25] These organizations were financed by the congregations within this movement and by donations received as a result of Slacum's radio broadcasts.

Anderson leaders and others regarded the new Watchman organizations to be in direct defiance of the 1947 resolutions. Therefore, a group of twenty-one ministers, mostly agency personnel, petitioned the Ordination and Yearbook Committee of Indiana to withhold the name of L. Earl Slacum from the 1948 *Yearbook*. The Indiana committee met on December 12, 1947, and agreed to the petition. They drew up a letter to this effect and mailed it to the registrar of the Clergy Bureau. The Clergy Bureau withheld Slacum's name, an act tantamount to official disfellowshiping. In June 1948 the Indiana Assembly followed this action with a resolution declaring Slacum no longer in fellowship.

A satellite center for the Watchman movement developed in Illinois with evangelists I. W. and Marie Gibson and Decatur pastor W. G. Finney as the principal leaders. The Gibsons' activities led to a 1948 resolution by the Executive Council of the Illinois Assembly recommending their names be withheld from the *Yearbook* "until such time as he [Slacum] should be readmitted to the fellowship of the ministers." The Illinois Assembly concurred in this action in early 1949. The Gibsons were restored to full fellowship, however, in September 1951. W. G. Finney's defection was much more complicated in that he pastored a large congregation and sought to take the whole group and its property with him into the Slacum camp. Some members objected, along with other ministers in the area. The result was a split in the congregation and court action regarding the property. The Finney faction lost. Eventually the congregation was restored to unity and Finney was disfellowshiped.[26]

Driven out of the only church he had ever known, Slacum put all of his energy into the new movement. Additional individuals and/ or congregations joined him. The Ministers and Missionaries Training School increased its enrollment, and the missionary work found good support. Ironically, this growth led to organizational expansion, and Slacum watched with alarm as this new reformed church body took on

25. Taped interview, January 26, 1976.
26. Minutes of the Illinois Ministerial Assembly, November 16, 1949. The court action also involved the Executive Council of the Church of God for an extended period.

the characteristics that had prompted his break with Anderson in the first place. Finally, in May of 1951, Earl Slacum could no longer stand the incongruity, and he wrote a letter that served as the death notice of the Watchman movement. In that letter Slacum pointed out that this new movement had developed more structure in five years than Anderson had in twenty-five. He emphasized that the very thing that had caused controversy to begin with was causing the same form of apostasy within their own ranks. He said that he could not continue on such a path and was resigning from all boards within the movement.[27] Later in that same year he contacted Andersonians Adam Miller, Gene Newberry, and Val Clear concerning his desire to refellowship with Anderson. His letter and subsequent conciliatory actions led to the speedy demise of the Watchman movement. Others, more radical than Slacum, tried to keep the splinter group going, but without its true leader the real force of the movement was gone. Slacum was refellowshiped by the Indiana Assembly in 1953, as were several others aligned with him. Some individuals and congregations, however, never attempted to be refellowshiped. The church in Bessie, Oklahoma, kept waiting for the entire Church of God reformation movement to repent.

One of the positive results of this controversial era was a serious reevaluation of many aspects of the movement's national organization. Significant in the process was the work of the Committee on Research and Improvement and its successor, the Committee on Revision and Planning. Even before there were any recommendations from a study committee one significant change had taken place in the national structure. The World Service Committee had been composed of the executives of each of the agencies participating in the distribution of budgetary funds. This committee met annually with each member requesting a dollar amount for the next year's operation of his agency. Determining which agency might get increases, keeping budget percentages in line with precedent, and limiting the total within the range of approval by the General Ministerial Assembly were difficult problems to handle in this head-to-head encounter. Certainly it did not foster good relations between the agencies. In 1945 the World Service Committee was reorganized and renamed. By vote of the Assembly it became the World Service Commission, and its membership was doubled by adding an equal number of elected individuals. The presence

27. Slacum, "An Open Letter" dated May 21, 1951, Anderson University and Church of God Archives.

of disinterested parties improved both the procedures and the climate of the budgeting process.

The Committee on Revision and Planning was to study certain suggestions and recommendations made by the Committee on Research and Improvement concerning the organization of the general boards and agencies and their relationship to the General Ministerial Assembly. In the process of study, the committee came to function as a bylaws revision committee. Each year, for no more than five years nor less than three , the Revision and Planning Committee was to present recommendations and suggestions to the General Assembly as needed changes were identified and agreed upon. In the course of the next two years the committee introduced changes such as restructuring the World Service Commission and creating the position of historian for the Church of God. It also recommended that the boards be aware of duplications in making their nominations and arranged for the appointment of a standing committee on public relations.[28] The committee's largest piece of work was a rather thorough study of a possible reorganization of the whole national structure for 1948–49.

In the 1948 report to the General Assembly, the consensus of all members of the committee was that problems lay mainly in three fields:

1. The desire for more direct rights and privileges on the part of the ministry in the making of nominations to the general boards
2. The desire for more direct control of the boards and their policies by the ministry
3. The desire for a more representative General Ministerial Assembly[29]

After the 1948 General Ministerial Assembly the Committee on Revision and Planning surveyed all ministers for their opinions in regard to several possibilities for reorganization of the national work:

1. A change in nomination procedures
2. A coordinating committee
3. A centralized board
4. A delegated assembly
5. A general church council[30]

---

28. Minutes of the General Ministerial Assembly, June 14, 1949.
29. Minutes of the General Ministerial Assembly, June 16, 1948.
30. Minutes of the General Ministerial Assembly, June 14, 1949.

In the 1949 session of the General Ministerial Assembly, the committee reported that over 44 percent of the questionnaires returned expressed the opinion that there should be no substantial change from current structures.[31] The committee still felt a bit uneasy, however, so they suggested that in order to establish better working relationships and understanding between general agencies, special times of dialogue should be set up by pastors or laypeople in the field. The boards should set up these times of discussion during Anderson Camp Meeting. This procedure was tried but did not meet with great success. At this point, the committee was somewhat at a loss for further suggestions since no clear-cut desire for change in any particular direction had surfaced.

Throughout its original term the Revision and Planning Committee was sensitive, first, to the apparent desire on the part of the ministry for a closer working relationship between themselves as members of the General Ministerial Assembly and the boards and, second, to better working relationships between the several boards. In its comprehensive, final report in 1952 the committee reviewed the six-year period since the original Committee on Research and Improvement had been appointed, presented ten generalizations that again noted problems and some possible solutions, and then recommended that the work of the Commission on Revision and Planning be continued for another five-year term. This recommendation was approved.[32]

The new commission continued to work cautiously, taking into account the major issues that had been identified by its predecessor. By 1954 there emerged a design for restructuring that was relatively simple but also addressed to many of the problems with which the commission had wrestled. The changes centered on the Executive Council, which had been created in 1932 as a continuing legal entity for the General Ministerial Assembly but had been delegated only a limited number of continuing responsibilities. By this 1954 action the council was enlarged, reorganized, and assigned more specific functions than previously, including some that were coordinative in nature. This was particularly true in revised budgeting procedures. The World Service Commission became a division under the council. The Clergy Bureau became another division and was renamed Church Service. Public relations functions were assigned to a third division designated as General Service. Various commissions and committees also were related

31. Ibid.
32. Minutes of the General Ministerial Assembly, June 18, 1952.

to the council. More importantly, perhaps, than any other function, the restructured Executive Council provided a neutral arena in which various agencies could relate to each other without the competitive climate inherent in the previous system. Since elected members, including some laypeople, would always outnumber the agency representatives, the power potential of the Anderson leadership was considerably curtailed. This realignment proved to be the major work of this second five-year term of the Commission on Revision and Planning.[33]

While all this agitation and study had been going on, several other significant developments had been taking place. One of these was to be the occasion for both fruitful outreach and severe internal friction. In 1946 Richard Meischke, an Anderson College student interested in radio and employed at a local station, conceived the idea of a nationally distributed Church of God radio broadcast. Conversations with W. Dale Oldham, pastor of the large Park Place Church in Anderson, and with the Board of Church Extension and Home Missions, which already had been discussing a similar idea, led to the launching of such a program on the first Sunday in January of 1947. With Meischke (later known as J. Richard Lee) as producer and announcer, Oldham as preacher, music by volunteer singers and instrumentalists, and sponsorship by the Board of Church Extension, the transcribed program was christened the *Christian Brotherhood Hour* and was initially heard on nineteen stations. Its slogan was "A united Church for a divided world." The program proved to be very successful, and by the end of its first month the number of stations airing it had increased to thirty.[34]

Over the course of the next five years the radio ministry continued to expand. Technical difficulties forced several changes in the production and distribution of transcriptions, but these problems were overcome. There was one aspect of the whole operation, however, that seemed to worsen rather than improve—personal relationships between the radio staff and the executive of the sponsoring Board of Church Extension and Home Missions, where offices that housed the *Christian Brotherhood Hour* were located. The deteriorating situation reached a crisis point on December 18, 1951, when the program staff presented a written statement to a meeting of the Board's board of directors declaring that "as of today the *Christian Brotherhood Hour* is a separate and distinct organization independent of other

33. When the second term of the commission ran out in 1957, there seemed to be no unfinished items on its agenda, so authorization was not renewed.

34. *Gospel Trumpet*, January 25, 1947.

Boards and taking its stand before the General Ministerial Assembly of the Church of God."[35] That night the radio office files and certain equipment were removed from the Church Extension Building to another location. The rift was now deep and did not heal easily. No solution appeared until June 1952 when the General Ministerial Assembly authorized the creation of a temporary commission to sponsor radio work.[36] A year later the Commission on Radio and Television became permanent, and after another year found a place in the national structure under the umbrella of the Executive Council.

W. Dale Oldham (1903–84), preacher. Church of God preachers took to the airwaves in the 1930s and '40s. Under the auspices of the Board of Church Extension and Home Missions, a national program was born in 1947. Oldham, pastor of Park Place Church of God, served as its first and longest-serving speaker, 1947–68. The program was first aired on KGGF, Coffeyville, Kansas.

Another important development raised the question of whether it was possible to have a nationally sponsored agency outside the cluster in Anderson, Indiana. Pacific Bible College in Portland, Oregon, supported mainly by congregations in western states, made an appeal for national support through the World Service budget on the basis that it was actually serving the whole church. President Albert F. Gray noted that Pacific Bible College students enrolled from across the nation, and likewise that its graduates found placement throughout the country. After considerable discussion this request was approved in 1947, and after proper funding agreements Pacific Bible College (name changed to Warner Pacific

The original *Christian Brotherhood Hour* quartet. From the very beginning, the movement's syndicated radio program featured fine musical groups. The quartet in particular became a mainstay. Pictured here are Homer Schauer, Gene Dyer, Doug Oldham, and Lowell Williamson.

35. As quoted in a mimeographed statement by the directors and members of the Board of Church Extension and Home Missions. Copy in the Anderson University and Church of God Archives.

36. Minutes of the General Ministerial Assembly, June 18, 1952.

Mid-Century Pain and Progress / 333

College in 1959) became a line item in the general World Service budget. It would take later action, however, to make the college a general agency.[37]

By the late 1940s there was considerable interest by congregations in many parts of the country in starting new colleges. In the central plains there had been talk of starting a new school ever since the demise of Warner Memorial University. Several possible locations in Kansas, Oklahoma, and Texas had been explored. Southern California leaders also were discussing the need for a Church of God institution of higher learning in that area. Likewise there were promoters of church-sponsored schools in the Deep South. All these expressed concerns for starting new educational institutions led to the belief that the time had come to give national attention to this regional enthusiasm.

In response to a petition signed by thirty-six ministers, the General Ministerial Assembly in 1948 authorized the creation of a Commission on Higher Education, later renamed the Commission on Christian Higher Education, and assigned to function under the Executive Council. The petitioning resolution defined the commission's purposes to be: "(l) To survey the needs and resources for higher education in the Church of God. (2) To plan an adequate national program of higher education."[38] Nothing was said about the commission's authority or its relationship to existing institutions; there was some fear on the part of these schools that the Assembly might be encroaching on their autonomy, but they were pleased to have some possible help in controlling competition.

With slender resources, little assistance, and considerable discouragement from the powerless commission, two new schools were launched in 1953—South Texas Bible Institute (renamed Gulf-Coast Bible College in 1955) in Houston, Texas, and Arlington College in Southern California. Each was regionally sponsored by area congregations and each succeeded in developing into a viable institution. In 1968 Gulf-Coast Bible College also was admitted into the family of national agencies, and in the same year Arlington College merged with Azusa Pacific College, an interdenominationally sponsored school located in the same area. Plans for a third school had been initiated in 1952, when J. Horace Germany, a white pastor from Muncie, Indiana, moved back to his native Mississippi for the purpose of starting a self-help program for the training of southern black ministers.

---

37. Pacific Bible College was first included in the 1947–48 World Service budget. *Yearbook of the Church of God*, 1948, 5.

38. Minutes of the General Ministerial Assembly, June 16, 1948.

Financial and racial problems delayed for almost a decade the development of what later became Bay Ridge Christian College in Kendleton, Texas.

All of these schools affirmed that their primary purpose was the training of ministers and other leaders in the Church of God. There had never been, however, any kind of educational requirement for ministerial ordination by the movement, so none of the colleges had found it necessary or perhaps even desirable to create a graduate program that would compare with seminaries offering the standard ministerial degrees.[39] Before and during World War I a stream of young Anderson College graduates flowed to Oberlin Seminary. In the immediate postwar period the changing educational climate produced a number of young people in the Church of God who felt a need for more specialized

J. Horace Germany (1914–2001), pastor and educator. In 1952, Germany returned to his native Mississippi to found a training school for African-American students for the ministry. In 1960, he became the target of white racists who beat Germany and left him for dead on the streets of Union, Mississippi. Germany's institute moved to Texas, where it became Bay Ridge Christian College.

training and, upon graduating from college, enrolled in various seminaries across the country. It was becoming increasingly apparent that a demand for this kind of training had developed. By 1948 Anderson College administrators and trustees began planning a three-year graduate School of Theology with 1950 as the target date for opening. Classes convened in October with an opening enrollment of thirty-two students.[40] Earl L. Martin was the first dean. The faculty that year consisted of Martin, Adam W. Miller, Charles E. Brown, Gene W. Newberry (the only full-time professor), Robert H. Reardon, Harold L. Phillips, and T. Franklin Miller. By 1952, John W. V. Smith and Robert Nicholson were added. Brown retired from teaching in 1952, and Adam Miller became dean in 1953. In 1954 Burt E. Coody joined the teaching staff in the field of Christian education. Enrollment

---

39. During a brief period in the mid-1930s Anderson College had offered the bachelor of divinity degree for one year of additional work above the bachelor of arts. Since regular seminaries required three years for this degree, the practice was deemed inappropriate and was discontinued.

40. News, *Gospel Trumpet*, October 21, 1950, 14–15.

continued to rise and reached a total of approximately seventy-five by 1955. Twenty-one students received degrees in the first three graduating classes of the years 1953–55.[41]

The postwar years brought a significant change in another aspect of the Church of God movement's national programming for young people. The first national youth convention had been held in 1924. After 1930 these conventions were held on a biennial schedule in different locations. At the 1936 Los Angeles meeting, the youth organization adopted the name Christian Crusaders and named several continuing commissions to give ongoing attention to youth camps, missions, education, and research. They also formed an advisory board made up of the presidents of all state and regional youth organizations. Keeping up with all the areas of work identified by these commissions considerably increased the work demands on the unpaid elected officers. By the 1942 convention in Cleveland, Ohio, there was a willingness to employ a full-time staff person. (This convention also voted to change the name of the organization to "Church of God Youth Fellowship;" Christian Crusaders never did really catch on.) By 1943 A. Leland Forrest left a pastorate in Lansing, Michigan, to become the first executive secretary of the national Youth Fellowship. He was followed in 1945 by Leslie E. Decker, who in turn was succeeded by Maurice J. Mauch in 1947 with the altered title of field secretary.[42]

During these years of development the national youth work had struggles with the problem of its relationship with the national church structure. National youth work had no organizational tie with the General Ministerial Assembly, the Executive Council, or any general agencies. This meant it was not included in any budget and had no entree for soliciting funds anywhere in the church except local youth groups and various conventions, which were considered financially successful if they paid their own expenses. After much discussion of many options it eventually seemed most logical and expedient to officially relate the Church of God Youth Fellowship to the Board of Christian Education, which already had a department of youth work into which the functions of the Youth Fellowship could be incorporated. The various necessary steps were taken in 1948 by the Board and the International Youth Convention in Denver, Colorado. Tom A. Smith of Oregon became the first director of youth work under the new arrangement.[43]

---

41. Bulletin, The School of Theology. Issues for years 1951–56.
42. *Yearbook of the Church of God* (years as indicated in text).
43. Ibid.

This period brought one other net addition to the number of national agencies functioning under the General Ministerial Assembly. For many years there had been discussion of a pension fund for ministers. Beginning in 1937 a small percentage of the national church budget had been designated for the Ministers' Aid and Pension Fund. Monies from this fund had been allocated mostly to hardship cases and emergency situations as they arose, but there was no participatory plan for any regular pension for retiring ministers. Following World War II discussion of such a plan accelerated and steps were taken to make the necessary preparation for a pension program. In June 1948 the General Ministerial Assembly authorized the creation of a nine-member Board of Pensions to implement and administer a ministerial pension fund. Lawrence E. Brooks was selected as the first executive secretary-treasurer. The plan began operation on January 1, 1949, and by June reported that two hundred ministers were participating.[44]

A major positive coordinated effort to pull the church together in a unified forward move was generated in the late 1940s and named "Mid-Century Evangelistic Advance." In February 1949 a group of about forty leaders, including local pastors, laypeople, and agency representatives, met to assess the pressing needs of the movement. They identified areas of special concern in regard to all aspects of the church's work—missions, evangelism, stewardship, education, spiritual life, and doctrinal understanding. During Anderson Camp Meeting that June, another group of about one hundred gave more attention to these needs and began to suggest goals and strategies. An unofficial committee was to assemble these ideas and place definite proposals before still another group of about fifty that met in November. Out of this meeting came the outline of a five-year program in which all of the general agencies, state organizations, and local congregations would cooperate in a planned strategy to push the movement ahead on all fronts.[45]

A coordinating committee was created and an attempt was made to secure a representative in each state to promote the program. The slogan, "Go—Make Disciples" was adopted as the overall directive for this special thrust to begin in the mid-century year of 1950. A particular emphasis was assigned to each of the five years outlined as follows:

44. Minutes of the General Ministerial Assembly, June 15, 1948, and June 14, 1949.
45. "The Church Faces Open Doors," News, *Gospel Trumpet*, December 3, 1949, 13.

1950–51	Achieving deeper levels of religious living
1951–52	Releasing the potential power of the local church
1952–53	Evangelizing the larger community
1953–54	Evangelizing the world community
1954–55	Strengthening the Christian fellowship[46]

The 1950 International Convention officially launched the Advance with great fanfare. Many sermons and conferences introduced and elaborated the themes. Pastor-musician Frederick G. Shackleton was commissioned to write a new song for the occasion, and great crowds joined in lustily singing the chorus:

Together we go to make disciples
For Jesus our Lord in ev'ry land;
We're reaching the lost for Christ, the Savior,
On far away shores and near at hand.
Together we go to tell our neighbors
The message of Christ, man's truest Friend.
All power is His, pow'r in earth and heaven,
And He will be with us to the end.[47]

The General Ministerial Assembly entered into the spirit of the occasion by approving the movement's first million-dollar budget for general causes. "So," said a brochure writer, "the Advance was begun, looking squarely at our challenge and our resources.... The Advance is all of us looking straight ahead at the job we have to do."[48]

In 1950 and succeeding years a great amount of supportive material was produced to highlight the general theme and to augment the annual emphases. The first year's focus was on personal evangelism. A flip chart titled "They Went Forth—Two By Two" was prepared for training laypeople in visitation evangelism. A sound filmstrip was available for use in motivating and instructing church members in soul winning. All kinds of enlistment and record keeping cards and forms gave the emphasis some structure and measurability. Even as the Advance moved

---

46. Brochure in Mid-Century Evangelistic Advance file, Anderson University and Church of God Archives.

47. *Hymnal of the Church of God* (Gospel Trumpet Company, 1953), no. 204.

48. Brochure in the Anderson University and Church of God Archives.

to other themes the evangelism emphasis continued through the whole five-year period.

Since the Advance centered on the local congregation, many of the materials produced were of a very practical nature. A series of four "How to Strengthen the Church" books were published with the titles completed respectively as follows: "—Spiritually," "—Financially," "—in Leadership," and "—in Management." In the last year of the Advance another series of six booklets was published under the emphasis for that year, "This We Believe—Together We Serve." Beliefs covered included the church, the Holy Spirit, health and healing, church membership in the Kingdom, and a general affirmation titled "Hold Fast to Those Basic Convictions." Many other pamphlets, leaflets, articles in the *Gospel Trumpet,* and posters were produced to further the "deep current of dedication, of service, of witness, of giving, of sacrifice, of daring courage, and of dauntless vision" that the brochure said was moving in the Church of God.[49]

As the Advance moved toward its conclusion some leaders noted that this special thrust was inopportunely concluding, for the movement would arrive at the seventy-fifth anniversary of its beginning in the year following. Consequently, some new members were recruited for the Advance Committee in order to make the final year blend into a new emphasis for the anniversary celebration. The culmination of the Mid-Century Advance put the church in a generally positive mood for the Diamond Jubilee in June 1955.[50]

These two special programs blended into each other, so there was never any summary report of the accomplishments of the Advance itself. A look at some *Yearbook* statistics tells something of the growth pattern during this five-year period. In 1950, estimated membership was listed at 96,749 people in 1,932 congregations.[51] The 1955 listing shows 121,655 members in 2,141 congregations.[52] Membership thus had increased by about 25 percent during this period, and the number of congregations was up over 10 percent. Compared to previous growth patterns these increases would not be deemed large, but they are creditable. Considering the internal turmoil of some of these years, it would have to be said that the Advance came at an opportune moment.

---

49. Ibid.
50. The Diamond Jubilee is reviewed in chapter 15.
51. *Yearbook of the Church of God*, 1950, 122.
52. *Yearbook of the Church of God*, 1955, 152.

Harold L. Phillips (1913–2006), fifth editor of the *Gospel Trumpet* (1951–77). During Phillips's tenure, the magazine's name was changed to *Vital Christianity* (1962). The editor was also the person finally responsible for Sunday school curriculum. Against the wishes of vocal critics, early in his tenure Phillips championed the curriculum's use of the new and, at points, controversial Revised Standard Version of the Bible.

The mid-century years brought several significant changes in national leadership. In 1951 Charles E. Brown, editor in chief for Gospel Trumpet Company publications for twenty-one years, was retired and Harold L. Phillips moved up from managing editor to take his place. Three other people who later were to become prominent national leaders were named to positions in the national offices. W. E. Reed became the secretary of evangelism for the Board of Church Extension and Home Missions; R. Eugene Sterner was named executive director of the Radio Commission; Tom A. Smith became the director of the Church of God Youth Fellowship and head of the Department of Youth Work for the Board of Christian Education. Gordon S. Schieck was named dean of Alberta Bible Institute. Max Gaulke of Gulf-Coast Bible College and C. Herbert Joiner of Arlington College took their places as college presidents.

This brief period in the movement's history saw an unusually large number of those who had been early prominent leaders pass from the scene. The year 1947 saw the untimely death of two very influential ministers, F. G. Smith and E. A. Reardon. J. W. Phelps, who had served as missions secretary and editor, and Thomas Nelson, a leader in the Scandinavian work, also died that year. In 1948 C. J. Blewitt, pioneer of the work in the East, L. E. Millensifer of western Canada, and J. D. Smoot, one of the most prominent of the black ministers, were called home. In 1949 it was Karl Arbeiter, well-known leader among German-speaking churches, who died. The list goes on: 1950—N. H. Byrum, W. E. Monk, and C. W. Naylor; 1951—Barney E. Warren and Nora Hunter; 1952—R. L. Berry; A. L. Byers, J. R. Hale, H. M. Riggle, and S. O. Susag; 1954—J. T. Wilson and Spanish-American leader M. F. Tafolla. Those young people who sparked the movement's development in its pioneer days were gone; new young faces rose to take their places.[53]

Evidence of growth and progress in the Church of God was apparent. Local church property values almost doubled in the years of the Advance. Anderson College, after long delays, occupied its first new building, Morrison Hall, in 1950. Dunn Hall, a men's dormitory, was completed in 1954. Pacific Bible College occupied its first new building, a women's dormitory, in 1946. Perhaps the most significant publication of the period was the *Hymnal of the Church of God*, which appeared in 1953, nearly twenty-five years after the previous *Hymns and Spiritual Songs*. In 1954 the General Ministerial Assembly approved a challenge goal of one and a quarter million dollars for World Service.

In summary, the period from 1946 to 1954 provided a time of recovery from the war, reevaluation, growth, and change for the movement. It will be remembered as a painful but significant era in Church of God history.

J. D. Smoot (1877–1948), pioneer African-American minister and pastor. Smoot was the second person to serve as pastor of the south Chicago congregation that became Langley Avenue Church of God. During the decade from 1910 to 1920, he successfully resisted proposals for a separate African-American worship service on the grounds of Anderson Camp Meeting.

53. Information gleaned from many sources but largely from the *Yearbook of the Church of God* (appropriate years).

CHAPTER 15

TOWARD SPIRITUAL DEMOCRACY
(1955–1962)

"Seventy-Five Years of Fellowship, Witness and Service." So summarized the content of a colorful brochure with the caption, "Church of God Diamond Jubilee." In June 1955 the Mid-Century Evangelistic Advance ended and the Jubilee began. This special anniversary celebration continued over an eighteen-month period, ending in December 1956. Through the combined Evangelistic Advance-Jubilee Committee, specific plans for a series of special events, programs, and publications had been under way for more than a year. The brochure, titled *Let's Get Acquainted,* was only one of the many items produced for the anniversary. It was designed for mass distribution by local congregations and at all appropriate mass meetings.[1]

The first and most spectacular event of the Diamond Jubilee was the premiere of a new historical motion picture about the Church of God at the 1955 International Convention in Anderson. This forty-five-minute film had been in the process of planning and production for much longer than other elements of the Jubilee. The Advance committee had conceived the idea almost four years earlier and activated it with concurrence of the World Service Commission by the appointment of a film study committee in 1951. This committee reported favorably, and a revamped committee was authorized to proceed with responsibility for all aspects from financing to production to utilization. Arrangements were made with the Jam Handy Organization for production, and the actual project was filmed in Anderson in a three-week period during the summer of 1954. By the following June *Heaven to Earth* was ready for showing and a sufficient number of 16-mm prints were available for bookings in local churches. The film, which attempted to capture the spirit of the movement as well as tell something of

---

1. First published as a brochure (copy in the Anderson University and Church of God Archives) and also by T. Franklin Miller, "Let's Get Acquainted," *Gospel Trumpet,* January 7, 1957, 3.

343

its history, was well received at the premiere and widely shown all during the Jubilee and afterward. Typical of many responses was that of one native son of the movement who wrote, "I became animated with the spirit, enthusiasm and vision of the movement more than I had ever been heretofore."[2]

A calendar of projected events designed to sustain momentum for the entire year-and-a-half period was assembled and rather closely followed. The Jubilee was emphasized in all the regularly scheduled national meetings and in all agency programming. After the introduction of the film the next most significant observance came in January 1956, when the *Christian Brotherhood Hour* celebrated its ninth anniversary, and the Gospel Trumpet Company observed its own seventy-fifth birthday. The latter made this a publishing occasion of considerable note.

In its first issue of the new year, the *Gospel Trumpet* noted, "The message first proclaimed seventy-five years ago by a tiny band of itinerant gospel workers has spread in 1956 to a movement reaching at least 277,534 people in 2,798 congregations around the world."[3] An editorial titled "The Year of Jubilee" observed:

> The idea of having a jubilee year roots back into the history of ancient Israel. It was customary to announce the arrival of the solemn moment of beginning that year by blowing a long and loud trumpet blast (see Lev. 25:9)....
>
> In the words of F. W. Boreham of Australia, "A year of jubilee, to be true to its traditions, should be a year of passionate evangelism....The year of jubilee must mark a new birth in every man's soul; a new era in every man's life; a new and delightful escape from all the forces that have heretofore hampered and enslaved us. Therein lies the enchanting music of the Silver Trumpets."[4]

The "enchanting music" of the Jubilee continued in many ways for the balance of the year. The Gospel Trumpet Company launched a $250,000 expansion and remodeling project that not only added new facilities but changed the whole appearance of the publishing plant and retail store. In

---

2. Comment by Warner Monroe, professor at Pacific Bible College. From a mimeographed sheet of testimonials regarding the film in the Anderson University and Church of God Archives.

3. News, *Gospel Trumpet*, January 7, 1957, 14.

4. Editorial, "The Year of Jubilee," *Gospel Trumpet*, January 7, 1957, 5. The quotation in the last paragraph is from F. W. Boreham, *Dreams of Sunset* (Valley Forge, PA: Judson Press, 1954), 32–33.

January 1956 the six-year-old School of Theology in Anderson was approved for associate membership in the American Association of Theological Schools, a first step toward full accreditation. A special Easter emphasis, captured in the slogan "Look with Christ on the Fields," was preceded by an unlabeled Lenten program called "Seven Weeks of Sacrifice." Many articles reviewed the past and assessed the teachings of the movement. Notable among these were two series: "The Legacy of Our Pioneers" by A. F. Gray[5] and "A Demonstration Reformation" by Gene W. Newberry.[6] John W. V. Smith published two historical works: *Heralds of a Brighter Day* (1955) and *Truth Marches On* (1956)[7]. F. G. Smith's classic work, *What the Bible Teaches,* was reissued in a condensed version prepared by Kenneth E. Jones.

A major event of the 1956 Jubilee year was the International Convention in June with over twenty thousand people in attendance. The program, built around the theme "Teach All Men These Things," highlighted the basic doctrinal emphases the movement had held from its beginning and projected the future task. In one sermon, A. R. Cochran, a pastor from Cleveland, Ohio, declared: "I believe without fear of contradiction that there is no body of people committed to teach and preach more fundamental Bible truth than we do. But I am not a Christian because I am affiliated with this reformation movement but because I accepted Christ as my personal Savior."[8] Harold Boyer, pastor in Springfield, Ohio, and chairperson of the General Ministerial Assembly, proclaimed, "God has always used minority groups.…He is counting on the reformation movement of the Church of God, and I pray we may have within our hearts a passion for the truth."[9] A generous Christ's World Service Day offering on the final Sunday pushed total giving for general causes for the year to a record total of $1,203,595, almost $100,000 more than any past performance.[10]

Later in the summer more than one hundred regularly scheduled area camp meetings across the country picked up the Diamond Jubilee theme. In August the biennial International Youth Convention was held

---

5. A. F. Gray, "The Legacy of Our Pioneers," *Gospel Trumpet*, January 7, 1956, 1; January 14, 3; January 21, 7.

6. Gene W. Newberry, "A Demonstration Reformation," *Gospel Trumpet*, March 3, 1956, 1; March 10, 9.

7. *Truth Marches On* was later revised and published as *A Brief History of the Church of God Reformation Movement.*

8. "Notes From Camp Meeting Sermons," *Gospel Trumpet*, July 28, 1956, 13.

9. Ibid., 3.

10. Ibid., 14.

in Springfield, Illinois, with the Jubilee-related theme, "One Lord—One Faith—One Task." In late October the Midwest Ministerial Assembly, largest of the regional assemblies, met in Kansas City with a program built around the theme "Counsel from the Word," which focused on basic Christian doctrine. The concluding Jubilee event was the annual Christ's Birthday Observance sponsored by the Woman's Missionary Society. Preceded by a twelve-day continuous prayer vigil for worldwide concerns, the occasion was climaxed by a churchwide offering for missions. The goal was set at $150,000; more than $162,800 was received.[11] The Jubilee ended on a note of great victory and the projection of new goals for the future.

In summing up the results of the six-and-a-half-year Mid-Century Evangelistic Advance and Diamond Jubilee program, T. Franklin Miller, who coordinated the work of the various committees, listed eleven specific accomplishments in a report to the Executive Council:

1. The revival of a sense of mission which has put new spiritual vitality and dedication into the Church of God.
2. A renewed emphasis upon the place of laymen in the evangelistic outreach of the church.
3. The groundwork was laid for a tremendous forward surge in the development of adequate programs of stewardship education.
4. The development of new tools to help in our common task…new ways to use filmstrips and motion pictures…many audio-visual resources that are speeding up the learning process.
5. The increase numerically was very significant. Members of congregations increased by 35,000 during the period and Sunday schools added 54,700 to their enrollment.
6. State boards of evangelism and Christian education were strengthened.
7. Many new people were won to the Lord.
8. Thousands of people for the first time really became acquainted with the Church of God—its history, purpose, and message.
9. The film *Heaven to Earth* was produced and shown to thousands of people around the world and helped acquaint the general public with the Church of God.

---

11. *Gospel Trumpet*, April 13, 1957, 14.

10. Local congregations became better acquainted with the church's missionary program.

11. The national boards and agencies of the church reviewed their own work and aims and received a clearer view of the task ahead.[12]

These years of a nationally directed program emphasis gave the movement both a positive focus and a forward momentum that was healthy and celebrative—a welcome change from the defensive posture of the late 1940s. Programs, however, do not tell the internal story of how the movement, during these years, worked its way toward solving the structural and relational problems that had fed the fires of agitation lighted by Earl Slacum and his followers. Decades earlier C. E. Brown had coined the phrase "spiritual democracy." The processes and progress toward that end were summarized in the long final report of the ten-year-old Commission on Revision and Planning given to the 1957 General Ministerial Assembly. By way of introduction the commission reviewed its purposes:

> The purpose of this commission was to study our plan of church organization, said study to include the relationship of this Assembly to the general boards, the possibility of a wider sharing of responsibility for formulating policies of our general agencies, more equitable representation in the Assembly, the methods of nomination to membership on our general boards and other organizational relationships of a general concern.[13]

The report listed twenty-one requests that had come to the commission from various sources and then responded with "our answer." These answers not only indicated the decisions but also explained the reasoning behind them. The first item referred to the 1954 action that enlarged and redefined the functions of the Executive Council. The explanation describes the new structure of the Executive Council and also expresses the felt urgency for democratizing procedures.

> *Request*—For a coordinating committee or Council from this Assembly. This request came both from the Commission on Research and Improvement and from ministers generally.

---

12. *Gospel Trumpet*, April 6, 1957, 14.
13. Minutes of the General Ministerial Assembly, 1957. Attached copy. Also in Annual Reports, 1957.

Our Answer—is the newly enlarged Executive Council. This Council is indeed your Council. Its office is your office. Its executive secretary is your executive secretary.

Let's take a look at its membership. First of all, 16 members are directly *your* members—nominated by your nominating committee elected directly by you in regular election. None of the 16 can be members of or be employed by any board or agency. In addition to these 16, your duly elected leaders—the three officers of this Assembly—the chairman, vice-chairman, and recording secretary—are members ex-officio making a total of 19 directly from this Assembly. These, together with the seven members representing our World Service agencies make a total of 26 members in the new Executive Council. We should like to observe that these seven in every case are appointed by board members whom you have elected. Therefore, you have indeed a coordinating council *from* this Assembly.[14]

The issue of broadening decision-making was more difficult. It impinged on the time-honored prerogative of the boards to make their own nominations. The commission recognized the problem but opted to recommend voluntary screening of nominees rather than legislating a limitation. Their report suggested such a policy was improving the situation.

Request—For some arrangement to prevent duplication of membership on Boards.

Our Answer—A request and recommendation was sent to all boards that this be done by common agreement. All boards and agencies are taking this seriously. Today there are only eight duplications. Three of these are laymen, three are ministers, and two are officers of this Assembly. This last duplication may be a desirable one. Of the 129 memberships available on all agencies, 121 different persons are serving.

Now as boards make nominations they are kept fully aware of nominations by other boards through the Executive Council Office.[15]

Westerners in particular also objected that a preponderance of board memberships were held by residents of the Midwestern states where the

---

14. Ibid., Request I. This quotation and subsequent indicated quotations are cited by "Request" number only since page numbers vary in different copies.

15. Ibid., Request II.

movement was most populous, leaving the more distant states underrepresented. The commission's recommendation minimally answered this objection by refusing geographical quotas in favor of voluntary management.

> *Request*—For more equitable distribution of board membership geographically.
> *Our Answer*—This request, too, is being taken seriously by our general agencies. Beginning this year the Executive Council office provides each board with a U.S. and Canadian map showing the geographical location of all Board members. Likewise, they have information on the location of our church membership. Thus, each board is able to work toward an equitable distribution of membership at the time nominations are made.[16]

It was further noted that the three West Coast states had a higher per capita representation than states east of the Rocky Mountains and that pastors moving from one region to another complicated the problem.

Two requests related to the membership/constituency of the General Ministerial Assembly itself—one suggesting the possibility of altered membership qualifications to include some laypeople and the other proposing an incorporated delegated assembly rather than an open temporary assembly that existed only when in session. The commission responded, or failed to respond, to the first in the following fashion:

> *Request*—For consideration of some sort of lay participation in the business affairs of the Assembly.
> *Our Answer*—The majority of the members of the Commission felt that any recommendation which we might make in this direction would not meet with a favorable response from the Assembly at this time. Hence no recommendation.
> It might be observed, however, that lay membership on the new Executive Council on a limited basis was provided for, and further, that various Boards are nominating laymen—the trend is in that direction. At present no less than 24 memberships are filled by laymen and women.[17]

---

16. Ibid., Request III.
17. Ibid., Request VII.

The commission dismissed the idea of an incorporated delegated assembly as unwanted and unnecessary. The commission explained:

—In two surveys which this committee has made and in a previous study many years ago, it was found that the majority of ministers do not look with favor on the possibility of losing their franchise in this Assembly. Most of them desired to retain the voluntary nature of this meeting.

With reference to the request for Incorporation—in our opinion the sentiment for this was never strong. We believe the new Executive Council meets the need for legal status; hence, no further recommendation.[18]

Requests had been made for the creation of two new permanent commissions under the Executive Council—one on evangelism and another on the ministry. In reply, the Commission on Revision and Planning expressed an awareness of the need for each of these and listed arguments favorable to constituting each. Evangelism, it was noted, was a broad concern affecting all agencies, and issues regarding the ministry such as recruitment and ordination procedures were of general importance to the whole church. No specific proposals were made, however, and so neither of these commissions was brought into existence.

A major portion of the commission's report dealt with the issue of finding some way to involve state leaders or representatives in national decision-making. In the absence of any standard polity such as episcopal, presbyterian or congregational, there seemed to be an omission of the opportunity to give voice to an intermediate level of organization between congregations and the national work. Various sources had suggested that there might be an unofficial planning group or advisory council that would be made up of representatives from the fifty or so state organizations. In response to this request, the commission replied at length:

Request—For a National Planning Committee and Advisory Council.

Our Answer—Soon after the Commission on Revision and Planning was first appointed, in June of 1947, the idea of the "Advisory Council" was suggested. The idea being simply that there should be a

18. Ibid., Request XI.

fairly large, geographically-representative group to guide our general work in terms of policy and objective; to keep alive the "grass-roots" viewpoint; to bring to bear upon our general work the most creative thinking from across the field; and thus, to achieve a closer working relationship among general agencies, state organizations, and local churches.[19]

After a further historical review, the commission lifted up six areas that an advisory council might address: (1) The need for a *broader planning base* for the general work and to bring the best creative thinking from across the field to bear upon such planning. (2) The *rising state* or *area-consciousness* in the work and the tendency to develop state organizations seemed to require more correlation between state and national work. This correlation involved promotion as well as planning. (3) The need for *geographical representation* was still felt. As pointed out in previous reports, there remained a certain amount of geographical representation in the Executive Council and also on the various boards. (4) There was a need for some *liaison work* in the church. The church at large needed to be represented in the general work, and the general work needed to be represented to the church at large. (5) There was a need for *elected representation* in order to offer a channel for expression. So far as practical there needed to be some means through which every minister could express his point of view and through which each state or section could have a representative to express the viewpoint of that group of ministers. Different points of view should be represented at the planning level. (6) There needs to be *more long-range general planning* in order to secure better cooperation, and to bring greater cohesion in the work as a whole, not merely in the agencies in Anderson, but in the *total* work involving state organizations and local congregations.

The commission then elaborated at length on the amount of broad planning that was already taking place voluntarily within the existing structure without any legislation to force it, thus presenting "evidence of desire on the part of all of us to make our general agencies more adequate expressions of the thinking, the spirit and the service of the entire Movement." This section of the report closed without making a specific recommendation: "Whether we need more structural relationships in this broader sense is a question still to be answered. The Commission…wishes to make these

---

19. Ibid., Request XVIII.

observations regarding an Advisory Council so that they may be a matter of record for any succeeding group to study."[20]

In summarizing its final report the Commission on Revision and Planning highlighted three major items that merited further consideration after the new Executive Council was better established. These were: (1) a commission on the ministry, (2) a commission on evangelism, and (3) an advisory council. With these considerations both the report and the commission came to an end.

That no further general revamping of the national structure was thought necessary for the quarter century following the commission's work testifies to its thoroughness and wisdom. Changes were made, of course, but these only modified the structure fashioned by the Commission on Revision and Planning. Nevertheless, this work must be seen as remarkable steps along a seventy-five-year pilgrimage from early charismatic organization to a twenty-five-page directory and description of the "nonecclesiastical" structure of the "family of believers" in 1956.[21]

Central to the national structure, ever since its creation in 1917, was the General Ministerial Assembly, a voluntary association consisting of ordained ministers, and unordained pastors or associates in recognized congregations. The Assembly met annually to conduct the general business of the Church of God. Much of this business was carried out through duly authorized boards and agencies subordinate to the Assembly.[22] In 1957 seven such agencies existed: Missionary Board, Board of Church Extension and Home Missions, Anderson College and Theological Seminary, Pacific Bible College, Board of Christian Education, Gospel Trumpet Company, and Board of Pensions. The Assembly gave guidance and direction to these agencies through (1) establishment of policies in charters, bylaws, and so forth, (2) election of board members, (3) ratification of chief executives, (4) review of annual reports, and (5) allocation of annual budgets.

The new aspect of the 1957 format was the redesign of the Executive Council, the legally incorporated functionary arm of the General Ministerial Assembly. In 1954 and again in 1956 the Assembly authorized changes

---

20. Ibid.

21. The phrases in quotes are the words of R. Eugene Sterner in his introduction to the Diamond Jubilee *Yearbook of the Church of God*, 1956, 4.

22. The boards are subordinate in the sense they are created by the Assembly, which approves their charter and exercises continuous control through the electing of members. The boards are legally incorporated entities, however, and are autonomous in the manner by which they carry out their authorized functions.

that redefined the council responsibilities and enlarged its membership. In addition to the scope of its work under the old arrangement, the enlarged council now assumed oversight of the work of the World Service Commission, the Clergy Bureau, and Ministers' Aid. Additional responsibilities also were assigned in the areas of coordination, public relations, and long-range planning.

The redesigned Executive Council now functioned in three areas through divisions. (1) The Division of General Service managed interagency relations, public relations, general coordination of national church work, and general long-range, creative planning for cooperative action. (2) The Division of World Service oversaw promotion and fundraising and bore primary responsibility for raising the annual budget to meet the needs approved by the General Ministerial Assembly. (3) The portfolio of the Division of Church Service included ministerial aid, registration, and the preparation of the yearbook. In this area it might conduct studies and surveys to place before pastors and leaders pertinent information on the life and work of the church, as well as coordinate the services offered to the church at large. For specific areas of work not assigned to other boards, divisions, or committees, the Executive Council was authorized to function through commissions approved by the Assembly. At the time of formation the only such agency in this category was the Radio and Television Commission. In 1958 the Commission on Christian Higher Education was given a permanent berth in the structure. Others would be added later. Generally, some commission members were elected by the Assembly and some were named by other agencies appropriate to the function.

The membership of the Executive Council was enlarged from fifteen to twenty-six individuals. Sixteen of these members, some of whom could be laypeople, were elected by the General Ministerial Assembly and were not to be members or employees of any of the general boards. In addition, three officers of the General Ministerial Assembly, the chairperson, vice-chairperson, and recording secretary, and one representative appointed by each general board comprised the Executive Council.

With nineteen members representing the General Ministerial Assembly and seven members representing the general boards, the Executive Council provided a round table where all the general interests of the church might converge for creative planning, for promotion of World Service, for better coordination of the work, and better service to the church. Thus did the enlarged Council provide an avenue by which the General Ministerial

Assembly and the boards could discuss mutual interests and share mutual concerns. The Council also served as an interim committee to carry out the directives and work of the General Ministerial Assembly throughout the year. By this means the cooperative work of the church on the national level could move forward in one unified effort.[23]

Diagram 1 shows the national structure as organized in 1958 with solid lines indicating direct relationships and dotted lines noting coordinative relationships:

DIAGRAM 1: Agency structure of the Church of God as organized in 1958

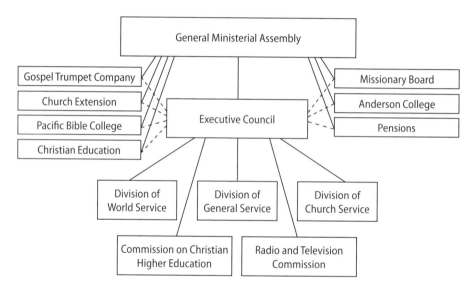

The 1955–62 period also saw considerably wider participation in the conduct of the national work of the church. Nowhere was this more evident than in fundraising. During 1955–56 a series of stewardship conferences was conducted in eighty-five districts throughout the United States and Canada. The stated purpose of these conferences was to help pastors and local leaders "broaden the base of stewardship response in the local church."[24] In the following year additional conferences were scheduled and a large number of stewardship rallies were conducted. In the two-year period a total of 258 conferences and rallies convened. Numerous pastors reported

---

23. Data regarding the national structure as of this date taken largely from the 1957 and 1958 *Yearbook of the Church of God*.

24. *Yearbook of the Church of God*, 1957, 14.

"increased attendance—more people working—more people giving—large increase in church income."[25]

An even more extensive grass roots involvement in national fundraising was the DAY-Men (Dollar-a-Year) program conducted and carried out by the World Service division. The DAY-Men program began in 1948, and by 1956 it was so much a part of World Service promotion that the roster of the approximately one hundred people involved was included in the *Yearbook*. DAY-Men were pastors selected from designated districts who met annually in Anderson for training in the promotion of the World Service causes among other pastors in their area. DAY-Men also provided a sounding board for reading general feelings toward the national work in the various areas. By 1960, however, staff people had come to assess this pastor-to-pastor emphasis, despite its obvious values, as not being the most effective way to reach the actual givers—the people in the congregations. Consequently, the DAY-Men program was discontinued by 1962, and alternate plans were laid to tell the story of the general causes to the movement's constituency. In the course of its more than a dozen years of operation the DAY-men program involved over one thousand pastors who, for a dollar a year, had helped to carry the burden and concern for the national work.[26]

Another segment of the Church of God targeted for broader involvement at this time were the racial minorities within the constituency. At this point African Americans were the most vocal. Clearly this was an issue affecting the entire movement and not a matter to be assigned to any single board or agency. The General Ministerial Assembly and the Executive Council had to give attention to it. The occasion that precipitated action was a visit to Anderson on January 16, 1957, by a group of black ministers representing the National Association of the Church of God. They met with general agency leaders and called attention to the fact that, despite the historic interracial stance of the movement, almost every level of the church from the local to national and international work had become significantly segregated. They presented a motion "that we as a voluntary group of key leaders representing the National Association and the general agencies of the international work of the Reformation movement recommend that a study commission be appointed to explore the varied facets of the integra-

25. "World Service Report," *Highlights of the General Ministerial Assembly of the Church of God*, 1957, 9.
26. "Division of World Service," Annual Reports, 1962, 33–34.

tion problem pursuant to correlating our Movement policies with the tenets of the gospel we preach."[27]

The proposed study commission was inaugurated in June 1957. Fifteen members were named by the Executive Council, with the National Association having submitted a list of recommended African-American leaders. Three agency-related individuals were named as resource persons. The commission included seven blacks, one Native American, one Hispanic American and six whites, plus the three white resource persons. Charles V. Weber was named chairperson and R. Eugene Sterner recording secretary and reporter. An interim working committee of five with Adam W. Miller as chairperson was named to prepare an agenda for the commission's work. In the first meetings of the entire group, specified studies were divided among four subcommittees:

1. To study Christian principles as applying to human relationships and adaptations made in New Testament times to the patterns of society then entrenched, and to ascertain how these principles and adaptations would bear upon our present problems.
2. A research committee to study what other religious groups have done with regard to race relations and an evaluation of their findings.
3. A committee to study present policies and problems within the Church of God, as they pertain to race relations.
4. A committee on organizational relationships which would be responsible for taking the findings of the previous three committees, and attempting to work out whatever organizational adaptations are necessary.[28]

The commission began boldly by reaffirming certain basic Christian theological and moral principles that they considered realistic and realizable in the church:

1. Our position in the Church of God has been always that there is one body in Christ. This does not admit of racial differences or cleavages.
2. As Christians we can do no less than endeavor with all our hearts to practice no difference but extend fellowship to all.

---

27. Final Report, The Study Commission on Race Relations. Minutes, General Ministerial Assembly, June 21, 1962, in *Annual Reports, 1962*, 22.

28. As reported in 1960 to the General Ministerial Assembly. Annual Reports, 1960, 16.

3. As Christians, we must exercise love toward those who fail to do this and pray for them.
4. We must guard against carnal and secular pressures such as are used by secular groups.
5. While we do not want to use carnal pressure, we are, nonetheless, waging a war, and we have to use moral weapons. We have to remember that yielding to evil is to strengthen evil.
6. We must not be frightened out. While a courageous stand may cause the loss of some people, to vacillate is to lose leadership and cause the loss of many other people.[29]

The commission further noted from its beginning that the movement had been essentially an interracial group. This fact should have made adjustment to the changes that were taking place in society much easier and should have enabled the Church of God to set a pace for other religious groups. The tone of the commission's language was forthright and optimistic.

In the course of its five-year tenure the commission submitted four reports to the General Ministerial Assembly. The first of these in 1958 was primarily a progress report but did include a resolution recommending that the Division of Church Service encourage the various state organizations to work toward integration and the setting up of single rather than segregated committees to ratify ministers for inclusion in the *Yearbook*.[30] Excerpts from subsequent reports indicate the scope of the study and the nature of specific recommendations made. In 1960 a list of six "actual steps toward the fuller integration of our work" was set forth:

1. We can and should achieve integrated ratification procedure for registration in our Yearbook. This should be realizable in the immediate future, even if ministerial assemblies must, for a time, be separate....
2. We should achieve the integration of ministerial assemblies in the not-too-distant future....It would seem that integration of ministers of the Church of God would be a necessary prerequisite to any serious attempt to achieve integration in our local churches and in the communities they serve.

29. Ibid., 17.
30. Highlights of the General Ministerial Assembly, 1958, 8.

3. We should encourage union meetings across racial lines for better understanding based upon better acquaintance.
4. The General Ministerial Assembly and the various state assemblies might appropriately take action to encourage movements toward integration which are on a high, ethical, and Christian plane.
5. Ministers of the Church of God could deal more vigorously with this issue and offer more positive teaching. To be sure, we should exercise wisdom and good strategy, but we ought to take a stand.
6. We should address ourselves seriously to our moral responsibility as Christians and to a realistic approach and strategy for achieving integration in the local church.[31]

In 1961 the commission repeated some of the previous recommendations but strengthened them with words and phrases like "deliberate speed," "immediately," and "positive stance." Some new items, however, were added to the list:

1. National leaders should enter into serious discussions toward the integration of national agencies, it being understood that leadership opportunity, representation, and expression would be on the basis of qualification, rather than with a racial bias.
2. Let recognition and support be given to certain experiences and developments where they are being carried out; that encouragement be given to local churches moving ahead with courage in this field; that the attention of the General Ministerial Assembly and of the church be directed toward these courageous moves in order to sharpen the concern of the church. And let our churches be encouraged to be churches of the community, whatever the racial situation may be.
3. Let the Executive Council and the General Ministerial Assembly pass resolutions directed to our own churches, urging interracial fellowship within the local church and among local churches, asking our people to press forward toward integration on a truly Christian basis.[32]

The report closed with the admonition: "This, therefore, is the time to take heart and practice the message we have taught."

31. Annual Reports, 1960, 18.
32. Annual Reports, 1961, 18.

The final report in 1962 was more of a summary and less categorical in tone. It sought to review the whole interracial situation in the Church of God at that time. Attention was called first to the many positive aspects of the picture:

> The General Ministerial Assembly, standing as it does at the very heart of this movement, has been interracial from the beginning. To be interracial at the point where the main direction of our work is established and where major policies are decided is very significant to say the least. Also, the international convention, representing as it does the high point in our total fellowship, has been interracial from the beginning. This too is significant. Our brethren, both ministers and laymen, know one another on a first-name basis across racial lines.
>
> It should be observed too that our church colleges, concerned as they are with the training of future leadership, have never turned a student away on the basis of race or color. And our Graduate School of Theology can point with justifiable pride to graduates of both races who have outstanding ability and promise to offer the Church.
>
> Our Missionary Board has, for many years, channeled the concern and service of the church to people of all races. It has engaged missionary personnel on the basis of fitness and motivation, regardless of race. The same thing is true of the Board of Church Extension and Home Missions, through which the church provides a spiritual ministry to many different races of peoples. Through the loan service we have helped several of our minority groups in large population centers to get the kind of facilities that would allow for rapid growth. Some of these churches have grown more rapidly because of the assistance they received. Also, our Board of Christian Education has bent every effort to bring service and training to the less developed churches and leaders without respect to race. Not only are the national agencies of the church alert to the needs of these minority groups, but also to the very astute and distinguished leaders among them, and the substantial contributions they are making to the church as a whole.[33]

The report then shifted attention to the points where great needs in race relations remained. In ten states there were separate black and white

---

33. Annual Reports, 1962, 23–24.

Lottie M. Franklin, Christian educator and publisher. Lottie Franklin is representative of the service of many women in the field of Christian education. She served for many years at the Gospel Trumpet Company as a Sunday school curriculum editor.

ministerial assemblies. In some of these, it was noted, "There is effort now being made to achieve an integrated Credentials Committee." But there were no marks on the accomplishment scorecard. Progress toward integration at the local congregational level was judged hopeless until barriers between ministers themselves were removed. Unhealthy conditions also remained at the movement's national level. Parallel organizations still existed at such central points as ministerial assemblies, missionary boards, boards of Christian education, youth work, and woman's missionary societies. Conversations were in progress but with few real achievements. Contritely, the commission stated, "We must admit that we have been too content and passive about some Christian standards. We have too much followed the population trends and shifts and have often moved our churches to fit those patterns."[34] The 1962 report ended with a plea for mutual understanding rather than a clarion call to revolutionary action. "This is a time to be patient with one another and to pray earnestly for one another that we may bear a positive Christian witness in such a time as this."

During these years of revising and testing new operational modes designed to broaden the base of participation in the national work of the church, there was no "wait to see how the wind blows" attitude on the part of any of the national agencies, the state organizations, or the local congregations. There was vigorous programming and progress in all areas. In the area of publications the best word was expansion. In 1961 the Gospel Trumpet Company for the second year in its history grossed over $4,000,000 in sales.[35] In addition to its best-known product, the *Gospel Trumpet*, it had over two hundred books on the market. The all-time best seller

34. Ibid., 24.
35. Ibid., 63.

was *Egermier's Bible Story Book,* first published in 1922. By 1955 it had gone through fifty-four printings and sold 1,117,900 copies. Sunday school curriculum and supplies, Christian art (including distribution rights on Warner Sallman pictures), religious greeting cards, and gift items made up the balance of merchandise available through the company.

A major transition in church-related publishing came with a double-barreled change in 1962—a change in the name of the major periodical and a change in the name of the company. During the previous year the Publication Board had discussed the possibility of finding a more contemporary name for the *Gospel Trumpet.* One suggestion was an adaptation of the subtitle already on the masthead, "A Weekly Journal of Vital Christianity." No action was taken at the time, but by its May 1962 meeting the Board was ready and approved the new name, *Vital Christianity,* with instructions to implement the decision as soon as possible. The first issue under the new title was dated June 10, 1962, in time for General Ministerial Assembly members and international conventioners to receive their first copy before coming to Anderson. Those who anticipated that the name change would be a central topic of conversation were not disappointed. Objections were raised, but no great uprising of protest occurred. Editor Harold L. Phillips smoothed some possible difficulty by making a public explanation to the Assembly.[36] The second change required action by the Assembly. The publishing company wanted to replace the historic corporation name, Gospel Trumpet Company, with Warner Press, Inc. It was noted that the name was not really new, for it had been used to designate the wholesale division of the company for approximately forty years. Company officials spoke in favor of the change, and the Assembly approved it by "an overwhelming vote."[37]

Important developments also occurred within the movement's institutions of higher education. On the Anderson College campus the most dramatic change came in June 1958 with the retirement of John A. Morrison, who had been associated with the institution for thirty-nine years. For thirty-five of those years he had been the school's chief executive officer and was the first to hold the title of president. His strong leadership in the college and church had contributed greatly to the success of both. The trauma of change normal to the departure of a leader with such long tenure was lessened considerably by the naming of Robert H. Reardon as his successor. Reardon, the son of prominent pastor and preacher E. A. Reardon, had been Morrison's assistant

---

36. Ibid., 16–17.
37. Minutes of the General Ministerial Assembly, Annual Reports, 1962, 17.

for nine years. He had previously completed graduate studies at Oberlin and had served as a pastor in Chester, Pennsylvania. Reardon held the title of executive vice-president; his appointment to the college presidency was no surprise. The leadership transition produced no upheavals.[38]

Before being named to his new office, Reardon had chaired a three-year intensive internal analysis task force. Known as the President's Study and Planning Commission, it had examined every aspect of the college's operation and projected goals for future development. Out of this commission's work there emerged a list of six major institutional objectives toward which the school should move in the next decade:

1. Exalt the spiritual and train for responsible Christian citizenship.
2. Improve instruction.
3. Attract qualified students.
4. Raise faculty salaries.
5. Build and conserve the physical plant.
6. Increase financial support.[39]

These objectives became the road map for the new president and his faculty-staff team. Within a short time, however, some plans had to be readjusted as three key individuals on the team fell victim to cancer within a span of two and a half years. Russell Olt, academic dean of the college for thirty-three years, died on June 28, 1958, just two days before Reardon officially took office. Robert Nicholson, head of the music department, was named as acting dean and then confirmed as dean by the trustees in October. The following year Carl Kardatzke, head of the education department and vice-president of the college, was stricken and died. Then just over a year and a half later, in November 1960, John H. Kane, vice-president for church relations and former alumni director, was taken.[40] During this same period two faculty members, Ruthven Byrum in art and Herman Reichenbach in mathematics, also died.

Despite these tragic losses in personnel, the college and its graduate School of Theology began a period of very rapid expansion. From 1957 to

---

38. Reardon was designated by the trustees as president elect and ratified by the General Ministerial Assembly in June 1957. He took office a year later when Morrison retired in June 1958. Reported in *Gospel Trumpet*, July 13, 1957, 15.

39. Annual Reports, 1959, 30–31.

40. Data confirmed in news stories in the *Gospel Trumpet*, July 19, 1958, 14 (Olt); February 7, 1959, 14 (Kardatzke); December 25, 1960, 14 (Kane).

1962 four major new campus buildings were constructed: a library (1957), a women's residence hall (1958), the School of Theology building (1961), and a gymnasium (1962). In addition, old Park Place Church was extensively remodeled for use as a music building, and many properties surrounding the campus were purchased. Three other major building projects were in final stages of preparation: a student center, a men's residence hall, and a science building.

Progress was also made in regard to other objectives. Student enrollment increased modestly from 1,111 in the 1956–1957 academic year to 1,250 in 1960–1961. Faculty salaries were advanced over 35 percent in the same period. A vigorous religious life department under the leadership of Bible professor Marie Strong was initiated with an emphasis on involvement in Christian service. A multifaceted program of increasing financial support from individuals, corporations, and foundations was not only underway but meeting with more than modest success. A significant personnel change came in June 1962 when Adam W. Miller retired as dean of the School of Theology, and Gene W. Newberry, professor of Christian doctrine, was appointed to succeed him.[41] In 1962 the seminary graduated twenty-seven people—the largest class in its twelve-year history.

Pacific Bible College in Portland, Oregon, also saw several significant changes in the late 1950s and early 1960s. Albert F. Gray, president of the school since its beginning, announced his retirement in the spring of 1957, climaxing a ministry in the Church of God which had begun fifty-two years earlier in Clarkston, Washington. Milo L. Chapman, then dean of the college, was named to succeed him. Faculty member Leslie Ratzlaff was appointed to the dean's position. The highly respected Gray, author of a two-volume work titled *Christian Theology,* continued to serve the church as a member of the Missionary Board and in many other capacities.[42]

In June 1956, Pacific Bible College had established a new status in the Church of God by becoming one of the national agencies related to the General Ministerial Assembly. For several years the school had received funds through the national World Service budget, but trustees had been elected by the regional West Coast Ministerial Assembly. The new arrangement gave this remotely located institution the same status as the other general agencies in Anderson. Trustees would henceforth be elected nationally, and

41. Summarized from Annual Reports and Anderson College catalogs for appropriate years.
42. *Gospel Trumpet*, May 25, 1957, 15.

Milo L. Chapman (1915–96), educator. Chapman served on the faculty of Arlington College from 1964 to 1967, but he is better remembered for his long years of service to Warner Pacific College. From 1950 to 1964 and again from 1967 until his retirement, Chapman served WPC as a professor, dean, provost, and, on two different occasions, president. He also chaired the Commission on Christian Higher Education from 1972 to 1978.

the president of the college would need to be ratified by the General Ministerial Assembly.[43] Another development with significant implications for both the school and the church was a change in the name of the institution in 1959 from Pacific Bible College to Warner Pacific College. This was more than a shift of labels. The new name allowed an enlargement of the curriculum to a full-orbed liberal arts program, which strengthened both student recruitment and the potential for approval by the regional accrediting association.[44] The latter goal was achieved in 1961 with accreditation by the Northwest Association of Schools and Colleges.

During these years this Western college expanded its campus by adding two new buildings: a men's residence hall in 1956 and a gymnasium-auditorium in 1961. Student enrollment reached a total of 217 for the 1961–62 academic year. In 1962 Chapman resigned as president of the institution to return to teaching. Louis F. Gough, a member of the faculty and a former professor of New Testament in the Anderson School of Theology, was named to succeed him.[45]

Growth, personnel changes, and program additions characterized all aspects of the national work. The Woman's Missionary Society observed its silver anniversary in 1957 with a series of celebrative occasions for its thirty-six thousand members. In 1960 Hollis S. Pistole, World Service staff member and former pastor in Baltimore, Maryland, succeeded retiring Lawrence E. Brooks as executive secretary of the Board of Pensions. Pistole left this position in 1962 to join the faculty of the School of Theol-

---

43. *Gospel Trumpet*, July 14, 1956, 14.
44. Annual Reports, 1960, 45.
45. Annual Reports, 1962, 73.

ogy and Ewald F. Wolfram, also from the World Service staff, assumed the Pensions post.[46] The *Christian Brotherhood Hour* was heard on a record 247 stations by mid-1962, with twenty-one of these being foreign outlets.[47] The Division of Church Service sponsored a series of three national consultations regarding various aspects of the general work. In 1960 the theme, "The Role of Church Service in Pastor-Church Contacts," was a timely one for any group with a congregational polity. The next year's topic, "The Right of Appeal," was a juridical issue, and in 1962 the session was simply called a "Consultation on the Ministry."[48] The monthly publication of the Board of Christian Education that had appeared under the name of *Planning Creatively* for more than twelve years was retitled *Christian Leadership* in January 1959, and the format was considerably expanded. In 1962 the board was in the midst of a special three-year project called "United Church School Advance" focused on leadership, learning, and redemptive fellowship.[49]

Expansion and accelerated activity also characterized Church of God missions. Fifty-five missionaries were at work in North America and ninety served overseas. The missions emphasis was given a considerable boost in September of 1961 with six world missions conventions in different cities within a period of two weeks.[50] The one really new development in foreign outreach was the beginning of the process of indigenizing missions work in various regions. In 1962 the Missionary Board announced that all properties belonging to the Board in Barbados were being deeded to the fifty-year-old church there. A similar transfer had occurred in Jamaica, and a similar move was under way in the large work in Kenya as well as in Egypt.[51]

Two unexpected events during this period forced the movement into radical unplanned adjustments. The first of these was the death of Clarence W. Hatch on January 29, 1960. Hatch had been involved in the national work for over twenty years in the area of fundraising. He had been a part of the changes from Associated Budgets to World Service Committee to World Service Commission to Division of World Service of the Executive Council. He was referred to as "Mr. Stewardship" in a *Gospel Trumpet* editorial:

---

46. *Gospel Trumpet*, January 10, 1960, 14; Minutes of the General Ministerial Assembly, Annual Reports, 1962, 19.
47. Annual Reports, 1962, 36.
48. Ibid., 32.
49. Ibid., 52–53.
50. *Gospel Trumpet*, October 22, 1961, 14.
51. Annual Reports, 1962, 68–69.

Mr. Stewardship has lifted our sights a long way up concerning the responsibility of every Christian, every pastor, every congregation, for every phase of the community, area, and world outreach of the church.…The day once was when the total World Service Budget was $165,000…and we weren't raising that.…We have come up and up and up since then…

Mr. Stewardship has left us a legacy.[52]

Hatch's legacy was largely completed, however, and he was moving into the newly created full-time position of executive secretary of the Executive Council of the Church of God. He had held this title since 1955, soon after the Executive Council had been restructured but in conjunction with his major responsibility as director of World Service. In its 1959 meetings the Executive Council recognized the increasing demands on the council and had asked Hatch to devote full time to this work. In June this step was approved by the General Ministerial Assembly, and Paul A. Tanner of Lansing, Michigan was ratified as director-elect of the Division of World Service to serve with Hatch for one year, after which Hatch would exclusively serve the Executive Council.[53]

Courtesy of Anderson University and Church of God Archives

Clarence W. Hatch (1903–60), agency executive. From 1955 to 1960, Hatch served as the first executive secretary of the Executive Council after its reorganization. Prior to his service there, Hatch had worked tirelessly in the cause of fundraising in support of the church's unified budget. Hatch's service extended from the early days of Associated Budgets through several reorganizations to the Division of World Service.

In preparation for this new assignment Hatch and his wife Mildred left Anderson at the end of June 1959 for a six-month world tour of the Church of God. They traveled to twenty-six countries, visited fifteen mission stations, and made personal contact with forty-one missionaries. They returned

52. Harold L. Phillips, "The Legacy of Mr. Stewardship." *Gospel Trumpet*, February 28, 1960, 3.
53. News, *Gospel Trumpet*, February 21, 1960, 14.

with a fresh world outlook on the church and in January began what was to be a dual-purpose nation-wide tour of American congregations to share their inspiration and also to learn more about the grassroots church at home. Only one month into that itinerary Hatch suffered a fatal heart attack and all the well-laid plans had to be adjusted.[54] The decision to staff the Executive Council with a full-time person remained firm, so the council set about the task of finding a suitable candidate. After extensive discussion an invitation was extended to Charles V. Weber of San Diego, California, who had worked with Hatch for several years in the World Service office. Weber accepted, was ratified by the Assembly in June 1960, and assumed his new responsibilities on October 1.[55]

The executive secretary's office had been vacant hardly a month after Hatch's death when the second traumatic event occurred. It involved not a person but a facility. In March 1960 heavy snow caused a portion of the roof on the campground tabernacle in Anderson to collapse. What seemed at first to be relatively simple repairs became more and more complicated as divergent

Paul A. Tanner (1923–), agency executive. In 1980, Tanner succeeded W. E. Reed as executive secretary of the Executive Council. Prior to holding that office, Tanner had served as director of the Division of World Service.

Charles V. Weber (1906–2004), agency leader. From 1960 to 1971, Weber served as executive secretary of the Executive Council. In that capacity, he presided over the planning and conduct of three successful World Conferences of the Church of God: Bochum, Germany; Zurich, Switzerland; and Oaxtepec, Mexico.

54. Ibid.
55. Annual Reports, 1960, 3–4.

opinions arose: Should the old building be repaired? A replacement constructed? Should a tabernacle be eliminated entirely in favor of a traveling convention? No decision could be made quickly, and no alternate facilities were available; so the June International Convention was canceled but the General Ministerial Assembly did meet that June. A major portion of the 1960 Assembly's agenda was devoted to a discussion of tabernacle issues. After lengthy deliberation the Assembly did arrive at some conclusions. Yes, it wanted to continue the annual meeting in Anderson, and thus a facility would be needed. It did not favor repairing the old tabernacle, but desired a new building with the cost not to exceed $150,000. If actual bid costs were higher, Assembly members wanted to vote on them by mail. The Assembly also wanted the whole campground facility to be titled to and managed by the Executive Council rather than the Gospel Trumpet Company.[56]

The task of determining the type of building, securing an architect, and obtaining bids fell to the Executive Council. A building committee composed of Steele C. Smith, W. E. Reed, and Adam W. Miller, along with Charles V. Weber, ex officio, was named to get the project under way. After exploring several options the committee and the council in a special September session agreed on the construction of a 240-foot concrete dome building with a seating capacity of approximately seven thousand. A mailing went to all ministers asking for approval. The response was overwhelmingly favorable (1481 to 101); however, costs considerably exceeded the earlier estimates. This became a major agenda item for the 1961 Assembly. Construction was already under way, but approval was needed to spend $417,740, rather than the original amount. After much discussion the Assembly voted to approve both the completion of the auditorium and a proposed plan of financing it. There were only two negative votes.[57] The Assembly also approved the transfer of ownership and management of convention facilities to the Executive Council.[58]

The construction of Warner Auditorium, as the building was named, attracted nationwide architectural attention. More than fifty journals discussed it, and multiple stories were distributed to six hundred newspapers. The feat of casting a 240-foot concrete dome on an earthen form and then raising it hydraulically to the top of thirty-six steel columns even made Rob-

---

56. Highlights of the General Ministerial Assembly, 1960, 3–5.
57. Highlights of the General Ministerial Assembly, 1961, 13.
58. Annual Reports, 1961, 40. The valuation of the property transferred was $239,194.56.

Warner Auditorium. From 1962 to 2004, Warner Auditorium, otherwise known as the Dome, housed the general services of the annual convention of the Church of God. Asbestos in the ceiling's sound insulation and other costly repairs forced the building's closure. The structure was demolished in 2006 and the land sold to Anderson University.

ert Ripley's worldwide syndicated feature, "Believe It Or Not."[59] Although not completely finished, the auditorium was ready for use by the 1962 convention. A dedication service for the new facility was held on June 24, the last Sunday of the convention. Final completion, including the solving of a stubborn acoustical problem, would not come until much later. This mundane project that had captured much of the movement's attention for over two years was at last ready to be used—and paid for.

As the movement concluded its eighth decade it continued to lose stalwart national leaders of the past to death. In 1956 it was P. J. Philip, who had been the most prominent of indigenous Church of God ministers in South India for forty years. Two missionaries, Nellie Olson and Rebecca Rather, who had served long years with their husbands in the Caribbean also died that year, as did Lucena Beardsley Byrum, widow of Enoch Byrum and a prominent writer of poetry and children's books. The year before it was W. J. Henry, one of the most prominent of the pioneer flying messengers; Charles E. Byers, evangelist and former pastor of one of the largest congregations of the movement in Springfield, Ohio; and James S. May, a leading nationally known black minister of Pittsburgh, Pennsylvania. In 1957 death claimed David W. Patterson, evangelist, home missionary in Alaska and Mexico, and onetime general manager of the Gospel Trumpet Company, and W. H. Hunt, president of the Board of Church Extension

---

59. Minutes of the General Ministerial Assembly, Annual Reports, 1962, 5–6.

and Home Missions and founder of Winchester Academy in Kentucky. George P. Tasker, a longtime missionary in India and a prolific and very able writer, died in 1958.

The list continues. 1959: J. J. M. Nichols-Roy, well-known preacher, writer, and political leader in Assam, North India; Sethard P. Dunn, black pastor of the movement's largest church in Chicago and benefactor through his estate of Anderson College; Noah S. Duncan, another of the pioneer evangelists who had traveled nationwide. 1960: H. A. Sherwood, member of the first faculty of Anderson Bible Training School and former pastor of Park Place Church in Anderson. 1961: William A. Bixler, well-known chalk-talk artist and a worker at the Gospel Trumpet office for half a century; Harry C. Gardner, president of Alberta Bible Institute for most of the time since its founding in 1933 and a veteran member of the Gospel Trumpet Publication Board; Mabel Hale, an early evangelist, author, teacher at the Kansas City Bible Training School, and writer of many materials for youth; Floyd W. Heinly, a thirty-one-year veteran missionary in India and Pakistan and one of the early leaders in the missionary home in New York City; Earl L. Martin, educator, author, and preacher for forty-five years. He was the first dean of the School of Theology in Anderson, was vice-president of Anderson College, had served on many of the national boards, and had authored several books.[60]

Underlying all these events and developments, however, was the continuing concern for making decision-making processes more participatory and to involve more people from the field in the national and international work of the church. Without a doubt it could be said that the period of 1955–62 was characterized by an active quest for spiritual democracy at all levels, including the rapidly developing state organizations.

However, this nagging structural concern did not override a persistent attention to the more important spiritual and personal matters. This was evident at any point one might choose to look. For example, the *Gospel Trumpet* continued its decades-old practice of carrying reader's prayer requests:

For the C. Jean Kilmers as they labor now in Kenya; for unsettled conditions in the Middle East, where they formerly served.

---

60. Data secured from appropriate yearbooks and respective news items in *Gospel Trumpet*.

Niece with cancer. Another niece has double curvature of the spine and needs a home; recently lost her mother. (A sister, N. Mex.)

Woman with three children who has had a nervous breakdown. (Mrs. L. O., Tex.)

Husband had hemorrhoid operation and trying to work but suffers much pain. (Mrs. O. W., Mo.)[61]

Dale Oldham's *Christian Brotherhood Hour* sermons were published regularly in the *Gospel Trumpet.* In 1960, he delivered a series of eight sermons on love. Oldham's warm and caring nature was communicated over the air and on the printed page in words such as:

If the Lord permitted you to lift but one prayer a day into his presence, what would that prayer be? For me, it would be, "O God, fill my heart so full of Thy love that it will overflow wherever I go." For love is the key to life, peace, joy, service, faith, and hope.[62]

This emphasis of personal concern was extended to many social issues. One example can be found in an article by William A. Hubbard in which he stated, "No, thank you, I don't drink because I need all of my faculties to do the job that God intends me to do."[63] Another article titled "Are We Failing Our Children?" reflected pointed interest in families, homes and schools.[64] One news note, titled "Aroused Church People Campaign Against Vice," told of a civic cleanup drive in Moundsville, West Virginia. Wyatt Weeks, pastor of the Ash Avenue Church of God, had been named to the city planning commission, which was working toward facilitating orderly growth in the Moundsville community.[65]

Personal news items frequently appeared in the *Gospel Trumpet.* One item featured in a January 1959 issue, titled "Ohio Pastor Is Named 'Woman of the Year,'" gave the news of Lillie McCutcheon's being honored by the *Newton Falls Herald.*[66] Other news notes announced pastoral changes, building dedications, and other items of personal and congregational interest, thus helping the movement feel united and informed about its local

61. *Gospel Trumpet*, May 18, 1957, 16.
62. Dale Oldham, "To Love Is to Pray," *Gospel Trumpet*, February 14, 1960, 12.
63. William A. Hubbard, "No, Thank You, I Don't Drink," *Gospel Trumpet*, March 18, 1958, 4.
64. Dale Oldham, "Are We Failing Our Children," *Gospel Trumpet*, May 10, 1958, 1.
65. "Aroused Church People Against Vice," *Gospel Trumpet*, August 3, 1957, 14.
66. *Gospel Trumpet*, January 17, 1959, 15.

congregations and people. In a 1957 *Trumpet,* a note from D. S. Warner's son stated, "D. Sidney Warner announces that the annual Trumpet Family reunion of former workers will be held during Anderson Camp Meeting."[67] Major articles in the *Gospel Trumpet* continued to treat doctrinal issues, particularly unity and the nature of the church. Practical emphases on prayer and the devotional life, as well as concern for missions and stewardship, were also characteristic of this era. Editor Harold L. Phillips stimulated thought and invited comment in his regular offerings on the editorial page. Vital, practical aspects of the Christian life were not neglected. In these years from 1955 to 1962, as the movement pressed boldly and decisively toward spiritual democracy, there was a strong sense of moving forward. In the words of Charles V. Weber in concluding his 1962 report to the General Ministerial Assembly, "In spite of the dangers and needs that are before us, I sincerely believe that the church has been making great progress and we have every reason to be encouraged."[68] The Assembly expressed its agreement by approving its largest budget ever: $1,600,950.

---

67. *Gospel Trumpet*, June 8, 1957, 15.
68. Report of the Executive Secretary of the Executive Council, Annual Reports, 1962, 7.

CHAPTER 16

FROM CONGRESS TO CONSULTATION
(1963–1972)

New York Times columnist C. L. Sulzberger characterized the years between 1963 and 1972 as "the age of mediocrity."[1] After interviewing most of the world's top leaders during that decade he concluded that historical events had not been shaped by towering giants. No Churchill, Roosevelt, or even a Kennedy dominated the stage; only average, capable business and government officials who sought to hold together world and society at a time when established systems and institutions were being challenged by nonleaders—youth, minorities, the poor, and the oppressed. The agenda was mostly in the hands of the challengers; leaders were forced to spend their time and energy reacting.

Whether or not one agrees with Mr. Sulzberger's judgment, a review of global events during this period lends considerable support to his overall analysis, even though one might want to cite certain exceptions. His assessment of world affairs could also apply to most institutions—corporations, labor unions, schools, and churches. All were thrust into the role of reactor rather than initiator. In a qualified sense this analysis also describes the Church of God during the age of mediocrity; in another sense it does not, for during these years national agencies—institutions—set and accomplished noteworthy goals. The period began and concluded with well-planned churchwide meetings aimed at self-assessment, projection of goals, and development of strategies for achieving them. The All Board Congress and Planning Council in 1963 and the 1970 Consultation undoubtedly contributed greatly to providing an agenda for the movement during the seven-year interlude between the two meetings and for the years immediately following. Events and developments in the Church of God during this period should reveal how well the movement fared during this age of mediocrity.

---

1. C. L. Sulzberger, *The Age of Mediocrity: Memoirs and Diaries, 1963–72* (New York: Macmillan, 1973.)

The All Board Congress and Planning Council was initiated by national leaders of the movement but, in the words of Findings Committee chairperson R. Eugene Sterner, it grew out of "a longfelt need for a reappraisal of our work, and for a dynamic new sense of mission and purpose."[2] The plan was to bring together board members of all the agencies under the General Ministerial Assembly. To this number were added selected staff members of these agencies, all full-time coordinators employed by the various state assemblies, and one other selected representative from each state. A total of 260 people participated in the meeting in Anderson from April 30 to May 2, 1963.

In preparation for this meeting a series of four sets of core questions regarding the nature, mission, message, and purpose of the church had been sent to all delegates months in advance with the request that participants give studied attention to each query and reply out of their deepest convictions. Responses were summarized in two papers presented at the beginning of the congress. These provided a stimulus for eighteen work groups, which focused on various areas of the church's task by asking three basic questions: (1) What is the Spirit saying to us? (2) How well are we obeying? (3) What, under God, shall we undertake together? A reporter observed, "It can be said that there was a frank and open discussion of basic questions in considerable depth. Real dialogue and communication did take place."[3]

The findings of the Congress were summarized at the close in a list of sixteen areas of consensus and concern. All were stated as "needs" for the Church of God under the following headings:

1. The need for clearer, stronger theological foundations
2. The need for Christian unity in teaching and practice
3. The need for redemptive fellowship to be realized more in the church
4. The need to sense whatever distinctive contribution we can make, as a Movement
5. The need for more adequate structure
6. The need for great, overarching goals

---

2. Report of the All Board Congress and Planning Council, Minutes of the General Ministerial Assembly, Annual Reports, 1963, 21.

3. Ibid., 22.

7. The need to strengthen the local church
8. The need to upgrade the pastor image and the pastor-congregation relationships
9. The need to enlist, train, and place ministers
10. The need to express the whole church as ministry and service
11. The need for social consciousness and conscience
12. The need for vital evangelism
13. The need for better communication of the gospel
14. The need for better stewardship
15. The need for stronger motivation and spiritual renewal
16. The need for self-awareness and analysis.[4]

A findings committee later reviewed these needs and summarized the consensus of the congress in five "overarching concerns" They were stated as follows:

1. There is a great need for a clarification of our teaching and for much more aggressive teaching throughout the church; for serious intellectual engagement and dialogue among our people, both the ministry and the laity. There is, furthermore, a need for a better understanding of our role and purpose as a movement; a new, fresh, clear sense of direction.
2. There is a great need for restructuring, to provide for much more adequate communication among us, permitting greater expression and also offering guidance and help, especially to the local church in times of stress and change.
3. We all sensed deeply and have spoken in many ways about the need for genuine spiritual renewal; fresh, strong motivations rooted in God's constraining love.
4. We are in great need of strong, vital evangelistic outreach. This is the main track of the church. We must be willing to make fresh approaches, think courageously about our theology of evangelism, and recover a sense of the individual person. We are more activistic than evangelistic.

---

4. Ibid.

5. We need to be much more deeply aware of social forces and influences around us which vitally affect human life. We need a social consciousness and conscience.[5]

A special effort was made to communicate these findings as widely as possible. Several conventions and state assemblies built their programs around them, and an international convention theme also emerged from the list of needs. Major developments in the remaining years of the decade reveal the magnitude of the impact this congress had on the Church of God. It came at a crucial time in the history of the movement and provided a climate of openness for discussing and handling some critical issues which the sixties thrust upon all social institutions—including the church.

In the light of such an auspicious beginning to this period the question immediately arises as to how the label "age of mediocrity" could apply. The term is applicable only in regard to certain aspects. It was true of the movement as of the political world that no towering giants emerged as leaders during those difficult days. But the fact of the matter is that for almost a generation the Church of God had been moving away from strong leaders in favor of more participatory decision making. The All Board Congress itself amply illustrates progress in this direction. Subsequent developments in the sixties were to show further advance along these lines. One point, however, to which "mediocrity" did apply was numerical growth.[6]

Since the earliest statistical records of the number of people in Church of God congregations, successive years had always shown increases, in some cases phenomenal. It was something of a shock, then, to discover that the "boom" was over and that in some tabulations there was even "negative growth." Available statistics indicate a decade-long plateau in almost all categories. From 1963 to 1972, the number of ministers (ordained and unordained) declined slightly from 3,341 to 3,293. There were thirty-two fewer missionaries in the field in 1972 than a decade earlier—down to 117 from 149. The total number of congregations in the United States and Canada also decreased by twenty-two. The largest drop came in Sunday school enrollment—down over 16,000 from 255,043 to 238,692. In the grassroots

---

5. As reported by R. Eugene Sterner for the Findings Committee to the 1970 Consultation of the Church of God. Included in the workbook for this consultation.

6. It should be noted that this was a period when all the major mainline Protestant denominations showed rather drastic declines in both membership and financial support. The Church of God was somewhat unique, along with other conservative churches, in that it did not experience this sharp decline in all statistics.

and leadership areas only the national "membership" figures showed an increase—modestly up 10,660 from 144,232 in 1963 to 154,892 in 1972.[7] In a very different vein, enrollment in the church's nationally supported colleges was also up significantly by about 80 percent during the decade.[8] Seminary enrollment increased markedly, more than 96 percent, from 62 in 1963 to a high of 122 in 1972. These figures would seem to indicate both a rapidly rising commitment to an educated leadership on the part of the Church of God, abetted considerably by the expanding economy, which also enhanced the total financial picture, and a willingness on the part of the church to put more money into higher education. Some of this increase is also attributable to sheer numbers; the first baby-boomers entered college in 1964. Vietnam also stimulated college attendance among males.

Financial figures also moved upward and certainly indicate something better than mediocrity about the Church of God. World Service income in this period rose from $1,485,363 in 1963 to $2,603,428 in 1972. In no year did the financial income fall behind that of a previous year, even though the projected budget was not always achieved.

Since World Service income is the single most important indicator of financial strength, its continual increase during the decade showed strong financial commitment to the national and international work of the Church of God. In the 1969 Annual Report by the Division of World Service, Director Paul A. Tanner made this observation: "Per capita giving of $15.09 broke the $15.00 barrier for the first time. Per capita giving growth from $10.00 to $15.00 has taken place during the last seven years, whereas, for eighteen years we varied between $5.00 to $10.00 per capita."[9]

A similar financial outlook is represented by the income of the national Woman's Missionary Society. From 1963 to 1967, income increased steadily from $484,813 to $579,306. In 1967, the income was off only

---

7. Figures from *Yearbook of the Church of God* for indicated years. Membership statistics have been something of an enigma for the movement since its beginning. After denying the capability of any human being to judge who is a member of the church and who is not and rejecting any membership procedures such as admission ceremonies or rolls, it has been difficult to get any accurate or consistent data about the number of people associated with the various congregations. The first attempt at listing figures of any kind was in the second *Yearbook* in 1918 where some of the entries included "Sunday School Attendance." The following year a few went further and entered a figure for "Number in Congregation." It was 1923, however, before responses to this question were sufficiently representative to total the number of "members" on the summary page.

8. Official enrollment data not available. Figures derived from Annual Reports for the designated years and files of the Commission on Christian Higher Education.

9. Annual Reports, 1969, 47.

slightly ($2,100), but off considerably in 1968, by nearly $61,000. This trend was reversed the following year, however, and rose to an all-time high of $652,000 in 1972.[10]

No single factor can be pointed out as the reason for such consistent financial growth. A greater dedication on the part of the membership toward God and the work of the church undoubtedly would be a significant element of the increase; however, a general improvement in economic conditions and individual financial status may be just as significant.

Real property value for the Church of God also showed considerable growth throughout the period. Local church property valuation climbed from $73,040,888 in 1963 to $149,144,810 in 1972. Many church building programs were also under way during this period. College and school property values rose from $5.1 million to $15.4 million during the decade. The value of the international campgrounds rose from $756,940 in 1963 to $956,613 in 1972. Property for general offices increased significantly also. In 1963 the approximate value was $345,000, but due to new building programs it reached $943,523 in 1972. It is thus apparent that the Church of God, along with the expanding economy, was showing strong growth in a variety of assets.[11]

Fidel Zamorano (1924–95), minister. In 1965, Zamorano founded *La Hora de Hermandad,* a Spanish-language version of the *Christian Brotherhood Hour,* and served as the program's speaker until 1995. Zamorano's program was the first of the non-English broadcasts. By 2000, CBH-affiliated programs were heard in Spanish, Swahili, Portuguese, Oriya, Russian, Arabic, and Mandarin.

Institutions expanded in ways other than financial growth. In the nine-year span between 1963 and 1972, the *Christian Brotherhood Hour* radio program also grew significantly. The English broadcast version was heard over 200 stations in 1960, but by 1969 it was aired over more than 340. In 1965, the Spanish-speaking version of CBH was launched in California by Fidel Zamorano, pastor of the Belvedere Church of God in Los Angeles, California. By 1969, the Spanish program was heard on forty-four stations.

10. Annual Reports, 1972, 79.
11. *Yearbook* (Summary page, designated years).

Developments in the Church of God within this context of plateaued numerical growth and expanding economic resources can well be categorized in the six areas of concern assigned to work groups in the 1970 Consultation that came near the end of this period. These six areas were social concerns, unity, lay ministry, evangelism, missions, and leadership. These were the issues that had moved to the front by that time. To understand what had brought them to the fore it is necessary to review some of the major events, undercurrents, and sequences of the seven preceding years.

Even a reader only minimally acquainted with this period in American history will understand why social concerns head the list. It also would be expected that racial issues were among the most prominent concerns in that category. Fortunately for the Church of God the issue of racial justice had not yet blossomed to crisis proportions when movement leadership began seriously to address the problem. In 1957 the General Ministerial Assembly had authorized a study committee on race relations. The final report of that committee was submitted in 1962 but the issue had not been dropped. Conversations had continued with the race relations committee of the National Association of the Church of God. These conversations produced a statement on race relations that was presented to the Executive Council in February 1964. The council adopted the statement and recommended it to the General Ministerial Assembly the following June. The Assembly adopted the statement with a resounding vocal approval. Its contents reviewed the work of the study committee, reaffirmed the interracial stance of the movement, and then moved on to note the climate of the time in relation to the problems yet unsolved:

In the year 1963, a new word was interjected into the whole movement for racial equality. That word was "now." It has changed the whole movement from one of a gradual process into a rapid revolutionary pace. Perhaps none foresaw such a rapid change in the whole picture. Suddenly words and declarations are no longer sufficient in this struggle. The plea to "slow down" or "wait" is no longer heeded. The problem will *not* wait. The voices of the past are drowned out with the cry for "now." This is true whether we like it or not. Up to now many have felt that gradual change in modest progress toward racial justice was acceptable. Whether this was a valid belief or not cannot be answered now because it is swept away by the fast moving changes that have been brought about during the past few months.

We are faced with the question of what the Church of God ought to do in light of the intensity of the present problem, and in light of our basic commitment to a message of unity and oneness in our common experience in Christ Jesus.[12]

After noting that the movement had been historically reluctant in making pronouncements or issuing directives since no person or body could speak for the whole group, the statement then observed, "Perhaps it is at this point that we have faltered and should confess with deep penitence that our performance as a church has not always kept pace with our profession."[13] This was followed by a forthright call to take a bold Christian stand, supporting it with Christian action:

We base our stand toward basic human rights on the teaching of the Scriptures. God has "made of one blood all nations of men" (Acts 17:6). "For we are all the children of God by faith in Jesus Christ…for we are all one in Jesus Christ" (Gal. 3:26, 28). The first of these speaks as to origin, the second as to relationship. We believe that in the Church of God there should be no racial barriers because we are all brethren in Christ. We believe that man was made in the image of God, that every person is of intrinsic worth before God, and that every individual has a right to the fullest possible opportunities for the development of life abundant and eternal. We believe that these rights are given by God and that the church has a responsibility to defend them and work for their guarantee.[14]

The remainder of the statement admonished congregations to make special efforts to integrate the races in their midst, to declare and practice an open door policy by fully welcoming into congregational life all people without regard to race, color, or nationality. State assemblies were urged to give special attention to including all races in their membership and in their nominations for offices. Where segregated assemblies existed they were encouraged to begin steps to bring them into one working fellowship. The statement's authors clearly believed that its endorsers and perhaps others believed their actions arose out of obedience to God's call.[15]

---

12. Minutes of the General Ministerial Assembly, Annual Reports, 1964, 10.
13. Ibid., 11.
14. Ibid., 12.
15. Ibid., 13.

There would be further official action on racial issues during the sixties, but in a slightly different context. That same year (1964) the General Ministerial Assembly brought into being a permanent Commission on Social Concerns. The enabling resolution, dated June 15, 1964, stated the commission's scope of responsibility to address a wide range of issues from temperance and vice to peace and world order to human relations:

> ...*temperance and general welfare,* particularly with alcohol problems, gambling, tobacco, pornographic literature; in areas of *peace and world order,* particularly with military policy and legislation for conscription, disarmament and nuclear weapon control; and in the area of *human relations* particularly in race relations, civil liberties, church-state relationships, housing, civic responsibility.[16]

Although "human relations" appeared near the end of the list of areas of concern the topic enjoyed high priority. The resolutions explicitly stated that it had been agreed upon by the Executive Council and the National Association of the Church of God (West Middlesex, Pennsylvania) through its standing committee on race relations.

The genius of the commission's membership lay in its constituency. Fifteen members were elected, five-to-seven of whom were to be blacks, with additional members from other races. Each of the general agencies was asked to name one member, and the executive secretary of the Executive Council and the director of the Division of Church Service served ex-officio. The three-year terms of elected members were staggered so as to provide continuity.

The new commission had as a primary purpose the coordination of efforts in the field of social concerns already undertaken by the several agencies of the Assembly. Many of these had been deeply involved in social service activities. Anderson College, for instance, sponsored many programs, including Tri-S (Summer Student Service) where volunteers traveled to many foreign countries often for the purpose of helping missionaries in teaching, serving, and building. Tri-S participants also went into the inner city, worked with migrants, Indians, Spanish Americans, Appalachians, and served in other home missions projects. In other programs students tutored disadvantaged youngsters. The Christianity-in-Action Program provided

---

16. Ibid., 14.

many service opportunities in local hospitals, nursing homes, jails, and ghetto areas. At Gulf-Coast Bible College in Houston, Texas, Christian Service was a major program involving the students in service learning, which usually meant conducting church services, musical ministries, literature distribution, visitation to the sick and imprisoned, and teaching—especially children. The college also maintained a housing project for low-income families.

Another group involved in social ministry was the Woman's Missionary Society. This organization helped to underwrite projects for the Urban Ministries department of the Board of Church Extension and Home Missions, assisted in alleviating world hunger problems, and encouraged study in social concerns and human needs. The women's organization also made efforts to establish closer ties with black women in local congregations.

The Division of Church Service sponsored meetings between black and white officers of assemblies in the southern states and encouraged wider participation of both races in those assemblies already integrated. The Board of Church Extension and Home Missions had appointed a full-time director for the newly created Department of Urban Ministries. The new appointment meant that two full-time executive staff people served in this area in addition to part-time assistance by others. They were responsible for considerable enlargement of the Metropolitan Mission Program and other urban programs.

The Missionary Board had been carrying out all its overseas work in closest harmony with the objectives and concerns of the Commission on Social Concerns. The Pensions Board had been helping older people, retirees, and widows. Warner Press continued a heavy schedule of publications, principally through *Vital Christianity,* devoted to topics such as racism, human relations, narcotics, urban challenges, war and peace, marriage and family relations, and calls to Christian action. Curriculum materials focused on social problems. Faster than other agencies, the company intentionally attempted to employ more blacks, and continued to encourage subscribers to read widely on race issues and in areas of "social sensitivity."

The Board of Christian Education incorporated social concerns into the church's educational ministry. The Board sponsored "awareness seminars," and continued to publish materials especially designed to focus attention on social needs such as racism, marriage, family life, and poverty. It also sponsored meetings between officers of the International Youth Convention and the Black Interstate Youth Convention.

In addition to coordinating the social concerns activities of other agencies, the commission was authorized to initiate studies and recommend action. In the light of internal controversy caused by social activists in other churches, the Assembly strongly felt that this commission's work should not include either programming or pronouncements. It could raise issues, it could study them, and it could recommend programs. Its prerogative was generally described as "speaking *to* the church, not *for* the church."

Despite these limitations, the commission set about its tasks. They divided membership into three work committees, each assigned to a specific area of concern: (1) temperance and general welfare, (2) peace and world order, and (3) human relations and economic affairs. Through the prodding of the Social Concerns Commission as well as a continuing general awareness and sensitivity on the part of the movement, many concerns were addressed and considerable activity initiated.[17]

In 1965 the Commission on Social Concerns sponsored three major resolutions related to race. One called "for support of Amendment XXV of the United States Constitution which guarantees equal voting rights without discrimination based upon racial, religious, or economic differences." The second resolution asked for greater personal involvement of every Christian in the quest for racial justice, and the third called on the general agencies to more directly involve the church in the struggle for equal rights. A fourth resolution urged a more positive stand against the use and advertising of tobacco.[18]

The commission sponsored four conferences at the 1967 International Convention. One of these, "What is it really like to be a Negro in the U.S.?" sought to sharpen the awareness of the individual to the problems faced by American blacks, and to bring into clearer focus the responsibilities of every Christian toward achieving racial justice. An additional four conferences were offered in 1968 at the International Convention—Racism: Black Power; Racism: Riots; Racism: Open Housing; and Racism: Law and Order.

In 1969, the commission reported extensively on actions being taken by the national agencies to address the race issue. Significant progress was reported by all. To illustrate the achievement made at the national level it was noted that in 1957 there were only six blacks serving on national boards

17. Report of Commission on Social Concerns, Minutes of the General Ministerial Assembly, Annual Reports, 1965, 34–40.

18. Annual Reports, 1967, 47; 1968, 48.

and agencies. By 1963 the numbers had increased to ten. In 1967 there were nineteen African-American board members, and in 1968–69 there were twenty-six, or 14 percent of the total board membership.[19]

Another area of the commission's concern was church-state relationships. Interest in this issue heightened in June 1963 when the United States Supreme Court handed down a decision declaring that compulsory Bible reading and prayer in public schools was unconstitutional. Coincidentally, the Assembly was in session at the time of the Court's decision. Only one year earlier, in 1962, the Assembly authorized the Executive Council to appoint a special study committee to address the area of church-state relationships. The committee was to give attention to many areas, among which were:

(1) The celebration of religious holidays, Bible readings and prayer in the public schools.
(2) Using school or other public property for religious services, religious displays or religious pageants.
(3) Sunday blue laws and the enforcement of such laws where they exist.
(4) Tax exemption for religious property and religious organizations.
(5) Exemption from military service for those of the clergy.
(6) Direct and indirect financial support to parochial schools and/or church-related colleges.[20]

In its report the committee noted the problem of church-state relationships was quite entangled: "Many churches, while maintaining the idea of separation on the one hand, have actually become entangled on the other... the Church of God is not an exception, but that we, too, have sought after and received favorable considerations from the State."[21]

In 1965, the study committee's assignment was turned over to the Commission on Social Concerns. However, in following years, the commission did not continue intensive work on the public school prayer issue. The committee's final report offers a possible explanation. Commission members declared their support for the Supreme Court and their willingness to abide by its decision. In the 1963 decision on prayer and public

19. Annual Reports, 1969, 49.
20. Minutes of the General Ministerial Assembly, Annual Reports, 1963, 17.
21. Ibid., 18.

schools the Commission saw an opportunity and a challenge. The church needed to re-examine its program to provide sound religious instruction. Furthermore, the commission stated, "We should not expect the public schools, or government, to do for us that which is the first responsibility of the family and the church."[22]

The committee report went on to state its reservations concerning the use of public funds to support elementary and secondary church-related schools. If done, then it must be without discrimination on the basis of race, religion, class, or national origin and with adequate safeguards against federal control of educational policy.[23] Regarding taxation, exemption, and deductions in relation to churches, the committee noted:

(1) Useful functions of religious institutions in society could be threatened, jeopardized by taxation.
(2) Religious institutions could be placed in a subservient position to the State through the payment of taxes.

Another area of great social concern during this seething decade was the issue of war and peace, brought on by the conflict in Vietnam. A *Gospel Trumpet* article early in 1960 titled "Serving God in the Military Service," sparked a fair degree of comment from the readers.[24] The article did not actually deal with the question of whether or not one should fight for one's country but encouraged those in any branch of the armed services to be solid in their Christian life and witness. Responses indicated that at least some members of the movement were very concerned about the issue of bearing arms for their country. About a month later editor Harold Phillips replied to comments by stating that his staff was not trying to take a stance for or against military service, but instead was trying to speak to the needs of those who were already in that position of service.[25]

In early 1966 *Vital Christianity* carried an article titled "Viet Nam: My View." Although not written by a Church of God person, the article appeared in the church's periodical and expressed a general approval of military actions of the United States in Vietnam. The author stated that "our

22. Minutes of the General Assembly, June 18, 1965. Exhibit AA, 2–4.
23. Ibid., 4–5.
24. A. Wayne Johnson, "Serving God in the Military Service," *Gospel Trumpet*, February 14, 1960, 9–10.
25. Harold L. Phillips, "Should a Christian Bear Armor?" *Gospel Trumpet*, March 20, 1960, 3–4.

military involvement there is morally right, just, and essential. I talked to no one in Vietnam who felt that there was a moral alternative to our troop buildup and increasing air strikes."[26] The incongruity of a prowar attitude in a magazine that represented a group of people with a significant pacifist commitment apparently was little noticed. Subsequent letters to the editor were not overwhelmingly negative, with at least as much support for the article as there was opposition. Apparently there was a significant amount of "God and country" sentiment in the churches during the sixties that tended to offset the traditional pacifistic Church of God position.

Prowar sentiment did not, of course, express the whole view of the Church of God. A "Statement of Conviction on War and Peace" was approved by the General Assembly in June of 1966 and included in the 1967 *Yearbook of the Church of God.* Along with the general support for the 1966 article, excerpts from the statement illustrate an almost bipolar attitude toward war and peace in the movement:

> Like all true Americans, we as members of the General Assembly of the Church of God meeting in regular session in Anderson, Indiana, this 16th day of June, 1966, view with deep concern the escalating military involvement and the conscription of our youth for military service. We believe that war represents our moral failures. We abhor the causes that lead to war. We stand by the teaching and example of our Lord who taught us and showed us the way of radical, sacrificial love.…
>
> We respect the right of each person to arrive at his own convictions. We believe in the principle of freedom of worship and freedom of conscience. We respect the rights of the individual conscience within our fellowship.…What we seek for ourselves we seek for every citizen of our land—the right of individual conscience which no governmental authority can abrogate or violate. We do not condemn or reject that person who differs with our position or participates in war. We shall seek to follow such persons with a ministry of help and guidance, but this is never to be construed as approval of war.…
>
> Let this statement of conviction be construed by any and all to mean that we fully support young men of the Church of God who sincerely and conscientiously are opposed to participation in military service.

---

26. Ben R. Hartley, "Viet Nam: My View," *Vital Christianity*, January 16, 1966, 5–6.

We encourage them to seek the constructive alternatives intended to bring health, healing, and understanding, and which serve the highest interests of our beloved country and of the whole world.[27]

There were numerous occasions in the following years to refer to this statement as the unpopularity of the Vietnam conflict increased and more young men refused to participate.

In the later years of the sixties the demands on the Commission on Social Concerns became so great that in November 1968 members requested from the Executive Council staff and office space to support the expanding work of the commission. After a year and a half of discussion by the council and the General Assembly the request was denied and the commission was instructed to continue "in its present assignment through the Council."[28] A resolution calling for the abolition of the commission also was rejected by that same Assembly.[29] Despite these thwarting actions the commission continued to press for racial justice and equal opportunity in both society and the church. Along with spokespersons for the movement's black constituency they urged the employment of more black persons in the offices of the general agencies and formulated a resolution asking congregations to sign an open door policy statement. On both points the commission was able to note significant progress.

Another area of extensive activity in the Church of God during this period was higher education. Anderson College continued to grow and add to its facilities. A new men's residence hall and a science building were completed in 1964. A coeducational dormitory, an apartment unit for married students, and a women's gymnasium were built in 1967. In 1968 the first college owned presidential residence was built. That same year saw the demolition of "Old Main" (the Trumpet Home from 1906 to 1917) and the beginning of construction for a new administration building. It was completed in 1970, the same year that an additional women's dormitory was built. In 1971 the Olt Student Center was doubled in size, and construction of a natatorium was begun. Enrollment topped the 2,000 mark in the 1971–1972 academic year. At the end of that year President Reardon

---

27. "Statement of Conviction on War and Peace," *Yearbook of the Church of God*, 1967, 151. A subsequent resolution on peace was adopted by the 1970 General Assembly that reaffirmed support of those who objected to the Vietnam war.

28. Minutes of the General Assembly, Annual Reports, 1970, 25.

29. Ibid., 43–45.

expressed his hope that "the turbulent 1960's with [their] rebellious, impatient, tuned-in, turned-on, tell-it-like-it-is, revolutionary approach to the world," were over and that the college might "recover something of the quiet thoughtfulness and balanced judgment which are marks of civil and refined people."[30]

Warner Pacific College also showed progress as well as encountering some severe problems. In 1963 the General Ministerial Assembly authorized a one-hundred-thousand-dollar World Service project to raise funds for a new administration building and additions to the college's library holdings. After having received provisional accreditation in 1961, the school worked diligently toward full endorsement by the Northwest Association of Secondary and Higher Schools and received that status in December of 1964. Enrollment that year climbed above the three hundred mark and a new coeducational residence hall was completed.[31]

Courtesy of Warner Pacific College

Louis F. Gough (1910–78), educator. Trained as a New Testament scholar, Gough moved back and forth between Portland, Oregon, and Anderson, Indiana, from 1952 to 1960, holding faculty positions at Warner Pacific College and Anderson School of Theology. In 1960, he returned to WPC and was elected its third president in 1962. Gough's plan to move WPC to San José proved short-lived and threw the institution into serious financial difficulty.

The college's board of trustees had appointed a Long-Range Planning Committee in 1963 to assess both the economic problems of the school and the availability of land for expansion. One year later, this committee determined that the eleven-acre campus in Portland could not be developed to handle the anticipated growth, that contiguous land was not available, that the area was already oversupplied with colleges, and therefore a more suitable site should be explored. In due course Warner Pacific College received an offer of a gift of one hundred acres of land at San José, California. The committee, with the strong support of President Louis F. Gough, recommended acceptance of the gift and a move to California. The trustees approved the recommendation in April 1965, and the matter was placed before the General Assembly in Anderson in

30. Annual Reports, 1972, 53.
31. Annual Reports, 1965, 80–86.

June for concurrent approval. After discussion regarding the possible merger of Warner Pacific College with Arlington College, the Southern California Association-sponsored school in Long Beach, the resolution to approve the move was passed.[32] It appeared the college was on the way to a new campus and rapid expansion.

Within a year the dream collapsed. In the course of preparing for the move and raising funds for the new facility various problems developed, both internally and externally. It became apparent that while all the official approvals had been received, many people—some faculty, alumni, and ministers and most of the Church of God constituency in the Portland area—opposed the move. Strong feeling led to a breakdown in goodwill and support. By midyear financial difficulties were beginning to mount and by spring they had reached the point of crisis. In a special meeting of the trustees on June 7, 1966, President Gough resigned, the move to San José was "temporarily" delayed, and the college set about raising $300,000 for unpaid bills due by late summer. With intense effort from trustees, the General Assembly, the Executive Council, the Anderson agencies, and many local congregations the school survived the financial crisis and continued operations in Portland under the leadership of E. Joe Gilliam, Indianapolis pastor and trustee, who was selected as president. In 1972 Warner Pacific received a major gift in trust which greatly abetted the college's future hopes even though it provided no immediate financial benefit. That year the total enrollment figure topped the five hundred mark.[33] The school had weathered a heavy storm. Plans for further development in Portland moved ahead. Before the end of the decade the college had completed construction of a major auditorium classroom complex.

At Gulf-Coast Bible College in Houston, Texas, there were also signs of growth but no major problems. In 1966 President Max Gaulke resigned his pastorate of First Church in Houston to give full time to the college. During that academic year the school received associate membership in the Accrediting Association of Bible Colleges and in 1968 was granted full accreditation. A new multipurpose building was dedicated in the spring of 1967 and that year enrollment reached a new high of 227 students. The 1968 General Assembly made the college a new general agency of the national church, thus making the school a participant in the national budget

32. Annual Reports, 1966, 90–93. Also, Minutes of the General Assembly, June 14, 1966, 12, 17.

33. Annual Reports, 1972, 56.

and the second general agency to be located outside Anderson. By 1971–1972 the cumulative enrollment had reached 332, and the college's net worth approached a half-million dollars.[34]

One of the more controversial aspects of the educational endeavors of the sixties manifested in a head-on encounter between the Commission on Christian Higher Education and members of the Southeastern Association of the Church of God who wished to found a college in that part of the nation. In 1967 the commission stated its opposition to such a proposal. Having assessed the status of existing institutions, potential numbers of students, likely levels of church support and the need of a general educational strategy, the commission could not support a proposal for another college:

Max Gaulke (1910–92), educator. The son of Church of God ministers in the upper Midwest, Gaulke was a pastor in Houston, Texas, when conversations began in earnest calling for a ministerial training center in the region. In 1953, with his church's facilities for its use, Gaulke founded the South Texas Bible Institute with himself as president. In this modest beginning, Gulf-Coast Bible College was born.

> We cannot claim infallibility of judgment in assessing the future of the Church or of higher education. We have endeavored, however, to seriously assess (1) the present and future status of our existing institutions, (2) evidence of student needs and potential, (3) levels of Church support, and (4) total educational strategy in the Church of God. We urge the brethren responsible for the future of the Southeastern Association of the Church of God to consider this counsel most seriously.[35]

The Southeastern Association refused to let the proposal die, but in 1968 the commission repeated its conviction, "This is not the time to attempt the beginning of a new college in the Church of God."[36] Again in 1969 the commission reaffirmed its stance by saying, "The commission continues to reiterate its firm belief that the church should not con-

---

34. Annual Reports, 1967, 51; 1968, 15; 1972, 59.
35. Minutes of the General Assembly, Annual Reports, 1967 13–14.
36. Annual Reports, 1968, 47.

tinue to start new colleges."[37] However, members of the Southeastern Association decided to proceed with a new college in Lake Wales, Florida, without the blessings of the Commission on Christian Higher Education. The first freshman class was enrolled in 1968, and Warner Southern College became a reality. Leroy M. Fulton of Drexel, North Carolina, was named as president.

There were also developments in the older regionally sponsored schools. Arlington College in Long Beach, California, sponsored by the Southern California Association of the Church of God, was merged with interdenominational Azusa Pacific College in 1968. The arrangement provided for the transfer of faculty and library holdings and for the association's limited participation in the control of the merged institution. Bay Ridge Christian College in Kendleton, Texas, controlled by the voluntary and mostly black Southern Association of the Church of God, had found its permanent location there on a 234-acre site in 1961 and graduated its first class of five men and three women in 1966.

Leroy Fulton (1931–), educator. In 1969, Fulton was named the first president of Warner Southern College. The school was the result of determined efforts to found a Church of God college in the South, even when those efforts were discouraged by the Commission on Christian Higher Education. Leslie Ratzlaff was appointed to direct the implementation of the new school between 1966 and the scheduled opening of classes in 1968. Fulton, the chair of the school's board of trustees and pastor of a church in Sarasota, Florida, took office the following January.

Perhaps the most controversial developments in higher education concerned Anderson College's School of Theology. In 1971 the Anderson College trustees authorized a special study committee to give attention to the School of Theology and its role in training ministers for the Church of God. The issue was more than academic, for enrollment in the seminary had declined to fewer than sixty (full-time equivalent), and net costs considerably exceeded World Service funds allocated to seminary support.

37. Annual Reports, 1969, 52.

The study committee dealt with the problem primarily by seeking means of cutting costs without markedly damaging the quality of training. Three measures were proposed. The first focused attention on new degrees that would require approximately half the credits of a regular three-year theological degree (master of divinity). This option could be considered because the Church of God had no specified educational requirement for ordination. It was believed that a shorter program would attract more students. Second, the proposal recommended that the School of Theology affiliate with the Foundation for Religious Studies in Indianapolis, a developing cluster of theological educational institutions that already included Christian Theological Seminary (Disciples of Christ) and a Roman Catholic school. Such a relationship would open opportunities for educational enrichment and enable those who desired to complete the standard theological degree. The third facet of the recommendation called for the creation of a Center for Pastoral Studies that would shift the locale of many educational opportunities from the campus to the local parish. The Center's emphasis was to be on an intern type of training and continuing education for those already in ministry. Trustees approved the proposal and it was placed on the agenda for the 1972 General Assembly.[38]

In his presentation of the proposal President Reardon reviewed the background of the study and listed the concerns that led to the suggested modifications of the seminary program. He expressed his belief that the proposed model would provide a solution to the major problems and asked support for a resolution from the board of trustees that presumed approval of the model. He also asked for the establishment of a special committee that would study the new program in its third year of operation in order to assess its effectiveness in the preparation of ministers for the Church of God. The Assembly had many questions, debated the matter at length, and rejected the resolution.[39]

Many issues were involved, but for an apparent majority of the Assembly the most significant one was affiliation with the Foundation for Religious Studies. To many this seemed like an alliance with "Babylon" and a contradiction of the movement's heritage. Accordingly, a new resolution was introduced the following day calling for a dissolution of any association with the Foundation for Religious Studies within three months or by the end of the first semester of the upcoming academic year. The debate was

38. Annual Reports, 1972, 55–52.
39. Minutes of the General Assembly, Annual Reports, 1972, 11–13.

long and intense. A ballot vote approved the resolution by a seventy-seven vote margin. That part of the seminary plan had to be abandoned.[40]

The next day still another resolution was presented by a group of younger pastors, mostly from the eastern United States. They called for the creation of a study committee composed of a representative from each of the church's six colleges, one from World Service and eight not related to any of the schools to be appointed by the Commission on Christian Higher Education. This committee would be asked to report the following year on a plan for the continuation of a Church of God seminary responsible to the General Assembly. Again debate was extensive, but the resolution was approved. Another motion charging "the Commission on Christian Higher Education to make a thorough and extensive study of theological and ministerial education in the Church of God, with a report of progress to be brought…in 1973" also passed.[41] Suddenly, and without great forethought, seminary education was under intensive scrutiny—the first time the movement as a whole had given serious and studied attention to this aspect of its program for training leaders.

Another topic of significant development during this period was Christian unity. Even though this had been a central theme during the movement's entire history it had been more of a sermon topic than a practice. During the 1950s, however, several contacts had been made with the Churches of God in North America, the group with which D. S. Warner had been associated in his early ministry. In order to respond to an invitation from their Commission on Christian Unity to engage in some fraternal dialogue, the Executive Council in 1959 had appointed a Committee on Conversations. This initiative began a series of exchanges that brought to light the fact that cooperation between the two groups was already taking place in several areas such as publications, missions, and curriculum; new avenues for working together were identified and implemented. In 1964 a resolution from the Michigan Ministerial Assembly was presented to the General Ministerial Assembly calling for the creation of a permanent Commission on Christian Unity.[42] This resolution was referred to the Executive Council, which responded by proposing in 1965 a four-year committee (not a permanent commission) on Christian unity. The motion to approve passed by a narrow margin, for many did not sanction the idea of carrying

---

40. Ibid., 19–20.
41. Ibid., 25–26.
42. Minutes of the General Ministerial Assembly, Annual Reports, 1964, 33–34.

on conversations that some feared could lead to the possibility of merger with another group.[43]

In its four-year history this committee was quite active, extending its range to conversations with several other groups. Annual reports highlighted both affinities and differences that had become apparent, and there were frequent statements to allay the fears of those who dreaded the awful specter of merger. They preferred rather to speak of mutual renewal through dialogue and cooperation.[44]

In 1969 the Committee on Christian Unity presented to the General Assembly a summary of its work. Highlights included: (1) The church groups with which the committee had met and carried on dialogue were the Churches of God in North America, the Church of the Brethren, the Brethren Church, and the Evangelical Covenant Church. (2) Committee chairperson James Massey had been invited to serve as a resource person at a retreat for the ministers of the Evangelical Covenant group, seeking to address their lack of black ministers. (3) The Churches of God of North America had been discovered to be most closely akin to the Church of God. They had utilized "our church school materials and have invited our leaders" to hold classes at their Summer Seminar in August in Findlay, Ohio. Cooperatively, ministers of both groups were found to have met in local geographical areas in ministerial retreats and district assemblies. The committee recommended that fellowship continue between "the local pastors and local congregations of the two movements."[45] The committee's work was to have ended with this report, but upon the recommendation of and as a result of a resolution from the committee, the Assembly extended the life of the committee for an additional three years with some modifications in personnel. In 1972 another three-year extension was approved with the provision that at the end of that period the matter of a possible recasting of the Committee on Christian Unity be addressed.[46]

While all these issues were under construction, the Church of God also was giving some additional attention to its structure. Back in 1958 the General Ministerial Assembly had approved a change in its constitution opening its membership to include also "laymen who are elected or appointed

43. Minutes of the General Assembly, Annual Reports, 1965, 19–21, 24–25.

44. Minutes of the General Assembly, Annual Reports, 1966–69. Each year the committee submitted an extensive report to the Assembly.

45. Minutes of the General Assembly, Annual Reports, 1969, 20.

46. Minutes of the General Assembly, Annual Reports, 1972, 17–18.

members of the Executive Council, a subordinate Board, committee, or commission of the Assembly."[47] This was immediately implemented, allowing some seventy-five to one hundred laypeople to become full voting members of the Assembly. Not until 1965, however, did awareness of the inappropriateness of the name, General Ministerial Assembly, become sufficiently evident to call for a deletion of the word *Ministerial*. In that year the change was made and the body henceforth was officially designated as "General Assembly."[48] Two years later the number of laypeople was further enlarged by providing that each state (district) or provincial assembly could select a layperson to attend the Assembly as an observer.

The democratizing process was advanced by two additional actions in 1971. One of these was a bylaws change that prohibited an employee of any general agency or the Executive Council from being nominated as a candidate for membership on the council or any division, commission, or board. This rather extreme reaction to the old problem of interlocking directorates worked a hardship on some agencies but was accepted as a valid principle. The second action was to allow the Executive Council to invite, for a five-year experimental period, state coordinators or state appointed representatives to attend Executive Council meetings with the privilege of voice but not vote.[49] As many as an additional fifty or more people could now sit with the council and influence its decisions.

This latter innovation was something of a culmination to a process that had begun in 1965 when the Assembly authorized a fifteen-member study committee to give attention to issues relating to state-national relationships. Drawing upon findings from three previous consultations on this matter in 1953, 1955, and 1961, the committee provided input for the 1970 Consultation and kept the issue in view. The 1971 proposal provided a channel to deal with problems arising in these relationships. Other adjustments in the mode of operation were made during this period and were generally regarded as improvements. In 1967 the Missionary Board of the Church of God and the Foreign Missionary Board of the National Association of the Church of God came to an agreement whereby all the work being carried out in the Caribbean area by the National Association would be administratively transferred to the Missionary Board. In effect this meant the dissolution of the separate board with the provision that the Missionary Board would

---

47. Highlights of the General Ministerial Assembly, 1958, 6.
48. Minutes of the General Assembly, Annual Reports, 1965, 23.
49. Minutes of the General Assembly, Annual Reports, 1971, 18.

R. Eugene Sterner (1912–2006), minister. From 1954 to 1961, Sterner worked as director of the *Christian Brotherhood Hour*. Widely respected as a preacher and a regular on the camp-meeting and revival circuits, he was asked to return to the radio program in 1968 as both director and speaker. In 1974, Sterner's workload was divided; he continued as speaker until 1977.

always have at least two black people as members.[50] The second adjustment was simply a recognition in 1970 of the statehood status of Hawaii, which called for transferring responsibility for the work there from the Missionary Board to the Home Missions Board.[51]

There was a considerable shuffle in national leadership in the period from 1963 to 1972. In 1965 the Assembly was asked to ratify T. Franklin Miller as president-elect of Warner Press to take office July 1, 1967, replacing Steele C. Smith who was retiring. In 1966 Donald Courtney replaced Miller as the Executive Secretary of the Board of Christian Education. In 1967 R. Eugene Sterner left the Division of Church Service and was ratified as speaker for the *Christian Brotherhood Hour*, replacing the retiring W. Dale Oldham. Roscoe Snowden was named to the Church Service post. Nineteen seventy was another year of change when W. E. Reed moved from the Board of Church Extension and Home Missions to replace retiring Charles V. Weber as executive secretary of the Executive Council. His vacated office at Church Extension was filled by Marvin J. Hartman. In the elected office category, Harold W. Boyer concluded fourteen years as chairperson of the General Assembly in 1968 when he voluntarily disallowed his name to be nominated. Arlo F. Newell was elected his successor.

This period was not devoid of special and exciting events in the movement. Three world conferences were held—the first in Bochum, Germany, in 1963; the second in Zurich, Switzerland, in 1967; and the third in Oaxtepec, Mexico, in 1971. Two of the general agencies celebrated fiftieth anniversaries—Anderson College in 1967 and the Board of Church Extension and Home Missions in 1971. The *Christian Brotherhood Hour* began a broadcast in Spanish, *Hora de Hermandad*, in 1965 and in 1971 moved

50. Minutes of the General Assembly, Annual Reports, 1967, 23.
51. Minutes of the General Assembly, Annual Reports, 1970, 34.

its offices from Los Angeles to Saltillo, Mexico. Special emphasis and fund-raising programs such as Mission: USA contributed to both financial and outreach gains. The church overseas was making good progress in all areas as the indigenizing process continued.

These years also saw the death of several more of the movement's national leaders including John A. Morrison, A. T. Rowe, Otto F. Linn, Thaddeus Neff, John S. Ludwig, Sidney Warner, E. E. Perry, N. Pearl Lewis, George Olson, H. B. Mitchell, David Meier, M. A. Monday, Ellen Olson, Wick Donohew, Minnie Riggle, and Charles E. Brown.

Reviewing all the developments of these years, it is evident that there was much to dispute the designation "age of mediocrity" for the Church of God. Even so, there was no way to ignore the statistical evidence that the movement was not growing numerically and even declining in some categories. Leaders, both local and national, were well aware of this situation and were deeply concerned. Executive Council Secretary Charles Weber called attention to the problem in his 1965 Report to the General Ministerial Assembly:

> During the past year there has been considerable concern expressed about our growth pattern. R. Eugene Sterner, Director of the Division of Church Service, has carefully analyzed this and it appears from his findings there is still a growing edge in our work. In the statistics this does not show because of adjustments in reporting and other factors. In spite of this explanation we must face the unpleasant fact that our growth has slowed radically in the past five years, and we should be deeply concerned about it....On February 11 this year approximately 70 persons…spent one day studying this situation…There were deep convictions that a strong evangelistic thrust must be initiated by our local congregations across the nation.… There is a need for stronger goals in the Church of God, and I think there is a need for a united advance program that will challenge and mobilize all our general agencies, all our local congregations, and even our missionary staff people and will help the church to fulfill its mission and realize its goals during the remainder of this century. It appears to me that this would be a good time to begin making plans. In just 15 years we will be celebrating our 100th year as a movement. Surely we should accelerate our speed and work to certain climactic goals at that time.[52]

---

52. Annual Reports, 1965, 10.

Out of this concern various agencies of the church developed national programs designed to stimulate growth. Warner Press sponsored massive literature distribution projects in both 1965 and 1966, which made large quantities of books and pamphlets available to congregations at low cost in order to stimulate outreach and growth at the local level. The Board of Church Extension and Home Missions developed an evangelistic program and asked the General Assembly to designate 1966 as the year for "Emphasis—Evangelism." Under the theme "God calls the church to care…to serve…to witness," congregations were urged to step up their efforts to reach new people. Approximately eight hundred congregations participated.

Programming to stimulate growth was extended by the Board of Christian Education when 1969–70 was designated as the Year of the Sunday School. Since declining numbers were most evident in the area of ministry, the Board enlisted congregations to set attendance goals and assisted them in achieving their objectives. The emphasis was on enlistment of new people, pupil participation, leadership enlistment and development, and effective administration and utilization of resources. Modest gains were reported.

Perhaps the most productive efforts toward progress were two attempts at general assessment and goal setting. The first of these was introduced in 1965 when a resolution calling for a long-range study of all aspects of the work of the Church of God was introduced in the General Assembly and referred to the Executive Council for action. As a result the council and all the general agencies were asked to project ten-year plans and goals. These were reported to the 1966 Assembly. No procedures were established for monitoring progress, but the process forced the establishing of long-range objectives and fostered improvement at many points.

The second event of consequence along this line was the 1970 Consultation.[53] Convening in Anderson, February 17-20, this meeting brought together almost two hundred people from the United States and Canada, all of whom were in positions of leadership in the Church of God movement. Unlike the 1963 All Board Congress, the participants in this consultation were mostly from among the leaders in the various states with a smaller number of people from the national agencies. The stated purpose of this consultation was "to find clear direction for the Church in the '70s." To accomplish this task a three-fold procedure was projected:

---

53. Data derived from the loose-leaf workbook of the 1970 Consultation of the Church of God.

1. We will seek to listen to Christ, the head of the church, to understand the unchanging mandate given to his disciples in this century, and reaffirm this mission. This calls for an honest study of scripture and sincere prayer for understanding.
2. We will seek to dig through the chaotic maze of needs now existing in our world to determine the ones where the church uniquely and primarily makes its contribution, and, by careful evaluation, attempt to find the priorities, goals, and objectives to which we will give ourselves.
3. We will search for the best methods to make our witness and work relevant and practical in achieving our goals.[54]

Preparation for the consultation was extensive with study papers and resource materials circulated ahead of time that were designed to stimulate thought, raise questions, and encourage discussion. This process began more than a year before the meeting, so there was ample opportunity for the participants to have given serious attention to the issues under consideration and to have formulated viewpoints to be shared and tested when the group assembled. In the consultation itself there were occasions for corporate worship and Bible study, papers read, and plenary sessions for whole group discussion. The major portion of the time, however, was spent in small groups of no more than twelve individuals who gave attention to one of six areas of concern. These were social concerns, unity, lay ministry, evangelism, missions, and leadership. In all of these, considerable attention was given to the role and work of the Holy Spirit in that particular aspect of the church's function and work. In many ways the work of this consultation provided the chief agenda items for the Church of God in the rest of the decade of the seventies—the crucial decade when the movement was approaching the first-century mark in its history.

---

54. Ibid.

CHAPTER 17

TARGET: CENTENNIAL
(1972–1980)

From the dawn of the 1970s there appears to have been a subtle awareness on the part of most people associated with the Church of God that the movement was approaching a historic milestone. Somehow the thought of rounding out a hundred years seemed to evoke reflection about the past and excitement about the future. These two tones intermingled in both delicate and sonorous ways to sound the notes that were to make up the symphony of the seventies. The centennial was thought of as something more than an anniversary—it was to be an event, a happening, a celebration, a target.

On the reflective side one leader looked back over the decade of the sixties just past and observed, "We do not seem to have such dominant figures now. We no longer have a 'daddy.' We just have a heavenly Father and we must learn better to act like brethren, to plan together and to achieve a more functional workable unity."[1]

Speaking in the context of the 1970 Consultation, R. Eugene Sterner also turned his rhetoric toward that present time and forthrightly declared:

> To update our thinking is imperative. The familiar and traditional can be deadening. We are always in danger of tramping around tooting our horns at the walls of a Jericho long since evacuated. What would God have us to be doing now? Can we sense his will for the 1970s? Are we sensitive enough? Are we dedicated enough? Do we care enough?[2]

Sterner's reflections typify the frame of mind prevalent in the movement during the last decade before its centennial. Recollection, evaluation, and celebration characterized this period in the history of the Church of God as

---

1. R. Eugene Sterner, "The Movement in 1970." Paper prepared for 1970 Consultation, 2.
2. Ibid.

confrontation with its own past, present, and future combined to stimulate development and change.

In 1966 the Division of General Service appointed a seven-person Special Committee on Centennial Proposal. This committee, which was instructed to offer recommendations and ideas but not to prepare formal plans, met twice and reported back to the division that they favored a "proper observance" of the approaching one hundredth birthday of the movement. Several suggestions were offered. The Division of General Service in turn recommended to the Executive Council in February 1967 that approval be given to the idea of a centennial celebration in 1980 and that the division be instructed to proceed in making plans. The council approved the recommendation.[3]

Informal discussion about plans for the centennial continued, but no formal implementation occurred until February 1972, when the board of directors of the Executive Council named five people to serve on a centennial committee: Adam W. Miller, John W. V. Smith, T. Franklin Miller, Harold L. Phillips, and W. E. Reed. Their first assignment was to do the necessary research and determine a proper date for the celebration. Other instructions included developing a "time line…and any other thoughts or suggestions in an over-all planning for such an event."[4] From that time specific planning was under way.

The 1966 committee had made one suggestion, however, which was to bear fruit and be carried out with success. Their minutes reported the following: "There was consensus that there should be some kind of general planning conference set up in 1969 or 1970.…It should provide an opportunity for us to look at the needs of the church and try to raise up some of the over-all objectives toward which we should be working in the decade ahead."[5] This notion materialized in the 1970 Consultation. The events of the balance of the seventies were strongly influenced by the assessments, projections, and intentional efforts generated in that consultation. It is well to review some of these and to note how they were translated into action.

It was not happenstance that the first in the list of areas to be explored by the work groups was social concerns. The ongoing intensity of issues raised during the 1960s is indicated by an unplanned development in this 1970 meeting. About midway through the consultation black participants

---

3. Minutes of the Executive Council, February 21, 1967.
4. Minutes of the Board of Directors of Executive Council, February 1, 1972.
5. Minutes of the Special Committee on Centennial, June 2, 1966.

held a caucus "requesting that the remaining sessions of the consultation raise those questions, and only those questions, that deal with the implications of race for: social concerns, unity, lay ministry, evangelism, mission and leadership."[6] Consultation delegates responded positively to this request and they agreed to give attention to racial questions in all the small groups but not to ignore other important aspects of each of the designated areas. This compromise proved satisfactory, and the consultation continued without incident.

In preparation for the meeting certain key leaders had been asked to prepare papers in which they projected future developments in the assigned areas. Writing the paper on social concerns, Hollis S. Pistole proved to be quite accurate in predicting future events and attitudes regarding race relations in the Church of God. He noted:

> The lure of "black power" will continue to attract a dynamic following among Negro youth: for it is both a search for identity and a way of life.
>
> Thus, while state assemblies, even in the south, will move toward full integration for functional purposes, black ministers will also maintain some form of separation for political purposes. Consequently, the West Middlesex meeting and the National Association will continue to serve for some time as a means of expression for black identity.
>
> We can expect to see continuing gains in many areas of cooperative action between the races.[7]

The record indicates that gains actually were made, for the Church of God made a concentrated effort in the 1970s to improve race relations by merging black and white state assemblies and by placing blacks in key positions of leadership. In June 1970, for instance, the Executive Council of the Church of God elected its first black chairperson, Marcus H. Morgan, pastor of Englewood Church of God in Chicago. Division of Church Service director Roscoe Snowden, in his report on race relations to the General Assembly in 1971, stated that observable progress had been too slow but also pointed out encouraging developments. Black and white assemblies in Northern Illinois had merged. North Carolina had developed a new credentials committee process fairer to blacks. Alabama

---

6. Harold L. Phillips, "Consultation of the Church of God," March 22, 1970, 22.
7. Hollis Pistole, "Social Concerns—A Projection for the '70s" (unpublished), 4–5.

had made considerable progress in race relations. Black and white youth were integrated in youth conventions and rallies in Georgia and Texas, and Arkansas had made a concentrated effort to overcome segregation of blacks and whites.[8]

Following up on the 1970 General Assembly's directive that the Division of World Service employ a black associate director, "one who can understand the needs of the Black community as well as…the urban crisis that faces the total church,"[9] in 1972 the division added Wilfred Jordan to the staff. As director of Interracial Affairs for Church of God World Service, his primary duties were to "build bridges of understanding across any existing racial boundaries so that our World Service agencies may be properly presented to local churches…and so special concerns of black churches may be brought to the attention of our national leaders"[10] Jordan almost immediately established a Schools of Stewardship program designed to meet the educational needs of black congregations. A year before Jordan's appointment Thomas J. Sawyer of Pittsburgh, Pennsylvania, had been added to the Anderson College faculty with special assignment as advisor to black students. Five years later he moved to an executive staff position with the Missionary Board. In 1972, Cauthion T. Boyd, Jr. was selected as president of the Missionary Board, the first black person to preside over a general agency of the Church of God.

In February 1974, the Executive Council authorized the establishment of the new office of associate executive secretary of the Executive Council, with the understanding that it would be filled initially by an African American. In June, the General Assembly approved this action and began a search. By the following June (1975) Edward L. Foggs had been selected. He was ratified and installed in this newly created office, the first black person to hold an administrative post of this stature in the Church of God. The same year Alvin Lewis, also an African American, was named associate secretary of the Board of Christian Education.[11] Additionally, as a gesture of goodwill and brotherhood, each of the general agencies agreed to contribute a proportionate share of $15,000 as a donation to the National Association of the Church of God for the purpose of assisting in the construction of a new tabernacle on the campgrounds at West Middlesex, Pennsylvania.

---

8. Roscoe Snowden, "Division of Church Service," in Annual Reports, 1971, 37.

9. Minutes of the General Assembly, June 18, 1970.

10. Paul A. Tanner, "Division of World Service," Annual Reports, 1972, 38.

11. Minutes of the General Assembly, June 18, 1975, in Annual Reports, 1975, 18.

Black leaders regarded these actions as highly significant in the promotion of good race relations.

Another milestone in opening top leadership posts to black people came in 1976 when James Earl Massey, pastor of Metropolitan Church in Detroit and campus minister at Anderson College, was ratified by the General Assembly as the speaker for the church's international radio program, the *Christian Brotherhood Hour*. There was considerable debate on Massey's approval, but the questions were related to doctrinal matters rather than race. After these were resolved, he was ratified, and a black person became the media voice for the Church of God. The same year Richard Goode was added to the staff of the Board of Church Extension and Home Missions.[12]

The issue of training black young people for leadership in the Church of God came to the fore in 1975 when the Southern Association of the Church of God requested that Bay Ridge Christian College be accorded national agency status with the attendant privilege of participating in the World Service bud-

James Earl Massey (1930–), preacher and educator. During the 1970s, several influential African-American leaders were called to positions in the national work of the Church of God. With a national reputation in American Protestantism, Massey was the most distinguished of these. From 1977 to 1982, he served as speaker for the *Christian Brotherhood Hour*. He also served as principal of Jamaica School of Theology, campus minister and a faculty member at Anderson College and the School of Theology, as well as dean of the seminary.

get.[13] The request was referred to the Commission on Christian Higher Education with instructions to give attention to the whole issue of black ministerial education. The commission enlisted the aid of eight black consultants, visited the Kendleton, Texas, campus and interviewed a number of southern black pastors. Two years later, in 1977, their report was presented to the General Assembly, the Commission recommended that Bay Ridge not be elevated to general agency status but that the 1977–1978 World

---

12. Minutes of the General Assembly, June 15, 1976, Annual Reports, 1976, 10–13.
13. Minutes of the General Assembly, June 17, 1975, Annual Reports, 1975, 16–17.

Service budget included a special project called the Fund for Black Ministerial Education. The first-year goal for this fund was $55,000 to be divided on a designated percentage basis among three areas of need: (1) Bay Ridge Christian College, (2) scholarships for eligible black ministerial students to attend Church of God colleges, and (3) the development of an in-service training program for black leaders through the Center for Pastoral Studies. This proposal was approved by the Assembly.[14]

The Fund for Black Ministerial Education became a continuing item in the special projects budget for the remainder of the decade. Even though amounts were increased, recipients—especially Bay Ridge—were not completely satisfied with the arrangement since the label of special project meant that only funds so designated by the donor were credited to the fund. The full amount established as a goal was not received in any year of the fund's existence, but the need was being recognized and channels for meeting it had been established. In this and in other areas black leaders continued to be vigilant. They developed an annual caucus in which progress—or regression—was reviewed and concerns were carried to the national executives, the Executive Council, or the General Assembly. Lines of communication were established and used. By the decade's end, rather than react to crisis, there was an obvious attempt to anticipate and plan regarding race relations in the Church of God.

Other social issues claimed the attention of the Church of God in the 1970s. The Vietnam War had forced renewed attention on world peace. The 1966 "Statement of Conviction on War and Peace" appeared in the *Yearbook* until 1973 when the military draft system was discontinued. While this statement affirmed the church's support of those of its members who were conscientious objectors to war, it also pledged support to members of the armed forces. A special "peace" issue of *Vital Christianity* in 1979 reaffirmed this right of conscience position by including articles from both pacifists and those in the military.[15] Throughout the 1970s the small but very active Church of God Peace Fellowship continued to keep the pacifist viewpoint before the church through publications and a series of conferences during the annual International Convention.

The 1970 Consultation had taken place in the context of an American society where protest marches, rallies, and demonstrations were common,

---

14. Minutes of the General Assembly, June 14, 1977, in Annual Reports, 1977, 12–13. Text of report and resolution, 50–53.

15. *Vital Christianity*, November 4, 1979.

especially concerning issues such as Vietnam, race, and human rights. At that time Hollis Pistole had stated, "The right to disagree and to engage in nonviolent protest should be supported by the church."[16] This view was generally held throughout the whole movement, and there were many from the Church of God who participated in demonstrations of this kind. Perhaps one of the most publicized examples of nonviolent protest by Church of God people took place in the mid-seventies in Anderson, Indiana. The city had proposed the building of a bridge across the White River at Third Street and the subsequent opening of a major thoroughfare down the middle of the Anderson College campus. College and church officials thought the project would cause considerable problems and dangers for Anderson College students and for the thousands of people attending the annual International Convention of the Church of God. It would also seriously mar much of the beauty of the Anderson College campus.

In protest of this proposal approximately one thousand Anderson College students led by W. E. Reed, executive secretary of the Executive Council of the Church of God, and Anderson College President Robert H. Reardon marched from the campus to the city building in downtown Anderson. Students carried signs and protested in a very peaceful and respectable manner. At the city building the crowd sang such songs as "Battle Hymn of the Republic" and "I Shall Not Be Moved." A press conference was held and the episode was reported on national television. Despite the protest the bridge was built and the thoroughfare opened but with a considerable number of concessions to the concerns expressed by the protesting students and church officials. For example,

William E. Reed (1915–85), agency executive. From the 1960s until the reorganization of the national offices in the 1990s, a pattern of promotion through the ranks shaped senior appointments to executive positions. Thus in 1971, W. E. Reed moved from his position as the president of the Board of Church Extension and Home Missions to succeed Charles V. Weber as the third executive secretary of the Executive Council. Reed retired from this position in 1980.

---

16. Pistole, "Social Concerns," 5. Paper presented at 1970 Consultation.

the state highway was re-routed rather than, as originally proposed, carried by the bridge through the campus.

Other social concerns mentioned by Pistole in 1970 proved to be major issues in churches generally as well as in the Church of God during the decade. He spoke to the issues of drug addiction and alcohol: "Of graver concern to the Church of God is the increasing acceptance in society of social drinking and the use of psychedelic drugs as a matter of personal choice. This places committed Christian young people in a perplexing situation."[17] By the end of the seventies many pastors were recognizing the magnitude of this problem in their congregations. Another concern addressed by Pistole was the issue of family solidarity. He stated, "The matter of sexual morality, premarital and marriage guidance, and family life must be a constant function of the church. The strength of a society is often drawn from an index based upon the integrity of its families."[18] In contrast, however, to the position on divorce so rigidly taught by the majority of the early Church of God pioneers, he declared, "The Church of God must take a closer look at its stringent attitude toward divorce….It must realistically face the fact that divorce is often preferable to an enforced state of marital discord."[19]

The Church of God gave considerable attention to the enhancement of family life and dealing with marriage problems during the seventies. The Board of Christian Education added a staff person, Alvin Lewis, who was a specialist in this field. The colleges offered a wide variety of courses in marriage and family relations. Marriage enrichment seminars in local churches and area meetings increased in popularity. Many conferences on related topics were conducted at the International Convention and at state and regional camp meetings and youth conventions. Problem issues such as abortion and homosexuality were discussed at length with a resolution relating to the latter being passed by the General Assembly.[20] Women's rights and the Equal Rights Amendment to the nation's constitution were widely discussed in relation to effects on family life.

This period also saw a heightened awareness on the part of the Church of God to special needs around the world. Disaster relief was quickly mobilized for victims of the Guatemala earthquake in 1976 and the civil war

---

17. Ibid., 8.
18. Ibid., 5–6.
19. Ibid.
20. Minutes of the General Assembly, June 20, 1979. In Annual Reports, 1979, 17. A resolution regarding the woman's role in the church was also passed in 1974. In the same year the Commission on Social Concerns adopted a "Statement of Concern" on abortion.

in Lebanon over several years. A Disaster Fund Committee was created to administer the distribution of this relief. World hunger funds were included in the general World Service budget throughout the decade with the amount being raised to one hundred thousand dollars in 1975. Cooperative arrangements for distribution of these funds were worked out with World Vision and other international agencies. Resettlement of refugees was encouraged by resolutions from the General Assembly in 1973, and in 1979 a design committee developed a model for Church of God participation in the worldwide program. The part-time services of Gwendolyn Massey were secured to coordinate and promote relocation sponsorship in congregations of the Church of God.[21]

One other development in social concerns is worthy of note. Changing times had seen the abandonment of old people's homes, orphanages, and other benevolent institutions by the Church of God. In 1974, however, Hope Hill Children's Home in Hope, Kentucky, an orphanage that had been started by Church of God people and supported by numerous interested congregations, was deeded to the Board of Church Extension and Home Missions.[22] Thereafter the Board assumed administrative and financial responsibility for the continuation of the orphanage at the high level it had already achieved. It was anticipated, and subsequent experience verified, that donors would continue their support under the new arrangement, which returned the national church to institutional benevolent service.

Leadership was another area given great attention in the 1970 Consultation and was the focus of significant developments in the next ten years. Gene W. Newberry, dean of the School of Theology, wrote a paper projecting developments during the coming decade. Among other things, he predicted, "Our theology of leadership will improve....Ministerial credentials will be clarified and heightened. More uniform practices of preparation for ordination, licensing and ordination proper, will develop."[23] The projection proved to be on target; within two years procedures were under way to regularize and strengthen variant standards in different parts of the country.

Concern in this area was being expressed by many state credentials committees who believed that some standards for ordination and guidelines

---

21. "Massey Administers Refugee Program," *Vital Christianity*, November 4, 1979, 19.

22. Minutes of the General Assembly, June 19, 1974. In Annual Reports, 1974, 17–18.

23. Gene W. Newberry, "Projections for the 70's—Leadership," in unpublished 1970 Consultation Workbook, pages 4–5 of paper.

for recognition and registration of ministers be adopted nationwide. The Division of Church Service was asked to sponsor a Consultation on Ministry following the Executive Council meetings in February 1974. To prepare for such a consultation a design committee of twenty people, representing state coordinators, state credentials committees, women, youth, pastors, and the School of Theology, was assembled. Surveys, work papers, a film presentation, and available statistical data on ministers of the Church of God were prepared. State leaders, people associated with the training of ministers, observers to the Executive Council, and members of the council were invited to share in this consultation involving approximately 125 participants.

Study papers furnished the consultation with carefully collated data, mind-stretching exploration into the future of ministry, and tender moments of reflection and gratitude for the call to ministry. The consultation underscored the mounting concern for standardized nationwide procedures for licensing and ordination, continuing education for the minister, the need for enlistment and encouragement of more women in the ministry, and knowledge of available support systems for ministers who find themselves or their families in stress situations. One year after the consultation a Workshop on Ministry convened for two days following the Executive Council meetings in February 1975. The goal of this workshop was to develop uniform procedures of ordination that, it was hoped, would be acceptable to all the state organizations. Four areas were given serious attention: (1) guidelines on recognition, licensing, and ordination; (2) training and ministerial education in preparation for ordination and the maintaining of credentials; (3) range of authority of credentials committees; and (4) guidelines for certification of ministers and churches.[24]

A critical issue, given the movement's early antipathy to theological education, was the question of minimum educational requirements for ordination. In the light of the historic position of the Church of God there was no disposition to set such a standard. Instead, alternative "tracks" toward ordination were suggested, the preferable one being the completion of the full seminary program of three years of graduate study. At least three other approaches to qualifying for ordination were offered, thus leaving the way open for those who felt called to ministry to be recognized regardless of their education, age, or family status.

24. Adapted from "Guidelines for Recognition and Ordination of Ministers." Unpublished paper in the Anderson University and Church of God Archives.

The major aspect of the leadership issue during the 1970s, however, focused on ministerial training and the role of the seminary. The actions of the 1972 General Assembly had thwarted certain features of a proposed revamping of graduate training for ministry but had set in motion a series of other actions that were to have a telling effect on the future of theological education in the Church of God. The first of these was the naming of a fifteen-member one-year study committee charged with the responsibility of bringing to the 1973 General Assembly "plans for the continuation of a Church of God Seminary responsible to the General Assembly rather than to any existing educational institution."[25] The second action was a resolution charging the Commission on Christian Higher Education "to make a thorough and extensive study of theological and ministerial training in the Church of God."[26] A progress report was to be brought to the Assembly the following year.

In 1973 the study committee made an extensive report. After a thorough investigation it was their judgment that a free-standing seminary unrelated to any existing educational institution was neither functionally desirable nor economically feasible. In that light, they offered a series of recommendations that included the following: (1) movement toward increased World Service support for the School of Theology with a separation of askings for the undergraduate and graduate programs of Anderson College; (2) promotion of scholarship funds for students; (3) establishment of a "blue ribbon" advisory committee composed of pastors who would give particular attention to the School of Theology; and (4) making the dean of the School of Theology one of the offices requiring ratification by the General Assembly. After lengthy debate the report, including the recommendations, was adopted.[27]

The Commission on Christian Higher Education made a progress report on its assignment in 1973, 1974, and 1975. Their final report on a study of theological education and ministerial training in the Church of God came in 1976 with the presentation of a nineteen-page document to the Assembly. After reviewing the picture of what was happening in these areas in all of the church's schools, the report concluded with a series of twelve proposals. These were of a general nature—encouraging support of all programs under way, urging the upgrading of the equality of education, giving attention to the actual needs of the Church of God, developing vari-

---

25. Minutes of the General Assembly, June 22, 1972, 22–23.
26. Ibid., 26.
27. Minutes of the General Assembly, June 19, 1973, 10–11. Text of the report, 75–87.

ous styles of continuing education, and identifying the particular needs of students from ethnic and minority groups. The report had been circulated ahead of the time of the Assembly; it was not read in its entirety but adopted without debate.[28]

As a result of all this intensive study and national attention a consensus emerged that the movement had been remiss in fulfilling its obligation to those preparing for leadership in the church, and steps were taken to remedy the situation. The 1974 General Assembly approved a resolution instructing the Division of World Service to raise $50,000 to aid Anderson School of Theology students with their tuition costs.[29] This amount was raised to $80,000 in 1975 and was increased again in 1976–77 to $100,000. Enrollment jumped from 68 in 1974 to 123 in 1975 and reached 188 by the 1977–78 school year. The School of Theology also witnessed the completion of the Adam W. Miller Chapel and a major library addition in 1975. Another significant event was the appointment of a new dean to the seminary. Barry L. Callen was installed in this position in a session of the General Assembly on June 19, 1974. He succeeded Gene W. Newberry, who had resigned while completing a sabbatical leave in Kenya, East Africa. Newberry was named the school's first "Distinguished Professor" and devoted his time to teaching and writing.

Another of the church's educational institutions experienced a leadership crisis near the end of the decade. Warner Pacific College, which under the leadership of President E. Joe Gilliam had recovered remarkably from its 1966 emergency, was again thrust into a leadership and financial crisis that precipitated the resignation of the president in January 1979. The college's trustees acted quickly and named former president and dean Milo Chapman as the acting head of the institution. While searching for a new president they requested and received a special dispensation from the Executive Council to solicit funds directly from congregations in the Western states for a period of three years. Trustees also instituted other plans to achieve financial security for the school and preserve its academic excellence. Efforts to find a new president were not immediately successful, and Chapman's status was changed from acting president to president, and the church's college in the Pacific Northwest was again on its road to recovery.[30] Widely respected up and down the West Coast, Chapman had previously

---

28. Minutes of the General Assembly, June 16, 1976, 14.
29. Minutes of the General Assembly, June 19, 1974, 14.
30. Minutes of the General Assembly, June 20, 1979, 19.

served as Warner Pacific's president and dean. His return to the presidency lent his good name to the school and provided a measure of stability.

The 1970 Consultation also gave considerable attention to the task of evangelism in the decade ahead. Isham E. (Joe) Crane, staff member of the Board of Church Extension and Home Missions, confronted the delegates with a projection of factors that would affect congregational evangelistic efforts in the United States. Among these were the increased urbanization of the American population, the higher educational attainment of American citizens, the younger median age level of church members, and a general concern with socioeconomic conditions. He suggested several ways to meet the challenge for greater evangelization. One was "through the gift of administrative evangelism."[31] He stressed consideration of many variables affecting church growth such as church building space, church school class organization, teacher-pupil ratio, and pastoral leadership. Appropriate adjustments to these factors made through administrative decisions would facilitate church growth. Another suggestion for more effective evangelism was cooperative planning and goal setting. Lastly, he suggested "new ministries designed to meet the basic issues of our day."[32]

E. Joe Gilliam (1929–), pastor and educator. Gilliam, a pastor from Indianapolis, Indiana, and Warner Pacific College trustee, was chosen as president of WPC following the departure of Louis Gough. Gilliam's tenure was marked by a successful broadening of academic programs, expansion of the campus, and intensive fundraising, all of which did much to reestablish confidence in the school, but the college continued to struggle financially, leading to his resignation in 1979.

Consultation delegates saw the need for projecting a strong thrust in personal witness evangelism with new materials and seminars to instruct and motivate both ministers and laypeople in this kind of outreach. Bible study and exploration of the theological foundations for evangelism were

31. Joe Crane, "Projections for the 70's: Evangelism in the Local Church," 1970 Consultation Workbook (unpublished), page 5 of paper.

32. Ibid., 6–7.

also recommended. Reexamination of the local church's mission to its community, whether ghetto or affluent suburb, was likewise stressed. These expressed concerns began to facilitate decisive action almost immediately and throughout the decade. Hardly had the consultation concluded when the "Asbury-Anderson Revival" emerged as "a new wind blowing"[33] in an unusual wave of evangelistic witness and response. Beginning in early February on the campus of Asbury College in Wilmore, Kentucky, the revival came to Anderson later in the month when seven Asbury students spoke in a meeting of the South Meridian Church of God, where Asbury alumnus Charles Tarr severed as pastor. This event began eight weeks of intense and spontaneous revival activity—meetings at all hours of the day and night and in many places, some of them attracting crowds of twenty-five hundred or more. Witness teams began forming to share the fervor abroad. Altogether 313 of these teams traveled to over thirty states and to Canada. The Anderson College campus was caught up in the momentum to such an extent that President Reardon reported:

> By all standards of measurement, the so-called "Asbury revival" was the most outstanding event of the year. For weeks the South Meridian Street Church of God was where the action was. At least a thousand students were caught up on this spontaneous outpouring of religious fervor. I know of no one who was hurt by it and hundreds who were helped.... Much better to have a campus shaken by a revival than a riot.[34]

The year 1970 also saw the beginning of a three-year broadly based program of evangelism and service dubbed "Mission: USA." (The initials were intended to mean United Social Action, but were commonly interpreted as being a mission to the nation.) A goal of $200,000 extra giving was set with the money designated to involve the whole church in urban ministries and provide educational opportunities for underprivileged youth. Training opportunities were offered for pastors and for laity employed by the churches. As of 1973, Mission USA money had gone to congregations in Chicago; Columbia, Maryland; Decatur, Illinois; Denver, Colorado; Detroit, Michigan; Houston, Texas; Miami, Florida; and Toledo, Ohio. In addition, metropolitan workshops were held in

---

33. This phrase became the title of a book by Charles R. Tarr (pastor of the South Meridian Church where the revival centered), *A New Wind Blowing* (Anderson, IN: Warner Press, 1972).

34. Annual Reports, 1970, 100.

Houston, Texas; Anderson, Indiana; Seattle, Washington; Milwaukee, Wisconsin; and Oakland, California.[35]

Early in the decade the Board of Church Extension and Home Missions employed Charles Tarr as secretary of evangelism. He developed a manual, conducted institutes, and promoted evangelism in area meetings and local congregations. Perhaps the greatest evangelistic thrust of the 1970s, however, was through "Key 73," a united interdenominational effort to present the gospel to every home in North America. It involved over 130 different Christian groups. Its general objectives were these:

(1) To forcefully and fully share with every person in North America the message and claims of the Gospel of Christ.
(2) To employ every means and method of communicating the gospel in order to create the conditions in which man more readily responds to God.
(3) To apply the message and meaning of Jesus Christ to the issues shaping man in his society in order that they may be resolved.
(4) To develop new resources for effective evangelism, for consideration, adoption or rejection by the participating churches or Christian groups.
(5) To assist in the efforts of Christian congregations and organizations to become more effective redemptive centers and more aggressive witnesses to God's redeeming power in the world.[36]

Although the Church of God historically was reluctant to join in ecumenical ventures, the 1970 General Assembly overwhelmingly agreed to participate in Key 73. The plan was simple: 1971 was the year of "presentation," 1972 was the year of "preparation," and 1973 was the year of "penetration."[37] Key 73 generated considerable interest in the Church of God. Plans were discussed in 1972 at the regional Central States Ministers' Meeting in St. Joseph, Michigan, at the 1972 Consultation on Evangelism and Doctrine for the state of Michigan and, later that same year, at the West Coast Ministerial Assembly in Portland, Oregon. Plans for the Church of God's participation had been coordinated through the Division of General Service. Tom A. Smith and Charles Tarr, both of the Department of

---

35. Annual Reports, 1973, 68.
36. Harold L. Phillips, "Report: What's Key 73?" *Vital Christianity*, November 28, 1971, 23.
37. Ibid.

Evangelism and Missions of the Board of Church Extension and Home Missions, did the actual work of publicizing the effort, making available resource materials, and representing the Church of God in cooperative planning. Many other people participated in the making and execution of plans.[38] Although the results of Key 73 could never be tabulated there can be little doubt that it was very effective in spreading the gospel of Jesus Christ and in encouraging Christian cooperation. In the words of Harold Phillips, "Key 73 is a historic venture because it [marked] the first time representatives of a number of leading North American Communions [had] agreed to work together in a major evangelistic effort."[39]

In the latter half of the decade general church programming for evangelism and outreach developed under the popular caption, "Church Growth." The Division of General Service took initial steps in 1975 to involve the Church of God in a church growth emphasis. Its first major undertaking was a church growth workshop conducted in February 1976. More than ninety people participated. In keeping with the interest voiced in the workshop, the Division of General Service recommended to the General Assembly in June 1976 the naming of the Church Growth Strategy and Planning Committee and the launching of an intensive two-year church growth program. A twenty-six-member committee was approved by the General Assembly and the following timeline was established:

1977–78   Year of Preparation and Enlistment
1978–80   Years of Implementation
          (the actual two-year emphasis period)
1980–81   Year of Evaluation and Projection

A central concern of the committee was to have a clear sense of purpose and direction so the church growth program it eventually developed would not be a mere echo of mounting church growth interest in the evangelical world. In keeping with this the committee felt the need to state a biblically and theologically sound definition of church growth:

Church growth is the increase in the number of persons who respond in faith and obedience to the leadership of the Holy Spirit and the authority of the Word of God, whose lives increasingly acknowledge

---

38. W. E. Reed, "Report of the Executive Secretary," Annual Reports, 1973, 29.
39. Phillips, "What's Key 73?"

the Lordship of Christ, and who commit themselves to the fellowship and mission of the Church.

Because of its awareness that church growth must represent a well-rounded, multidimensional emphasis, the committee identified six strategic areas as basic to the goals congregations need to establish. The six sought church growth through (1) numerical increase—a 10 percent projected gain, (2) personal and family spiritual enrichment through small groups, retreats, and so forth, (3) leadership enlistment and training—a 50 percent increase in leadership personnel, (4) community involvement through service programs and public relations, (5) new church development—finding areas where new churches are needed, and (6) mission outreach or local involvement in worldwide ministries.[40] These areas were further described in a brochure, "With Faith…We Grow!" which emphasized the spiritual nature of this endeavor and wigged a solid undergirding of all efforts with prayer, Bible study, and other spiritual disciplines.

The program was launched in June 1978 with its first workshop scheduled for the beginning of the International Convention. A comprehensive workbook was introduced. Other workshops were held later in the year in Seattle and Atlanta. Under the leadership of Edward L. Foggs there was an attempt to get the program operational in every congregation of the Church of God.

While all these efforts in evangelistic outreach were in progress some major developments also were proceeding in the area of home and foreign missions. In the early 1970s there were many instances of former mission projects' becoming indigenous and self-supporting. For example, a Caribbean ministers' meeting at Antigua voted to establish a Church of God Assembly encompassing the West Indies. Further plans were developed at a later meeting on Grenada Island. Second, missionary Thomas Pickens, Jr. and his family returned to America from pastoral duties in London. Composed largely of West Indians, the congregation took the name Tottenham Court Church of God. They became self-supporting and called their own minister. Third, the Home Missions Board no longer furnished personnel for the Crow Agency project in Montana. This congregation likewise became responsible for securing its own leadership.[41]

---

40. Essential data on the church growth program secured from the Report of the Church Growth Strategy and Planning Committee to the General Assembly, June 20, 1978 (*Annual Reports*, 1978, 24–26) and from the workbook *With Faith…We Grow!*

41. Annual Reports, 1972, 45.

The overseas programs of the Church of God continued to develop in all areas where work had been established, but the major thrust of the 1970s was deliberately directed toward advance in Latin America. Plans for this special effort were carefully laid. In early 1969 a committee composed of Lester A. Crose and Donald D. Johnson from the Missionary Board and David L. Lawson from the World Service staff toured and surveyed Central and South American countries for six weeks. They talked with many leaders in both religion and government, established contacts, and began to lay plans. Undergirding those plans was a proposal to the 1969 General Assembly that a special fund-raising project labeled "Mission Latin America" be approved with a goal of an extra $150,000 to be gathered over a period of two years. The Assembly accepted the challenge. The funding phase of the program thrust was more than successful. By 1971 a total of $214,725 had been subscribed, and thus signaled implementation of all plans. The program was shaped by seven goals:

1. Identify the extant work of the Church of God in Latin America.
2. Provide limited term capital fund assistance.
3. Assist in the planting of churches in strategic centers.
4. Aid in literature and leadership development.
5. Provide specialized missionary personnel, but emphasize a low profile approach.
6. Significant operational budget involvement to support the advance.
7. Cooperation with specialist mission groups to avoid overlap and costly duplication.[42]

By 1974 active programs were under way toward the accomplishment of all of these goals, and by the end of the decade the list of accomplishments was impressive. In 1970 the Church of God was functioning in six Latin American countries; by 1980 that number had almost tripled. Native leadership was being trained in four active Bible schools, one each in Mexico, Peru, Brazil, and Argentina. The *Christian Brotherhood Hour* was being broadcast by radio to the hemisphere in Spanish and Portuguese. By planting churches at strategic places in Amazonia, the Church of God had moved in on the ground floor of the vast development project for

---

42. Annual Reports, 1971, 66–67.

the interior jungle area of Brazil made possible by the construction of the new trans-Amazon highway. The leadership of Latin American churches had been drawn together and motivated by four Inter-American Conferences held at different locations during the decade. A Christian Center had been established in San José, Costa Rica, the first in Latin America for the Church of God. In addition to work in rural areas an emphasis on important population centers led to definite strategies for enlarging the witness of the Church of God in Mexico City, Guatemala City, Panama City, Lima, São Paulo, and Buenos Aires. Maurice Caldwell, Missionary Board associate secretary for Latin America, and his wife Dondeena were heavily involved throughout this decade of advance, both as missionaries and Maurice as an administrator for the later phases of the program.[43]

The success of the Latin American venture prompted the launching of another "over-and-above" program for the 1980s. This time the focus was broadened to include home missions projects as well as foreign, and the goal was set to raise $1,000,000 over a three-year period. The Million for Missions special project was approved by the 1977 General Assembly and launched on July 1 of that year. One fourth of the total was allocated for home missions and targeted toward expanding and developing Spanish-speaking congregations of the Church of God, extending the Christian witness among Native Americans, assisting inner-city congregations and establishing urban mission centers, launching a new congregation in Hawaii, and developing models for full-time ministries in the rural South.[44]

The project list for foreign missions was worldwide in scope and included special needs in Latin America, the Caribbean, Africa, and Australia. The main thrust, however, was toward Asia, which became the special area focus for the 1980s. It was selected because this is the part of the world where most of the earth's people live—over one-half of the globe's population live in twenty-two countries surrounding Thailand—excluding mainland China. Less than 4 percent of the people in any of these countries are Christian and in some it is less than 1 percent. Population growth rates of Asian nations are among the highest in the world. Missionary Board Secretary Donald Johnson observed, "Our mission is to the whole world.

43. Data summarized from a handout sheet titled "Servants of God and of His Church in Latin America" prepared by Maurice Caldwell for the Missionary Board.

44. Marvin J. Hartman, "Unique Opportunities: Home Missions," *Church of God Missions*, July 1977, 3.

This does not exclude those hard places in the world where planting the church is difficult and where Christian growth is slow."[45]

In preparation for the Asian effort the Missionary Board initiated two major consultations. The first was Tokyo 1978, which was a meeting of all area missionaries and Missionary Board personnel. The second was Bangkok 1979, which included national leaders of existing Church of God work in seven countries of South and East Asia along with representatives from the Missionary Board. The two consultations gave detailed statements of their deliberations and recommendations that were compiled in a publication titled "Asia in the 80s." By June 1979, the second year of the project's fundraising element, approximately one-half of the million-dollar goal had been raised, and projections were that the total amount would come in with a slight extension of the time frame.

An additional aspect of the missions picture in the Church of God during the 1970s was the proliferation of independent missionary ventures. The number and scope of paramissionary groups, volunteerism, and separately sponsored crusades and work camps grew rapidly. Beginning in the sixties a number of these groups had emerged and some had developed very extensive programs. By the early seventies a number of problems of relationships had surfaced, so the General Assembly in 1974 authorized the naming of a twelve-member Mission Study Committee to investigate the situation. In its 1975 report this committee, which included representatives of independent groups, reviewed the problem areas and set forth some general guidelines for paramission organizations. It made recommendations that urged continued conversation, cooperation, and coordination of all independent efforts with the long-range work of the authorized mission boards. All agreed that the basic World Service budget should have financial priority in the giving of both individuals and congregations. The report was adopted.[46] In the meantime the Missionary Board had initiated its own program of volunteer enlistment that was labeled Ventures in Missions (VIM). Statistically, during the 1970s the Church of God overseas grew impressively. The number of congregations increased from 1,003 to 1,574, an increase of 573 during the decade. The membership figures had

---

45. Donald D. Johnson, "The Value of a Special Project," *Church of God Missions*, July 1977, 8–9.

46. Minutes of the General Assembly, June 18, 1975. In Annual Reports, 1975, 15. Text of report, 26–34.

more than doubled, from 63,102 in 1970 to 141,738 in 1980.[47] Observers predicted that the constituency of the movement in other countries would likely exceed that in the United States by the mid-1980s.

The 1970 Consultation also projected advancement during the decade regarding lay involvement in the work of the church. Robert Reitz, an insurance company president with many years of lay participation in the Church of God both locally and nationally, wrote the projective paper regarding the coming role of laypeople in the church. He optimistically stated, "The present situation is encouraging. Laymen are deeply concerned about the needs of others. They are getting involved increasingly in small groups. Creative leadership can take advantage of the situation."[48] The consultation agreed that laypeople should be more involved and urged that arrangements be made in the various states for lay-clergy dialogue in order to create feelings of mutual trust and ways to work toward the same goals. There were also suggestions regarding the opportunities laypeople have for their own unique Christian witness in the world of business and work.

Unlike the other concerns discussed in this meeting, there was no General Assembly-related program board or commission to pick up the recommendations and implement them. Likewise, lay involvement was an area in which national programming was more difficult since that involvement had to be related to some task—and tasks were assigned to a multitude of agencies. Even so, two national organizations, unattached to any of the official structures but cooperative with all, gave major attention to the functional role of laypeople in the church. Women of the Church of God and Church of God Men, International, each had established their respective structures at the local, state, and national levels. Of the two, the women's organization had the longer history and the more extensive development. Beginning in 1932 as the Woman's Home and Foreign Missionary Society, its founder, Nora Hunter, had defined its objectives as being first "to cooperate with all recognized agencies of the Church of God in promoting missionary work at home and abroad; to make the cause of missions a heart interest rather than a passing fancy." Other objectives included: "…to study the spiritual, moral and social needs of the world; to encourage liberality and wisdom in the stewardship of prayer, the stewardship of personality, and the stewardship of

---

47. *Yearbook of the Church of God*, summary page in respective years.
48. Robert Reitz, "Projections [for] the 70's: The Role of Laymen," unpublished paper in workbook, page 5 of paper.

possessions."[49] In succeeding years the society enjoyed a succession of strong, effective leaders: Hunter, Ocie Perry, Hallie Patterson, and Nellie Snowden.

The society met its objectives by developing a comprehensive organizational structure. By the early seventies membership reached approximately forty thousand women functioning in eighteen hundred local units. By 1980 over $16,000,000 had been raised and relayed to the church's national agencies, plus considerable additional amounts for scholarships and other tangible expressions of interest and support. In 1978 the annual Christ's Birthday Offering topped $1,000,000 for the first time. In its pattern of annual programming, the organization offers abundant opportunities for laywomen to be involved not only in missions-related activities but also in a wide variety of service projects and self-improvement ventures. In 1974 the society changed its name to Women of the Church of God in order to reflect the broader focus of its slogan, "United in Mission, Friendship, Personal Growth and Service."[50] In 1977 they sponsored the first national Church of God convention for women in Louisville, Kentucky, with over eleven hundred participants.

Church of God Men, International, had its beginnings around 1960 when the Board of Church Extension and Home Missions employed retired army officer A. Wayne Johnson on a part-time basis to develop a national men's organization. The groundwork was laid, and within a few years Men of the Church of God was a functioning fellowship in the church. Donald C. Ritchey of Findlay, Ohio, became the new organization's national president and general executive. In 1976 a new office in Findlay was dedicated.[51] The objectives of Church of God Men focused on challenging men to accept Christ and be effective witnesses in both the local community and around the world. Great stress was placed on personal prayer, Bible reading, development of the spiritual life, and a deeper commitment in regard to the investment of time, money, and talents. Programming has emphasized fellowship and participation in service projects at home and wherever else special needs can be addressed. Through publications, workshops, conferences, retreats, and conventions the work of educating and involving laymen in the work of the church has been promoted.

Despite concern, organization, and enthusiasm, lay involvement in the national agencies of the church showed only slight gains during the

49. Nora Hunter, as quoted in the WCG brochure *From Dream to Reality.*
50. As stated in Ibid.
51. Annual Reports, 1976, 39.

decade of the seventies. In 1975 the elected membership on the Executive Council was increased from seventeen to twenty-five and the maximum number of laypeople raised from six to eight. Lay membership on the national boards remained approximately the same for a total of around one hundred people. These people also, by virtue of having been elected by the Assembly, became full members of the General Assembly. However, by the decade's end, and despite extended discussion, the Assembly still had not approved any plan for enlarging the number of laypeople included in its membership.[52] Perhaps the greatest change in established patterns of leadership came in 1975 when Donald A. Noffsinger, a layperson, was named to succeed T. Franklin Miller as the president of Warner Press. Noffsinger's selection by the Publication Board and his subsequent ratification by the Assembly marked the first time that a layperson had headed any of the national agencies.[53]

The one other area that the 1970 Consultation addressed was Christian unity. At this point in the history of the Church of God concern was expressed both for unity among all Christians and for unity within the movement itself. The former had been a central emphasis from the beginning; the latter had been a matter of continuing concern also, but the presence of potentially disruptive issues usually was not openly discussed. However, both in the consultation itself and in subsequent developments there was a deliberate attempt to identify threatening clouds on the horizon that might gather into storms. Most polarities fit on the conservative versus liberal spectrum common to many religious groups. Some, however, were unique to the Church of God. Chief among these would be the "Reformationists" versus the "Inclusivists."[54]

The Reformationists formed around the desire for mutual encouragement and fellowship and, most importantly, to emphasize what they identified as the historic, biblical message of the Church of God. The early catalysts of this group, William Neece, Lilly McCutcheon, O. L. Johnson, and John Conley, stood in the theological tradition of F. G. Smith, H. M. Riggle, and E. E. Byrum. Before 1972 these individuals had informally discussed the possibility of a group organized around these concerns. How-

---

52. The Bylaws Committee was scheduled to report in 1980 on the response to a proposed model circulated to congregations prior to the meeting of the Assembly.

53. Minutes of the General Assembly, June 18, 1975, 18.

54. Neither of these terms were ever used to label any separate "parties" but are descriptive of the generally divergent stances regarding the nature of the movement and its mission.

ever, it was Anderson College's proposal that its seminary join a theological consortium that sparked the creation of the Pastors' Fellowship. Its leaders were particularly opposed to the possibility that Church of God ministerial students might be instructed by Roman Catholic professors. The Pastors' Fellowship developed a considerable following in the seventies and eighties, eventually sponsoring annual events from Winchester, Kentucky, to Pryor, Oklahoma, to Seattle, Washington.

While the Pastors' Fellowship movement got under way, people at the opposite end of the theological spectrum also began informal discussions. Many of them the product of college and seminary training during the sixties, these men and women were ecumenically oriented and concerned for a social agenda driven by the civil rights and anti-war crusades of that era. A group of pastors known colloquially as the "Columbus Caucus" for their meeting place in Columbus, Ohio, kept these and other issues alive, but it was an intellectually gifted group of students and recent alumni of the School of Theology: Roger Hatch, Frank Watkins, Ray Brennen, and others who were the driving force behind the Inclusivist position and the development of a small magazine to publish that viewpoint.

In the 1970s these variant positions were articulated in print by the appearance of two ad hoc periodicals, *The Reformation Witness* and *Colloquium,* both underwritten by supporters and distributed free. The first, with the slogan, "Earnestly contending for the faith once delivered to the saints," declared in its masthead, "Our position and support will be from those who are Bible-believing, conservative, and evangelical. Further, we believe in the biblical concepts which brought the Church of God reformation movement into existence. We feel that theological conservatives need to have some kind of voice, and we will seek to provide that… with integrity, gentleness and concern."[55] *Colloquium,* on the other hand, declared itself to be:

> A publication of contemporary Christian comment for both leaders and lay members of the Church of God—seeks to relate itself and its leaders to the whole spectrum of the human situation from Christian perspectives. In these pages we hope to raise questions, to provide awareness, to appraise answers, and to suggest possible alternatives. *Colloquium* hopes to provide and promote a many-sided discussion of

55. From the masthead of the *Reformation Witness*, Alan Tinnerstet, editor. Published in 1979 from Big Springs, Texas.

issues in its articles, among its readers, and in their written responses to the articles.[56]

No war of words developed between the two journals, but each provided a platform for expressing views and airing concerns. To some degree their very presence kept channels of dialogue open and mitigated tendencies for the adherents of the different camps to move further apart. The Reformationists did go one step further and began holding annual regional Pastors' Fellowship meetings in Kentucky and Oklahoma. There may have been some early expectation that meetings usually held in May would discuss strategies for influencing actions of the General Assembly in June. However, the May sessions became largely inspirational and instructional. Many national agency leaders attended, and some appeared on the program.

The most extensive national attempt to deal with these internal polarizing tendencies came from a resolution originating in the Committee on Christian Unity passed by the General Assembly in 1970. This resolution, noted that there had been "expressed differences" that could create "a possible problem of attitudes as well as opinions" and that "many of the differences reflect theological and doctrinal problems that need to be openly and honestly faced by this Assembly." Thus the resolution proposed that "the Executive Council and the graduate School of Theology examine the feasibility of calling a Consultation on Doctrine to allow mutual discussion among us as leaders in faith and practice."[57] The resolution passed, and in the following year it was reported that such a consultation was feasible. The Division of General Service was charged with responsibility for preparing and distributing the necessary guidance information for conducting the consultation.

In order to carry out its assignment, the Division of General Service appointed a thirty-member design committee for advice regarding the best method to conduct the consultation and to arrange for and evaluate the necessary resource materials. No budget was appropriated, so the whole committee was never able to meet. It did its work by mail and determined that instead of having one nationally representative meeting this consultation should be conducted in many area meetings, primarily in state and regional assemblies throughout the Church of God. The committee's stated purpose for this multi-meeting consultation:

---

56. From the masthead of *Colloquium*, James R. Cook, John E. Stanley, Susie C. Stanley, eds. Published in 1979 from Corona, California.

57. Minutes of the General Assembly, June 19, 1970, in Annual Reports, 1979, 48–49.

To explore biblically and historically the church's nature, mission, polity, and unity in order to find a common ground for the commitment of old and the nurturing of newer members of our churches. In order to accomplish this, we will:

1. Examine our biblical and theological rootage.
2. Identify doctrinal distinctives and their meaning and application today.
3. Appraise our affinities with other religious groups, and the nature of the unity we seek.
4. Evaluate the doctrine of the Holy Spirit as it relates to the church as the people of God.
5. Express programmatically the challenges to the church for evangelism and mission.[58]

To encourage the participants to dig deep into the issues a resource book was prepared for the consultation. This booklet contained brief essays written by five ministers: "Development of Corporate Procedures in the Church of God" by John W. V. Smith, "The Nature of the Church" by Keith Huttenlocker, "The Mission of the Church" by R. Eugene Sterner, "The Polity of the Church" by Arlo F. Newell, and "The Unity of the Church" by James Earl Massey.[59] The latter four became the main themes of the consultation. In addition, the Executive Council also circulated questionnaires seeking responses on key issues in order to find out what the rank-and-file ministers of the church believed concerning certain doctrines.

W. E. Reed collated all results and reported that from 1971 to 1974 thirty ministerial assemblies and over 2,200 ministers had participated in the consultation. The novel methodological approach made possible the highest level of participation in any national consultation. Several outcomes were achieved, notably:

1. An increased appreciation for the heritage which is ours in the Church of God.
2. An increased awareness of the relationship between sound doctrine and authentic experience.

---

58. "Consultation on Doctrine: Report to the General Assembly of the Church of God," June 18–20, 1974, 3.
59. Ibid., 4.

3. Some areas of polarization have been identified.
4. The consultations have also provided a vehicle which has encouraged openness in discussion.
5. An awareness that recognition in the church should be predicated on participation in the church's broader ministries.[60]

Reed added that the Church of God seemed to be universally upholding the following three teachings: (1) To be a genuine Christian one must have a life-changing relationship with God. (2) The church is both human and divine and is composed only of true believers. (3) Christian unity is to be sought.[61]

By design the consultation focused attention on aspects of ecclesiology—the church's nature, mission, polity and unity. This focus minimized or eliminated formal discussion of some of the polarizing issues, for example the doctrine of biblical inerrancy. As another example, in Reed's 1973 executive secretary's report to the General Assembly, he recognized another teaching that was receiving a great deal of attention and leading to some dissension: the doctrinal practice of speaking in tongues. He wrote, "In some states there is a lot of controversy about speaking in tongues and the charismatic movement. A few of our congregations have encountered serious schisms over this issue."[62] This matter continued to be a concern for many throughout the rest of the decade. The attitude of most ministers was to permit *glossolalia* as a private devotional language. Above all, the practice was not to be allowed to become divisive either in congregations or in the movement.

The commitment to Christian unity continued to find new and singular ways of expression. Neither the General Assembly nor the Executive Council held any formal relationships with any interdenominational organization. Thus participation by the Church of God at the national level in either programs or meetings of this nature continued to be through the various agencies (including divisions, commissions, and committees) or interested individuals. The Committee on Christian Unity served as a reminder of this ongoing concern. After its elevation in 1975 to the status of a commission under the Executive Council, it was in a position to establish relationships

---

60. Ibid., 4–6.
61. Ibid., 35.
62. Annual Reports, 1973, 28.

of its own with appropriate groups. In 1979 the commission authorized two individuals to serve with the Commission on Faith and Order of the National Council of Churches and named two observers to participate in the January 1980 plenary session of the Consultation on Church Union.

Christian unity was one of the major themes of the Consultation on Doctrine, and consequently a great deal of attention was given to a discussion of this issue during those three years. The focus was more on the meaning and nature of unity rather than strategies for implementing it. Even so, significant involvement in interchurch activities occurred at many levels. For instance, in July 1974 seventeen representatives from the Church of God (only four of them from the United States) attended the International Congress on World Evangelization in Lausanne, Switzerland. One of these, James Earl Massey, was named as a member of the Lausanne Continuation Committee. In 1975 the Church of God sent one delegated observer and several visitors to the Fifth Assembly of the World Council of Churches in Nairobi, Kenya. Dialogue with the Churches of God in North America and the Church of the Brethren continued at a modest level. A significant number of individuals also participated in activities of the National Association of Evangelicals, the Christian Holiness Association, and various other interdenominational organizations. In 1979 Massey's *Concerning Christian Unity* appeared as one of the eight volumes in the Church of God Doctrinal Library being published in preparation for the movement's centennial.[63]

The last two-thirds of the seventies was marked by many other special events, conventions, personnel changes, and anniversaries. International youth conventions were held in Denver (1974), Cincinnati (1976), and Seattle (1978). Anniversaries were celebrated by the School of Theology (Twenty-fifth in 1975), Bay Ridge Christian College (Twenty-fifth in 1978), the Church of God in Argentina (Fiftieth in 1977), and the Board of Christian Education (Fiftieth in 1973). A feature of the observance by the latter agency was a consultation on the future of Christian education in the Church of God held in Kansas City, Missouri, in May 1973. Sixty-five participants studied a list of thirty-seven goals that had been developed from responses to a survey sent out by the Board before the conference. Some of the high-priority goals were Bible-centered curriculum, development of teachers and other leaders, and Christian family life. Other tangible goals were: (1) working toward a 10 percent increase in average Sunday school at-

---

63. James Earl Massey, *Concerning Christian Unity* (Anderson, IN: Warner Press, 1979).

tendance and enrollment during 1973–74; (2) developing a more effective teacher training program; and (3) providing scholarships and other forms of encouragement for Christian educators.[64] The Board also sponsored a round of regional meetings of state and area boards of Christian education to try to implement the goals set by the consultation and further such programs as CARE Labs and Effective Teaching Labs.

In 1976 the Radio and Television Commission became the Mass Communications Board of the Church of God and a new addition to the family of general agencies. A new staff person was added in 1977 when Maurice Berquist became the executive secretary of this new board. Staff changes in other agencies included the retirement of Max R. Gaulke as president of Gulf-Coast Bible College in 1975 and the selection of John W. Conley to succeed him. The same year Donald D. Johnson replaced retiring Lester A. Crose as executive secretary of the Missionary Board. A year earlier, upon the retirement of Ewald E. Wolfram, Harold A. Conrad had been named to head the Board of Pensions. In 1977 Arlo F. Newell succeeded Harold L. Phillips as editor in chief of Warner Press. Then in 1979 Paul A. Tanner left his position as director of the Division of World Service to become executive secretary-elect of the Executive Council and successor to W. E. Reed upon his retirement in 1980. David L. Lawson was named to Tanner's post in the World Service office. There were also notable losses by death. Among the most prominent leaders who died in the last eight years of the decade were J. Edgar Smith, Ivory Downer, Axchie Bolitho, C. Herbert Joiner, Boyce Blackwelder, Nick Zazanis, Louis F. Gough, and Irene Caldwell.

Running through all the other events and changes, however, was the awareness that the centennial was approaching. The committee appointed to frame the celebration made its report to the Executive Council, which in turn passed on the recommendation to the General Assembly:

> WHEREAS the Church of God, with General Agencies in Anderson, Indiana, and with congregations in forty or more countries of the world, will reach its centennial at the end of this decade; and
>
> WHEREAS the Church of God around the world will want to celebrate its centennial in a way that pays tribute to those who have preceded us in this work and, at the same time, present an appropriate challenge to those in generations to come: therefore, be it

---

64. "Christian Education Leaders Set Goals, " *Vital Christianity*, July 8, 1973, 19.

RESOLVED that the General Assembly, on this 21st day of June, 1972, concur in the recommendation of its Executive Council in confirming the time period for the Centennial Celebration as beginning with June 1980 and extending through October 1981; and be it further

RESOLVED that the Executive Council be instructed to proceed through its committee on planning for an observance of the Centennial in a manner commensurate with our spiritual heritage and our unrealized hopes.[65]

The committee drafted the following purpose:

It is our firm conviction that in the nineteenth century the early leaders of this movement were led by the Holy Spirit in the recapturing of a vision of God's one Holy Church and that those responsible for the launching and development of the Church of God reformation acted on the impetus of a divine commission to help restore the Church to its intended wholeness, purity, and unity....We further believe that the essential message and spirit of these pioneers has great meaning for our present witness in the world and lays a solid foundation for our mission to the future. Therefore, it shall be the purpose of this Centennial Celebration to pay tribute to those who have preceded us in this work and, at the same time, present an appropriate challenge to those who shall follow in generations to come. In order to accomplish this overall purpose, we set forth the following specific objectives:

(1) To relate significantly to our heritage of faith and witness
(2) To reassess our heritage
(3) To project our heritage.[66]

For the first two years, the committee enlisted the thinking of several hundred people in the planning process. In the spring of 1974 the Committee began to address attention to drafting a master plan for the centennial's observance. After securing many suggestions the following sequence of possible program and publication accents was developed for the six years preceding and including the centennial celebration:

---

65. Minutes of the General Assembly, June 21, 1972, 18–19.
66. Adapted from "Centennial Observance of the Church of God" (unpublished).

1976: REMEMBERING OUR ROOTS
- key idea here is to link up with religious and heritage aspects of the U.S. Bicentennial (both CBH and VC have such emphases already planned and in process).
- a biblical base: "Lest You Forget…." (Deut 4:9).

1977: REPENTANCE and RENEWAL
- historically, linkage with the great revivals, particularly those in the nineteenth century. Proclaim the always needed biblical call to repent and be renewed.
- a biblical base: "If my people, which are called by my name, shall humble themselves, and pray, and seek my face…." (2 Chron 7:14 KJV).

1978: A CLOUD OF WITNESSES
- recall of and re-acquaintance with reformer and pioneer figures in the history of the church *and* in Church of God reformation movement. Agency heritage and key figures.
- a biblical base: "Wherefore seeing we also are compassed about with so great a cloud of witnesses…." (Heb 12:1 KJV).

1979: "WE HOLD THESE TRUTHS"
- biblical-doctrinal affirmations. Studies series to be available, combining biblical, historical, and current insights into key doctrinal areas.
- a biblical base: "Speak thou the things which become sound doctrine…" (Titus 2:1 KJV).

1980: WE'VE COME THIS FAR
- specific celebration of Church of God history and heritage; our journey and where we are now.
- a biblical base: "Rejoice with joy inexpressible and full of glory" (1 Pet 1:8 NASB).

1981: JOURNEY ONWARD
- specific attention to goal-setting for the road ahead; a time both to acquaint with current program and projected planning.
- a biblical base: "Be on the alert, stand firm in the faith,…be strong" (1 Cor 16:13 NASB).[67]

---

67. Ibid.

Details soon began to fall into place. Historical projects were identified and dates projected. The first of these was a revision and enlargement of an earlier work by John W. V. Smith which was published in 1976 under the title, *A Brief History of the Church of God Reformation Movement. Where the Saints Have Trod: A Social History of the Church of God Reformation Movement* by Val Clear was published in 1977. This was followed by a six-volume paperback sourcebook series (later reissued as a two-volume hardback) edited by Barry L. Callen and released between 1977 and 1979 under the general title, *A Time to Remember.*[68] In 1979 Harold L. Phillips' *Miracle of Survival* and Robert H. Reardon's, *The Early Morning Light,* were published. Phillips' book was a history of the Gospel Trumpet Company. Reardon wrote "a friendly reflection on some of the main events in the life of the Church of God reformation during the first thirty years." The committee also recommended the preparation and publication of the movement's first documented history and placed the project in the hands of the movement's historian and the Publication Board. The present volume is a response to that trust.

Included in publication projections was an eight-volume doctrinal series, the Church of God Doctrinal Library, to begin in 1978 and be completed by 1980. The titles indicate the themes to which the movement has given major emphasis during its one-hundred-year history:

Receive the Holy Spirit by Arlo F. Newell
Healing and Wholeness by R. Eugene Sterner
God, Can I Get to Know You? by Keith Huttenlocker
The Life of Salvation by Gilbert W. Stafford
A Kingdom of Servants by Dwight L. Dye
Concerning Christian Unity by James E. Massey
The Word of God by Kenneth E. Jones

In order that the centennial might become a grassroots as well as a national and international celebration, every functioning unit in the Church of God around the world was encouraged to research, prepare, publish, and utilize its own history. Local congregations, state organizations, camp meetings, assemblies, regional meetings, boards and other national agencies, and the work in the various countries were all the objects of intensive

---

68. The two-volume hardback edition (with some added material) was retitled *The First Century.*

attempts to recover and record the story of the movement's past. Another facet of the recovery process was an oral history project for the Church of God Archives consisting of taped interviews with people who by experience or knowledge were able to recall significant aspects of the movement's history. Various other procedures for collecting and preserving historical materials such as diaries, journals, photo albums, correspondence files, and significant memorabilia were implemented. A logo was designed for use on all centennial publications and for souvenir items relating to the occasion. W. E. Reed chaired the Centennial Committee, and T. Franklin Miller was named as coordinator for the developing plans and activities.

A significant part of the launch of this sixteen-month celebration was the Sixth World Conference of the Church of God. For the first time the conference was scheduled in the United States. Appropriately, its location was Anderson at approximately the same time as the usual International Convention in June 1980. The previous World Conference had been held in Oaxtepec, Mexico, in 1971. The scheduled location for the 1975 conference was Beirut, Lebanon, but this event had to be canceled because of civil war in that country. Fortunately, the decision about the 1980 World Conference in Anderson had been made in 1971, and so continuity was preserved. To lay specific plans for the conference, which was to launch the centennial celebration, a World Strategy and Planning meeting was held in Nairobi, Kenya, in October 1977. This meeting of twenty-five representatives from twenty-one countries not only outlined the program for 1980, but also proposed the formation of a "World Forum of the Church of God," a continuing global organization made up of representatives from all of the countries in which the church has functioning structures. This organization would give attention to worldwide concerns and develop international strategies for the movement.[69]

Nearing the century's end, the Church of God in comparison with other Christian bodies was neither large nor wealthy but it had made considerable strides in number of adherents and assets. Table 4 tells its own story in wide-ranging statistics.[70] In regard to its geographic extensiveness the comparison with other groups was more favorable. The sixty countries listed in table 5 were a solid witness to the movement's continuing zeal for outreach and sharing the message of Christ and the church.[71]

---

69. Annual Reports, 1978, 29.
70. *Centennial Yearbook of the Church of God, 1880–1980*, 305.
71. Ibid., 135.

Paving the way for the road ahead, the 1970 Consultation guided the movement through this last decade of its first century. Anticipation of a very meaningful and significant celebration at the one-hundred-year mark created the kind of atmosphere and feeling to make the 1980 World Conference a dramatic launching pad for the months of festivity that would mark the period of the centennial observance. With two thousand guests from overseas, the estimated forty thousand hosts from the "home church" would join in celebrating the past and the present—and in looking thoughtfully and prayerfully toward the future.

TABLE 4: Summary Statistics United States and Canada 1980

Ministers
Ordained	3,063
Unordained	670
Missionaries	100
Retired ministers	587
Retired missionaries	18

Congregations
United States	2,259
Canada	49
* Other countries	1,574

Membership
Sunday School Enrollment (U.S.)	228,380
Sunday School Enrollment (Canada)	3,398
Sunday School Attendance (U.S.)	153,194
Sunday School Attendance (Canada)	2,453
Membership (U.S.)	175,113
Membership (Canada)	2,623
* Membership (Other countries)	141,738
Morning Attendance (U.S.)	191,566
Morning Attendance (Canada)	3,131

Property

Local church property (U.S.)..........$337,650,288
Local church property (Canada) 5,749,654
Colleges and schools 34,804,398
Publishing work 5,789,591
International campground and buildings....2,588,564
General Offices 1,921,300
Agency-owned mission property 467,830

*includes only areas of work under the administration of the Missionary Board.

TABLE 5: International Summary 1980

Country	Congregation	Membership
Antigua	5	400
Argentina	20	1,500
Australia	3	50
Bangladesh	35	1,200
Barbados	20	1,200
Bermuda	2	280
Bolivia	96	7,000
Brazil	34	2,500
Bulgaria	2	40
Cayman Islands	5	150
Colombia	4	110
Costa Rica	5	121
Cuba	6	150
Curaçao	2	225
Czechoslovakia	?	?
Denmark	4	175
East Germany	?	300
Egypt	12	600
El Salvador	6	240
England	5	250
Germany	33	3,000
Greece	1	60
Grenada	4	250
Guam	1	100

Guatemala	61	5,600
Guyana	9	600
Haiti	20	1,500
Holland	4	100
Honduras	3	120
Hong Kong (New Mission)	0	3
Hungary	10?	300
India	436	44,000
Ireland (North)	0	5
Italy	3	250
Jamaica	90	5,000
Japan	18	800
Kenya	400	50,000
Korea	27	5,500
Lebanon	6	350
Mexico	31	1,000
Nicaragua	24	2,000
Panama	22	750
Paraguay	1	25
Peru	25	500
Philippines	65	5,000
Poland	?	?
Puerto Rico	3	200
Russia	60?	3,000
St. Kitts and Nevis	7	550
St. Vincent	2	60
Singapore (New Mission)	0	2
Switzerland	3	100
Taiwan	2	100
Tanzania	54	2,650
Thailand	5	80
Trinidad	18	700
Uganda	?	?
Uruguay	1	30
Venezuela (New Mission)	0	2
TOTALS	1,715	150,778

CHAPTER 18

COUNTERWEIGHTS
(1980–1992)

In 1980 voters elected Ronald Reagan as the fortieth president of the United States. Pundits and commentators observed that Reagan's election was more than the defeat of incumbent Jimmy Carter; in their view it signaled a turn toward conservatism in the American electorate. Although in eight years Reagan never presented a balanced budget to Congress nor delivered a live speech opposing abortion, he endeared himself to political and cultural conservatives. His election signaled the beginning of a conservative shift in American political life that continued through his two terms and beyond. (After Democrat Bill Clinton was elected twelve years later, he quickly moved to govern from the center of the political spectrum rather than to espouse classic, liberal Democrat positions.) The so-called "Reagan Revolution" emboldened religious and cultural conservatives such as James Dobson, Jerry Falwell, and Pat Robertson who claimed that evangelicals and a "Moral Majority" had been instrumental in securing a Republican victory. During the 1970s and 1980s conservative Protestants took to the march in pursuit of a Christian America, but also a more theologically consistent evangelicalism.

In 1976 Harold Lindsell, a former member of the Fuller Theological Seminary faculty and subsequently Editor of *Christianity Today*, published a book titled *The Battle for the Bible*. While at Fuller, Lindsell and other conservative members of the faculty became troubled by the attitudes of some of their colleagues and members of the student body toward the doctrine of biblical inerrancy. Fundamentalist Protestants regard the doctrine of inerrancy as the cornerstone of biblical authority on which all other doctrine rests; in their view other means of grounding the Bible's authority are insufficient. Fuller Seminary had adopted a position on biblical authority called "infallibility," but Lindsell and others believed that any doctrine other than inerrancy threatened to undermine the authority of the Bible and eventually the church as well. This position he championed in *The Battle for the Bible*. With a popular religious magazine for a platform the doctrine of inerrancy stirred American evangelicals and other conservative Protestant readers.

While Lindsell and others fanned the flames of inerrancy among evangelicals similar issues were coming to a head among Southern Baptists. In the late 1970s noted Baptist conservatives Paige Patterson, W. A. Criswell, and Paul Pressler were determined to elect Adrian Rogers as the Southern Baptist Convention's (SBC's) president. Rogers shared their belief that the denomination had fallen under the control of moderates—to their minds, liberals—and that it was time for conservatives to regain control. Like beauty, whether their effort constituted a conservative resurgence or a fundamentalist takeover rests in the eye of the beholder. It is not disputed that in 1979 the convention elected Rogers president on the first ballot, and the word *inerrancy* was used for the first time to define an SBC doctrine of inspiration. These and subsequent developments among Southern Baptists were widely reported even in secular news media. They could not fail to draw the attention of many non-Baptist conservative Christians and encourage them to similar action.

The Reagan political revolution, the battle for the Bible among evangelicals, and the fundamentalist takeover of the Southern Baptist Convention inspired and reinforced conservative voices in the Church of God. In several cases they espoused causes that significantly broadened the understanding of what it meant to be a conservative in the Church of God. Since the early 1970s the Pastors' Fellowship had championed conservatism in the Church of God. But that position was defined by the traditional doctrinal themes of holiness and the church-historical interpretation of the books of Daniel and Revelation. It went without saying that these traditional conservatives took a high view of the authority of the Bible, but historically it had not been necessary to anchor that view to a doctrine of inerrancy. Nevertheless, the broad-based social and religious conservative movements of the seventies and eighties influenced some Church of God conservatives to adopt inerrancy language and other stances, but conservatives of all stripes spoke out during the period between 1980 and 1993 to define what they believed should be the chief commitments of the Church of God reformation movement.

Conservatives, traditional or otherwise, were not the only voices to speak out during the decade of the eighties and following. Issues not typically associated with theological, political, or social conservatism found advocates within some quarters of the Church of God constituency. Moderates, often located in the church's educational institutions and in the Commissions on Higher Education, Social Concerns, and Christian Unity, may have been initially surprised at the depth of conservative criticism, but they refused to be cowed. They refused to allow the Church of God to be defined by an exclusively conservative agenda, whether political or theological. Moderates believed in the authority of the Bible but not the doctrine of inerrancy, advocated the cause of Christian unity by encouraging ecumenical participation, called for nuclear disarmament, and championed their own version of "family values." They also espoused policies that supported racial and gender equality. That moderates in the church took positions in some cases contrary to the conservative agenda ensured that the bulk of the period from 1980 to 1992 would feature a sustained conversation, often a debate, between counterweighted positions at opposite ends of a continuum spanning nearly the entire breadth of the Church of God reformation movement.

The Open Letter and Anderson College

Church of God folk journeyed to the International Convention of the Church of God in Anderson, Indiana, in June 1980 from all across the United States and Canada, and, quite literally, from around the world to join in the celebration of the centennial anniversary of the Church of God movement. For several years a Centennial Planning Committee had been laying groundwork for the best possible celebration, but they could not have imagined the events that unfolded in the months preceding the convention in a manner so contrary to the committee's expectations. Those events not only cast a shadow over the centennial celebration; they also shaped attitudes and discussions in the church for nearly a decade.

In the Spring of 1980 ministers of the Church of God in the United States and Canada opened the mail to find an open letter from Rev. Leroy Oesch, a former professor at both Warner Pacific College and Gulf-Coast Bible College. In 1980 Oesch was the pastor of St. Andrew Church of God in Camden, South Carolina, and chairperson of the South Carolina Assembly of the Church of God. His letter was addressed to Robert Reardon, president of Anderson College. Prior to mailing his letter, Oesch had sought meetings with Reardon in order to air a list of grievances. Oesch's efforts proved unsuccessful, and out of a sense of frustration he felt he had no alternative but to publish his concerns throughout the church. Using the standards of resurgent conservative evangelicalism, Oesch believed Anderson College to be sliding down a liberal slope. To him one indication of this slippage was the fact that the doctrine of inerrancy was not taught either in the School of Theology or by the members of the undergraduate Department of Religious Studies. To be sure, inerrancy had not been taught for decades, if ever, at Anderson College or at Warner Pacific College, but that absence had not been due to liberalism. Historically, theology in the Church of God has not been articulated in a manner that rests on the doctrine of inerrancy. This is not to say that Church of God teachers have not held the Bible in high regard; quite the contrary has been true. However, as authoritative as they may have held the Bible, that authority has been grounded elsewhere than in a doctrine of inerrancy.[1] It is also historically the case that Church of God ministers have enjoyed a degree of latitude on a doctrines such as inerrancy. Leroy Oesch and others, perhaps several, could and did teach the doctrine of inerrancy, but that did not make it the historic position of the Church of God. In some sense this had been an academic dispute among theologians, but Oesch's letter and its supporters took the absence of inerrancy teaching to be the germ of doctrinal and moral decay at Anderson College and the adjoining Anderson School of Theology.

Further complaints in the "Open Letter," as it came to be called, served to illustrate the decay created by neglect of inerrancy. Oesch took offense to the use of coarse language uttered on stage in theatrical productions on the Anderson campus. His letter cited several vulgar or profane words and phrases typically not part of the speech of Holiness groups like the Church of God. More inflammatory, however, were Oesch's charges concerning an undergraduate Anderson College course in human sexuality. One target of his criticism was required course reading, which did not treat sexuality from a Christian moral perspective. Textbooks included explicit line drawings or illustrations of human beings engaged in various positions of sexual intercourse. Oesch photocopied these and included them in his letter. In the eyes of some readers the drawings were little more than an academic

---

1. See, for example, H. C. Wickersham's dynamic definition cited in chapter 5 (p. 83). One would have difficulty equating this definition with inerrancy. For a study of doctrines of biblical authority among past and then contemporary Church of God teachers see Stephen Wayne Stall, *The Inspiration and Authority of Scripture: The Views of Eight Historical and Twenty-One Current Doctrinal Teachers in the Church of God (Anderson, Indiana)* (master's thesis, Anderson School of Theology, 1985).

venture into pornography.[2] But the most incendiary complaint in Oesch's letter was drawn from an interview with M. Lavern Norris, professor of sociology and the teacher of the course in question. Norris's open views on human sexuality, criticism of traditional church condemnation of masturbation, and candid endorsement of the limited use of pornography by married couples Oesch presented as evidence of moral decline at Anderson College. That Norris's course used a textbook that treated homosexuality as an alternative lifestyle appeared to many as his personal dismissal, if not a blatant disregard of church teaching. Only the year previous the General Assembly had adopted a resolution recognizing "the biblical admonition that homosexuality is sin and that we oppose the ordination of any ministers who are homosexual."[3] Oesch also found insufficient the textbook's tendency to base sex education on the findings of professional societies of therapists and counselors rather than on the Bible. Included in Oesch's letter was the transcript of an interview in which Norris equated biblical truth and the best of human wisdom.[4] No statement could have cemented any more strongly Oesch's assertions about the doctrine of inerrancy and Anderson College.

The Open Letter's late arrival in the mail ensured an emotionally charged General Assembly that June. Time did not permit a rebuttal before the convention, so Assembly members arrived in Anderson having read only Oesch's side of the story, and he had allies. Since the early 1970s the Pastors' Fellowship had criticized the college because its Bible professors did not teach F. G. Smith's exegesis of Daniel and Revelation. That interpretation portrayed the Roman Catholic Church, especially the papacy, as apostate. In the early 1970s Anderson College's proposal to link its graduate School of Theology with a Catholic seminary in a theological school consortium had galvanized the Pastors' Fellowship into opposition. Furthermore, in 1971 the college invited Father Theodore Hesburgh, president of the University of Notre Dame, to address graduates at commencement. The combination of these circumstances perpetuated the Fellowship's suspicion of the college and seminary, a suspicion that the Open Letter served only to deepen.

---

2. Only the Anderson College course on human sexuality came under Oesch's guns. A similar course and the same textbook were also taught at Warner Pacific College, but the Open Letter took no notice.

3. The resolution originated in the Pryor, Oklahoma, meeting of the Pastors' Fellowship, May 15, 1979. Minutes of the General Assembly, Annual Reports, 1979, 17.

4. The interviewer was a woman named Marjorie Rauner. It appeared in the Open Letter as "Exhibit VI."

In 1979 other conservatives, some affiliated with the Pastors' Fellowship but many not, inaugurated a new grassroots publication under the title *Crossroads: Christian Insight on Crucial Issues*. The magazine linked the rising conservative tide in the United States with its call for a similar resurgence in the Church of God, adopting some of the issues of the former into the life of the Church of God. For example, *Crossroads* painted conservative evangelical issues such as inerrancy, opposition to abortion, endorsement of capital punishment and opposition to the Equal Rights Amendment with Church of God colors. The criticisms of *Crossroads*, the Pastors' Fellowship, and the Open Letter dominated the movement's attention in the weeks before the convention. Members of the General Assembly, the vast majority of them ministers, arrived in Anderson with questions about Anderson College. The absence of any rebuttal by college administrators seemed to lend credence to the charges.

Chairperson Paul Hart scarcely gaveled the 1980 General Assembly into its opening session before the Open Letter controversy hit the floor. Customarily the Assembly convened in Park Place Church of God, but a larger-than-usual attendance was anticipated because of the centennial celebration. Church leaders moved the meeting location to O. C. Lewis Gymnasium on the Anderson College campus. Given the tenor of much of the debate, some Assembly members later observed ironically that it was appropriate to hold such sessions in a gym. At Hart's request, a somewhat chastened President Reardon followed his annual welcome with a reply to the Open Letter. He dismissed some charges as based in outdated or limited information. For example, to Oesch's charge that a professor had shown stag films on campus Reardon answered that a temporary teacher had indeed shown one such film but that this action suffered faculty censure, the teacher had been dropped from the faculty, and the film was never again shown. The Open Letter also called into question the college's teaching on homosexuality, charging that some professors viewed it as an alternate Christian lifestyle. Speaking for the administration and the professors in question, Reardon stated that such teaching was contrary to his understanding of the Bible and that he had made it clear in writing that Anderson College would not condone such teaching. Concerning the textbooks used in the human sexuality course, he distinguished explicit illustrations from pornographic illustrations and defended the use of such materials in courses preparing students for professional work as counselors, social workers, and ministers. Finally, Reardon said, student opinion held that the college faculty did not have a liberal bias but fairly presented conservative views as well. However, he conceded that the college may need further, serious discussion on this point.

Courtesy of Anderson University and Church of God Archives

Robert H. Reardon (1919–2007), educator. The son of E. A. Reardon, Robert was groomed for the Anderson College presidency. After brief pastorates in the mid-forties, he returned to his alma mater as assistant to the president in 1947. In 1952, he was named executive vice president, succeeding John Morrison in 1958 as the institution's second president. Until retirement in 1983, Reardon presided over a dramatic expansion of personnel, programs, and facilities at Anderson College.

Anderson College may have been the focal point of Assembly concern, but it was by no means the only target to come under conservative guns. The Commissions on Social Concerns and Christian Unity also were sharply questioned and criticized from the Assembly floor. Some members took the Commission on Social Concerns report to task for its use of "liberal language," for a preference for public schools over private Christian schools, and for a veiled endorsement of the Equal Rights Amendment. When commission chairperson Wayne Harting replied that they had not taken a position on the E.R.A., he was chided by an Assembly member who declared, "The Bible has taken a stand on the E.R.A., therefore the Church of God has a position."[5] Sharp exchanges also characterized the discussion of the report of the Commission on Christian Unity. Richard Bradley, a frequent critic of Anderson and outspoken defender of conservative views, questioned whether commission members should have attended a meeting of the Consultation on Christian Union (COCU), given that Christian unity is not the same as such denominational church unions. He was joined in a declaration of opposition to further attendance at such meetings by Gene Miller, a professor at Gulf-Coast Bible College who believed that such associations made the movement appear to be a denomination with views on union similar to COCU's. His Gulf-Coast colleague Everett Carver expressed parallel concerns, but when he asserted that ecumenical observers

5. Minutes of the General Assembly, Annual Reports, 1980, 17–18.

must stand for the historic position of the church rather than repudiate it, Carver earned the sharp rebuke of John W. V. Smith. A member of the National Council of Churches Commission on Faith and Order, Smith insisted that his view of the church was precisely that of D. S. Warner and that no member of the Christian Unity Commission wanted to join any of the ecumenical bodies to which Church of God representatives were delegated. The discussion's heated tone prompted Forrest Robinson, a pastor from Sikeston, Missouri, to plead, "We must not leave this Assembly being suspicious of one another."[6]

Pastor Robinson's admonition was tested later when the Assembly gathered in its final session to consider the adoption of the World Service budget for the 1980–81 fiscal year. Anderson College had a line item in that budget for nearly a half-million dollars, and some Assembly members, dissatisfied with Reardon's earlier reply, were in a mood to hold the entire budget hostage until a more satisfactory statement was forthcoming. Previous Assemblies had sometimes seen pointed budget debates, but by and large these had been orderly affairs that were easily chaired. Of an angular spirit with which Chairperson Hart had little experience, the 1980 Assembly's budget consideration was marked by accusations that were at points inflammatory. Hart was unprepared for sharp, overly personal charges and struggled to control the session. The Assembly seemed in a mood to veto any measure having anything to do with Anderson or the national church organization. Thus, for example, the Assembly voted down each section of a resolution from the Executive Council that would have restructured the three commissions of the General Assembly—Higher Education, Social Concerns, and Christian Unity. In this climate Rev. Marvin Baker, chairperson of the Anderson College trustee board, stepped to the microphone to announce the creation and membership of a select committee to inquire into the charges concerning the college.[7] Many Assembly members desired something more than this. They had been urged to attend the Assembly in expectation of dealing firsthand with the charges in Oesch's letter, and Baker's announcement appeared to some a tactic to forestall further discussion from the floor. Frustrated, they called on the Rev. Lillie McCutcheon, pastor of the Church of God in Newton Falls, Ohio and a leader of the Pastors' Fellowship, to air their feelings.

---

6. Ibid, 19–20.

7. Members of the committee included: James C. Burchett, David Cox, David Grubbs, Samuel Hines, Kenneth Jones, Fred Menchinger, Wilma Perry, Harold Phillips, Kenneth Schemmer, and Willard Wilcox. Grubbs was the lone college trustee on the committee.

Lillie McCutcheon was a churchwoman who held a deep loyalty to the Church of God. Of a strongly conservative viewpoint, she championed the apocalyptically grounded view of the church with which her mentor F. G. Smith had been closely identified. From this perspective she often disagreed with the college and decisions made by Anderson-based agencies. Unlike some ministers, however, she never withheld her congregation's support of the World Service budget in protest of national policies. McCutcheon spoke for many of those who had come to believe that Assembly procedures effectively silenced grassroots members who wanted to get their views or proposals before the entire body. Some were unclear about the Assembly's rules of procedure and the means by which items could be added to the agenda from the floor, and they were restive under what they perceived as the Business Committee's control of the agenda. Clearly, many members believed that the Assembly itself should exercise closer, if not direct control over agencies such as Anderson College and commissions such as Social Concerns and Christian Unity. To the degree that they could not influence the agenda or control the agencies, some Assembly members felt disconnected and ignored in the national work of the church. In their eyes neither the college nor the Commission on Social Concerns had responded adequately to the Assembly's resolution on homosexuality adopted the previous year. McCutcheon contended that this failure had necessitated the Open Letter as a means of getting church leadership's attention.[8]

Signs of both accord and discord were apparent in the final session of the 1980 General Assembly. At the conclusion of her comments McCutcheon expressed her faith in the Select Committee on Anderson College and issued a plea for the adoption of the World Service budget. Later Robert Reardon offered his approval of her proposal and the committee constituted to inquire into the theological and moral stances of the institution over which he presided. The Assembly voted the adoption of the World Service budget by a margin of more than ten to one. However, by adjournment a host of members had risen to the microphone, sometimes to speak to the item at hand but more often to attack Reardon and the college, commend Oesch, challenge the credentials of another speaker, offer suggestions for the recruitment of college faculty members, call for a point of order, propose revisions in Assembly bylaws, and so forth. It is understandable that, just prior

---

8. Minutes of the General Assembly, Annual Reports, 1980, 22–23.

to adjournment, pastor and missionary Oscar Borden asked the Assembly to rise in appreciation for its long-suffering and harried chairperson.

New Watchmen on the Wall

The discussion and debate of the spring and summer surrounding the 1980 General Assembly set a tone for the better part of the decade following the Open Letter controversy. Despite Forrest Robinson's solicitude, suspicion and frustration percolated through the Assembly and, by extension, the church. Discussions about the educational program at Anderson College had been dominated by charges from the church's conservatives. During the summer and following months, college officials took measures to rebut some charges and debate the premises of others. The Select Committee was to report its findings and recommendations to the 1981 Assembly. Neither the college nor its critics passively awaited the report. Both sides were determined to employ all the measures at their respective disposal to shape the attitude of the Assembly and church.

Shortly after the conclusion of the 1980 International Convention each registrant in the *Yearbook of the Church of God* received a letter over the signatures of some of the most respected and distinguished elder statesmen in the movement.[9] Enclosed with the letter was an unedited transcript of Reardon's remarks in the opening session of the General Assembly. Rumors about the Assembly had flown across the church, and the letter of these elders was intended to address what it characterized as "misunderstandings and uncertainties."[10] The letter was also at pains to dispel any rising doubts about church leadership in the various agencies and commissions. Its signers vouched for the integrity, doctrinal loyalty, and devotion to Christ of all the national leaders of the Church of God. Finally, the letter affirmed the wisdom of Baker and Hart in naming the Select Committee and the unquestioned integrity of its members. The letter expressed a hope that the committee's work would "resolve uncertainties and make recommendations which will enable us to lock hearts and arms in true unity. . ."[11]

---

9. Signatories included: Milo L. Chapman, Lester A. Crose, Leroy M. Fulton, Sidney Johnson, Darold H. Jones, Adam W. Miller, T. Franklin Miller, M[arcus]. H. Morgan, Dale Oldham, W. E. Reed, A. D. Semrau, and Charles V. Weber.

10. A copy of the letter, dated, June 26, 1980, and its enclosure are included in the file "Open Letter" in the Anderson University and Church of God Archives.

11. Ibid.

Members of the School of Theology faculty also entered the church-wide discussion. Jerry C. Grubbs, professor of Christian Education, devoted an entire issue of a newsletter titled *Centering on Ministry*[12] to the topic of biblical inspiration. The issue was both educational as well as a polemic directed at those who wished to make inerrancy the standard view of inspiration in the Church of God. Theologian Gilbert Stafford offered a carefully nuanced glossary of terms associated with the authority of the Bible—inspiration, authority, inerrancy, infallibility, and so forth. Of the last of these he wrote, "Those using it in this latter sense [infallibility as contrasted with inerrancy] stress that that which God has spoken is perfectly trustworthy and as such is to be accepted as absolutely authoritative, not because it passes the test of our human understanding regarding a perfect, original manuscript but because of the witness of the Holy Spirit."[13] Stafford was joined in this issue by John W. V. Smith, professor emeritus of church history and Church of God historian, who concluded a historical overview of the doctrine of biblical inspiration in the Church of God by stating:

> Despite the fact that many of them [Church of God teachers and preachers] were writing in the early decades of the twentieth century when the 'fundamentalist' controversy over biblical inerrancy was splitting churches apart, there is practically no evidence that any of them, with the possible exception of C. E. Brown, felt that their high view of the Bible needed to be supported by legalist definitions applied to the text such as 'inerrancy' and 'verbal inspiration.' They simply saw no need to enter into that debate. In terms of the Bible's message, however, the adjectives 'infallible,' 'unerring,' 'eternal,' 'inspired,' and 'authoritative' were, and still are, perfectly appropriate.[14]

Neither were conservatives idle in the months before the 1981 Assembly. The editors of *Crossroads* devoted the majority of space in the magazine's Spring 1981 issue to biblical inspiration. Jerry Kolb attributed many of the day's pressing social and political problems to a rejection of biblical authori-

---

12. The newsletter was a publication of the School of Theology's Center for Pastoral Education.

13. Gilbert W. Stafford, "What We Really Mean to Say: A Glossary of Terms," *Centering on Ministry* 6, no. 3 (1981), 3.

14. John V. W. Smith, "The Bible in the Church of God Reformation Movement: A Historical Perspective," *Centering on Ministry* 6, no. 3 (1981), 6.

ty.[15] As far as he was concerned, biblical authority had to be grounded in a doctrine of inerrancy; no other view was adequate. Kolb conceded that not all evangelicals were inerrantists, but he granted little if any legitimacy to the alternatives. In this he followed Harold Lindsell's argument in *The Battle for the Bible.* Leroy Oesch was of one mind with *Crossroads* on the inerrancy issue. In mid-winter he wrote to the General Assembly's Business Committee asking for a resolution on biblical inspiration to be put on the floor before the motion to adopt the World Service budget. That portions of his letter were quoted in *Crossroads* strongly suggests that Oesch and the magazine's editors had come to regard each other as allies. Using the inerrancy issue as a springboard, *Crossroads* editors also fanned the flames of discontent among readers who believed themselves silenced by manipulative leadership. For example, an article reported on the "Dialogue on Internal Unity" held the previous January in Winona Lake, Indiana, at the initiation of Paul Tanner, newly elected executive secretary of the Executive Council. The magazine characterized dialogue participants in the following language: "This group was said to represent a cross-section of the movement philosophically, racially, and geographically. But only <u>eighteen</u> ministers were invited to represent <u>forty-eight states</u> where the Church of God has congregations, while <u>twelve represented Anderson, Indiana</u>. Eleven of the thirty invited were executives of general agencies in Anderson."[16] Gathered around a cluster of issues—at some points moral, at others theological, and still others concerned with polity—conservatives kept alive the protest that had galvanized so many a year earlier. As the convention and Assembly of 1981 approached they were determined to let neither Anderson College nor church leaders off the hook.

Conservative intentions were clear from the very first minutes of the 1981 General Assembly, but college advocates also were prepared. Assembly members approved a motion to amend the agenda by moving the World Service budget consideration to the last item, in other words, following the Anderson College report. The Committee's findings and recommendation were made in the form of a report from the Anderson College trustees, which suggests that the board had been given the Select Committee's findings

---

15. Nearly verbatim, Kolb's list included: homosexuality as an acceptable lifestyle, abortion as a morally valid means of birth control, extra-marital sexual activity as a legitimate fulfillment of a God-given need, communism as a success story, authority as an infringement on the right of self-assertion, the miracles of Jesus as fanciful creations by first century preachers, the words of Jesus as artificial constructions by the early church, and the virgin birth denied. *Crossroads*, Spring 1981, 2.

16. Ibid., 7, magazine's emphasis.

sufficiently in advance to discuss and prepare recommendations. Almost 1,300 delegates then turned their attention to this document. Distributed and read by college trustees, the report was discussed with Board chairperson Ronald Fowler, pastor of Robert Street Church of God in Akron, Ohio, moderating. Conservatives questioned the absence in the report of a plan to combat secular humanism. Of the view that only Christian professors should teach at a Christian college, conservatives also asked whether a Mormon and a Hindu were college faculty members. From the outset it was clear that college advocates were better prepared to defend the institution than had been the case a year earlier. When asked whether a Mormon and a Hindu taught on the faculty, Fowler acknowledged with a simple yes. Also unlike the 1980 debate, pro-college Assembly members spoke in greater numbers from the floor in defense of the human sexuality course, specifically characterizing the course professor's attitude toward homosexuality as redemptive compassion.

The report was structured in five sections, each a reply to charges made in the Open Letter. The report considered: (1) the relationship between the college and the church; (2) the integration of faith and academic subject matter; (3) personnel policies; (4) the relationship between the trustees and the college administration; and (5) the human sexuality course. Conservative critics had repeatedly charged that secular humanism had found a home at Anderson, but the report specifically denied that accusation, explicitly stating that the college approached "the human condition in the light of God's revelation of himself and his will in Jesus Christ."[17] Mention of the word *revelation* opened the topic of biblical authority, perhaps the most critical issue in the entire controversy. The report refused to adopt the language of inerrancy, while it simultaneously affirmed the central authority of the Bible in the Church of God and the college. The theological heritage of the Church God also was invoked in the trustees' refusal to apply a doctrinal test as a condition of faculty appointment. They appealed to the movement's historic opposition to written creeds as a standard that should be followed. However, administrators did revise the college's employment application form to state an intention to employ men and women whose lives "reflected a belief in and commitment to Jesus Christ and the Christian faith as these are interpreted through the historic witness of the Bible and

---

17. Report of the Anderson College Board of Trustees to the General Assembly of the Church of God, June 16, 1981, 7.

the contemporary witness of the Holy Spirit."[18] Concerning the course in human sexuality, college trustees affirmed the decision that had removed LaVern Norris as its professor. However, they refused demands that the textbooks be changed but suggested that a supplemental text with a Christian perspective on sexuality be added to the course reading list.

College president Reardon believed that the bulk of the General Assembly's constituency were theological moderates. Furthermore, he believed that a determined minority had seized control of the 1980 Assembly. Amidst the charges and rumors that had flown throughout the church during that spring and summer it was understandable that moderates would be alarmed. Reardon's belief that these moderates would see things differently in the light of reason was affirmed by actions of the 1981 Assembly. In the first case it overwhelmingly accepted the Anderson College Trustees Report. Secondly, an interesting coalition of liberals and traditional conservatives joined in opposition to a resolution originating among other conservatives.

The trustees' report had included recommendations intended to mollify conservative critics. However, it refused to apply a doctrinal test for faculty appointment. Conservatives seem to have anticipated such a step, for they had placed on the agenda a resolution titled "Biblical Authority in the Life of the Church." If adopted, the resolution would have required church leaders and agency personnel to affirm the doctrine of inerrancy. In essence the resolution called for the imposition of a doctrinal standard or creed on some but not all members of the Church of God community. Recognizing this step as unprecedented in the movement's history and alien to its non-creedalism, conservative pastor O. L. Johnson offered an amendment substituting the word *expectation* for *requirement*. Debate on Johnson's amendment exposed a key difference among conservatives. Those who opposed the amendment and favored required inerrancy language were conservatives influenced by such evangelical voices as Harold Lindsell. Along with others, traditional Church of God conservatives, such as Johnson and Lillie McCutcheon, favored the amendment because the original resolution would bind people to a doctrinal position. Traditional conservatives may have favored the language of inerrancy, but they were unwilling to impose it on the church or any part of it through a statement that smacked of a creed. Thus they joined with moderates and those who could be termed liberals in

---

18. Ibid., 18.

the Assembly to overwhelmingly pass Johnson's substitutions. As amended, the key paragraph of the resolution reads:

> Resolved, that this Assembly state its requirement that governing boards and elected officials, charged with oversight of the operational policies of agencies and the credentials of ministers related to this Assembly, will act responsibly and forthrightly in establishing the central significance of the authority of the Bible and in interpreting and implementing the teachings and directives of the Bible in their respective areas of work of the Church.[19]

Authors of the original resolution opposed its amended form, but it passed by virtually the same margins as the amendment vote and the vote to accept the Anderson College report.

The Open Letter controversy of 1980–81 pushed the Church of God movement in a more clearly conservative direction on theological and socio-political issues throughout most of the 1980s. In a real sense the Church of God movement has always been, in the main, theologically conservative although not fundamentalist. But opponents of any contact with ecumenical Christianity questioned reports from the Commission on Christian Unity more loudly through the eighties. Likewise, critics of the Commission on Social Concerns—often the same people who opposed ecumenism—also continued to question its positions. Perhaps most significantly, under the administration of Robert A. Nicholson, who assumed the presidency in 1983, Anderson College joined the Coalition of Christian Colleges and Universities, a conservative and mostly evangelical group. Following the successive retirements of the Sikh and Mormon faculty members it also became clear that the institution sought to appoint only those who were Christians to the faculty.

Where Do Authority and Control Lie?

The successful motion to move the adoption of the World Service budget to the bottom of the agenda in the 1981 General Assembly also exposed rank-and-file members' growing sense of frustration with national church structures. Many members were increasingly impatient with rules and procedures

---

19. The entire resolution, as adopted, can be found in Barry L. Callen, ed., *Following the Light*, (Anderson, IN: Warner Press, 2000), 203–4.

Edward L. Foggs (1934–), agency executive. In 1988, Foggs succeeded Paul Tanner as executive secretary of the Executive Council. Prior to this appointment, Foggs had served as associate executive secretary, the first person to hold the position newly created in response to criticism of the fact that senior agency executive positions were held exclusively by whites. As executive secretary Foggs presided over the council that called into being the Task Force on Governance and Polity. He retired in 1999.

that at times seemed to block the will of the majority. Some of this frustration arose from misunderstandings about the Assembly's nature and lines of authority in the church. Many members believed that the Assembly should play a more direct role in determining the qualifications of candidates for key national offices. During the decade of the eighties several sessions featured debates over Assembly bylaws and procedures by which business could be brought to the floor.

Leadership transitions signal the possibility of changes in direction, and like most decades the eighties witnessed several changes in national office. In 1981 Paul Tanner succeeded W. E. Reed as executive secretary of the Executive Council, serving until 1988 when he was in turn succeeded by Edward Foggs. That same year Marshall Christensen was elected and ratified as the fifth president of Warner Pacific College. Also in 1981 Doris Dale succeeded Nellie Snowden as executive secretary-treasurer of Women of the Church of God. In the decade of the eighties, the role of speaker on the *Christian Brotherhood Hour* changed four times. It was held by R. Eugene Sterner until 1982, then David Grubbs, followed by Sterner again, and finally Gilbert W. Stafford in 1986.[20] During the fiscal year 1986–87 Donald Courtney died while serving as executive secretary-treasurer of the Board of Christian Education, and Marvin Hartman, president of the Board of Church Extension and Home Missions, also died in office. They were succeeded by Sherrill Hayes and J. Perry Grubbs, respectively. In 1988 Norman Patton took the assignment of president of the Missionary Board following the successive resignations of Donald Johnson and Thomas Pickens. In 1989

20. David Grubbs resigned without completing a full term; Sterner accepted a temporary appointment until a successor could be named.

Donald Noffsinger retired from the presidency of Warner Press and was succeeded by James Edwards, who one year later assumed the same office at Anderson University following the retirement of Robert Nicholson. Perhaps more than other decades, the eighties witnessed frequent leadership transitions.

The positions to which these individuals were elected were not generally considered to be theologically sensitive, and the General Assembly ratified each candidate without major debate. An exception to this trend occurred in 1983 when Anderson College trustees elected Jerry C. Grubbs as the fifth dean of the graduate School of Theology, the movement's only seminary. The election of a seminary dean required ratification by the Assembly, and some members wanted an opportunity to determine for themselves the dean-elect's orthodoxy. Jerry Grubbs was an alumnus of the seminary and returned to his alma mater to teach Christian Education prior to his

election as dean. Grubbs was widely known across the church, having led conferences and workshops in a host of state and national settings. He had a reputation as a progressive thinker at the opposite end of the theological continuum from the Pastors' Fellowship. It was about matters related to this reputation, whether fact or rumor, that some Assembly members wished to question Grubbs from the floor. However, established procedure made no provision for the direct questioning of candidates; such matters were left to search committees and governing boards. Anderson's trustees' election of Grubbs was to be understood as vouchsafing that he had satisfactorily answered a thorough questioning. However, in the climate of the eighties this understanding did not satisfy some conservative members of the Assembly who wanted to determine Grubbs' theological orthodoxy for

Courtesy of Anderson University and Church of God Archives

J. David Grubbs (1935–), minister. A thoughtful and dynamic preacher popular with college students in the 1960s, Grubbs served as pastor of Salem Avenue Church of God, Clayton, Ohio. In 1982, he was elected speaker of the *Christian Brotherhood Hour* radio program, a position he filled until 1986.

themselves.[21] Anderson College trustee chairperson Ronald Fowler, who presented the dean-elect for ratification, was at some pains to defend both candidate and procedure, in the end refusing Assembly members the opportunity to put questions to Grubbs. In the end, he was ratified but by a margin narrower than typical. The episode stands as an illustration of Assembly members' desire to take more direct control of the movement's affairs and their belief that the Assembly as a body had that right.

Assembly and agency procedures may have denied grassroots ministers much control over appointments and elections, but these local leaders could direct congregational giving to the movement's national causes. Beginning with the veiled threat in 1981 (i.e., the motion to move the budget vote to the end of the Assembly agenda, after all agency reports had been received and discussed), a growing tendency developed among congregations to designate their financial support to specific line items or special projects of the World Service budget rather than to support the budget as a whole. The budget was divided into two categories. For fiscal year 1981–82 the primary category, the so-called "basic budget," represented the approved requests of twenty-one agency line items, from the Missionary Board to the World Service staff. However, congregations could also receive World Service credit for contributions designated to special projects or a specific agency line item. For example, the Mass Communications Board requested a special line amounting to slightly more than $211,000 in the 1981–82 budget to fund a one-time television program, *The Doctor Is In*. Individuals or congregations could contribute directly to the "television special" and receive World Service credit for this support, regardless of any contributions they made to the basic budget. For fiscal year 1980–81 total giving to World Service reached a record level of more than $7,047,000. However, the basic budget failed to reach its goal by $135,000. Throughout the eighties there emerged a pattern wherein World Service total giving often achieved record levels yet left the basic budget underfunded. The most striking example occurred in fiscal year 1986–87, when giving exceeded the total goal by more than $290,000 but the basic budget goal was missed by 4 percent, and some agencies were forced to cut programs. The shortfall generated considerable

21. Would-be questioners sought Jerry Grubbs's responses on topics such as biblical inerrancy, the virgin birth, the "literal" resurrection of Jesus, the "literal interpretation" of miracles, and the "literal" existence of Satan. Minutes of the General Assembly, Annual Reports, 1983, 16–17. It should be noted that the topics on which people wished to question the dean-elect closely paralleled some fundamentalist lists of nonnegotiable doctrinal loci. The parallel illustrates the influence of fundamentalism and conservative evangelicalism on an essentially Wesleyan-Pietist group.

discussion in the 1987 General Assembly. Cutting funds and programs of the Missionary Board struck at the heart of the movement's evangelistic concerns. The pattern of shortfalls suggests a growing willingness by some ministers and congregations to direct their giving to lines in the budget they supported while withholding support for the basic budget, thus penalizing national agencies or programs with which they disagreed. Perhaps the most striking illustration of this pattern occurred in a motion from the Assembly floor during discussion of the 1986–87 World Service report. As a means of dealing with the shortfall in the Missionary Board's budget, an Assembly member moved that all the funding for the Commission on Social Concerns be redirected to the Missionary Board.[22] The motion died for lack of a second, but it made a point. Designated giving to the World Service budget was increasingly a tool that grassroots ministers, frustrated by what they felt was a lack of voice, could use to get the attention of church leaders.

Grassroots ministers thus seemed determined to have a voice in national church policy. Throughout the eighties and into the nineties they kept the pressure on agency and commission leaders from the floor of the Assembly with resolutions on a range of social issues of particular concern to conservatives. In 1983 they brought a resolution from the Alabama chapter of Church of God Men calling for support of prayer in public schools and further supporting the efforts of President Reagan and members of Congress to "turn the country back to God."[23] Through several resolutions the General Assembly also expressed its disapproval of the relaxed sexual mores of American society. In 1984 the Assembly adopted the first of several statements on pornography, this one calling on all congregations to actively oppose pornography and obscenity in the media by changes in law. In 1988 the Assembly adopted a resolution calling for more extensive ministry to parents and their adolescent children regarding responsible sexual behavior. In 1993 conservatives brought a more extensive, more strongly worded statement on homosexuality to the Assembly, where it was adopted.[24] In 1987

---

22. Minutes of the General Assembly, Annual Reports, 1987, 18–19.

23. The text of the resolution as adopted appears in Annual Reports, 1983, 25.

24. Among other points the resolution states: (1) "we in the Church of God are committed to biblical holiness and hold in high regard scriptural injunctions related to homosexuality and, therefore, cannot accept, endorse, or condone homosexual behavior". . .; (2) "we are a redemptive body and seek to express love, compassion, and concern for those who struggle with sexual identity or homosexual orientation to assist them in a chaste relationship with Christ". . .; (3) "the General Assembly of the Church of God go on record reaffirming our conviction that, biblically, homosexual behavior is sin . . ." Callen, *Following the Light*, No. 140, 260–61.

the Assembly had adopted a resolution in which it called for the following fiscal year to be one of regular fasting and prayer for a revival in America, because "there is much disorientation about the morality, testimony, and lifestyle of Christians currently being witnessed by the world."[25] The fact that some Christians appreciated rock music or made it easily accessible was a case in point. In 1988, once again during the discussion of the World Service budget, objections were raised to the fact that the box office at Anderson University's Reardon Auditorium was connected to Ticketmaster, an electronic automated purchasing service through which "all sorts of rock groups sell their tickets."[26] Steven Williams, a rising figure in the Pastors' Fellowship, moved to amend the World Service budget motion with the statement "that we are opposed to Ticket Master [sic] being in Reardon Auditorium and ask for the Trustees of Anderson University to sever any and all connection with it."[27] Assembly chairperson Sam Hines noted that Williams' motion was technically a grievance and thus not in keeping with established procedure. However, he allowed the motion to stand, and it passed by a vote of 442–275 with nineteen abstentions. Whether concerning sexual permissiveness, the legality of abortion, prayer and Bible reading in public schools, or rock music, conservatives in the Church of God were determined to state their views and bring action in the General Assembly whereby the church stood on record as opposing these trends.

Conservatives were also disturbed by the association of members of the Commission on Christian Unity with the ecumenical movement, particularly with program units of the National Council of Churches. For several decades individuals and agencies of the Church of God had enjoyed associations with many different National Council committees and boards.[28] Until his death in 1984 John W. V. Smith was a member of the Commission on Faith and Order. He was succeeded by Gilbert Stafford, who continued membership on the commission until his death in 2008.[29] Smith and Marshall Christensen attended meetings of the World Council of Churches in Vancouver, British Columbia. Participants at such meetings were not official representatives of the Church of God. Christensen was the delegated member-observer to the

---

25. The text of the statement can be found in Annual Reports, 1987, 33.

26. Minutes of the General Assembly, Annual Reports, 1988, 19.

27. Richard Bradley seconded the motion. Ibid.

28. For a discussion of this point on the agencies and their associations see Merle D. Strege, *I Saw the Church*, (Anderson: Warner Press, 2002), 299–302.

29. Stafford's seat on the commission was taken over by James Lewis, a professor in the School of Theology and its associate dean.

Vancouver meeting; Smith paid his own way to attend with press credentials. Nevertheless, in 1987 conservatives called for a special committee to investigate into the circumstances of such participation and what endorsement it may imply of the interests and commitments of ecumenical Christianity.

In 1988 the Special Committee on National/World Council Relationships made its report to the General Assembly. That report included a set of guidelines that defined relationships between Church of God agencies and the National or World Councils: (1) the Executive Council, acting as representative of the Church of God was not to join the NCCC; (2) agencies were to enter into relationships only with those interchurch bodies committed to the lordship and divinity of Jesus Christ; (3) relationships with interchurch bodies were to be seen as opportunities to serve and witness to the movement's unique heritage on Christian unity; (4) interchurch relationships were to be severed if they were construed as support for beliefs or actions that violated the doctrinal and ethical commitments of the Church of God; (5) participants in interchurch relationships should make it clear that they function in those relationships by individual or agency choice and do not necessarily speak for the movement; and (6) Church of God agency or staff funds invested in any interchurch relationship were to be limited to the ministries justifying that relationship.[30] Clearly the guidelines limited, even restricted relationships with the conciliar Christian community. Nevertheless, conservatives in the Assembly called for another year of study "to further investigate the claims made which make the NCCC suspect to millions of Americans and that a full report be made . . . as to the strength and fallacy of those allegations." However, the Assembly rejected this call and by a voice vote adopted the committee's report with the stated guidelines. This was a sign that some ministers and laypeople were growing weary of the same voices asking the same questions about the same issues year after year. Authority, decision-making, and relationships between local congregations and ministers continued among the Assembly's major concerns, but other church constituents let it be known that they did not share the conservative agenda.

Point, Counterpoint

Traditional conservatives and others influenced by evangelical and fundamentalist issues changed agendas and demanded answers throughout the

---

30. Minutes of the General Assembly, Annual Reports, 1988.

eighties, but theirs were not the only voices articulating issues and insisting on action. Public issues more often the concern of social and political liberals also found expression in the church. Still within the ranks of the Church of God, but frequently at the opposite end of the social and theological continuum could be found women, ethnic minorities, and ministers with a particular concern for evangelism who insisted that the movement consider issues of importance to them. These men and women may have not spoken as loudly as conservatives, but their presence and voices would not be denied.

Ever since the Soviet Union became an atomic power Americans had lived with the threat of nuclear war. Nuclear disarmament had been the constant desire of some, but the Reagan government's increased military spending prompted a new intensity in calls for disarmament in the early 1980s. A special session of the United Nations addressed the issue. Many Americans, Christians or otherwise, spoke out for an end to the arms race. American Catholic bishops issued a formal paper calling for the same. It was not very surprising, then, that the Church of God Commission on Social Concerns drafted a resolution calling on President Reagan and Soviet Premier Leonid Brezhnev to reject the policy of brinkmanship and reduce their governments' stockpiles of nuclear weapons. The resolution concluded:

> Our deliberate choice is to be faithful to Jesus Christ and his gospel of reconciliation. His purpose for all people is life that is abundant and eternal. To place our trust in weapons of mass murder and destruction is irresponsible and idolatrous. We encourage Church of God people to accept our historical imperative to choose life and to find and support alternatives to the nuclear arms race.[31]

The commission placed the strongly worded resolution on the agenda for the 1982 Assembly. Discussion of the motion revealed deeply divided opinion. Its supporters saw arms reduction as a moral issue threatening the entire planet. Opponents worried that it might be interpreted as going soft on communism. Others were concerned about the issue but felt they could not support the resolution as written. In the end, by a 2-to-1 majority the Assembly voted to "receive as a helpful guide to the individual conscience of the members of the Assembly for their personal and moral decisions

---

31. "Nuclear Arms Reduction: The Choice Is Ours," *Annual Reports*, 1982, 23-24.

and reactions to this world crisis."[32] Thus qualified, the reception—not adoption—of the resolution was victory for liberals, but rather modest in its scope.

As might be expected, the Peace Fellowship of the Church of God strongly supported the nuclear arms reduction resolution. In fact some members of the fellowship sat on the Commission on Social Concerns. But the Peace Fellowship carried on its own program and asserted its concerns with growing confidence through the eighties and beyond. It sponsored an annual set of conferences at the International Convention of the Church of God in Anderson, often bringing to the convention nationally recognized speakers, writers, and scholars such as Ron Sider, Tom Sine, Bernice King, and Mennonite theologian John Howard Yoder. In 1997 peace activists and retired missionaries Maurice and Dondeena Caldwell established the Mack and Irene Caldwell Peacemaking Fund at Anderson University by an initial gift of $10,000. With an original goal of $100,000 the fund was intended to support courses and seminars on conflict resolution and a range of justice and peace issues.[33] The Caldwells were deeply committed to peacemaking and in the next decade could often be seen on Saturday mornings standing near a war memorial in front of Anderson City Hall alongside other protestors of the Iraq war.

It would not be quite accurate to state that women in the Church of God found a voice in the eighties and nineties. Equally with men, women's call to ministry had been accepted and recognized through ordination since the movement's inception. A long list of women have left distinguished marks on Church of God ministry—Lena Shoffner Matthesen, Nora Siens Hunter, Lillie McCutcheon, Irene Smith Caldwell, Ivory and Hattie Downer, Ann Smith, Wilma Perry, Gertrude Little, and E. Marie Strong, to name some of the most familiar. However, it has also been the case that the decades from 1930 to 1970 witnessed a marked decline in the number of women pastors in the movement. That decline, and perhaps one of its causes, is illustrated by the call of a woman to be associate pastor of First Church of God in Vancouver, Washington.

In spring 1980 the Vancouver church began a search for a new associate pastor that led them to Jeannette Flynn, who was to graduate that year from the School of Theology at Anderson College. When Flynn's name was proposed, objections to a woman minister were raised that left older

---

32. Minutes of the General Assembly, Annual Reports, 1982, 20.
33. Maurice Caldwell to Merle Strege, July 12, 2008.

members of the congregation at something of a loss. The senior pastor, Gerald Marvel, was himself a product of his grandmother's spiritual leadership and unsympathetic to objectors. Many of them were unaware that the pastor whose work had laid the foundation for the thriving congregation was none other than Minna Jarrett, the sweet little nonagenarian who sat on the third pew every Sunday morning and evening. More recent members of the congregation, many of them from denominations that refused to ordain women, were unaware of Mrs. Jarrett's years of pastoral service.[34] Their objections to Flynn were rejected by the elder members of the congregation who remembered Sister Jarrett's pastorate with fond appreciation. Their vote carried the day and Flynn was extended a pastoral call, which she accepted.

A significant means of Church of God congregational growth has been the transfer of believers from other church communions. This influx had introduced beliefs as well as people, and in some cases they stand in opposition to established doctrinal practice. The ordination and call of women pastors is a case in point. Furthermore, as fewer women were seen in pastorates the idea of a woman pastor became less imaginable. As mainstream Protestant denominations ordained growing numbers of women, some people in the Church of God associated the ordination of women with theological liberalism. The experience of the Vancouver church again makes the point. First Church of God had a reputation in the community as a "Bible-believing church." Its call to Jeannette Flynn seemed to some the kind of step that liberal churches might take. In point of fact, the congregation and its pastor hewed tightly to their interpretation of the New Testament, and it was this conservative reading that prompted them to call a woman to the pastoral staff. The Vancouver episode notwithstanding, in many segments of the United States the trend was toward less support for women in ministry. In 1985 only two per cent of Church of God pastorates were filled by women. However, late in the decade of Flynn's call, women in the Church of God confronted this situation.

In 1989 several individual women contributed essays to a collection published under the title *Called to Ministry, Empowered to Serve*.[35] Edited by Juanita Evans Leonard, a professor in Anderson's graduate School of

---

34. The influx of individuals unaware of the role that women have played in the Church of God explains, in part, the decline in the number of women pastors in the Church of God.

35. Juanita Evans Leonard, ed., *Called to Ministry, Empowered to Serve* (Anderson, IN: Warner Press, 1989).

Theology, the essays presented a formidable case for women on warrants from biblical exegesis, historical precedent, and theology. The authors came from all walks of life in the movement; professors of New Testament, theology and ethics, and the history of Christianity; missionaries; and pastors were among the contributors. Articles covered the history of women in ministry, examining it in various ethnical contexts as well as in the mainstream American church. Marie Strong and Sharon Pearson put the case for women in ministry on the solid exegetical footing to be expected of two fine scholar-teachers. Strong taught New Testament at Anderson, and Pearson was a professor of biblical studies at Azusa Pacific College. Cheryl Sanders, on the other hand, took the offense in her essay. She was a professor of ethics at Howard University's Divinity School in Washington, DC, and drew on the themes of holiness and unity to call into question the "privileged status of the White male in the Church of God."[36] Taken together, the volume's essays illustrated their authors' determination to reclaim the movement's heritage of women in ministry and make a strong case in its behalf.

Called to Minister, Empowered to Serve was originally prepared for a national Consultation on Women in Mission and Ministry held in 1985. Leonard served as the consultation's convener. Although the consultation did not quickly reverse the trend toward fewer women in ministry, it stimulated a continuing conversation from which emerged additional measures in support of the original consultation's cause. At the turn of the century Church of God Ministries created a Task Force on Women in Ministry. Originally composed of eighteen women, the Task Force met five times between 2001 and 2003. After the first meeting three additional women and twelve men were added to the group. Its mission was to educate and be an advocate for women in ministry in the Church of God and beyond. By the conclusion of its term the Task Force had published a study booklet titled *Go, Preach My Gospel* and sponsored the production of an evocative video by the same title.[37] A member of the Task Force, Randal Huber, proved to be a stalwart advocate of women. Pastor of the Chapel Hill Church of God in York Springs, Pennsylvania, his School of Theology doctoral thesis was published in 2006 by Warner Press under the title, *Called, Equipped, and No Place to Go*. He specifically attacked the problem of placement, and offered creative

---

36. Cheryl Sanders, "Ethics of Holiness and Unity in the Church of God," 142, in Leonard, *Called to Minister, Empowered to Serve*, 131–46.

37. Erin Moss Taylor, ed., *Go Preach My Gospel* (Anderson, IN: Church of God Ministries, 2004).

suggestions, as well as a direct challenge, to area administrators and pastoral search committees aimed at overcoming congregations' reluctance to call a woman to the pastorate. The issue of women in ministry transcended liberal-conservative distinctions, at least where traditional Church of God conservatives were concerned. Their regard for the movement's theological history and McCutcheon's leadership in the Pastors' Fellowship meant that most traditional conservatives believed that God calls both women and men to the ministry without respect to gender.[38]

Along with women's issues and the agenda of the Commission on Social Concerns, evangelism stepped into the spotlight in the latter half of the eighties. Traditionally, the revival had been the movement's dominant evangelistic vehicle. However, some began to discard revivals as an outmoded measure from the previous century. The call for new forms of evangelism grew louder as the decade approached 1990 and ministers took note of an unprecedented decline in aggregate morning attendance in Church of God congregations in the United States and Canada. Although Sunday morning attendance actually declined for the first time, membership continued to grow throughout the decade. From 1980 to 1990 the North American (United States and Canada) constituency of the Church of God grew from 177,700 to 203,200, an increase of more than 13 percent. However, during the same period membership in the Church of God beyond North America grew by 77 percent, from 141,700 to 268,500. For the first time ever, in 1985 the constituency outside North America surpassed that in the United States and Canada. By comparison, the church's North American growth seemed modest. Worse, the growth of the American church had not even kept pace with the general population's growth rate. The lagging growth rate combined with declining attendance on Sunday mornings led to concern on the part of Church of God ministers.

The attendance trend troubled Assembly members, who responded by calling for a new dedication to evangelism. In 1986 the Assembly adopted a two-year church planting project, to begin July 1, 1987. In support of this project the Assembly approved a special funding of $500,000 in the World Service budget. After deducting promotional expenses, 50 percent of the funds were to be used at the discretion of state ministries; the Board of Church Extension was to receive the other half of the funds for the support of church-planting projects and programs that it supervised. By 1988, 106

---

38. For a biography of Lillie McCutcheon, see Barry L. Callen, *She Came Preaching*, (Anderson, IN: Warner Press, 1992).

new congregations had been started, but only $110,000 had been raised in support of the project. Evangelism continued to be a concern of key individuals such as Oral Withrow, a successful pastor and vocal national leader who advocated institutionalizing the effort. Withrow and his wife, Laura, wrote a widely distributed booklet called *Meet Us at the Cross* intended for use as an evangelistic tool and an introduction to the Church of God. His advocacy was a key stimulus in the creation of a national program of evangelism called "Vision-2-Grow." The program, which called for pastoral mentoring in church growth as well as new congregational development, began in 1991 under the direction of the Committee on Long Range Planning. Rolland Daniels became its first director.

The Vison-2-Grow program is an example of the growing influence that the Church Growth movement exerted on Church of God ministers in the late eighties and throughout the nineties. Originated by Donald MacGavran, the Institute of Church Growth was incorporated into the School of World Mission at Fuller Theological Seminary in 1965. One of the chief characteristics of the Church Growth Movement was its pragmatic approach to church planting. It also laid great stress on *measurable* results. A church planter widely regarded as among the most successful was Bill Hybels, founding pastor of Willow Creek Community Church, which opened in 1975 in suburban Chicago. Willow Creek has frequently been named the most influential church in the United States, and that influence certainly extended to the Church of God.[39] Willow Creek and others in the Church Growth Movement tended to downplay doctrinal distinctions in favor of pragmatic approaches to attracting the unchurched. Such techniques might include removing the cross from the exterior of a church building, replacing organs with more contemporary musical instruments, dropping the use of hymnals in favor of contemporary praise choruses projected on screen, or eschewing a denominational title in favor of "Community Church." The techniques and vocabulary of this pragmatic approach were adopted by a segment of Church of God ministers in the decade of the eighties.

One of the most successful Church of God applications of Church Growth techniques occurred on the south edge of Phoenix, Arizona, where Robin Wood planted a congregation that came to be known as Mountain Park Community Church. Wood was a relentless bundle of energy who quickly formed relationships with a host of people across the Phoenix area.

---

39. Shortly after the turn of the twenty-first century, Bill Hybels was invited to speak in one of the general services at the North American Convention of the Church of God.

His intention from the outset was to reach the lost and build up a congregation of the newly saved. As the congregation grew, it attracted the interest of members of other churches in the community, but Wood often discouraged such folk from affiliating with his congregation. Founded in 1987, by the end of its first decade the Mountain Park congregation had grown to a morning attendance of more than nine hundred. People were attracted to the professional quality of contemporary music and the frequent use of drama as elements of worship. The congregation also proved to be very generous in its support of missionary projects in Latin America and the city of Phoenix, and of its young people who enrolled at Church of God colleges. This was particularly true of those who elected to attend Anderson University, where Wood was a trustee. Yet Wood also realized that a large segment of those who attended on Sunday mornings were not part of a group he came to call "The Community of Faith at Mountain Park." Although listed in the *Yearbook of the Church of God*, the congregation had few people, even lay leaders, who knew much about its connection with the movement's national work or its doctrinal tradition or history.

The approach that created Mountain Park and other similar congregations troubled traditional conservatives in the Church of God even as it was enthusiastically embraced by others. Conservatives had formed the Pastors' Fellowship in order to lift up doctrinal themes they believed were languishing. Now a successful evangelism strategy was being employed to raise up new congregations ostensibly as part of the Church of God reformation movement, but at the apparent price of minimizing, if not suppressing, the very heritage that the Pastors' Fellowship sought to recover and emphasize.

Growing Pains in Missions and the International Church[40]

In the 1980s "partnership" became the watchword for missions and the Church of God outside North America. Donald Johnson, Executive Secretary of the Missionary Board from 1975 to 1985 believed that genuine partnership between the North American church and national churches was absolutely crucial. He found a strong theological ally in Douglas Welch,

---

40. My discussion in this section is deeply indebted to Cheryl Johnson Barton and Donald D. Johnson, who generously permitted me to read the prepublication manuscript of *Into All the World* (Anderson, IN: Warner Press, 2009), their revised and enlarged edition of Lester A. Crose's *Passport for a Reformation*, (Anderson, IN: Warner Press, 1981).

a veteran missionary in Kenya and after 1978 professor of missiology at Anderson College's School of Theology. On the eve of the centennial celebration each man wrote a paper suggesting new structures in the national churches that would prompt stronger partnerships with the North American church. For example, they suggested that rather than relying on the North American church's Missionary Board, the national churches should develop their own sending agencies. This idea and others were the subject of earnest conversations during the World Forum that met in Anderson prior to the 1980 International Convention.

The encouragement to develop national church structures led to several new regional and international agencies throughout the decade. Thus, for example, in 1980 the Caribbean-Atlantic Assembly was formed and a year later appointed Victor Babb as part-time regional director; five years later the position was expanded to full time. Also in 1980 Latin American church leaders assembled for the Inter-American Conference, a meeting that in the opinion of Maurice Caldwell was a major unifying force in the Church of God in Central and South America. Asian church leaders met in Taipei, Taiwan, in November 1982 for the first in a series of meetings that led to the formation of the Asia-Pacific Church of God Conference. In 1984 Fouad Melki founded Mediterranean Bible College in Beirut, Lebanon. Gifted and in many cases well-educated national leaders were crucial to the emerging partnership. Carlton and Theodosia Cumberbatch in the Caribbean, Kozo Konno in Japan, Byrum Makokha in Kenya, Asim Das in India, the aforementioned Melki in Lebanon and others proved to be effective national church leaders who could make genuine partnership work. The extent of such partnerships was strikingly exemplified in Meghalaya, India.

Meghalaya was home to Borman Roy Sohkhia, Leaderwell Pohsngap, and Leaderwell's wife, Rivulet. Sohkhia studied at the School of Theology in Anderson in the late 1970s, and after earning a graduate degree returned to India. In 1980 he was a key organizer of the Missions Committee of the Church of God in Meghalaya. In this capacity Sohkhia approached the Pohsngaps about taking an assignment to teach at the Church of God pastoral training school in Kenya, Kima Theological College, and in 1981 they moved to Kima to take up this work. The Pohsngaps' presence in Kenya was the product of a joint venture of the Church of God in India and the Missionary Board in the United States. Three years after moving to Kenya the Pohsngaps moved to Kentucky in order to pursue further graduate study at Asbury Theological Seminary. Following study there they returned to Meghalaya, where Leaderwell became the founding president of Nichols-Roy Bible College. He later served two terms as president of Union Biblical Seminary and also sat on the national and international boards of World Vision. In 1983 the Meghalayan church sent another native-born couple, Amos and Semper Moore, to Nepal, a very dangerous assignment given that Hindu country's restrictions on Christian conversion. Unlike the Pohsngaps' assignment in Kenya, the mission to Nepal originally received no financial assistance from the American Missionary Board. However in 1984 the Church of God in Japan began some financial support of the Nepal project. These examples of missionary partnership depended not only on a willingness to partner, but also on the presence of dedicated, gifted, and well-educated national church leaders such as Soh5khia, the Pohsngaps, and the Moores.

Halfway around the world another example of the growing trend toward global partnership in missions developed in a set of relationships that produced a Russian language version of the *Christian Brotherhood Hour*. The key individual in these relationships was Walentin Schüle, born to German parents living in the Soviet republic of Kazakhstan. Decades before the Bolshevik Revolution migrations of ethnic Germans established large settlements deep in Russia as well as in borderlands like Wollenia. As the message of the Church of God reached Germany in the early twentieth century it was only to be expected that German converts would carry the message of holiness and unity to their friends and relatives in these German colonies. Schüle's family had been among the first generation of German Church of God immigrants to the Russian Caucasus. After experiencing conversion himself, the adolescent Walentin began translating German sermons into Russian for the spiritual benefit of his neighbors.

As an adult Schüle and his wife Irma moved to West Germany in 1974, where he founded a Church of God congregation dedicated to ministering to repatriated Germans such as himself. The Russian people remained his spiritual burden, however, so he founded a Russian language radio program beamed by short wave radio deep into his former homeland. Through his efforts *CBH-Russian*, known in the Soviet Union as *The Voice of the Gospel*, went on the air in the summer of 1984. Congregations in Kalamazoo, Michigan, and Fort Wayne, Indiana,[41] financed production costs, and the

---

41. Westwood Church of God and Sherman Street Church of God, respectively.

Women of the Church of God gave the program $10,000 to expand the range of its broadcasts. Although the American Missionary Board was not directly involved in these developments, Cheryl Johnson Barton and Donald D. Johnson assert in their history of Church of God missions that *CBH-Russian* prepared the environment for "a significant evangelistic thrust from the [Missionary] Board into Russia during the next decade after the fall of the Berlin Wall in 1990 and the breakup of the Soviet Union in 1991."[42]

Enterprises such as the Meghalayan mission and *CBH-Russian* illustrated the growing pattern of partnerships among Church of God congregations around the world. Characteristic of these partnerships was a larger role for so-called national churches and a smaller role for the original sending church in the United States and Canada. The move to partnerships approximating equal roles did not happen without some stresses and strains. The seventh World Conference of the Church of God convened in Nairobi, Kenya, on August 11–14, 1987. Edward Foggs, then associate secretary of the Executive Council, told the assembled delegates, "If we do not understand we are partners, if we do not act as partners, we are without justification for claiming that we are the body of Christ."[43] Ironically, Fogg's comments were delivered in the context of a Kenyan national church that had an uneasy partnership with the Missionary Board. In a real sense missionaries bore the real burden of defining partnership as they worked within a set of several relationships—the Missionary Board, their sending churches, and the national churches to which missionaries were sent. Missionaries sometimes chafed within this set of relationships, as in the case of Kenya in the late seventies and into the eighties.

Money was one important index of the strength of global partnership in missions. Was the Missionary Board willing to put budgeted funds directly in the hands of the national churches, or would the Board insist on budgetary oversight by missionaries in the field? Answers to those questions were partially responsible for straining the Board's relationship with the Kenyan national church. Missionaries in East Africa criticized the Kenyan church for a lack of accountability in its use of monies disbursed by the Missionary Board. After meetings between Johnson and Byrum Makokha, the leader of the Kenyan church, a new budgeting system was subsequently introduced to the national church in Kenya. Furthermore, in fiscal year 1980–81 George Buck, a missionary in East Africa, was assigned by the

---

42. Crose, Barton, and Johnson, *Into All the World*, 219.
43. Quoted in ibid., 225.

Board to the role of administrative assistant to the secretaries of the Kenyan General Assembly; part of Buck's assignment included responsibility for the Assembly's financial administration. The Board's action did not sit well with the Kenyan national church, which demanded the suspension of missionary staff meetings in the belief that missionaries were acting too independently of the Kenyan church.[44] The situation had reached a crisis stage when Johnson and the Board solicited the consultation of Paul Dietterich, director of the Center for Parish Development in Naperville, Illinois.

Dietterich's consultation helped create a review process that was in place by 1982. However, in the course of this review, it had also become apparent to the Board that its staff was too small to oversee a program of global missions. By 1985 the supervisory staff had been enlarged to six individuals, in addition to Johnson and his associate Oral Withrow. Associate secretaries with responsibilities for Africa and Latin America remained in Anderson for the time being. The enlarged staff meant that some of Johnson's oversight responsibilities could be shared, which resulted in improved relationships between the Board and field missionaries, the Board and national churches and their leadership, and between missionaries and national churches.

Committees and Colleges

Changes in the intellectual life of the Church of God were expressed in its academic institutions and also in the work of a special study committee appointed in the theological aftermath of the Open Letter controversy. The letter's concern for doctrinal standards resulted in a call for the Assembly to consider the practice of *glossolalia* or speaking in tongues. Two of the movement's colleges faced serious financial challenges during the decade of the eighties. Anderson College had to deal with the ramifications of the Open Letter and the subsequent report of its trustees. Throughout the decade, each of the church's schools experienced at least one and sometimes more presidential transitions.

In 1985 the Ohio General Assembly brought a resolution to the General Assembly requesting the formation of a committee to study the doctrine of the Holy Spirit with particular reference to the practice of speaking in tongues, a practice closely identified with Pentecostalism. After the Azusa Street revival in 1906 and consequent birth of Pentecostalism it was

---

44. Ibid., 226.

not always easy to demarcate holiness and Pentecostal worship services; in fact, distinctions between the two movements were often blurred. Early Church of God worship sometimes included speaking in tongues, but in other instances the practice was discouraged or strictly controlled.[45] One implication of this close historic connection was the practice, sometimes welcome but more often not, of speaking in tongues in some contemporary Church of God congregations. Because the phenomenon was sometimes claimed as necessary evidence of the gift of the Holy Spirit, the potential for divisiveness was present and in some cases realized. Concern for the potentially disruptive effects of glossolalia in congregational life led to the Ohio Assembly's resolution, which was referred to the Executive Council.

The Council appointed a steering committee that recommended the membership of the study committee, assigned research projects to several of its members, and designed a process for the discussion of issues. Steering committee members included Ronald Fowler, Leonard Snyder, W. E. Reed, and Paul Tanner. Barry Callen was appointed to the committee following Reed's death, and Sherrill Hayes was invited both to join the committee and serve as coordinator and facilitator of the study committee's discussions. The Board of Directors of the Executive Council determined the study committee's membership.[46] During the first half of 1986 the committee met twice, in January and May, and in the second meeting completed a report that went to the General Assembly the following June. The report noted differences in attitudes toward glossolalia across the movement, from complete avoidance to cautious permission to a welcome endorsement as with any other spiritual gift. However, the committee also observed that "to the degree the Church of God movement has functioned with a 'consensus theology,' speaking in tongues in the classic pentecostal sense has *not* been part of that generally agreed upon and proclaimed consensus."[47] The study committee was not in complete agreement within itself on the issue. Committee members disagreed on the exegesis of key New Testament texts as well as whether all glossolalia should be regarded as counterfeit.

---

45. For a historical discussion of glossolalia in the Church of God see Merle D. Strege, *I Saw the Church: The Life of the Church of God Told Theologically*, (Anderson: Warner Press, 2002), 121–31.

46. Members included: John E. Boedecker, Barry L. Callen, Milo L. Chapman, John W. Conley, Edward L. Foggs, Ronald J. Fowler, Sherrill D. Hayes, Keith E. Huttenlocker, Donald D. Johnson, Ernie R. Lopez, Lillie S. McCutcheon, Arlo F. Newell, Leonard W. Snyder, Gilbert W. Stafford, Merle D. Strege, Paul A. Tanner, and Lawrence P. Wyatt.

47. Report of the Study Committee on Glossolalia, June 18, 1986, 4.

Despite significant disagreements, Hayes' skilled facilitation of the sessions helped the committee identify significant areas of accord. Many members also attributed this accord to the work of the Spirit himself. Among the areas of agreement were that: (1) the believer's quest for the infilling of the Holy Spirit and a holy life is to be encouraged; (2) the gifts of the Spirit are to be understood as primarily intended for service in and to the church that it might be strengthened and made more effective in its mission; (3) a life of love, not glossolalia, is the essential evidence of the infilling of the Holy Spirit; and (4) which gift, or the number of gifts, are not factors in a person's salvation or sanctification.[48] The committee also qualified the conditions under which the practice of glossolalia was to be accepted by the church. They urged appropriate bodies to credential only those candidates for licensure or ordination who "by belief and practice" live within the stated guidelines. However, the committee noted that while its own report was appropriate for the North American church, churches in other regions possessed different understandings and practices.[49] When the committee's report was read to the General Assembly the following June, the Assembly voted unanimously to receive the report and recommended that it be published in *Vital Christianity* and made available to the church at large.[50] It was extraordinary that the Assembly acted with unanimity on a topic of such potential divisiveness during an era when virtually all official statements were meticulously scrutinized.

In 1980 Gulf-Coast Bible College (GBC) resided in Houston, Texas, the city where it had been founded. John Conley, a former pastor, had succeeded the school's founding president, Max R. Gaulke. Conley dreamed of the day when GBC could leave its problematic location in Houston for a more attractive setting. In 1980 he sought the sale of the campus, but high interest rates and a sluggish economy frustrated his plans. The sale of the Houston campus remained a persistent problem for Conley. By 1986 he could wait no longer. Despite the fact that the Houston campus had not sold, he moved the college to Oklahoma City, where it was renamed Mid-America Bible College. The move precipitated a financial crisis that was partially resolved only when Church of God World Service agreed to sponsor the "Giant Leap Campaign," which earmarked $300,000 in special giving for Mid-America. In fact, the campaign generated nearly $400,000, to which

---

48. Ibid., 5.
49. Ibid., 8.
50. Minutes of the 1986 General Assembly, 26.

the Women of the Church of God gave an additional $50,000.[51] Mid-America weathered the crisis and achieved the unique status of dual accreditation by the National Association of Bible Colleges and the North Central Association of Secondary Schools and Colleges. The college's teacher education program was also certified by the Oklahoma Department of Education. Conley resigned the Mid-America presidency in 1989. Forrest Robinson, a pastor from Sikeston, Missouri, and a college trustee was appointed interim president. Robinson was eventually elected as Mid-America's third president and served in that capacity until 1999, when he was succeeded by John Fozard.

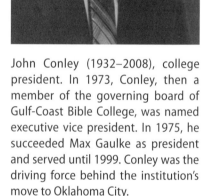

John Conley (1932–2008), college president. In 1973, Conley, then a member of the governing board of Gulf-Coast Bible College, was named executive vice president. In 1975, he succeeded Max Gaulke as president and served until 1999. Conley was the driving force behind the institution's move to Oklahoma City.

Another of the movement's colleges also experienced leadership transitions and financial challenges during the eighties. In 1987 Warner Pacific College (WPC) celebrated the fiftieth anniversary of its founding. Marshall Christensen, formerly a professor of history and vice-president for academic affairs had succeeded the avuncular Milo L. Chapman as WPC's president in 1981. A former Fulbright Scholar, Christensen was widely respected by the Warner Pacific community as a scholar-teacher. In the mid-seventies, along with friend and colleague Arthur Kelly, he had developed an innovative general studies program that won a major grant from the Lilly Endowment, virtually the first award of its kind for the school. Chapman's stature in the church and Christensen's strong work ethic restored a measure of stability to Warner Pacific in the wake of the turmoil surrounding the resignation of E. Joe Gilliam in the late seventies.

---

51. The gifts did not completely resolve Mid-America's financial problems. In fiscal year 1988-89 the Executive Council used the leverage gained by the campaign to aid Mid-America, at the time under threat of foreclosure, in negotiations that restructured its indebtedness on much more favorable terms.

Marshall K. Christensen (1941–), educator. Christensen joined the Warner Pacific College faculty in 1966. In 1975, he was appointed vice-president for academic affairs and served in that capacity until 1978. He was elected president in 1981, a post he held until 1996. A Fulbright Scholar, Christensen was the most able academic to hold the presidency at any Church of God institution of higher education.

Gilliam had wanted the college to be respected in the wider community. He courted the support of political and civic leaders such as Edith Green, representative of Oregon's third congressional district, and U.S. Senator Mark Hatfield. Toward this end Gilliam scored a remarkable coup when President Gerald Ford delivered Warner Pacific's commencement address in 1976. Gilliam also secured a multimillion dollar donation that created the Visbeck-Lee trust, and with that as a future addition to its endowment Warner Pacific's future looked bright. The challenge before the school was to survive until the dawn of a happier day. However, while Gilliam sought wider recognition for Warner Pacific, its relationship with the Church of God was left somewhat unattended.

Christensen worked hard to restore that relationship and sought measures to stabilize institutional finances. During his tenure, Warner Pacific entered a formal agreement with GEOS Language Corporation, a Japanese firm specializing in teaching English as a second language. In exchange for sizeable loans to the college, GEOS acquired in WPC an affiliated English-language campus and a strong interest in the institution. The arrangement eventually became little more than a financial relationship that enabled the college to negotiate a particularly difficult period, but by the end of the eighties Executive Secretary Edward Foggs found himself and the Executive Council once again involved in shoring up Warner's financial situation. Financial problems plagued the school through Christensen's tenure and were instrumental in the college being placed on probationary status by the Northwest Association of Schools and Colleges. Financial issues dogged Christensen's administration until his resignation in 1996, and they obscured a noteworthy legacy as a president at home with and among academics, one who strengthened the school's academic standing. Despite financial challenges Christensen pushed forward important upgrades of Linn Library and led the way to connecting the school to the Internet. More controversial, however, was his decision to eliminate the college's intercollegiate athletic program. Schlatter Chapel, a small chapel and multipurpose building, was constructed during Christensen's tenure.

In 1983, after a twenty-five year presidency at Anderson College, Robert Reardon retired. He was succeeded by long-time friend and close working associate Robert A. Nicholson. Only a few years Reardon's junior, it was widely believed that Nicholson's tenure would not be long. In fact he remained in office until 1990, when he was succeeded by James Edwards. Until assuming the presidency Nicholson had served as dean at Anderson since 1958. Educated in Anderson's liberal arts curriculum, he nonetheless possessed an engineer's concern for precision and orderliness. At his encouragement the institution changed its name to Anderson University in 1987. The change reflected an increasing diversity of programs and the growing professionalization of the curriculum. During Nicholson's tenure, for example, the institution began offering a graduate business degree in addition to the degrees offered in the graduate School of Theology. Also during Nicholson's administration Anderson University joined the Coalition of Christian Colleges and Universities,[52] and he formed a personal friendship with its president, Myron Augsburger. The Coalition gathered together institutions that were mainly evangelical in theological orientation, and its membership in this association signaled a shift at Anderson. From the sixties through much of the seventies a number of social and political liberals

Robert A. Nicholson (1923–), educator. After one semester and a summer of graduate study, at age twenty-one Nicholson joined the faculty of Anderson College as an instructor in music. Founder of the Anderson College Chorale, in 1958 he became dean of the college and then president in 1983 until retirement in 1990. Nicholson also chaired the Commission on Christian Higher Education (1963–68, 1983–84).

52. The organization later changed its name to the current Council of Christian Colleges and Universities.

had visited Anderson College; Jesse Jackson was perhaps the most widely-known of these individuals, who typically spoke in college chapel. Perhaps the most significant outcome of the college's membership in the Coalition was that such invitations became a thing of the past. A shift toward a more conservative stance was one consequence of the Open Letter controversy.

The younger of the two colleges whose names memorialize D. S. Warner, Warner Southern College, also experienced a presidential transition in the eighties. In 1989 Leroy Fulton, the school's founding president retired. Gregory Hall chaired the presidential search committee, whose search led them to Hall. Throughout the decade Warner Southern continued to grow and expand its programs, but it remained outside the family of general agencies and on its own financially; without agency status, Warner Southern did not have a line item in the World Service budget.

Reinvigorating an Old Polity or Envisioning a New?

In 1987 the Executive Council created a Task Force on Governance and Polity for a term of three to five years.[53] After the General Assembly approved this action Robert Nicholson chaired the task force from its inception until 1992. It had come into being as a result of Executive Council discussions about the disconnect between local pastors and congregations and the national church offices. Formally stated, the purpose of the Task Force was ". . . to undertake a wide-ranging analysis of present governance and polity traditions, assumptions, structures, and relationships; to develop recommendations for enhancing the effectiveness of governance and polity—local, state, and national—to the end that mission and ministry are strengthened."[54] Early on the Task Force held regional forums where pastors were invited to share their perceptions about issues of vital importance to the movement. The concern repeatedly identified across the United States was pastors' belief that the work of the national agencies was in disarray if not dysfunctional. This concern also expressed the climate of suspicion that was manifestly evident in the General Assembly in the wake

---

53. Members were Robert Nicholson, chair; Sherrill Hayes, vice-chair; Gerald Nevitt, secretary; Edward Foggs, Executive Council; Wayne Anderson; Merv Bennett; Milo Chapman; James Coe; Robert Culp; Gilbert Davila; Ronald Fowler; Samuel Hines; Keith Huttenlocker; O. L. Johnson; Betty Lewis; Maxine McCall; Arlo Newell; Jordan Smith; and Gilbert Stafford. Additionally, George Blough served on the Task Force until his death, and Ben Chandler and Robert Lawrence served until their respective resignations after four years of service.

54. Report of the Task Force on Governance and Polity, Annual Reports, 1989, 58.

of the Open Letter controversy.[55] The Task Force believed that polity issues also affected the life of local congregations and state ministries, but local ministers repeatedly identified the national agencies as the arena where the largest problems existed. Consequently the Task Force devoted the bulk of its attention to finding or developing means of making the national work more efficient and strengthening communication between the grassroots church and the national agencies.

After its first year of work the Task Force made several affirmations. Among these it noted that no biblical mandate exists for any specific form of polity over others and that in fact all forms can be found in the Church of God around the world. Although some attention was given to state work, the bulk of the Task Force's affirmations concerned the role of the movement's national ministries. It asserted that "much work" needed to be done at that level to clarify the roles and relationship of the national agencies, Executive Council, and General Assembly. The debates of the previous decade had served to illustrate widespread confusion concerning this aspect of the work of the Church of God. The Task Force also affirmed a need for closer working relationships between state and national offices and that "throughout the movement and at every level, we must work to strengthen trust and communication."[56]

By the conclusion of the third year of its work the Task Force had reached some preliminary conclusions about the national work of the Church of God. Three of these conclusions eventually shaped the Task Force's final recommendations. First, the Task Force addressed the persistent confusion about the nature and role of the General Assembly, reminding Assembly members that by its own bylaws it functioned as a "temporary presbytery in the conduct of the business of the Church of God." The Task Force concluded that the Assembly's "real strength would appear to be more as a consultative than a legislative body."[57] Secondly, Task Force members sought a more balanced geographical representation in the national work. For many years it had been the case that the states west of the Mississippi were underrepresented in the Assembly, and this was particularly true of California, Oregon, Washington, and Alaska. At the same time, however, it was also the case that during the decade of the eighties one or more of these states was disproportionately overrepresented on the various trustee

---

55. Robert A. Nicholson to the author, April 8, 2008.
56. Report of the Task Force on Governance and Polity, Annual Reports, 1989, 58.
57. Report of the Task Force on Governance and Polity, Annual Reports, 1990, 67

boards of the national agencies. Thirdly, the Task Force had concluded that the Executive Council's work was largely procedural in nature and that the Council itself was not constituted to address major issues confronting the national church or develop and assess goals for the entire movement. By 1990 the Task Force was considering a new model through which the corporate work of the Church of God might be more centralized and directed. Whatever its final shape, the new model would need to address several issues: (1) a larger, more geographically diverse body than the Executive Council, (2) an increase in the number of state-based ministers, one that included more area administrators and laypeople, and (3) a stronger body than the Executive Council. Along with these three concerns the Task Force hoped that the new model would meet twice a year rather than the old Executive Council pattern of one annual meeting and that meetings be conducted more toward the goal of achieving mission-oriented goals than hearing annual reports and amending the manual of operations.

In 1992 the Task Force brought a series of resolutions to the General Assembly in its final report. Along the way, the Task Force had made some interesting and prescient observations about the paradoxical nature of the movement and its way of being together. For example, the Task Force noted a desire for better national processes but a reluctance to accept more structure or connections; a jealous regard for local congregational autonomy but a desire for greater accountability to the whole body; and both a desire for and yet distrust of strong leadership.[58] Nobody could accuse the members of the Task Force of being out of touch. Their observations of some of the movement's paradoxical attitudes were insightful, to the point, and clarified the challenge confronting those who sought change across the length and breadth of the Church of God movement. To address problems of polity and other issues the Task Force recommended the adoption of nine resolutions on matters ranging from congregational mission statements to a study of the possibility of holding the convention at some location outside Indiana, to the establishment of a triennial visioning conference on mission and ministry to the reorganization of the various boards and agencies of the national work of the Church of God.[59] After presentation to the 1992 Assembly an attempt was made to delay adoption and any implementation of the resolutions for one year, but the Assembly was ready to act and

---

58. Report of the Task Force on Governance and Polity, Annual Reports, 1990, 64.
59. The full text of the final report and all nine resolutions can be found in Annual Reports, 1992, 33–57.

resoundingly defeated the delaying tactic.[60] Considering each resolution separately, the Assembly adopted eight of the nine recommendations; only the resolution calling for a triennial visioning conference failed to be approved. In addition to the nine resolutions the Task Force also suggested a time line for implementation between 1992 and 2000. It called first for new efforts at collaboration between and among the various national boards and agencies. The Task Force also envisioned the creation of a unified board of mission and ministry and asked that the period from 1992 to 1994 be devoted to movement-wide discussions about that idea. Following those discussions and any structural changes growing out of them, the Task Force called for a transitional period for any dissolution of existing structures and the creation of their successors in the new, unified model to conclude by 2000.

The adoption in principle of the final report of the Task Force on Governance and Polity brought to a close a fractious period in the history of the Church of God movement. The period had begun with a conservative challenge to the direction it perceived was being taken by the movement's oldest and largest academic institution. Articulated in language broader than traditional Church of God conservatism, the challenge illustrated the growing influence of American evangelicalism and even fundamentalism on elements of the movement's ministry and laity. Part of that challenge also included an insistence on the part of the grassroots church that it be heard and its concerns taken seriously by national leadership. These insistent voices were by no means the only ones to speak up during this period. Women and African Americans also called for attention to be given to their concerns. Many ministers adopted the new measures of the Church Growth movement in place of traditional revivals as the means of evangelism. The international Church of God experienced unprecedented growth, and after 1985 could claim more adherents than the sending churches of North America. Leadership in the Church of God outside North America was maturing at a pace that in some sense made obsolete the very idea of a "sending church." It was also an era when some of the movement's educational institutions faced serious problems and overcame challenges to their health while others prospered and one aspired to the status of "university." Most periods of comparable length will witness some degree of leadership change. But from 1980 to 1992 leadership transitions in the Church of God

---

60. The motion (Richard Bradley/Earl Wheatley) was defeated, 325–521.

were unusually frequent and represented a passing of the baton from an entire generation to another. In a real sense, the work of the Task Force on Governance and Polity was the final gift of the passing generation of leadership to its children. It remained to be seen how they would implement it.

19

AT A CROSSROADS
(1993–2006)

Across North America and around the world people anticipated the arrival of the year 2000 with a mixture of hopefulness and technological dread. Any New Year's Day typically engenders hope for a better future; the arrival of a new century and indeed a new millennium gave birth to even greater expectations and a sense of change. The term *millennium* also gave its name to a rising generation with aspirations very different from those of their baby-boomer parents.[1] On the other hand, people who believe that the end of time must occur in a year that ends in double zero speculated aloud that the year 2000 must certainly usher in the Last Day. A technological twist was added to these apocalyptic worries in widespread warnings that "Y2K" (Year 2000) threatened to shut down systems that depended on computers programmed with calendars limited to the twentieth century.

In the year 2000 Warner Press published a slender volume by Gilbert W. Stafford, professor of systematic theology at Anderson University's School of Theology, titled *Church of God at the Crossroads*. The book attracted a degree of attention disproportionate to its size, generating discussion across the United States. Stafford was the senior member of the seminary faculty. Prior to his appointment there he had served as senior pastor at East Ashman Church of God in Midland, Michigan, for several years. He had also served for ten years as speaker on the *Christian Brotherhood Hour*. Widely respected across the church, he touched a nerve in this book, which spotlighted troublesome issues. Throughout the Church of God, people felt that the movement was at a crossroads. That sense of being at a pivotal point in the movement's history characterizes the period 1993 to 2006.

---

1. The term *millennial* was applied to the generation born between 1982 and 2003. According to some, millennials represent a more civic-minded approach to politics than their idealist boomer parents.

Reorganization

During the period from 1992 to 2000 local, state, and national leaders of the movement worked at the task of reorganization. The General Assembly had adopted all but one of the proposals made by the Task Force on Governance and Polity. Adoption was fairly simple compared to the discussions, implementation, and legal steps necessary to bring about the most sweeping reorganization of national structures in half a century. Not since the expansion of the Executive Council in the 1950s had the national boards undergone such change. In both instances restructuring occurred as the result of perceptions that more efficient procedures combined with stronger and broader lines of communication would lead to more effective ministry. Although the adoption in principle of the Task Force report committed the movement to structural change, the precise form that change might take had not yet been determined in 1992.

To help movement leaders envision the shape of a reorganized structure the renamed Leadership Council (formerly the Executive Council) retained the services of Dr. Leith Anderson. Pastor of Wooddale Church in Eden Prairie, Minnesota, Anderson was a national leader and consultant in evangelical circles. He thought that reorganization along the lines of his recommendations would lead to a certain degree of downsizing and help the Church of God—in his view now a denomination—recapture some of its former characteristics as a movement.[2] By 1996 initial work had been completed and a report with Anderson's recommendations made to the General Assembly

Courtesy of Anderson University and Church of God Archives

Gilbert W. Stafford (1938–2008), preacher and educator. Stafford left a successful pastorate in Midland, Michigan, to become professor of systematic theology at Anderson University School of Theology. Admired and popular with seminarians, Stafford was also a respected preacher who served as speaker of the *Christian Brotherhood Hour* from 1986 to 1996. Strongly committed to Christian unity, Stafford succeeded John W. V. Smith on the Commission on Faith and Order of the National Council of Churches.

---

2. Minutes of the General Assembly, Annual Reports, 1996, 18.

that June.[3] Still not precisely certain of the changes that might follow from the report, Leadership Council President Merv Bennett moved that the Assembly approve the recommendations in concept and that a task force by appointed to implement them. Clearly, the vagueness of the phrase "in concept" worried some Assembly members. In response to this uneasiness General Secretary Edward Foggs[4] outlined principles that would guide change. First, the intent of any change was to enhance the service of the national agencies to local congregations. Second, the General Assembly's central governing role was affirmed. Third, the Leadership Council or its successor would become a single board responsible for executing the movement's business. Fourth, current ministry boards could anticipate being combined into two or three major divisions.[5]

Speaking mainly for an older generation of ministers and leaders, Robert Reardon observed that Anderson's recommendations concentrated power.[6] In addition to the Leadership Council, under the current structure the affairs of the movement were the responsibility of no fewer than ten general agencies, three commissions and two divisions. Anderson's recommendations would reduce the number of key executives, in effect pushing broad participation vertically. To Reardon and others the vertical organization of power seemed an odd means of broadening participation and improving communications with the grassroots church. In opposition to Reardon's views, soon-to-be-elected *CBH* speaker James Lyon, pastor of North Anderson Church of God, offered the opinion that the old structure was breaking down and that immediate change was necessary.[7] In the end more than 90 percent of the Assembly members agreed with Lyon, and Bennett's motion passed.

The debate on structural reorganization overshadowed a motion from Anderson University as well as changes in Assembly membership and procedures. The relatively easy passage of these measures and the adoption of the Bennett motion indicated a noticeable change in the Assembly's attitude. That change was born out further in 1997 with the comparatively easy adoption of the Implementation Task Force report. In contrast to its attitude during much of the eighties, the General Assembly seemed no

---

3. The report was titled, "Movement for the 21st Century."
4. In 1993 Foggs' title had been changed from executive secretary to general secretary.
5. Minutes of the General Assembly, Annual Reports, 1996, 18.
6. Ibid.
7. Ibid.

longer interested in closely scrutinizing agenda items. In 1996 several measures passed on voice votes with comparatively little discussion. Absentee balloting for national church offices, expanded lay membership in the Assembly, and a statement limiting the meaning of Assembly ratifications were among the measures that passed. Given that issues such as lay Assembly participation had a rather lengthy history of discussion but no action, the Assembly's easy expansion of lay membership is striking. Most interesting among these several actions was the Assembly's approval of changes in the corporate bylaws of Anderson University. The university was quick to seize on some of the implications of restructuring. With regard to trustee nominations and elections, these changes moved in the direction of creating a self-perpetuating board and thus reducing Assembly involvement in the selection process; after bylaws revision the Assembly would ratify trustees but no longer elect them. When the motion was brought to the floor Edward Beasley offered a substitute motion that would have required votes on each individual bylaws change, but the motion was defeated, again, on a voice vote. All the bylaws changes subsequently were approved. A decade earlier Assembly members sought a direct hand in the selection of AU administrators; in the mid-nineties they seemed willing to give away some of the control they did possess. There was less enthusiasm for direct oversight, and that lack of enthusiasm would become increasingly apparent as more serious issues subsequently arose. The first appeared only months after the General Assembly adjourned.

The first step in national reorganization was more a matter of necessity than design. In autumn 1996 the venerable Church of God magazine, *Vital Christianity*, the successor to the *Gospel Trumpet*, ceased publication after a run of more than a century. The magazine's disappearance was the latest and loudest signal that Warner Press was in serious financial difficulty. Questions concerning the company's executive leadership had dogged Donald Noffsinger, president, from the mid-eighties until his retirement in 1989. No improprieties were ever suggested, but the Warner Press executive salary structure differed markedly from other agencies. In the early eighties, when the publishing house enjoyed record sales and income its president was paid a salary of $84,400 to which was added a ten per cent performance incentive. In 1984 each officer of the company received the same incentive. Noffsinger was a layman who tended to a greater appreciation of the 78 percent of sales that were wholesale or commercial than the 22 percent of company sales to the Church of God, primarily in the form of Sunday school curriculum, books, and other resources. However, most ministers thought of Warner Press and its products as the church's publishing house. That its president should command such a comparatively high salary raised eyebrows. In some respects it was a dispute based on different comparisons. Measured against the business world from which Noffsinger had come to Warner Press his salary seemed reasonable; compared to the salaries of many pastors, however, it was a king's ransom. In 1985 a special study committee reported that the practice of giving executive bonuses had been halted and executive and managerial salaries frozen for one year. A year later executive salaries were cut between eight and ten per cent. Nevertheless, at $78,200 the president's salary remained double that of some agency executives and at least $30,000 more than the salaries of the two next highest paid agency leaders.[8] In the watchful climate of the mid-eighties the study committee also limited Publication Board memberships to no more than three terms.

Warner Press salaries became an issue partially because the company reported a deficit for the fiscal year 1985–86. Executives had decided to modernize printing capability by purchasing a state-of-the-art press. In hindsight the decision proved a major mistake because publishing, like many other enterprises was about to be revolutionized by computer technology. Company leaders had assumed that long runs printed on very large presses would continue to be the most efficient means of production. Computer-driven publishing stood that assumption on its head, and the company soon found itself with a new, very large, and almost obsolete printing press. Sales continued to be strong, however, approximating $20,000,000 in 1988. Fueled by such figures expansion continued. In fiscal year 1987–88 Warner Press acquired a greeting card company and the firm of Kriebel and Bates, owners of the famed paintings of Christ by Warner Sallman.[9] However, the company also finished the year with losses in excess of $678,000. Noffsinger believed the company would be profitable (although a not-for-profit corporation) were it not saddled with the obligation of providing resources for the Church of God.[10]

Elected editor of Warner Press only two years following Noffsinger's election to the presidency in 1976 was Arlo F. Newell. Coming from a pastorate

8. Salary data can be found in the Warner Press reports and the report of the Warner Press Study Committee in Annual Reports for the years 1985 and 1986.

9. Annual Reports, 1988, 115–16. The Sallman paintings were given to Anderson University, where they remain on periodic display.

10. In the company's 1988 report, Noffsinger claimed that costs associated with Church of God sales exceeded income from those sales by $1,177,213. Ibid.

Courtesy of Anderson University and Church of God Archives

Arlo F. Newell (1926–), editor in chief of Warner Press from 1977 to 1993. Following very successful pastorates, Newell, also a popular revival preacher, adopted an editorial policy that attempted to include the increasingly diverse voices speaking out in the movement. Well-read and strongly supportive of graduate theological education, Newell founded a lectureship in biblical studies in honor of his wife Helen at Anderson University's School of Theology.

at Maiden Lane Church of God in Springfield, Ohio and a popular preacher throughout the church, Newell presided over a flowering of books and other publications that either studied the Church of God or advanced its theology. Several book-length studies were published in connection with the movement's centennial celebration in 1980, but the list of books published on Newell's watch continued to lengthen throughout the eighties.[11] He also encouraged a policy of evenhandedness concerning the content of *Vital Christianity*, publishing contributions from writers across the movement's theological spectrum. Always respectful of scholarship and learning, in 1982 Newell established an endowed lectureship in biblical studies at Anderson University's School of Theology. The list of scholars invited to this series has included Bruce Metzger, Walter Brueggemann, and James D. G. Dunn.

Arlo Newell retired in 1993, four years after Donald Noffsinger's retirement. Noffsinger was succeeded by James L. Edwards, who served only one year before assuming the presidency of Anderson University. He was succeeded at Warner Press by Robert Rist. Newell was succeeded as editor in chief by David Shultz, pastor of North Anderson Church of God. For the next several years Rist and Shultz were saddled with the continuing problem of company debt. Reports to the church in the early nineties became less specific; the income and sales figures that characterized Noffsinger's reports no longer appeared. The company searched high and low for cost-saving

---

11. Notable titles published during Newell's tenure include the first edition of the present volume; *Miracle of Survival*, by Harold L. Phillips; *A Time to Remember*, edited by Barry L. Callen; *Passport for a Reformation*, by Lester A. Crose, *Tell Me the Tale* and *Tell Me Another Tale*, by Merle D. Strege; a multi-author series titled The Church of God Doctrinal Library; and *Called to Ministry, Empowered to Serve*, edited by Juanita Evans Leonard.

measures. Early in 1996 their presses fell silent; changes in the printing business had made it less expensive for Warner Press to send out jobs rather than print on their own presses; even *Vital Christianity* was sent out to be printed. Nevertheless such measures did not halt the flow of red ink, and Rist departed when the magazine ceased publication. Shultz remained as acting president in addition to editor.

Warner Press was in a deep financial crisis, but leaders in the company and church sought to avoid dissolving the corporation. In addition to the suspension of *Vital Christianity*, the company sold two retail stores and a major section of its wholesale division. The number of employees was reduced from approximately 250 to 55, and the number of executive positions from seven to one. The Publication Board also cut salaries and suspended contributions to employee pension accounts. From 1995 to 1996 the Warner Press balance sheet dropped from more than $15.5 million to slightly over $10 million, and the company began searching for prospective purchasers of its real property. Very much on Shultz's mind were agency and individual lenders who held Warner Press notes worth $4.7 million; his first priority was to see that they suffered no loss. The result was the "Warner Press Strategy." In its original form the plan called for the Board of Church Extension and Home Missions to assume the Warner Press notes in exchange for title to company buildings and land. However, in the end the Ministries Council (successor to the Leadership Council) assumed the company's indebtedness. Through this step Shultz and church leaders hoped to achieve several goals: (1) satisfy financial obligations to individual noteholders, (2) provide for long-term repayment to agencies holding Warner Press notes, (3) continue paying benefits to company retirees, (4) continue production

David Shultz (1944–), minister. The son of missionaries, Shultz graduated from Warner Pacific College and served the church in a number of minister-at-large positions. In 1993, he was elected editor in chief of Warner Press. The resignation of Robert Rist as president left Shultz to preside over some of the most difficult days in the history of the publishing house, itself older than the Church of God movement. Shultz's resignation as editor in 1998 vacated that office permanently.

of Warner Press church resource products, and (5) develop in the former Warner Press building a new home for all Church of God ministries staff.[12] The strategy was adopted, and David Shultz resigned the editor's chair in July 1998 to return to pastoral ministry. The segment of the company that produced resources for the Church of God was reassigned under Church of God Ministries (see below) as "Church of God Publications."[13] Under the leadership of Eric King Warner Press continued as a producer of greeting cards, church worship folders, and other church supplies. With Shultz's resignation the office of editor in chief was formally retired.

As the Warner Press affair unfolded, members of the General Assembly returned to Anderson in June 1997 to hear the report and recommendations of the Implementation Task Force.[14] The report recommended sweeping changes in the national organizational structure. From the present arrangement of boards and agencies structured as independent corporations the Task Force recommended moving to a single corporate entity, Church of God Ministries, Inc., with a chief executive officer to be selected by the Ministries Council and ratified by the General Assembly. The colleges and university remained independent corporations, the election of their presidents and the dean of the School of Theology still subject to Assembly ratification. But the Missionary Board, the Board of Christian Education, the Mass Media Board, the home missions facet of the Board of Church Extension's work, the divisions of Church Service and World Service all were brought into Church of God Ministries, Inc., and organized into three "teams": Congregational Ministries, Resource and Linking Ministries, and Outreach Ministries. Oversight of each ministry team was assigned to a team director. In its original form the report called for team directors to serve at the will of the general director, but a successful amendment to the report's enabling motion subjected the appointment of team directors to ratification by the Assembly. During the vigorous floor discussion of the report additional attempts were made to modify or even delay implementation of the new structure, but all failed on voice votes. In the end, the Task Force report was accepted as amended by an overwhelming majority.

---

12. Annual Reports, 1998, 109.

13. Church of God Ministries, Inc., continues to publish material released under the Warner Press imprint. Warner Press, Inc., is a subsidiary of Church of God Ministries.

14. Task Force members included: David Cox (chairperson), Timothy Clarke, David Cotto, Esther Cottrell, Doris Dale, Melvyn Hester, Don Johnson, Maxine McCall, Robert Moss, Gerald Nevitt, Robert Nicholson, Frank Ramey, and John Zerkle. Minutes of the General Assembly, Annual Reports, 1997, 13.

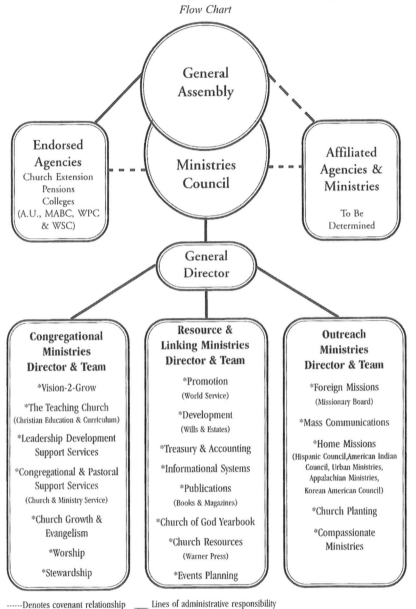

After Restructure (A Working Document)

CHURCH OF GOD MINISTRIES, INC.

Flow Chart

General Assembly

Endorsed Agencies
Church Extension
Pensions
Colleges
(A.U., MABC, WPC & WSC)

Ministries Council

Affiliated Agencies & Ministries
To Be Determined

General Director

Congregational Ministries Director & Team

*Vision-2-Grow

*The Teaching Church
(Christian Education & Curriculum)

*Leadership Development
Support Services

*Congregational & Pastoral
Support Services
(Church & Ministry Service)

*Church Growth &
Evangelism

*Worship

*Stewardship

Resource & Linking Ministries Director & Team

*Promotion
(World Service)

*Development
(Wills & Estates)

*Treasury & Accounting

*Informational Systems

*Publications
(Books & Magazines)

*Church of God Yearbook

*Church Resources
(Warner Press)

*Events Planning

Outreach Ministries Director & Team

*Foreign Missions
(Missionary Board)

*Mass Communications

*Home Missions
(Hispanic Council,American Indian
Council, Urban Ministries,
Appalachian Ministries,
Korean American Council)

*Church Planting

*Compassionate
Ministries

------Denotes covenant relationship ____ Lines of administrative responsibility

DIAGRAM 2: Reorganized national structure as it appeared in the 1999 *Yearbook of the Church of God*. The structure continues to evolve.

From its earliest days Church of God ecclesiology took the form of a radical congregationalism. Early adherents believed that no form of human organization could or should exercise control of the church. To do so would usurp the divine authority of Christ, the only true Head of the church. A corollary of this was a belief that the only true church was the visible church, the gathered local congregation of believers. The movement did not deny that a worldwide fellowship of Christians existed, but people were members of that fellowship by virtue of their personal experience of salvation in Christ, evidenced by their life in a local body of believers. Congregationalist polity placed a premium on the local gathering of believers. At the same time, this polity made cooperation between congregations somewhat problematic. If the church is governed by Christ and the local congregation is the prime manifestation of the church, it was difficult to see how local congregations might cooperate in larger efforts. In fact, such a vision was impossible in the Church of God for the first thirty years of its life. Only after 1910 did a large-scale effort begin to organize, as was often said, not the church but the church's business. The effort spurred the organizational revolution from 1910 to 1928 and the creation of the movement's first set of national agencies.[15] The relationship of those agencies with the church and with each other continued to evolve until the early 1950s with the creation of the restructured Executive Council. Other than additions such as Warner Pacific College and Mid-America College, the Council's structure remained substantially the same until the report of the Task Force on Governance and Polity.

After nearly twenty years of study and discussion the Church of God through its General Assembly had enthusiastically embraced change in its national structure. Those who resisted the move were told that the new structure would eliminate unnecessary duplication, simplify, and make the work of the church more effective. It was also the case that "change" had become something of a watchword among a sizeable element of the ministry. Doris Dale expressed the opinion of many when she said, "Remaining the same is not feasible when everything around you is changing."[16] The national organization was restructured in the name of increasing grassroots participation as well as for the belief that change was necessary. People in the church talked of the need for a "new vision." It was believed that broader participation would lead to a common perspective, largely lacking since

15. See chapter 10.
16. Minutes of the General Assembly, Annual Reports, 1997, 14.

the fractious days of the early eighties. The preponderance of the elected membership of the Ministries Council, now much larger than those who held membership by virtue of office, was emblematic of this democratizing change and its associated hope. Even more illustrative of this belief in the value of broad participation was the creation of a triennial visioning conference. The idea of such a meeting had first been broached in the final report of the Task Force on Governance and Polity. That proposal was formally rejected but never really died. The Implementation Task Force picked up the idea and gave it new life as one of their recommendations. As adopted, the triennial meeting was to assemble nearly 260 men and women from across the Church of God in North America—laypeople, ministers, national leaders—for discussions of matters of importance to the future of the movement. An enthusiasm for change, a desire to streamline national structures, and a hope that broader participation would lead to a common vision were the key factors behind the reorganization adopted in 1997.

The Laidback, Traditional, and Sanctified Church of God

The second half of the sixties and then the seventies introduced Americans to the word and the idea of a *counterculture*. During that era many believed that the "Age of Aquarius" led young people to become devotees of Eastern religions. In fact, the popularity of a photo of the Beatles clad in Asian dress and bedecked in flowers distorts rather than portrays the reality. While it is true that the counterculture influenced many forms of religion in America, historian Mark Oppenheimer notes that its influence appeared in forms very different from the popular image.[17] The counterculture did broadly influence American culture and religion, and some of those effects came to be felt somewhat belatedly in the Church of God as well. In several different aspects of its life in the nineties, elements of the Church of God began to relax; in a word, they became "laidback."

For much of the eighties and early nineties formality still governed social convention and institutions in the Church of God. In 1980 male General Assembly members assembled in Park Place Church of God, typically attired in suit and tie even in the Indiana summer heat and humidity. They sat on unpadded wooden pews arranged in two rows on either side of the center aisle of the nave. Scarcely more than a decade later Assembly

17. See Mark Oppenheimer, *Knocking on Heaven's Door: American Religion in the Age of the Counterculture* (New York and London: Yale University Press, 2003).

members settled into the padded theater seats of Reardon Auditorium. All but the most traditional members had by then adopted "business casual" dress, even though the hall was air-conditioned. Changes in clothing styles were obvious indicators of growing informality in the life of the church. A similar change expressed itself in the conduct of public worship.

By the middle of the nineties many leaders had adopted a form of worship that complemented the relaxed, laidback atmosphere of the culture at large. Worshipers found themselves opening hymnals less frequently in favor of singing lyrics projected on a screen. Sometimes the lyrics were to a familiar hymn, but increasingly they were the praise choruses or songs taken from the contemporary Christian music business. Printed folders (often called "bulletins" by older worshipers) disappeared, along with any semblance of formal liturgy. In newer church buildings, pulpits were never part of the platform furniture or were soon removed. In not a few instances communion tables also disappeared; in place of "In Remembrance of Me," worshipers might read "Yamaha" or "Bose" on the most prominent pieces of platform furniture—audio speakers. Some congregations were sharply divided by the question of whether the church organ should accompany singing; others simply replaced it with synthesizers and electric guitars. Often dressed in khakis and sport shirts, male laidback pastors delivered sermons that were designed to establish a warm, human relationship between speaker and listeners, while short on biblical exegesis. In all its elements this description could be applied to a significant number of Church of God congregations. Others adopted some elements of this shift in the worship culture, while a minority rejected most of these in favor of traditional worship. However, in many circles, the label "traditional worship" was equated with "outmoded"; instead, "contemporary worship," as described above, became the form of choice.

Change in music styles led to a particularly significant conversation within the Church of God. More was at stake than the so-called "worship wars" of contemporary American Protestantism. Especially during the days of come-outism but even in later years the movement's musicians and poets had written a remarkably large body of gospel songs and hymns that were the staple of congregational worship. Songs such as "He's Just the Same Today," "Back to the Blessed Old Bible," or "Crown Him Lord of All" conveyed vital aspects of the movement's theology. Without a confession or catechism, the Church of God historically had depended heavily on congregational singing as a means of theological instruction. As the so-called heritage hymns disappeared from worship, some in the church feared a corresponding loss of a basic knowledge of the movement's theological commitments. A few of the more talented musicians and music ministers rearranged some of these songs in an effort to contemporize their musical idioms.[18] Older constituents nevertheless felt that the music so familiar to them was fading into the past and they worried that the movement's distinctive theological tradition was also disappearing.

A pragmatic approach to evangelism accompanied the counterculture's laidback style. In fact, it is not easy to say whether pragmatic evangelism or the counterculture exercised the greater influence on the church. A rising generation of pastor-leaders quite intentionally adopted the methods of Willow Creek Church or Saddleback Church. The recent history of Madison Park Church of God is a case in point. In 1991 James D. Lyon arrived from Seattle to take the pastorate at North Anderson Church of God in conservative, traditionally inclined Indiana. After moving to Anderson, Lyon visited Willow Creek at least once and clearly was impressed with its building and program. Like others influenced by this model, Lyon wanted to reduce or remove "church language" in an effort to attract people who were put off or intimidated by traditional terminology. Thus *auditorium* replaced *sanctuary* as the name of the room where worship was conducted. Lyon also sought the modification of North Anderson's architecture to incorporate some of the features of Willow Creek's building. An imaginative and

James D. Lyon (1952–), minister. A native of Seattle, Lyon moved to Anderson, Indiana, to assume the pastorate of North Anderson Church of God. A gifted communicator who used popular culture to connect with his audiences, Lyon was elected speaker of the *Christian Brotherhood Hour* in 1996. He quickly moved to change the program name and format, adopting the title *ViewPoint.*

creative leader, Lyon studied the culture at large and borrowed ideas he believed could serve the church's evangelistic purpose. For example, drawing on an idea that originated with Starbuck's Coffee, he wanted to make

---

18. Joe Gregory, associate minister of music at First Church of God in Vincennes, Indiana, has done some of the most extensive work in the area of rearranging Church of God songs.

space in the church building for informal conversation and social interaction. Another example of Lyon's adaptation of the culture to the aims of the church occurred after his election as speaker on the movement's radio program in 1996, when he refashioned its format to resemble an eyewitness news program. Formerly known as the *Christian Brotherhood Hour,* the program was renamed *ViewPoint.*[19] His ultimate goal for North Anderson was a new building that incorporated the physical features of a "seeker-friendly" church, and in 2004 construction began on new facilities located at the opposite end of town from the congregation's current location. Since the name "North" did not apply to a church at the south end of town, the new edifice was christened "Madison Park Church of God" and occupied in the summer of 2007.

At Madison Park, Sunday morning worship occurs in the main auditorium and worship leaders gather in the green room. The congregation's seeker-friendly pragmatism also appears in programming. Even before relocation, a commercially equipped coffee bar, the Holy Grounds Café was introduced in the church lobby. To be sure, the coffee bar existed for reasons other than to provide refreshments and a gathering place; proceeds from sales were contributed to designated missions projects. A gifted and charismatic speaker in wide demand, Lyon often presented his sermons in series under catchy titles such as "Vitamin C for the Soul." Sermons were always connected to a biblical text, but there was no mistaking Lyon's search for a relevant cultural hook to catch listeners' attention. For instance, on the occasion of the fortieth anniversary of its release, cuts from the Beatles' album *Sgt. Pepper's Lonely Hearts Club Band* provided topics for a sermon series. There was no gainsaying the apparent success of this strategy. In the year prior to Lyon's arrival, North Anderson's average morning attendance was 970; by 2008 that number had increased to 1,839. Moreover, the congregation committed itself extensively to missions and ministry, in the latter case founding a shelter for women and children as well as arranging for adoptions.

Madison Park was by no means the only example of the laidback church style of the nineties. Mountain Park Community Church and North Hills Church of God, both in Phoenix, possessed many of the same characteristics, as did Mt. Scott Community Church in Portland, Oregon, Crossings Community Church in Oklahoma City, Indian Creek Community Church

---

19. While the congregation was still at North Anderson, Lyon, a self-described "news junkie," dubbed its foreign missions travel program "Eyewitness North."

in Olathe, Kansas, The Church at Rancho Bernardo in San Diego, Fairfax Community Church in Fairfax, Virginia, Cornwall Church in Bellingham, Washington, and Bayside Community Church in Safety Harbor, Florida to name some of the most prominent. This list includes some of the largest Church of God congregations in the United States. At a time when the average Sunday morning attendance of all American congregations was 113, among these churches the average was 1,505. Laidback congregations typically dropped the traditional Sunday evening service. Their pastors also largely abandoned the revival sermon in favor of a more relational preaching style. The evangelism of the unsaved remained their primary goal, but the altar rail at the conclusion of worship was less and less likely the place where people would experience conversion.

One of the most imaginative and, perhaps, laidback of all the churches was Hope Community Church in Andover, Kansas. Pastored by Steve Weldon, Hope Community was among the earliest Church of God congregations to make extensive use of the Internet. From a gathering of eight families in 1988 the church grew to a constituency of one thousand and launched a new church in central Wichita. Titled "mosaic church," the new church plant intentionally adopted a laidback, open approach to evangelism illustrated by this quotation from its Web site: "What would happen if Christ walked into a church and had long hair and smelled like a homeless person and said, 'Listen everybody, I want you all to quit your jobs, renounce your worldly goods, and give away everything you have, and come walk around with me?' I don't think he'd get very far. People would look at him and say, 'This is not the form of God we're used to.'"[20]

It would be a serious misrepresentation of the Church of God to take any single congregation or even a group as typical of the entire movement at the turn of the twenty-first century. Madison Park and Hope Community were no more representative of the church as a whole than First Church of God in Greeneville, Tennessee, a congregation where the traditional ethos of the Church of God remained clearly present. Pastored by H. Gerald Rudd, a leading member of the Pastors' Fellowship, the Greeneville congregation continued holding services on Sunday evenings. Rudd preached in the familiar revival style, concluding his sermons with invitations to come forward to the altar. Worship music tended to blend heritage hymns with contemporary choruses. Recorded music sometimes accompanied congre-

---

20. www.mosaicchurch.org

gational singing as well as the more traditional piano and organ. Rudd wore a coat and tie, like many parishioners; one would have been very surprised to see him leading worship clad in an open-collar shirt and khaki slacks. He delivered traditionally structured, exegetical sermons from a pulpit and referred to the "sanctuary" rather than an auditorium. The coffee bar, which was a staple of many laidback churches, was absent from the narthex of the Greeneville church. Although parishioners might well find a cup of coffee in a Sunday school classroom, they would never dream of carrying it into the sanctuary for morning worship. Thriving and certainly traditional, the Greeneville congregation was nevertheless not the most conservative of churches in the movement.

Traditional Church of God conservatism continued to be articulated by the Pastors' Fellowship. However, the force of its influence seemed to have diminished in the nineties. During the eighties, regional meetings of the Pastors' Fellowship were held across the United State, from Kentucky to Oklahoma to the state of Washington. By the turn of the millennium, only the annual meeting in Winchester, Kentucky remained, and the fellowship's magazine, *The Reformation Witness*, was published with decreasing frequency and increasing irregularity. One of the group's leaders, Steven Williams, learned how to cost-effectively publish small runs of books and was able to maintain a catalogue of classic Church of God books available through Reformation Publishers. His enterprise focused on preserving and enlarging the theological heritage of the Church of God. In one sense the traditional Church of God informed the North American Convention, which many people still referred to as "Anderson Camp Meeting." But even here aspects of the laidback church appeared in the musical instruments that often accompanied congregational singing and the high entertainment values of the worship leaders *cum* performers on stage.

Another caution against assuming the laidback church was typical of the whole movement is the phenomenon of the Heritage Hymn Sing-a-long. The brainchild of Paul Yerden, a veteran minister of music and a former accompanist for the *Christian Brotherhood Hour*, the first Sing-a-long occurred at the North American Convention in 2000. It was an instant success and became an annual feature of the convention. The program featured gospel songs written and composed by Church of God songwriters, music that had been the staple of the movement's several general hymnals. The event had to be moved to larger and larger venues, but regardless of their size seats were hard to find. People came to listen and to sing the songs of the Church of

God. Event organizers began recording the evening's program and selling copies across the church. Proceeds supported the education of ministerial students at the Kima International School of Theology in Kenya. By 2008, sales had funded the education of forty-five students.

Still another prominent and distinctive element of the Church of God at the turn of the millennium was, to borrow a term from scholar-pastor Cheryl Sanders, the "Sanctified church."[21] Sanders succeeded the late Samuel Hines as pastor of Third Street Church of God in Washington, DC, while she simultaneously held a faculty post at Howard University Divinity School. She developed the phrase to refer to African-American elements in the Holiness-Pentecostal traditions. It has been observed that aspects of Pentecostal worship have influenced worship practices in Holiness and evangelical bodies. Perhaps nowhere do Pentecostal and Holiness traditions of worship converge closer than in the Sanctified church. Worship in that church, as Sanders argues, has been formed not only by Pentecostalism but primarily by the African-American experience of exile. Thus she writes, "The distinctive songs, speech, and dances of the Sanctified church symbolically 'usher' the saints 'out' of this world and into a more authentic one discerned within sacred time and space. . . . When the saints sing 'Holy' unto the Lord, lift up holy hands, or do the holy dance, in effect, they are expressing their allegiance to a world in which God has determined who is accepted and

Photo by Dale Pickett

Cheryl Sanders, educator and pastor. Sanders is professor of Christian ethics at Howard University's Divinity School. Since 1997 she has also held the pastorate at Third Street Church of God in Washington, DC. A noted preacher, scholar, and author in the tradition of her predecessor in that pulpit, Samuel Hines, Sanders critiques the Church of God for a failure to practice its teaching on Christian unity, especially concerning ethnic minorities and women.

---

21. Sanders develops the term in her book *Saints in Exile: The Holiness-Pentecostal Experience in African American Religion and Culture* (New York: Oxford University Press, 1996). The book analyzes dimensions of the African-American experience of exile as it impinges on black Holiness-Pentecostal religion as opposed to the perhaps more familiar black Baptist and Methodist groups. Sanders uses the African-American experience in the Church of God as a principal example.

who will receive power."[22] At points, tension arose between some in the African-American church and those in more traditional Church of God congregations when the latter perceived worship in the churches of the former as beginning to take on too many characteristics of Pentecostalism. Addressing this tension had been one of the motives behind convening the Study Committee on Glossolalia in 1986–1987.

If differences appeared in forms of worship, so also many African-American congregations of the Church of God differed from other congregations in their location. Nearly all larger white congregations of the Church of God were located in suburbs or medium-sized towns. No large white congregation was located in a major American city. By contrast, nearly all large black or primarily black congregations were located in major metropolitan areas: New Covenant Church of Philadelphia, two congregations in Chicago—Covenant Faith and Vernon Park—and First Church of God Inglewood in Los Angeles. Differences more significant than geographic location surfaced in the late nineties and early years of the new century as reconciliation, especially between black and white Church of God groups, became a topic of serious conversation.

Courtesy of Anderson University and Church of God Archives

Samuel G. Hines (1929–95), minister. A native of Jamaica, Hines served a long pastorate at Third Street Church of God in Washington, DC. Passionately committed to the causes of equality and racial unity, Hines formed friendships that transcended racial and economic divides. Hines was the first African American to chair the General Assembly (1983–89).

For much of his ministry until his death in 1995 Samuel Hines had preached a message of ethnic as well as Christian unity. Ever since the Caucus of Black Churchmen in the Church of God met in 1970, African Americans had noted the irony of racial divisions within a movement committed to Christian unity. Hines made this irony the theme of his preaching, especially in the latter stages of his ministry. He insisted that authentic Christian unity must lead to overcoming ethnic divisions. Hines practiced what he preached. He and the Reverend Louis Evans, pastor

22. Ibid., 63–64.

of Washington's predominantly white National Presbyterian Church, led their respective congregations in a covenant that committed both groups to embodying racial reconciliation. This goal became a dominant theme in Hines's preaching to the wider Church of God. He was fond of saying that the Church of God got an A for its message of unity but an F in its practice. In the late nineties Hines's call was taken up by other black leaders, who issued their own calls for reconciliation with some considerable justification. Old wounds had not healed, and some people had long memories. It was remembered, for example, that national Church of God leaders had once decided that the movement needed to have a congregation in Washington, DC. Rather than committing financial resources and other support to the predominantly black Third Street congregation, which had been founded in 1910, national church leaders planted National Memorial Church of God on NW Sixteenth Street in 1970 as the movement's flagship congregation in the national capital.

In an age when cultures came to be increasingly appreciated for their distinctiveness, the National Association of the Church of God and other similar organizations took on a greater role. Calls for reconciliation among the major ethnic groups and organizations within the movement became more urgent. Neither the Association's mission statement nor its Web site claimed that any part of its purpose was to affirm African-American culture. Nevertheless, that the Association's primary mission was with and among black congregations was acknowledged throughout the movement. The Association's stated purpose has been to support "member congregations, pastors, and ministers . . .," the vast majority of which were African American. Concilio Hispano de la Iglesia de Dios specifically targeted the Hispanic population and congregations. People who could not read Spanish would be lost in the Web site of the Concilio, an outgrowth of home missions work among Hispanics. A third ethnically oriented association of the Church of God was the American Indian Council, the result of earlier home missions among Native American peoples. In the late nineties and after the turn of the millennium, these three associations took on greater importance as representatives of their respective ethnic groups. In 2004 calls for reconciliation brought together representatives of these associations and Ronald V. Duncan, general director of Church of God Ministries. The group observed, à la the old theme of Sam Hines, that unity was often discussed but with little to show for it. Two additional meetings that year produced a common commitment to the unity articulated in John 17, especially concerning a common vision across the movement. Out of these meetings was created a working group called "Partners in Ministry." Its goal was not the amalgamation of all into one, but a nonhierarchical working relationship in which common goals could be determined and partnerships forged.[23]

Alongside the enthusiasm for the laidback church, First Church of God, Greeneville and the Heritage Hymn Sing-a-long illustrate the continuing pull of the traditional Church of God. In contrast to the stated purpose of Church of God Ministries, Inc., to "Transform Culture by Being the Body of Christ," the three ethnic ministry associations indicate a countervailing pull according to culture and ethnicity. Together these several pulls portray a diversity in the Church of God that almost defies generalizations about the church as a whole. Gilbert Stafford saw this diversity as deeply problematic, especially with respect to what he called the "culture" of the Church of God.[24] Stafford observed that the movement was at a crossroads from which it would become either an increasingly loose association of congregations or a distinctive Christian fellowship. He worried that "the evidence decreases year by year that we are truly such an identifiable fellowship united by common doctrine, practice, mission, ministries, and worship. Instead, increasing evidence points to each congregation doing its own thing and going its own disconnected way in all the areas just mentioned."[25] Stafford's published ideas articulated a concern that had been expressing itself in a variety of ways, from questioning the church affiliation of candidates for board trusteeships to noting the diminishing congregational support of the World Service basic budget. In the years after the publication of Stafford's book, people began asking what it was that did—or could—hold the Church of God together.

Autonomy

Gilbert Stafford had reason to worry about the eroding culture of the Church of God. His wide travels and numerous contacts across the church lent veracity to his perceptions. Over the years significant elements of the movement's culture kept disappearing or were otherwise ignored. Fewer congregations used the Warner Press Sunday school curriculum, especially

---

23. Minutes of the Partners in Ministry, December 7, 2007.
24. See his *Church of God at the Crossroads* (Anderson, IN: Warner Press, 2000), 9.
25. Ibid., 15.

at the younger age levels. The use of Church of God hymnals also diminished in favor of generic praise choruses and contemporary Christian music. For decades regional ministers meetings counterbalanced the independent tendencies of the movement's congregationalist polity. One by one, however, declining attendance forced the closure of these meetings and the network of face-to-face relationships that they sustained. In addition to these factors, developments in publishing, the women's organization, and giving to World Service combined to force the conclusion that Stafford's observations were on target.

The suspension of *Vital Christianity* removed some of the glue that had historically held the movement together. However, it might be argued that the demise of the magazine was more an effect of a growing spirit of autonomy than it was the cause. Readership had been declining for several years and reflected a divide between an older generation that acquired information through print media versus younger people who read from computer monitors. The magazine's loss nevertheless was a symbolic blow felt so keenly that an attempt was made to publish a successor under the title *ONEvoice!* The General Assembly's enthusiasm for the project was apparently expressed more through its vote of approval than by encouraging subscriptions, however, because its circulation fell far short of that needed for the magazine's financial viability. *ONEvoice!* enjoyed a brief run of only three years, from May 2004 through May 2007.

The loss of the magazine was also symptomatic of another aspect of the erosion of the movement's culture. Until the 1970s constituents of the Church of God primarily read literature from the Gospel Trumpet Company, later Warner Press. As the movement shed some of its stronger sectarian tendencies its adherents read more and more widely. This development coincided with the explosion of evangelical publishing, beginning with the founding of *Christianity Today* in 1956. It took a while, but Church of God people eventually noticed the literature coming from evangelical houses such as Eerdmans and Zondervan. Competition diluted the cultural literacy of Church of God readers concerning their own tradition. Along with books, the growing availability of audio cassettes, videos, compact discs, DVDs, and access to the Internet further added to the chorus of voices with which Church of God speakers, musicians, writers, and producers competed. Similarly, the missionary work of the Church of God increasingly had to compete with independent or para-church missions for the dollars of the movement's adherents or congregations. After the nineties it was not as likely that the representative of a foreign missions project standing before a congregation was a missionary of the Church of God.[26] Nobody argued for a return to the old sectarianism, but it was also the case that these developments contributed to a thinning church culture.

Over the years, important elements of the culture of the Church of God had been shaped by the formidable women's organization. But here also there were signs of weakening influence. For decades known as the Woman's Missionary Society, it had taken a new name in 1974 that indicated a broadening sense of purpose: Women of the Church of God. The organization expanded its attention to women's issues even as it continued to support missions and missionaries. Two historic expressions of that support had been the Penny-a-Day calendar and the Christ's Birthday Observance, and both were woven deeply into the movement's culture. The brainchild of the first generation of society leaders, the venerable calendar held twelve small packets, one per month, for daily contributions of one cent to be accompanied by a prayer for missionaries. The calendars hung in Church of God homes across the United States and Canada, and one by-product of this pervasiveness was their practical, everyday unifying force in the movement. Eventually the calendar gave way to the Missionary Prayer Calendar, minus the envelopes, which were replaced by coin boxes; in time even the modified calendar disappeared. The women's organization also contributed to the movement's culture through the Christ's Birthday Observance (CBO). Accompanied by a set of Advent devotions produced by the Society, the CBO culminated in an annual offering designated for missions in the World Service budget. From the nineties onward, dwindling interest from a number of congregations in primarily the Society's activities but also the CBO contributed to the weakening church culture. Although a congregation might tithe its annual income to the World Ministries Budget, a decision not to participate in the CBO signified more than an unmade contribution; it also meant that a historically important element of the movement's common life went unnoticed. It was also the case, however, that the women's organization itself suffered significant membership losses. From a high point of 40,000 in 1982 membership declined by almost 50

---

26. These examples illustrate that the Church of God, like many American Protestant groups, experienced the decline in constituent loyalty described in Robert Wuthnow's seminal work, *The Restructuring of American Religion* (Princeton, NJ: Princeton University Press, 1988).

percent in the years after 2000.[27] As the number of women working outside the home grew, participation in the women's society or its projects retreated or remained on a plateau.

Aspects of giving to Church of God World Service also indicated a weakening of the culture. The directorship of World Service had passed through the successive care of Paul Tanner, David Lawson, and James Williams, who retired in 1998. He was succeeded by James Martin, who, as director of the new Resource and Linking Ministries Team carried a portfolio that included oversight of what had formerly been known as the World Service Division. Like Tanner and Lawson before him, Williams had been nurtured by years of work in the division and took his stewardship of it and the budget very seriously. He provided carefully detailed reports that called attention to serious problems in the movement's responsiveness to the overall World Service budget. In fiscal 1995–1996 giving to World Service increased by 7.4 percent, but Williams noted that the predominant increase came in designated giving rather than the basic budget. From 1988 to 1995 giving to the basic budget had increased by only 7 percent while designated giving had almost doubled. For the entire period of Williams' study the priority budget had grown modestly, and in fact trailed the national rate of inflation by two percentage points.[28] Not only was the basic budget barely growing and rarely met, Williams also noted that a minority of congregations were giving the lion's share of contributions. Of 2,359 congregations in North America,[29] 663 gave more than 78 percent of World Service income in fiscal 1995–96. These statistics strongly suggest that many individual congregations and their pastoral leaders were less and less inclined to contribute to the movement's cooperative ministries.

James Williams' issues with the budget were relatively minor compared to the problems faced by James Martin. The budget committee continued to increase the basic budget, even though it was annually underfunded. This problem was magnified by the Warner Press strategy, which left Church of God Ministries with the responsibility to raise almost a half-million dollars of additional funds for the basic budget each year. In agreeing to that strategy, Church of God Ministries assumed Warner Press obligations to pay off its indebtedness as well as $200,000 a year in retirement benefits. When

---

27. In 2008 membership was put at over fourteen thousand. Arnetta Bailey, executive director of Women of the Church of God, to Merle Strege, August 12, 2008.

28. Division of World Service Report, Annual Reports, 1996, 53–54.

29. The figure is taken from the *Yearbook of the Church of God*, 1996.

Martin stated that he anticipated a 1998–99 budget shortfall of somewhere between two and three hundred thousand dollars, Assembly members wanted to know how the 1999–2000 budget could be increased by 6.5 percent and also assume the Warner Press obligations. The full implications of the Warner Press strategy were realized when the Assembly learned that payments would continue for fifteen years. The financial burdens appeared staggering, especially when fewer than half the movement's congregations were supporting the cooperative budget.

Gilbert Stafford's observation that the culture of the Church of God was wearing thin had been confirmed by a wide variety of data. Small wonder, then, that General Secretary Edward Foggs played the role of prophet in his 1996 Annual Report when he stated, "I am prepared to argue that the way we exercise our autonomy in the Church of God has brought us to undue grief in local congregations, in state and regional ministries and in national ministries." Foggs continued, "I am . . . pleading for a consultative, conferring autonomy that seeks counsel beyond itself for the good of the whole body. Without such a partnering autonomy, we are at risk for fractured persons, congregations, ministries, and relationships."[30]

Steps Backwards and Forwards

The transition from the old national structure to the new was scheduled for completion by the end of December 1999. Transitions at the top of the structure included the retirement of Edward Foggs as general secretary and the election of Robert Pearson in 1998 as the first general director of Church of God Ministries. The two men spent a year working side-by-side ushering in the new organizational structure while the organization it was to replace maintained ministry. Pearson had come to Anderson from Southern California where he had served as an area administrator. His first report to the Assembly detailed a very ambitious program, significantly imposed on him by the demands of transition and the new national structure. Pearson was not overly troubled by self-doubt, and thus he reported the accomplishments of his first year in office: (1) completion of an orderly transition; (2) selection and ratification of directors for the three ministry teams; (3) facilitation of the first triennial visioning conference; (4) oversight of the mergers associated with the creation of Church of God Ministries, Inc.;

---

30. Report of the General Secretary, Annual Reports, 1996, 29.

(5 and 6) organized and staffed the new ministry teams; (7) defined the relationships between Church of God Ministries, Inc., and several entities such as the colleges and universities, Women of the Church of God, area administrators, what Pearson termed "cultural groups" such as the National Association and the *Concilio*, and the regional assemblies of the Church of God in Canada; (8) implemented the Warner Press Strategy; (9) "articulate a compelling vision for the national, North American, and international ministries of the Church of God"; and (10) build the fiscal 1999–2000 World Service budget.[31]

It is often the case that incoming executives are overly ambitious in their plans for the first year in office, and Pearson fell prey to that tendency. The ninth point of his report was the only one where he could state goals for the movement that he had not inherited from previous decisions. That one point contained more than thirty goals to be accomplished in addition to the

Robert Pearson (1955–), minister. Coming from Southern California, where he had served as an area coordinator, in 1998 Pearson took office as the first general director of Church of God Ministries. The transition required by national restructuring proved to be more demanding than anticipated, complicated as it was by financial difficulties at Warner Press and with the World Ministries Budget. Pearson resigned after two years in office.

demands imposed by the organizational transition. In some cases those new demands, specifically the appointment of team directors, raised other issues that had to be addressed. Racial reconciliation had been a live issue even before the General Assembly adopted a resolution on that topic in 1998; African Americans were keenly interested in Pearson's nominations for the three team director positions, especially after it was learned that no African American was on the original short list of possible appointees. Women also watched with a very attentive eye. Pearson informed critics that in fact

---

31. Annual Report of the General Director, Annual Reports, 1999, 23–45. The sheer size of Pearson's report reflects something of his ambition for the church. General Secretary Foggs' report for 1998 was less than a third the length.

several African Americans had been offered a team director's position but all had declined. In the end his nominations included a woman and two men, one of whom was an African American. The selection of Michael Curry, a black pastor, did not occur without considerable effort, which Pearson took some pains to defend.[32]

The new general director's interest in visionary leadership made him keenly concerned with events such as the visioning conference, the first of which convened in Colorado Springs in autumn 1998. Leonard Sweet, dean of Drew University's School of Theology and a leading futurist, served as guest speaker. Participants identified 275 visioning statements which were organized into five topics—leadership development, communications/resource development, outreach/mission/evangelism/church planting, and reconciliation. Pearson took the statements very seriously; many of them informed his annual report. He clearly wanted to integrate the product of the visioning conference into the agenda of Church of God Ministries. Nevertheless, Pearson was shackled by the demands of the present and the serious Warner Press financial problems, coupled with the declining trend of giving to the World Ministries Budget, which did not meet the goals of the basic budget. Those demands became acute in fiscal year 1999–2000, when Church of God Ministries went into debt. After the close of that fiscal year and a dismal report of Church of God Ministries' financial condition, Robert Pearson resigned. In a letter intended for public announcement, he cited his belief that he had become a lightning rod for several problems besieging Church of God Ministries and that its work could not go forward as long as he continued in office.[33] Forrest Robinson, veteran pastor and former president of Mid-America Bible College, was appointed interim general director. Scarcely more than a year into its existence the new structure once argued as necessary to the movement's future was floundering. In this gloomy climate rumors began circulating about problems at the Board of Church Extension.

In August 2000 six Church Extension executives, including its controller, abruptly resigned while citing their fears over questionable investment practices at the not-for-profit corporation. Indicators were present that might have alerted watchful observers. Church Extension had changed

---

32. Pearson elaborately detailed a process in which African-American church leaders were consulted and their recommendations used to generate a list of qualified candidates for team director positions. Ibid., 26.

33. Robert W. Pearson to Ministries Council of the Church of God, October 4, 2000.

auditors four times between 1991 and 1997. In 1991 its auditors had stated that Church Extension was in critical financial condition. Inexplicably, in 2000 the corporation failed to renew its license to register securities in the state of Indiana. Nevertheless it continued to sell investments and therefore incurred a civil fine of $10,000. In that same year Church Extension did not file a public audit, but president Perry Grubbs assured General Assembly members that "the most recent audited financial statement indicates that progress continues to be made."[34] However, after investigating the corporation's activities, in 2002 the Securities and Exchange Commission filed a civil action in United States Federal Court against Church Extension, a subsidiary (United Management Services, Inc.), Grubbs, and Vice President Shearon L. [Louis] Jackson. No criminal charges were brought against any of the defendants, but the truth about more than $81 million in investments was at stake as well as the credibility and reputation of the Church of God and its various ministries.[35]

The investigation had revealed that Church Extension's assets did not come close to covering its liabilities. Nevertheless, in January 2003 the corporate defendants and the SEC reached an amicable settlement. A new board of directors was created to liquidate all holdings for the benefit of Church Extension's creditors and note holders. Also, a new corporation called Church Builders Plus was created to serve the church's needs for loans, capital fund campaigns, and planned giving. It was also agreed that 10 percent of the proceeds of loans solicited by the new corporation would be used to repay Church Extension's creditors. Five years from the date of the agreement Church Builders Plus was also to execute a note payable to creditors in the amount of $10 million. The case against Grubbs and Jackson proceeded, and in 2004 a jury found each of them "guilty of misleading investors through inaccuracies in financial statements and written information sent out to investors; and guilty of negligence for allowing the said information to be included in the circulars sent to investors and potential investors."[36]

Trial testimony disclosed serious shortcomings in the two men's management of the corporation and its investments. In point of fact, Church

34. Report of Church Extension, Annual Reports, 2000, 53.

35. The defendants were accused of (a) artificially inflating income statements, (b) misleading investors about the use of their investments, and (c) misstating the safety and risks associated with investment notes.

36. Quoted in John M. Brutlag, "Jury Rules Against Church Extension Officials," *Indianapolis Star*, July 16, 2004.

Extension had become a holding company with so many subsidiaries that a working knowledge of each and oversight of all would have been difficult for the most attentive manager. This long list of diverse and sometimes little-known holdings occasionally led to embarrassing revelations, such as the disclosure that a Caribbean hotel owned by Church Extension served alcoholic beverages. Nevertheless, it was investors who lost the most through the whole affair. In the end, note-holders were repaid at a rate of approximately 64 percent. In June 2004 Church of God Ministries created a special fund, the Action and Assistance Plan for Church Extension Noteholders,[37] which eventually repaid 82.5 percent of the investments of more than 250 individuals with critical needs and succeeded in soliciting more than $2 million in support of that end.[38]

Ronald V. Duncan (1946–), minister and agency executive. After graduating from Anderson College, Duncan earned graduate degrees from Christian Theological Seminary and Ashland Seminary. He held several pastorates prior to his election to the Ministries Council. In 2002, he took office as the second general director of Church of God Ministries, Inc. Duncan's personal leadership style returned the element of face-to-face relationships between national leaders and the grassroots church.

While the problems at Church Extension slowly came to light, Ronald V. Duncan was elected and ratified as the new general director of Church of God Ministries, taking office in January 2002. Duncan's extensive record of experience included pastorates at Mansfield, Ohio, Park Place Church of God in Anderson, and Pasadena Church of God in Houston, Texas. He was also a United States Army Reserve chaplain, and along with his irrepressible optimism and transparency brought an almost military sense of order and accountability to his assignment. Church of God Ministries staff members and directors were not required to salute their new "general," but he did expect clear, precise answers and brought a new level of accountability to the office and the General Assembly. In his first report Duncan declared his intention

37. Colloquially known as the Church Extension Compassion Fund.
38. Figures cited here are as of summer 2008.

to "commend, build up, and assess—with honesty and candor—where we are, where we hope to go, and the crucial importance of [the Assembly's] partnership."[39] He resisted the temptation to make large promises, other than hard work. Duncan expected no less of himself and in time undertook an extensive travel schedule. Although the organizational structure had changed, in some respects Duncan's leadership style reverted to that of T. Franklin Miller and other leaders of the forties and fifties; there was a greater likelihood that communication would once again be more personal, perhaps face to face. This personal style translated into congregations' and ministers' slow but steady return of confidence in Church of God Ministries. At a moment when some asked whether the Church of God was experiencing its darkest days, Duncan's personal style and the conduct of his office provided the movement with a much needed ray of light.

Jay Barber (1941–), educator. After a successful pastorate in Red Bluff, California, Barber joined the Warner Pacific College administration as vice president for development in 1981 and served his alma mater in that capacity until 1988. In 1996, he succeeded Marshall Christensen as president and continued in that post until retirement in 2008. During his tenure, Barber was able to relieve the institution of nagging long-term debt and restore lost campus programs.

Financial difficulties at Church Extension and Church of God Ministries, which now included a portion of the Warner Press indebtedness, cast a shadow over the national work of the Church of God at the turn of the millennium. Meanwhile, the church's institutions of higher education were not without their own financial problems. After a tenure of fifteen years Marshall Christensen stepped down as president of Warner Pacific. He was succeeded by Jay Barber in 1996. A WPC alumnus, Barber had served as a pastor before joining the WPC staff from 1981 to 1988 as a vice-president in development. Upon his return as president, Barber's principal task was the management and ultimately the elimination of the institution's long-term debt. Through several large gifts Warner Pacific achieved this goal in 2007. Barber also successfully negotiated the

---

39. Annual Reports, 2002, 21.

termination of the college's relationship with GEOS Language Corporation. Improved institutional finances also contributed significantly to the lifting of its probationary status with the regional accrediting association. Along the way, Barber reinstituted intercollegiate athletics, and the school also launched an adult degree program.

Mid-America Bible College also experienced financial hardships that it eventually weathered. John Fozard had succeeded to the Mid-America presidency in 1999. Fozard held degrees from Southern Illinois University and the School of Theology at Anderson College. He also held a doctorate in theological distance education and applied both his education and experience to implement a distance learning program at Oklahoma City. Online and distance learning opportunities expanded the student base, and as in Warner Pacific's case large gifts enabled Mid-America to achieve financial stability. During Fozard's tenure the institution eliminated its indebtedness and made more than a half-million dollars worth of capital improvements. His first year in office marked the beginning of annual record increases in fall semester enrollment. Program expansion eventually led to a name change, and in 2003 the school became Mid-America Christian University.

Only Anderson escaped operating deficits during the period, but it needed to weather a financial crisis of a different sort. During Robert Reardon's tenure the school had received a gift in kind that resulted in financial obligations. College officials did not convert the gift to cash but retained it as a business venture and as a result the school was entangled in a web of financial liabilities. To his credit, James Edwards confronted the situation and succeeded in extracting the institution from serious economic threat. However, the school paid a high price for its freedom in the form of a multimillion dollar loss to its endowment. As part of its recovery, during the same period Anderson embarked on a major capital campaign and eventually emerged from its financial challenge.

After 2003 the movement's educational institutions presented a sunnier picture. Riding the echo generation of the baby boom, Anderson, Mid-America, Warner Pacific and Warner Southern reported expanding and even record enrollments. In 1997 Warner Southern had joined its sister schools with general agency status and a line in the World Ministries Budget. Each campus witnessed the addition of major new construction projects, from Schlatter Memorial Chapel in Portland to the Pontious Learning Resource Center at Lake Wales to the $15 million Kardatzke Wellness Center in Anderson. In the case of Warner Southern, however, campus development did not occur without a very serious interruption. In the summer of 2004 four hurricanes swept through Florida with devastating effect, three striking Polk County, the location of Warner Southern College. Hurricane Charlie hit about a week before entering students were scheduled to arrive for the opening of the new academic year. The campus suffered serious damage; nearly all structures required some repair or rebuilding, the gymnasium remained closed until the following autumn, and two buildings were total losses. College officials delayed the opening of the academic year by four weeks, and when courses began, students attended some classes in buildings while repairs were ongoing. An entire calendar year elapsed before the campus was able to resume normal operations. The school was not left alone in her efforts to rebuild. Warner Southern's sister institutions in the Church of God rallied to her support with donations and offers of help in the rebuilding effort.

The support for Warner Southern (now Warner University) was but one indicator of a growing cordiality in relationships between the educational institutions and particularly their leaders. Prior to 1998 the Commission on Christian Higher Education had provided a formal structure for inter-institutional relationships, but as part of the reorganization transition the commission's life came to an end along with the commissions on Christian Unity and Social Concerns. Participation on the Commission for Higher Education aside, however, competition between the schools had been historically keen, made even sharper by the comparatively low number of Church of God students who elected to attend one of the church's colleges or the university. At Anderson University, which enjoyed the highest enrollment percentage among the schools, no more than one-third of the traditional student body came from Church of God congregations. The schools' enrollments grew during the period by recruiting more students from beyond the Church of God and through various programs such as degree completion, adult education, and distance learning. It may have been the development of such programs that allowed relationships between the schools' presidents to warm after 1998. This warming seemed almost paradoxical, since the very entity that had existed to promote dialogue between them had disappeared in the wake of reorganization. However, the four presidents—Warner Pacific's Jay Barber, Anderson's James Edwards, Mid-America's John Fozard, and Warner Southern's Gregory Hall—formed genuine friendships that led to an ad hoc presidential conversation group subsequently enlarged to include John Howard of Gardner College in Canada, the president of Bay

Ridge Christian College, as well as the presidents of the movement's international ministerial training schools. Members of the group engaged one another in honest dialogue on issues of common concern. The demise of the commissions as part of reorganization had unintentionally eliminated three important locations for church-wide conversations on areas of special interest to the Church of God. The presidents' discussions became a means of continuing conversations at least where they concerned higher education.

General Director Duncan was a strong advocate of higher education. He himself held graduate professional degrees in theology and ministry and was keenly interested in the advancement of the movement's schools. Church leaders also were increasingly concerned about the advancing age of Church of God ministers and their impending retirements. Leadership development in higher education and beyond became a lively topic of discussion. Duncan initiated a series of annual meetings that brought together administrators, professors, and trustees of each of the movement's schools in North America. On occasion students were also invited to participate in conversations on matters of concern to all of Church of God higher education. Principal among these was leadership development for the church. The first Visioning Conference had identified leadership development as an issue to be addressed through programming, and in 1999 a Task Force on Leadership Development came into being. One of its most significant products was a college-level textbook, *First Steps to Ministry*.[40] David Markle, a former pastor and a professor of Christian ministry at Warner Pacific College had identified the absence of such a textbook as a serious gap in ministerial education. Accordingly, he served as the general editor of this collection of essays written by some of the movement's leading ministers and scholars. The International Youth Convention also became an arena for leadership recruitment and development. A challenge to consider the ministry as a calling became a regular feature of the biennial event. In these ways the issue of leadership development strengthened working relationships between the church with its concerns for ministry and the educational concerns of the several colleges.

Following reorganization, Church of God Ministries faced serious shortfalls in operating expenses. However, while it was short of cash Church of God Ministries held title to extensive tracts of land surrounding the old Warner Press building—now the Church of God Ministry Center—as

---

40. David Markle, ed., *First Steps to Ministry* (Anderson, IN: Warner Press, 2001).

well as adjacent to the Anderson University campus. Beginning in 1999 Church of God Ministries and Anderson University negotiated a series of purchases involving land and buildings. Through these land sales Church of God Ministries was able to reduce the size of its operating losses. Among the properties was the building that formerly housed the executive offices for the church and the Women of the Church of God. In fiscal year 2000–2001 the university bought this building and its land for slightly less than $500,000. However, the church's land holdings were finite; some means had to be found to eliminate the long-term debt Church of God Ministries had incurred through the Warner Press strategy. Not long after the sale of the old Church of God Ministries building, Ronald Duncan learned of still another problem with large financial implications. In the summer of 2004, an inspection of Warner Auditorium revealed that some of its concrete was deteriorating and its roof leaking. Much worse, sound insulation on the ceiling was found to contain asbestos. Church of God Ministries was given 180 days to submit a plan to clean the auditorium of the dangerous material. On May 4, 2005, the building was temporarily closed, and Anderson University was forced to shift its commencement exercises to the field house of Kardatzke Wellness Center.

Duncan and the Ministries Council were faced with yet another serious financial dilemma. Estimates varied, but asbestos clean-up and refurbishing the auditorium would cost well in excess of a half-million dollars. The Church of God Ministries budget was already strapped and could not sustain such an expenditure. Warner Auditorium remained sealed, and beginning in 2005 the general worship services for the North American Convention were held in the same location as Anderson University's commencement exercises. Then Duncan went to work on a comprehensive plan to resolve not only the problems in Warner Auditorium but also Church of God Ministries' long-term indebtedness. After some months of consideration he offered Anderson University officials three options for the purchase of Warner Auditorium and adjacent land. In the end, they selected a proposal by which Church of God Ministries would sell to the school the auditorium and the surrounding land between Third and Fifth Streets east to Nursery Road—in other words, the campground used by convention delegates and their families. Anderson University agreed to leave the campground in its existing configuration for an unspecified future.

In a deal completed in September 2006 the university paid $2,185,000 for slightly less than forty acres of land along with Warner Auditorium and its problems. Additionally, the University agreed to contribute $700,000 for asbestos abatement and demolition of the structure and another $1.2 million in a gift to Church of God Ministries. The transaction completed, Warner Auditorium was razed in the autumn of 2006 after a life of forty years. Onlookers watched with mixed emotions. The building had been the hub of the Anderson Camp Meeting, especially for the events and celebrations that occurred inside but also for the gatherings, personal reunions and conversations that took place around its vast circumference. On the other hand, the building's demise was a key element in negotiations that lifted many of the financial clouds that had darkened the horizon of the national church work for a decade. With a total of nearly $4.1 million in hand, the church's leadership was able to resolve all major outstanding financial issues. As those clouds lifted, the mood at Church of God Ministries and among the national church leadership perceptibly brightened.

Planning for the Future

Ronald Duncan longed for the opportunity to plan for future ministries of the Church of God. Until the Warner Auditorium land sale, however, crisis management had taken up much of his time. In anticipation of that sale, Duncan was free to plan strategically for future ministry and assembled a committee to shape the third visioning conference, scheduled for August 2006 in Nashville, Tennessee.[41] A signal of the changing climate in the church was the renaming of the meeting to "Strategic Planning Conference." Its goal was "to engage invited leaders in addressing the strategic questions facing the Church of God and suggesting how the church might best carry out its strategic goals."[42] In cooperation with the Ministries Council and others, Duncan had developed five strategic goals in advance of the conference: (1) announcing God's good news to the world; (2) relating as God's Spirit-born children, (3) investing for the sake of God's kingdom; (4) sharing in response to God's call; and (5) empowering God's gifted people in ministry. These goals formed the acronym ARISE, which was the conference theme. Pre-conference planners also identified four strategic questions to be addressed by conferees:

---

41. Members included Jay Barber; Robert Davis; Robert Dulin; Ron Elkins; Vernon Maddox, chair; Don Medley; Rebecca New-Edson; J. Thomas Pelt; Ray Rood, facilitator; Gerald Rudd; David Shrout; and Church of God Ministries staff members Ronald Duncan and Sue Baird.

42. Minutes of the Strategic Planning Conference of the Church of God, August 23–25, 2006, 1.

1. What should be the biblical and healthy role of leadership (national, state, and local) for a group of churches that practice congregational polity and the priesthood of all believers?
2. How does leadership (national, state, local) honor the traditions (e.g., doctrine, governance) of a group of churches, interpret the culture and the implications of a changing postmodern culture, and lead the churches forward in changing the culture?
3. What should be the paradigm (design) best suited for the harmonious work among national leadership, state leadership, and churches in a congregationalist polity system to provide integrated solutions to common needs, challenges, problems, and opportunities?
4. How can the vision (missional and relational) of national leadership be best presented to all stakeholders?

For two and a half days 143 delegates addressed these questions and discussed issues rising out of the process.

Duncan believed that the Nashville meeting was occurring at a crucial moment in the movement's history. He had high hopes for the gathering and saw it as different from any previous national meeting of this kind. He candidly acknowledged the effects of three financial crises, leadership transitions, and the stress of reorganization. He also recognized changes occurring in American culture and their effects on church life. But the promise of a vastly improved debt structure in the national church allowed Duncan to view the Nashville meeting as an opportunity to build a foundation for what he called a "flexible ministry future" for the movement.[43] Elements of the conference were the product of his wide travel through the church. In this both Duncan and the movement benefited from his return to a face-to-face leadership style. From many conversations with the grassroots church he had concluded that people in the movement wanted leaders to set a direction for the church that would excite it and engender support.[44] Personal conversations also enabled ministers and lay people to get to know Duncan and on that basis trust him. This allowed Duncan to address conferees with confidence and optimism, and this spirit proved infectious.

In terms of both process and planning the Nashville meeting was a marked improvement over its two predecessors. The Colorado Springs

43. The phrase is taken from the printed version of Duncan's opening presentation to the conference, August 23, 2006, 2.
44. Minutes of the Strategic Planning Committee, April 3–4, 2006, 1–2.

conference as well as the second triennial meeting in Phoenix three years later were each overshadowed by problems associated with reorganization and various financial burdens; an uncertain present made it difficult for conferees to contemplate and plan for the future. However, during these years the reorganization plan slowly found traction and began to find its stride. General Director Duncan seized the initiative and found the means to eliminate the long-term indebtedness of Church of God Ministries. The Nashville conference thus presented movement leaders with an opportunity largely beyond the experience of the Church of God during the previous decade. There they could legitimately contemplate goals and ministry that could respond with flexibility to the demands of the future.

During the period from 1993 to 2006 the Church of God movement had stood at a crossroads. During these years questions were raised about the identity and cohesiveness of the movement. A variety of serious financial problems threatened the viability of several agencies and program units and forced the demise of one. Other agencies were forced to redefine their purpose. The problems also changed the way in which the organized overseas missions work of the Church of God was funded through Global Missions, the successor within Church of God Ministries to the Missionary Board.[45] People wondered whether the church could overcome financial and ethical obstacles that effectively obscured a vision of the future. After the turn of the millennium the movement's future became brighter. One by one national agencies worked through their problems. At the same time, ministry in and with local congregations had continued despite challenges to the national offices, and the number of adherents in the North American church and around the world continued to grow. By the end of the period, and after a century and a quarter of existence, the Church of God reformation movement had appeared to find a way forward.

---

45. For a complete history of the work of the Missionary Board and Global Missions, see *Into All the World: A Century of Church of God Missions*, by Lester A. Crose, Cheryl Johnson Barton, and Donald Johnson (Anderson, IN: Warner Press, 2009).

20

A SEMI-HISTORICAL POSTSCRIPT

Those who believe that history is a mere record of the past see the task of history writers as documentation. Accordingly, they are regarded as men and women who face backward while braver souls confront the challenge of the future. However, historians are keenly interested in the present and in understanding the processes, attitudes, and decisions by which we have arrived at the present moment. Moreover, historians write the story of our arrival at the present in order to be of service to those who confront the future. People ignorant of the narrative of their own lives are inadequately prepared to think about the kind of people they might become, whether as individuals or as a group. Indeed, those who are unclear in their identity can hardly be expected to know how to go forward well. Understanding the present and determining a path through the future become risky and subject to great error when divorced from historical understanding.

The vital connection between historical knowledge and the ability to act wisely in the future poses two occupational hazards for the historian: preachy moralism or reckless prognostication. The author of the first edition of this study studiously avoided both temptations all the way through that work to its conclusion. By way of summation, nevertheless, from his perspective as the historian of the Church of God and preeminent student of its life he identified three items of unfinished business on the movement's agenda. Almost three decades after their original publication and in light of some of the events of those years, one cannot help noticing his prescience and wondering whether some problems might have been avoided had Professor Smith's summary been read more attentively.

It would violate the spirit of a revision to reprint Smith's conclusion. Thirty years should have taught us something about one or more of the items he noted. To keep faith with the original edition, however, they should at least be noted before offering a new summation. In point of fact, Smith's unfinished agenda will serve as a springboard to that summary. As the Church of God celebrated its centennial and contemplated its future,

Smith's three items were: (1) establishing a consistency between ecclesiology and organizational practice, (2) determining new expressions of the movement's historic commitment to Christian unity in an increasingly dynamic religious setting, and (3) recovering a clear sense of identity and, with it, a reason for being.

Since the proposal for a missionary committee in 1908, the Church of God lived uncomfortably with bureaucratic organization. Over time that uneasiness has relaxed. The thought that "the church's work" was being organized rather than the church itself provided sufficient comfort to allow the further development of organization. The Earl Slacum controversy of the forties and fifties illustrated the persistence of that uneasiness. However, a half century later, the rather ready acceptance of the recommendations of the Task Force on Governance and Polity indicated that a majority had become comfortable with bureaucratic forms of organization. At the turn of the millennium some even believed them a panacea for the church's ailments.

Smith's second item of unfinished business, the need to find expressions of Christian unity, has fared quite differently. To the delight of some, reorganization disbanded the Commission on Christian Unity, but with that the movement lost its most significant forum for continuing discussion of the topic. For a good measure of its life the Church of God movement wove holiness, Christian unity, and evangelism together in a whole cloth. In the seventies and eighties evangelism alone seized the center stage. Key 73 and the Vision-2-Grow program combined with the mushrooming influence of the Church Growth movement to emphasize evangelism to the near disregard of Christian unity or anything else. Added to the loss of the commission, these developments left the movement's original generative theological idea largely to be discussed by those individuals for whom it remained important. Thus, while it is certainly a crucial element of any church's mission, evangelism came to dominate the agenda of the Church of God so much that the movement largely forgot that it had come into being to call a divided church to unity.

As for the third of Smith's agenda items, the publication and ensuing discussion of Gilbert Stafford's *Church of God at the Crossroads* strongly suggest that mission and identity have now become matters perpetually demanding the attention of church leaders. Mission statements and a vision are now expected of all leaders and organizations. However, we see according to who we are, and that identity is formed as we answer the question, "Of what stories are we a part?" Aside from the requirement that we have more than a passing acquaintance with our constitutive narratives, the operative word in that question is *we*. The entire church—ministers and laypeople alike—must own those narratives as theirs if history is to have any formative influence.

Smith's three unfinished agenda items ultimately call attention to ecclesiology. Running through Church of God history is the topic of the church. Indeed, scratch the surface of several theological debates in that history, and one frequently discovers that the doctrine of the church was the real issue. From D. S. Warner's vision that holiness could not prosper on sectarian soil to H. M. Riggle's debates with premillennialists, from *Our Ministerial Letter* to Earl Slacum, from E. A. Reardon's opinion that Jesus would not work solely with the Church of God to the Assembly's ambivalence about executives' participation in ecumenical meetings, from the Task Force on Governance and Polity to the present attempts to streamline the restructured national organization, the church has always been the underlying topic of conversation among Church of God people. Indeed, it is not too much to say that the Church of God movement is an extended conversation—some might prefer argument—about the implications of the doctrine of the church as the community in which Christians live out their discipleship.

In the early decades Church of God people who had recently joined the fellowship often testified that they had "seen the church" or discerned the body of Christ. This vision prompted them to forsake their former fellowships and "sign up," so to speak, in common cause with other Christians equally committed to a holy church beyond division. Early ideas about the church allowed for a very loosely connected fellowship bound together by their belief that God was at work among them and by the *Gospel Trumpet* as a witness to that divine activity. Although loosely connected those early saints were bound together in a common commitment to the church. The common cause—"seeing the church"—remained a unifying force through decades of change, even the organizational revolution from 1913 to 1930. Admittedly, a fair degree of sectarianism characterized this era. When editor C. E. Brown declared that all who were saved in Christ were members of the church of God, regardless of their denominational home, that sectarian tendency was checked; however, the church seen by Church of God people simultaneously began to take on wider and more disparate interpretations.

It is not at all incorrect to describe the Church of God movement as an extended conversation—in W. B. Gallie's phrase, an "essentially contested concept"—about the church.[1] Until recently, Church of God folk have strived to be the kind of church that they found in the pages of the New Testament. Not long after the first issues of the *Gospel Trumpet* came off the press, however, it became apparent that the saints were not in unanimity concerning their understanding of the church. Differences deepened after the turn of the twentieth century. Despite opposing viewpoints that sometimes erupted into open conflict, those who held divergent views managed to remain in fellowship with each other, in large measure because they shared a common commitment to "the church." They may not have "seen" quite the same church, but nearly all believed it was important to seek and be the body of Christ.

The movement's ministers have been the primary although not exclusive participants in this conversation. For much of its life the policy-making body of the Church of God was called the General *Ministerial* Assembly. The middle term was eventually dropped, which obscures the fact that ministers were the primary participants in theological conversations. At the annual meeting in Anderson and at regional ministerial meetings such as the Central States Ministers Meeting, clergy gathered for encouragement and enrichment, but also for theological engagement. It should be remembered, after all, that one of the sparks that lit the Anderson College controversy of the late twenties and early thirties was Professor Russell Byrum's theological paper read to the Indiana State Ministerial Assembly. Recent years have witnessed the demise of most regional ministers' meetings. Moreover, the tenor of General Assembly meetings has shifted from the intense theological debates of the eighties to an agenda dominated by largely procedural matters. If the Church of God movement is an extended conversation about the meaning and doctrinal practice of the church, but the venues for such conversations have largely disappeared, one is left to ponder the cohesiveness of the larger body beyond the local congregation. Today, the polity of the extended conversation called the Church of God is less vital due to dwindling ministerial interest in continuing the conversation about being the church.

One sign of the movement's weakening polity is the perennial problem of insufficient funding of the World Service (now World Ministries) Budget. Since its division into basic and designated categories, national

---

1. Stephen Sykes explores the implications of Gallie's idea in *The Identity of Christianity* (Philadelphia: Fortress Press, 1984), 251–52. Sykes applies the idea to Christianity; in the context of the history of the Church of God, I have restricted Gallie's idea to the concept of the church.

church leaders have been vexed by the problem of underfunded ongoing operations. While giving to the total budget continued to grow, sometimes at record levels, giving to basic operations went begging. Congregations and individuals gave generously, but to the projects in which they had some interest. Such giving patterns reflect the growing influence of a market mentality in the church. Rather than giving as members of a body, congregations contribute to the national budget much as customers, determining where they will spend their dollars—and in the American consumer culture, the customer is always right. That local congregations often relate to national ministries in terms of the market should not be surprising, for that is the metaphor of the Church Growth movement. However, emergence of the market mentality threatens to radically alter the conception of the church, for the market transforms the church from a cause to a provider of services. This trend begs for a discussion of the market's appropriateness as a metaphor for the church, but that discussion would require another book. After the Strategic Planning Conference of 2006, it appeared that the Church of God had begun to step beyond a crossroads, but ensuing budget crises made it apparent that the movement had not moved very far beyond them.

Jesus said that people's treasure lies next to their hearts. The statement might be inverted to ask whether the absence of treasure means that the heart is also absent. Along with its congregationalist polity, the history of the Church of God points to the local congregation as possessing the hearts of ministers and laypeople alike. This is perhaps to be expected. On the other hand, the jealously guarded autonomy of the local church has proved a hindrance to national church efforts ever since C. E. Brown observed that little cooperation can be expected from a people who believe that all forms of organization are sin. Pride in the fact that no national church leader can dictate to the local church is finally a thin justification to belong to the Church of God movement. Moreover, local autonomy and the insistence on being "sold" the World Ministries Budget before supporting can lead in some sense to a practical schism. Remember that, classically defined, *schism* is the sin against Christian love. The problems of finance and autonomy thus are symptomatic of a larger issue. Stated in question form, "What are the bonds which tie the Church of God movement together? Wherein does the movement's unity lie?"

Answers to these questions are not overly abundant, but some possibilities can be identified. One hopeful sign is the discovery by some pastors that the autonomy conferred by a radical congregationalist polity is not as desirable as many have thought. Ministers who have enrolled in the SHAPE program have in many instances recovered the concept and practice of brotherly and sisterly collegiality. Generated by a grant from the Lilly Endowment, SHAPE is an acronym for a program called "Sustaining Pastoral Health and Excellence." It organizes participants into clusters where they are coached by a seasoned minister. Study and the formation of peer relationships are central elements of the SHAPE program. Although not an original program goal, participants repeatedly point to their discovery of pastoral loneliness and the consequent need for a genuine collegiality. We have long understood that the church is the body of Christ, but if ministers understand that they too can be connected within that body, perhaps we will find the seeds of a revitalized conversation about the church.

A second hopeful sign is the determination of the present general director and the staff of Church of God Ministries to be present in the life of the church. Historically, the Church of God has depended on its publications and face-to-face relationships as key components of its way of being together. Face-to-face polity eroded in the last three decades of the twentieth century in favor of more bureaucratic leadership. In several instances there was good justification for this shift, but it also weakened the movement's polity. This is evident in the calls from the grassroots church to be heard and the findings of the Task Force on Governance and Polity. The loss of periodical publications and several venues where face-to-face relationships were nurtured remains cause for serious concern. But the present general director and staff are determined to keep those relationships alive. The driving force behind this determination is a commitment to what they see as the common cause of the church. They believe that the church is not bound together by programs or consumer choices, but by the love of God poured into the hearts of believers by the Holy Spirit. It is a belief as old as Paul's insistence that Christians in Europe and Asia Minor contribute to the relief of the saints in Jerusalem.

A third hopeful sign is a remarkable ministry that stretches around the earth. Shortly after his retirement from the pastoral staff of Park Place Church of God in 1999, David Coolidge inaugurated what became an Internet prayer ministry. In 2000, Coolidge used e-mail to solicit prayer in behalf of a gravely ill friend and former colleague. Word of the particular request spread and attracted wide support. Before long, Coolidge was being contacted by others who sought the prayers of the church beyond their local congregations. What began as a simple prayer request grew into a ministry;

Coolidge's e-mail address book now contains well over 1,500 entries, and scarcely a day passes but what those on his mailing list learn of an illness, crisis, or death and respond with encouragement and assurances of prayer. This technological web of concern may weave through cyberspace, but its ligaments are the Christian virtues of faith, hope, and love. Not unlike the *Gospel Trumpet* of yesterday, David Coolidge's ministry is some of the glue holding the Church of God together. The people who are connected by this ministry are not attracted to a program. They do not think of the church as a provider. Nor are they solicited as if potential consumers who must be sold on an idea before they would give of their time and energy. David Coolidge's ministry reminds people in the Church of God that the Bible, not the market, is the standard from which the church draws the images that guide its discipleship. Finally, this ministry is shaped by the metaphor of a body bound together by the Love that moves the stars and forms the people of God in such a way that, when one suffers, all do—and so too may all rejoice. In David Coolidge's ministry, in the determination of a small group of servants, in the growing awareness that ministers must have true, honest friends we can see hopeful, ecclesiologically healthy signs that the Church of God movement will step forward.

BIBLIOGRAPHY

Adcock, Elver. *Our American Missions*. Anderson, IN: Board of Church Extension and Home Missions of the Church of God, [1934].

Ahlstrom, Sydney E. *A Religious History of the American People*. New Haven, CT: Yale University Press, 1972.

Anderson, Beverly Carvin. "A History of the Church of God in Ontario." BDiv thesis, Anderson College and Theological Seminary, 1955.

Andrews, Edward G. "Address of Welcome." In *National Perils and Opportunities; The Discussions of the General Christian Conference Held in Washington, D.C., December 7th, 8th and 9th, 1887*, under the auspices and direction of the Evangelical Alliance for the United States, 13. New York: Baker and Taylor, 1887.

Berry, Robert L. *Constructive Evangelism*. Anderson, IN: Gospel Trumpet Co., 1934.

———. *The Golden Jubilee Book*. Anderson, IN: Gospel Trumpet Co., 1931.

———. *Guide to Christian Stewardship*. Anderson, IN: Gospel Trumpet Co., 1940.

Bolitho, Axchie A. "National Woman's Missionary Society of the Church of God: A Brief Survey 1932–1946." Anderson, IN: National Woman's Missionary Society, 1946.

———. *To the Chief Singer: A Brief Story of the Work and Influence of Barney E. Warren*. Anderson, IN: Gospel Trumpet Co., 1942.

Boreham, F. W. *Dreams of Sunset*. Valley Forge, PA: Judson Press, 1954.

Brenton, Howard. *Friends for 300 Years*. New York: Harper and Brothers, 1952.

Brown, Charles E. *Adventures in the Spiritual Life*. Anderson, IN: Warner Press, 1946

———. *The Church Beyond Division*. Anderson, IN: Gospel Trumpet Co., 1939.

———. *The Meaning of Salvation*. Anderson, IN: Gospel Trumpet Co., 1944.

———. *The Meaning of Sanctification*. Anderson, IN: Warner Press, 1945.

———. *A New Approach to Christian Unity*. Anderson, IN: Gospel Trumpet Co., 1931.

———. *The Way of Faith*. Anderson, IN: Warner Press, 1943.

———. *The Way of Prayer*. Anderson, IN: Warner Press, 1940.

———. *When Souls Awaken*. Anderson, IN: Gospel Trumpet Co., 1954.

———. *When the Trumpet Sounded*. Anderson, IN: Gospel Trumpet Co., 1951.

Byers, Andrew. L. *Birth of a Reformation, or the Life and Labors of D. S. Warner*. Anderson, IN: Gospel Trumpet Co., 1921.

———. *The Gospel Trumpet Publishing Work*. Anderson, IN: Gospel Trumpet Co., 1907.

Byers, Andrew L., and Barney E. Warren, eds. *Hymns and Spiritual Songs for Christian Worship and General Church Work*. Anderson, IN: Gospel Trumpet Co., [1930].

Byrum, Enoch E. *The Boy's Companion, or a Warning Against the Secret Vice and Other Bad Habits*. Grand Junction, MI: Gospel Trumpet Co., 1893.

———. *The Christian's Treasure*. Anderson, IN: Gospel Trumpet Co., 1937.

———. *Divine Healing of Soul and Body: Also, How God Heals the Sick*. Moundsville, WV: Gospel Trumpet Co., 1892.

———. *The Great Physician and His Power to Heal*. Moundsville, WV: Gospel Trumpet Publishing Co., 1899.

———. *Life Experiences*. Anderson, IN: Gospel Trumpet Co., 1928.

———. *Thoughts on the Life of Faith*. Anderson, IN: Gospel Trumpet Co., 1940.

Byrum, Noah H. *Familiar Names and Faces*. Moundsville, WV: Gospel Trumpet Co., 1902.

Byrum, Russell R. *Christian Theology: A Systematic Statement of Christian Doctrine for the Use of Theological Students*. Anderson, IN: Gospel Trumpet Co., 1925.

———. *Problems of the Local Church*. Anderson, IN: Gospel Trumpet Co., 1927.

Callen, Barry L. *She Came Preaching*. Anderson, IN: Warner Press, 1992.

Callen, Barry L., ed. *A Time to Remember*. Anderson, IN: Warner Press, 1977–78.

———. *Following the Light*. Anderson, IN: Warner Press, 2000.

————. *The First Century.* 2 vols. Anderson, IN: Warner Press, 1979.

"Christian Education Leaders Set Goals, " *Vital Christianity*, July 8, 1973, 19.

Clark, Elmer T. *The Small Sects in America.* New York: Abingdon Cokesbury, 1950.

Clear, Valorous B. "The Church of God: A Study in Social Adaptation." PhD diss., University of Chicago, 1953.

————. *Where the Saints Have Trod: A Social History of the Church of God Reformation Movement.* Chesterfield, IN: Midwest Publications, 1977.

Courtney, Donald Addison. "A Study of the Development of the Sunday School in the Church of God." (BDiv thesis, Anderson College and Theological Seminary, 1954).

Crose, Lester A. *Passport for a Reformation.* Anderson, IN: Warner Press, 1981.

Crose, Lester A., Cheryl Johnson Barton, and Donald D. Johnson. *Into All the World.* Anderson, IN: Warner Press, 2009.

Davis, Katie R. *Zion's Hill at West Middlesex.* Corpus Christi, TX: Christian Triumph Press, n.d.

Dawson, I. K. *Working Together in an Enlarged Program of State Evangelism.* Anderson, IN: Board of Church Extension and Home Missions, 1944.

Delory, George E., ed. *The World Almanac and Book of Facts* (New York: Newspaper Enterprise Association, 1978.

Dieter, Melvin E. *Revivalism and Holiness.* Ann Arbor, MI: University Microfilms, 1973.

Dye, Dwight L. *A Kingdom of Servants: The Kingdom of God.* Anderson, IN: Warner Press, 1979.

Edwards, Jonathan. *Apocalyptic Writings.* Edited by Stephen J. Stein. Vol. 5 of *The Works of Jonathan Edwards.* New Haven: Yale University Press, 1977.

Elliott, Benjamin F. *Experiences in the Gospel Work in Lower California, Mexico.* LaPaz, Mexico: Office of "The Gospel," 1906.

Fisher, Joseph C., ed. *Songs of Victory.* Williamston, MI: Gospel Trumpet Co., 1885.

Forney, Christian H. *History of the Churches of God in the United States of North America.* Harrisburg, PA: Publishing House and Book Rooms of the Churches of God, 1914.

Forrest, Aubrey L. "A Study of the Development of the Basic Doctrines and Institutional Patterns in the Church of God (Anderson, Indiana)." PhD diss., University of Southern California, 1948.

Gaddis, Merrill E. "Christian Perfectionism in America." PhD diss., University of Chicago, 1929.

Gray, Albert F. *Christian Theology*. 2 vols. Anderson, IN: Warner Press, 1944–46.

————. *Time and Tides on the Western Shore*. N.p., privately published, 1966.

Hartley, Ben R. "Viet Nam: My View." *Vital Christianity*, January 16, 1966, 5–6.

Hartman, Marvin J. "The Origin and Development of the General Ministerial Assembly of the Church of God, 1917–1950." BDiv thesis, Butler University, 1958.

————. "Unique Opportunities: Home Missions." *Church of God Missions*, July 1977, 3.

Heffren, Henry C. *Voices of the Pioneers*. Camrose, AB: privately published, [1968].

Hofstadter, Richard. *Anti-intellectualism in American Life*. New York: Random House, 1963.

Howe, Daniel Walker, ed. *Victorian America*. Philadelphia: University of Pennsylvania Press, 1976.

Huber, Randal. *Called, Equpped, and No Place to Go: Women Pastors and the Church*. Anderson, IN: Warner Press, 2003.

Huttenlocker, Keith. *God, Can I Get to Know You?* Anderson, IN: Warner Press, 1979.

Hymnal of the Church of God. Anderson, IN: Gospel Trumpet Co., 1953.

Johnson, Donald D. "The Value of a Special Project." *Church of God Missions*, July 1977, 8–9.

Jones, Kenneth E. *The Word of God*. Anderson, IN: Warner Press, 1980.

Kern, Richard. *John Winebrenner, Nineteenth-Century Reformer*. Harrisburg, PA: Central Publishing House, 1974.

Khan, A. D. *From Darkness to Light: The Testimony of A. D. Khan—Converted Mohammedan* (Anderson, IN: Mission Board of the Church of God, 1954).

————. *India's Millions*. Moundsville, WV: Gospel Trumpet Co., 1903.

Koglin, Anna E. *History of the Church of God in Minnesota*. N.p., privately printed, 1976.

Latourette, Kenneth Scott. *A History of the Expansion of Christianity.* 7 vols. New York: Harper and Brothers, 1943.

Leonard, Juanita Evans, ed. *Called to Ministry, Empowered to Serve: Women in Ministry.* Anderson, IN: Warner Press, 1989.

Lindsell, Harold. *The Battle for the Bible.* Grand Rapids, MI: Zondervan Publishing House, 1976.

Linn, Otto F. *The Gospel of John: An Exposition.* Anderson, IN: Gospel Trumpet Co., 1942.

———. *The Gospel of Mark: An Exposition.* Anderson, IN: Gospel Trumpet Co., 1944.

———. *Gospels and Acts.* Vol. 1 of *Studies in the New Testament.* Anderson, IN: Warner Press, 1941.

———. *Hebrews to Revelation.* Vol. 3 of *Studies in the New Testament.* Anderson, IN: privately published, 1942.

———. *Romans to Philemon.* Vol. 2 of *Studies in the New Testament.* Anderson, IN: Warner Press, 1942.

Lynch, Denis T. *"Boss" Tweed: The Story of a Grim Generation.* New York: Boni and Liveright, 1927.

———. *The Wild Seventies.* New York: Appleton-Century, 1941.

Markle, David, ed. *First Steps to Ministry.* Anderson, IN: Warner Press, 2001.

Martin, Earl L. *The Gospel of Luke: An Exposition.* Anderson, IN: Gospel Trumpet Co., 1944.

———. *Toward Understanding God.* Anderson, IN: Gospel Trumpet Co., 1941.

"Massey Administers Refugee Program," *Vital Christianity*, November 4, 1979, 19.

Massey, James Earl. *African-Americans and the Church of God, Anderson, Indiana.* Anderson, IN: Anderson University Press, 2005.

———. *Concerning Christian Unity.* Anderson, IN: Warner Press, 1979.

McAllister, Lester G., and William E. Tucker. *Journey in Faith: A History of the Christian Church (Disciples of Christ).* St. Louis: The Bethany Press, 1975.

Miller, Adam W. *The Gospel of Matthew.* Anderson, IN: Gospel Trumpet Co., 1944.

———. *An Introduction to the New Testament.* Anderson, IN: Gospel Trumpet Co., 1943.

Morgan, H. Wayne. *Victorian Culture in America, 1865–1914*. Itasca, IL: F. E. Peacock Publishers, 1973.

Morrison, John A. *As the River Flows*. Anderson, IN: Anderson College Press, 1962.

———. *The Preacher of Today*. Anderson, IN: Warner Press, 1937.

Naylor, Charles W. *The Secret of Being Strong*. Anderson, IN: Warner Press, 1941.

———. *The Teachings of D. S. Warner and His Associates*. Anderson, IN: privately printed, n.d.

Neal, Hazel G., and Axchie A. Bolitho. *Madam President*. Anderson, IN: Gospel Trumpet Co., 1951.

Newell, Arlo. *Receive the Holy Spirit*. Anderson, IN: Warner Press, 1978.

Oldham, W. Dale. *Giants Along My Path*. Anderson, IN: Warner Press, 1973.

Oppenheimer, Mark. *Knocking on Heaven's Door: American Religion in the Age of the Counterculture*. New York: Yale University Press, 2003.

Orr, Charles. E. *Christian Conduct, or the Way to Heaven*. Moundsville, WV: Gospel Trumpet Co., 1903.

———. *Not a New Movement*. Guthrie, OK: Faith Publishing House, n.d..

———. *The Rule of a Saintly Life*. Aberdeen, Scotland: Herald of Truth Publishing Co., n.d..

Outler, Albert C., ed. *John Wesley*. New York: Oxford University Press, 1974.

Phillips, Harold L. *Miracle of Survival*. Anderson, IN: Warner Press, 1979.

———. "Report: What's Key 73?" *Vital Christianity*, November 28, 1971, 23.

Pruitt, Fred. *God's Gracious Dealings*. Guthrie, OK: Faith Publishing House, 1955.

Reardon, Robert H. "The Doctrine of the Church and the Christian Life in the Church of God Reformation Movement." Master's thesis, Oberlin Graduate School of Theology, 1943.

———. *The Early Morning Light*. Anderson, IN: Warner Press, 1979.

Reed, Harold W. "The Growth of a Sect-Type Institution as Reflected in the Development of the Church of the Nazarene." PhD diss., University of Southern California, Los Angeles, 1943.

Riggle, Herbert M. *The Kingdom of God and the One Thousand Years' Reign.* Moundsville, WV: Gospel Trumpet Publishing Co., 1899.

———. *The New Testament Church.* Anderson, IN: Gospel Trumpet Co., 1937.

———. *Pioneer Evangelism.* Anderson, IN: Gospel Trumpet Co., 1924.

Roark, Warren C., comp. *Divine Healing.* Anderson, IN: Warner Press, 1945.

Rowe, Ida Byrd. *At Work with Young People.* Anderson, IN: Warner Press, 1939.

Sanders, Cheryl J. "Ethics of Holiness and Unity in the Church of God." In *Called to Minister, Empowered to Serve: Women in Ministry*, edited by Juanita Evans Leonard, 131–46. Anderson, IN: Warner Press, 1989.

———. *Saints in Exile: The Holiness-Pentecostal Experience in African American Religion and Culture.* New York: Oxford University Press, 1996.

Schell, William G. *The Better Testament.* Moundsville, WV: Gospel Trumpet Publishing Co., 1899.

———. *The Biblical Trace of the Church.* Grand Junction, MI: Gospel Trumpet Publishing Co., 1893.

———. *Is the Negro a Beast?* Moundsville, WV: Gospel Trumpet Co., 1901.

Schlesinger, Arthur M., Sr. *A Critical Period in American Religion, 1875–1900.* Philadelphia: Fortress Press, 1967.

Select Camp-meeting Sermons: Preached at the International Camp-meeting of the Church of God, Anderson, Indiana, June 16–24, 1928. Anderson, IN: Gospel Trumpet Co., 1928.

Sherwood, H. A., comp. *Reformation Glory.* Anderson, IN: Gospel Trumpet Co., 1923.

Smith, Frederick G. "Church of God Reformation Movement." In *The Church*, compiled by Warren Roark, 78–84. Anderson, IN: Warner Press, 1946.

———. *The Last Reformation.* Anderson, IN: Gospel Trumpet Co., 1919.

———. *The Revelation Explained: An Exposition, Text by Text, of the Apocalypse of St. John.* Anderson, IN: Gospel Trumpet Co., 1908.

———. *What the Bible Teaches: A Systematic Presentation of the Fundamental Principles of Truth Contained in the Holy Scripture.* Anderson, IN: Gospel Trumpet Co., 1914.

———. *What the Bible Teaches: A Systematic Presentation of the Fundamental Principles of Truth*. Condensed by Kenneth E. Jones. Anderson, IN: Warner Press, 1955.

Smith, Irene Catherine. *Solving Church School Problems*. Anderson, IN: Warner Press, 1944.

Smith, John W. V. "The Bible in the Church of God Reformation Movement: A Historical Perspective." *Centering on Ministry* 6, no. 3 (1981): 6.

———. *A Brief History of the Church of God Reformation Movement*. Anderson, IN: Warner Press, 1976.

———. *Heralds of a Brighter Day*. Anderson, IN: Gospel Trumpet Co., 1955.

———. "Mileposts of Multiplication." *Planning Creatively*, October 1956, 3.

———. *Truth Marches on: A Brief Study of the History of the Church of God Reformation Movement*. Anderson, IN: Gospel Trumpet Co., 1956.

Smith, Uriah. *Thoughts on the Prophecies of Daniel and the Revelation*. Battle Creek, MI: Review and Herald Publishing Co., 1897.

Songs of Zion: A Compilation of Favorite Hymns and Songs Intended for All Kinds of Religious Services. Anderson, IN: Gospel Trumpet Co., 1940.

Stafford, Gilbert W. *Church of God at the Crossroads*. Anderson, IN: Warner Press, 2000.

———. *The Life of Salvation*. Anderson, IN: Warner Press, 1979.

———. "What We Really Mean to Say: A Glossary of Terms." *Centering on Ministry* 6, no. 3 (1981): 3

Stall, Stephen Wayne. *The Inspiration and Authority of Scripture: The Views of Eight Historical and Twenty-One Current Doctrinal Teachers in the Church of God (Anderson, Indiana)*. Master's thesis, Anderson School of Theology, 1985.

Sterner, R. Eugene. *Healing and Wholeness*. Anderson, IN: Warner Press, 1978.

Strege, Merle D. *I Saw the Church: The Life of the Church of God Told Theologically*. Anderson: Warner Press, 2002.

———. *Tell Me Another Tale: Further Reflections on the Church of God*. Anderson, IN: Warner Press, 1993.

———. *Tell Me the Tale: Historical Reflections on the Church of God*. Anderson, IN: Warner Press, 1991.

———. "Where Scandinavian Is Spoken." ThD diss., Graduate Theological Union, 1982.

Sulzberger, C. L. *The Age of Mediocrity: Memoirs and Diaries, 1963–72.* New York: Macmillan, 1973.

Susag, S. O. *Personal Experiences of S. O. Susag.* Houston, TX: Ambassador Press, n.d.

Sykes, Stephen. *The Identity of Christianity.* Philadelphia: Fortress Press, 1984.

Tarr, Charles R. *A New Wind Blowing.* Anderson, IN: Warner Press, 1972.

Taylor, Erin Moss, ed. *Go Preach My Gospel.* Anderson, IN: Church of God Ministries, 2004.

Teasley, D. Otis. *How to Conduct a Sunday School.* Anderson, IN: Gospel Trumpet Co., 1912.

Walker, Williston. *A History of the Christian Church.* 3rd ed. New York: Charles Scribner's Sons, 1970.

Warner, Daniel S. *Bible Proofs of the Second Work of Grace.* Goshen, IN: E. U. Mennonite Publishing Society, 1880.

———. *The Church of God, or What Is the Church and What Is Not.* Anderson, IN: Warner Press, n.d.

———. *Must We Sin?* Grand Junction, MI: Gospel Trumpet Publishing Co., n.d.

———. *Salvation: Present, Perfect, Now or Never.* Grand Junction, MI: Gospel Trumpet Publishing Co., [1896].

Warner, Daniel S., and Herbert M. Riggle. *The Cleansing of the Sanctuary.* Moundsville, WV: Gospel Trumpet Publishing Co., 1903.

Warner, Daniel. S., and Barney. E. Warren, eds. *Anthems from the Throne.* Grand Junction, MI: Gospel Trumpet Publishing Co., 1888.

Warren, Barney E., and Andrew L. Byers. *Songs of the Evening Light.* Moundsville, WV: Gospel Trumpet Co., 1897.

Warren, Barney E., Andrew L. Byers, Clara M. Brooks, and D. Otis Teasley, eds. *Select Hymns for Christian Worship and General Gospel Service.* Anderson, IN: Gospel Trumpet Co., 1911.

Warren, Barney E., Andrew L. Byers, Clarence E. Hunter, and D. Otis Teasley, eds. *Salvation Echoes.* Moundsville, WV: Gospel Trumpet Publishing Co., 1900.

———, eds. *Truth in Song*. Anderson, IN: Gospel Trumpet Co., 1907.

Warren, Barney E., and Daniel S. Warner. *Echoes from Glory*. Grand Junction, MI: Gospel Trumpet Publishing Co., 1893.

Weisberger, Bernard A. *The Age of Steel and Steam*. New York: Time, Inc., 1964.

Western Holiness Association. *Proceedings of the Western Union Holiness Convention*. Bloomington, IL: Western Holiness Association, 1881.

Wickersham, Henry C. *A History of the Church*. Moundsville, WV: Gospel Trumpet Publishing Co., 1900.

———. *Holiness Bible Subjects*. Grand Junction, MI: Gospel Trumpet Publishing Co., 1894.

Wiebe, Robert H. *The Search for Order, 1877–1920*. New York: Hill and Wang, 1967.

Winebrenner, John. *Doctrinal and Practical Sermons*. Lebanon, PA: General Eldership of the Church of God, 1868.

Withrow, Oral and Laura. *Meet Us at the Cross: An Introduction to the Church of God*. Anderson, IN: Warner Press, 1999.

Worship the Lord: Hymnal of the Church of God. Anderson, IN: Warner Press, 1989.

Wuthnow, Robert. *The Restructuring of American Religion*. Princeton, NJ: Princeton University Press, 1988.

Yahn, S. G. *History of the Churches of God in North America*. Harrisburg, PA: Central Publishing House, 1926.

Yanik, Paul. *Through the Years*. Sharon, PA: Hlasnik Publishing Co., 1956.

Zoff, Otto. *They Shall Inherit the Earth*. New York: John Day Co., 1943.

INDEX

Anderson Bible Training School: establishment of, 203, 213, 235; name change, 247; reorganization as independent entity, 213, 247; WWI-era challenges, 246. *See also* Anderson College and Theological Seminary; Anderson University; School of Theology

Anderson Camp Meeting: auditorium construction for, 148; missionary work, 120, 207, 276; necktie resolutions, 194; organization acceptance debate, 209; organization reform efforts (1948–52), 331, 337; tabernacles, 149, 258, 512; WWII restrictions on, 303; and youth ministry, 222, 279. *See also* North American Convention; International Convention

Anderson College and Theological Seminary: accreditation process, 290–92; Anderson city bridge project through, 407–8; Asbury-Anderson revival (1970), 414; building construction and expansion, 341, 387; Byrum's heresy trial aftermath, 261–62; conservative challenges to, 250, 289–90, 423–24, 439–51, 453–54; Depression-era challenges for, 281, 288–90; fiftieth anniversary, 396; growth in 1960s, 387–88; and inerrancy doctrine challenge, 439–46; Morrison-Reardon transition, 361–62; name change to, 248; Reardon-Nicholson transition, 473–74; social concerns activity, 381. *See also* Anderson Bible Training School; Anderson University; School of Theology

Anderson University: Caldwell fund, 459; and Coalition of Christian Colleges and Universities, 473; land acquisitions from Church of God Ministries, 369, 510–12; name change to, 473; Nicholson-Edwards transition, 453; restructuring (1996), 482; shifting enrollment demographics, 509; Ticketmaster controversy, 456. *See also* Anderson Bible Training School; Anderson College and Theological Seminary; School of Theology

Andrews, Edward Gayer, 9, 16, 22, 31

Angelos, Chris, 178

Anthems from the Throne, 64

anti-cleansing heresy, 104, 106, 179–86, 206

Antigua, 417, 435

apocalyptic perspective, 92–98, 445

apostolic succession, 2, 88

Arbeiter, Karl, 116, 167, 340

Argentina, 418, 419, 428, 435

Arkansas, 404

Arlington College, 334, 389, 391

"Asbury-Anderson Revival," 414

Ashenfelter, Edith, 119

Ashenfelter, Mabel, 129, 130, 370

Asia: Bangladesh, 435; China, 113, 120–21, 302, 306, 318–19; fundraising for, 419–20; Hong Kong, 436; Japan, 266, 306, 436, 465, 466; Korea, 436; Nepal, 466; Singapore, 436; Taiwan, 436. *See also* India

Asia–Pacific Church of God Conference, 465

Assam, India, 119

Associated Budgets: Depression-
era challenges, 284–86;
establishment of, 256–57;
growth of giving (1940–46),
286–88; Hatch's role in, 285–86.
See also World Service
Attercliff, Ontario, 100, 103
Australia, 113, 121, 435
authority of Scripture: as basic tenet
of CHOG, 81–83, 87, 91; and
Christian unity, 249; inerrancy
issue, 24, 437–46, 447–48, 449–
51; vs. inner revelation, 199
Azusa Pacific College, 334, 391
Babb, Victor, 465
"Babylon," sectarianism as, 38, 94,
183, 219–20, 392
Bailey, George W., 119, 135, 170, 234
Baja California, 111–12
Baker, Marvin, 444
Baldwin, W. J., 170
Ballinger, William, 37
Bancroft, Ontario, 105
Bangladesh, 435
Bangor, Michigan, 62, 72, 75, 152
Barbados, 120, 302, 365, 435
Barber, Jay, 507–8, 509
Barton, Cheryl Johnson, 467
Bass, Hayden, 127
Bastin, Albert, 273
Battle Creek, Michigan, 68
Bay Point, California, 178
Bay Ridge Christian College, 335,
391, 405–6, 428
Beasley, Edward, 482
Beaver Dam, Indiana, 35–37, 53
Beecher, Henry Ward, 22
Beirut, Lebanon, 433, 465
Belgrade, Minnesota, 170
Benevolent Budget (1922), 218
Bennett, Merv, 481
Bennett family, 126

Berghouse, Nettie, 220
Berlin, Ontario, 103
Bermuda, 113, 435
Berquist, Maurice, 429
Berry, Robert L.: death of, 340;
educational work, 220, 243, 247,
278; on evangelism, 271, 272;
on general budget idea, 222; and
Golden Jubilee, 265, 267, 271,
272; stewardship program, 288
Berry, Mrs. T. A., 275
Bertelson, B. Olaf, 219
Bessie, Oklahoma, 327, 329
Bible. *See* Scripture
Bible Proofs of the Second Work of Grace
(Warner, D. S.), 46, 49, 81
Birdsall, S. M., 103–4
Bixler, Abram, 103
Bixler, Adelbert, 126
Bixler, William A., 370
Black Interstate Youth Convention,
382
blacks. *See* African Americans
Blackwood, Lottie, 72
Blaney, J. C., 103, 104, 106–7, 245
Blewitt, Charles J., 118, 170, 232,
276, 340
blind, publishing work for the, 148
Block Chapel, Indiana, 127
Bloomington, Indiana, 273–74
Blore, F. C., 220
Board of Christian Education:
awareness seminars for social
concerns, 382; Board of
Religious Education and Sunday
Schools, 220, 222, 277–79;
and Church of God Youth
Fellowship, 336; contribution
to growth (1969–70), 398;
establishment of, 279; fiftieth
anniversary, 428; and General
Ministerial Assembly, 352;

Brunk, J. B., 324
Brush College, Indiana, 127
Buck, George, 467–68
Bucyrus, Ohio, 57–60, 132, 189
Buenos Aires, Argentina, 419
Buettner, Eleanor, 319
Buettner, Milton A., 319
Bulgaria, 435
Bullocksville, Alberta, 110
Burgess, O. A., 220, 234, 247
Burleigh, George W., 14
Business Committee, 269
Byers, Andrew L.: death of, 340;
    educational work, 137; on move
    to Anderson, 146; and necktie
    controversy, 194; photo, 65;
    on racial justice, 65; on second
    cleansing doctrine, 183; as
    songwriter, 65, 136; on Trumpet
    family operations, 141–42; on
    Warner and church's beginnings,
    32, 37, 159; writings on the
    pioneers, 65
Byers, Charles E., 269, 369
Byers, Jacob W., 74, 207, 219, 229,
    233
Byers, Jennie M., 74, 220, 229, 233
Byers, Mollie, 114
Byrum, Bessie Hittle (Mrs. R. R.),
    220, 221, 244, 278
Byrum, Enoch E.: and anti-cleansing
    heresy, 181–82, 183–84, 186;
    and Articles of Agreement,
    152; death of, 151; and divine
    healing, 136; on Edmonton
    work's difficulties, 110;
    educational work, 137, 213,
    228; and Golden Jubilee, 267;
    on growth of Movement, 76;
    and holiness behavior and dress,
    189, 190, 192–93, 194–95, 197,
    199; at Jordan Harbor camp

meeting (1901), 76–77; minister
list development, 131–32;
missionary work, 116, 119, 207,
276; move to Anderson, 146–48;
photos, 133, 193; publishing
work, 62–64, 132–36; and
race relations, 160–61, 162;
resignation from editorship, 151,
211–12; and Trumpet family
culture, 137–39, 140–41, 143,
145; and youth movement, 279
Byrum, Lucena Beardsley (Mrs. E. E.),
    275, 369
Byrum, Myrl, 219
Byrum, Noah H., 132, 134–36, 137,
    140, 152, 340
Byrum, Russell R.: Christian unity
    controversy, 246–50, 253–54,
    322; on congregational
    organization, 223; educational
    work, 244; photo, 245; Tasker as
    inspiration for, 242
Byrum, Ruthven, 362
Byrum Hall, 149
Calcutta, India, 117–19
Caldwell, Dondeena, 459
Caldwell, Irene Smith, 293, 294, 318,
    429, 459
Caldwell, Maurice, 419, 459, 465
California: Arlington College, 334,
    389, 391; congregation building
    in, 178; early missionary work
    in, 74, 111, 228–29, 273; lack
    of organizational representation,
    475; Spanish language outreach,
    219, 378
Called to Minister, Empowered to Serve,
    460–61
Callen, Barry L., 412, 432, 469
Campbell, Alexander, 31
Campbell, J. E., 244
Campbell, Ohio, 174

education, 405; and collegiality growth among colleges, 509; establishment of, 334; ministerial education evaluation, 393, 411; organizational role of, 353; and Southeastern Associations' desire for a college, 390–91

Commission on Social Concerns, 381–87, 443, 445, 451, 455, 458–59

Committee of 14, 264

Committee (Commission) on Christian Unity, 393–94, 425, 427–28, 443–45, 451, 456–57

Committee on Conversations, 393–94

Concilio Hispano de la Iglesia de Dios, 497

congregations. *See* local congregations

Conkis, William, 178

Conley, John, 470, 471

Conrad, Harold A., 429

conscientious objectors, 259–60, 299–302, 317–18, 406

conservative perspectives: inerrancy, biblical, 438, 439–42, 445, 448; and laidback church style, 464; necktie controversy, 189–91, 192–201, 206; social concerns, 439–42, 445, 449, 450, 455. *See also* Pastors' Fellowship

Constitution and Bylaws Committee, 215–16

constructive evangelism, 267–68, 271–72

Constructive Evangelism (Berry), 271–72

Consultation (1970): areas of concern, 379, 409, 413–14, 421, 423; the event, 398–99, 401–3; findings, 375–76; introduction, 373; missionary work, 395–96; summary, 434

Consultation on Church Union (COCU), 428, 443

Consultation on Doctrine, 425, 428

Consultation on the Ministry, 365

Consultation on Women in Mission and Ministry, 461

Coody, Burt E., 335

Coolidge, David, 520–21

Cooper, George S., 272

Corey, Bruce R., 219

Costa Rica, 410, 435

Coston, Isabel, 137

Courtney, Donald, 396, 452

Cox, Columbus, 127, 128

Crane, Isham E. (Joe), 413

Crose, John D., 233

Crose, Lester A., 297, 418, 429

Crose, Pearl, 233

Crossroads: Christian Insight on Crucial Issues, 442

Crow Agency, Montana, 417

Crowland, Ontario, 101

Cuba, 328, 435

Cumberbatch, Carlton, 465

Cumberbatch, Theodosia, 465

Curaçao, 435

Cuttack, India, 119

Czechoslovakia, 176, 435

Dale, Doris, 452, 488

Dallas, George, 178

Daniel, book of, 96, 212, 438, 441

Daniels, Rolland, 463

Danville, Illinois, 229

Darwinism, 21–22

Das, Asim, 465

Daugherty, J. W., 107, 114, 128

Davis, Alice, 62

Dawson, I. K., 322

DAY-Men program, 355

Deachman, William, 103, 107

Decatur, Illinois, 328

Decker, Leslie E., 336

change, 394–95; ordination eligibility and certification, 316; race relations, 345, 355–60, 379–80; reorganization proposal (1931), 268–69; reorganizations, 316, 329–32, 352–54; social concerns, 259–60, 301, 318, 381, 384, 386; supervision of agencies, 223; and Watchman doctrinal challenge, 323–30; *Yearbook* publication, 215–16. *See also* General Assembly; Executive Council; Leadership Council

General Service, Division of, 331, 353, 416, 425

Georgia, 157, 160, 404

German-language work (in North America), 64, 110, 136, 164–68, 231

German Reformed Church, 29–30, 31

Germany, 114–16, 121, 299, 435, 466

Germany, J. Horace, 334–35

Germany, R. A., 253

Giant Leap Campaign, 470–71

Gibson, I. W., 324, 328

Gibson, Marie, 324, 328

Gilded Age, 8–9, 13

Gilliam, E. Joe, 389, 412, 413, 471–72

Global Missions, 514. *See also* Missionary Board

glossolalia, 28, 427, 468–70, 496

Gloucester, New Jersey, 271

Golden Jubilee (1931), 255, 265–68, 270–73, 275, 280–81

"Go—Make Disciples," 337–38

Goode, Richard, 405

Gordon, J. G., 128

Gordon Bible School, 253

Gospel Ark, 72

Gospel Trumpet: blind readers, publishing work for, 309; buildings and equipment, 63, 134–35; Byrum-Warner partnership, 62–64; and democratization, 315–16; early business developments, 56–57, 60–64; early circulation of, 146; early contributors, 64–65; as evangelical tool, 52, 53, 67, 69, 70, 73, 75–76, 99, 100; expansion of reach, 133–34, 135; as fellowship tool, 84; Fisher-Warner partnership, 38, 54–55, 61–62; foreign language publications, 165–66, 169, 171, 175, 178; masthead and banner, 82; as missionary tool overseas, 117–19, 121; name change to *Vital Christianity,* 361; 19th-century expansion of, 64; seventy-fifth anniversary, 344; Smith-Brown editorial transition, 250, 261–64; songbooks, 60–61, 64; Warner's editorship, 36–37, 49, 54–55, 204

Gospel Trumpet Company: and Anderson Bible Training School, 242–47; Anderson move, 146–48; book production, 136, 151, 307–8, 360–61; buildings and equipment, 144–45, 146, 147–48, 150; Byrum brothers' role in, 132; Byrum-Smith transition, 211–12; children's books, 137; church's organization beyond, 210–17; Diamond Jubilee, 344–45; early 20th-century expansion, 148, 150; educational role, 137, 151, 220, 278, 296; family-to-employment culture shift, 213, 243–44; financial ups and downs, 139, 264–65, 284, 360–61; Golden Jubilee, 265; in Grand Junction, 63, 132; incorporation of, 152–53; as missionary funds relay, 207; Moundsville sojourn, 135, 143–46, 152–53; name change to Warner Press, 361; organizational development, 133–37, 152–53; Patterson-Rowe transition, 264; songbook production, 136; Sunday school materials, 137, 151, 220, 278; tracts, 135–36; *Yearbook* establishment, 215–16. *See also* Trumpet family; Warner Press, Inc.

Gospel Van, 115

gospel workers, 65, 69, 142, 234, 243, 272

Gough, Louis F., 364, 388–89, 429

governance. *See* human organization

Grand Forks, North Dakota, 169–70

Grand Junction, Michigan, 61–63, 112, 132–35, 138–44

Grand Junction Camp Meeting Association, 152

Grant, Charles A., 170, 171

Gray, Albert F.: and doctrinal challenge (1947), 326; educational work, 235, 247, 292, 333, 363; gospel workers' training, 234; ministerial training of, 232; photo, 292; reorganization proposal (1931), 268–69; and Woman's Home and Foreign Missionary Society, 275–76; writings, 345

Great Britain, 33, 77, 114, 115–16, 181, 417, 435

Great Depression. *See* Depression, Great

Greece, 435

Greek work (in North America), 178

Greer, Hester, 274

Grenada, 417, 435

Grubbs, David, 452

Grubbs, Jerry C., 447, 453

Grubbs, J. Perry, 452, 505–6

Guam, 435

Guatemala, 408, 436

The Guide, 101–2

Gulf-Coast Bible College, 334, 340, 382, 389–90, 429, 470–71. *See also* Mid-America Bible College

Gustafson, Oscar, 127

Guthrie, Oklahoma, 161, 201

Guyana, 436

Hahn, Fred, 64, 166–67

Haines, G., 49

Haiti, 436

Halbesleben, Brother, 167

Haldeman, Walter, 278

Hale, Alice V., 119

Hale, J. R., 106, 130, 340

Hale, Mabel Ashenfelter, 129, 130, 370

Hall, Gregory, 474, 509

Hamburg, Germany, 115–16, 167

Hanak, A., 175–76

Harrington, J. M., 184

Hart, Paul, 442, 444

Harting, Wayne, 443

Hartman, Marvin J., 211, 396, 452

Hartman, William, 73, 75

Hartselle, Alabama, 158, 161

Hatch, Clarence W., 285–86, 288, 309, 311, 365–67

Hatch, J. D., 120

Hatch, Ralph V., 253

Hauge, Hans Nielsen, 168

Hawaii, 396, 419

Hayes, Sherrill, 452, 469, 470

Haynes, W. A., 106, 181, 184–85

Heaven to Earth (film), 343, 346

Heffren, H. C., 109
Helms, Mabel, 244
The Helper, 148
Hendricks, Dick, 302
Henry, Mollie, 114
Henry, William J.: and anti-cleansing heresy, 181, 184, 186; death of, 369; local congregational development, 188; missionary work, 103, 113–14; photo, 114
Herald of Gospel Freedom, 14, 48
The Herald of Truth, 195, 199–201
Heritage Hymn Sing-a-long, 494
higher education: black ministerial education, 405; collegiality growth (1990s–2000s), 509–10; conservative perspective, 440–46; editorial conflict (1930), 261–62; establishment of, 334; liberal perspective, 440–41, 443; ministerial education evaluation, 393, 411; organizational role of, 353; state-national relationships, 333–34. *See also individual institutions*
Hillard, James R., 273
Hines, Samuel, 495, 496–97
Hispanic Council of the Church of God. *See* Concilio Hispano de la Iglesia de Dios
Hlasnik, 175–76
Hoboken, New Jersey, 170
holiness: and anti-cleansing heresy, 180–86; and ascetic lifestyle, 189–201; and authority of Bible, 81; as central tenet of Movement, 6, 24–25, 54; and early evangelical ministry, 54, 58–60, 66–67, 125, 129; and experiential religion, 85; as manifested in all the people, 88–89; and Open Letter

challenge (1980), 440–41; and Pentecostalism, 469, 495; as premise for early reformers, 24–25, 88–89; Reformation-era restoration of, 4; second cleansing, 85–86, 104, 106, 179–86, 206; and sexuality, 59; and unity, 89; Warner's adoption of, 38, 40, 45–48, 52; Warner's developing doctrine, 85–86, 89, 135–36. *See also* sanctification; worldliness, avoiding
Holiness Movement, 5–6, 24–31, 32, 36, 45–52
Holland, 44, 436
Holy Spirit leadership: and authority of Bible, 447; and avoidance of human organization, 88–89, 208, 216, 219, 223–24; as central tenet of Movement, 31, 39, 40, 82, 206; and criticism of organization (1940s), 320; and democratic processes, 314–15; and education, 220–21, 225–27, 253; and evangelistic call, 270–71; with formal organization, 222, 223–24, 225, 313, 399, 416–17; and *glossolalia,* 468–70; ministerial inspiration role, 204–5, 217, 226–27, 253; and openness to new truth, 90–91; sanctification role, 86, 180, 182–83
homes, missionary. *See* missionary homes
homosexuality, 408, 441–42, 445, 449, 455
Honduras, 436
Hong Kong, 436
Hope Community Church, 493
Hope Hill, Kentucky, 409
Hope Hill Children's Home, 409

Jubilee events, 343, 345; family life issues, 408; international partnerships, 465; Mid-Century Evangelistic Advance, 338; and Open Letter challenge, 439; pacifism, 406, 459; race relations, 383. See also Anderson Camp Meeting; North American Convention

International Youth Convention, 279–80, 311, 336, 345–46, 382, 510

Iowa, 169

Ireland, 113, 115–16, 436

Italy, 436

Jackson, Shearon L., 505–6

Jacobson, Fred N., 75

Jamaica, 113, 365, 436

Janes, L. Y., 201

Japan, 266, 306, 436, 465, 466

Jarrett, Minna, 460

Jarvis, Robert, 119

Jerry City, Ohio, 67–68, 114, 181

Johnson, A. Wayne, 422

Johnson, Donald D., 57, 418–19, 429, 452, 464, 467–68

Johnson, L. H., 59

Johnson, Morris C., 116, 172

Johnson, O. L., 423, 450–51

Johnson, Pearl, 278

Johnstown, Pennsylvania, 174

Joiner, C. Herbert, 340, 429

Joiner, Samuel W., 324, 327

Jones, Andy and Mrs., 127

Jones, Kenneth E., 345, 432

Jones, Sam, 33

Jordan, Wilfred, 404

Jordan Harbor, Ontario, 106–7

Jubilees: Diamond (1956), 339, 343–47, 345; Golden (1931), 255, 265–68, 270–73, 275, 280–81

Kane, John H., 362

Kansas, 127, 167

Kansas City, Missouri, 128, 231, 235–36, 242, 346, 428

Kansas City Bible Training School, 235, 370

Karamitros, Anestes, 178

Kardatzke, Carl, 318, 362

Kaser, Lodema, 73–74

Kaumeyer, C. L., 101–2, 137

Keagy, Rhoda, 61

Keeling, George P., 181–83, 185–86

Kelly, Arthur, 471

Kendleton, Texas, 335, 391, 405

Kentucky, 409

Kenya, 428, 433, 436, 465, 467

Key, Elihu, 172

Key, Enos, 172

"Key 73," 415–16, 516

Khan, A. D., 107, 116–19, 207, 232

Kigar, Nannie, 68, 100

Kilpatrick, Alexander J., 66–67, 103, 114, 158

Kima International School of Theology, 465, 495

Kima Theological College, 465

King, Eric, 486

King, William W., 325

Kirkpatrick, Celia, 61

Kitchener, Ontario (formerly Berlin), 103

Koglin, Anna E., 169, 171, 173, 247, 278

Kohns, Gottfried, 167

Kolb, Jerry, 447–48

Konno, Kozo, 465

Korea, 436

Krause, Fred, 37

Kriebel, James, 114

Kurseong, India, 119

Lahore, India, 119

laidback church style, 463–64, 489–95

Lake Wales, Florida, 391, 508

Makokha, Byrum, 428, 465
Markle, David, 510
Martin, Earl L.: on conscientious
    objection status, 299; death of,
    370; educational work, 220, 247,
    278, 335; Golden Jubilee, 265;
    Spanish-language publications,
    219; on Washington, DC,
    church, 311
Martin, James, 501–2
Marvel, Gerald, 460
Maryland, 323, 414
Mashue, Henry, Sr., 188
Mashue, Mary, 187–88
Mass Communications Board of the
    Church of God, 429
Massey, Gwendolyn, 409
Massey, James E., 157, 394, 405, 426,
    428, 432
Mast, Jennie I., 72
Mast, L. C., 72
Masters, E. G., 106, 184, 234, 268
Matthesen, Lena Shoffner, 114, 129–
    31, 158–59, 161
Mauch, Maurice J., 336
May, Flemming, 108
May, James S., 369
May, R. W., 110
Mayer, Mary, 107
Mayfield, Charles, 128
Mazatlán, Sinaloa, Mexico, 112
McCann, Frank, 184
McClive, Thomas, 100
McCoy, I. S., 173–74
McCreary, W. Burgess, 220, 260, 278
McCrie, Josephine, 108
McCully, Price, 184
McCurry, Everett, 273
McCurry, Marie, 273
McCutcheon, Lillie Sowers, 371, 423,
    444–45, 450, 459, 462
McElmmerry, S. R., 127

Medicine Hat, Alberta, 167, 293
Mediterranean Bible College, 465
Meier, David, 397
Meischke, Richard Lee, 312, 332
Melki, Fouad, 465
membership (statistics), 434–36
Mennonites, 23, 30–31, 40, 49, 459
Meridian, Mississippi, 125, 160
The Messenger of Love, 185
Methodist churches, 18, 24–26, 29,
    67, 189, 190
Methodist Episcopal Church, 67
Metropolitan Mission Program, 382
Mexico, 111–13, 312, 397, 418–19,
    436
Mexico City, Mexico, 419
Michels, Sebastian, 62–63, 73, 75,
    112, 152–53
Michigan: call for Christian
    Unity Commission, 393;
    congregational development,
    152, 178; early evangelical work,
    68, 72, 73, 75, 101, 126; Fishers'
    conflict with Churches of God,
    38; and founding of CHOG, 1;
    publishing work in, 60–63, 74,
    132–44; race relations, 161–62;
    Warner's holiness and unity
    preaching in, 38–39, 53
Mid-America Bible College/Christian
    University, 470–71, 508. *See also*
    Gulf-Coast Bible College
Mid-Century Evangelistic Advance,
    337–39
Midland, Michigan, 187
Midwest Bible School, 253
Midwest Ministerial Assembly, 346
Miller, Adam W.: on Centennial
    Planning Committee, 402;
    educational work, 278, 335;
    Missionary Board work, 298;
    National Woman's Home

proposal, 276; and race relations, 356; reorganization proposal (1931), 269; retirement of, 363; and Warner Auditorium construction, 368; World Peace and Post War Problems Committee, 318

Miller, Frances (Frankie), 68, 100, 280

Miller, Gene, 443

Miller, T. Franklin: on Centennial Planning Committee, 402, 433; Diamond Jubilee report, 346; educational work, 294, 335; leadership style, 507; at Warner Press, 396, 423

Miller, William, 96

Million Campaign, 286, 310–11

Million for Missions, 419

Mills, Benjamin F., 33

Milwaukee, Wisconsin, 64, 166–67, 415

ministerial lists, 65, 132

ministerial training: of African Americans, 334–35, 405–6; initial organization of, 225–28; missionary homes' role in, 205, 228, 232, 234; as primary purpose of colleges, 247; seminary reassessment, 411–12; and state-national relationships, 263–64, 409–10. *See also* Anderson College and Theological Seminary

Ministers and Missionaries Training School, 327–28

Ministers' Benefit Association, 280–81

Ministers' Pension Fund, 288

Ministries Council, 485, 489, 511–12. See also Leadership Council; Executive Council

Minnesota, 169–73, 214, 233–34

Missionary Board: Asian work, 419–20; budgeting issues, 222–23, 455; Caribbean area, 395–96; Depression-era reach of, 274–75; focus on overseas work, 217–18; hospitality service, 242; and international partnerships, 464–68; Latin American work, 418–19; need for, 206–7; Scandinavian work, 172–73; in team organization, 486; women's missionary society, 275–76; WWII challenges, 298

Missionary Committee, 207–9, 213

Missionary Herald, 148, 207

missionary homes: Chicago, Illinois, 229–31; criticism of method, 236–37; decline of, 242; early development of, 128, 205, 217–19; expansion of, 231; Kansas City, Missouri, 235–36; listing of, 238–41; ministerial training function, 205, 228, 232, 234; New York, New York, 120, 232, 235, 236; Oakland, California, 229, 233; Oklahoma City, Oklahoma, 128–31; and Spanish-language outreach, 219; Spokane, Washington, 234–35; St. Paul Park, Minnesota, 171–72, 233–34; youth training function, 242. *See also* Board of Church Extension and Home Missions

missionary work, early: ad hoc methods of, 121–22; Australia, 121; Canada, 99–111; China, 120–21; Eastern Europe, 116; Egypt, 120; England, 114, 115–16; Germany, 114–15, 116; India, 117–19; Japan, 120; Latvia, 116; Mexico, 111–13; Scandinavia, 116–17; Scotland, 116; West Indies, 113, 120

New Testament church, principles of, 3–4
Newton Falls, Ohio, 444
New York Bible Training School, 232
New York City, New York, 15, 120, 161, 232, 235, 236
Nicaragua, 436
Nicholaou, Constantine (Gust), 177–78
Nichols, Evalyn (Mrs. J. J. M. Nichols-Roy), 119, 275
Nicholson, Robert A., 335, 362, 451, 453, 473, 474
Nichols-Roy, J. J. M. (also J. J. M. Roy), 119, 370
Nichols-Roy Bible College, 466
Niels, C. G., 171
Nieman, Johanna, 116
1970 Consultation. *See* Consultation (1970)
Noffsinger, Donald A., 423, 453, 482–84
non-creedalism, 449, 450
Norris, LaVern, 450
North American Convention, 494, 511. *See also* Anderson Camp Meeting; International Convention
North Carolina, 391
North Dakota, 169–70
Northern Indiana Eldership of the Churches of God, 36, 48–49, 50, 51
Northern Ireland, 436
Northern Michigan Eldership of the Churches of God, 38
Northwest Ministerial Assembly, 292
Norway Lake, Minnesota, 170
nuclear disarmament, 458–59

Oak Grove, Mississippi, 160
Oakland, California, 178

Oaxtepec, Mexico, 367, 396, 433
Oberlin College, 41, 225
Oden, D. F., 162, 207
Oesch, Leroy, 439–42, 445, 448
Ohio: Churches of God in, 30, 43; congregational development, 273, 325; early evangelical work, 57–60, 66, 67–68, 73, 103, 181; Pastors' Fellowship in, 424; Slovak work in, 174, 177; as Warner's birthplace, 41; Warner's coming-out process in, 43–47
Oklahoma: Mid-America Bible College, 470–71, 508; missionary home in, 128–31; and necktie controversy, 201; Pastors' Fellowship in, 425; and race relations, 161; and Slacum's challenge, 327
Oklahoma City, Oklahoma, 128–30, 470–71, 492, 508
Oldham, Doug, 333
Oldham, W. Dale, 136, 312, 332–33, 371, 396
Old Main, 147
old people's home, 73, 148, 173, 214, 234, 409
Olive Bethel, Indiana, 74, 127
Oliver, W. H., 46
Olsen, Ellen, 172
Olsen, Lars, 172, 297
Olson, Ellen, 397
Olson, George W., 120, 397
Olson, Mary, 120
Olson, Nellie, 369
Olt, George Russell: and conscientious objector support, 318; death of, 362; educational work, 213, 247, 278, 291, 293; photo, 291
"One Thousand New Sunday Schools" Campaign, 278
ONEvoice!, 499

radio program, 491–92. See also *Christian Brotherhood Hour*

raison d'être, 80

Rather, Rebecca, 369

Ratzlaff, Leslie, 363, 391

Reardon, Eugene A.: at Chicago mission home, 230; death of, 340, 517; educational work, 244, 247; missionary work, 116, 120, 177, 207; necktie controversy, 195; reorganization proposal (1931), 268–69

Reardon, Robert H.: in bridge protest, 392; educational work, 335, 361–62, 387–88, 407, 414; and Open Letter controversy, 439–40, 442–46, 450; photo, 291, 443; on reorganization (1990s), 481; retirement of, 473; on sanctification doctrinal adherence, 323; writings, 432

Reed, William E.: in bridge protest, 407; building project, 368; on Centennial Planning Committee, 402, 433; death of, 469; and doctrinal assessment (1970s), 426–27; on Executive Council, 396; home missions work, 340; photo, 407; retirement of, 429

Reformationists, 423–24

The Reformation Witness, 424, 494

Reichenbach, Herman, 362

Reitz, Robert, 421

Renbeck, Edel, 170

Renbeck, Nels, 116, 170, 172, 280

Research and Improvement Committee, 325–26, 329, 330

restorationism, 2–6, 24–31, 32, 36, 45–52

Revelation, Book of, 94, 96–98, 212, 248–49, 438, 441

The Revelation Explained (Smith, F. G.), 98, 248

Revision and Planning Committee (Commission), 329, 330–32, 347, 350–52

revivalism, 17, 29, 33–34, 84, 149, 462

Rice, Mister, 59

Riga, Latvia, 116

Riggle, Herbert, M.: and Bible training school idea, 246; on church governance, 209; death of, 340; editorial work, 262; on flying ministry disadvantages, 77; as Gospel Trumpet Co. president, 284; on missionary home concept, 236–37; missionary work, 116, 207; and necktie controversy, 193–95; pastoral ministry, 130, 170, 173; photo, 193; reorganization proposal (1931), 269; on women's organization, 276

Riggle, Minnie, 397

Right of Appeal, 365

Ring, Otto T., 116, 170–72, 233

Rist, Robert, 484, 485

Ritchey, Donald C., 422

Roark, Warren C., 307, 311–12

Roberts, John E., 193

Robinson, Forrest, 444, 471, 504

Rogers, Harry, 71

Rolla, Missouri, 125–27

Roman Catholic Church, 441

Roush, O. A., 234

Rowe, Alexander Thomas: death of, 397; educational work, 247, 278, 295–96; on formal organization idea, 210; Golden Jubilee role, 268–70; at Gospel Trumpet Co., 264–65; and necktie controversy, 195

Rowe, Ida Byrd (Mrs. A. T.), 220, 318

Roy, J. J. M. (also J. J. M. Nichols-Roy), 119, 275, 370

Rudd, Gerald H., 493

Rupert, Hattie, 114–15

Rupert, J. H., 114–16, 167

Russia, 113, 133, 436, 466

Rutty, Jennie C., 116

Saint Kitts and Nevis, 436

Saint Vincent, 436

Saltillo, Mexico, 397

Salt Lake City, Utah, 177

Salvation Army, 22, 50, 75, 108, 115

Salvation Echoes, 136

sanctification: and anti-cleansing heresy, 104, 106, 179–86, 206; denominations' attempts to co-opt, 25–26; as rebellion against mainline churches, 24; and sexuality, 59; theological basis, 85–86, 89; and unity, 5–6, 89; Warner on, 81–82, 85–86; Warner's experience of, 45–46

Sanctified church concept, 495

Sanders, Cheryl, 460, 495

San Diego, California, 228–29

San José, California, 388

San José, Costa Rica, 410

Sankey, Ira D., 33, 35

Santa Barbara, California, 111

São Paulo, Brazil, 419

Saskatchewan, Canada, 108

Saskatoon, Saskatchewan, 108

Sauk County, Wisconsin, 167

Sawyer, Thomas J., 404

Scandinavian countries, 116–17, 168, 170, 173, 435

Scandinavian work (in North America), 168–73, 233–34

Schauer, Homer, 333

Schell, William G.: on anti-cleansing heresy, 182–83; ministry of, 75; missionary work, 103; on race relations, 156–57; writings, 64, 82, 98, 136, 156–57, 182–83, 248

Schieck, Gordon S., 340

Schield, Wilbur, 291

Schlatter, H. A., 268

School of Theology: accreditation of, 345; assessment of (1971–73), 391–93, 411–12; endowed lectureship, 484; establishment of, 335–36; expansion of, 362–63; and Open Letter controversy, 440–41, 447

Schools of Stewardship, 404

Schüle, Irma, 466

Schüle, Walentin, 466

Scotland, 116, 195

Scripture: biblical criticism's threat to, 22; and human rights, 380; vs. inner revelation, 199; as locus of truth, 44; and New Testament basis for restorationism, 3–4; prophetic, 94, 96–98, 212, 248–49, 438, 441; re-dedication to, 287; and unity, 208; and Warner's search for holiness, 45, 52. *See also* authority of Scripture

Seattle, Washington, 234, 292, 415, 417, 424, 428

second cleansing doctrine, 85–86, 104, 106, 179–86, 206

sectarianism. *See* denominationalism

secular humanism, 449

Securities and Exchange Commission (SEC), 505

"seeing the church," 517–18

Select Hymns, 151

seminary. *See* Anderson College and Theological Seminary

sexual morality, 408, 440–42, 445, 449, 450, 455

Shackleton, Frederick G., 338
SHAPE program, 520
Sharon, Pennsylvania, 163, 173–74
Shaw, E. E., 268
Sheefel, Olive, 275
Sheldon, A. Leroy, 74, 280
Shelly, A. J., 75, 187–88
Sherwood, H. A., 244, 247, 267, 370
Shillong, India, 119
The Shining Light, 64
Shively family, 101
Shoffner, Lena (Mrs. Mattheson), 114,
    129–31, 158–59, 161
Shoot, W. H., 195
Shultz, David, 484, 485, 486
Singapore, 436
Slacum, L. Earl, 321–29, 347, 516
Sloan, E. S., 184
Slovak work (in North America),
    173–77
Smith, Birdie (Mrs. F. G.), 247
Smith, Frederick George: vs. Byrum,
    211, 250; editorial work,
    211–12; educational work, 244,
    246–48; missionary work, 116;
    and necktie controversy, 194;
    and organizational dangers, 216;
    as prophecy authority, 136; on
    race relations, 156; vs. Tasker,
    207; writings, 82, 151
Smith, Irene C. (Mrs. Caldwell), 293,
    294, 318, 459
Smith, J. A., 184
Smith, J. Edgar, 429
Smith, Jennie, 61, 74
Smith, J. M., 125
Smith, John E., 100–101, 103, 105
Smith, John W. V.: on Centennial
    Planning Committee, 402; on
    ecumenism, 444; educational
    work, 335; on Faith and Order
    Commission, 456–57; on

inerrancy, 447; writings, 345,
    426
Smith, Joseph, 73
Smith, Sarah, 67–68, 100, 114, 164,
    181
Smith, Steele C., 130, 368, 396
Smith, Thomas A., 336, 340, 415
Smith, Uriah, 96, 98
Smith, William H., 108–11
Smith, William N., 61, 74
Smithfield, Pennsylvania, 174
Smoot, J. D., 340–41
Snowden, Nellie, 422, 452
Snowden, Roscoe, 396, 403
Snyder, Leonard, 469
social concerns: church-state relations,
    384–85; Commission on Social
    Concerns, 381–87, 443, 445,
    451, 455, 458–59; disaster relief
    work, 408–9; family life and
    values, 296, 408, 439; marriage,
    62, 306, 408; prayer in public
    schools, 384–85, 455; sexual
    morality, 408, 440–42, 445, 449,
    450, 455. *See also* peace and war;
    race relations; temperance
social gospel, 22–23, 31–32
Society of Friends (Quakers), 40
Sohkhia, Borman Roy, 465
songs. *See* music
Songs of Victory, 60
Songs of Zion, 175, 307
South America, 113, 418–19, 428,
    435, 436, 465
South Carolina, 157
Southeastern Association of the
    Church of God, 390–91
Southern Association of the Church of
    God, 391, 405
Southern Baptists, 438
Southern California Association, 389,
    391

South Haven, Michigan, 62, 73

South Texas Bible Institute. *See* Gulf-Coast Bible College

Sowers, Mary, 102

Spanish Evangelical Association, 219

Spanish Fork, Utah, 178

Spanish-language outreach, 497

Spanish Literature Company, 219

Spaulding, John, 61

speaking in tongues, practice of, 28, 427, 468–70, 496

Speck, Samuel L., 75, 135

Spiritual Workers Training School. *See* Anderson Bible Training School

Spokane, Washington, 234–35, 242, 292

Spokane Bible Institute, 234–35. *See also* Pacific Bible College

Stafford, Gilbert W.: on Commission on Faith and Order, 456; on erosion of CHOG culture, 498–99, 502; on inerrancy, 447; photo, 480; as radio broadcaster, 452; writings, 432, 479, 516

St. Ann, Ontario, 101

"Statement of Conviction on War and Peace," 386, 406

state-national relationships: and asceticism, 194; Assembly representation, 374, 395; early national guidance, 124, 194; and educational boards, 294; and higher education, 333–34; and ministerial training, 263–64, 409–10; and national leadership composition, 349–51; and national-level education focus, 251; 1930s decentralization moves, 281; 1960s assessment, 395–96; 1980s conservative challenge, 448; state organizational growth, 315–16,

322, 370; Strategic Planning Conference (2006), 512–13; Task Force on Governance and Polity, 474–76; and *Yearbook* inputs, 357

Stavropoulos, Constantine, 178

Stergiou, Nick, 178

Sterner, R. Eugene: church reassessment (1963), 374; growth pattern analysis, 397; looking to the future, 401; photo, 396; and race relations, 356; as radio broadcaster, 396, 452; on Radio Commission, 344; writings, 426, 432

Stevenson, Alex L., 108

stewardship initiatives, 285–88, 354–55, 365–66, 404. *See also* fundraising

Stewart, E. Faith, 328

St. Kitts and Nevis, 436

St. Louis, Missouri, 11, 33, 161

Stockwell, R. S., 59–60

Stoll, Emma, 111

Stone, Barton W., 31

Stoneboro, Pennsylvania, 170

Stone-Campbell movement, 4–5, 31, 40

Stories for Children, 137

St. Paul Park, Minnesota, 169–73, 214, 233–34

Strang, S. P., 73, 135

Strategic Planning Conference (2006), 512–14

Strong, Marie, 363, 459, 460, 461

St. Thomas, Ontario, 103

Student Summer Service (Tri-S), 381

St. Vincent, 436

Sunday, Billy, 33

Sunday schools: and children's home ministry, 73; early opposition to, 219–20; governing board

for, 220, 222, 277–79; growth
of, 277–78, 294–95; in India,
119; interdenominational,
31; in local congregation,
273–74; local move away from
national curriculum, 498–99;
organization of, 220–21;
publications for, 101, 137,
151, 296, 340, 361; refocus on
(1970s), 376–77, 398, 428–29;
Slovak, 174
Susag, Martha, 171
Susag, Sven O., 168, 170–72, 340
Swayze, Mister, 104
Sweden, 173
Swinehart, E. V., 292
Swiss Brethren, 40
Switzerland, 367, 396, 436
Syria (Lebanon), 151, 302, 409, 433,
436, 465
tabernacle, Anderson campground,
148, 149, 258, 367–68
Tafolla, M. F., 219, 340
Taiwan, 436
Tallen, James R., 267
Tanner, Paul A., 366–67, 377, 429,
448, 469, 501
Tanzania, 436
Tarr, Charles, R., 414, 415
Tasker, George P., 105, 116, 120, 207,
232, 370
Task Force on Governance and Polity,
474–78, 488, 489
Task Force on Women in Ministry,
461
team organization, 486–87
Teasley, D. Otis, 151, 194–95, 198,
199, 207
temperance: alcohol, 144, 191–92,
260–61, 384, 408; drug use and
addiction, 189, 408; tobacco,
159, 189, 381, 383

Tennant, E. C., 327
Terre Haute, Indiana, 51, 322–23
Texas: higher education, 252–53,
334–35, 382, 389, 391, 405,
470; race relations, 335, 404,
405
Thailand, 436
theology: divine destiny for humanity,
92–98; experiential religion,
Christianity as, 84–86; vision
of the Church, 86–91. *See also*
authority of Scripture; doctrines;
unity, Christian
Thomas, William, 101
Thompson, C. A., 268
Titley, W. W., 71
tobacco, 159, 189, 381, 383
Toledo, Ohio, 11, 414
tongues, speaking in, 28, 427, 468–
70, 496
Torrey, R. A., 33
Travencore, India, 119
Trinidad, 436
Tri-S (Student Summer Service), 381
La Trompeta Evangelica, 113
Trumpet family: at Anderson home,
147, 151, 242; early communal
lifestyle of, 61, 137–43; as model
for missionary homes, 228; at
Moundsville home, 143–45,
181; racial integration in, 157
Tubbs, C. H., 170, 172
Tubbs, Mary, 170, 172
Tucker, Isaac B., 274
Tufford, Emma, 106
Tufts, Gorham, 105, 118, 206,
229–30
Turner, John, 73
Turner, Pearl B., 267
Uganda, 436
United Brethren church, 66, 72–73,
74, 135, 170

publishing work, 36–37, 49, 54–55; and race relations, 159–60; and sanctification, 45–46, 81–82, 85–86, 183; separation from Churches of God, 46–48; on suicide lecture, 14; on Sunday schools, 219–20; unity doctrine, 5–6, 43–45, 89; writings, 46, 49, 81, 96–97, 98, 135

Warner, Frances Miller (Mrs. D. S.), 280

Warner, Sarah (Mrs. D. S.), 59–60

Warner Auditorium, 368–69, 511–12

Warner Memorial University, 252–53, 265, 334

Warner Pacific College: expansion plans, 388–89; fiftieth anniversary, 471; financial struggles, 472–73; lack of inerrancy teaching, 440; leadership crisis (1979), 412–13; name change to, 364. *See also* Pacific Bible College

Warner Press, Inc.: financial struggles, 482–86, 501–2, 504, 507; increased production for evangelism, 398; leadership transitions, 423, 429, 453; name change to, 361; and social concerns agenda, 382. *See also* Gospel Trumpet Company

Warner Southern College, 391, 474, 508–9

Warner University. *See* Warner Southern College

Warren, Barney E., 68–70, 100, 136, 151, 195

Warren, Kitty, 126

Warren, William E., 105–6

Washington, DC, 495

Washington state, 234–35, 242, 292, 424, 428

"Watchmen on the Wall," 328–29, 446–51

Waterloo, Ontario, 229

Weber, Charles V., 356, 367–68, 372, 396–97, 407

Welch, Douglas, 464–65

Weldon, Steve, 493

Welland, Ontario, 101

West Coast Ministerial Assembly, 363, 415

Western Union Holiness Convention, 50, 67

West Indies, 113, 120, 302, 365, 435, 436

West Middlesex, Pennsylvania, 163–64, 381, 403–4

West Ohio Eldership of the Churches of God, 43, 46, 47, 94, 180

West Virginia, 143–46

Whaley, William T., 185

What the Bible Teaches (Smith, F. G.), 82, 151, 178, 248, 345

White, Eliza, J., 100

White, John, 140

White, L. W., 127

Wickersham, Henry C., 62, 74, 82, 85, 98, 138

Wiens, Jacob, 293

Williams, Ethel, 108

Williams, George S., 119

Williams, James, 501

Williams, Jane, 157–58

Williams, Steven, 456, 494

Williamson, Lowell, 333

Williamston, Michigan, 60–62, 74

Willow Creek Community Church, 463

Wilson, Charles E., 291

Wilson, Joseph Turner, 147, 195, 213, 243–44, 246–47

Wimbish, Earnest E., 163

Winchester Academy, 252, 265, 370

Winebrenner, John, 29–31, 43
Winebrennerian Church of God.
    See Churches of God in North
    America
Winona, Ontario, 103
Winters, Pina, 120
Wisconsin, 64, 166–67, 415
Wiseman, Peter, 324
Withrow, Oral, 468
Wolfram, E. E., 365, 429
Woman's Missionary Society, 275–76,
    312, 346, 364, 377, 382, 500.
    See also National Woman's Home
    and Foreign Missionary Society;
    Women of the Church of God
women in ministry, revival of, 459–62
Women of the Church of God, 421–
    22, 452, 467, 471, 500, 503,
    511. *See also* National Woman's
    Home and Foreign Missionary
    Society; Woman's Missionary
    Society
Wood, Robin, 463–64
Wooden, Byron, 137
Woods, J. C., 127
World Conference, 433–34, 467
World Forum of the Church of God,
    433
worldliness, avoiding, 31, 189, 191,
    201, 248. *See also* plain dress

World Peace and Post War Problems
    Committee, 317–18
World Service Commission (Division
    of World Service), 329–31, 343,
    353, 365
World Service Day, 286, 288, 303–4,
    309–11, 345
World War I, 246, 259
World War II, 283–84, 290, 297–306
Wright, Walker, 247
Yajima, Ukichi, 120
Yanik, Paul, Jr., 175–76
Yanik, Paul, Sr., 175–76
Yeaman, Elizabeth, 129, 131
Yeaman, Powhatan, 129
Yearbook of the Church of God, 69,
    153, 168, 215–16
Year of the Sunday School, 398
Yerden, Paul, 494
Yoder, John Howard, 459
Yoder, Lydia, 120
Young People's Friend, 279–80
youth work, 279–80, 303, 311, 336,
    345–46, 382, 510
Zamorano, Fidel, 378
Zaugg, Ira, 119
Zazanis, Nick, 178, 429
Zinn, David, 106
Zinzendorfism, 104, 181–85
Zurich, Switzerland, 367, 396, 436